A
Reference
Grammar
of Modern
Italian

A Reference Grammar of Modern *Italian*

MARTIN MAIDEN &
CECILIA ROBUSTELLI

NTC Publishing Group

Library of Congress Cataloging-in-Publication Data

Maiden, Martin, 1957–
    A reference grammar of modern Italian/Martin Maiden & Cecilia Robustelli.
        p. cm.
    Text in English and Italian.
    Includes bibliographical references and index.
    ISBN 0-658-00430-1
    1. Italian language—Grammar.   I. Robustelli, Cecilia.   II. Title.

PC1112.M26 2000
458.2*421—dc21
                                                                        99-047884

This edition first published 2000 by NTC Publishing Group,
a division of NTC/Contemporary Publishing Group,
4255 West Touhy Avenue, Lincolnwood (Chicago), Illinois 60712-1975, U.S.A.

Originally published by Edward Arnold, a member of the Hodder Headline Group.

International Standard Book Number: 0-658-00430-1

Printed in Malta

MAY 0 4 2001

Contents

Abbreviations and symbols

Most abbreviations used in this book should be transparent (masc. = 'masculine', fem. = 'feminine', sg. = 'singular', pl. = 'plural', pres. = 'present', etc.). 'Lit.' is the abbreviation for 'literally' (*not* literary). The symbol * placed in front of an example means that what follows is *ungrammatical*; in the relatively few cases where examples preceded by * are used, we have tried to be careful to make it clear in words, as well, that the relevant example is not grammatical. Sources for the examples, where given, are abbreviated as follows:

www = website www.alice.it (a database of contemporary Italian literature, including interviews with authors)
Cal. I. Calvino 1964. *Il sentiero dei nidi di ragno*. Turin: Einaudi.
Cas. C. Cassola 1960. *La ragazza di Bube*. Milan: Rizzoli.
Chia. R. Chiaberge 1999. *Navigatori del sapere*. Milano: Raffaello Cortina.
Dur1. F. Duranti 1988. *Effetti personali*. Milan: Rizzoli.
Dur2. F. Duranti 1996. *Sogni mancini*. Milan: Rizzoli.
Esp. *L'Espresso* (magazine) 8 March 1996
Gal. E. Galli della Loggia 1998. *L'identità italiana*. Bologna: Il Mulino.
Gin. C. Ginzburg 1976. *Il formaggio e i vermi*. Turin: Einaudi.
Gua. G. Guareschi 1948. *Mondo piccolo don Camillo*. Milan: Rizzoli.
Lam. G. Lampedusa 1957. *Il Gattopardo*. Milan: Feltrinelli.
Mar. D. Maraini 1990. *La lunga vita di Marianna Ucrìa*. Milan: Rizzoli.
Ogg. *Oggi* (magazine) 13 March 1996
Pan. *Panorama* (magazine) 15 March 1996
Rep. *La Repubblica* (newspaper) 19 June 1997
Rio1. G. Riotta 1991. *Cambio di stagione*. Milan: Feltrinelli.
Rio2. G. Riotta 1995. *Ombra*. Milan: Rizzoli.
Tut. *Tuttosport* (newspaper) 25 September 1995

Glossary of key grammatical terms

Items given in bold in the definitions are also defined in this glossary. Where a particular term is defined in the text of this grammar, the appropriate reference is supplied.

Adjectival phrase – See **phrase**

Adjective – (see also **phrase**) A class of words whose characteristic function is to modify a noun, expressing some property of that **noun**. E.g., the underlined elements in *la ragazza intelligente* 'the intelligent girl', *il tempo era bello* 'the weather was nice'.

Adverb – A class of words whose characteristic function is to modify a **verb** or **verb phrase**. Often, but by no means always, ending in *-mente* in Italian and '-ly' in English. E.g., the underlined elements in *canta sempre* 'he's always singing', *mangia lentamente* 'she eats slowly'. An adverb which modifies a verb phrase is sometimes called a 'sentence adverbial' (see 13.12): e.g., *Finalmente, ti vediamo* 'At last, we can see you.'

Agreement – The phenomenon whereby adjectives (and also articles and demonstratives) vary in form according to the gender and number of the noun they modify, and verbs vary in form according to the person, number (and sometimes the gender – see 6.32) of their subject. E.g., *Il gatto nero mangia* 'The black [male] cat eats' (masculine third person singular), *I gatti neri mangiano* 'The black[male] cats eat' (masculine third person plural),, *La gatta nera mangia* 'The black[female] cat eats'(feminine third person singular), *Le gatte nere mangiano* 'The black [female] cats eat' (feminie third person plural). Pronouns also agree in gender and number with the noun they stand for: *Viene lei = Viene la maestra.*

Animate – Any entity that can be perceived as acting, or being capable of acting, of its own will, is 'animate'. Typically, human beings, but sometimes also animals.

Antecedent – Typically, an element already mentioned to which a **pronoun** (and especially a **relative** pronoun) 'refers back'. E.g., *Vidi molte cose quel giorno, le quali non ti posso raccontare* 'I saw many things that day, which I canot tell you about', where *molte cose* / 'many things' is the antecedent of *le quali* / 'which'.

Apodosis – In a conditional construction, the apododis is the clause that expresses what will happen if the condition expressed in the **protasis** is fulfilled. The protasis is the 'if' clause, which stipulates the condition that needs to be fulfilled for something to come about. In *Se viene, lo vedremo* 'If he comes, we'll see him', *Se viene* is the protasis and *lo vedremo* the apodosis.

Article – Words equivalent to English 'the' (the 'definite article': Italian *il/lo/l' la le/ i/gli*) and 'a / an' (the 'indefinite article': Italian *un/uno/un' una*).

Attenuative – Form tending to attenuate or 'play down' the full meaning of some word. Like 'a bit. . . .', 'rather. . . .', '. . .-ish'.

Augmentative – A form that indicates large size relative to the norm (e.g., *un sassone* 'a big stone' – cf. *sasso* 'stone').

Auxiliary verb – A verb such as *avere, essere, stare* (see 14.19-21,30,33;15.17) used in combination with a **past participle** or a **gerund**. The auxiliary does most of the grammatical 'work', indicating person and number of the subject, mood (i.e., subjunctive or indicative) and to some extent tense, whereas the accompanying past participle or gerund signals the basic meaning of the verb. E.g., (with auxiliaries underlined) <u>Ho</u> *cantato* 'I've sung', <u>Sono</u> *arrivato* 'I've arrived', <u>Sono</u> *visto* 'I'm seen', <u>Sto</u> *cantando* 'I'm singing'.

Cardinal number – a number in the series *uno* (1), *due* (2), *tre* (3), etc.

Clause – Any string of words seen as constituting, or corresponding to, a sentence. A 'subordinate clause' is such an element within a larger sentence (and is often introduced by *che*). E.g., in *Dico che Mario canta* 'I say that M. sings', the subordinate clause is *che Mario canta* (corresponding to *Mario canta*). But in *Ti dico di cantare* 'I tell you to sing', the subordinate clause is *di cantare* (corresponding to *Tu canti*), and in *Giani comincia a cantare* 'G. starts to sing' it is *a cantare* (corresponding to *Gianni canta*).

Comparative – Comparative constructions involve modifications of adjectives or adverbs to indicate, for example, 'more' or 'less' than. . ., or 'as much as. . .' (the latter are called 'comparisons of equality').

Complement – (see 17.1)

Coreferent(ial) – Referring to the same person or entity. Used especially in describing the relation between the subject of a main clause and that of a **subordinate clause**. In *Gianni ha detto che cantava* 'G. said he was singing', the subjects of *ha detto* and *cantava* are 'coreferent' if they both refer to the same individual, *Gianni*, but not coreferent if the subject of *cantava* is a different individual, say *Paolo*.

Demonstrative – A word whose basic function is to locate something in relation to the speaker or addressee. E.g, *questo* 'this' vs. *quello* 'that', *qua* 'here' vs. *là* 'there'.

Determiner – Word, such as the **articles** and the **demonstratives** which limit the range of entities a noun phrase refers to.

Diminutive – Form indicating relative smallness. The suffixes *-ino* and *-etto* are often described as 'diminutives' (e.g., *ragazzino* 'little boy' from *ragazzo*).

Direct Object – (see Object)

Discourse marker – Any element whose function is to indicate the relationship between sentences forming part of a coherent, linked succession of sentences. Such things as *dunque*, or *però*: *Non ha visto nessuno. Dunque ha deciso di partire.* 'He saw nobody. So he decided to leave'; *Mangia molto. Però non ingrassa mai.* 'He eats a lot. Yet he never puts on weight.'

Dislocation – Moving some element of a sentence out of the position it would normally be expected to occupy. For example the position to the left of the verb of the direct object *Gianni* in *Gianni non lo vedo mai* (a case of 'left-dislocation') as opposed to the more 'normal' *Non vedo mai Gianni*, with the object to the right of the verb.

Durative – A durative form of the verb expresses a process normally viewed as unfolding over an appreciable stretch of time.

Elative – Form indicating 'very. . .', 'highly. . .', 'extremely. . .' or 'most. . .'. E.g., the ending *-issimo* in *Era altissimo* 'He was extremely tall'.

Finite – A finite verb-form is one which contains specifications of person, number and tense unlike, say, an infinitive. *Cantate* is finite (2nd person plural present indicative) in *Sento che cantate* 'I can hear that you're singing', but *cantare* is not finite in *Vi sento cantare* 'I hear you sing'.

Gender – Every Italian noun has either masculine or feminine gender, manifested in the form of the **determiner** that a noun takes, the form of the pronouns that represent it, and frequently in the form of modifying adjectives. Although nouns denoting females are usually femine and those denoting males usually masculine, there is often no way of predicting gender from the meaning of a word, and the gender of each noun needs to be learned individually. See 3.9-24.

Gerund – see 14.17, 15.20.

Imperative – Form of the verb used for giving commands, orders, instructions. E.g., *Sii bravo*! 'Be good!', *State attenti* 'Be careful'.

Inalienable – An 'inalienable' possession is an inherent part of some entity, without which that entity may be viewed as incomplete, e.g., *gli occhi* in *Paola apre gli occhi* 'P opens her eyes', as opposed to *il libro che le avevo mandato* in *Paola apre il libro che gli avevo mandato in regalo* 'P opens the book I had sent her as a present.'

Indicative – see 15.25

Indirect Object – see **Object**

Infinitive – non-**finite** form of the verb, ending in Italian in *-re*, and used in dictionaries, etc., as the 'name' or 'citation form' of the verb.

Interjections – Forms that express 'states of mind', and do not form part of larger grammatical constructions. E.g., *Eh?* 'Eh?', 'What?'.

Interrogative – Concerned with asking questions, for example the interrogative **pronoun** *chi?* 'who?', or interrogative sentences such as *Viene Paolo?* 'Is P coming?'

Intransitive (and **transitive**) – A 'transitive' verb is one which is associated with two **nouns** or **noun phrases** one of which is the **direct object**, typically undergoing the action or process expressed by the verb, while the other is the **subject**, which typically expresses the agent, controller or causer of the action or process expressed by the verb. Some typical transitive sentences are: *Il cane* [subject] *morde il gatto* [direct object] 'The dog bites the cat', *Mario* [subject] *apre la porta* [direct object] 'M. opens the door', *Tu* [subject] *guardavi la partita* [direct object] 'You were watching the match'. An 'intransitive' verb, in contrast, is one that has no direct object, and is associated with a single noun which is always the verb's subject: e.g., *Il gatto* [subject] *muore* 'The cat dies', *Paolo* [subject] *piange* 'P is crying', *Le ragazze* [subject] *stavano giocando* 'The girls were playing'.

Noun – A class of words characteristically denoting 'things' or 'notions', and capable of appearing as the subject or object of the verb. E.g., the underlined elements in *Il cane* / *Il vapore* / *La linguistica non fa male* 'The dog / The steam / Linguistics doesn't hurt', or *Odio il cane* / *il vapore* / *la linguistica* 'I hate the dog / the steam / linguistics'.

Noun Phrase – see Phrase

Object – A **noun**, **noun phrase** or **pronoun**, other than the **subject**, which is· involved in or undergoes the state or action expressed by a verb. E.g., the underlined elements in *Paolo vede Gianni* 'P. sees G.', *Gianni adora la matematica* 'G. adores mathematics', *Non li voglio* 'I don't want them'. The preceding examples illustrate 'direct objects'; the 'indirect object' (preceded by the preposition *a*, or represented by the pronouns *gli, le, loro*), typically represents the 'recipient' of some action, to whom/which or to for whom/which the action of the verb takes place. E.g., the underlined elements in *Do il libro a Gianni* 'I give the book to G.', *Lo dico ai ragazzi* 'I say it to the boys', *Le duole un dente* 'A tooth is hurting (to) her'.

Ordinal number – Number in the series *primo* (1st), *secondo* (2nd), *terzo* (3rd), etc.

Participle – name for certain non-**finite** forms of the verb. The past participle is a form of the verb occurring in a variety of constructions with **auxiliary** verbs, and characterized by the endings *-to* or *-so* (see 14.14,15) in the masculine singular. For the so-called 'present participle', see 3.32.

Passive – See 14.30.

Pejorative – A form used to refer to someone or something unfavourably. E.g., the suffix *-accio* in *vinaccio* 'bad, unpleasant wine'.

Person – Category of verbs (and pronouns) indicating speaker or speakers (1st person: e.g., *io parlo, noi parliamo*), addressee or addressees (2nd person: e.g., *tu parli, voi parlate*) or neither (3rd person: e.g., *lui parla, loro parlano*).

Phrase – A 'noun phrase' is a noun taken together with the elements (**articles, demonstratives, adjectives, relative clauses**) which modify it: e.g., the underlined element in *I turisti sono già partiti* 'The tourists have already left', *I turisti svedesi sono già partiti* 'The Swedish tourists have already left', *I turisti svedesi di cui mi hai parlato sono già partiti* 'The Swedish tourists you spoke to me about have already left', *I turisti svedesi simpatici di cui mi hai parlato sono già partiti* 'The nice Swedish tourists you spoke to me about have already left'. Similarly, an adjectival phrase comprises an adjective and its modifiers (usually adverbs): *Era ancora più bello di quanto pensassi* 'It was even more beautiful than I thought.' A 'verb phrase' comprises a verb, together with any or all of auxiliaries, modifying adverbs, and the verb's **complement**. E.g., the underlined elements in *Mario ha cantato bene* 'M. sang well', *Mario ha sempre cantato bene questa canzone* 'M. has always sung this song well.'

Possessive – Form which indicates the relation between a possessor and the thing possessed. See 10.1-7.

Predicative – A 'predicative adjective' represents that property which asserted about some noun, and is usually introduced by a verb such as *essere, diventare, sembrare*. E.g., *Il ragazzo è intelligente* 'The boy is intelligent', *Diventavano stanchi* 'They were becoming tired'.

Prefix – An element added to the beginning of one word forming another word: e.g., *anti* in *anticomunista*.

Preposition – A word that precedes a noun or noun phrase and which typically expresses spatial relations, e.g., *su, con, sotto, senza, contro*. Prominent among prepositions are also *di, a, per*.

Privative – Indicating absence or removal. E.g., the prefix *s-* in *sdentato* 'toothless'.

Productive – The property of permitting the creation of new forms, not heard or written before.

Pronoun – A form used to stand for a noun or noun phrase (e.g., *lui, lei, loro*), or to stand for the participants in discourse (e.g., *io noi tu voi*). The pronominal elements are underlined in *Giorgio vede spesso suo nipote ma <u>noi</u> non <u>lo</u> vediamo mai e non <u>ne</u> parliamo mai* 'G. often sees his grandson but we never see him and never speak about him'. There are also pronouns which stand for a preposition + noun (e.g., *Va spesso a Roma ma noi non <u>ci</u> andiamo mai* 'He often goes to Rome but we never go there'), or for whole clauses (e.g., *Dice di essere stato a Roma, ma <u>ciò</u> mi pare poco probabile* 'He says he's been to Rome but that strikes me as unlikely.'). See Chapter 6.

Proper name – Name of person or place, e.g., *Paolo, Milano*.

Protasis – See 'apodosis'

Quantifier – Any word or expression indicating quantity. E.g., *tutto, poco, alcuni*.

Reciprocal – Constructions of the type 'each other', 'one another': E.g., *Si rispettano l'un l'altro* 'They respect each other'.

Reflexive – Construction in which the **subject** of the verb is seen as carrying out some action on or to itself (e.g., *Mario si lava* 'M. washes himself'). The 'reflexive pronouns' are *si* and *sé*.

Register – Set of linguistic features deliberately used for speaking or writing for particular purposes or in particular contexts. Features pertaining to 'formal' registers might be used in making an official public announcement, an academic address, addressing the President of the Republic, etc., etc.

Relative – A 'relative clause' is a subordinate **clause** which modifies a noun **phrase** or a **pronoun**. It is usually introduced by a 'relative' pronoun, such as *che* 'who/which/that', *il quale*, etc. E.g., *Ho visto entrare l'uomo <u>che conosci</u>* 'I saw the man whom you know come in'. For the distinction between 'restrictive' and 'non-restrictive' relatives, see 7.4.

Rheme – See 17.1

Root – That part of a verb, noun or adjective, minus grammatical endings, which indicates its basic meaning. So the 'roots' of *vedevate, cani* and *gialla* are *ved-, can-* and *giall-*, those parts of the word that carry the meanings 'see', 'dog' and 'yellow'.

Subordinate clause – See 'Clause'

Subject – Noun or noun phrase with which the verb **agrees** in **person** and number. In a **transitive** sentence the subject is typically the agent, causer or controller of the action expressed by the verb. See 'intransitive' above.

Subjunctive – See 15.25.

Suffix – An element added usually to the **root** of one word forming another word. E.g., *giallastro* 'yellowish' from *giallo*.

Superlative – Grammatical form expressing 'the most. . .', 'the . . .est': *Mario è il più alto* 'M. is the tallest.'

Tense – The tenses are forms of the **verb** associated with the time, in relation to the time of speaking, at which the event expressed by the verb occurs. E.g., 'present tense' *parlo* 'I'm speaking', 'past tense' *ho parlato*, 'future tense' *parlerò*. It is perfectly possible, however, for tense-forms to indicate times other than those suggested by their grammatical label. So 'present tense' *dico* in *Te lo dico domani* 'I'll tell you tomorrow' actually refers to future time.

Theme – See 'Rheme'

Transitive – See 'intransitive'

Verb – A class of words typically indicating actions, states or processes (e.g., *cantare* 'to sing', *rimanere* 'to remain', *dormire* 'to sleep', *invecchiare* 'to grow old'), with forms indicating **tense**, **person** and so forth. Italian verbs are normally cited in dictionaries, etc., in the **infinitive** form, ending in *-re*.

Verb phrase – See 'Phrase'

1

Introduction

This book aims to provide a comprehensive work of reference for learners of Italian whose native language is English, or who possess a very good knowledge of English. It is not intended as a course in Italian grammar, but it is meant to be accessible to all learners of Italian, whatever their level of knowledge of the language. So a beginner who needs to check the distinction between the forms of the article *il* and *lo* should find this book as useful as an advanced learner who is interested, say, in the finer points of use of the subjunctive. The fact that we are aiming at English-speaking learners means that we do not usually comment on those aspects of Italian grammar which happen to be identical to English, and over which an English-speaking learner is unlikely ever to make a mistake; thus, for example, while we mention that it is possible in Italian, unlike English, to form adverbs from certain adjectives of nationality (e.g., *italianamente*), we do not bother to state that in Italian one cannot form adverbs from adjectives of colour (*giallamente) – for no more can one say 'yellowly' in English.

A 'reference grammar' should, precisely, facilitate 'reference', so this grammar has a detailed index and list of contents. In the latter, section headings are designed, as far as possible, to give the user a clear idea of what the section deals with, often including brief examples of the type of structure involved, with English translation where appropriate. On the whole, the meaning of grammatical terminology, if unfamiliar, should be obvious from the illustrative examples but, where necessary, explanatory notes have been given. There is also extensive cross-referencing within the text, a fact which should help obviate some of the problems of organization which can affect works of this kind: it is debatable, for example, whether a section on 'negative adverbs' should appear in the chapter on adverbs or in the chapter on negatives, but this should matter little so long as there is good cross-referencing between the two.

We have tried to give ample exemplification of the grammatical points discussed and, to avoid the monotony of invented examples in the *'plume de ma tante'* tradition, we have taken as many as possible from current newspapers, magazines, from novels, political, historical, sociological and scientific works and from radio and television broadcasts. We have also made use of the database of contemporary Italian literature available on the Internet at *www.alice.it*. We have not, however, felt it necessary to give the source of each example, except for cases where we believe that the source may have some real bearing on the grammatical structure at issue, and for passages which constitute substantial quotations from literary works or whose content is, taken out of context, so striking that readers might actually wish to see the original. Virtually all examples have been translated (by Maiden) into English, in as natural and idiomatic a way as is compatible with illustrating the grammatical point in question.

There are some 'grey areas' between what should be contained in a dictionary and what should be contained in a grammar. A good example of this appears in Chapter 20, on word formation: a comprehensive account of the semantic and structural idiosyncrasies of word formation is beyond the scope of a reference grammar, and one can do little more than indicate some of the problems and structures associated with word formation. Arguably, Chapters 12 (on numerals) and 21 (on time expressions), barely belong in a 'grammar' at all, but the inclusion of such things (apparently on the grounds that, like morphological paradigms, they often constitute closed sets of forms) is a time-honoured tradition, and we make no exception here.

As far as we have been able, we have attempted to bear in mind potentially significant differences at least between United States English and British English. We apologize in advance to readers in other parts of the Anglophone world, if we have labelled as 'British', or 'United States', usages which are actually more widespread, or have neglected to mention features of English in other parts of the world which might be relevant to learners of Italian in those places.

The differences between varieties of English are much less dramatic than those between varieties of Italian. The 'Italian language' (based on a late-medieval form of just one of the dialects of Italy, that of Florence) was for many centuries primarily a written language and chiefly the preserve of intellectuals. The adoption of Italian as a versatile everyday language by the mass of the population is really a phenomenon of the twentieth century. The dialects which until recently were the native speech of Italians were often so profoundly different from Italian (and from each other) as to constitute 'different languages', and these differences have left their mark on the way in which the Italian language is used in different regions of Italy.[1] This reference grammar makes no attempt at a systematic account of the regional varieties of Italian but points out some of the more salient regional differences which might be encountered in the speech or writing of educated speakers of Italian. There are also considerable differences of register between the kind of Italian used in formal discourse (such as making a public address, academic or bureaucratic writing, etc.) and informal (particularly spoken) usage. It is simply beyond the scope of this book to give a detailed characterization of such differences, but we have attempted where possible to point out major differences between formal and informal discourse, as far as they impinge on grammatical structure.

This book is the joint work of both authors. However, Martin Maiden is principally responsible for Chapters 2, 3, 4, 5, 6 (1–28, 37–38), 7, 8, 9, 10, 11, 12, 13, 14 (1–24), 15 (1–11, 17–57), 16, 20 and 21, and the glossary, and Cecilia Robustelli for Chapters 6 (29–36), 14 (25–35), 15 (12–17), 17, 18, 19 and 22.

Many native speakers and/or specialists in Italian linguistics have been consulted – some of them will feel that they have been pestered – in the preparation

---

[1]Brief accounts of the historical and dialect background (with suggestions for further reading) appear in Part One of Lepschy and Lepschy (1988), Maiden (1995, Chapters 1 and 3), and the articles under 'Italy' variously by Benincà, Maiden, Parry and Vanelli, in Price (1998: 251–76).

of this book. A complete list of names would be lengthy, but our thanks go to all of them. Among those who have particularly gone out of their way to be helpful, we should like to mention Michela Cennamo, Roberta Middleton, Anna Morpurgo Davies and Nigel Vincent. But our greatest debt of gratitude goes to Giulio Lepschy, who has patiently and painstakingly commented on a large part of this book, making countless acute suggestions for improving it. The authors alone are responsible for the defects of this grammar, but many of its strengths are due to Giulio.

Martin Maiden
Cecilia Robustelli

e-mail: martin.maiden@mod-langs.ox.ac.uk
uhlj004@lara.rhbnc.ac.uk

2

Spelling and pronunciation

2.1 The relationship between letters and sounds

The relationship between Italian letters and the sounds they represent is relatively straightforward. By and large, one letter corresponds to one sound, and vice versa. But there are also respects in which this relationship is less transparent and, in certain cases, highly unpredictable. Sections 2 to 6 throw some light on these more problematic areas. Pronunciation, and especially that part of pronunciation which is not unambiguously indicated by spelling, is a domain in which standardization of Italian is at its weakest and most fluid: even educated speakers vary considerably from region to region and deviation from a norm which is based, historically, on Tuscan, and particularly Florentine, pronunciation, is widespread and often perfectly acceptable. After all, only a minority of Italians are Tuscan, leave alone Florentine (and there are differences in the pronunciation of standard Italian even within Tuscany), and although some general rules can be supplied for the pronunciation of the notoriously ambiguous letters *e*, *o*, *s* and *z*, to know the notionally 'correct' pronunciations of these one often has to learn them word-by-word from a good dictionary, or ask a Tuscan. One may agree with the many Italians who feel that there is no reason to insist rigidly on a model of pronunciation based historically on Florentine, but for the benefit of those who feel that they want a model to imitate, we give in what follows some guidelines reflecting that model (while also giving some general indications about other regional variations). For further information on regional variation see particularly Lepschy and Lepschy (1988: Chapter 4), Maiden (1995: 229–57).

2.2 The letters c, (q), g, h, i, u

C and *g* are pronounced [k] and [g] except when immediately followed by *i* or *e*, in which case they are pronounced [tʃ] and [dʒ] (*cc* and *gg* are correspondingly pronounced [ttʃ] and [ddʒ]). In the same circumstances, the combination *sc* is pronounced [ʃ] ([ʃʃ] between two vowels).

caro ['karo]	'dear'	*pago* ['pago]	'I pay'
dica ['dika]	'let him say'	*fugga* ['fugga]	'let him flee'
lacuna [la'kuna]	'lacuna'	*anguria* [aŋ'gurja]	'water melon'
nasco ['nasko]	'I am born'	*sguardo* ['zgwardo]	'look'
scuro ['skuro]	'dark'	*sgarbo* ['zgarbo]	'discourtesy'
etc.			

cito ['tʃito]	'I cite'	*giro* ['dʒiro]	'tour'
dice ['ditʃe]	'he says'	*fugge* ['fuddʒe]	'he flees'
concedi [kon'tʃɛdi]	'you concede'	*argilla* [ar'dʒilla]	'clay'
nasce ['naʃʃe]	'she is born'		
scemo ['ʃemo]	'silly'	*sgelo* ['zdʒɛlo]	'thaw'
etc.			

The sound [kw] is usually written *qu* (*quando, quiete, quota*, etc.), but note *cuore* ['kwɔre], *cuoco* ['kwɔko], *scuola* ['skwɔla]. Long [kkw] is always spelled *cqu* (*acqua, piacque*), with the sole exception of *soqquadro* (in *mettere a soqquadro* 'to turn upside down', 'make chaotic').

How does one write the *sounds* [ki], [ke] and [gi], [ge], given that *ci, ce, gi, ge* have a different value? The solution is to add *h* after *c* and *g*. This *h* is a 'diacritic' letter, having no pronunciation of its own, but simply serving to indicate that preceding *c, g* are pronounced [k], [g]. Note that the letter *k* is rarely used, and restricted to a few words borrowed from other languages (e.g. *kepì, karaoke, karaokista*): one does occasionally encounter spellings such as *kilo, kilometro, kerosene*, but *chilo, chilometro, cherosene* are preferred.

chilo ['kilo]	'kilo'
stanchi ['staŋki]	'tired' (pl. of *stanco*)
pescherò [peske'rɔ]	'I'll fish' (future of *pescare*)
scherzo ['skɛrtso]	'joke'
bianchiccio [bjaŋ'kittʃo]	'whitish' (from *bianco*)
ghiro ['giro]	'dormouse'
paghi ['pagi]	'you pay' (2sg. of *pagare*)
pagherò [page'rɔ]	'I'll pay' (future of *pagare*)
sghignazzare [zgiɲɲat'tsare]	'sneer'
laghetto [la'getto]	'little lake' (from *lago*)
etc.	

The letter *h* has three other uses: it is written (but not pronounced) in the singular and third person plural present indicative of *avere*: *ho, hai, ha, hanno*, and thereby serves to distinguish these words from *o* 'or', *ai* 'to the', *a* 'to', *anno* 'year'. It appears in certain exclamations, such as *ehi! ahi!, mah!*, where the *h* corresponds to a frequently audible glottal catch or a slight aspiration (approximately [maʔ] to express surprise, and [mah] or [maː] for casual indifference), also *boh!* [bɔʔ] for surprise or indifference; laughter is conventionally written *ah ah!* but pronounced [ha ha]. *H* also appears in words imported from foreign languages (particularly English, e.g., *hobby, handicap, hacker*), where it may be pronounced if speakers attempt to reproduce the pronunciation of the source language, but usually is not.

The combination *gn* is pronounced [ɲ] ([ɲɲ] between vowels): *gnomo* 'gnome' ['ɲɔmo], *ragno* 'spider' ['raɲɲo]; the combination *gn* + unstressed *i* (for example in the subjunctive *sogniate* vs. indicative *sognate*) is also pronounced [ɲɲ]. *Gl*, when followed by the letter *i*, is pronounced [ʎ] ([ʎʎ] between vowels): *gli* [ʎi] 'to him', *figlia* 'daughter' ['fiʎʎa], except that it is always [gl] at the *beginning* of a word (apart from the pronoun *gli*):[1]

---

[1] Another exception is *gliommero* ['ʎommero], an archaic type of verse form. But the word is so little used (and so little known) that even highly educated speakers, on seeing the written form, tend to say ['gljommero].

glicine ['gliʧine]	'wisteria'
glicerina [gliʧe'rina]	'glycerine'
glissando [glis'sando]	'glissando'

Gl is also pronounced [gl] inside a few other words, e.g.:

anglicano [aŋgli'kano]	'Anglican'
geroglifico [ʤero'glifiko]	'hieroglyphic'
ganglio ['gaŋgljo]	'ganglion'

The letter *i* is always [i], except when it *does not represent a stressed vowel and is immediately followed by a vowel*. In this case, unstressed *i* is usually pronounced [j] (but see below), but is generally *not pronounced at all* if it is immediately preceded by *c, g, sc, gl* (where *gl* = [ʎ] – see above):

odiavo [o'djavo]	'I hated'	*più* [pju]	'more'
siamo ['sjamo]	'we are'	*chiaro* ['kjaro]	'clear'
etc.			

già [ʤa]	'already'	*scià* [ʃa]	'shah'
faccio ['faʧo]	'I do'	*aglio* ['aʎʎo]	'garlic'
etc.			

Likewise, the sequences *gi, gni,* and *gli* which appear in first person plural present and second person plural present subjunctive verb forms such as *mangiamo, mangiate; sogniamo, sogniate; cogliamo, cogliate* are usually pronounced, respectively, [ʤ, ɲɲ, ʎʎ]: thus [man'ʤamo, man'ʤate; soɲ'ɲamo, soɲ'ɲate; koʎ'ʎamo, koʎ'ʎate], even though the relevant endings are pronounced ['jamo, 'jate] in other verbs. In all these cases, *i* is simply another 'diacritic' letter, which serves to indicate that the preceding *g, c, sc, gl* are pronounced [ʤ, ʧ, ʃ, ʎ].

In some words an *i* followed by a vowel may occur both stressed and unstressed, for example when the *i* is part of the root of a verb, and carries stress in the singular persons and third person plural of the present, but not elsewhere. In such cases, the unstressed *i* tends also to be pronounced [i] (i.e., it retains the same vowel quality as when it is stressed).

scio ['ʃio]	'I ski'	*spio* ['spio]	'I spy'
scii ['ʃii]		*spii* ['spii]	
scia ['ʃia]		*spia* ['spia]	
sciano ['ʃiano]		*spiano* ['spiano]	

sciavo [ʃi'avo]	'I skied'	*spiavo* [spi'avo]	'I spied'
scierò [ʃie'rɔ]	'I'll ski'	*spierò* [spie'rɔ]	'I'll spy'
sciando [ʃi'ando]	'skiing'	*spiando* [spi'ando]	'spying'
etc.			

The same principle sometimes applies to nouns, where *i* becomes unstressed as the result of adding a stressed suffix:

via ['via]	*viuzza* [vi'utsa]	'alley'
Pio ['pio]	*piano* [pi'ano]	(pertaining to Pius)
etc.		

Prefixes ending in unstressed *-i* normally retain [i], even when a vowel follows:

antiaerea [antia'ɛrea]	'anti-aircraft'
semiaperto [semia'pɛrto]	'half open'

If *i* is preceded by *sc-*, *c-* or *g-*, and followed by an *e* which is part of an inflectional ending (such as feminine plural *-e* or future and conditional tense *-er-*), then the *i* must be omitted in verbs, and may be omitted in nouns and adjectives:

baciare	*bacerò*	'I shall kiss'
mangiare	*mangerei*	'I would eat'
lancia	*lance* (or *lancie*)	'lances'
valigia	*valigie* (or *valige*)	'suitcases'

The plural spellings *-cie* and *-gie* are preferred after a vowel, while *-ce* and *-ge* are strongly preferred after a consonant. The *i* is never written after *c* and *g* before the suffixes *-etto* and *-ese*:

lancia	*lancetta*	'small lance', 'hand of clock'
Francia	*francese*	'French'
etc.		

A particular problem arises where unstressed *i* is followed by another unstressed *i*. This is a situation which potentially occurs 'across morpheme boundaries', e.g., where the root of a word ends in unstressed *i* and a following inflection begins with unstressed *i*. One might predict that the result would be pronounced [ji], but *[ji] does not exist in Italian, and the actual pronunciation is [i]. The spelling is therefore normally a single *i* so that the plural of *studio* (plural ending *i*) and the second person singular/present subjunctive of *studiare* (inflection *i*) are usually spelled: *gli studi, tu studi, che studi, che studino, studiamo, che studiate*. In more old-fashioned spellings one may however encounter, in the plural of nouns and adjectives, the types *studii, studî* (the only case where one finds a circumflex accent in Italian spelling) or the now extremely rare *studj* or *studij*. Note that if the first *i* is stressed, the pronunciation is ['ii] and the spelling is accordingly *ii*: *scii* ['ʃii], *sciino* ['ʃiino]; but in those verbs (see above) where *i* remains [i] even when unstressed and followed by a vowel, the pronunciation is [i], and the spelling is always a single *i*: *sciamo* [ʃi'amo], *spiate* [spi'at e], etc.

Some of what is said here for *i* is also true for the letter *u*, which is usually pronounced [w] when unstressed and followed by a vowel: *suora* ['swɔra] 'nun', *sguardo* ['zgwardo] 'look', *quale?* ['kwale] 'which?', etc. But in certain words the *u* tends to be pronounced [u]: e.g., *lacuale* [laku'ale], 'pertaining to lakes', *arcuato* [arku'ato] 'arch shaped', *acuità* [akui'ta] 'acuity'.

2.3 The letters e and o

E and *o* present few problems in unstressed syllables, where they are generally [e] and [o] (but see 2.11). A difficulty arises in stressed syllables, where they may have either the value [e], [o] ('closed mid vowels') or [ɛ], [ɔ] ('open mid vowels'). This distinction is not indicated in spelling (e.g., *venti* ['venti] '20', *botte* ['botte] 'barrel' vs. *venti* ['vɛnti] 'winds', *botte* ['bɔtte] 'blows'), except for *e* [e] 'and' vs. *è* [ɛ] 'is'. Very many native speakers of Italian do not systematically make the distinctions between these vowels (except *e* vs. *è*) as prescribed by more conservative grammars, and based on central Italian (particularly Florentine) pronunciation. Indeed it has been argued[2] that learners should not be required to

---

[2] See Lepschy (1964); also Lepschy and Lepschy (1988: 90).

acquire these distinctions, and the foreign learner is hardly ever likely to be misunderstood for using the 'wrong' vowel. But a problem for those who aim to achieve an authentically 'native speaker' pronunciation of Italian is that it is not the case that outside Tuscany and central Italy the closed-mid and open-mid vowel qualities can simply be used indifferently. Some areas prefer the open value (e.g., Sicily), but in most both vowel qualities exist yet are distributed according to different criteria from Florentine: for example, in many northern varieties the open vowels tend to occur in syllables which end in a consonant, and the closed vowels in other stressed syllables (this especially where [e] and [ɛ] are concerned); in Sardinia we have [ɔ] and [ɛ], except that [o] and [e] occur if and only if the following syllable contains the vowel [i]. For the benefit of those who would like to conform to the Florentine-based model, the following are some general guidelines. It should be borne in mind that, for the most part, there is no way of knowing which pronunciation these vowels have, short of consulting a good dictionary, asking a Tuscan, or consulting a manual such as Canepari (1992: 100–8).

- If *o* is followed by a nasal consonant *n* or *m* which is followed in turn by another consonant, it will always be [o]: *ponte* ['ponte] 'bridge', *compra* ['kompra] 'he buys', *vongola* ['voŋgola] 'clam' (*nn* is an exception: *donna* ['dɔnna] 'woman', *gonna* ['gɔnna] or ['gonna] 'skirt').
- Stressed -*ò* at the end of a word is always pronounced [ɔ]: *porterò* [porte'rɔ] 'I'll carry', *oblò* [o'blɔ] 'porthole'.
- In the stressed diphthongs *ie* and *uo* the *e* and *o* are *usually* open: *viene* ['vjɛne] 'she comes', *fiero* ['fjɛro] 'proud', *vuole* ['vwɔle] 'he wants', *cuore* ['kwɔre] 'the heart', etc.
- As a broad generalization, *e* and *o* will be pronounced *open* in words which belong to the sphere of 'learned', 'religious', 'scientific', 'technical', 'intellectual' vocabulary. The relevant words frequently have easily recognizable counterparts in other languages, such as English: *elettrico* [e'lɛttriko] 'electric', *filosofo* [fi'lɔzofo] 'philosopher', *il credo* [il 'krɛdo] 'the creed', *elicottero* [eli'kɔttero] 'helicopter', *eccetera* [et'ʧɛtera] 'etcetera', etc. The fact that stressed *e* and *o* are pronounced [ɛ] and [ɔ] when followed by 'single consonant + unstressed *i* + vowel': *Antonio* [an'tɔnjo], *astemio* [as'tɛmjo] 'abstemious', etc., arises because 'single consonant + unstressed *i* + vowel' happen characteristically to belong to 'erudite' vocabulary.
- Clues may also be available from related English and modern Italian words, originally 'borrowed' from Latin,[3] which contain *i* and *u*:

vetro ['vetro]	*vitreous*	*molto* ['molto]	*multitude*
	vitreo		
capello [ka'pello]	*capillary*	*corrotto* [kor'rotto]	*corrupt*
	capillare		*corruzione*
legno ['leɲɲo]	*ligneous*	*corro* ['korro]	*current*
	ligneo		

---

[3] A knowledge of Latin itself is helpful, since Latin words containing stressed short *i* and *u*, or long *e* and *o*, generally show closed mid vowels [e] and [o] in Italian, whilst Latin words in short *e* and *o* usually have [ɛ] and [ɔ] in Italian. For details see, for example, Maiden (1995: 28–30).

meno ['meno]   *m<u>i</u>nus*   *prodotto* [pro'dotto]   *prod<u>u</u>ction*
                                                                 produ<u>z</u>ione
    etc.

In compound words made up of two independent words, or whose first element has 'autonomous secondary stress' (see 2.11), the vowels [ɛ] and [ɔ] may occur, even if they are not part of the primary stressed element:

perditempo [ˌpɛrdi'tɛmpo]   'time-waster'
portachiavi [ˌpɔrta'kjavi]   'key ring'
elettromagnetico [eˌlɛttromaɲ'ɲɛtiko] 'electromagnetic'
eterosessuale [ˌɛteroses'swale]   'heterosexual'
tossicodipendente [ˌtɔssikodipen'dɛnte] 'drug addict'

2.4 The letters *s* and *z*

The letter *s* has two pronunciations, [s] and [z]. With two kinds of exception, *s* is pronounced [s] (e.g., *sano* ['sano] 'healthy', *spacco* ['spakko] 'I split'). Immediately before a voiced consonant, however, it is always [z]: *smetto* ['zmetto] 'I stop', *slitta* ['zlitta] 'sled', *snervato* [zner'vato] 'nerveless', *sbudellare* [zbudel'lare] 'disembowel', *sdentato* [zden'tato] 'toothless', *svenire* [zve'nire] 'faint', *sregolato* [zrego'lato] 'unruly'. The pronunciation of *s* <u>inside a word and flanked on either side by vowels</u>, is more problematic, at least for learners wishing to reproduce the Florentine-based model of pronunciation prescribed by conservative grammars. In this pronunciation, *s* between vowels usually stands for [s] (e.g., *naso* ['naso] 'nose', *cosa* ['kɔsa] 'thing', *chiese* ['kjɛse] 's/he asked', *inglese* [iŋ'glese] 'English' and most words in *-ese*, *fuso* ['fuso] 'spindle'), but in certain, unpredictable, cases, it may be [z]: e.g., *fuso* ['fuzo] 'melted', *chiese* ['kjɛze] 'churches', *francese* [fran'tʃeze] 'French'. There is little alternative to consulting a good dictionary or a native Tuscan to establish the correct pronunciation but, as a rule of thumb, (cf. 2.3), it is the sphere of 'learned', 'scientific', 'technical', 'intellectual', and religious, vocabulary in which [z]-pronunciations tend to prevail: e.g., *psicosi* [psi'kɔzi] 'psychosis', *filosofo* [fi'lɔzofo] 'philosopher', *quaresima* [kwa'rɛzima] 'Lent', *Gesù* [dʒe'zu] 'Jesus', *crisi* ['krizi] 'crisis'. Alternatively, word-internal *s* between vowels may be pronounced [z] in all cases (normal in northern Italy, and generally gaining ground as a prestigious pronunciation), or [s] in all cases (normal in southern Italy, but less prestigious). *S* should be pronounced [s] in compound words where it is the first letter of the second element: e.g., *semiserio* [semi'sɛrjo] 'half serious', *risalutare* [risalu'tare] 'to greet again'. See further Canepari (1992: 109–11).

The letter *z* also has two pronunciations, [ts] and [dz]. There is a strong and growing tendency to pronounce *z* as [dz] at the beginning of a word, even where the traditional Tuscan pronunciation would be [ts] (e.g., *zio* ['dzio] 'uncle', *zuppa* ['dzuppa] 'soup'). But, inside the word, pronunciation is highly unpredictable. The usual pronunciation is [ts], but [dz] is often found, especially in words which belong to the sphere of 'learned', 'religious', 'scientific', 'technical', 'intellectual' vocabulary. Thus: *azoto* [ad'dzɔto] 'nitrogen', *romanzo* [ro'mandzo] 'novel', *zebra* ['ʣɛbra], *zoologo* [ʣo'ɔlogo] 'zoologist', all verbs[4] in *-izzare* (e.g., [realid'ʣare]). Note also *pranzo* ['prandʒo] 'lunch', *mezzo* ['mɛdʣo] 'half'.

2.5 Spelling and pronunciation of 'double' consonants

In general, written double consonants stand for phonologically long pronunciations: *pala* ['pala] 'spade' vs. *palla* ['palla] 'ball', *cane* ['kane] 'dog' vs. *canne* ['kanne] 'reeds', etc. But certain letters and combinations of letters always represent long consonants when they occur between two vowels; this applies both inside words and at the beginnings of words:

- Both *z* and *zz* represent a long consonant (each can be either [tts] or [dʣ]) when written between vowels: there is no distinction of pronunciation between them, and single [ts] or [dʒ] never occur between vowels: *spazzi* ['spattsi] 'you sweep', *spazi* ['spattsi] 'spaces', *realizzazione* [realidʣat'tsjone] 'realization', etc. Also *la zebra* [la d'ʣebra] 'the zebra', *lo zoologo* [lo dʣo'ɔlogo] 'the zoologist', *la zia* [la t'tsia] 'the aunt'.
- *gn* is always [ɲɲ] between vowels: *ragno* ['raɲɲo] 'spider', *lo gnomo* [lo ɲ'ɲɔmo] 'the gnome'.
- *gli* is [ʎʎ] between vowels (but see 2.2 for the pronunciation [gl]): *aglio* ['aʎʎo] 'garlic', *sceglieva* [ʃeʎ'ʎeva] 'she chose'.
- *sc* + *e/i* is always [ʃʃ] between vowels: *pesce* ['peʃʃe] 'fish', *la sceglie* [la ʃ'ʃeʎʎe] 'he chooses it', *lascia* ['laʃʃa] 'he leaves'.

2.6 Lengthening of consonants at the beginning of words: *rafforzamento (fono)sintattico*

There is a major and systematic feature of Italian pronunciation which is almost never represented in writing, and tends therefore to be neglected by non-natives. This is so-called 'syntactic doubling', variously known in Italian as *raddoppiamento sintattico, rafforzamento sintattico, rafforzamento fonosintattico*. *Rafforzamento fonosintattico* (henceforth RF) is a phenomenon whereby a consonant at the beginning of a word receives a 'double', or a little more accurately a 'lengthened', pronunciation when preceded by certain other words within the same phrase. This occurs principally when the immediately preceding word (including all monosyllabic verb forms, monosyllabic nouns, monosyllabic adverbs, monosyllabic numerals and monosyllabic pronouns of all kinds other than clitics) *ends in a stressed vowel*:

città persa [tʃit'ta p'pɛrsa]	'lost city'
Sarà bello. [sa'ra b'bɛllo]	'It'll be nice.'
Che fai? [ke f'fai]	'What are you doing?'
Chi sei? ['ki s'sɛi]	'Who are you?'
Ciò ti piace. ['tʃɔ tti 'pjatʃe]	'You like that.'
A me la mandi? [a m'me l'la 'mandi]	'Are you sending it to <u>me</u>?'
le cose che fai [le 'kɔse ke f'fai]	'the things that you are doing'
lunedì prossimo [lune'di p'prɔssimo]	'next Monday'

---

[4]Except *rizzare* [rit'tsare] 'to stand up, on end'.

colibrì blu [koli'bri b'blu]	'blue humming bird'
già preparato ['ʤa pprepa'rato]	'already prepared'
oblò chiuso [o'blɔ k'kjuso]	'closed porthole'
Parlò forte. [par'lɔ f'fɔrte]	'He talked loudly.'
caffè turco [kaf'fɛ t'turko]	'Turkish coffee'
virtù naturale [vir'tu nnatu'rale]	'natural virtue'
gnu selvatico ['ɲu ssel'vatiko]	'wild gnu'
più grosso ['pju g'grɔsso]	'larger'
qui sotto ['kwi s'sotto]	'down here'
scià morto ['ʃa m'mɔrto]	'dead shah'
tre giorni ['tre d'ʤorni]	'three days'
Va bene. ['va b'bɛne]	'It goes well.'
Ho fame. ['ɔ f'fame]	'I'm hungry.'
È vero. ['ɛ v'vero]	'It's true.'

Note that RF does NOT operate in the following circumstances:

- At the beginning of words where a consonant is immediately followed by another consonant (e.g., *ho studiato* ['ɔ stu'djato] 'I've studied'; *a psicologi* [a psi'kɔloʤi] 'to psychologists'); but if the second consonant is [r] or [l], RF applies (e.g., *è troppo* ['ɛ t'trɔppo] 'it's too much', *è fluido* ['ɛ f'fluido] 'it's fluid').
- After the stressed diphthongs *ai, au, ei, eu, oi, ui* (e.g., *lui viene* ['lui 'vjɛne] 'he comes', *poi parto* ['poi 'parto] 'then I leave').
- After words ending in stressed vowel + apostrophe (e.g., *un po' caldo* [um 'pɔ 'kaldo] 'a bit hot'); this category includes notably those monosyllabic second person singular imperatives[5] written with an apostrophe (see 14.9) (e.g., *sta' fermo* ['sta 'fermo] 'stand still', *va' sotto* ['va 'sotto] 'go under', *di' la parola* ['di la pa'rɔla]).

RF is further caused by the prepositions and conjunctions *a, come, da, dove, e, fra/tra, ma, né, o, sopra, su,* and by the words *se* ('if'), *che* 'that' (complementizer) and *qualche* 'some':

a me [a m'me]	'to me'
Vedo che vieni. ['vedo ke v'vjɛni]	'I see that you are coming.'
come lui ['kome l'lui]	'like him'
da capo [da k'kapo]	'from the start'
Dove vai? ['dove v'vai]	'Where are you going?'
io e te ['io e tte]	'I and you'
ma sai [ma s'sai]	'but you know'
né Mario né Luigi [ne m'marjo ne l'lwiʤi]	'neither M nor L'
me o lui ['me o l'lui]	'me or him'
qualche volta ['kwalke v'vɔlta]	'sometimes'
Se canti. [se k'kanti]	'If you sing.'
sopra Milano ['sopra mmi'lano]	'over Milan'

Note that *come* meaning 'like', 'as' causes RF when followed by a noun phrase or a pronoun or an adjective, but not when followed by a verb phrase, an adverb phrase or a conjunction:

---

[5]It is a nice object lesson in the extent to which the rules of RF can vary regionally that one of the authors of this book (Robustelli, herself a Tuscan) reports that in her speech RF *does* occur after these imperatives (as it also does after *come,* regardless of what follows. In contrast, RF does not occur for her after *sopra.*

come me ['kome m'me]   'like me'
come sindaco ['kome s'sindako]   'as mayor'
come tanti altri ['kome t'tanti'altri]   'like so many others'

but

come fai ['kome 'fai]   'as you do'
come se fosse ['kome se f'fosse]   'as if it were'
come già ti dissi ['kome 'dʒa tti 'dissi]   'as I already told you'

The word *Dio*, with its plural *dei* (see 3.6) and feminine *dea, dee*, undergoes RF *whenever it is preceded by a vowel*, stressed or unstressed. The double consonant appears to have its origin in *Iddio*, a Tuscan form (also sometimes encountered in the standard language) derived historically from *il Dio*.

Parla di Dio. ['parla di d'dio]   'He speaks of God.'
gli dei [ʎi d'dɛi]   'the gods'
queste dee ['kweste d'dɛe]   'these godesses'

Note also *Spirito Santo* often pronounced ['spirit o s'sant o] 'Holy Spirit'. For many speakers, monosyllabic names of letters of the alphabet also trigger RF: e.g., *la P* [la p'pi], *due C* ['due t'tʃi].

RF may impinge upon spelling if a word triggering RF and the following word undergoing it are written as a single word. In this case, the long consonant generally appears as a double consonant in spelling. Included here are certain prefixes (*contra-, sovra-*), and monosyllabic second person singular imperatives followed by clitic pronouns (see 6.3):

contraddire   'contradict'
dappoco   'worthless'
daccapo   'from the beginning'
frapporre   'interpose'
giacché   'since', 'because' (*già* + *che*)
il daffarsi   'what is to be done' (*da* + *farsi*)
piucchepperfetto   'pluperfect' (*più* + *che* + *perfetto*)
sebbene   'although'
sennò   'if not', 'otherwise'
soprattutto   'above all'
sovrapporre   'superimpose'
sovrapprezzo   'surcharge'
vabbene   'OK'
Fallo.   'Do it.'
Vattene.   'Go away.'
Dimmi.   'Say to me.'
Stacci.   'Stay there.'
etc.

Exceptions are *tremila* '3000' and *trecento* '300' which show RF neither in spelling nor in pronunciation. The spellings *piuccheperfetto, sopratutto, sovraprezzo* are also possible.

For a more detailed account of RF and its regional variants, see Canepari (1992: 138f.).

Mention should also be made of lengthening at the *end* of words. Words (usually borrowed from foreign languages) which end in a consonant, especially if they are stressed on the final syllable, often lengthen their final consonant when the following word begins with a vowel: e.g., *tram elettrico* ['tramm e'lɛttriko] 'electric tram', *radar egiziano* ['radarr edʒit'sjano] 'Egyptian radar', *ras etiopico* ['rass e'tjɔpiko] 'Ethiopian chieftain'.

2.7 The type *Isvizzera* for *Svizzera*

In old Italian, words beginning with *s* + consonant sometimes developed an *i* in front of the *s* (e.g., *istrada, ispalla, iscuola, Isvizzera*). Such pronunciations are now considered archaic, but are sometimes still encountered in phrases such as *in Isvizzera* 'in Switzerland', *per isbaglio* 'by mistake', etc.

2.8 Optional removal of final unstressed vowels: *aver fatto* vs. *avere fatto*, etc.

Unstressed vowels at the ends of words may optionally be omitted if (a) they are preceded by a vowel + the consonants *r, n, l* and sometimes *m* and (b) they are not at the end of a sentence or followed by a pause. It is difficult to give precise rules for such omission of the vowel (for the obligatory deletion of the final vowel of infinitives followed by clitics, see 6.3), but it tends to occur particularly in the following circumstances:

- In infinitives of auxiliary verbs followed by participles or infinitives:

Mi esprimeva infinita gratitudine per aver cantato il dramma del suo popolo.	'He expressed infinite gratitude to me for having sung the drama of his people.'
Non ti far vedere.	'Don't show yourself.'

The following example is interesting because although the final *-e* is omitted before the first two participles it is not before the third, probably because the words *nato cristiano* are a quotation and are therefore preceded by a slight pause:

Dopo aver ammesso di aver detto in passato di essere «nato cristiano . . .»	'After having admitted having said in the past that he had been "born a Christian . . ."'

- Where the infinitive forms a 'set phrase' with the element that follows it. What constitutes a 'set phrase' is a little difficult to define, but they are frequently combinations of infinitive and its complement which are potentially expressible by a single word in English, such as *dar lavoro* 'employ', *far finta* 'pretend', *portar via* 'remove', and cases where the complement is very frequently encountered after the infinitive in question:

Sono serviti a dar lavoro a centinaia di persone.	'They served to employ hundreds of people.'
Ma non si può far finta che non sia successo nulla.	'But we can't pretend nothing's happened.'
Senza pronunciar parola, diede ai ragazzi ciò che avevano chiesto.	'Without saying a word, he gave the boys what they'd asked for.'
Difatti Pin faticava a tener gli occhi aperti.	'Indeed P was having trouble keeping his eyes open.'
Mi voleva portar via anche i mobili.	'He even wanted to take away my furniture.'

- Virtually always in titles in -*re*, when they are followed by a name: *signore, professore, ingegnere*, but *il signor Rossi* 'Mr Rossi' (*signore*), *il professor Coletti* 'Professor Coletti' (*professore*), *l'ingegner Prodi* 'engineer Prodi'. But the final vowel is often retained in the usage of southern Italians (*il professore Coletti*, etc.).
- The -*o* of the third person plural verb forms is always deleted in the (nowadays rare) circumstances in which they are followed by a clitic (e.g., *Vendonsi libri* 'Books for sale' – see also 6.17). In other cases, such deletion is now restricted almost entirely to poetic or deliberately archaizing language. But deletion of the final -*o* of *hanno* and *sono* is characteristic, also, of informal spoken language (e.g., *Han detto di no* 'They said not', *Son tutti rossi* 'They are all red', etc.).

In general, deletion of the final vowel tends to convey an elevated and somewhat old-fashioned tone:

È stata la maggior tragedia di tutta questa storia.	'It was the greatest tragedy of all this story.'
Intanto l'attenzione del mondo politico [...] è tutta concentrata sulla figura di Vittorio Cecchi Gori, [...] protagonista di questa vicenda che profuma molto, par [= pare] di capire, di intrighi all'italiana.	'Meanwhile the attention of the political world is all concentrated on the figure of VCG, the protagonist of this affair which, so it would seem, has a distinct whiff of Italian-style intrigue about it.'
Siam tutti tuoi servitori.	'We are all your servants.'

Deletion is particularly common in some set phrases, such as *vita natural durante* 'throughout one's natural life', *amor proprio* 'amour propre', etc. For deletion of the final vowel of *quale* (*qual*), see 8.5.

2.9 Primary stress

The primary stressed syllable of an Italian word may be defined as the syllable whose vowel is loudest or most prominent within a word (indicated below by underlining the vowel). In certain cases, differences of primary stress may distinguish the meaning of two words:

ancora	'anchor'	*ancora*	'still'
subito	'immediately'	*subito*	'undergone'
principi	'princes'	*principi*	'principles'
volano	'they fly'	*volano*	'flywheel'
impari	'odd' (number)	*impari*	'you learn'
altero	'I alter'	*altero*	'haughty'
tendine	'tendon'	*tendine*	'curtains'
capitano	'they turn up'	*capitano*	'captain'

As a rule, main stress may fall on any one of the last three syllables of a word. Italian has special names for each of these stress positions: words stressed on the final syllable (e.g., *tribù* 'tribe') are called 'parole tronche'; those stressed on the last syllable but one (e.g., *amante* 'lover') 'parole piane', and those stressed on the last syllable but two (e.g., *logico* 'logical') 'parole sdrucciole'. How far is it possible to predict where main stress falls? Spelling helps us only in the case of those 'parole tronche' which comprise more than one syllable and end in a vowel; here the stressed vowel of the final syllable always carries a written accent:

amer<u>à</u>	'she will love'	pens<u>erò</u>	'I shall think'
caff<u>è</u>	'coffee'	pens<u>ò</u>	'she thought'
carib<u>ù</u>	'caribu'	pot<u>é</u>	'she could'
casin<u>ò</u>	'casino'	scimpanz<u>é</u>	'chimpanzee'
citt<u>à</u>	'city'	sent<u>ì</u>	'she felt'
colibr<u>ì</u>	'humming bird'		

In non-final syllables, the position of main stress is predictable, but only up to a point. Main stress almost *never* falls more than three syllables from the end of a word:

acr<u>o</u>bata	'acrobat'	inimit<u>a</u>bile	'inimitable'
aerop<u>o</u>rto	'airport'	lacrim<u>o</u>geno	'tear gas'
caratter<u>i</u>zzo	'I characterize'	ninf<u>o</u>mane	'nymphomaniac'
centr<u>i</u>fugo	'centrifugal'	r<u>e</u>duce	'veteran'
di<u>a</u>gnosi	'diagnosis'	rep<u>u</u>to	'I think'
etan<u>o</u>lo	'ethanol'	stere<u>o</u>tipo	'stereotype'
ge<u>o</u>metra	'surveyor'	term<u>o</u>stato	'thermostat'

The sole exception to this rule concerns the third person plural of certain first conjugation verbs, which are *parole bisdrucciole* (stressed on the last syllable but three). This occurs in verbs whose third person *singular* is a 'parola sdrucciola'. The result:

Third person singular	**Third person plural**	
br<u>o</u>ntola	br<u>o</u>ntolano	'grumble'
l<u>i</u>tiga	l<u>i</u>tigano	'argue'
man<u>i</u>pola	man<u>i</u>polano	'manipulate'
pr<u>e</u>dica	pr<u>e</u>dicano	'preach'
pr<u>o</u>voca	pr<u>o</u>vocano	'provoke'
r<u>e</u>gola	r<u>e</u>golano	'regulate'
r<u>o</u>tola	r<u>o</u>tolano	'roll'
sc<u>i</u>vola	sc<u>i</u>volano	'slip'
tel<u>e</u>fona	tel<u>e</u>fonano	'telephone'

The second major principle for the prediction of primary stress concerns the structure of the penultimate syllable of a word. In words whose penultimate syllable ends in a consonant (see rules for syllabification in 2.14), if primary stress does not fall on the final syllable then it must fall on the penultimate:

camm<u>e</u>llo	'camel'	entusi<u>a</u>sta	'enthusiast'
elef<u>a</u>nte	'elephant'	palins<u>e</u>sto	'palimpsest'
bast<u>a</u>rdo	'bastard'	inchi<u>e</u>sta	'inquiry'

There are just a handful of exceptions to this principle, namely certain 'parole sdrucciole' in which the penultimate syllable none the less ends in a consonant. These are the place names *T<u>a</u>ranto, <u>O</u>tranto, L<u>e</u>panto, <u>A</u>gordo, <u>A</u>gosta* (in Lazio), the surname *<u>A</u>lbizzi*, and the nouns *pol<u>i</u>zza* '(insurance) policy', *<u>a</u>rista* 'chine of pork', *m<u>a</u>ndorla* 'almond', *m<u>a</u>ndorlo* 'almond tree', *c<u>o</u>riz(z)a* 'coryza'.

Clitic pronouns (6.3) following the verb are irrelevant to the rules of stress placement. In (theoretically possible) forms such as *f<u>a</u>bbricamicene* 'make me some of them there', or *app<u>i</u>ccicaticelo* 'stick it to yourself there', the stress may appear to be six syllables from the end, but it is only three syllables from the end of the 'host' words (*f<u>a</u>bbrica* and *app<u>i</u>ccica*) to which the clitics are attached.

In words ending in a consonant – usually, 'loans' from foreign languages – it is much more difficult to predict the position of stress (note that stress on the final syllable is not obligatorily indicated by an accent). Sometimes, but not always, Italian preserves the stress pattern of the source language; in a number of cases, stress is variable:

> tronche: *agitprop, Aldebaran, bazar, boutique, Interpol, Intersind, samisdat*
> piane: *amburger, babysitter, Niagara, pirex, pullman, pullover, Volkswagen*
> sdrucciole: *Aldebaran, amburger, festival, Interpol, permafrost*

A number of surnames (especially from the Veneto) have final stress, without written accent: e.g., *Marin, Manin, Padoan.*

There are also various morphological clues as to primary stress placement. Most noun and adjective suffixes (e.g., *-one, -ino, -ano, -oso, -ese, -iere, -aio, -uolo*) have penultimate stress, as do most two-syllable inflectional endings on verbs, such as *-avo, -iamo, -ate, -ete, -ite.*

minestrone	'minestrone'	*irlandese*	'Irish'
ragazzino	'little boy'	*forestiero*	'stranger'
americano	'American'	*macellaio*	'butcher'
favoloso	'fabulous'	*faccenduola*	'little business'
etc.			
amavo	'I loved'	*finite*	'you finish'
cantiamo	'we sing'	*amavamo*	'we loved'
pensate	'you think'	*finivate*	'you finished'
etc.			

However, third person plurals in *-ano, -ono, -ino, -ero*, and first person plural imperfect subjunctive forms in *-ssimo* are 'parole sdrucciole'.

amano	'they love'	*facevano*	'they did'
vendono	'they sell'	*amassimo*	'we loved (subjn.)'
pensino	'they think (subjn.)'	*facessimo*	'we did (subjn.)'
tacquero	'they fell silent'		

Words ending in three-syllable suffixes (e.g. *-issimo, -errimo, -evole, -abile, -ognolo, -icolo, -ag(g)ine, -ologo*) are typically 'sdrucciole':

bellissimo	'most beautiful'	*verdognolo*	'greenish'
simpaticissimo	'extremely nice'	*ridicolo*	'ridiculous'
miserrimo	'most wretched'	*stupidaggine*	'idiocy'
deplorevole	'deplorable'	*geologo*	'geologist'
probabile	'probable'	etc.	

Words ending in *-ico, -ica* are predominantly 'sdrucciole':

scientifico	'scientific'	*panico*	'panic'
medico	'doctor'	*manica*	'sleeve'
matematica	'mathematics'		

A few of them are, however, 'piane':

lombrico	'earthworm'	*mollica*	'crumb'
pudico	'modest'	etc.	

The suffix *-olo* and plural *-oli* can be problematic. It is usually *unstressed* (e.g., *spiccioli* 'small change', *mostricciattolo* 'little monster', etc.), but it is also a variant of stressed *-uolo* often found after 'consonant + *i*' (e.g., *bracciolo* 'armrest', *figliolo* or *figliuolo* 'son').

2.10 Variable primary stress

There are a number of cases in which native speakers hesitate over the positioning of main stress. Some of these variants can be labelled (following the judgements of Canepari [1992]) as 'deliberate' and used to display one's education, or archaic or literary (both classes are grouped together below with the symbol †). There is variant stress in all singular and in third person plural forms of some first conjugation verbs, e.g.:

adula	*adula*†	'adulates'
evapora	*evapora*†	'evaporates'
separa	*separa*†	'separates'
travia	*travia*†	'strays'
valuta	*valuta*†	'evaluates'

also

diatriba	*diatriba*	'diatribe'
edile	*edile*	'building' (adj.)
incavo	*incavo*	'hollow'
leccornia	*leccornia*†	'titbit'
mollica (esp. in the Veneto)	*mollica*	'soft part of bread'
salubre	*salubre*	'salubrious'
sanscrito	*sanscrito*†	'Sanskrit'
scandinavo	*scandinavo*†	'Scandinavian'
utensile	*utensile*	'utensil'

Some placenames and personal names frequently have variant stresses:

Nuoro	*Nuoro*†
Salgari	*Salgari*†

2.11 Secondary stress: 'regular' and 'autonomous'

In words of three or more syllables, certain syllables carry a 'secondary' stress. The position of 'regular' secondary stress is predictable in terms of three simple principles (the effect of which is to confer a kind of undulating rhythm on the word):

(a) No two stresses (be they 'primary' or 'secondary') may be adjacent.
(b) No two stresses ('primary' or 'secondary') may be more than two syllables apart.
(c) When the primary stressed vowel is preceded by two or more syllables, the initial syllable of the word usually receives a secondary stress.

Within these constraints, the position of secondary stress is free. Therefore, certain words may have variable secondary stress patterns (secondary stress is here indicated by double underlining):

caratterizzabile	OR	*caratterizzabile*	'characterizable'
encefalogramma	OR	*encefalogramma*	'encephalogram'
claustrofobia	OR	*claustrofobia*	'claustrophobia'
dipsomania	OR	*dipsomania*	'dipsomania'

However, these principles are overridden in compound words whose elements also exist as independent words. In such compounds, the last element always carries the primary stress of the whole word, but in the preceding element (or elements) a secondary stress *must* fall on the same syllable which would carry the primary stress outside the compound. For example:

m*a*cina 'grind' + *caffè* 'coffee'	*macinaffè* 'coffee grinder' (never **macinacaffè*)
asp*i*ra ' breathe' + *polvere* 'dust'	*aspirapolvere* 'vacuum cleaner' (never **aspirapolvere*)
t*o*ssico ' toxic' + *dipendente* 'addict'	*tossicodipendente* 'drug addict' (never **tossicodipendente*)
dial*e*tto 'dialect' + *fobia* 'phobia', 'dislike'	*dialettofobia* 'dislike of dialects' (never **dialettofobia*)
Eg*i*tto 'Egypt' + *mania* 'mania'	*egittomania* 'Egyptomania' (never **egittomania*)

etc.

In some compound words, the second element may be an independent word, preceded by a first element which appears only in compounds. In such cases, the first element sometimes none the less has a fixed secondary stress. For example: *elettroterapia* (never **elettroterapia*), *psicoanalitico* (never **psicoanalitico*), *eterosessuale* (never **eterosessuale*) – where *terapia, analitico, sessuale* all exist as independent words: but, for example, *eterogeneità* or *eterogeneità* (where neither the first nor the second element exists as an independent word).[6]

2.12 Written accents

The role of written accents in indicating a stressed final vowel has been discussed in 2.9. Monosyllables having the shape 'consonant + written unstressed *i* or *u* + vowel' also bear a stressed accent on the final vowel: *giù, più, ciò, già, può*. Note also *è* 'is' vs. *e* 'and', *sì* 'yes' vs. *si* (reflexive pronoun), *là/lì* 'there' vs. *la/li* (article and pronouns), *dà* 'gives' vs. *da* 'from', 'by' and *sé* (stressed reflexive pronoun) vs. *se* 'if', and unstressed reflexive pronoun, *né* 'nor' vs. *ne* (clitic pronoun), *ché* 'for' (conjunction) vs. *che* 'that'. On non-final vowels, accents may *optionally* be written to distinguish homographs (two words which are spelled identically but stressed differently): e.g., *sùbito* 'immediately' vs. *subìto* 'undergone', *prìncipi* 'princes' vs. *princìpi* 'principles'.

The most commonly used accent in Italian is the grave (`` ` ``), which can safely be used wherever a written accent is required. But there is a convention (by no means consistently followed) that an accent is written acute (´) on the vowel [e], and grave on [ɛ], which is why *né, sé, perché* are usually written with an acute, but *è* with a grave.

Accents cannot be omitted from capital letters in Italian (unlike French or Spanish). In printing, if the capital letter leaves no space above it for an accent, an apostrophe may be used instead: ANTICHITA', PIU', etc.

---

[6]For a more detailed account of secondary stresses (using a slightly different terminology), see particularly Lepschy (1992 and 1993).

2.13 Punctuation

The full stop (period) *punto*, colon *due punti*, semicolon *punto e virgola*, comma *virgola*, inverted commas *virgolette* are used broadly as in English.[7] In lists, commas may optionally be omitted:

Aveva trovato nel cassetto matite penne cartoline carte da visite francobolli e varie altre cose.	'He had found in the drawer pencils, pens, postcards, visiting cards, stamps and various other things.'

Turns in dialogue, usually presented in English between inverted commas, are often preceded in Italian by a long dash *lineetta* (and separated from phrases such as 'he said' by a further long dash):

—Posso prendere questa sedia?— chiese nel silenzio il pesce dai capelli bianchi.	'"May I take this chair?" asked, during the silence, the fish-like individual with the white hair.'
—Oh,— disse De Palma, —mi scusi, Eminenza. Si accomodi.	"Oh," said DP, "forgive me Your Eminence. Do sit down."'

2.14 Hyphens and syllabification

If a word is broken at the end of a line, a hyphen may be inserted, but as a rule only between syllables. This raises the question of where the syllable boundaries occur. Every syllable must contain a vowel, and in a sequence 'vowel + consonant + vowel' the consonant will always be assigned to the same syllable as the following vowel, so that the syllable division occurs between the first vowel and the consonant. *Patata* and *amore* may therefore be hyphenated as *pa-tata a-more* or *pata-ta amo-re*, but not in any other way. In a sequence of two vowels, the syllable division occurs between the vowels, allowing hyphenations such as *a-ereo aere-o* (or *ae-reo*), *line-etta* 'dash', *sci-a, pro-a*, etc. However, the sequences 'unstressed *i, u* + vowel' or 'vowel + unstressed *i, u*' form part of a single syllable and cannot be divided: *pie-de, vuo-le, a-ia, ai-rone, au-to, fi-nii* (never **pi-ede, *vu-ole, *ai-a, *a-irone, *a-uto, *fini-i*), except in those cases (discussed in 2.2) where unstressed *i* and *u* are pronounced [i] and [u] before a vowel (*spi-avo, lacu-ale*, etc.).

In clusters of two or more consonants, however, the principle is that the hyphen precedes any cluster which can also appear at the beginning of the written form of a word:[8] e.g., *ba-sta* (cf. *stava*), *a-stro* (cf. *strano*), *o-ptare* (cf. *pterodattilo*), *ra-psodico* (cf. *psicologo*), *a-pre* (cf. *prato*) – and likewise all other clusters of consonant + *r*, *Empedo-cle* (cf. *clamore*), *ri-tmo* (cf. *tmesi*). In any cluster which cannot appear at the beginning of a word, the hyphen is placed between the first and second consonant: e.g., *ter-ra, pal-la, op-zione, con-tro, al-tro* (no Italian words begin *rr, ll, tl, pz, ntr, ltr*). But note that *vr*, although it never occurs at the beginning of a word, is hyphenated *-vr* (e.g., *a-vrò*). The cluster *tl* may be hyphenated either as *t-l* or *-tl* (e.g., *at-leta* or *a-tleta*).

---

[7]An extensive list of Italian names of punctuation signs, and related terminology, is available in Canepari (1992: 400f.).
[8]But the *syllable* boundary in such clusters falls between the first and the second consonant: ['bas-ta], ['as-tro], etc.

2.15 Capital letters

In titles of books, plays, organizations, etc., only the first word usually bears an initial capital letter (*maiuscola*):

Società internazionale di linguistica e filologia italiana	'International Society for Italian Linguistics and Philology'
Guerra e pace	'War and Peace'
I promessi sposi	'The Betrothed'

This does not apply to newspapers and magazines (e.g., *La Stampa, Il Corriere della Sera, Il Resto del Carlino*).

Adjectives and nouns of place or nationality are not written with a capital: *il governo tedesco* 'the German government', *Arrivano i tedeschi* 'The Germans arrive', although a capital is sometimes encountered when the noun refers to the people as a whole (*I Tedeschi/tedeschi sono molto puntuali*).

'God' is normally written with a capital (*Dio*) and pronouns referring to God tend, correspondingly, to take a capital (*Egli, Lui*, etc.):

Mi rivolsi a Dio, pregandoLo che mi aiutasse. E ringrazio Lui della mia buona fortuna.	'I turned to God, praying to Him to help me. And it's Him I thank for my good fortune.'

Unlike English, Italian does not employ capital letters for names of days of the week (*lunedì, martedì*, etc.), months (*gennaio, febbraio*, etc.), compass points (*nord, sud, est, ovest*).

For the use of capital letters in address forms (*La, Lei*, etc.), see 22.3.

2.16 Names of letters of the alphabet

The Italian names of the letters of the alphabet are (in phonetic representation):

A	[a]	N	['ɛnne]
B	[bi]	O	[ɔ]
C	[tʃi]	P	[pi]
D	[di]	Q	[ku]
E	[ɛ]	R	['ɛrre]
F	['ɛffe]	S	['ɛsse]
G	[dʒi]	T	[ti]
H	['akka]	V	[vu] or [vi]
I	[i]	W⁹	['doppjo 'vu]
J	[i l'luŋga]		['doppjo 'vi]
K	['kappa]	X	[iks]
L	['ɛlle]	Y	['ipsilon] or [i 'grɛko]
M	['ɛmme]	Z	['dzɛta]

Note that, because Y and J are little used some Italians are apt to confuse them, so that care should be taken in ensuring that surnames, etc., containing these letters are correctly spelled by Italians.

---

⁹There are no less than three variables in the name of this letter: (i) [vi] or [vu], (ii) gender – for some speakers [vi] or [vu] is feminine, like the names of most letters of the alphabet, hence [doppja vu], (iii) [vi] or [vu] may precede [doppjo] ([vu ddoppjo], etc.).

3

Nouns and adjectives

3.1 Three general principles for plural formation

Almost all Italian noun and adjective plurals are formed according to one of three general principles:

(i) If a *feminine* singular noun or adjective ends in *unstressed -a*, then that *-a* is replaced by *-e* in the plural.
(ii) *All other* singular nouns and adjectives *that end in an unstressed vowel*, replace that vowel with *-i* in the plural.
(iii) Nouns and adjectives that *do not end in an unstressed vowel* are invariant: i.e., their plural is identical to their singular.

Plurals of feminines in *-a*:

Singular	Plural	
bianca	*bianche*	'white'
buia	*buie*	'dark'
gialla	*gialle*	'yellow'
dottoressa	*dottoresse*	'female doctor'
foglia	*foglie*	'leaf'
gamba	*gambe*	'leg'
lampada	*lampade*	'lamp'
larga	*larghe*	'broad'
matta	*matte*	'mad'
pallida	*pallide*	'pale'
ragazza	*ragazze*	'girl'
rossa	*rosse*	'red'
ruota	*ruote*	'wheel'
socialista	*socialiste*	'socialist'
tavola	*tavole*	'table'
zia	*zie*	'aunt'
etc.		

Plurals of other nouns and adjectives ending in an unstressed vowel:

Singular	Plural	
amico	*amici*	'friend'
aroma	*aromi*	'aroma'
banana verde	*banane verdi*	'green banana'
bianco	*bianchi*	'white'
botte	*botti*	'barrel'
brindisi	*brindisi*	'drinking toast'
buio	*bui*	'dark'
carne	*carni*	'meat'

Singular	Plural	
crisi	*crisi*	'crisis'
giallo	*gialli*	'yellow'
immagine	*immagini*	'image'
luce	*luci*	'light'
mano	*mani*	'hand'
matto	*matti*	'mad'
mese	*mesi*	'month'
pallido	*pallidi*	'pale'
parte	*parti*	'part'
poeta	*poeti*	'poet'
posizione	*posizioni*	'position'
problema	*problemi*	'problem'
ragazzo	*ragazzi*	'boy'
rosso	*rossi*	'red'
socialista	*socialisti*	'socialist'
studente	*studenti*	'student'
telefono	*telefoni*	'telephone'
telegramma	*telegrammi*	'telegram'
vite	*viti*	'screw'
volume	*volumi*	'volume'
zio	*zii*	'uncle'
etc.		

Note that in words that end in *-i* in the singular (e.g., *crisi*), the plural is identical to the singular.

It can be seen from the above that in adjectives, and many nouns, a feminine in *-a* – *-e* corresponds to a masculine in *-o* – *-i*, and vice versa (see 3.9 on gender):

	Singular	Plural	Singular	Plural
M	*bianco*	*bianchi*	*ragazzo*	*ragazzi*
F	*bianca*	*bianche*	*ragazza*	*ragazze*
M	*rosso*	*rossi*	*zio*	*zii*
F	*rossa*	*rosse*	*zia*	*zie*
	etc.			

The plurals of words which do not end in an unstressed vowel, and are consequently invariant, may be illustrated as follows:

Words ending in a consonant:

sport	*sport*	'sport'
album	*album*	'album'
film	*film*	'film'
laser	*laser*	'laser'
pullman	*pullman*	'coach'
Fiat	*Fiat*	'Fiat (motor car)'
gas	*gas*	'gas'
ananas	*ananas*	'pineapple'
etc.		

Words ending in a stressed vowel (including stressed monosyllables):

città	*città*	'city'
tribù	*tribù*	'tribe'
scimpanzé	*scimpanzé*	'chimpanzee'
oblò	*oblò*	'porthole'
blu	*blu*	'blue'
scià	*scià*	'shah'

tè	*tè*	'tea'
gru	*gru*	'crane'
etc.		

3.2 Spelling of plurals

The following rules for spelling of plurals are discussed in more detail in 2.2. Briefly, in words which in the singular end in *-co, -go, -ca, -ga*, the *c* and *g* change to *ch* and *gh*, respectively, before the plural endings *-i* or *-e*. This *always* applies before the feminine plural ending *-e*, and *usually* applies (for some very important exceptions, see 3.6) before plural *-i*:

	Singular	**Plural**	**Singular**	**Plural**
M	*bianco* 'white'	*bianchi*	*largo* 'broad'	*larghi*
F	*bianca*	*bianche*	*larga*	*larghe*
M	*tacco* 'heel'	*tacchi*	*lago* 'lake'	*laghi*
F	*gerarca* 'hierarch'	*gerarchi*	*strega* 'witch'	*streghe*
	etc.			

Some complications arise in the spelling of the plural of words which, in the singular, end in *unstressed i* + vowel:

- In words ending in *-cia* and *-gia*, where the *i* is not stressed and is merely acting as a diacritic (see 2.2), the spelling convention is that *i* is usually omitted in the plural where *c* or *g* are preceded by another consonant, but retained when these consonants are preceded by a vowel (*arancia – arance* 'orange', *spiaggia – spiagge* 'beach', etc. but *camicia – camicie* 'shirt', *ciliegia – ciliegie* 'cherry', etc.).
- See 3.3 below for the plural of nouns ending in *-cie* and *-gie* in the singular.
- As for masculines in *-io*, the plural is formed in the regular way (*-ii*) if the *i* is a stressed vowel (*zio – zii*, etc.), but is normally written as the single letter *-i* if *i* is unstressed in the singular, as in *buio – bui* 'dark', *vizio – vizi* 'vice', etc., or merely a diacritic (2.2) as in *bacio – baci* 'kiss', *raggio – raggi* 'ray', etc. See also 2.2 for alternative spellings in *-ii, -j, î*.

3.3 Exceptions to the general principles: nouns and adjectives with irregular plural endings

Nouns and adjectives may be regarded as having 'irregular' plural endings if they do not conform to the principles mentioned above. It is noteworthy that virtually all of the 'irregularities' concern nouns rather than adjectives.

- Two feminine nouns with singular *-a* form their plural in *-i*:

ala	*ali*	'wing'
arma	*armi*	'weapon'

- Abbreviated, or 'truncated', words, from which the final syllables have been deleted, are invariant. It might be argued that these words really belong to the class of words that do not 'end in an unstressed vowel', their final syllable having been removed. However, it is not necessarily obvious, even to the native speaker, that such forms are abbreviations, and they are best listed as exceptions, some of the commonest of which are:

Full form		**Abbreviated**		
cinematografo	*cinematografi*	*cinema*	*cinema*	'cinema'
automobile	*automobili*	*auto*	*auto*	'car'
fotografia	*fotografie*	*foto*	*foto*	'photo'
(fucile) mitragliatore	*(fucili) mitragliatori*	*mitra*	*mitra*	'machine gun'
televisione	*televisioni*	*tele*	*tele*	'television'
motocicletta	*motociclette*	*moto*	*moto*	'motorcycle'
etc.				

- Some feminine nouns ending in *-ie* have invariant plurals: *la serie – le serie* 'series', *la congerie – le congerie* 'congeries'; other words ending in *-gie*, *-cie*, such as *effigie* 'effigy', *superficie* 'surface' and *specie* 'species', may none the less have variant plurals: *le superfici* and *le effigi* are more commonly used than *le superficie* and *le effigie*, and *le speci* is sometimes encountered instead of *le specie*. The reason why certain words in *-gie* and *-cie* may have variant plurals is a matter of pronunciation: their *i* is not pronounced (for an explanation, see 2.2), so that the singular is [ef'fiʤe], [super'fiʧe], ['spɛʧe] and the plurals tend to be formed, just like other nouns ending in *-e*, in 'regular' *-i*. For the same reason (that the *i* is not pronounced)[1] *moglie* 'wife' has the regular plural *mogli*.

- Some masculine nouns in *-a* (particularly those taken from exotic languages) have invariant plurals. Among these are:

delta	*delta*	'delta'
boia	*boia*	'executioner'
lama	*lama*	'llama'
lama	*lama*	'lama'
paria	*paria*	'pariah'
sosia	*sosia*	'identical twin'
vaglia	*vaglia*	'postal order'
gorilla	*gorilla*	'gorilla'
panda	*panda*	'panda'
puma	*puma*	'puma'

  Vaglia was originally a verb (the third person singular subjunctive of *valere*, now *valga*), not a noun.

- *Contralto* and *soprano*: These words, which normally denote women, are invariant: *le contralto*, *le soprano*; in the rare cases where they denote men, their plural may either be regular (*i contralti*, etc.) or invariant (cf. 3.11).

- Invariance of nouns used as adjectives (especially colour adjectives): If any word which is not normally a noun is used as a noun, or any word which is not normally an adjective is used as an adjective, it is invariant. The most prominent example of this involves the use of nouns as adjectives of colour, e.g. (where *rosa* and *viola* originally designate the flower with which their colour is conventionally associated):

---

[1] In this word the *i* is a mere diacritic, indicating that *gli* is pronounced [ʎʎ].

due vestiti rosa	'two pink suits'
delle camicie viola	'some purple shirts'
delle cravatte crema	'some cream coloured ties'

- Invariance of names: Surnames are invariant for number, and this is usually the case with forenames as well:

Sono arrivati gli Spataro.	'The Spataros have arrived.'
Ci sono due Giorgio e due Antonella	'There are two Georges and two Antonellas
in questa classe.	in this class.'

In Italian the names, or 'citation forms', of words are also invariant. To illustrate what is meant here, one may consider such possible English utterances as: 'There are too many "Gods" in this sentence', 'His speech is full of "OK"'s', 'He uttered six "neverthelesses"', meaning the *words* 'God', 'OK', 'nevertheless'. In Italian, words are cited in the form in which they actually appear, and are not modified for number: *Ci sono troppi «Dio» in questa frase, Il suo discorso è pieno di «vabbene», Disse ben sei «nondimeno».*

- Occasional plurals of foreign words in *-s*: Words borrowed from foreign languages, and especially those ending in a consonant, are generally invariable (*lo sport – gli sport, il leader – i leader, lo handout – gli handout,* etc.). But one also encounters *optional* final *-s* in imitation of the plural in the source language (largely English, French, e.g., *i leaders, gli champagnes* also *i gauchos, gli indios* '(South American) Indians'.

3.4 Nouns in masculine singular -o, and feminine plural -*a*

A number of nouns with masculine singulars in *-o* have plurals which end in *-a* and, unlike the singular, are *feminine*:

il centinaio	*le centinaia*	'hundred or so' (see 12.10)
il migliaio	*le migliaia*	'thousand or so' (see 12.10)
il membro	*le membra*	'limb' (of body; *i membri* are 'members of an organization', etc.)
il miglio	*le miglia*	'mile'
il paio	*le paia*	'pair'
il riso	*le risa*	'laugh' (plural = 'laughter')
l'uovo	*le uova*	'egg'

Several other nouns in masculine singular *-o* have 'double' plurals: a feminine plural in *-a*, and a 'regular' masculine plural in *-i*. It is difficult to generalize about when the feminine *-a* forms should be used, and when the masculine *-i*. As a broad rule, the feminine *-a* plural is used in these nouns if they denote a pair of body parts or a class of objects usually occurring as a set; otherwise the masculine *-i* plural is used. But Brunet's very detailed critical survey (1978: 30–90) shows this to be a considerable oversimplification. What follows are general indications for the use of the alternative plurals. We exclude such plurals as *le vestimenta* 'clothes', *le anella* 'curls of hair' (cf. *l'anello* 'ring'), *le castella* 'castles', *le carra* 'cartloads' (cf. *il carro* 'cart'), *le gomita* 'elbows', now considered archaic or regional.

Body parts characteristically occurring in pairs or sets:

- *il braccio*   *le braccia*   *i bracci*   'arm'

The feminine plural is principally associated with the pair of arms of a human body (or, marginally, with the 'arms' of an object seen as resembling the arms of a human):

Mi consolo stringendolo tra le braccia.	'I console myself by squeezing him in my arms.'
I pali telegrafici balzavano l'uno dopo l'altro incontro alla macchina con le braccia spalancate.	'The telegraph poles came bounding one after the other towards the car with their arms out wide.'

The feminine *braccia* is also used as a measure of depth: *È profonda tre braccia* 'It's three fathoms deep'. In other cases the masculine is employed: one usually talks of the *bracci* of an armchair, a candelabrum, a basket. Note also that the plural of diminutive *braccino* may also be feminine (in *-e*):

Pin ha due braccine smilze smilze.	'P has two spindly little arms.'

- *il budello*   *le budella*   *i budelli*   'intestine'

Le budella are anatomical intestines (also *le budelle* in colloquial usage); *i budelli* are long, narrow tubes or passages in general.

- *il cervello*   *le cervella*   *i cervelli*   'brain'

I cervelli is the generally preferred form, although one encounters *cervella* in certain expressions such as *farsi saltare le cervella* 'to blow one's brain's out' and *cervella* is the form used of brain served as food.

- *il ciglio*   *le ciglia*   *i cigli*   'eyelash'

The feminine plural is usually preferred (including the microbiological sense of 'cilia'):

L'aceto le cola fra le ciglia bruciandole gli occhi.	'The vinegar seeps through her eyelashes burning her eyes.'

But the masculine is used in the figurative sense of 'edge', as in *i cigli della strada* 'the edges of the road'. For many speakers the singular, like the plural, is however *(la) ciglia*.

- *il corno*   *le corna*   *i corni*   'horn'

Corno is generally feminine in the plural when indicating the body parts, but masculine in the meanings 'pointed extremities' (of some object), and 'horn' (musical instrument).

- *il dito*   *le dita*   *i diti*   'finger'

The plural is generally *le dita*, even when the word is used to indicate a measurement (e.g., *Ci metta due dita di vino* 'Put a couple of fingers of wine in'). *I diti* is employed when fingers are considered not as a group or set, but as separate, detached, entities, e.g.:

Nello stesso momento, in due città lontanissime, due diti facevano lo stesso numero.	'At the same moment, in two far distant cities, two fingers were dialling the same number.'

●   *il ginocchio*   *le ginocchia*   *i ginocchi*   'knee'

In modern usage *i ginocchi* can safely be used in most cases, although *le ginocchia* is still frequently encountered, especially in certain idioms, such as *sedere sulle ginocchia di qualcuno* 'to be sitting on someone's lap', *Fa venire il latte alle ginocchia* 'He's a crashing bore'. But there seems to be no clear, systematic, difference in meaning between the two.

●   *il labbro*   *le labbra*   *i labbri*   'lip'

Le labbra is usual for anatomical lips:

Ma ha le labbra che gli tremano, le labbra da ragazzo malato.	'But his lips are trembling, the lips of a sick boy.'

But both *i labbri* and *le labbra* may be used in the figurative sense of 'lips', 'edges of a wound', 'cave', etc.

●   *il midollo*   *le midolla*   *i midolli*   'marrow' (of bone)

The feminine plural, the sole form normally used, often corresponds to English 'bones': e.g., *Il freddo mi entra nelle midolla* 'The cold gets into my bones'; note also *Era fradicio fino alle midolla* 'He was soaked to the skin'.

●   *l'osso*   *le ossa*   *gli ossi*   'bone'

Le ossa usually denotes the set of bones in a body:

Mi fanno male le ossa!	'My bones are aching!'

Gli ossi are separate, loose, bones, not viewed as forming an anatomical set. For example:

Le bandiere erano nere e avevano nel centro l'immagine d'un teschio tra quattro ossi.	'The flags were black and in the centre they had the image of a skull amid four bones.'

●   *il sopracciglio*   *le sopracciglia*   *i sopraccigli*   'eyebrow'

The feminine plural is the more commonly used, and there is no obvious distinction of meaning between the masculine and the feminine.

Other words with feminine plural -*a* are:

●   *il fondamento*   *le fondamenta*   *i fondamenti*   'foundation'

The feminine is used of the foundations of a building; the masculine in the sense 'basic, elementary notions' (e.g., *fondamenti di matematica*).

●   *il lenzuolo*   *le lenzuola*   *i lenzuoli*   'sheet'

The feminine plural is *preferred* for the pair of sheets on a bed; otherwise the masculine is employed.

●   *il muro*   *le mura*   *i muri*   'wall'

Le mura denotes the perimeter walls of a town, building or room, viewed as a set or collectivity (e.g., *fra queste quattro mura* 'within these four walls'). If the collective sense is absent, or simply not regarded as important, the masculine is used:

Erano andati a stare in una casa nuova, situata fuori delle mura della città.	'They had gone to live in a new house, outside the city walls.'
Sui muri di Napoli apparvero grandi manifesti.	'On the walls of Naples appeared large posters.'

● *lo staio* *le staia* (*gli stai*) 'bushel', 'grain container'

The plural is almost always *staia*, although some dictionaries state that the feminine refers to the measurement and the masculine to the container.

Le cuoia is an archaic plural of *cuoio* 'leather', 'hide', but still used in the idiom *tirare le cuoia* 'to kick the bucket'.

In certain words, native speakers accept either kind of plural indifferently; where the feminine seems to be the predominant form, the masculine is given in brackets:

il ferramento	*le ferramenta*	(*i ferramenti*)	'tool', 'ironware'
il grido	*le grida*	*i gridi*	'shout'
il moggio	*le moggia*	(*i moggi*)	'grain measure' = 5 bushels
lo strido	*le strida*	(*gli stridi*)	'shriek'
l'urlo	*le urla*	*gli urli*	'howl'
il vestigio	*le vestigia*	*i vestigi*	'vestige'

The plural of *fuso* 'spindle' is *le fusa* only in the idiom *fare le fusa* 'to purr' (of a cat); the plural of *filo* 'thread', *le fila*, is limited to senses associated with plots or conspiracies (e.g., *Ha in mano lui le fila della congiura* 'He has the threads of the plot in his hands'). Also *fare le fila* 'to be stringy', 'grated' (of cheese). The feminine plural of *calcagno* 'heel', *le calcagna*, seems to occur principally in phrases indicating 'being at somebody's heels', 'in pursuit', 'following' (e.g., *Non sapeva che il padre gli aveva messo alle calcagna un investigatore privato* 'He didn't know his father had set a private detective to tail him').

The feminine plural ending -*a* occurs in nouns only: modifying adjectives have their ordinary feminine form in the plural (thus *l'uovo fresco* 'the fresh egg' vs. *le uova fresche*). A peculiarity of agreement is that a singular pronoun referring to such feminine plural nouns will take a *feminine singular* form:

Queste uova costano dieci lire ciascuna.	'These eggs cost 10 lire each one.'
Di sopra, a circa quattrocento metri,	'Above, at about 400 metres, on a little
sopra un piccolo piazzale, stavano le ossa	terrace, were D's bones, one here, one
di Darrio, una qui una lì.	there.'

A pronoun referring to a plural of these words may have feminine form (although this rule is not obligatory, and some speakers prefer *venderli* in the following example):

Dice che sua madre non gli dà mai un	'He says his mother never gives him an
uovo perché deve venderle.	egg because she has to sell them.'

3.5 Other nouns which differ in gender between singular and plural

fem. sg.	*la eco*	'echo'	masc. pl.	*gli echi*	
masc. sg.	*il carcere*	'jail'	fem. pl.	*le carceri*	
masc. sg.	*il rene*	'kidney'	fem. pl.	*le reni*	
		'small of back	'masc. pl.	*i reni*	

Orecchio 'ear' is problematic (see particularly Brunet 1978: 91), in that both masculine *orecchi* and feminine *orecchie* are used in the plural, with no obvious distinction of meaning. There is also an alternative, and less common, *feminine singular orecchia*.

3.6 Irregularities in the plural root: *porco – porci, amico – amici, dio – dei, uomo – uomini,* etc.

In general, the *root* of a noun or adjective is invariant, i.e., the same in the plural as in the singular; only the *ending* varies. This is *always* the case for feminine nouns and adjectives, but in certain masculine words the root varies between singular and plural.

- Plurals of masculines in *-co, -ca, -go, -ga*:

  Masculines ending in *-co* and *-go* (or *-ca* and *-ga*) are generally invariant *in the root*. As with feminines, this invariance entails, however, a spelling adjustment, insertion of *h* (see 2.2; 3.2), in the plural:

antico	*antichi*	'ancient'
carico	*carichi*	'loaded'
il cosacco	*i cosacchi*	'cossack'
il demagogo	*i demagoghi*	'demagogue'
il dialogo	*i dialoghi*	'dialogue'
l'incarico	*gli incarichi*	'charge'
il monarca	*i monarchi*	'monarch'
il pizzico	*i pizzichi*	'pinch'
prodigo	*prodighi*	'prodigal'
pudico	*pudichi*	'modest'
il rammarico	*i rammarichi*	'regret'
sacrilego	*sacrileghi*	'sacrilegious'
lo strascico	*gli strascichi*	'dragging'
il solletico	*i solletichi*	'tickle'
sporco	*sporchi*	'dirty'
il valico	*i valichi*	'(mountain) pass'
etc.		

  In a number of cases, the [k] and [g] sounds of the singular are replaced by a palatal consonant (respectively [tʃ] and [dʒ]) in the plural – but the *spelling* of the plural root must remain identical to that of the singular, and there is no addition of *h*. Root variability of this kind is commoner for words in *-co* than for those in *-go*. Among variant words in *-co* are:

l'amico	*gli amici*	'friend'
il nemico	*i nemici*	'enemy'
il porco	*i porci*	'pig'
il greco	*i greci*	'Greek'

To these we may add the rare and erudite *falisco – falisci* or *falischi* 'Faliscan' and *osco – osci* or *oschi*, 'Oscan'.

A large class of *parole sdrucciole* (i.e., words stressed on the last syllable but two, see 2.9), ending in an unstressed vowel + *-co*, also form their plurals in *-ci*:

fanatico	*fanatici*	'fanatical' / 'fanatic'
matematico	*matematici*	'mathematical' / 'mathematician'
monaco	*monaci*	'monk'
romantico	*romantici*	'romantic'
sindaco	*sindaci*	'mayor'
maniaco	*maniaci*	'maniacal'
equivoco	*equivoci*	'equivocal'
etc.		

The plurals in unstressed vowel + *ci* are principally characteristic of 'learned' or 'cultivated' vocabulary (contrast *solletichi* 'tickles' which is not 'learned', and *pudichi* 'modest', which (arguably) *is* learned, but is stressed on the *i*). In such words the ending *-co* continues Latin (unstressed vowel +) *cus* or Greek (unstressed vowel +) -κος. As a rule, words taking plural *-ci* tend to be part of 'international' vocabulary, and also have counterparts in *-c* or *-cal* in English (e.g., 'fanatical', 'mathematical', 'romantic', 'maniacal'); words such as *valichi*, *solletichi*, *dimentichi* have no such counterparts in English. One exception to this rule is *manico manici* '(broom) handle', which clearly does not belong to 'learned' discourse, yet usually has plural *manici*.

Many unstressed *-ico* and *-aco* words may form their plurals either in *-ici* and *-aci* or in *-ichi* and *-achi*. Where one variant is regarded as more acceptable than the other (cf. Brunet 1978), this is indicated by the symbol [†].

farmaco	*farmaci / farmachi*	'drug'
fondaco	*fondaci / fondachi*	'warehouse'
manico	*manici*[†] */ manichi*	'handle'
mendico	*mendici / mendichi*	'beggar'
traffico	*traffici / traffichi*	'traffic', 'trade'
intonaco	*intonaci / intonachi*	'plaster'
stomaco	*stomaci / stomachi*[†]	'stomach'
parroco	*parroci*[†] */ parrochi*	'parish priest'
etc.		

There is only *one* word in *-go* in modern Italian which *always* forms its plural in *-gi*:

asparago	*asparagi*	'asparagus'

Most masculine words in *-go* or *-ga* words form their plurals in *-ghi*:

catalogo	*cataloghi*	'catalogue'
collega	*colleghi*	'colleague'
dialogo	*dialoghi*	'dialogue'
fiammingo	*fiamminghi*	'Flemish'
lago	*laghi*	'lake'
largo	*larghi*	'broad'
mago	*maghi*	'wizard'
naufrago	*naufraghi*	'shipwrecked person'
transfuga	*transfughi*	'deserter'
ramingo	*raminghi*	'wandering'
etc.		

The noun *mago* has the plural *magi* when it denotes (biblical) Magi. Masculine *belga* 'Belgian' always forms its plural as *belgi*. Words ending in the suffix *-ologo*, referring to *persons* (and equivalent to English *-ologist* or *-ologer*), may form their plurals either with *-ologi* or with *-ologhi*. Most grammars (e.g., Battaglia and Pernicone 1954: 123f.; Brunet 1978: 14f.) indicate that *-ologi* is preferable:

astrologo	*astrologi / astrologhi*	'astrologer'
biologo	*biologi / biologhi*	'biologist'
filologo	*filologi / filologhi*	'philologist'
sociologo	*sociologi / sociologhi*	'sociologist'
etc.		

Words in *-ofago*, and *chirurgo*, behave similarly, although *chirurghi* is more common than *chirurgi*:

antropofago	*antropofagi/antropofaghi*	'cannibal'
sarcofago	*sarcofagi/sarcofaghi*	'sarcophagus'
chirurgo	*chirurghi/chirurgi*	'surgeon'

● Some other words have idiosyncratic irregularities in the root:

uomo	*uomini*	'man'
dio	*dei*	'god'
bue	*buoi*	'ox'
tuo	*tuoi*	'your'
suo	*suoi*	'his'/'her'/'its'
mio	*miei*	'my'

Note: in addition to the plural *dei* the form of the plural definite article occurring with this word is *gli*. *Gli dei* is, by the way, pronounced [ʎi d'dɛi].

3.7 Forming the plural of compound nouns: *il capogruppo – i capigruppo*, etc.

Many compound nouns (cf. also 3.13, 20.1) are transparently made up of a 'head' noun modified by some other element: for example, *terracotta* is obviously *terra* 'earth' modified by the adjective *cotta* 'baked', whence the meaning 'earthenware', 'terracotta'. Grammatically, these behave much as they would if they were ordinary phrases made up of separate words. Provided that the head noun is of the same gender as the compound in which it appears, then it is the head noun which generally distinguishes number, and any adjectival modifiers duly agree for number with it: (e.g., *mezzaluna – mezzelune* 'half moon'; *terracotta – terrecotte* 'baked earth' = 'terracotta'; *altopiano – altipiani* 'high plain' = 'upland plateau'; *roccaforte – roccheforti* 'strong fortress' = 'stronghold'; *cassaforte – casseforti* 'strong box', 'safe', 'box (which is) strong', etc.). If the modifier is a noun which stands in apposition to the head (i.e., 'an X which is a Y'), then both nouns may inflect for number (e.g., *cassapanca – cassepanche* 'settle', 'chest [which is also a] bench'). All other kinds of modifier remain invariant, and only the head noun distinguishes number (e.g., *capogruppo – capigruppo* 'head(s) (of a) group' = 'group leader' (cf. *capi di gruppo*); *pescespada – pescispada* 'fish(es) [part of whose anatomy resembles a] sword', 'swordfish'; *grillotalpa – grillitalpa* 'cricket(s) [which live(s) underground like] the mole' = 'mole cricket'; *nerofumo – nerifumo* 'black [pigment(s) made from] smoke' = 'lampblack'; (*ferrovia – ferrovie* 'road(s) [made of] iron' = 'railway'; *capostazione – capistazione* 'head(s) [of a] station' = 'stationmaster'; *ficodindia – fichidindia* 'fig(s) of India' = 'prickly pear', etc.

Some of these compound nouns may also be treated like 'ordinary' nouns: i.e., they form their plural solely by modifying the ending of the word. Unfortunately, there is no easy rule to predict which compounds can be treated in this way. Some, notably a number of those containing *capo-*, vary as to whether they pluralize both elements or only the end of the word:

capocuoco	*capocuochi / capicuochi*	'head chef'
capocomico	*capocomici / capicomici*	'actor manager'
capomastro	*capomastri / capimastri*	'master builder'
bassorilievo	*bassirilievi / bassorilievi*	'bas relief'
cassaforte	*casseforti / cassaforti*	'strong box'
terracotta	*terrecotte / terracotte*	'terracotta'

Many others are treated as simple nouns, so that they change the end of the compound only, even though their internal structure may be quite transparent; for example *belvedere* 'view', 'panorama' is obviously *bel* 'beautiful' + *vedere* 'sight', 'seeing' yet its plural is not *beivederi*, but *belvederi*:

arcobaleno	*arcobaleni*	'rainbow'
camposanto	*camposanti*	'cemetery'
capolavoro	*capolavori*	'masterpiece'
francobollo	*francobolli*	'stamp'
palcoscenico	*palcoscenici*	'stage'
pianoforte	*pianoforti*	'piano'
pescecane	*pescecani*	'shark'
porcospino	*porcospini*	'porcupine'
cartapecora	*cartapecore*	'parchment'
madreperla	*madreperle*	'mother of pearl'
etc.		

The plural of *pomodoro*, literally 'fruit of gold' = 'tomato', is now usually *pomodori*, although *pomidoro* and even *pomidori* are sometimes encountered.

Any element of a compound noun which is not a noun or an adjective is invariant for number: *dopopranzo – dopopranzi* 'afternoon', *sottaceto – sottaceti* 'pickle', *parafulmine – parafulmini* 'lightning conductor', *portachiave – portachiavi* 'key ring', *scendiletto – scendiletti* 'bedside mat', *fabbisogno – fabbisogni* 'necessity', *tergicristallo – tergicristalli* 'windscreen wiper', etc.

Any noun or adjective element within a compound which is of a different gender from the compound itself (typically, a feminine element within a masculine compound, but sometimes masculines within feminine compounds) is invariant for number. Examples below (feminine elements underlined).

il *barbanera*	i *barbanera*	'astrological calendar'
il *battiscopa*	i *battiscopa*	'skirting board'
il *cavalcavia*	i *cavalcavia*	'flyover'
il *guardaroba*	i *guardaroba*	'wardrobe', 'cloakroom'
il *paracadute*	i *paracadute*	'parachute'
il *portafortuna*	i *portafortuna*	'good luck charm'
il *retroterra*	i *retroterra*	'hinterland'
il *tagliacarte*	i *tagliacarte*	'paper knife'
lo *scansafatiche*	gli *scansafatiche*	'idler'
lo *spartiacque*	gli *spartiacque*	'watershed'
il *retroscena*[2]	i *retroscena*	'developments behind the scenes'
il *retrocucina*	i *retrocucina*	'pantry'
etc.		

For the same reason, the masculine *capo-* is invariant in feminine compounds:

---

[2]But cf. *la retroscena – le retroscene* 'backstage'. *Retrocucina* may also be feminine, in which case the plural is *le retrocucine*.

la capocuoca	*le capocuoche*	'head cook'
la capogruppo	*le capogruppo*	'group leader '
etc.		

However, masculine compounds whose second element is a feminine noun with the singular inflection *-e* or *-o*, may optionally form their plural with *-i*:

il caccia<u>vite</u>	*i caccia<u>vite</u>/caccia<u>viti</u>*	'screwdriver'
il salva<u>gente</u>	*i salva<u>gente</u>/salva<u>genti</u>*	'life jacket'
il porta<u>cenere</u>	*i porta<u>cenere</u>/porta<u>ceneri</u>*	'ashtray'
il bacia<u>mano</u>	*i bacia<u>mano</u>/ bacia<u>mani</u>*	'hand-kissing'
etc.		

In some cases, invariance of a noun element within the compound may be motivated by meaning. In the following examples, the underlined element is clearly a 'mass' noun (i.e., a noun of a kind that cannot normally have a plural):

il buca<u>neve</u>	*i buca<u>neve</u>*	'snowdrop'
il mangia<u>pane</u>	*i mangia<u>pane</u>*	'scrounger'
il trita<u>tutto</u>	*i trita<u>tutto</u>*	'all-purpose grinder'
il trita<u>carne</u>	*i trita<u>carne</u>*	'meat grinder'
il lascia<u>passare</u>	*i lascia<u>passare</u>*	'pass'
etc.		

Note also *il senzatetto – i senzatetto* 'homeless person' (i.e., '[people each of whom is] without [a] roof').

In general, in compound adjectives only the second element varies, e.g., *idee piccolo-borghesi* 'petit-bourgeois ideas' (but see also 3.3 for colour adjectives).

3.8 Number mismatches between languages: English plurals for Italian singulars, and vice versa

It is possible to view some entities (e.g., the hair of the head) either as 'singular' or as 'plural', a fact which can lead to differences between languages, such as:

i capelli	'hair'
l'uva	'grapes' ('a [single] grape' is *un chicco d'uva*)
La gente canta.	'People sing.'
gli interessi	'interest (on a loan, investment)' (cf. *senza interesse* 'uninteresting'; *senza interessi* 'interest-free')
Gli spaghetti sono pronti.	'The spaghetti is ready.'
i soldi	'money'
il pigiama	'pyjamas'

Italian stands with English and against French in having plural *i pantaloni* 'trousers'. For the use of the plural *i frutti* 'fruit', 'fruits', see 3.18.

A major difference between the two languages concerns nouns referring to items of which each of a number of individuals has only one. This is noticeable particularly, but by no means exclusively, with body parts and items of clothing. In a sentence such as 'The boys all opened their mouths', it is of course the case that each boy has only one mouth and it is this fact which determines the use of an Italian singular, rather than a plural, of *bocca*: *I ragazzi aprirono tutti la bocca*. Similarly, compare 10.2, 13 for the use of the article and the indirect object in these examples:

Avevano tutti il naso rosso.	'They all had red noses.'
Io e mio fratello indossavamo la camicia di seta.	'My brother and I wore silk shirts.'
Le porte avevano la maniglia di rame.	'The doors had brass handles.'
La lingua si era gonfiata in bocca a tutti gli atleti.	'All the athletes' tongues had swollen up in their mouths.'

The singular is typically used where the 'possessor' of the noun is the subject or indirect object (10.13, 14) of the verb and could easily and naturally be qualified in English by the phrase 'each (one)': 'They each had a red nose', 'My brother and I each wore a silk shirt', etc. In other cases, a plural would be used in Italian as in English:

Le maniglie di rame delle porte erano sporchissime.	'The doors' brass handles were filthy.'
Ammiravo moltissimo le camicie di seta degli invitati.	'I greatly admired the guests' silk shirts.'

With *cambiare* 'change', Italian frequently uses a singular where English employs a plural:

Sono bilingui e cambiano lingua ogni cinque minuti.	'They are bilingual and switch languages every five minutes.'

3.9 Three principles for predicting the gender of nouns

Every Italian noun has either masculine or feminine gender. The gender of many nouns is predictable from three simple general principles:

(i) Nouns denoting males are almost always masculine and those denoting females are overwhelmingly feminine:

il cane	'dog'	*la cagna*	'bitch'
il dio	'god'	*la dea*	'goddess'
il fratello	'brother'	*la sorella*	'sister'
il gallo	'cock'	*la gallina*	'hen'
il padre	'father'	*la madre*	'mother'
il portiere	'porter'	*la portiera*	'female porter'
il ragazzo	'boy'	*la ragazza*	'girl'
il re	'king'	*la regina*	'queen'
il toro	'bull'	*la mucca*	'cow'
l'asino	'donkey'	*l'asina*	'she-donkey'
l'infermiere	'male nurse'	*l'infermiera*	'female nurse'
l'uomo	'man'	*la donna*	'woman'
lo stallone	'stallion'	*la giumenta*	'mare'
etc.			

(ii) Nouns ending in *-o* are almost always masculine:

il carro	'cart'	*il popolo*	'people'	*l'uomo*	'man'
lo scoiattolo	'squirrel'	*il polpo*	'octopus'	*il cuoio*	'leather'
il ragazzo	'boy'	*il gomito*	'elbow'	*il volto*	'face'
lo spazio	'space'	*il dito*	'finger'	*il gancio*	'hook'
etc.					

(iii) Nouns ending in *-a* are usually feminine (but there is a significant minority of exceptions):

la casa	'house'	*la paglia*	'straw'	*la donna*	'woman'
l'anatra	'duck'	*la seppia*	'cuttlefish'	*la spiaggia*	'beach'
la cosa	'thing'	*la data*	'date'	*la nuvola*	'cloud'
l'arma	'weapon'	*la sella*	'saddle'	*la vasca*	'bathtub'
etc.					

However, there are some words (discussed in 3.4) in which the plural is, or may be, different in gender from the singular.

3.10 Nouns (notably those in -e) whose gender is not predictable from the three general principles for gender

Any noun which does not denote a male or female, and does not end in *-o* or *-a*, evidently lies outside the three principles outlined above. In such cases, there is usually no alternative to learning the gender of each individual word separately. The principal class of nouns of this type ends in *-e*:

Masculine		**Feminine**	
dente	'tooth'	*dote*	'dowry'
fiele	'gall'	*felce*	'fern'
germe	'germ'	*gente*	'people'
indice	'index'	*incudine*	'anvil'
larice	'larch tree'	*luce*	'light'
mese	'month'	*messe*	'harvest'
pesce	'fish'	*pece*	'pitch', 'tar'
rene	'kidney'	*rete*	'net'
seme	'seed'	*selce*	'flint'
ventre	'stomach'	*volpe*	'fox'
etc.			

Also:

Masculine		**Feminine**	
bambù	'bamboo'	*tribù*	'tribe'
sofà	'sofa'	*società*	'society'
brindisi	'drinking toast'	*analisi*	'analysis'
sport	'sport'	*gag*	'gag' (joke)
club	'club'	*leadership*	'leadership'
caffè	'coffee'	*gang*	'gang'
etc.			

For further discussion of ways of predicting the gender of nouns in *-i*, a stressed vowel, or a consonant, see below.

3.11 Nouns which contradict the general principles for gender (feminine gender for males; masculine gender for females; masculines in -*a*; feminines in -*o*)

A problem is presented by nouns in which sex and grammatical gender do not correspond (feminines denoting males, and masculines denoting females). Many of these denote living creatures whose sex is not evident, or at any rate not considered important; thus *volpe* is feminine, regardless of whether a fox or a vixen is denoted, and *serpente* is masculine, even if a female snake is denoted. Use of masculine nouns such as *soprano* to denote human females may reflect the fact that they traditionally denoted males; use of feminine nouns such as *guardia* to denote a male person is sometimes partly explicable by the fact that the noun originally denoted not the person, but the activity (represented by a feminine noun) carried out by the person:

Masculine

pesce	'fish'	*pidocchio*	'louse'	*serpente*	'snake'
leopardo	'leopard'	*scarafaggio*	'beetle'	*ghiro*	'dormouse'
gorilla	'gorilla'	*panda*	'panda'	*eremita*	'hermit'
soprano	'soprano'	*contralto*	'contralto'		
etc.					

Feminine

quaglia	'quail'	*pulce*	'flea'	*volpe*	'fox'
aquila	'eagle'	*formica*	'ant'	*tigre*	'tiger'
spia	'spy'	*guardia*	'guard'	*guida*	'guide'
recluta	'recruit'	*vittima*	'victim'	*persona*	'person'
sentinella	'sentinel'	*vedetta*	'lookout'		
etc.					

Lepre 'hare' is generally feminine, although a masculine variant is sometimes encountered. The masculine *il tigre* existed in old Italian and regained a brief currency in the world of advertising in the 1960s, with the Esso slogan *Metti un tigre nel motore* 'Put a tiger in your engine', where a masculine form was apparently thought consonant with an image of power and dynamism.

A number of nouns ending in *-o* are feminine (some of them abbreviations of longer nouns). Most prominent among these is *mano* 'hand'. Also:

moto (*motocicletta*)	'motorcycle'	*eco*	'echo'
auto (*automobile*)	'car'	*virago*	'virago'
dinamo	'dynamo'	*radio*	'radio'

Eco is generally feminine, but one encounters occasional masculine uses, such as *eco telefonico* 'telephone echo'; the plural is always masculine.

A sizeable minority of nouns ending in *-a* is masculine. Prominent among these are nouns in final *-ma*. Those who know Greek will recognize that the majority (but not all) of them originate in Greek neuter nouns. A useful, but not infallible, rule of thumb, is that if the *-ma* word has an obviously related equivalent, of the same or similar meaning, in English, then it is probably masculine in Italian, as in the following examples:

amalgama	'amalgam'	*dramma*	'drama'
apoftegma	'apophthegm'	*emblema*	'emblem'
aroma	'aroma'	*enigma*	'enigma'
cataplasma	'poultice', 'cataplasm'	*enzima*	'enzyme'
carisma	'charisma'	*fantasma*	'phantom'
clima	'climate'	*lemma*	'lemma', 'dictionary entry'
coma	'coma'	*morfema*	'morpheme'
diadema	'diadem'	*panorama*	'panorama', 'view'
diagramma	'diagram'	*pigiama*	'pyjamas'
dilemma	'dilemma'	*plasma*	'plasma'
diploma	'diploma'	*poema*	'poem'
dogma	'dogma'	*prisma*	'prism'

problema	'problem'	*sperma*	'sperm'
proclama	'proclamation'	*stemma*	'coat of arms'
programma	'programme'	*stratagemma*	'stratagem'
radiogramma	'radiogram'	*telegramma*	'telegram'
rizoma	'rhizome'	*tema*	'theme', 'essay'
sisma	'earthquake'	*teorema*	'theorem'
sistema	'system'	*trauma*	'trauma'
schema	'scheme'		

There is also *il cinema*, which is an abbreviated form of *il cinematografo*. *Lo zigoma* 'cheekbone', has now been replaced by *lo zigomo*.

However, the following nouns in *-ma* are feminine:

arma	'weapon'	*lima*	'file' (tool)
asma	'asthma'	*melma*	'mud'
calma	'calm'	*norma*	'norm'
crema	'cream'	*palma*	'palm' (tree, hand)
dracma	'drachma'	*quaresima*	'Lent'
fiamma	'flame'	*rima*	'rhyme'
firma	'signature'	*risma*	'ream'
flegma	'phlegm'	*salma*	'corpse'
forma	'form', 'shape'	*somma*	'sum'
gamma	'gamut', 'range'	*stima*	'esteem', 'estimate'
gomma	'rubber', 'tyre'	*tema*	'fear' (literary and archaic)
lacrima	'tear'	*trama*	'plot' (of book, etc.)

Some nouns in *-a* are masculine if they denote male persons, and feminine if they denote female persons. Notable among these are nouns in *-ista*:

artista	'artist'	*oltranzista*	'political extremist', 'hardliner'
autista	'driver'		
comunista	'communist'	*ottimista*	'optimist'
menefreghista	'person who doesn't give a damn' (from *me ne frego*)	*pessimista*	'pessimist'
		professionista	'professional'
		solista	'soloist'
nazionalista	'nationalist'	*tennista*	'tennis player'
normalista	'student of the Scuola Normale Superiore'	*teppista*	'vandal'
etc.			

suicida	'suicide' (person)	*patricida/parricida*	'parricide'
matricida	'matricide'	*idiota*	'idiot'
etc.			

The following nouns in *-a*, and denoting persons or creatures, are always masculine:

apostata	'apostate'	*papa*	'pope'
boia	'executioner'	*paria*	'pariah'
camerata	'comrade'	*patriarca*	'patriarch'
eremita	'hermit'	*pilota*	'pilot'
gerarca	'hierarch'	*pirata*	'pirate'
gorilla	'gorilla'	*puma*	'puma'
monarca	'monarch'	*sosia*	'identical twin'
panda	'panda'		

Some further masculine nouns in *-a* are:

colera	'cholera'	*vaglia*	'postal order'
delta	'delta' (of river)	*via*	'go-ahead' (*dare il via*
mitra	'machine gun' (short for *il*		'give the go-ahead')
	fucile mitragliatore)	*insetticida*	'insecticide'
nirvana	'nirvana'	*yoga*	'yoga'
pianeta	'planet'		

Names of countries and regions in *-a* are generally feminine (*la Nigeria*, *l'Uganda*, *l'Alaska*, *l'Italia*, *la Spagna*, *la Francia*, *la Cina*), but some are masculine: *il Nicaragua*, *il Sahara*, *il Venezuela*, *il Canada* (also *il Canadà*), *il Kenia*.

3.12 Other clues to the gender of nouns (endings and suffixes)

Nouns ending in *-tà* and *-tù* are almost always feminine:

età	'age'	*cecità*	'blindness'	*realtà*	'reality'
onestà	'honesty'	*nazionalità*	'nationality'	*società*	'society'
unità	'unity'	*nobiltà*	'nobility'	*sordità*	'deafness'
capacità	'capacity'	*qualità*	'quality'	*verità*	'truth'
virtù	'virtue'	*schiavitù*	'slavery'		
etc.					

However, *podestà* (the head of a medieval commune, or the head of local administration during the Fascist period) is masculine.

Most nouns in *-i* in the singular are feminine (especially those, of Greek origin, which correspond to English nouns in *-is*):

analisi	'analysis'	*crisi*	'crisis'	*tesi*	'thesis'
oasi	'oasis'	*esegesi*	'exegesis'	*genesi*	'genesis'
paralisi	'paralysis'	*dialisi*	'dialysis'	*prostesi*	'prosthesis'
etc.					

But masculine *il brindisi* '(drinking) toast', *lo spermaceti* 'spermaceti'. *Genesi* may be masculine when it refers to the first book (cf. *il libro*) of the Bible.

Nouns in *-zione* are feminine:

azione	'action'	*nazione*	'nation'
comunicazione	'communication'	*operazione*	'operation'
direzione	'direction', 'management'	*quantificazione*	'quantification'
elezione	'election'	*trazione*	'traction'
frizione	'friction', 'clutch' (of car)	*produzione*	'production'
manifestazione	'manifestation'	*respirazione*	'breathing'
etc.			

Nouns in *-ore* are masculine:

colore	'colour'	*grigiore*	'greyness'	*rossore*	'redness'
dolore	'pain'	*orrore*	'horror'	*vapore*	'steam'
valore	'value'	*radiatore*	'radiator'	*sudore*	'sweat'
etc.					

In literary and archaic usage the noun *fòlgore* 'thunderbolt' is also masculine, but in modern usage it is generally feminine.

Nouns ending in *-trice* are feminine:

cucitrice	'sewing machine' / 'female sewer'	*trebbiatrice*	'threshing machine' / 'female thresher'
etc.			

The (usually augmentative) suffix *-one* confers masculine gender on any feminine noun to which it is attached (but see 3.19):

la porta	'door'	*il portone*	'front door'
la palla	'ball'	*il pallone*	'large ball', 'football'
la donna	'woman'	*il donnone*	'large/big woman'
la minestra	'soup'	*il minestrone*	'minestrone'

3.13 Gender of compound nouns

Compound nouns are those made up of two (or sometimes more) independently existing words (cf. 3.7; 20.1). They are overwhelmingly masculine:

asciugamano	'towel'	*passamontagna*	'balaclava helmet' (lit. 'pass mountain')
battiscopa	'skirting board' (lit. 'beat broom')	*pellerossa*	'redskin' (native American)
bucaneve	'snowdrop'	*pescespada*	'swordfish'
cacciavite	'screwdriver'	*portacenere*	'ashtray'
cavalcavia	'flyover'	*portafortuna*	'good luck charm'
cruciverba	'crossword'	*retroterra*	'hinterland' (lit. 'behind land')
dopoguerra	'the post-war period' (lit. 'after war')	*salvagente*	'life jacket' (lit. 'save people')
dormiveglia	'doze' (lit. 'sleep wake')		
girasole	'sunflower' (lit. 'turn sun')	*sottaceto*	'pickle'
grillotalpa	'mole cricket' (lit. 'cricket mole')	*scolapasta*	'colander'
		spartiacque	'watershed' (lit. 'divide waters')
guardaroba	'wardrobe' (lit. 'keep stuff')	*tritacarne*	'meat mincer' (lit. 'mince meat')
nontiscordardimé	'forget-me-not'		
parabrezza	'windscreen/shield' (lit. 'parry breeze')		

Compound nouns are feminine only in the following cases:

- They specifically denote a female (they remain masculine when they denote a male):

capofabbrica	'female factory head'
rompiscatole	'annoying, troublesome woman'
pellerossa	'female redskin'

- They are analysable as comprising a feminine 'head' noun modified by the other element of the compound, which will be either an adjective or another noun. As a rule of thumb (cf. 3.7), such compounds are analysable of having the meaning 'an X (where X is a feminine noun) which is (or is like, or functions as, or is used for, or is made of) Y (where Y is an adjective or noun)'.

acquaforte	'etching '(lit. 'strong water')	*belladonna*	'deadly nightshade'
banconota	'bank note'	*cartapecora*	'parchment' (lit. 'paper [of] sheep')

cassaforte	'strong box', 'safe'	*manodopera*	'workforce'
cassapanca	'bench chest'	*mezzaluna*	'half moon'
ferrovia	'railway'	*mezzanotte*	'midnight'
grancassa	'chest'	*terracotta*	'terracotta'
madreperla	'mother of pearl'	*terraferma*	'mainland'
etc.			

Other feminine compound nouns are:

sottogonna	'underskirt'	*sottoveste*	'petticoat'
sottocalza	'underhose'	*retromarcia*	'reverse gear'
retroguardia	'rearguard'	*compravendita*	'sale and purchase'
retrostanza	'backroom'		
etc.			

Sottocoppa 'saucer' and *retrocucina* 'pantry' may have either gender. *Sottogola* 'chinstrap', and *retroscena* 'backstage' may have either gender but are usually masculine. Note, however, *il crocevia* crossroads, *il sottoscala* 'cupboard under the stairs'. Also, *il barbanera* 'astrological calendar' (so called because of a popular representation of the astrologer as having a black beard); *il barbagianni* 'owl' (based on regional *barba* meaning 'Uncle', lit. 'Uncle John'); *il testarapata* 'man with shaven head'; *il barbarossa* 'redbeard'.

In compound adjectives, generally only the second element varies for gender: e.g., *le truppe austro-ungariche* 'the Austro-Hungarian troops', *una presentazione storico-geografica* 'a historical-geographical presentation'.

3.14 Gender of acronyms (*sigle*)

Acronyms (*sigle*) normally take their gender from the gender of the phrase for which the acronym stands (*l'ONU* (f.) = *la Organizzazione delle nazioni unite*; *le FS* = *le Ferrovie dello Stato*; *il PCI* = *il Partito comunista italiano*). This principle generally applies also to acronyms based on foreign words, where the equivalent in Italian would be feminine: *la NATO* = 'North Atlantic Treaty Organization' (*la organizzazione*); *la NASA* = 'National Aeronautic and Space Administration' (*l'amministrazione*), *la CIA* = 'Central Intelligence Agency' (*l'agenzia*), etc.

3.15 Gender of parts of speech other than nouns

Sometimes forms which are not normally nouns may be used as nouns; when so used they have masculine gender.

Adjectives used as nouns:

il verde	'green'	*il falso*	'that which is false'
il rosso	'red'	*il vero*	'that which is true'
l'azzurro	'blue'		
etc.			

Interjections used as nouns:

il via	'the go-ahead' (from *via!* 'off you go')	*l'alleluia*	'alleluia'
etc.			

Infinitives used as nouns (cf. 15.24):

il cantare	'(the fact of) singing'	*il naufragare*	'(the fact of) getting
lo sperare	'(the fact of) hoping'		shipwrecked'
etc.			

Conjunctions and discourse markers used as nouns:

Voglio capire il perché.	'I want to understand (the reason) why.'
Nella tua promessa ci sono troppi 'purché'.	'There are too many "provided thats" in your promise.'

The same principle applies when whole phrases or parts of phrases are employed as nouns:

Il francese apostrofa il team manager della Ferrari con un esplicito: «Questa volta mi hai rotto . . .»	'The Frenchman rounds on the Ferrari team manager with an explicit: "This time you've broken my . . .".'
In questo caso, 'intonazione' è usato in senso piuttosto lato.	'In this case, [the word] "intonation" is used in a rather broad sense.'

3.16 Gender of names of cities, cars, rivers, valleys and wines

The gender of certain nouns may be predictable from the gender of the word denoting the class of entities to which the noun in question belongs. For example, names of motor cars are feminine, apparently because the generic word for 'motor car' is itself feminine (*la macchina* or *l'automobile*).

Names of cars are feminine:

la Rolls Royce	*la Topolino*	*la Uno*	*la Ritmo*	*la Bravo*
la Bentley	*la Jeep*	*la Ford*	*la Renault*	*la Fiat*
etc.				

Names of towns and cities are feminine (cf. *la città*) in standard Italian (although this may not always be true in dialects and regional varieties of Italian):

La Hollywood italiana è miracolosamente risorta.	'The Italian Hollywood has miraculously risen again.'
Avrebbero fatto ridere tutta Berlino.	'They would have made all Berlin laugh.'
Milano mi è sempre parsa poco accogliente.	'Milan has always seemed to me unwelcoming.'
Cercava d'immaginarsi la Zurigo del tardo Ottocento.	'He tried to imagine the Zurich of the late nineteenth century.'
Nell'ultimo decennio Sarajevo è stata martoriata dall'artiglieria serba, snaturata nella sua vita quotidiana da continui bombardamenti, tagliata fuori dal mondo da un assedio implacabile.	'In the last ten years Sarajevo has been tormented by Serb artillery, distorted in its daily life by continual bombardments, cut off from the world by a ruthless siege.'

The two major exceptions are *Il Cairo* and *Il Pireo* (Piraeus), both of which are usually accompanied by the definite article.

Names of rivers *tend* to be masculine (cf. *il fiume*), unless they end in *-a*: *il Tevere*, *il Tamigi*, *il Mississippi*, *la Senna*, *la Loira*, *la Dora*, etc. However: *il Volga*; *il* or *la Livenza*; *il* or *la Magra*; *il* or *la Brenta*. *Il Piave* is now normal, but *la Piave* was used until the time of the First World War. Names of valleys containing the feminine noun *valle* (or *val*) tend to be feminine: *la Valsesia, la Val Camonica, la Valbondione*, etc. But *il Valdarno*.

Names of wines are usually masculine (cf. *il vino*): *il Regaleali, il Donnafugata, l'Etna rosso*, etc. *Barbera* and *Marsala* may have either gender. *Malvasia* and *Vernaccia* are usually feminine (but masculine gender is also possible).

Names of letters of the alphabet (including those of the Greek alphabet) are usually feminine: *la B, la C, la D, la U, la delta*, etc., although masculine gender is sometimes encountered.

Most names of football teams are masculine (e.g., *il Milan*). Names derived from adjectives, and those which do not correspond to names of towns, are usually feminine: *la Juventus, la Sampdoria, la Fiorentina, la Pistoiese, la Cremonese* (but *la Roma*). In a number of cases the name of the team is of the opposite gender to that of the town or region represented: *la Lazio, il Pisa, il Perugia, il Bologna, il Torino, il Napoli*.

3.17 Other meaning differences associated with gender (trees vs. fruits; size)

There are a number of cases where different meanings are expressed by the distinction between masculine and feminine forms of the 'same' word. A masculine noun often denotes a fruit-bearing tree while a feminine form of the same noun denotes the fruit:

Tree	Fruit	
il ciliegio	*la ciliegia*	'cherry'
il melo	*la mela*	'apple'
il prugno	*la prugna*	'plum'
il nespolo	*la nespola*	'medlar'
il pero	*la pera*	'pear'
l'olivo	*l'oliva*	'olive'
il noce	*la noce*	'nut'/'walnut tree'
il pesco	*la pesca*	'peach'
il banano	*la banana*	'banana'

Il limone 'lemon', *il fico* 'fig' and *l'arancio* 'orange' each denote both the tree and the fruit. *La fica*, in modern Italian, has become a taboo word indicating the female sexual organ. While *l'arancio* appears to be the predominant modern form, *l'arancia* was formerly used for the fruit, and occasionally even for the tree.

In some cases, the masculine word indicates smaller size than the feminine:

il buco	'hole'		*la buca*	'deep (usually excavated) hole'
il terrazzo	'terrace' (often a balcony)'		*la terrazza*	'large terrace' (often on roof)
il carretto	'(hand)cart'		*la carretta*	'large cart', generally drawn by animals
il sacco	'sack', 'bag'		*la sacca*	'large sack', 'pocket/zone' (of territory)
il vitello	'calf' (in first year of life)		*la vitella*	'young cow'

Frequently a diminutive suffix is accompanied by a change to masculine gender:

la finestra	'window'	*il finestrino*	'window of train, aeroplane', etc.
la festa	'holiday', 'feast day'	*il festino*	'party'
la capra	'goat'	*il capretto*	'kid'
la calza	'sock', 'stocking'	*il calzino*	'short sock'

There is no particular difference of size between *il tavolo* and *la tavola*, but *tavolo* tends to be used where the table has a particular and specific use (*tavolo da stiro* 'ironing board', *tavolo operatorio* 'operating table'); *tavola* is always used in the phrases *a tavola* 'at table' and *a capotavola* 'at the head of the table'. Note that *la mattina* is the general term for 'morning' (as opposed to, say, *sera* 'evening'), but *mattino* tends to be preferred when a specific time of the morning is indicated: *di buon mattino* 'early in the morning' (yet *di prima mattina* 'first thing'), *alle nove del mattino* 'at 9 in the morning'.

3.18 Other pairs of words differentiated by gender

There are a number of further cases where gender distinguishes words whose meanings are, however, much less closely connected than those listed above:

il fine	'aim', 'purpose'	*la fine*	'end', 'termination'
il capitale	'capital' (finance)	*la capitale*	'capital city'
il fronte	'(battle) front'	*la fronte*	'forehead'
il mitra	'machine gun'	*la mitra*	'mitre'
il fonte	'(baptismal) font'	*la fonte*	'fount', 'source'
il camerata	'comrade'	*la camerata*	'ward', 'dormitory'
il pianeta	'planet'	*la pianeta*	'chasuble'
il comune	'commune'	*la comune*	'commune' (in the history of Paris, Communist China)
il cappuccino	'Capuchin monk', 'type of coffee'	*la cappuccina*	'type of lettuce'
il caccia	'fighter aircraft'	*la caccia*	'hunt'

Masculine *il frutto* is fruit (figuratively, as a product or result of something: *il frutto della mia ricerca* 'the fruit of my research'); *la frutta* is (a) fruit (as foodstuff: *Devo mangiare molta frutta* 'I have to eat a lot of fruit', *Qual è la tua frutta preferita?* 'Which is your favourite fruit?'). In the plural Italian uses masculine *i frutti* to mean 'individual fruits growing on a plant', or 'different types, species of fruit' where English might use singular 'fruit':

Nel giardino c'è un albero con strani frutti verdi e rugosi.	'In the garden there's a tree with strange, green, wrinkled fruit.' [i.e., individual fruits growing on it]
La foresta li nutriva con frutti, semi, bacche e noccioline.	'The forest nourished them with [different kinds of] fruit, seeds, berries and hazelnuts.'

3.19 Sex: ways of expressing 'male' and 'female' in nouns denoting living beings

In nouns denoting living beings, distinctions of sex are often made 'lexically', as in English, so that the 'male' noun has a wholly or partly different root from the 'female' noun: e.g., *toro* 'bull' vs. *mucca* 'cow', *uomo* 'man' vs. *donna* 'woman', *gallo* 'cock' vs. *gallina* 'hen', *re* 'king' vs. *regina* 'queen'. In many other cases, the 'male' and 'female' forms share the same root, but differ simply in gender: e.g., *il francese* 'the Frenchman' vs. *la francese* 'the Frenchwoman', *il ballerino* 'male ballet dancer' vs. *la ballerina* 'female ballet dancer', *il gatto* 'cat' vs. *la gatta*, *l'asino* 'donkey' vs. *l'asina*. Another strategy involves the use of special suffixes:

- Masculine nouns in *-tore* (except *dottore*, *pastore* whose feminines are *dottoressa*, *pastorella*) denoting males, have counterparts in *-trice* denoting females:

cantatore	'singer'	*cantatrice*
venditore	'seller'	*venditrice*
lettore	'reader'	*lettrice*
etc.		

  Note *fattore* 'creator', feminine *fattrice*, but *fattore* 'farmer', feminine *fattoressa* 'farmer's wife' (also *fattora*).

- A few masculine nouns in *-e* have counterparts denoting females in *-a*:

signore	'lord', 'sir'	*signora*	'lady', 'madam'
priore	'prior'	*priora*	'prioress'
infermiere	'male nurse'	*infermiera*	'female nurse'
marchese	'marquis'	*marchesa*	'marchioness'
padrone	'master'	*padrona*	'mistress'

- The 'augmentative/pejorative' suffix *-one* has the effect of conferring masculine gender onto a noun, even if it denotes a female (e.g., *il donnone* 'great big woman'). As a rule, however, the augmentative ending for nouns denoting persons is *-ona* (plural *-one*):

spendaccione	*spendaccioni*	'(male) spendthrift'
spendacciona	*spendaccione*	'(female) spendthrift'

  The *-ona* suffix may also be used to make it transparent that what is intended is simply a 'big', 'large' variant of the unsuffixed form, whereas *-one* does not necessarily have this effect: *minestrone* is not exactly a 'big' version of *minestra*, but a different sort of soup; the true augmentative of *minestra* in the sense 'big soup' would be *minestrona*.

- Some female nouns are formed by adding *-essa* to the root of the masculine, but there is no way of predicting where this suffix applies, so examples have to be learned word-by-word:

barone	'baron'	*baronessa*
campione	'champion'	*campionessa*
conte	'count'	*contessa*
dottore	'doctor'	*dottoressa*
leone	'lion'	*leonessa*
poeta	'poet'	*poetessa*
presidente	'president'	*presidentessa* (or *la presidente*)
prìncipe	'prince'	*principessa*
professore	'teacher'	*professoressa*
sacerdote	'priest'	*sacerdotessa*
studente	'student'	*studentessa*
duca	'duke'	*duchessa*
etc.		

The *-essa* suffix cannot be applied at will, because sometimes the result, even if it actually occurs, is considered jocular or pejorative. Thus *avvocatessa* (*avvocato* 'lawyer'), seems to suggest a 'talkative, opinionated woman', and *filosofessa* (*filosofo* 'philosopher') has mocking or ironic overtones for some speakers.

There are many nouns denoting living beings of either sex which normally have only one gender. This can create a clash between grammatical gender and sex, and there may be some cases in which it becomes necessary to indicate the sex clearly. Few reliable general rules can be given for such cases (but an excellent survey is Brunet 1982: 125–57), and there is often a risk – especially in creating explicitly 'female' forms of normally masculine nouns – that the result may have undesirable pejorative connotations for some speakers.

In some cases one may simply change the gender of the noun: e.g., *la ministra* 'female minister' corresponding to *il ministro*, *la preside* 'female head (of school)' corresponding to *il preside*, *la deputata* 'the member of Parliament', corresponding to *il deputato*, etc. But these forms, too, may be considered ungainly or slightly pejorative (*deputata, la preside* and also *la presidente* seem to be widely accepted however). Such nouns are often best left in the masculine, even when they refer to females (e.g., *l'ex-Primo Ministro britannico, Thatcher*). Feminine forms of *cassiere* 'cashier' and *tesoriere* 'treasurer' (namely, *la cassiera* and *la tesoriera*) occur but are best avoided (*cassiera* is liable to be interpreted as 'the woman who works at the cash till' (*cassa*), but, it seems, never as a female 'cashier' in the sense of 'senior financier'.

Another possible approach is to preserve the original noun intact, adding the nouns *femmina* or *maschio* (or *uomo* and *donna*,[3] for people). Note that because these are *nouns*, they will not agree for gender.

la guida	'guide'	*la guida maschio/uomo*	'the male guide'
il soldato	'soldier'	*la donna soldato*	'woman soldier'
la tigre	'tiger'	*la tigre maschio*	'the male tiger'
il bisonte	'bison'	*il bisonte femmina*	'the female bison'
la felce	'fern'	*la felce maschio*	'male fern'

Uomo and *donna* may either precede or follow the noun: the difference between a *donna soldato* and a *soldato donna* is roughly that between 'a woman who is a soldier' and 'a soldier who is a woman'. *Soldatessa* is also sometimes used.

To conclude, if in doubt about the appropriate way to indicate mismatches between gender and sex of a person, the best advice is to avoid any of these solutions and to find some other way – if absolutely necessary – of indicating sex. For 'They wanted only female architects' one might say for example *Come architetti volevano solo delle donne.*

3.20 Apparent anomalies of gender where a noun is understood but not expressed

Nouns sometimes appear to have the 'wrong' gender (and even the wrong number) where the gender (and number) actually refers to a noun which is not expressed:

---

[3]Some people may find specification of *donna* in cases such as this in principle objectionable.

una second'anno	'a second year [female student]'
	= *una [studentessa] di second'anno*
uno zuppa di verdura	'a [plate of] vegetable soup'
	= *un [piatto] di zuppa di verdura*
Preferisco il vaniglia.	'I prefer the vanilla [ice cream].'
	= *Preferisco il [gelato di] vaniglia.*
etc.	

3.21 Masculine plurals of nouns denoting relatives may refer to both sexes

The masculine plurals *figli, cugini, nipoti, zii, nonni,* and also *suoceri* and *fratelli,* may refer to *both sexes*:

Quanti fratelli hai?	'How many brothers and sisters do you have?'
Sono gli zii/i nonni di Marco.	'They are M's uncle and aunt/grandparents.'
Domani arrivano i suoceri.	'Our in-laws get here tomorrow.'

3.22 Gender and adjectives

Adjectives always agree in gender with the noun they refer to. This applies both when they directly modify the noun and when they are in the predicate of the noun. Adjectives whose masculine singular ends in *-o* distinguish gender according to the following pattern:

	Singular	Plural
Masculine	*-o*	*-i*
Feminine	*-a*	*-e*

l' uomo furbo	'the crafty man'	*L'uomo è/diventa/ sembra furbo.*	'The man is/ becomes/seems crafty.'
la donna furba	'the crafty woman'	*La donna è/diventa/ sembra furba.*	'The woman is/ becomes/seems crafty.'
gli uomini furbi	'the crafty men'	*Gli uomini sono/ diventano/sembrano furbi.*	'The men are/ become/seem crafty'.
le donne furbe	'the crafty women'	*Le donne sono/ diventano/sembrano furbe.*	'The women are/ become/seem crafty.'

Adjectives that end in *-a* in the masculine singular also have *-a* in the feminine singular, and so distinguish gender only in the plural (*-i* vs. *-e*):

l'uomo pessimista	'the pessimistic man'	*L'uomo è/diventa/ sembra pessimista.*	'The man is/ becomes/seems pessimistic.'
la donna pessimista	'the pessimistic woman'	*La donna è/diventa/ sembra pessimista.*	'The woman is/ becomes/seems pessimistic.'
gli uomini pessimisti	'the pessimistic men'	*Gli uomini sono/ diventano/sembrano pessimisti.*	'The men are/ become/seem pessimistic.'
le donne pessimiste	'the pessimistic women'	*Le donne sono/ diventano/sembrano pessimiste.*	'The women are/ become/seem pessimistic.'

Just as masculine nouns in *-tore* form their feminine in *-trice* (3.12, 19), so do adjectives in *-tore*:

uno sguardo ammiratore	'an admiring look'
degli sguardi ammiratori	'admiring looks'
un'occhiata ammiratrice	'an admiring glance'
delle occhiate ammiratrici	'admiring glances'

All other kinds of adjectives, including those that end in *-e* (plural *-i*), a stressed vowel or a consonant, show no distinction for gender:

un uomo cortese	'a polite man'	*Quest'uomo è cortese.*	'This man is polite.'
una donna cortese	'a polite woman'	*Questa donna è cortese.*	'This woman is polite.'
due uomini cortesi	'two polite men'	*Questi uomini sono cortesi.*	'These men are polite.'
due donne cortesi	'two polite women'	*Queste donne sono cortesi.*	'These women are polite.'
il vestito blu	'the blue suit'	*Il vestito è blu.*	'The suit is blue.'
la gonna blu	'the blue skirt'	*La gonna è blu.*	'The skirt is blue.'
i vestiti blu	'the blue suits'	*I vestiti sono blu.*	'The suits are blue.'
le gonne blu etc.	'the blue skirts'	*Le gonne sono blu.*	'The skirts are blue.'

3.23 Agreement patterns with nouns of different gender: *Aveva le mani e i piedi legati* 'His hands and feet were bound'

Adjectives (and past participles) which qualify two or more nouns of different gender take the *masculine* plural form if those nouns denote non-human entities:

Ho comprato penne e astucci rossi.	'I bought red pens and pen cases.'
Mangiavamo allora anatre, faraone e polli tutti allevati dal fattore.	'Then we used to eat ducks, guinea fowl and chickens all raised by the farmer.'

But for most Italians, the masculine plural form of the adjective is used in such cases only if the last noun is masculine; thus *anatre, polli e faraone tutti allevati ...* would tend to be avoided. In lists of non-human nouns where feminines considerably outnumber masculines, feminine agreement is not unusual:

La rosa, la viola, la mimosa, il tulipano, la primula e la petunia, tutte profumate ...	'The rose, the violet, the mimosa, the tulip, the primula and the petunia, all scented ...'

Masculine or feminine agreement with a number of conjoined nouns most of which are feminine tends to be avoided where those nouns denote persons. The pattern

Carla, Franca, Enrico, Lucia e Sara sono simpatici.	'Carla, Franca, Enrico, Lucia and Sarah are nice.'
Carla, Franca, Enrico, Lucia e Sara sono partiti.	'Carla, Franca, Enrico, Lucia and Sarah have left.'

is possible, but it is generally preferable to say:

Carla, Franca, Enrico, Lucia e Sara sono tutte persone simpatiche.

or

Carla, Franca, Lucia e Sara sono simpatiche, ed è simpatico anche Enrico.
Carla, Franca, Lucia e Sara sono partite, ed è partito anche Enrico.

3.24 Gender strictly determined by the noun

Native speakers of English often seem to assume that in cases where the grammatical gender of a noun is in some sense 'in the background', it ought to be acceptable to use masculine gender, even if the noun is feminine. Imagine, for example, that you are eating in a restaurant and have found that the knife is dirty; you then pick up the fork and want to ask 'Is this clean?' Clearly what is in the 'foreground' is the 'cleanliness' of the cutlery, rather than the fact that you are referring specifically to a fork, yet you *cannot* ask (without producing confusion) *È pulito questo?*, in the masculine, because *forchetta* is feminine. The question must be *È pulita questa?* Similarly, if you wish to talk about 'a colleague', known to you but completely unknown to your audience and whose identity you consider immaterial, it is not possible to use a kind of 'generic' masculine if that colleague is a woman. You could not in such a case start off *Un mio collega, che voi non conoscete . . .* for 'A colleague of mine whom you don't know . . .'. One has to specify *Una collega* from the beginning, otherwise one creates the expectation that the colleague is a man, and any subsequent information indicating that she is a woman may cause confusion or surprise.

3.25 The position of the adjective

Italian adjectives may either follow or precede the noun which they modify (except that 'specificational' adjectives [3.29] and demonstrative adjectives always precede). Adjectives following the noun ('postposed' adjectives) have a particular *delimiting* function: they serve to identify, pick out, highlight, place in the foreground, focus attention on, a subset of the entities referred to by the noun. An adjective placed in front of the noun ('preposed'), in contrast, is simply 'neutral' in this respect: it does not necessarily have any delimiting, highlighting, focusing function. The phrase *Ho conosciuto uno studioso giovane che lavora sugli insetti* 'I met a young scholar working on insects' marks the scholar out as being young (and may imply that other scholars in the field are old); *Ho conosciuto un giovane studioso che lavora sugli insetti* states, simply, both that he is a scholar and also that he is young.

A number of consequences flow from this distinction:

(i) Adjectives follow the noun when there is an explicit or implicit contrast with other entities:

Ho invitato i colleghi giovani, non i colleghi anziani.	'I invited my young colleagues, not my old colleagues.'
Apri la scatola grande e prendimi la matita verde.	'Open the big box [rather than any other box] and get me the green pencil [rather than any of the other pencils].'
Mi avevi detto che ti piace la cucina indiana, ma io avevo capito 'cucina italiana'.	'You'd told me you like Indian cooking, but I'd thought you'd said "Italian cooking".'

(ii) Italian adjectives overwhelmingly *follow* the noun; this may be viewed as a natural consequence of the fact that adjectives tend to single out a subset of the entities referred to by the noun as possessing some particular property:

A volte il fare uno scherzo cattivo lascia un gusto amaro.	'Sometimes making a bad joke leaves a bitter taste.'
Ricordatevi di essere concreti e di parlare con battute brevi e pungenti.	'Remember to be concrete and to speak in short, pithy phrases.'
È certo una congettura arrischiata, trattandosi di un testo molto complesso.	'It certainly is a daring speculation, since we're dealing with a very complex text.'

(iii) 'Defining', 'delimiting' functions of the adjective are only possible when there is a possibility of *contrast*. If there is no such possibility, the 'defining' function of the adjective becomes inappropriate, and the adjective tends to precede the noun. This occurs, for example, when the noun denotes an inherent characteristic of a unique individual, or where the adjective expresses some inherent, essential, quality associated with the noun (such as the whiteness of snow – there is no such thing, normally, as snow which is not white):

Aprirà la serie il simpaticissimo Braccobaldo, con la storia di Braccobaldo pompiere.	'The series will be opened by the delightful B, with the story of B the fireman.'
Li guardò con materna dolcezza.	'She looked at them with maternal sweetness.'
Contemplavo la bianca neve delle montagne.	'I was contemplating the white snow of the mountains.'

If one were to say *Aprirà la serie il Braccobaldo simpaticissimo*, this might be taken to imply that B is only sometimes *simpaticissimo*, but that he will be on this occasion, or that there is some rival *Braccobaldo* who is not *simpaticissimo*, but that the one opening the series is the one who is *simpaticissimo*. *Li guardò con materna dolcezza* tends to imply that the subject actually *is* their mother, and that her *dolcezza* is natural to her as a mother; the alternative *Li guardò con dolcezza materna* merely tells us that the sweetness is of a kind typical of mothers, 'like a mother's'. As for a sentence such as *Contemplavo la neve bianca delle montagne*, its effect would be to especially highlight and emphasize the whiteness of the snow, to draw the reader's/hearer's attention to its whiteness, to make it clear that this was snow that was particularly prominent by its whiteness. The sense is not too distant from 'I was contemplating the snow of the mountains. How white it was!'

In a sentence such as

Gli uomini sono delle disgraziate creature condannate al progresso.	'Men are wretched creatures condemned to progress.'

the preposing of *disgraziate* implies that 'wretchedness' is an inherent, necessary characteristic of *creature condannate al progresso*. An alternative *Gli uomini sono delle creature disgraziate condannate al progresso*, *disgraziate* would simply define men as creatures who are 'wretched' and also 'condemned to progress'. In fact, preposing is typical of adjectives expressing properties which the speaker asserts as being inherent or characteristic of the noun, among them particularly those expressing attitudes of sympathy and antipathy: *Odio quel maledetto professore* 'I hate that blasted professor'; *Amavo infinitamente il mio santo professore* 'I loved my saintly teacher infinitely'.

In the following example, the effect of postposing *eccitatissimo* is to indicate that Bendicò (a dog) is, at that moment, in a very excited mood, which is not his inherent state (a fact also indicated by the use of the indefinite article).[4] But the preposed adjective *breve* suggests that there is only *one* 'flight of steps leading to the garden', and therefore no possibility of contrast with any other 'flight of steps leading to the garden':

Preceduto da un Bendicò eccitatissimo discese la breve scala che conduceva al giardino.	'Preceded by a very excited Bendicò, he came down the short flight of steps leading to the garden.'

In the following, the preposing of *oscuri* probably reflects the fact that 'pine woods' tend naturally to be 'dark':

Sono saliti per oliveti, poi per terreni gerbidi, poi per oscuri boschi di pini.	'They climbed through olive groves, then through barren land, then through dark pine woods.'

Adjectives which indicate common and inherent characteristics, such as *bello*, *brutto*, *buono*, *cattivo*, *grande*, *piccolo* are often placed before the noun:

È una bella ragazza.	'She's a beautiful girl.'
Non venga a dirci che è il buon Dio a infilargli la carta falsa nel polsino.	'Let him not try and tell us that the good Lord is slipping the false card up his sleeve.'
Ha varcato il portone di Palazzo Chigi di buon passo.	'He walked briskly through the front door of Palazzo Chigi.'
Il vecchio contadino inglese pensava a Dio come a un «buon vecchio», a Cristo come a un «bel giovanotto», all'anima come a un «grosso osso confitto nel corpo» e all'aldilà come a un «bel prato verde».	'The old English peasant thought of God as a "nice old man", Christ as a "fine young man", the soul as a "big bone stuck in the body" and the afterlife as a "nice green meadow".'
Non modificano un bel niente, perché, un bel giorno, tutto andrà a catafascio.	'They don't change a damned thing, because one fine day everything will go to pieces.'
Ho scoperto un piccolo problema.	'I've discovered a little problem.'
C'è un cattivo odore qui dentro.	'There's a bad smell in here.'

The effect of preposing adjectives may require special attention when translating Italian into English. For example, adjectives of place and nationality virtually always follow the noun in Italian, and preposing them creates a highly marked stylistic effect, so that a phrase such as *Il lombardo scrittore di queste pagine non avrebbe mai usato una espressione così tipicamente siciliana* is not just 'The Lombard writer of these pages would never have used such a typically Sicilian expression', but 'The writer of these pages, as a true Lombard/in his capacity as a Lombard, would never have used such a typically Sicilian expression' or 'The

---

[4]This example is slightly complicated by the fact that the use of the indefinite article alone would suffice to show that being excited was a temporary state, independently of the position of the adjective. But if we substitute *da un Bendicò* with *dal cane Bendicò*, there emerges a clearer distinction between *dall'eccitatissimo cane Bendicò* which would tend to imply that excitedness was an expected characteristic of the dog, and *dal cane Bendicò eccitatissimo* which would suggest that on this occasion he was very excited.

essentially Lombard writer of these pages would never have used such a typically Sicilian expression.'

(iv) Because the adjective tends to be preposed when it expresses an inherent quality of the noun, use of a preposed adjective may in turn *suggest* that the quality expressed by the adjective is inherent to the noun, whilst postposing the adjective could imply that this was not so. This fact is noticeable, for example, in the language of political propaganda and of advertising:

Le nostre eroiche truppe hanno salvato la vita a molti bambini.	'Our heroic troops have saved the lives of many children.'
Ammirerete i delicati colori delle bluse Armani.	'You'll admire the delicate colours of Armani blouses.'

To have used a postposed adjective in these examples would have been to suggest that our troops are not all or inherently heroic, that not all the colours of Armani blouses are delicate. Note that the force of a postposed adjective in these examples might well be expressed in English by stressing the adjective: *Le nostre truppe eroiche hanno salvato la vita a molti bambini* and *Ammirerete i colori delicati delle bluse Armani* are equivalent to saying 'Our <u>heroic</u> troops have saved the lives of many children', 'You'll admire the <u>delicate</u> colours of Armani blouses', possibly leaving the implication that our less-than-heroic troops, on the other hand, did not do so, or that some of the colours are not delicate, and those you won't admire.

Other examples of a preposed adjective implying that the referent of the noun intrinsically has the quality expressed by the adjective are:

Ho sempre ammirato i tuoi affascinanti quadri.	'I've always admired your fascinating paintings.'
Odio quegli orribili posti.	'I hate those horrible places.'
Entrò il terribile dittatore, Stalin.	'In walked the terrible dictator Stalin.'

On the other hand, there are cases where the effect of preposing the adjective would be strange. Phrases such as *la tedesca invasione dell'Austria* or *l'italiano patto con il nemico* are odd in the extreme. But they are not absolutely impossible, and might conceivably be used where the implication or background belief was that there was something characteristically and uniquely German about invading Austria, and Italian about making pacts with the enemy.

(v) Complex adjectival phrases (for example those consisting of an adverb and an adjective, or conjoined adjectives – see 3.27) tend to follow the noun. In fact, the longer the adjectival phrase the more likely it is to follow. Adjectives such as *buono* which usually precede the noun, tend to follow when they are modified by an adverb. Adjectival phrases containing a preposition (including such things as *d'oro* 'golden', or *a fiori* 'flower patterned' – see 11.23, 25 – which consist of a preposition + noun) always follow the noun they modify:

Una miriade di minuscoli pesci argentati risalgono il flusso.	'A myriad minute silvery fish swim back up the stream.'

but

Una miriade di pesci minuscoli e argentati risalgono il flusso.	'A myriad minute, silvery fish swim back up the stream.'

Pin ha due braccine smilze smilze.	'P has two spindly little arms.'
Aspetta di vederne uscire un colombello nuovo e voglioso di vivere.	'He is expecting to see emerging from it a new little dove keen to live.'
Si recarono nelle vie solitamente frequentate da prostitute, spacciatori e drogati.	'They made their way into the streets usually frequented by prostitutes, pushers and addicts.'
Era una cosa davvero straordinaria a vedersi.	'It was a truly extraordinary thing to see.'
È certo una congettura arrischiata, trattandosi di un testo molto complesso.	'It's certainly a hazardous conjecture, since we're dealing with a very complex text.'
Mi sembra un'idea proprio stupida.	'It seems a really stupid idea to me.'
Ricordo che comprasti un orologio d'oro.	'I recall you bought a gold watch.'
Conosco una donna dai capelli rossi.	'I know a red-haired woman.'
Ho degli amici appassionati di musica.	'I have some friends [who are] mad keen on music.'
È stato un risultato abbastanza/molto buono.	'It was a fairly/very good result.'

In elevated and rather archaic styles adjective phrases consisting of *poco/molto/alquanto/quasi/pressoché/assai/bene* + adjective may occasionally precede the noun:

Apprezzo i molto eleganti scritti di Dalmazi.	'I appreciate D's very elegant writings.'
i quasi ignoti ruderi di questa zona	'the all but unknown ruins of this area'
una pressoché totale sintonia di vedute	'a nearly total harmony of views'

3.26 Adjectives are next to the noun they modify

Adjectives almost always immediately precede or immediately follow the noun they modify. Usually, the only element that can separate an adjective from its noun is another adjective or an adjective phrase modifying the same noun. Thus one could say:

Ammiro gli eloquenti discorsi del presidente.	'I admire the president's eloquent speeches.'
Ammiro i discorsi eloquenti del presidente.	'I admire the president's eloquent speeches.'

but not **Ammiro i discorsi del presidente eloquenti*, where *discorsi* would be separated from *eloquenti* by a non-adjectival phrase (*del presidente*). This last example raises the question of when a phrase comprising a 'preposition + noun' counts as an adjective, and when it does not. The simplest rule is to see whether the preposition + noun can be expressed in English as an adjective, or the noun can in English be used like an adjective simply by placing it in front of the noun which it modifies. On this criterion, the phrases *d'oro, di nailon, a fiori* clearly count as adjectives (cf. also 11.5), whereas *del presidente* (a possessive phrase) or *sul tavolo*, do not:

un vaso a fiori	'a flower-patterned vase'
un orologio d'oro	'a gold watch'
una camicia di nailon	'a nylon shirt'
l'orologio del presidente	'the president's watch' (not *'the president watch')
l'orologio sul tavolo	'the watch on the table' (not *'the table watch')

It is a hallmark of erudite discourse (and scarcely ever found in informal usage) that a preceding adjective may sometimes be separated from the noun:

la prima, in ordine cronologico, espressione poetica di quel mondo	'the first poetic expression of that world, in chronological order'
Grazie alla sua esaustività e nonostante una certa – peraltro necessaria, almeno dal punto di vista editoriale – semplificazione dell'analisi lessicografica . . .	'Thanks to its exhaustiveness and despite a certain – albeit necessary, at least from the editorial point of view – simplification of the lexicographical analysis . . .'

3.27 The order of adjectives in combination: *molti bei libri* 'many fine books', *tavole rotonde verniciate* or *tavole rotonde e verniciate* 'round painted tables', etc.

Specificational (3.29) and demonstrative adjectives always precede other adjectives:

questi bei quadri	'these fine pictures'
alcune piccole cose	'some small things'
etc.	

In other cases the order of combinations of adjectives is usually the mirror image of their order in English:

impianti nucleari moderni	'modern nuclear installations'
fiori carnivori esotici	'exotic carnivorous flowers'
un ingegnere elettronico giapponese bravissimo	'an excellent Japanese electronic engineer'
etc.	

The basic principle is that a (postposed) Italian adjective modifies *everything to its left*, in other words it treats the preceding 'adjective + noun(s)' as a 'block':

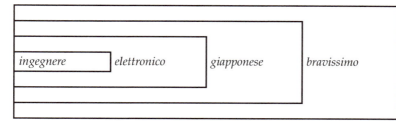

It is usually possible for the 'outermost' adjective to be placed in front of the noun and its other modifying adjectives, according to the principles outlined earlier:

moderni impianti nucleari
esotici fiori carnivori
un bravissimo ingegnere elettronico giapponese

But Italian regularly makes a distinction not always made in English: phrases such as 'exotic carnivorous flowers' or 'elegant tapering fingers' are ambiguous between on the one hand 'carnivorous flowers which are exotic'/'tapering fingers which are elegant', where 'exotic' and 'elegant' define a subset of 'carnivorous flowers' and 'tapering fingers', and on the other hand 'flowers which are carnivorous and also exotic'/'fingers which are tapering and also elegant', where 'exotic/elegant' define a subset of 'flowers' and 'fingers', but not of 'exotic flowers' or 'tapering fingers'. In cases of the latter kind, in fact, English often inserts a comma between the two adjectives, but Italian obligatorily inserts the conjunction *e* between them:

Cerca fiori carnivori ed esotici.	'He is looking for carnivorous, exotic flowers.'
Ha le dita affusolate ed eleganti.	'He has elegant, tapering fingers.'
Ricordatevi di essere concreti e di parlare con battute brevi e pungenti.	'Remember to be concrete and to speak in brief, pithy phrases.'

When two adjectives are combined, and one of them is itself modified (e.g., by an adverb), the modified adjective normally follows the unmodified ones:

una tavola elegante molto lunga	'a very long elegant table'
una tavola lunga molto elegante	'a very elegant long table'

3.28 The forms of preposed adjectives *bello, buono, grande* (and *santo*)

Bello, when it precedes the noun, has variant forms exactly parallel to the variant forms of the definite article (see 4.1) and the demonstrative adjective *quello* (see 5.1): *bel* is the masculine singular form used before most following consonants (*bel tempo, bel giorno*, etc.); *bello* appears before *s* + consonant, *z-*, *ps-*, etc. (*bello sguardo, bello zio*, etc.), and *bell'* before vowels (*bell'uomo, bell'orsacchiotto*, etc.). In the masculine plural *bei* corresponds to singular *bel*, and *begli* to singular *bello* or *bell'* (*begli sguardi, begli zii, begli uomini, begli orsacchiotti*, etc.). In the feminine singular, *bella* is used before consonants, and *bella* or *bell'* before a vowel (the latter being especially common if the following vowel is *a*): *bella cosa, bell'anima*. The feminine plural is always *belle*.

Gli uomini si illudono di dare un corso diverso alla storia, ma non modificano un bel niente, perché, un bel giorno, tutto andrà a catafascio.	'Men like to think they can change the direction of history, but they don't change a damned thing, because one fine day everything will go to pieces.'
Gli diede un bello schiaffo.	'She gave him a good old slap.'
Che begli occhi che hai!	'What lovely eyes you have!'

Buono before the noun has variant forms exactly parallel to those of the indefinite article (see 4.1): *buon* is the masculine form used when the following word begins with a vowel or a consonant other than *s* + consonant, *z-*, *ps-*, etc., in which case *buono* is used (*buon pane, buon bevitore, buon architetto, buono studente, buono zio, buono psicologo*, etc.). In the feminine singular, either *buon'* or *buona* may be used before a vowel if the following word begins with a vowel but in modern Italian, especially in writing, the non-elided forms are often preferred. The plural is always masculine *buoni* and feminine *buone*.

Grande has an optional variant *gran* (invariant for number and gender) which may be used when the adjective precedes the noun: *gran cose/grandi cose; gran cane/grande cane; gran studio/grande studio*, etc. It seems (see Brunet 1983: 148–75 for a very detailed analysis) that, overall, *grande* is *preferred* (but not obligatory) before words beginning with a vowel and before *s* + consonant, *z*- etc. *Grandi* is generally *preferred* over *gran* in the plural: *grande abilità* 'great ability', *grande studio* 'great study', *grandi reti* 'big nets', etc. rather than *gran abilità, gran studio, gran reti*, etc. But *gran* tends to be used in certain set expressions and geographical names: *gran voglia* 'great desire', *gran cosa* 'something special', *gran parte* 'much of'. One finds only *gran* in *gran che* 'something special' (e.g., *Non vale gran che* 'It's not much to write home about'). Also the proper names *Gran Sasso, Gran Bretagna*, etc. *Gran* is frequent as a kind of intensifying adverb: *È una gran brutta cosa* 'It's a really nasty thing', *È una gran bella donna* 'She's a fine looking woman', etc. Elision of the final vowel of *grande* is optional before a word beginning with a vowel (and is particularly common in the phrase *grand'uomo* 'great man').

The title *Santo* 'saint' is shortened to *San* before the names of saints beginning with a consonant: *San Francesco, San Giorgio*, etc.[5] When the name begins with *s* + consonant or *z*-, the rules are less clear: we find *Santo Stefano* but *San Stanislao, San Zenone, San Zaccaria*. Before a vowel, *Santo* and *Santa* are frequently shortened to *Sant'*: *Sant'Egidio, Sant'Anna*, etc.

3.29 The position of specificational adjectives: *diverse idee* (vs. *idee diverse*), etc.

'Specificational' adjectives define a subset of the entities indicated by the noun, but do not assert any property of the noun. 'Specificational' adjectives comprise quantifiers such as *poco* 'not much', *molto* 'much', *tanto* 'so much', *troppo* 'too much', *tutto* 'all', *certi* 'some', 'an indeterminate number' and 'identifiers' such as *altro*[6] 'other', *stesso* 'same', (*un*) *certo* 'a certain', ordinal numerals (12.8, 9), such as *primo, secondo*. These regularly precede the noun and its other modifying adjectives:

Ho molti bellissimi cani.	'I have many lovely dogs.'
Sono diplomata maestra d'asilo, ma pur avendo bussato a tante porte nessuno mi ha dato un lavoro.	'I'm qualified as a nursery school teacher, but although I've knocked on so many doors nobody has given me a job.'
Le mani le sono diventate robuste per il tanto impastare.	'Her hands have become sturdy through so much kneading.'
La signora Anna Maria è una bella donna dai capelli rossi e dai molti gioielli.	'Mrs AM is a beautiful woman with red hair and many jewels.'
i pochi ma giustamente famosi documenti rumeni del Cinquecento	'the few but rightly famous Romanian documents of the 16th century'
Abbiamo molte bellissime cose da raccontarvi.	'We have many very lovely things to tell you.'
Furono scoperti certi curiosi oggetti, di cui nessuno riusciva a spiegarsi l'uso.	'Certain curious objects were discovered, whose use nobody could figure out.'

A number of adjectives have a 'quantifier' function in addition to their basic meaning. As quantifiers, they always precede the noun (cf. also 9.8 for the indefinite quantifiers); as 'ordinary adjectives' they may either precede or follow

---

[5]This is not always true in place names, for example *Santo Pietro Belvedere*.
[6]Exceptionally, one may encounter *altro* after the noun, with the sense of 'different, alternative': *una cultura altra* 'a different culture'.

the noun (but usually follow it). Such quantifier adjectives – some of which only have this function in the plural – are: *diversi, vari* ('a number of', 'several'),[7] *numerosi* ('many', 'numerous'), *certo* '(a) certain', 'unspecified', *leggero* ('slight'), *vecchio* ('old', 'of long standing' – a kind of 'temporal' quantifier), *nuovo* ('some more', 'further'), *unico* ('sole', 'only one'), *semplice* ('no more than', 'just, mere'):

Non tutti i miei amici sono giovani. Ho sì un amico vecchio che però conosco da solo qualche mese.	'Not all my friends are young. I do have an old friend, but I've only known him for a few months.'
È un vecchio amico che conosco da sessantacinque anni.	'He's an old friend [a friend of long standing] whom I've known for 65 years.'
Ha trovato dei libri nuovi.	'He's found some new [e.g., newly published] books.'
Ha trovato dei nuovi libri.	'He's found more/further books.'
Io sono un falegname semplice.	'I'm a simple [unsophisticated] carpenter.'
Io sono un semplice falegname.	'I'm a simple carpenter/just a carpenter/no more than a carpenter.'
C'è una valigia leggera.	'There's a light suitcase.'
C'è una leggera differenza.	'There's a slight difference.'
Ci vivono numerose famiglie.	'Numerous/many families live there.'
Ci vivono famiglie numerose.	'Large families [families with many members] live there.'
Si tratta di una proposta unica.	'It represents a unique proposal.'
Si tratta di una unica proposta.	'It represents just one/a single/a sole proposal.'

Note also the distinction between *unico figlio, unica figlia* and *figlio unico, figlia unica*:

Sono figlia unica.	'I'm an only child.'
Sono l'unica figlia della signora Tozzi.	'I'm Mrs T's only daughter.' (She has sons, but I'm the only daughter.)

As for *vari* and *diversi*, the meaning 'of different kinds' is possible either preceding or following the noun, but the sense 'various', 'a number of' is only possible when *vari* precedes:

Ha dei coltelli diversi.	'He has different knives/other sorts of knives.'
Ha diversi coltelli.	'He has a number of knives.'
poter ammirare i toni vari ed armonizzanti delle due diverse porpore e la marezzatura delle pesantissime sete	'to be able to admire the varied harmonizing shades of the two different purples and the moiré effect of the very heavy silks'
Vendono delle camicie di colori vari/vari colori.	'They sell shirts of varied colours.'
Vendono delle camicie di vari colori.	'They sell shirts in a number of colours.'

---

[7]Note that when plural *diversi, vari, numerosi* and *certi* with 'quantifier' function precede the noun, they cannot be used with a 'partitive' article (see 4.20): one can say *diverse case* 'several houses' or *delle case* 'some houses', but not **delle diverse case*, etc.

3.30 The type *la povera donna* vs. *la donna povera*

The adjective *povero* can mean either 'poor', 'deserving of sympathy', 'pitiable', or 'impecunious'. In the former sense it precedes the noun:

La mia povera sorella ha perso marito e figlia nel giro di sei mesi.	'My poor sister lost her husband and her daughter within six months.'
È inutile chiedere soldi alla mia sorella povera; andiamo da mio fratello, che lui è ricco.	'It's pointless to ask my poor sister for money; let's go to my brother; he's rich.'

Note that *povero* can also refer to someone who has died:

La mia povera madre amava molto la campagna.	'My poor mother did like the countryside.'

Grande precedes when the sense is 'moral greatness', 'admirability': *È un grand'uomo* 'He's a great man' vs. *È un uomo grande* 'He's a big man.' *Grande* also precedes agent nouns when it serves to intensify the noun (cf., 'He's a great walker = He walks a lot' – see also 3.33 below):

È un grande camminatore.	'He's a great walker.'
Sono dei grandi esploratori.	'They're great explorers./They like to explore a lot.'
Era un gran bugiardo.	'He was a big liar.'

Of course *Sono dei grandi esploratori* could also mean 'They are distinguished, famous, admired explorers'.

Alto in the sense of 'important', 'high placed' precedes the noun:

Mi riferivo a quell'alto funzionario del Ministero della Pubblica Istruzione.	'I meant that high-ranking civil servant in the Ministry of Education.'
Mi riferivo a quel funzionario alto del Ministero della Pubblica Istruzione.	'I meant that tall civil servant in the Ministry of Education.'

3.31 The type *Trovo questo libro interessante* 'I find this book interesting' (vs. *Trovo interessante questo libro*)

Just as in English it is possible to say 'I find/think/consider this book interesting' for 'I find/think/consider that this book is interesting', so one can say in Italian *Trovo/Considero/Credo questo libro interessante*. It is equally possible to say *Trovo/Considero/Credo interessante questo libro*. However, the order *Trovo interessante questo libro* is particularly likely to be used if the speaker/writer wants to avoid ambiguity with *Trovo questo libro interessante* 'I find this interesting book.' Note that in a structure such as *Trovo interessante questo libro* the adjective (*interessante*) is usually the most stressed element in the sentence with the following noun phrase (*questo libro*) being noticeably less emphatically stressed.[8]

A similar principle of ordering holds for sentences such as *Lascio la porta aperta* 'I leave the door open' or 'I leave the open door', and *Lascio aperta la porta* 'I leave the door open', the latter being available to avoid the possible interpretation 'I leave the open door'.

---

[8]This goes against a general principle that the most emphatically stressed constituent in an Italian sentence tends to be the final one.

3.32 The 'present participle'

Italian has a number of adjectives which were, originally, derived from verbs and often remain close in meaning to the verb from which they came. In form these 'present participles' are usually identical to the gerund (see 14.17), except that while the gerund ends in *-do* the 'present participle' ends in *-te* (plural *-ti*):

Gerund	'Present participle'
occupando	*occupante*
parlando	*parlante*
volendo	*volente*
richiedere	*richiedente*
etc.	

There is a tradition in Italian grammars for listing 'present participles' as part of the conjugation of the verb, alongside the gerund, the infinitive and so forth. But this is misleading, because:

- By no means all verbs have 'present participles' (whereas all verbs have, for example, gerunds and infinitives): e.g., *essere*, *dare*, *sapere* lack a present participle. 'Present participles' only exist for verbs which indicate properties or states; thus *comprendente* corresponds to *comprendere* only in the sense 'comprise', 'be composed of' (*un opuscolo comprendente tre sezioni* 'a little work comprising three sections') but not *comprendere* in the sense 'understand', 'grasp'.
- There are several adjectives which have the appearance of 'present participles', and were, historically, derived from verbs, but correspond to no verb in modern Italian. For example: *arcaicizzante* 'archaizing' (but also *arcaizzante* corresponding to *arcaizzare*); *carente* 'lacking'; *chiaroveggente* 'clairvoyant'; *eloquente* 'eloquent'; *impudente* 'impudent'; *insufficiente* 'insufficient'; *nolente* 'not wanting' (effectively limited to the expression *volente o nolente* 'willy nilly'); *presente* 'present'; *prudente* 'prudent' (vs. *prudere* 'itch'); *urgente* 'urgent' (*urgere* exists but is, in contrast, very rare), etc.
- 'Present participles' in fact have no particular connection with *present* time or the present tense (any more than an ordinary adjective like *rosso* is connected with any particular time or tense).
- There are frequently idiosyncratic and unpredictable differences of *meaning* between 'present participles' and the verbs to which they are related: *arrogare* 'arrogate' vs. *arrogante* 'arrogant'; *costare* 'cost' vs. *costante* 'constant'; *dolere* 'ache', 'cause pain' vs. *dolente* 'grieving', 'unhappy', 'hurt'; *potere* 'be able' vs. *potente* 'powerful' (also *possente*), etc.
- There are frequently idiosyncratic and unpredictable differences of *form* between 'present participles' and the verbs to which they are related: *puzzolente* 'stinking' vs. *puzzare*; *appariscente* 'prominent', 'standing out' vs. *apparire* (but also *apparente* 'apparent', 'seeming'); *abbiente* 'wealthy' vs. *avere* (but also *avente* 'having'); *empiente* 'filling' vs. *empire*; *adempiente* 'fulfilling' vs. *adempire*.

The best approach is to observe that adjectives in *-nte* may very well be derived from verbs and often, but not always, have a meaning close to English verbal adjectives in *-ing*:

Sono stati sessantanove i colpi partiti, nella sconvolgente mattinata del primo marzo.	'Sixty-nine shots were fired, on the dreadful/upsetting morning of 1 March.'

Il capo dello Stato ha avvertito che se l'Ulivo uscirà vincente dalle prossime elezioni, l'incarico per la formazione del nuovo governo dovrà essere affidato al leader di quello schieramento.	'The head of state has warned that if the Olive Tree emerges victorious from the forthcoming elections, the job of forming the new government will have to be entrusted to the leader of that grouping.'
Ho invitato tutti i colleghi appartenenti al club 'Gatto rosso'.	'I invited all my colleagues belonging/who belonged to the "Red Cat" club.'
La vista di quel cadavere era impressionante. Un padre e una figlia eccoli lì: lui biondo, bello, sorridente, lei goffa, lentigginosa, spaventata.	'The sight of that corpse was striking.' 'There they are, a father and daughter: he fair, handsome, smiling, she gauche, freckled, frightened.'

'Present participles' are very frequently employed as nouns:

Questo esercizio è riservato ai principianti.	'This exercise is reserved for beginners.'
Sono un rappresentante della Lloyd Adriatica.	'I am a representative of LA.'
Avvertì l'ispettore Henry, suo conoscente, che la raggiungesse immediatamente.	'He told inspector H, an acquaintance of his, to get to it immediately.'
Ti sono così fedele, che se il Signore volesse togliermi al mondo dei viventi e portarmi via, continuerei a esserlo anche dal Cielo.	'I am so faithful to you that if the Lord wanted to remove me from the world of the living and take me away, I would still be even from Heaven.'

Many, indeed, are principally used as nouns: *dirigente* 'manager', *credente* '(religious) believer', *governante* 'governess', *scrivente* 'writer' (e.g., *lo scrivente vi supplica* 'the writer/the undersigned begs you'; compare with *lo scrittore* '[professional] writer', 'author'), *tenente* 'lieutenant', etc.

There are two respects in which some 'present participles' (often used as nouns) remain vestigially verb-like. Namely, that they may sometimes take an object, and that clitic pronouns (but not usually third person direct object clitics – see 6.2) may be attached to them:

Una Madonna di Andrea del Sarto sembrava stupita di trovarsi contornata da litografie colorate rappresentanti santi di terz'ordine.	'A Madonna by AS seemed astonished to be surrounded by coloured lithographs representing third order saints.'
Sono stati riletti i documenti riferentisi al progetto.	'The documents referring to the project have been reread.'
Immaginavo una serie di esplosioni, succedentisi nel tempo.	'I imagined a series of explosions, following each other through time.'
la ricompensa spettante ad ognuno	'the recompense due to everyone'
le ricompense spettantici	'the recompenses due to us'
un quadro raffigurante la Firenze di Dante	'a picture representing D's Florence'

The use of direct objects and clitics with certain present participles used as nouns (see above) is largely restricted to elevated, formal registers:

In quanto presidente la commissione, dichiaro . . .	'In my capacity as president of the committee [i.e., the 'one who presides over'], I declare . . .'
Gli aventi diritto alla tessera dovranno fare richiesta presso . . .	'Those who have the right to a card must apply to . . . .'
i componenti della commissione	'the members of the commission'
ginnastica tonificante i muscoli della schiena	'gymnastics which tones up the back muscles'

Note also *prospiciente* 'looking on to', which 'takes a direct object' even though there is no corresponding verb:

> *i balconi prospicienti il giardino*   'the balconies overlooking the garden'

Some 'present participles' (*stante* 'standing', 'being given', *vivente* 'being alive', *regnante* 'reigning', *consenziente* 'agreeing', *permettente* 'permitting', *volente* 'willing') may be used 'absolutely', in the sense 'if', 'when', 'while' + 'verb', as follows:

> *Stante questa legge, hanno dovuto*   'This law being the case/With this law
> *acconsentire.*   as it stood, they had to agree.'
> *Dio volente, ritornerà la pace.*   'God willing, peace will return.'
> *Vivente l'autore, sembrava impossibile*   'With the author alive, it seemed
> *negli anni 50 che un simile testo potesse*   impossible in the 50s that such a text
> *venire stampato.*   could get printed.'
> etc.

3.33 The type 'I'm a slow eater' *Sono uno che mangia lentamente*, etc.

In English it is often possible to convert the structure 'verb + adverb of manner', such as 'I eat slowly', into 'adjective + agent noun', such as 'I am a slow eater'. Such conversions are also sometimes encountered in Italian, but they cannot be made nearly so readily as in English: Italians seem to find *Sono un lettore lento* 'I'm a slow reader' fairly acceptable, but apparently much less so *Sono un mangiatore lento* in the sense 'I'm a slow eater'. *Sono un mangiatore lento* would tend to be interpreted as 'I am an eater who is slow', and need not indicate that I am slow specifically at eating. The commonest and most reliable way of changing the verb + adverb structure into a noun is to say, literally, 'I am (some)one who eats slowly', *Sono (qualc)uno che mangia lentamente*, etc.

4
The articles

4.1 The forms of the definite and indefinite articles

The definite and indefinite articles vary not only according to the gender and number of the noun they precede but also, as will be explained below, according to the nature of the sound at the beginning of the following word:

Definite article

	Masculine	Feminine
Singular	il lo l'	la l'
Plural	i gli	le

Indefinite article (singular)

Masculine	Feminine
un	una
uno	un'

The variant forms of the masculine singular and plural articles and of the feminine singular articles, illustrated above, depend exclusively on the nature of the sound at the beginning of the immediately following word, regardless of the nature or function of that word:

il presidente	l'ex-presidente
lo studioso famoso	il famoso studioso
gli Stati Uniti	i lontanissimi Stati Uniti
etc.	

- Masculine *il, i, un* and feminine *la, le, una* are used before words beginning with a consonant (with a series of important exceptions for the masculines, as explained below): *il gatto – i gatti – un gatto; la gatta – le gatte – una gatta*, etc.
- Masculine *lo, gli, uno* are selected before any word beginning with:
  - s + consonant: *lo spazio – gli spazi – uno spazio; lo scoglio – gli scogli – uno scoglio; lo svizzero – gli svizzeri – uno svizzero*, etc.
  - [ʃ] (principally those beginning with *sc* followed by *i* or *e*): *lo scippo – gli scippi – uno scippo; lo champagne – gli champagne – uno champagne; lo show-man – gli showman – uno showman*, etc.

- z: *lo zio – gli zii – uno zio; lo zero – gli zeri – uno zero; lo zaino – gli zaini – uno zaino; lo zaffiro – gli zaffiri – uno zaffiro,* etc.

● Masculine *lo, gli, uno* are usually selected before the following sounds or combinations of sounds (although exceptions using *il, i, un* are sometimes encountered, especially in informal, non-literary speech and writing):

- gn: *lo gnu – gli gnu – uno gnu; lo gnaulio – gli gnaulii – uno gnaulio; lo gnocco – gli gnocchi – uno gnocco,* etc.
- ps: *lo psichiatra – gli psichiatri – uno psichiatra; lo pseudonimo – gli pseudonimi – uno pseudonimo.*
- i + vowel; j + vowel; y + vowel: *lo iodio – gli iodi – uno iodio; lo iugoslavo – gli iugoslavi – uno iugoslavo; lo Yorkshire; lo yacht – gli yacht – uno yacht.* This rule applies when *i, y* or *j* are pronounced [j]; it does not apply where *j-* is pronounced [ʤ] (e.g., *il jazz, i jeans*).

● Masculine *lo, gli, uno* are selected – but by no means consistently – before words beginning with consonants and consonant clusters which are otherwise rare at the beginnings of Italian words:

- pn: *lo pneumatico* (but frequently *il pneumatico*)
- x: *lo xilofono* or *il xilofono*
- pt: *lo ptialismo*
- ct: *lo ctenidio*
- ft: *lo ftalato*

etc.

● Masculine *lo, gli, uno* are selected before [ʎ]: *lo gli* (i.e., 'the pronoun *gli*'), and the extremely rare *lo gliommero*. Other words beginning with *gli-* are pronounced [gl-], and therefore regularly take *il, i, un*: *il glicine,* etc.

● Masculine *lo, gli, uno* tend to be selected before foreign words beginning with *h* + vowel, if the *h* is aspirate (pronounced [h]) in the language from which they are taken (particularly English and German). This use of *lo,* etc. can occur regardless of whether the aspirate *h* is actually pronounced by Italians: *lo Hegel; lo Heine; lo Hampshire; uno handout.* But if the *h* is not pronounced it is equally acceptable to use the forms of the article normally occurring before vowels, and this is especially the case where the relevant words have Italian suffixes attached: *l'Heine, l'heinismo; un handoutaccio,* etc.

● Masculine singular *lo* is used in the set expressions *per lo più* (or *perlopiù*) 'generally', 'as a rule', *per lo meno* (or *perlomeno*) 'at least'. Outside these set expressions, the ordinary forms of the article are used: *per il più bello,* etc.

● Masculine *l', gli* and *un* are used before any word beginning with a vowel: *l'orso – gli orsi – un orso; l'uomo – gli uomini – un uomo; l'angelo – gli angeli – un angelo; l'imbecille – gli imbecilli – un imbecille; l'unico rimasto – gli unici rimasti – un unico rimasto; l'eccezionale studio – gli eccezionali studi – un eccezionale studio,* etc.

● *gl'* for *gli* before the vowel *i*:
The use of *gl'* before *i-* (as in *gl'italiani*) is archaic. *Gli* (e.g., *gli italiani*) is now generally used.

● *Gli dei*:
Dei plural of *dio* 'god' exceptionally takes the plural article *gli* (see also 2.6): *gli dei.*

● Feminine *la, una* are used before any consonant: *la ruota, la zingara, la cosa, la strada,* etc.

c Feminine *la* and *una* are generally used before *i* + vowel, *y* + vowel and *j* + vowel: *la Iugoslavia, la Juventus*, etc. Note that *un'* is feminine only; the masculine indefinite article before a vowel is always *un*.

c Feminine *l'* and *un'* are generally selected before words beginning with a vowel, particularly in speech *l'idea – un'idea; l'ora – un'ora; l'arte – un'arte*. But in print (especially in journalistic usage) *la* and particularly *una* have become increasingly common before vowels: *una enorme clientela, una ora*, etc.

c A now little-observed typographical rule maintains that no line of print should end in an apostrophe. In such cases, *l'* or feminine *un'* can usually be run on to the next line; alternatively they may be kept on the preceding line, with feminine *l', un'* being replaced by *la, una* and, very occasionally, masculine *l'* being replaced by *lo* . But the use of *lo* at the end of the line, in this context, is best avoided altogether.

c Feminine plural *le* is used regardless of the nature of the following sound: *le cose, le zingare, le anatre, le unghie*, etc. The feminine plural form *l'* before a vowel (e.g., *l'arti, l'erbe*) sounds archaic and is now very little used.

c The articles before letters of the alphabet and numerals:
The principles stated above also apply when the following word is written as a numeral or a letter of the alphabet. The form of the article depends on how the numeral or letter is *pronounced*:

gli RPG 80 [*erre pi gi ottanta*] *ritrovati a San Giuseppe Jato*	'the RPG 80s found at San Giuseppe Jato'
gli USA	'the USA'
Cancello i 7 [*sette*] *e gli 8* [*otto*]*, ma voglio lasciare i 9* [*nove*].	'I'm cancelling the sevens and the eights, but I want to leave the nines.'
Lo 007 [*zero zero sette*]	'Double O Seven'

4.2 Combinations of preposition + definite article

When the prepositions *a, di, in, su* (and sometimes *con*) are immediately followed by a definite article, they combine with the article in the following ways:

TABLE 4.A

+	*il*	*lo*	*l'*	*i*	*gli*	*la*	*le*
a	*al*	*allo*	*all'*	*ai*	*agli*	*alla*	*alle*
da	*dal*	*dallo*	*dall'*	*dai*	*dagli*	*dalla*	*dalle*
di	*del*	*dello*	*dell'*	*dei*	*degli*	*della*	*delle*
in	*nel*	*nello*	*nell'*	*nei*	*negli*	*nella*	*nelle*
su	*sul*	*sullo*	*sull'*	*sui*	*sugli*	*sulla*	*sulle*
con	(*col*)	(*collo*)	(*coll'*)	(*coi*)	(*cogli*)	(*colla*)	(*colle*)

c The combined forms with *con* are nowadays little used (*con la, con i*, etc. being preferred). The masculine singular form *col* remains however fairly frequent, and is regularly used in certain set expressions such as *col che* 'whereupon' and *col cavolo!* (an exclamation of denial). In old-fashioned usage *per* + definite article sometimes yields *pel, pello, pell', pei, pegli, pella, pelle*. Even more archaic are combinations with *tra /fra* (*fral, frai*, etc.).

When the definite article is an integral part of the title of a book, play, film, etc., there is a tendency to keep the form of that title invariant by separating preposition and article.

> *Leggerete ne* La Nazione …
> *il redattore de* Il Tempo
> *la prima pagina de* Gli indifferenti
> *i corsi de* L'inglese per executives

The preposition may also appear in its unmodified form:

> *i protagonisti di* La Terra Trema
> *in* La Terra Trema

But it is acceptable, and even recommendable (according to Serianni 1988: 162), to combine preposition and article in the normal way:

> *Leggerete nella* Nazione
> *il redattore del* Tempo
> *Nella* Terra Trema

4.3 Uses of the definite article

There are many similarities between the use of the definite article in English and its use in Italian. But there are also a number of situations in which the article would be required in Italian but inappropriate in English. Very broadly speaking, the Italian definite article is used with common nouns (i.e., not proper names) denoting entities or classes of entities which are part of the 'common universe of experience' of both speaker and hearer. As in English, this includes unique entities (or unique sets of entities) which are simply part of common human experience:

Il sole è una stella come le altre.	'The sun is just another star.'
Adoro il mare.	'I adore the sea.'
Di giorno non si vedono le stelle.	'By day the stars can't be seen.'

and also entities which have become part of interlocutors' 'common experience' simply because they have previously been mentioned:

—*Sappiamo che c'è una donna che porta cocaina dal Brasile. E sei tu, vero?*	'"We know that there's a woman bringing in cocaine from Brazil. It's you, isn't it?"
—*No! La donna che porta cocaina non sono io.*	"No! I'm not the woman bringing in cocaine."'

But we shall see below that Italian takes these general principles much further, so that it frequently requires an article (usually, the definite article) where English requires none, or a definite article where English employs an indefinite.

4.4 The definite article with nouns having 'generic', 'universal' reference: *Il vino fa male alla salute* 'Wine is bad for your health', etc.

Nouns which refer generically to 'wholes' or 'totalities' – whether the 'whole' is a mass, a substance or an abstract concept, or the universal class of some set of entities – are preceded by the definite article.

Gli uomini si illudono di dare un corso diverso alla storia.	'Men kid themselves that they can change the course of history.' (men generally, history in general)
La sorella di Pin è sempre stata sciatta nelle faccende di casa.	'P's sister has always been slovenly at housework.' (household chores in general)
E poi i cani, che siano grandi o piccoli, che stia alla larga dai cani.	'And dogs, whether big or small, she should steer clear of dogs.' (dogs in general)
Temo la vecchiaia.	'I fear old age.' [old age generally]
Lo zucchero fa male ai denti.	'Sugar is bad for the teeth.' (sugar in general)
L'odio è forse la più potente delle passioni umane.	'Hatred is perhaps the most powerful of human passions.' (hatred generally, human passions as a whole)

The adjective *tutto*, by its very meaning ('all', the 'complete set' of), will normally be followed by the definite article:

Tutti i giocatori di calcio rispettano un grande giocatore come Pelé.	'All football players respect a great player like Pele.'
Tutta la vita è preziosa.	'All life is precious.'

For the type *tutto italiano* 'any Italian', see 9.9.

4.5 The article with names of body parts and other 'inherent attributes'

Some things may be viewed as 'part of common experience' by being inherent, 'normally expected' entities – either in general or in some particular context. For example, every normal human is expected to have a head, hair, a pair of feet, a pair of arms, a heart, and so forth. Italian usually places the definite article before the names of body parts where the part referred to is a unique entity, or a complete set; but body parts which do not form the complete set (say, one arm or one tooth) are usually preceded by the indefinite article. Note that the English equivalent is normally preceded not by an article but by a possessive adjective (see 10.13 for the role also played by indirect object forms in indicating the 'possessor' of the body part):

Si è fatto male al naso.	'He hurt his nose.'
Maria si dipinge le unghie.	'M paints her nails.'
Maria si dipinge un'unghia.	'M paints her nail.'
Mi dolgono i denti.	'My teeth ache.'
Mi duole un dente.	'My tooth aches.'/'I have an aching tooth.'
Ha i capelli bianchi.	'He has white hair.'
Ha dei capelli bianchi.	'He has (some) white hairs.'
Le anguille si possono acchiappare con le mani.	'Eels can be caught with your hands.'
Le anguille si possono acchiappare con una mano.	'Eels can be caught with your hand.'

but note that *la mano* is frequently used in those contexts where only one hand would be expected to be used:

Ciascun alunno deve alzare la mano per chiedere di uscire.	'Every pupil must raise his hand to ask to go out.'

Ha dovuto smettere di dipingere perché gli tremava troppo la mano.	'He had to give up painting because his hand was shaking too much.'

The definite article is also used in a wide variety of cases where the noun is a normal, expected (even if not necessary) attribute of persons and their everyday life (for example, clothes, physical conditions and illnesses, family members, possessions, documents, social rituals, civil procedures). In many of these cases, English uses an indefinite article or a possessive adjective:

Era rimasto a letto perché aveva la tosse.	'He'd stayed in bed because he had a cough.'
Ha la febbre.	'He has a fever.'
Ci si toglie la maglia per cercare i pidocchi.	'One takes off one's jersey to look for lice.'
Spalancò i piccoli occhi da talpa dietro le spesse lenti simili a fondi di bottiglia.	'He opened wide his little mole's eyes behind his thick lenses like bottle-ends.'
Cammina con tanta disinvoltura, incurante che la gonna si alzi e lasci scoperti i calcagni callosi e macchiati.	'She walks so unselfconsciously, unconcerned that her skirt rides up to reveal her callused, stained heels.'
La signora Anna Maria è una bella donna dai capelli rossi e dai molti gioielli.	'Mrs AM is a beautiful woman with red hair and many jewels.'
Hai la macchina?	'Do you have a car?'
Devo prendere la patente.	'I have to get a driving licence.'
Rita Rusic è alta almeno 15 centimetri più del marito.	'RR is at least 15 cm taller than her husband.'
Conobbe la moglie nei primi anni Sessanta grazie alla sorella Maruzza.	'He met his wife at the beginning of the 60s thanks to his sister M.'

But note *prendersi un* (or *il*) *raffreddore* 'to have a cold'.

In other cases, the 'normality' or 'expectedness' of the attribute is determined by the situation. In the context, say, of going to the theatre, or riding on a bus, a 'ticket' is a normal attribute, and the definite article is likely to be used: *Devi fare il biglietto* 'You must get a/your ticket', etc.

4.6 The article with proper names (of places, countries, persons, etc.)

Names of countries, regions and continents are generally preceded by the definite article:

Viva l'Italia!	'Long live Italy!'
Il Brasile attraversa un periodo di crisi.	'Brazil is going through a period of crisis.'
Voglio vedere il Galles e la Scozia.	'I want to see Wales and Scotland.'
Dove va la Gran Bretagna dopo la vittoria di Blair?	'Where is Great Britain going after B's victory?'
Abbiamo fatto il giro della Spagna.	'We made a tour of Spain.'
Ma dovete anche vedere un po' il Veneto.	'You should also have a look at the Veneto.'
Dove finisce l'Europa e dove comincia l'Asia?	'Where does Europe finish and Asia begin?'

Note that *Israele, Cuba, Andorra, San Marino, Malta, Monaco* never take the definite article (but see 4.7).

When the name of a country is singular, and preceded by *di*, the article may be omitted – more readily with feminines than with masculines:

Ecco entrare la regina d'Inghilterra.	'Here is the Queen of England coming in.'
il sole d'Africa or *dell'Africa*	'the sun of Africa'
i buoni vini di Francia or *della Francia*	'the fine wines of France'
l'imperatore del Messico	'the emperor of Mexico'
Arrivammo alla frontiera dell'Iran.	'We arrived at the frontier of Iran.'

Where the article is omitted before feminine names of countries, the sense is often closer to that of an adjective (cf. also 4.20). The presence of the article tends to put the identity of the country into the foreground, while its absence gives it rather less prominence: for example, the phrase *il re dell'Italia* implies that it is true of Italy that it has a king, whilst *il re d'Italia* might just as well be used of a king in exile, or a claimant to the throne, as of any real king of Italy. Similarly, *i vini d'Italia* might be 'Italian wines', while *i vini dell'Italia* might be the wines that Italy produces.

The article is always omitted after *in* with feminine singular names of countries and regions: *Vive/Lo mando in Italia, in Calabria, in Nigeria*, etc. The position with masculine names of countries is much less clear. Some names always dispense with the article (e.g., *in Egitto*). Most allow either possibility:

Vive nel/in Portogallo.	'He lives in Portugal.'
In Messico non ci sono mai stato.	'Mexico I've never been to.'
Fu uno dei primi insediamenti europei nel Messico.	'It was one of the first European settlements in Mexico.'

Names of countries that are plural, or consist of a noun modified by an adjective, normally have the definite article after *in* and *di*:

Vive negli Stati Uniti.	'He lives in the United States.'
Mosca era la capitale della Unione Sovietica.	'Moscow used to be the capital of the Soviet Union.'

A rule often given is that singular names of 'large' islands require the definite article, and those of 'small' islands do not: *Capri, Ischia, Ponza, Procida, Pantelleria*; but *la Sardegna, la Sicilia, la Corsica*. It is debatable whether *Malta* should count as 'small', but in any case its name does not take the article. And the names of many incontestably 'large' islands, especially those outside Italy, do not take the article, e.g., *Cuba, Sumatra, Timor, Formosa, Creta, Giava, Ceylon, Zante, Maiorca, Cipro, Corfù*. Note that in some cases (e.g., *il Giglio, l'Elba, la Capraia*) the definite article is actually an inherent part of the name:

Andiamo domani all'Elba.	'Tomorrow we're going to Elba.'
I fiori della Capraia.	'The flowers of Capraia.'

But note *l'isola d'Elba.*

Particularly in the case of exotic islands, usage seems to vary (see Brunet 1979: 89, 91). One may say either *Era in Madagascar* or *Era nel Madagascar* (but always *partire per il Madagascar*).

With compass points, the article tends to be used when they denote a region, but not when they denote a direction.

Ora vive nel sud.	'Now he lives in the south.'
Andando verso nord vedrai la torre sulla montagna.	'Going north you'll see the tower up on the mountain.'

È situato ad ovest di Matera.	'It's situated to the west of Matera.'
Ha viaggiato in quasi tutti i paesi dell'est.	'He has travelled in almost all the countries of the east.'

4.7 The article with names of cities, towns, villages, streets, rivers

Names of cities, towns and villages do not normally take the definite article (*Vado a Roma, Vivo a Parigi, le strade di Londra*, etc.), except in the following cases where the article is an integral part of the name: *Il Cairo; L'Aquila; La Spezia; L'Aia; La Valletta; Il Pireo* 'Piraeus'; *La Mecca; L'Avana* 'Havana'.

Names of streets usually lack the definite article:

Vivo in vicolo Bovi.	'I live in vicolo Bovi.'
C'è un negozio in via Garibaldi.	'There's a shop in via Garibaldi.'
Ritornavo da Piazza Nuova.	'I was coming back from Piazza Nuova.'

Names of rivers, lakes and mountains normally require the article:

Ho nuotato nel Tamigi.	'I have swum in the Thames.'
le acque del Volga	'the waters of the Volga'
Ha un castello vicino alla Loira.	'He has a castle near the Loire.'
la prossima eruzione dell'Etna	'the next eruption of Etna'
la vetta del Cervino	'the peak of the Matterhorn'
una gita sul Trasimeno	'a trip on lake Trasimene'

However, *in Tamigi, in Po*, etc., is possible in literary language.

Note that an article is normally used with all place names if the name is modified by an adjective or adjectival phrase:

Parigi ha oggi un po' gli stessi problemi della Parigi medievale.	'Paris today has rather the same problems as medieval Paris did.'
Anch'io amo Roma, ma non la Roma del turismo di massa.	'I love Rome too, but not the Rome of mass tourism.'

But note *in Gran Bretagna, in Alta Italia, in Bassa Italia, ad Ascoli Piceno*, etc. where the adjective is regarded as an integral part of the name.

Plural names of islands and groups of islands take the article: e.g., *le Egadi, le Antille, le Tremiti*, etc.

4.8 The article with names of persons

When women are referred to by surname alone, the surname is usually preceded by the definite article:

Hai visto la Quacquarini?	'Have you seen Q?'
Devo parlare con la Pisani.	'I have to speak to P.'
Ebbi una telefonata dalla Tibiletti.	'I had a phone call from T.'
etc.	

However, attempts to achieve a 'gender-free' style (notably in academic publications) often lead to omission of the article from women's surnames, as for men. The article is not generally used with surnames of men, unless their bearer is 'famous', but the precise criteria are elusive. The article tends not to be used with the names of Italians who are both familiar and either disliked or well-liked, one might almost say 'household names': *Garibaldi, Cavour, Mazzini, Puccini, Mussolini,* etc. Use of the article tends to imply greater emotional detachment and/or distance in time from the person: *il Manzoni, il Leopardi, il Bembo, il Savonarola,* etc. But its use with the names of famous foreigners (e.g., *lo Shakespeare*) is nowadays regarded as old-fashioned. The article is never used for famous people known by their forename (e.g., *Dante, Michelangelo* as opposed to *l'Alighieri, il Buonarroti*) or for names from classical antiquity (e.g., *Cesare, Virgilio, Aristotele*). But it is usually required where the name is a nickname, or indicates the bearer's place of origin (e.g., *l'Aretino, il Grechetto, il Perugino, il Tegghiaio*).

The article is not used when giving one's own surname, either by men or women, nor after *casa* when it is equivalent to French *chez*:

Buongiorno, sono Rossi.	'Hello, it's Rossi here.'
Pronto, parla Pisani.	'Hello, Pisani speaking.'
Qui casa Pennacchi.	'Pennacchi household here.'
Vado a casa Rossi.	'I'm going to the Rossis' place/chez the Rossis.'

Use of the article with forenames is a largely regional phenomenon: its use with female forenames is predominantly characteristic of Tuscany and northern Italy, whilst its use with male forenames is largely restricted to parts of northern Italy.

A teatro ci andavano di solito mia madre, la Paola e Mario.	'My mother, Paola and Mario usually went to the theatre.'

The article is not usually used before *Cristo* (e.g., *la nascita di Cristo* 'the birth of Christ'; *avanti Cristo* 'BC', *dopo Cristo* 'AD', *fratelli in Cristo, addormentarsi in Cristo*), or before *Gesù* 'Jesus'.

The article is optional with the titles *re, regina* and *papa* when followed by the name:

un ritratto di/del re Fernando	'a portrait of King Ferdinand'
Fu presentata a/al papa Giovanni Paolo II.	'She was presented to Pope John Paul II.'

Professional and civic titles (such as *professore, ingegnere, signore, signora*) + name are preceded by the article: *l'ingegner Ubaldini; il dottor Rossi; il professor Prodi; la signora Gigli*. The titles *frate, suora, compare, comare, prete, don* do not take the article: *Frate Giacomo; Compare Beppe,* etc. The article is never used with titles when the title is used to address an individual:

Buongiorno, professor Prodi.	'Hello, Professor P.'
Ingegner Ubaldini, che piacere rivederla!	'Engineer U, how nice to see you again!'

The article must be used with plural names and titles: *i compari Giacomo e Matteo; i maestri Claudio e Filippo; i signori Gigli; i professori Bellini,* etc.

4.9 The article with names of languages

The names of languages are usually preceded by the article:

Come si può capire il Giappone senza studiare il giapponese?	'How can one understand Japan without studying Japanese?'
L'arabo è una lingua sotto molti aspetti simile all'ebraico.	'Arabic is a language in many respects similar to Hebrew.'

But the article may be omitted if the language is part of an official course of study (cf. English 'to do' a language):

Nelle scuole australiane molti studenti 'In Australian schools many students do
studiano giapponese. Japanese.'

The article is omitted after the preposition *in*:

L'ho tradotto in italiano. 'I translated it into Italian.'
Stavano parlando in russo. 'They were talking in Russian.'

After *parlare* the article tends to be omitted where the sense is closer to 'speak *in* the language', whereas it is present if the sense is 'be able to speak'/'know the language':

Tutta la mia famiglia parla il russo anche 'All my family can speak Russian even
se di solito parliamo inglese. though we usually speak (in) English.'

4.10 Omission of articles in verbal expressions: *aver sonno, far piacere*, etc.

The bare noun (unaccompanied by articles) is frequently encountered in verb constructions where what is relevant is the basic meaning of the noun, rather than any specific entities denoted by the noun (for this distinction, see also section 4.20 on partitives). Thus *far piacere a qualcuno* is 'to please someone' (with inanimate subject), whereas *far un piacere a qualcuno* is 'to do someone a favour' (i.e., something that pleases). A few examples are:

aprir bocca	'speak', 'open one's mouth'
aver fame/sete	'be hungry/thirsty'
aver paura (di)	'fear', 'be afraid (of)'
aver ragione/torto	'be right/wrong'
cambiar colore/idea, etc.	'change colour/one's mind'
chiudere bottega	'shut up shop'
dar carta bianca	'give carte blanche'
dar ragione/torto (a)	'say that someone is right/wrong'
far caso	'notice'
far fronte (a)	'face up to'
far paura (a)	'frighten'
far scalo	'stop off/over'
prender/dare fuoco	'catch/set fire'
prendere nota	'take note'
prendere sonno	'fall asleep'
etc.	

4.11 The type *Faccio il falegname* = 'I'm a carpenter': the construction *fare* + definite article + noun

To express a person's habitual function, activity or profession, the following construction is very common:

Mio padre fa il professore. 'My father is a teacher.'
Ai tempi faceva il contrabbandiere. 'In the old days he was a smuggler.'
So perché fa il partigiano. 'I know why he's a partisan.'

Fare + definite article + noun can also mean 'to behave in the manner typical of a . . .'. In this construction, the 'noun' may be an adjective used as a noun:

Era meglio se lo lasciavi libero di fare l'uccello rapace.	'It was better to leave him free to act like a bird of prey.'
Non fare lo scemo.	'Don't be an idiot.'
Giorgio comincia a fare il difficile.	'G is beginning to be/act awkward.'

4.12 English genitive -'s and the Italian article: the type *la casa del professore* 'the teacher's house'

English structures of the type:

'noun phrase A + -'s (plural -s') + noun phrase B'
e.g., 'the teacher's house'

correspond to Italian

'article + noun phrase B + *di* + noun phrase A'
la casa del professore

l'amico di Carlo	'Carlo's friend'
il padre di una vittima	'a victim's father'
Sono andati persi tutti i vestiti dei miei amici.	'All my friends' clothes have been lost.'

For the type 'It's Carlo's' = *È quello di Carlo*, see 5.9; 10.1.

An English sentence such as 'It is fascinating to study a poet's life' is ambiguous between 'the life of a (particular) poet' (where the indefinite article modifies the word 'poet') and 'a life (typical) of a poet, the life of any poet, generally' (where the indefinite article modifies to the whole phrase 'poet's life'). In Italian this distinction tends to be made explicit:

Abbiamo già studiato la vita di un poeta (Leopardi), adesso studiamo la vita di uno scultore.	'We've already studied a poet's life (Leopardi), now let's study a sculptor's life.'
Ho vissuto una vita da poeta, e ho conosciuto solo miseria.	'I've lived a poet's life, and found only wretchedness.'

For the use of *da* to mean 'characteristic of' in the last example, see 11.28.

4.13 Italian *quello, questo* = English 'the'

The more limited use of the definite article in English is a potential source of ambiguity if 'the' is rendered in Italian simply by the definite article. Consider the following sentences:

'I always let him play tennis, because I knew he loved the sport.'
'I always gave him Camembert, because he liked the cheese.'

'The sport' and 'the cheese' in these sentences unambiguously refer back to 'tennis' and 'Camembert' respectively. But use of the definite article would be inadequate in such cases in Italian. The sentences

Lo facevo sempre giocare a tennis, perché sapevo che amava lo sport.

and

Gli davo sempre del camembert, perché gli piaceva il formaggio.

both receive the 'generic' interpretations 'he loved sport' and 'he liked cheese'. To indicate that the 'sport' and the 'cheese' are the specific ones previously referred to, Italian resorts to some other device, such as a demonstrative:

> *Lo facevo sempre giocare a tennis, perché sapevo che amava questo sport.*

and

> *Gli davo sempre del camembert, perché gli piaceva questo formaggio.*

Quel corresponds to English 'the' in expressions of the type 'like the idiot he was':

Lasciò la porta aperta, da quell'imbecille che era.	'He left the door open, like the idiot he was.'

4.14 Omission of the article in appositive and predicative constructions: the type *È studente* 'He's a student'

The article (definite or indefinite) is generally omitted with nouns whose function is to explain the function or nature of a previously introduced noun. The article-less 'explaining' noun may be introduced by 'predicative' verbs such as *essere, diventare, farsi, diventare, cambiarsi in, nominare, eleggere a*; in many other cases, it occurs where a relative clause of the type 'who is . . .' might be inserted in front of it:

L'accusato era X, studente all'Università di Bologna.	'The accused was X, [who is] a student at Bologna University.'
X era studente all'Università di Bologna.	'X was a student at Bologna University.'
Le presento Franco Rossi, sindaco della città.	'I present FR, [who is] the mayor of the city.'
Ma c'era da combattere la malaria, principale ostacolo alla conquista della zona.	'But there was malaria to be fought, [which was] the main obstacle to the conquest of the area.'
Si riferiva al fascismo, dogma politico odioso ma stranamente pervicace.	'He meant fascism, [which was] an odious but oddly persistent political dogma.'
Ripartimmo per Perugia, capoluogo della regione.	'We left for Perugia, [which is] the capital of the region.'
Il mio amico Giovanni è professore.	'My friend G is a teacher.'
Aldo è diventato azionista della società.	'A became a shareholder in the company.'
Speriamo Giorgio sia nominato professore di genetica.	'Let's hope G is appointed professor of genetics.'
Chirac è stato eletto presidente della Francia.	'C has been elected president of France.'
Il bruco si trasforma in farfalla.	'The caterpillar changes into a butterfly.'

Note also *cominciare* in the sense 'begin as':

Ha cominciato bambino e lavora ancora oggi.	'He started as a child and he's still working today.'

The article is also omitted after certain prepositions and phrases which function to define a function or an identity, such as *da, come, in quanto, in qualità di*:

Ma Aldo parlava da dottore, non da paziente.	'But A was talking as a doctor, not as a patient.'
Come/In quanto/In qualità di preside di questa scuola, il professor Rossi non può permettere questo comportamento.	'As the headmaster of this school, Professor R cannot allow this behaviour.'

However, the definite article may be used where it has the function of individuating, or picking out from among a number of possibilities. In such cases the second noun does not tell us 'what something/somebody is', but 'which, or of which kind, something/somebody is'. If the *indefinite* article is employed, the implication is that the noun represents one among several:

Il mio amico Giovanni è il professore.	'My friend G is [the one who is] the teacher.'
Aldo è diventato un presidente della società.	'A became a president of the society.' [i.e., one of the presidents]

Verbs such as 'call', 'consider', which in English may be followed by an indefinite article, need not take an indefinite one in Italian:

Mi ha chiamato ladro.	'He called me a thief.'
Lo consideravamo esperto di matematica.	'We considered him an expert on mathematics.'

4.15 Omission of the article in exclamations

The article is not generally used in exclamations consisting of an adjective + noun:

Povera madre!	'The poor mother!'
Fortunati giovani!	'The lucky youngsters!'
Bella cosa!	'A fine thing!'

4.16 Omission of the article in lists and conjoined expressions

When nouns which, individually, would require the article form a list, the article may optionally be omitted:

Riprende a grattarsi mattina e sera.	'He starts scratching again morning and night.'
Aveva portato con sé cappello, camicia, pantaloni e scarpe.	'He had brought with him a hat, a shirt, trousers and shoes.'

The article is frequently omitted from pairs of nouns coordinated by *e*, especially where the two nouns form a commonly occurring set:

Sono venuti padre e figlio.	'The father and the son came.'
Casa e chiesa sono sempre state al centro della loro vita.	'The home and the church have always been the centre of their life.'
Il fumo brucia gola e occhi ai soccorritori.	'The smoke burns the rescuers' throats and eyes.'

Omission is also common where the coordinated nouns are preceded by *tra/fra*:

I rapporti tra Francia e Germania sono pessimi.	'Relations between France and Germany are terrible.'

Fra vestiti e libri aveva speso due milioni.	'What with the clothes and the books he had spent 2 million.'

Where the first item in a list begins with the definite article, the article may be removed from remaining items if they are of the same number and gender as the first:

Lo ringraziano i colleghi, amici, aiutanti e alunni.	'His colleagues, friends, assistants and pupils thank him.'

4.17 Omission of the article in book and chapter titles

Titles of books, articles, chapters, sections, plays and films usually appear without the article:

Grande grammatica italiana di consultazione
Storia della lingua italiana
Psicopatologia della vita quotidiana
Capitolo ventitreesimo
Sezione 7

While *Psicopatologia della vita quotidiana* is what appears on the cover of the Italian translation of Freud's book, one would normally allude to it with the definite article:

Hai letto la Psicopatologia della vita quotidiana *di Freud?*	'Have you read Freud's *Psychopathology of Everyday Life*?'

4.18 Omission of the article after prepositions: the type *in ufficio* 'at the office'

The article is very frequently absent from singular nouns when they are preceded by the prepositions *a* and *in*. In such cases, preposition and noun form a kind of 'set phrase', often expressing well-known, commonplace, familiar or habitual locations and positions, or destinations (e.g., 'the home', 'the bank', 'the office' and even 'in heaven'). A comprehensive definition of such cases is, however, extremely elusive. Some examples are listed below:

a scuola	'to/at school'
a teatro	'to/at the theatre'
a cavallo	'on horseback'
a tavola	'to/at the table'
in banca	'to/at the bank'
in comune	'to/at the town hall'
in paradiso	'to/in heaven'
in mano	'in one's hand'
in tasca	'in one's pocket'
in autobus	'by bus'
in macchina	'by car'
in ufficio	'to/at the office'

● Omission of the article in the type *a semaforo rosso* 'when the traffic light is red':

A conti fatti quanto ti rimane?	'How much have you left when the calculations are done?'
A semaforo rosso non attraversare.	'Don't cross when the light is red.'

● Omission of the article after *dietro, su, previo*:
When *dietro* and *su* mean 'at', 'as a consequence of', the definite article is omitted:

Lo feci dietro suggerimento di un mio amico.	'I did it at the suggestion of a friend of mine.'

The preposition *previo* (limited to bureaucratic and official usage) behaves similarly:

La tessera verrà rilasciata previo versamento della somma richiesta.	'The card will be issued on payment of the sum requested.'

● The article is usually omitted with *giocare a* 'to play (at)': *giocare a scacchi; giocare a tennis; giocare a calcio; giocare a nascondino*, etc. But *giocare al tennis*, etc., with the article, is also possible.

● Adverbial expressions (notably after *senza*):

Ha parlato con rabbia.	'He spoke angrily.'
Il problema fu risolto senza difficoltà.	'The problem was solved without difficulty [= easily]'.
Scrive senza interesse.	'He writes in an uninterested fashion.'
Ti ho risparmiato per pietà.	'I saved you out of mercy.'
Sai per caso dov'è la banca?	'Do you know, by any chance, where the bank is?'
Allora ci rendemmo conto che l'avevano accusata a torto.	'Then we realized they'd accused her wrongly.'
Scrivilo a matita.	'Write it in pencil.'
Scrivilo a stampatello.	'Write it in capitals.'
Arrivò di corsa.	'He came running.'

When *senza* means 'without any' and is followed by a generic noun, the article is usually omitted:

Se ne sono andati senza speranza.	'They left without hope.'
La sua era una vita randagia, senza donne né amici.	'His was a wandering life, without women or friends.'
Così mi trovai a Parigi a mezzanotte senza soldi.	'So I found myself in Paris at midnight penniless.'

When the noun following *senza* is specified (i.e., identified as a particular member or subclass of the set of entities referred to by the noun), then the article (definite or indefinite) is used according to the ordinary rules for use of the article:

Come faccio a costruire una sedia senza un martello per i chiodi?	'How am I to make a chair without a hammer for the nails?'
Non devi uscire senza un cappotto che ti protegga dalla neve.	'You mustn't go out without an overcoat to protect you from the snow.'

4.19 The articles frequently absent in proverbial expressions

Gallina vecchia fa buon brodo.	'An old hen makes good broth.'
A caval donato non si guarda in bocca.	'Don't look a gift horse in the mouth.'
etc.	

4.20 The 'partitive' type *Voglio del vino, Porto dei fiori* with *di +* article + noun and the 'zero article' type *Voglio vino, Porto fiori*[1]

The so-called partitive article consists of the preposition *di* + definite article. In the singular, the partitive is the counterpart of the indefinite article *un*. Where *un* would be used with a 'count noun' (i.e., a noun capable of appearing in the plural), *del* is used with 'mass nouns' (nouns that cannot normally take a plural and indicate substances or abstract concepts) to indicate an *unspecified quantity or part of the whole denoted by a noun*:

C'è una mosca dentro la bottiglia.	'There's a fly in the bottle.'
C'è dell'acqua dentro la bottiglia.	'There's (some) water in the bottle.'

In the plural, the partitive article has a double function: it serves as a plural form of the indefinite article and it serves to indicate an unspecified quantity or part of the whole denoted by the plural noun:

Ci sono delle mosche dentro la bottiglia.	'There are (some) flies in the bottle.'

But the partitive construction has an apparent rival, the so-called 'zero article', i.e., the bare noun not preceded by any article at all:

C'è acqua dentro la bottiglia.	'There's (some) water in the bottle.'
Ci sono mosche dentro la bottiglia.	'There are (some) flies in the bottle.'

The difference between partitive article and zero article is, up to a point, regional: northern Italians tend to prefer the partitive article, southerners the zero article. But there exists, none the less, a fine distinction between the two possibilities. Note that the 'bare noun' is also the form in which nouns are cited when one is simply *defining their meaning* (e.g., in dictionaries) – for example:

'Autarchia' è un indirizzo di politica economica che, sfruttando le risorse proprie di uno stato, tende a renderlo autosufficiente.	'"Autarchy" is an economic policy which, by exploiting a state's own resources, tends to make it self-sufficient.'
'Lendine' significa l'uovo del pidocchio dell'uomo.	'"Nit" means the egg of a human louse.'

It is no coincidence that, in general, the bare noun tends to be used where the focus is on the *concept expressed by the noun*, rather than on entities denoted by the noun. This principle goes some way to explaining why the bare noun also appears (instead of the definite article) in 4.10, 14, 16, 17, above, where what is involved is principally a matter of defining, listing or naming. The partitive construction, in contrast, focuses more on *entities denoted by the noun*, not merely on the concept expressed by it. The distinction may in part be illustrated through the English translations we suggest for the following sentences:

Dava lavoro ai ragazzi.	'He employed the boys.'
Dava del lavoro ai ragazzi.	'He gave the boys some work.'
Dice bugie.	'He lies.'/'He's a liar. '
Dice delle bugie.	'He's telling lies.'
Mi dava consigli.	'He advised me.'/'He was my advisor.'

---

[1]For detailed background to much of the discussion in this section, see Korzen (1996).

Mi dava dei consigli.	'He was giving me some bits of advice.'
Vendono fiori.	'They sell flowers.' / 'They're flower-selling.' / 'They are flower-sellers.'
Vendono dei fiori.	'They sell some flowers.' / 'They're selling flowers.'
Bevo tè.	'I'm a tea-drinker.' / 'I'm tea-drinking.' / 'I drink tea.'
Bevo del tè.	'I'm drinking tea.'

The 'bare' nouns do not denote *specific* 'work', 'lies', 'advice', 'flowers', 'tea', but the *concepts* of 'work', 'lies', 'advice', 'flowers', 'tea'. The partitive forms, in contrast, denote actual entities ('work', 'lies', 'pieces of advice', 'flowers', etc.). The above examples also show that the distinction may be reflected in a difference in the form of the verb in English: the progressive form in '-ing' ('I'm drinking tea') in fact suggests that there is an actual (cup of) tea which I am drinking; the simple verbs forms, such as 'I drink', indicate the general property or characteristic of tea-drinking, and can be truthfully uttered when one is drinking no tea at all. The distinction is also apparent in the following example, where what is expressed is the general notion of, so to speak, 'Italian-book-having'. Consequently, a response indicating that the subject has only one Italian book might be acceptable:

Sì, ho libri inglesi ma vedi che ho anche libri italiani: Il Gattopardo di Lampedusa, per esempio.	'Yes, I have English books but you can see that I also have Italian books: Lampedusa's *The Leopard*, for example.'

In fact, those cases in which Italian tends to use the zero article constructions lend themselves very easily to paraphrasing in English by the verbal noun construction of the type 'lie-telling', 'flower-selling', 'tea-drinking' (even if the effect is often strained and ungainly in English). Thus *Mangio piselli freschi, Leggo manoscritti antichi, Vendo francobolli egiziani* indicate that I perform the activities of 'fresh-pea-eating', 'ancient-manuscript-reading', 'Egyptian-stamp-selling'; in contrast, *Mangio dei piselli, Leggo dei manoscritti antichi, Vendo dei francobolli egiziani* mean simply that I 'eat some peas', 'read some ancient manuscripts', 'sell some Egyptian stamps'.

Adjectives and other 'delimiting' expressions (such as relatives) usually serve to single out entities or subvarieties, and therefore tend to occur with the partitive article:

Qui vendono birra.	'They sell beer here.'
Qui vendono della birra ottima.	'They sell excellent beer here.'
Ho portato della birra che ho assaggiato ieri.	'I've brought some beer I tried yesterday.'

The bare noun, rather than the partitive, is particularly common in negative constructions (including after *senza*):

Non mangio pane.	'I don't eat bread.'
Non ho visto sangue sul tappeto.	'I didn't see any blood on the carpet.'
Non ci sono serpenti nel giardino.	'There are no snakes in the garden.'
Sono rimasto senza soldi.	'I was left penniless.'

In negative constructions, the partitive article is used, however, where what is being negated is precisely the notion of 'a certain amount', 'a certain quantity', 'some', which is implicit in the use of the partitive article. In speech, *delle* and *dei* in the following examples would be likely to receive heavy stress:

Non ho delle fidanzate, ho solo una fidanzata a cui sono sempre rimasto fedele.	'I don't have <u>some</u> girlfriends/I don't have "girlfriends" plural, I have just one girlfriend to whom I have always been faithful'.
Non raccolgo dei funghi, raccolgo i funghi che Luigi mi ha indicato.	'I'm not picking <u>some</u> mushrooms/I'm not picking just any mushrooms, I'm picking the mushrooms L has pointed out to me.'

Equivalent sentences with the zero partitive would be at best peculiar. For example, *Non raccolgo funghi* would assert that I am 'not mushroom-picking', while a following *Raccolgo i funghi che Luigi mi ha indicato* would assert, in blatant contradiction, that I *am* picking mushrooms.

There is a strong tendency to prefer the partitive article when the noun is the subject of the sentence and is positioned before the verb:

Crescevano fiori gialli tra i binari. OR *Dei fiori gialli crescevano tra i binari.*	'Yellow flowers grew between the tracks.'
Viene versato latte nel bicchiere. OR *Del latte viene versato nel bicchiere.*	'Milk is poured into the glass.'

The type *Fiori gialli crescevano tra i binari* is possible, but strongly associated with elevated, formal styles. The zero partitive is, however, perfectly normal at the beginning of a sentence if the noun is modified by restrictive phrases (such as '*così* + adjective', or *di questo tipo*):

Chiodi di questo tipo si usavano già nel Duecento.	'Nails of this kind were already being used in the thirteenth century.'
Proposte così assurde sono inammissibili.	'Such absurd proposals are inadmissible.'

The zero partitive is used to avoid potential sequences of *di + del, dei, della, delle*, etc., and is preferred over *da* or *a + del, dei, della, delle*, etc:

Sanno storie di spie che muoiono nude dentro fosse di terra. [never **di delle spie*]	'They know stories of spies who die naked in earth ditches.'
L'ho saputo da [preferable to *da dei*] *colleghi spagnoli.*	'I learned this from some Spanish colleagues.'
E lo fece davanti a [preferable to *a degli*] *scienziati di tutti i paesi.*	'And he did it before scientists from all over the world.'

Occasionally, the partitive article may be used in preference to the bare noun in order to make it clear that the noun is plural (with nouns which are invariant in singular and plural – cf. 3.1), or that an adjective is being used as a noun:

Voglio avere delle possibilità di vincere.	'I want to have possibilities of winning.'
Siete dei privilegiati.	'You are privileged people.'
Siete privilegiati.	'You are privileged.'

Mention should be made of a case where neither the zero article nor the partitive is necessarily used. There is a tendency for names of body parts that come in pairs to be preceded by *due*:

Ha due braccia lunghissime.	'He has very long arms.'
Mi fissavano due occhi bellissimi. Era Paola.	'Beautiful eyes were staring at me. It was P.'

For use of the partitive where an adjective stands for a noun (e.g., *Ho dei rossi* 'I have some red ones'), see 5.9 and 17.2.

4.21 The partitive construction *di* + noun phrase: the type *Di rose ne ho colte tante*

There is a further (never obligatory) partitive construction *di* + noun phrase (without the definite article), principally encountered in those structures in which an element moved from its normal position to the left of the noun phrase is also expressed by the partitive pronoun *ne* (see further 17.2). This construction with *di* is especially common where the moved element is an adjective used as a noun.

Di ragazze ne conosceva tante.	'He knew so many girls.'
Ne avrai visti, d'incidenti stradali.	'You must have seen a few traffic accidents.'
Ce ne sono in giro, di ladri.	'There are thieves about.'
Di latte se n'è versato nel bicchiere.	'Milk was poured into the glass.'
Ne abbiamo anche troppe, d'idee.	'We even have too many ideas.'
Ce n'erano di alti e di bassi.	'There were tall ones and short ones.'

4.22 The indefinite article

The indefinite article is broadly similar in use and function to the English indefinite article: typically, it accompanies a 'count' noun (i.e., a noun which can also take a plural form, as opposed to a 'mass' noun like 'air', 'rice' or 'blood'), and serves to introduce into the discourse a 'new' (hitherto unmentioned) entity whose identity is unknown at least to the addressee:

Cerco un albergo.	'I'm looking for a hotel.'
Hai una matita?	'Have you a pencil?'

For the plural form corresponding to the singular indefinite article, see 4.20.

The indefinite article can be employed with singular mass nouns to indicate a particular type/variety of some entity:

Il Murfatlar è un vino rumeno.	'Murfatlar is a Romanian wine.'
Questo è un riso che mi piace moltissimo.	'This is a kind of rice I like very much.'

Placing the indefinite article before what would normally be a bare noun, without article, can also, in informal usage, have the effect of intensifying the noun in exclamations, in a way roughly equivalent to English 'such'/'so':

È di una forza!	'He's so strong!'
Ho una fame!	'I'm so hungry!'
Mi è venuta una rabbia!	'I got so angry!'

The indefinite article can also be used with proper names where the person or thing referred to is being presented as being in a particular state or condition:

Preceduto da un Bendicò eccitatissimo discese la breve scala.	'Preceded by a very excited Bendicò, he came down the short flight of stairs.'
Non avrei mai immaginato un Mario così disinibito.	'I would never have imagined such an uninhibited Mario/Mario so uninhibited.'

Note also:

Ho parlato con un Franco Rossi.	'I spoke to a Franco Rossi/to someone called Franco Rossi.'

> *Qua ci vuole un Einstein!* — 'We need an Einstein/someone like Einstein here!'

In the sense of 'some more', 'some other', 'further', rather than 'another', *altro* lacks the indefinite article:

> *Ha versato altro latte.* — 'He poured more milk.'
> *Ha versato un altro latte.* — 'He poured another [glass of] milk.'

In the sense 'a further', 'yet another', the article may optionally be omitted with *altro*, particularly in elevated and literary registers:

> *In realtà queste idee non hanno la minima importanza. Altro errore è credere che la Chiesa sia stata responsabile della diffusione di questa dottrina.* — 'Actually these ideas do not have the slightest importance. Another mistake is to believe that the Church was responsible for the diffusion of this doctrine.'

In negative constructions, the indefinite article may be omitted where the sense is equivalent to *nessun* (see 9.11), or English 'no'/'not any', + noun:

> *Ci sono dei giorni dell'anno in cui non c'è rete, non c'è velo, non c'è essenza che possa tenere lontane le zanzare.* — 'There are some days of the year when there's no net, no veil, no oil that can keep the mosquitoes off.'
> *Non ho mai visto vestito più elegante.* — 'I've never seen a more elegant suit.'

This omission of the indefinite article is typically associated with more formal registers of Italian, and is generally only possible where the noun follows the verb: the type *Vestito più elegante non è mai stato visto* is extremely unusual.

5

Demonstratives

5.1 Forms of the demonstrative adjectives and pronouns: *questo* (and *sto*), *quello*, etc.

TABLE 5.A

	Singular	Plural
Masc. adjective	questo/quest'	
Masc. pronoun	questo	questi
Masc. human subject pronoun	questi	
Fem. adjective	questa/quest'	queste
Fem. pronoun	questa	

	Singular	Plural
Masc. adjective	quel/quell'/quello	quei/quegli
Masc. pronoun	quello	quelli
Masc. human subject pronoun	quegli	
Fem. adjective	quella/quell'	quelle
Fem. pronoun	quella	

The demonstrative adjectives have a number of variant forms: *quel, quell', quello, quei, quegli, quella, quelle*. These have *exactly* the same distribution as the variant forms of the definite article (*il, l', lo, i, gli, la, le*), for which see 4.1. Thus *quel*, like the definite article *il*, occurs before nouns and adjectives beginning with a consonant – unless the consonant is *s* + consonant, *z-*, *ps-*, etc., in which case *quello* (like *lo*) is used. Plural *quei* occurs before most consonants or before vowels, and *quegli* before *s* + consonant, *z-*, etc., exactly like the plural articles *i* and *gli*. For *questo* and *questa* elision of the vowel before another word beginning with a vowel is optional, but particularly common where a sequence of two identical vowels (e.g., *questa anima*) would otherwise arise:

questo libro	'this book'	*questi libri*
quest'uomo	'this man'	*questi uomini*
questo spazio	'this space'	*questi spazi*
questa cosa	'this thing'	*queste cose*
quest'anima	'this soul'	*queste anime*
quel libro	'that book'	*quei libri*
quell'uomo	'that man'	*quegli uomini*
quello spazio	'that space'	*quegli spazi*
quella cosa	'that thing'	*quelle cose*
quell'anima	'that soul'	*quelle anime*

The adjective *sto* = *questo*

Sto (*sti, sta, ste*) is perceived by most Italians as a shortened form of the adjective *questo*, to which it is identical in meaning (it is often spelled as '*sto*). It is extremely frequent in informal speech, but avoided in formal discourse and writing (apart from its appearance in the words *stasera* 'this evening', *stamane*, *stamattina* 'this morning', *stanotte* 'last night', *stavolta* 'this time'):

Non mi piace mica sta macchina.	'I really don't like this car.'
Sti cretini non ci capiscono un fico secco.	'These idiots don't understand a damned thing about it.'

5.2 Meaning of *questo* vs. *quello*

The demonstrative *questo* corresponds by and large to English *this*, and is distinguished from *quello* (roughly 'that') in that *questo* is 'first-person oriented': it is applied to anything which the speaker(s) or writer(s) view as *close* to them in space or time, or with which they present themselves as in some way closely concerned or associated). In writing and speaking, such 'closeness' may simply constitute 'that which is most recently mentioned', for example:

Cosa sia stato quel trauma lo espresse poeticamente un altro giovane, meno che ventenne, Ugo Foscolo, nell'ode 'Bonaparte liberatore'. Lo descriverà nuovamente, in prosa questa volta, due anni dopo, in una dedica a Bonaparte.	'What that trauma was, was expressed poetically by another young man, still not twenty, UF, in the ode "BL". He describes it again, this time in prose, two years later, in a dedication to Bonaparte.'

Questo and *quello* can also mean, respectively, 'latter' and 'former':

Insomma, sembra che il peccato sia regolato dalla stessa legge che regola la virtù; sia anche quello, non meno di questa, una forma di virtù.	'So it seems that sin is regulated by the same law as virtue; that the former, just as much as the latter, is a kind of virtue.'

The next example involves simple spatial proximity to the speaker, who is giving directions from the steps on which she stands towards some shops in the distance:

Deve scendere questa scaletta, sempre dritto, e poi continuare fino a quei negozi laggiù.	'Go down these steps, straight ahead, and go on until those shops down there.'

Quest'ultimo is also sometimes used for 'the latter':

Proprio la settimana avanti andava al campo insieme a una zia e a un'altra donna, e quest'ultima aveva messo il piede su una mina ed era saltata in aria.	'Just the week before she was going to the field with an aunt and another woman and she [the latter] had stepped on a mine and been blown up.'
Un giorno si verificò l'allagamento dei locali di cui la Casa editrice era conduttrice e la maggior parte dei libri subì notevoli danni. Dopo avere invano richiesto il risarcimento del condominio, essa si decise ad intraprendere una azione legale contro quest'ultimo.	'One day the premises run by the publishing house were flooded, and most of the books were seriously damaged. After unsuccessfully seeking compensation by the condominium, it [i.e., the publishing house] decided to sue the latter [i.e., the condominium].'

Noun phrases containing *questo* and *quello* can be reinforced, respectively, by *qui/qua* and *lì/là* (see 5.15):

Vuoi questo tovagliolo qui o quello lì?	'Do you want this napkin (here) or that one (there)?'
Quelli là non hanno la minima idea di quello che pensiamo noi.	'Those people (there) haven't the faintest idea what we think.'

For the use of *questo* where English might employ a definite article (e.g., *Amava questo sport* 'He loved the sport'), see 4.13.

5.3 *Codesto*

The difference between *questo* and *quello* might broadly be described as 'first-person oriented' vs. 'not first-person oriented'. But there is another demonstrative, *codesto* (sometimes also *cotesto*), which is now generally considered archaic (and limited in current usage to bureaucratic language), except by many Tuscans, in whose usage it remains current. It is a 'second-person oriented', being centred on the *addressee* in much the same way that *questo* is centred on the speaker/writer.

Togliti cotesta camicia, è zuppa di sudore!	'Take off that shirt [you're wearing], it's soaked with sweat.'
Per carità, signora mia, non dica codeste cose.	'Please, madam, don't say those things [that you're saying].'

Use of *codesto*, rather than *questo*, may also serve simply to maintain the addressee's interest in what is being said, or as a way of involving the addressee in this discourse: *codesta idea* might be 'this idea [that I'm going to tell you about]':

Mi stia a sentire un attimo, che le volevo proporre codesta idea che mi è venuta in mente l'altro giorno.	'Just listen to me a moment: I wanted to show you this idea which I had the other day.'

Codesto/cotesto also corresponds, sometimes, to English 'such a . . ., such . . .':

Si mise a fare un discorso trotskista, ma suo padre gli obiettò che codeste idee non avevano nessun valore.	'He started talking Trotskyism, but his father protested that such ideas had no value.'

5.4 The demonstratives *questo* and *quello* as personal pronouns

We see in 6.26 that the third person pronouns *lui, lei* and *loro* principally refer to persons, and *esso* and *essa* are restricted to elevated discourse. So what pronom-

inal forms serve to represent 'non-persons' in ordinary discourse? In fact extensive use is made of *questo* and *quello*:

Nel passaggio ci sono delle fotocopiatrici e queste stanno sempre accese.	'In the passage there are photocopiers and they are always on.'

Questo and *quello* may also be used of persons, in informal speech, although
the effect may sound slightly discourteous and even derogatory, especially if the
demonstratives are accompanied by *lì* or *là* (e.g., *quello lì* 'that bloke').

A factor in the choice between *lui*, *lei*, etc. and the demonstratives seems to be
the speaker's attitude towards the person referred to. *Lui* and *lei* may express
sympathy for, or particular interest in, the person; *questo*, *questa*, etc. suggest a
negative attitude towards, or lack of interest in, the person.

Calabrese (in Renzi 1988: 624), observes that use of the demonstrative pronouns with reference to persons is less acceptable if the noun is a proper name,
in which case *lui*, *lei*, etc. tend to be preferred:

Dopo che Carlo m'ha visto con la fidanzata, lui [not *questo*] *è scoppiato a ridere.*	'After Carlo saw me with my girlfriend, he burst out laughing.'

5.5 The pronouns *questi* 'he', 'the last mentioned [person]', 'the latter', *quegli* 'he', 'the former'

The demonstrative pronouns *questi*, and the now rare *quegli*, have in common
with the pronoun *egli* that they are (i) singular only, (ii) refer only to male
humans and (iii) are encountered mainly in formal registers; most grammars also
state that they should be used only as subject pronouns. They refer to a person
previously mentioned in the discourse ('this man', 'he'), and *questi* often serves
to indicate the most recently mentioned:

In un articolo su Giovanni Paolo II, per evitare troppe ripetizioni, questi verrà menzionato di volta in volta come «il papa», «il pontefice». [Serianni 1988: 207f.]	'In an article on John Paul II, to avoid excessive repetition, he will be called variously "the pope", "the pontiff".'
Arrossì e pregò il portiere di guidarlo; quegli acconsentì volentieri.	'He blushed and asked the porter to lead the way; he [the porter] willingly agreed.'

Questi may sometimes be opposed to *quegli*:

. . . e che l'occasione serva a riconciliare i due ex amici [. . .] *sperano sia George Eastman sia Alessandro Haber: questi, modestissimo critico di provincia, stretto dalla solitudine, quegli, titolare di uno squallido club sportivo.*[1]	'. . . and that the occasion should help to reconcile the two former friends is the hope both of GE and AH: the latter, a very minor provincial critic, constrained by solitude, the former, the owner of a squalid sports club.'

5.6 The type *quelli del municipio* = 'the town hall people'

The phrase *quello/quelli di* + X is colloquially used to mean 'the X man'/'the X
people':

---

[1]Example cited by Serianni (1988: 237).

| *Sono venuti quelli del gas.* | 'The gas people have come.' |
| *Ho parlato con quello dello scarico.* | 'I talked to the man at the rubbish dump.' |

5.7 The pronouns *questo*, *quello*, *ciò* 'this', 'that', referring to assertions/propositions

Both *questo* and *quello* (always masculine singular) can be used to refer to a previous assertion, proposition or question. Italian tends to use *questo* in such cases, where English more readily employs 'that':

—*Si rifiuta di rimborsarci.*	'He's refusing to refund us.'
—*Questo proprio non lo sopporto!*	'I'm just not having that!'
—*Ognuno ha i suoi difetti.*	'We all have our faults.'
—*Questo è vero.*	'That's true.'
—*Il suo intervento giova o nuoce alla causa per la quale egli si batte, o dice di battersi?*	'Does his intervention help or hinder the cause he's fighting for, or claims to be fighting for?'
—*Questo sì che è un interrogativo fondato.*	'That certainly is a valid question.'

The pronoun *ciò* might also have been used in the above examples. Apart from its use as a declarative marker (19.9) in *cioè*, *ciò* is mainly characteristic of formal and literary registers:

| *Il principe aveva troppa esperienza per offrire a degli invitati siciliani, in un paese dell'interno, un pranzo che si iniziasse con un* potage, *e infrangeva tanto più facilmente le regole dell'alta cucina in quanto ciò corrispondeva ai propri gusti.* | 'The prince was too experienced to offer Sicilian guests, in a village in the interior, any lunch that started with a *potage,* and he broke the rules of *haute cuisine* all the more readily because that suited his own tastes.' |
| *Firmò silenziosamente la lettera e con ciò se ne andò, senza dire una parola.* | 'He signed the letter in silence, and with that he left, without saying a word.' |

Note also *per questo* ... or *perciò* = 'that's why ...', 'for that reason':

| *Mi hanno richiamato inaspettatamente a Roma. Per questo non ho potuto telefonarti.* | 'I was unexpectedly called back to Rome. That's why I couldn't phone you.' |
| *La loro risposta è insolente e perciò inaccettabile.* | 'Their answer is insolent and therefore unacceptable.' |

The Italian equivalent of English 'that means ...', where 'that' does not carry contrastive stress, is usually simply *vuol dire*:

| *'Energumeno'. Che vuol dire?* | '"Energumen". What does that mean?' |

5.8 The type *La situazione è sempre quella* 'The situation is still the same'

| *Povero Carlo, non sembra più quello* (or *lui*). | 'Poor C, he no longer seems himself.' / 'Poor C, he isn't what he used to be.' |
| *Purtroppo la situazione è sempre quella.* | 'Alas the situation is what it always has been / is just the same as ever / hasn't changed a bit.' |

5.9 Pronominalization of adjectives: the type *quello francese* = 'the French one'

English 'pronominalizes' adjectives by using the structure 'article + adjective + one(s)', or 'that/those + adjective'. The Italian equivalent is usually '*quel*, etc., + adjective':

Questi fatti piacevano parecchio alla gente, perché erano molto più verosimili di quelli veri.	'People really liked these facts, because they were much truer than the real ones.'
Poi abbiamo reso l'ambiente più caldo sostituendo i mobili moderni con quelli antichi.	'Then we made the ambience warmer by replacing modern pieces of furniture with antique ones.'
Io ho sempre pensato che il Paese dovesse risolvere la questione comunista, la questione fascista e la questione cattolica. Quelle comunista e fascista sono ormai archiviate.	'I always thought that the country should resolve the communist question, the fascist question and the Catholic question. The communist and fascist ones are now cut and dried.'

Note the following differences between 'demonstrative adjective + noun' and 'demonstrative pronoun + (nominalized) adjective':

demonstrative adjective + noun		demonstrative pronoun + (nominalized adjective)	
quel francese	'that Frenchman'	*quello francese*	'the French one'
quegli austriaci	'those Austrians'	*quelli austriaci*	'the Austrian ones'

Note that it is also possible (though less common) to express 'the French one', etc., by means of the definite article + noun:

Di questi vini mi piace più il francese che l'italiano.	'Of these wines I like the French one better than the Italian one.'

But in partitive constructions (see 4.20, 21), e.g., 'some French (ones)', the preposition *di* + article is normally used:

Ho del francese e dell'italiano.	'I have some French and some Italian [wine].'
Ci sono dei brutti e dei belli.	'There are some ugly ones and some beautiful ones.'

5.10 'Verbless' uses of *questo*

—*Ma ti hanno pagato, vero?*	'But they did pay you, didn't they?'
—*Questo sì, ma i soldi non bastano.*	'That's true,/They did, but the money isn't enough'.
—*Hai anche pulito gli stivali di Massimo?*	'Have you cleaned M's boots, too?'
—*Questo no, ma pazienza!*	'I haven't done that, but I'll get round to it!'

Usually characteristic of formal discourse is the following structure, with *questo* following the noun. In effect, this is a kind of relative structure, equivalent to 'which is a . . .', etc.:

Ebbi una telefonata dalla Tibiletti che mi faceva le sue rimostranze perché aveva saputo che io avrei portato la cocaina, circostanza questa non vera.	'I had a call from T who told me off because she'd heard I was supposed to have been bringing in cocaine, but this was not the case.' [lit. 'a circumstance this not true']

Volevano ballare in mezzo alla strada, comportamento questo davvero scandaloso agli occhi dei vicini.	'They wanted to dance in the street, which was really scandalous behaviour in the eyes of the neighbours.'

5.11 Some idioms and expressions with *questo* and *quello*

- *In quel di* + name of place or region = 'in the region of':

È nato cinquant'anni fa in quel di Perugia.	'He was born 50 years ago in the Perugia region.'
Ci fu una volta un paesino in quel di Verona.	'Once upon a time there was a little village in the Verona region.'

- *In quella* = 'at that moment':

In quella il telefono squillò.	'At that moment the phone rang.'

- *Questa* often appears in ironic or jocular exclamations:

Questa è bella!	'There's a fine thing!'
Questa è nuova!	'Here's a turn up for the books!'
Ci mancava anche questa!	'That was all we needed!'

- *Questo di . . .* or *questa di . . .* 'all this about':

Questo dei polli è un mucchio di cavolate.	'This story about the chickens is a pack of lies.'
Questa dell'IVA è una fregatura.	'All this stuff about VAT is a rip-off.'

5.12 The demonstrative pronoun *costui* (and *colui*), etc.

The following pronouns refer to human beings only, and are restricted to formal and written language. In particular, the use of *colui*, etc. as a demonstrative pronoun (corresponding to *quello*) is now extremely rare and old-fashioned, and *quello*, etc. is preferred instead (but *colui* is regularly used in relative constructions – see 7.17). They may function as subjects or non-subjects.

	Masculine	**Feminine**
Singular	*costui*	*costei*
	(*colui*)	(*colei*)
Plural	*costoro*	*costoro*
	(*coloro*)	(*coloro*)

È venuto il momento di parlare della padrona di casa. Se finora non ho detto niente di costei, è perché . . .	'The time has come to talk of the landlady. If I have said nothing about that lady hitherto, it is because . . .'
E costui ebbe per due o tre giorni un bel da fare nel seguirli di ristorante in ristorante.	'And this fellow [that I'm telling you about] for two or three days was saddled with following them from restaurant to restaurant.'

Costui may have a pejorative ring when it is used 'deictically' (i.e., not to refer to somebody just mentioned but to point to a person: 'that person over here'):

Ma chi si crede di essere costui?	'Just who does that bloke over there think he is?'

5.13 Demonstratives of kind and manner: *così, tale*

Così is an adverb meaning 'thus', 'so', 'to such a degree', 'in that way', 'such (a) + adjective'. It usually precedes the adjective; the structure 'such (a) + adjective + noun' is '*un* + noun + *così* + adjective'. It may also be used as an adjective 'like that', 'of that kind', in which case it always follows the noun:

Era così lontano che non si vedeva nemmeno.	'It was so far away you couldn't even see it.'
Quando noto una contraddittorietà così palese, ne resto turbato.	'When I notice such an obvious contradiction, I am disturbed by it.'
Noi a un pastrocchio così non parteciperemo mai!	'We will never take part in such a farce!'
Non lo avrei mai creduto così.	'I should never have thought him [to be] like that.'

Less commonly, *così* may also follow the adjective. The effect is to emphasize *così*:

Bello così non credevo che fosse.	'I didn't think he was *that* handsome.'
Cose grandi così non ne ho viste mai.	'I've never seen things *that* big.'

Tale is an adjective, and usually precedes the noun; 'such (a) + noun' is '*un tale* + noun'. It also has an adverbial form, *talmente*, which may be used in much the same way as adverbial *così*:

Non avrei mai creduto a una tale storia.	'I would never have believed such a story.'
Ma vanno evitati il tabacco e l'alcol. Tali sostanze nuociono sicuramente alla salute.	'Tobacco and alcohol should be avoided. Such substances are certainly damaging to one's health.'
Non lo avrei mai creduto tale.	'I should never have thought him [to be] like that.'
Menocchio, venutone a conoscenza, ne rimase talmente scosso da esporla diffusamente.	'M, having come to learn of it, was so affected by it as to expound it far and wide.'

When *tale* is itself modified by *che . . .* or *da . . .*, it follows the noun:

È di una bontà tale che non te la puoi neanche immaginare.	'He is of a goodness such as you can't even imagine.'
Era un urlo tale da far venire i brividi.	'It was a shriek such as to make you shudder.'

Alternatives to *tale* are *simile, siffatto, del genere,* and the now archaic *cotale*:

Fra marito e moglie è impensabile un simile litigio.	'Such an argument is unthinkable between husband and wife.'
Siffatte stupidaggini sono ormai finite. etc.	'This kind of silliness has now stopped.'

5.14 'Text-internal' demonstratives: *suddetto* 'above mentioned', etc.

Peculiar to written texts and chiefly characteristic of bureaucratic and legal usage are *suddetto, summenzionato, anzidetto, suesposto*:

Per i motivi suddetti non posso accettare.	'For the above-mentioned reasons I cannot accept.'

Il suddetto si presentava in condizioni pessime.	'The above-named presented himself in an extremely poor condition.'

5.15 Demonstratives of place:[2] *qua, là*, etc.

qui/qua 'here'   (*costì/costà* 'there')   *lì/là* 'there'

The relation between *qui/qua* and *lì/là* is very close to that between *questo* and *quello: qui/qua* is 'first person oriented', and *lì/là* are 'non-first-person oriented'. *Costì/costà* are mainly used in Tuscany and are 'second-person oriented', like *codesto* (see 5.3); outside Tuscany, they are likely to be perceived as antiquated:

È meglio che io rimanga qua e che tu rimanga là.	'It's better for me to stay here and you to stay there.'
Là in America ne combinerà di tutti i colori.	'He'll be up to goodness knows what (over) there in America.'
Da qui a lì saranno ottocento chilometri.	'It must be 800 km from here to there.'
Resta costà, non ti muovere, vengo a prenderti io.	'Stay there and don't move; I'll come and get you.'

These demonstratives can also be used to refer to points in time 'here', 'at this point' vs. 'then', 'at that point':

Vorrei continuare il mio lavoro ma qui mi devo fermare un attimo.	'I'd like to continue my work but here [i.e., now] I must stop a moment.'
Di qui a un po' ci siamo.	'We'll be there shortly.' [lit. 'A little from here we're there.']
Di lì a poco incontrano un mulo.	'Shortly afterwards they meet a mule.' [lit. 'A little from there they meet a mule.']

There is a further difference between the forms with the vowel *a*, and those with *i*. Those with *i* are essentially 'punctual': they refer to clearly defined, focused, 'points' in space or time; those in *a* are 'areal', and have a vaguer, more diffuse reference, which helps to explain why only the *a* forms are encountered in certain expressions denoting general but not specific position, or general motion in a particular direction: *qua e là* 'here and there' (as in *girava qua e là* 'he wandered hither and thither'), *di là* 'over there', 'over that way', 'beyond', *di qua* 'over here', 'this way', 'on this side', *più in là* 'further away', *più in qua* 'closer in', *quaggiù* 'down here', *laggiù* 'down there', *quassù* 'up here', *lassù* 'up there'. There is thus a distinction between *Non passare di là* 'Don't go that way', and (the rather unusual) *Non passare di lì* 'Don't go through that specific spot'.

Si diceva che avesse un'altra famiglia in una città di là dal mare.	'He was said to have another family in a city over the sea.'
Infatti eccolo lì che esce dalla porta delle scale.	'There he is, just there coming out from the stairway door.'
E lì conobbi l'uomo più dolce e grande che abbia mai incontrato.	'And there [in that place] I met the sweetest and greatest man I've ever known.'

---

[2]Temporal demonstratives, such as 'then', 'now', etc., are dealt with in 13.16.

5.16 *Qui, qua, lì, là* + locative term: *lì vicino* 'near there', etc. *Laggiù/quaggiù* 'down there/here'

The words *qui, qua, lì, là* may be followed by the locative terms *accanto, addosso, davanti, fuori, intorno, vicino, dentro, contro, dietro, oltre, presso, sotto, sopra,* These correspond to English 'locative term + here/there':

C'è un bar qui vicino?	'Is there a bar near here/nearby?'
Li trovammo lì dietro.	'We found them behind there.' [or 'behind that']
Là dentro ci sarebbe un cinghiale.	'There's supposed to be a boar in there.'
Qua sotto non c'è niente.	'There's nothing down here.'

Su and the locative adverb *giù* combine with *qua* and *là* to form *quassù* 'up here', *lassù* 'up there', *quaggiù* 'down here', *laggiù* 'down there':

Quella pietra laggiù potrebbe essere quella che cerchiamo.	'That stone down there could be the one we're looking for.'
Portateli quassù!	'Bring them up here.'

5.17 Demonstratives of identity: *l'albero stesso* 'the very tree', 'the tree itself'

The demonstrative adjective and pronoun *stesso* serves to underline *identity*. It corresponds to English 'the self same . . .', 'the very . . .', or 'the . . . itself', 'that . . . (and no other)'. In this use, *stesso* has a more literary counterpart *medesimo*.

È morto il giorno stesso in cui tu sei nata.	'He died the very day you were born.'
Mia madre stessa non mi vuole più a casa.	'Even my mother won't have me at home any more.'
È sempre la stessa storia: non vuoi mai metterti sotto a studiare.	'It's always the same old story: you just won't buckle down to studying.'

Also, with personal pronouns:

Io stesso preferisco rimanere a casa.	'I, too, prefer to remain at home'.
Me l'avete detto voi stessi di non toccare i fili.	'You yourselves told me not to touch the wires'.
L'hanno visto loro stessi.	'They saw it themselves.'

In the sense of 'the self same . . .', *stesso* (*medesimo*) precedes the noun; in the sense of emphatic 'him-/her-/itself, themselves' it may precede or follow:

Avevano letto lo stesso articolo.	'They'd read the same article.'
Avevano letto l'articolo stesso.	'They'd read the article itself.'
Ha offeso gli dei stessi./Ha offeso gli stessi dei.	'He's offended the very gods.'

Stesso may serve to add emphasis to possessive adjectives, and is then roughly equivalent to English 'own':

Ti presterò la mia stessa barca.	'I'll lend you my/my very own boat.'
Aveva dimenticato il suo stesso nome.	'He had forgotten his own name.'

5.18 What is the difference between *stesso* and reflexives?

English uses 'him-/her-/itself, themselves' for two different purposes: to emphasize identity, or as reflexives. English-speakers are liable to confuse these two functions in Italian. The Italian reflexive pronouns are used where the subject of the sentence carries out some action on (or for) himself/herself/itself:

Anna parla di sé.	'A talks about herself.'
I giudici lo fanno per sé.	'The judges do it for themselves.'

Stesso, on the other hand, is an emphatic adjective which simply emphasizes identity and is *not* reflexive.

Anna stessa parla.	'A herself [and no other] speaks.'
I giudici stessi lo fanno.	'The judges themselves do it.'

Pronouns corresponding to English emphatic 'his-, her-, itself', etc., are formed simply by placing *stesso* after an ordinary personal pronoun:

Lei stessa lo fa.	'She herself does it.'
I giudici lo fanno loro stessi.	'The judges themselves do it.'

Of course it is perfectly possible for *stesso* to modify a genuinely reflexive pronoun. In the following examples the underlinings in the English translations express the fact that the reflexive pronoun in English would also carry heavy, emphatic, stress. Note that when *stesso* is combined with *sé*, *sé* usually loses its accent:

Capisco te, ma non capisco me stesso.	'I understand <u>you</u>, but I don't understand <u>myself</u>.'
Lei parla di se stessa.	'She talks about <u>herself</u>.' [i.e., 'her very self']
I giudici criticano se stessi.	'The judges criticize <u>themselves</u>.' [i.e., 'their very selves']

Note that *se stesso*, rather than *sé*, must be used in the following cases:

● where the pronoun is the predicate of *essere, sembrare, diventare*:

Non sembra più se stesso.	'He no longer seems himself.'
Potrai ridiventare te stessa.	'You'll be able to become yourself again.'

● where the pronoun refers to the direct or indirect object of a main clause, rather than to the subject:

Giovanni lo costringeva a parlare di se stesso.	'G forced him to talk about himself.' [Where 'him' and 'himself' both refer to, say, Marco.]

5.19 *Stesso* not equivalent to English '-self' where '-self' means 'as far as X is concerned' or 'on his/her/its own'

English '-self' can also serve to focus or contrast some noun as opposed to others. Thus 'I myself' might be equivalent to 'as far as I'm concerned', 'for my part', 'I personally', etc., and in such cases Italian uses not *stesso* but other devices for focusing or highlighting the noun. For example:

Marco personalmente preferisce rimanere a casa. OR	'M himself prefers to remain at home.'
In quanto a/Per quanto riguarda M, preferisce rimanere a casa.	'As for M/As far as M is concerned, he prefers to stay at home.'

Where English 'him-, her-, itself', etc., means 'alone', 'on his own', etc., 'unassisted', 'single-handed', the equivalent Italian expression is usually *da* + stressed reflexive pronoun', or *da solo*:

La porta si chiude da sé.	'The door closes itself/is self-closing/closes automatically.'
I miei amici mi hanno abbandonato e ho dovuto fare tutto da me.	'My friends left me and I had to do everything myself/on my own.'
Non puoi farlo da solo.	'You can't do it yourself/on your own.'

5.20 The difference between *stesso* and *uguale*

Both words correspond to English 'same'; the difference is that *stesso* can mean either 'the very same' or 'just like', whereas *uguale* is 'just like' (but not 'the same one'). *Stesso* is normally accompanied by the definite article, and *uguale* by the indefinite:

Io e lei avevamo lo stesso foulard.	'She and I had the same scarf.' [either 'shared a scarf' or, simply, 'wore a scarf of the same design']
Io e lei avevamo un foulard uguale.	'She and I had the same scarf.' [i.e., 'of identical design']

6

Personal pronouns

For demonstrative, relative and interrogative pronouns, see Chapters 5, 7 and 8.

6.1 The differences between stressed and clitic ('unstressed') pronouns

Italian, unlike English, has two sets of pronouns: the 'stressed' pronouns and the 'unstressed', more commonly called 'clitic', pronouns. Some major differences between these two sets are:

(i) Clitics are not independent words: they are always 'attached' to a verb (i.e., they either immediately precede the verb or immediately follow it), and their position in relation to the verb, and in relation to each other when more than one clitic is combined, is subject to special rules of ordering (see 6.3, 4, 5, 6). Stressed pronouns, in contrast, are words which behave in many respects like independent nouns. They have virtually the same freedom of position within a sentence as ordinary nouns, and can stand independently of any verb.

(ii) Clitics are subject to special variations in their form when they are combined together (see 6.2), quite unlike anything encountered in ordinary nouns or in stressed pronouns.

(iii) Unlike nouns and stressed pronouns, clitics cannot normally be emphasized by stressing them, nor can they be contrasted with other pronouns or nouns.

(iv) In standard Italian there are *no* clitic pronouns representing the subject of a verb (which is indicated simply by the verb's ending). The subject pronouns have stressed forms only, and are used for purposes of emphasis, drawing attention or contrast.
   Examples:

Ebbi una telefonata dalla Tibiletti che mi faceva le sue rimostranze perché aveva saputo che io avrei portato la cocaina.	'I had a phone call from T, telling me off because she'd heard that I had been bringing in the cocaine.'

The subject pronoun does not appear with *ebbi*, and the first person indirect object pronoun *mi* is clitic because there is no implied contrast with any other person. But the stressed (subject) pronoun *io* appears with *avrei portato* probably to emphasize the writer's distress at the accusation that she, of all people, should be accused of importing cocaine.

La NASA ci teneva molto all'esperimento, tanto che ha pagato la maggior parte delle spese: l'equivalente di 800 miliardi di lire. Noi ne abbiamo investiti 242.	'NASA was very keen on the experiment, so much so that it paid most of the costs: the equivalent of 800 billion lire. <u>We</u> invested 242 [billion].'
Io non voglio dirlo allo zio, diteglielo voi.	'<u>I</u> don't want to tell uncle, <u>you</u> tell him.'

In the first example, *noi* is contrasted with *la NASA*. In the second the stressed pronouns are both subjects, are contrasted with each other (indicated by underlining in the English translation), and show similar freedom of position within the sentence as ordinary nouns (the first pronoun precedes the verb, but the second follows). The same freedom of positioning is apparent in the next two examples, where the subject pronoun is dislocated (17.2) to the beginning of the clause, some way from its verb:

Noi a un pastrocchio così non parteciperemo mai!	'<u>We</u>'ll never get involved in a farce like that!'
Io i posti del fossato li conosco palmo a palmo e tutte le ragazzine che ho coricato per quelle rive tu non lo immagini nemmeno.	'<u>I</u> know every inch of the area around the ditch and <u>you</u> can't even imagine how many young girls I've had on the banks.'

In the last example there is also an emphatic contrast between *io* and *tu*.

In the sentence

Bisogna vedere, chi fa prima, se loro a fucilare me o io a fucilare loro.	'We'll have to see who acts first, if <u>they</u> (act) to shoot <u>me</u>, or <u>I</u> (act) to shoot <u>them</u>.'

the stressed subject pronoun *loro* is contrasted with stressed subject *io*, and the stressed object *me* with the stressed object *loro*.

It is a consequence of the emphatic nature of the stressed pronouns that they are regularly used after 'focusing' words, such as *pure*, *proprio* and *anche*, whose function is precisely to focus attention on the pronoun:

Han preso anche te in un rastrellamento.	'They captured you, too, in a raid.'
Ho capito che se avessi avuto paura, anche io ero finita.	'I realized that if I got frightened, I too was finished.'
Hanno visto proprio lui.	'It was actually him they saw.'

An example of the ability of stressed pronouns (this time object forms) to stand independently of the verb is:

E chi fucileranno, allora? Me. O forse te.	'So who will they shoot? Me. Or maybe you.'

Another reflection of the emphatic, contrastive, nature of the stressed pronouns is their frequent use with certain forms of the subjunctive. The present subjunctive verb forms (see 14.6) are identical to each other in the first, second and third persons singular; the past subjunctive forms are identical in the first and second persons singular (see 14.11). A consequence of this is that stressed subject pronouns are often required in order to distinguish the persons. As a rule, a singular subjunctive form without a subject pronoun will tend to be interpreted as third person (unless it is clear from the context that this cannot be so); and if the verb is first or second person, a subject pronoun will be employed:

Io non ho nulla in contrario che bari al gioco, purché non venga a dirci che è il buon Dio a infilargli la carta falsa nel polsino. [Ogg.]	'I don't mind him cheating, as long as he doesn't try to make out that the dummy card gets up his sleeve by divine intervention.'
E finché non lo farete e non lo avrete dimostrato a me resterete in peccato mortale, che io conosca le vostre azioni, o no. [Lam.]	'And until you do it, and show me that you have, you'll remain in mortal sin, whether I know what you've done or not.'
Poi conobbi una ragazza, e allora passavo le giornate pensando a come si sarebbe comportata quella ragazza se io fossi diventato imperatore del Messico o se fossi morto. [Gua.]	'Then I met a girl, and spent my days wondering how she would react if I became emperor of Mexico or died.'

The last example shows that the pronoun need not be employed once the identity of the subject is established.

(v) A clitic can never be governed by a preposition. If a preposition is used, then an appropriate stressed pronoun must follow it.

Infine Marianna aveva ottenuto che di mattina, solo a pranzo, il bambino sedesse accanto a lei. [not *a la] [Mar.]	'At last M had managed, in the morning, just at lunchtime, to have the child sit next to her.'
E quando i piccoli non possono lasciare il letto, sono le maestre ad andare da loro. [not *da li]	'When the little ones can't leave their beds, the schoolmistresses go to them.'
L'immagine più viva è di me a letto. [not *di mi]	'The most striking picture is of me in bed.'
Il settimo proiettile l'ha riservato a sé. [not *a si]	'The seventh bullet he kept for himself.'

While the clitics cannot be preceded by any preposition, they can often stand for a noun preceded by a preposition: *Gli mando il pacco* = *Mando il pacco allo zio*, etc.

(vi) Third person stressed pronouns, but not the clitics, can vary according to such things as the 'humanness' or 'maleness' of the noun they represent (see 6.26), and according to register and style.

(vii) Many clitics have multiple functions (cf. *ci* in 6.10, 11, 12), and in certain set expressions (e.g., 6.9) they do not obviously 'stand for' any noun.

6.2 Forms of the clitics: *mi, ti, gli*, etc., vs. *me, te, glie*, etc.; elision; avoidance of repetition

The first and second person clitic pronouns are:

TABLE 6.A

1sg.	*mi* (*me*)
2sg.	*ti* (*te*)
1pl.	*ci* (*ce*)
2pl.	*vi* (*ve*)

These forms also function as reflexive pronouns:

Mi lavo.	'I wash myself.'
Guardati!	'Look at yourself.'
Ci sentiamo male.	'We feel ill.'
Vi vedete allo specchio.	'You see yourselves in the mirror.'
etc.	

The system of third person clitics is more complex, in that there are distinctions for case (i.e., direct vs. indirect object of the verb) and for gender. There is no gender distinction in the plural indirect object form. But the reflexive pronoun has its own special form, which does not distinguish case, gender or number:

TABLE 6.B

	Direct object	Indirect object	Reflexive
3sg.	M. *lo* F. *la*	M. *gli* (*glie*) F. *le* (*glie*)	
3pl.	M. *li* F. *le*	*loro*[1] or *gli* (*glie*)	*si* (*se*)

There is also a 'partitive' (*ne*), and a 'locative' (*ci* – which has a stylistically more elevated variant, *vi*) whose precise functions will be explained in 6.13. These do not distinguish gender or number:

TABLE 6.C

Partitive	*ne*
Locative	*ci* (*vi*)

Most clitics optionally elide ('drop') their final vowel before a following word beginning with a vowel. Elision is much more common in speech than in writing, but the following are indications for the written language:

- *Mi* and *ti* commonly elide before a vowel, especially *i* and *e*.
- *Ci*, *vi* elide principally before *essere*, *è* and the imperfect indicative forms of *essere* (*c'è*, *c'ero*, etc.); this is obligatory for *ci* but only optional for *vi*.
- *Li* and *le* (plural and indirect object) never elide. Elision is optional with *lo* and *la*, but is especially common in *l'ho* and *l'ha* (rather than *lo ho*, *la ho*, *lo ha*,

---

[1]The third person plural indirect object pronoun *loro* is a special case, and will be discussed (together with its relationship to third person plural *gli*) in 6.7.

la ha). But these pronouns tend not to elide before other verbs beginning with a stressed vowel (e.g. *lo ami* rather than *l'ami*), especially if that verb is *essere* (*lo è, lo era,* etc., rather than *l'è, l'era*).

- *Gli* only elides before a following *i*.
- *Si* elides most commonly before a following *i*.
- *Ne* rarely elides, except before *essere, è, era,* etc. It sometimes elides before words beginning with *i* and *e*, especially when preceded by another clitic (e.g., *Se n'intendeva*).

The clitics *mi, ti, gli, le, si, ci, vi* obligatorily change to *me, te, glie, glie, se, ce, ve,* respectively, when they are immediately followed by the third person direct object clitics *lo, la, li, le,* or by *ne*. These changes principally involve substitution of the vowel *i* by *e* (but *gli* becomes *glie*). Note that the feminine indirect object form *le* becomes *glie*, and so becomes identical to the masculine:

TABLE 6.D

Normal form	Form when followed by any of *lo,/la,/li,/le,/ne*
mi	*me*
ti	*te*
gli	*glie*
le	*glie*
si	*se*
ci	*ce*
vi	*ve*

Chiedimelo.	'Ask me it.'
Te la offro.	'I offer it to you.'
Diteglielo voi.	'You tell her.'
Se lo mangia.	'He eats it up.'
Se le ricorda tutte.	'He remembers them all.'
Ce lo mando.	'I send it there.'
Non ce ne sono.	'There aren't any.'
etc.	

Sequences of two identical clitics are not allowed. Potential sequences of **vi vi* or **ci ci* are usually replaced by *vi ci*:

Vi ci portano. [not **ci ci*]	'They take us there.'
Vi ci portano. [not **vi vi*]	'They take you there.'
Vi ci rivolgiamo. [not **ci ci*]	'We turn [*rivolgersi*] to it.'
Vi ci rivolgete. [not **vi vi*]	'You turn to it.'

Potential sequences of **si si* are always *ci si* (e.g., *Ci si lava* 'One washes oneself'). For more details, see 6.31.

When a clitic is attached to a monosyllabic second person singular imperative (see 14.9), its consonant is lengthened (but *gli, glie* undergo no change):

Dillo.	'Say it.'
Fammelo.	'Do it for me.'
Vallo a sotterrare!	'Go and bury him!'
Stammi bene.	'Stay well (for me)!'
etc.	

but

Daglielo.	'Give it to him.'

The *i* of the clitics may optionally be deleted before a following word beginning with a vowel. This is particularly, but not exclusively, true of spoken Italian:

L'accampamento s'indovina prima d'arrivarci.	'The camp can be guessed at before you get to it.'
Fossi andato dove so io il giorno che t'ho conosciuta!	'I wish you'd gone to a place I know the day I met you!'

However, omission of *i* from *ci*, while perfectly common in speech, is avoided in writing simply because of the difficulties of representing the sound [ʧ] in writing without a following *i* (2.2). Thus what is written *Ci hai visti* may be pronounced [ʧai̯ visti].

6.3 Position of clitics in relation to their verb

Clitics *precede* all first person, second person and third person forms of the verb (but some imperatives are an exception, see below):

Ce li troverai.	'You'll find them there.'
Mi alzo alle sette.	'I get up at 7.'
Ne conosceremo la causa.	'We'll know the reason for it.' [lit. 'of it']
Glielo manderebbe.	'He'd send it to him.'
Ti ce ne vorranno migliaia.	'You'll need thousands of them.'
Ci si addormentò.	'He fell asleep there.'
etc.	

Note that *loro* behaves differently, and will be discussed in 6.7.

With imperative verb forms, the clitics *follow* the verb forms corresponding to *tu*, *voi* and *noi*, but *precede* the verb where the third person (*Lei* and *Loro* 14.8 and 22.3) imperative is used:

Alzati subito!	'Get up immediately!'
Prendine pure!	'Do take some!'
Alzatevi subito!	'Get up immediately!'
Prendetene pure!	'Do take some!'
Alziamoci subito!	'Let's get up immediately!'
Prendiamone pure!	'Do let's take some!'
etc.	

Si alzi subito (lei)!	'Get up immediately!'
Ne prenda pure (lei)!	'Do take some!'
Si alzino subito (loro)!	'Get up immediately!'
Ne prendano pure (loro)!	'Do take some!'

But in negative imperatives, the clitic tends to precede rather than follow the verb. The negative imperative corresponding to *tu* is identical to the infinitive:

Non ti alzare! or *Non alzarti!*

Non ne prendere! or *Non prenderne!*
Non vi alzate! or *Non alzatevi!*
Non ne prendete! or *Non prendetene!*
Non ci alziamo! or *Non alziamoci!*
Non ne prendiamo! or *Non prendiamone!*

Note, however, that with the negative of the 'generic' or 'indefinite' imperative as used in public instructions, recipes, etc. (see 14.8), which also employs an infinitive, the clitic must follow the infinitive:

Non tagliarla prima che sia cotta.   'Do not cut it before it is cooked.'

Clitics *follow* all those forms of the verb whose endings do not indicate the person of the subject. As these examples show, when clitics follow the verb they are joined to it in writing. The final *-e* of the infinitive (the final *-re*, with infinitives in *-rre*) is removed:

an infinitive	*mandarglielo*	*produrla*
a gerund	*mandandoglielo*	*producendole*
a past participle	*mandatoglielo*	*prodottone*
a present participle	*riguardantelo*	*producentili*

Attachment of the clitic to the past participle, e.g., *Ricevutolo, entrò* 'Having received it, he entered', occurs only where the participle is used 'absolutely' (without an accompanying auxiliary verb), roughly with the sense of English 'having + past participle':

Consegnatolo all'editore, ritornò a Zagabria.   'Having handed it to the publisher, he returned to Zagreb.'

The absolute use of the past participle is much more common with verbs which would normally take *essere* as their auxiliary (see 14.20), and such constructions frequently occur with reflexive and passive verbs:

I cacciatori, alzatisi prima dell'alba,   'The hunters, having risen before
si misero a seguire il cinghiale.   dawn, started to trail the boar.'
Ho studiato attentamente tutti i documenti   'I have carefully studied all the
mandatimi.   documents sent to me.'

6.4 Position of clitics in relation to constructions comprising more than one verb: *L'ho lavato, Lo devo lavare, Devo lavarlo,* etc.

The clitic is always attached to the *auxiliary* in constructions consisting of *avere* or *essere* + past participle, and to *fare* in causative structures (see 15.25–9):

Si erano alzati alle tre.   'They had got up at three.'
L'avevo fatto.   'I'd done it.'
Glielo faccio scrivere.   'I make him write it.'
Fatemelo vedere!   'Show it to me!'
etc.

In combinations of verb + gerund (*stare, andare, venire* + gerund) or verb + infinitive (*venire, potere, volere, dovere, sapere, andare a, venire a, tornare a, cominciare a, continuare a, stare a, finire di, stare per* + infinitive), the clitic may be attached either to the first verb, or to the gerund/infinitive. There is no clearly identifiable difference in meaning between these variant possibilities, although many speakers seem to feel that when the auxiliary is attached to the first verb there is a closer link between the two verbs, and the first verb is 'subordinate' or 'ancillary' to the first. For further discussion of this point, see 14.20 on auxiliary selection. The type with clitic attached to the first verb is more frequently encountered in northern Italy, and the type with clitic attached to the infinitive or gerund tends to be favoured in central and southern Italy.

Li sta lavando./Sta lavandoli.	'He's washing them.'
Lo andava dicendo./Andava dicendolo.	'He was going round saying it.'
La veniva costruendo./Veniva costruendola.	'He was building it.'
Dovendolo fare./Dovendo farlo.	'Having to do it.'
etc.	
Ne posso fare./Posso farne.	'I can do some.'
Glielo voglio mandare./Voglio mandarglielo.	'I want to send it to him.'
Ne comincio a scoprire./Comincio a scoprirne.	'I'm beginning to discover some.'
Li sarebbero andati a prendere./Sarebbero andati a prenderli.	'They would have gone to get them.'
Ti vengo a trovare./Vengo a trovarti.	'I'm coming to see you.'
Lo sta a fare ora./Sta a farlo ora.	'He's doing it now.'
Si stava per aprire./Stava per aprirsi.	'It was about to open.'
Vallo a sotterrare!/Va a sotterrarlo!	'Go and bury him!'
etc.	

There is one case in which the position of the clitic in the above 'verb + infinitive' construction is not optional. If the first verb is one that *normally* takes *avere* as its auxiliary (i.e., *volere, potere, dovere, sapere, cominciare a, finire di*), and the auxiliary *avere* is the one used, then *the clitic must attach to the following infinitive*. But if the auxiliary *essere* is used instead of *avere*, then *the clitic must attach to the auxiliary*, and not to the infinitive:

Avevo dovuto andarci./C'ero dovuto andare.	'I'd had to go there.'
Not **Ci avevo dovuto andare./*Ero dovuto andarci.*	
Ha voluto andarsene/ Se n'è voluto andare.	'He wanted to go away.'
Not **Se ne ha voluto andare./*È voluto andarsene.*	
Ha potuto diventarlo./Lo è potuto diventare.	'He managed to become it.'
Not **Lo ha potuto diventare./*È potuto diventarlo.*	
etc.	

6.5 *Ecco* + clitic

Clitics can also be attached to the presentative particle *ecco*. With a direct object clitic, the meaning is '(t)here he/she/it is', etc.; with an indirect object clitic, the clitic often serves to indicate that the thing indicated is of interest or concern to the person indicated by that clitic, and very often there is no easily expressible English equivalent:

Dov'è ? Ah, eccola!	'Where is she? Oh, there she is!'
Eccoci arrivati!	'Here we are, we've arrived.'
Eccomi.	'Here I am.'
Eccoti il disastro che avevo previsto!	'There you are, that's the disaster I predicted!'
L'ho trovata! Eccole la patente!	'Found it! Here's your driving licence!'

6.6 Order of combinations of clitics

The order of combinations of clitics is also rigidly fixed and is the same whether the combined clitics precede or follow the verb. Combinations of clitics can never be 'split up': i.e., one may say either *Devo mandarglielo* 'I must send him it' or *Glielo devo mandare* but never **Gli devo mandarlo*. The sole exception involves indefinite personal *si* used as a subject personal pronoun (e.g., *Si voleva farlo* 'One wanted to do it'), for which see 6.31.

Combinations of more than two clitics are fairly rare (but see 6.31), and possible combinations of more than three barely ever occur. Most of our examples will contain only two. The rules are especially complex – and native speakers' judgements of acceptability by no means clear-cut – where 'locative' and first and second person clitics are concerned. Non-native speakers are best advised simply to avoid trying to combine more than two clitics, or first person clitics with second person clitics, or 'locatives' with first or second person clitics: it is often better, and clearer, to resort to stressed pronouns or locative forms instead. Thus, instead of *Mi gli presento* 'I present myself to him' one might say *Mi presento a lui*; for *Ti ci ho incontrato* 'I met you there', one might say *Ti ho incontrato lì*, and so forth.

Of the many theoretically possible combinations of clitics, the following are the ones that most commonly occur, and can confidently be used without sounding strange or contrived:

me lo	*te lo*	*glielo*	*se lo*	*ce lo*	*ve lo*
me la	*te la*	*gliela*	*se la*	*ce la*	*ve la*
me li	*te li*	*glieli*	*se li*	*ce li*	*ve li*
me le	*te le*	*gliele*	*se le*	*ce le*	*ve le*
me ne	*te ne*	*gliene*	*se ne*	*ce ne*	*ve ne*

The combinations *mi si, ti si, gli/le si, lo si, la si, li si, le si, ci si* and *vi si* are also current where the *si* is the indefinite personal pronoun meaning 'one' (see 6.31).

The ordering of the most commonly encountered combinations in modern Italian is:

> indirect object + direct object + 'indefinite personal' *si* (*se*) + *ne*

Direct object clitics immediately follow indirect object clitics:

Diteglielo voi.	'You say it to him.'
Toglitelo dalla testa.	'Get it out of your head.' (cf. 10.13)
Se glielo trovi, faccelo sapere.	'If you find it for him, let us know [it].'
Decise di avvicinarsela.	'He decided to draw it to himself.'

The last example, with *avvicinare una cosa* 'to draw something near' might be contrasted with

Decise di avvicinarlesi.	'He decided to go up to her.'

which corresponds to *avvicinarsi a qualcuno* 'to approach someone'. Although grammatically possible, the sequence indirect object *le* + *si* is felt to be rather awkward (cf. the list of common combinations above): a more likely formulation might be *Decise di avvicinarsi a lei*.

Ne is always the last element in any sequence of clitics in which it occurs:

Devo parlarvene.	'I have to speak to you about it.'

Mi ce ne vogliono quattro.	'I need four of them.'
Ci se ne accorge.	'One realizes it.'

In principle, one may have the combination *ne* + *lo/la/li/le* (e.g., *Non sapeva come tirarnelo* 'He didn't know how to pull him out of it'). However *ne lo*, etc., is scarcely ever encountered.

Si, when it is the indefinite personal pronoun 'one', but *not* when it is a reflexive pronoun, is always the last element in any sequence of clitics (apart from *ne*). Details are given in 6.31.

There are some important exceptions to the general principles of ordering:

(i) First person singular clitics (direct or indirect object) generally precede all others.

(ii) Combinations of third person direct object pronouns (*lo/la/li/le*) and *ne* must simply be avoided (archaic, literary usage in fact has *ne lo*, etc.), and some other mode of expression found. For example:

Tu l'hai accusato di orgoglio, ma io l'ho mai accusato di questo?	'You accused him of pride, but did I ever accuse him of it?'
S'era impantanato nel fango, e non riuscivo a tirarlo fuori.	'He got stuck in the mud and I couldn't get him out [of it].'

(iii) 'Locative' clitics (see 6.10 for their various uses) behave as follows:

Ci precedes third person direct object clitics:

Ce lo porteranno domani.	'They'll take it there tomorrow.'

Ci follows other direct and indirect object clitics:

Le ci vorranno almeno otto ore.	'It'll take her at least eight hours.'
Ti ci porteranno domani.	'They'll take you there tomorrow.'
Ti ci ruberanno la borsa.	'They'll steal your purse there.'

Combinations of *vi* and *ci* generally have the order *vi ci* regardless of the functions of *vi* and *ci*. See 6.2 for examples.

6.7 The 'semi-clitic' *loro*: *Do loro il libro* vs. *Gli do il libro* 'I give them the book'

Use of third person plural indirect object *loro* is largely restricted to formal speech and writing. In everyday usage *gli* (identical to the masculine singular) is used instead, and many educated Italians now regard *gli* as acceptable both in speech and writing.

Avevo il loro numero di telefono e gli telefonai.	'I had their phone number and I phoned [to] them.'

Use of *gli* also has the advantage of avoiding the characteristics which make *loro* different from other clitics, namely that:

● *loro* almost always follows the verb (in very formal usage it is occasionally found preceding the present or past participle: e.g., *i diritti loro spettanti* 'the rights due to them').

- in combinations of auxiliary + past participle *loro* generally *follows* the past participle. Some Italians feel that the type *Ho loro detto*, with *loro* between the auxiliary and the past participle, is possible in formal usage, especially if *loro* is very lightly stressed; others reject this possibility altogether.
- *loro* always follows other clitic pronouns.
- *loro* is always written as a separate word (and not attached to the preceding verb or other clitics).

Ordina loro di fermarsi e di scavare la fossa.	'He orders [to] them to stop and dig the ditch.'
Faremo loro vedere l'ingiustizia della proposta.	'We'll show [to] them the injustice of their proposal.'
Si è dimostrato molto generoso nel ritirarsi per preparare loro la strada.	'He proved very generous in withdrawing to prepare the way [for] them.'
Voleva comunicarlo loro.	'He wanted to communicate it to them.'
Abbiamo indicato loro la presenza di elementi estranei.	'We indicated to them the presence of alien elements.'
Forse qualcosa era loro sfuggito.	'Perhaps something had escaped [from] them.'

6.8 *Lo* standing for clauses and phrases: *Lui è italiano e lo sono anch'io* = 'He's Italian and I am too'

The clitic *lo* can stand not only for a masculine noun or noun phrase, but for whole clauses and for adjective and predicate phrases (underlined in the following examples). It is especially common in dislocated structures (see 17.2, 4). It also has to be used after predicative verbs such as *essere, diventare, sembrare, parere* where English might either delete the predicative phrase or replace it with 'to be':

Tutte le ragazzine che ho coricato per quelle rive tu non lo immagini nemmeno.	[lit]. 'All the young girls I've had on those banks, you can't even imagine it.'
Cosa sia stato quel trauma lo espresse poeticamente un altro giovane . . . [Esp.]	'What that trauma was, was poetically expressed by another young man.'
So che si sono rifiutati di ricevermi, e proprio non lo capisco.	'I know they refused to receive me, and I really don't understand it.'
La pianura era spesso avvolta nella nebbia, ma quel giorno per fortuna non lo era.	'The plain was often shrouded in fog, but luckily that day it wasn't.'
Dovevano essere buffi a vedersi, stupidi come possono esserlo coloro che ripetono un dovere che non capiscono. [Mar.]	'They must have been ridiculous to see, stupid in the way that people who repeat a duty they don't understand are.'
Lui è italiano e lo sono anch'io.	'He is Italian, and I am too.'
Lei è inglese ma non lo sembra.	'She's English but she doesn't seem to be.'
Vuole diventare infermiera, ma non lo diventerà mai.	'She wants to become a nurse, but she never will.'

Lo also stands for the complement of *sapere*:

—*È professore.*	'He's a teacher.'
—*Lo so.*	'I know [it = that he's a teacher].'

> *Oggi è festa,* non *lo sapevi?* 'Today's a holiday, didn't you know [it = that it's a holiday]?'

6.9 Idioms with feminine *la*

A large number of idiomatic expressions contain an apparently meaningless feminine singular pronoun *la* (sometimes combined with other clitics, such as *ci* and *si*). Among these are:

farcela 'to manage', 'succeed':

> *Proprio non ce la faceva più a sopportare la nostra condizione.* 'He just couldn't manage to put up with our condition any more.'

cavarsela 'to manage', 'get by', 'muddle through':

> *Me la cavo in inglese.* 'I can get by in English.'

smetterla 'to stop', 'leave off':

> *La vuoi smettere di fare lo scemo?* 'Will you stop being a fool?'

sentirsela 'to feel up to (doing something)':

> *Te la senti di fare due passi?* 'Do you feel up to taking a stroll?'
> *'Proprio non me la sento.* 'I really don't feel up to it.'

prendersela 'to take offence':

> *Non te la prendere, stavo scherzando.* 'Don't be offended, I was joking.'

avercela con qualcuno 'to be annoyed with/have a grudge against somebody':

> *Non ce l'ho con te ma con Alifano.* 'It's not you I'm annoyed with, it's Alifano.'

godersela 'to have a good time':

> *E io devo lavorare mentre voi ve la godete.* 'And I have to work while you enjoy yourselves.'

squagliarsela 'to high tail it', 'run off'

> *Hanno approfittato del suo starsene assorta sulla tela per squagliarsela.* 'They took advantage of her standing engrossed over the canvas to beat it.'

6.10 'Locative' *ci* and *vi* '(t)here'

In addition to being first and second person plural pronouns, *ci* and *vi* also stand for noun phrases indicating 'location in/at/under/on/between/through' or 'motion to(wards)'. There is no difference of meaning between *ci* and *vi*, but there is one of register, *vi* being relatively rare and characteristically associated with formal language.

Both are close in meaning to English 'there', except that they can only be used with reference to a location or direction previously mentioned in the discourse. Thus one may say *Guarda sotto il tavolo e ci troverai il fazzoletto* 'Look under the table and you'll find the handkerchief there', where *ci* stands for *sotto il tavolo*, but, in answer to a question *Dov'è il fazzoletto?* one would normally say not *Ce *lo troverai* but *Lo troverai là* 'You'll find it there' (probably accompanied by an appropriate gesture).

When a noun phrase preceded by the preposition *a* denotes a *person* the indirect object pronouns *gli, le, loro* are preferable: *Gli racconto la storia* 'I tell him the story' = *Racconto la storia al ragazzo* 'I tell the boy the story'. Use of *ci* with reference to persons is characteristic of popular and colloquial styles (*glielo dico* rather than *ce lo dico*, etc.).

Ci or *vi* may stand for *da* + noun phrase where *da* = 'to', or 'through'. But where *da* means 'from', or 'by' in passive constructions, *ne* is usually employed.

Penso sempre alla mia patria.	'I always think of my country.'
Ci penso sempre.	'I always think of it.'
Ritorno a Roma domani.	'I'm going back to Rome tomorrow.'
Ci ritorno domani.	'I'm going back there tomorrow.'
Si fermò davanti al negozio.	'He stopped in front of the shop.'
Ci si fermò davanti.	'He stopped in front of it.'
È pericoloso pescare nel pozzo.	'It's dangerous to fish in the well.'
È pericoloso pescarci.	'It's dangerous to fish there.'
Mi disse d'averla lasciata sul tavolo, ma non ce l'ho trovata.	'He told me he'd left it on the table, but I didn't find it there.'
Dentro quella biblioteca, non c'era mai entrato.	'Inside that library, he had never been [there].'
Lo lascerai sotto il ponte?	'You'll leave it under the bridge?
Sì, certo che ce lo lascerò.	Yes of course I'll leave it there.'
Sono appena stata dal dentista, e per un anno almeno non voglio tornarci!	'I've just been to the dentist's, and I don't want to go back for at least a year.'
Devo andare dal medico, ma non ci voglio andare per niente.	'I have to go to the doctor's, but I don't want to go there at all.'

The use of *ci* to stand for *con* + noun phrase is commonly heard, but considered out of place in formal discourse:

Mia madre mi aveva vietato di parlare con i militari, ma ci parlavo lo stesso.	'My mother had forbidden me to speak to [lit. 'with'] the soldiers, but I spoke to them anyway.'
Non esco mai con Carlo.	'I never go out with C.'
Non ci esco mai.	'I never go out with him.'

More acceptable alternatives would be *Ma parlavo con loro lo stesso* and *Non esco mai con lui*.

6.11 The type *Ci camminava sopra* 'He was walking on it'

With the prepositions *contro, dentro, sopra, sotto, su*, the *ci* or *vi* may substitute just the noun. Because *ci* and *vi* are clitics, they must occur next to the verb, but these prepositions remain in the position immediately before the position where the noun would occur. Thus:

Rimase dentro la grotta.	'It stayed in the cave.'
Ci rimase dentro.	'It stayed inside it.'
Si lanciò contro la porta.	'He flung himself against the door.'
Ci si lanciò contro.	'He flung himself against it.'
Aveva rimuginato sulla cosa per anni.	'He'd been mulling the matter over for years. '
Ci aveva rimuginato su per anni.	'He'd been mulling it over for years.'

Lo nascosero sotto il sasso.	'They hid it under the rock.'
Ce lo nascosero sotto.	'They hid it under it.'
Vai dietro alla macchina.	'Go along behind the machine.'
Vacci dietro.	'Go along behind it.'

6.12 The types c'è 'there is', *ci vuole* 'is necessary', *ci ha* 'he has'

Ci (or *vi*) are also used with *essere* (*c'è, ci sono, c'era*, etc. 'there is', 'there are', 'there was', etc.):

C'è qualcuno alla porta.	'There's somebody at the door.'
Ci saranno altri motivi, dei quali non ha parlato.	'There may be other reasons he didn't talk about.'
Ci sono le mie sei lenzuola ricamate e le sei di cotone stampato. C'è il mio piccolo conto in banca. C'è il mio tavolo di noce. C'è il mio abbonamento al cinema d'essai dei preti. Ci sono persone, strade, pentole, tram, scale, alberi, che in tutto o in ogni parte mi appartengono. [Dur1.]	'There are my six embroidered sheets and the six printed cotton ones. There's my little bank account. There's my walnut table. There's my subscription to the priests' experimental cinema. There are people, roads, saucepans, trams, stairs, trees, which wholly or in every part belong to me.'

Note that, unlike English 'there', which can be used in a variety of 'presentative' constructions, *ci* in this sense can only be combined with *essere*. Constructions such as 'There arrived ...', 'There appeared ...', 'There followed ...', 'There arose ...', etc., consist in Italian merely of the verb (without *ci*) *followed* by the subject (cf. also 17.1 on this word order):

Arrivarono due uomini.	'There arrived two men.'
È sorto un problema.	'There has arisen a problem.'

To say 'There seems/appears to be ...', *ci* must be attached to *essere* not to *sembrare* or *parere*:

Sembravano esserci dei problemi.	'There seemed to be problems.'
Sembra esserci una soluzione.	'There seems to be a solution.'

But presentative *ci* cannot be attached to *essere* if *essere* is the auxiliary of a passive verb. Constructions such as 'There was heard an explosion', 'There were seen two boys' simply consist of the passive verb (without *ci*) followed by the subject:

Fu sentita una esplosione.	'There was heard an explosion.'
È stata dichiarata la tregua.	'There has been declared a truce.'

Ci is also combined with *volere* to give *volerci* ('to be necessary'). In the spoken language, the verb *avere* is frequently, if redundantly, combined with *ci* (*averci*) where the sense is 'have', 'possess' (never when *avere* is an auxiliary). Note that when *ci* is directly followed by *ho, hai, ha*, etc., in this case, it is always pronounced [ʧ], never [ʧi]:

Ci ho [ʧɔ] *una pistola tedesca.*	'I've got a German pistol.'
Ci hai [ʧai]*le chiavi? Sì, ce le ho.*	'Have you got the keys? Yes, I've got them.'

6.13 The functions of *ne* and restrictions on its use

Ne is a pronoun which may stand for prepositional phrases consisting of *di* + noun. (For the many uses of the preposition *di*, see 10.1; 11.5; also 10.10 for differences between *ne* and possessive adjectives.)

Solo io ho la chiave della porta.	'Only I have the key to the door.'
Solo io ne ho la chiave.	'Only I have the key to it.'
Sono contento del tuo lavoro.	'I'm happy with your work.'
Ne sono contento.	'I'm happy with it.'
Conosco il segreto di Roberto.	'I know R's secret.'
Ne conosco il segreto.	'I know his secret.'
Ti parlerò domani dei miei problemi.	'I'll tell you about my problems tomorrow.'
Te ne parlerò domani.	'I'll tell you about them tomorrow.'
Ammiro l'intelligenza di Marco.	'I admire M's intelligence.'
Ne ammiro l'intelligenza.	'I admire his intelligence.'
Conosco un sacco di ragazze.	'I know loads of girls.'
Ne conosco un sacco.	'I know loads (of them).'
Hanno scritto migliaia di parole.	'They wrote thousands of words.'
Ne hanno scritte migliaia.	'They wrote thousands (of them).'
Non m'importa di quello che lui pensa.	'I don't care about what he thinks.'
Non me ne importa.	'I don't care about it.'
etc.	

Ne can be equivalent to English 'some' or 'any', standing for partitive noun phrases (for these see 4.20):

Ho bevuto del vino.	'I've drunk some wine.'
Ne ho bevuto.	'I've drunk some.'
Ho bevuto vino.	'I've drunk wine.'
Ne ho bevuto.	'I've drunk some.'
Prendi degli spaghetti!	'Take some spaghetti!'
Prendine!	'Take some!'
Ho amici a Perugia.	'I've friends in Perugia.'
Ne ho a Perugia.	'I have some in Perugia.'
Volevo comprare una bicicletta, ma non ne avevano in vendita.	'I wanted to buy a bicycle but they didn't have any for sale.'

Ne corresponds to nouns preceded by a quantifier (e.g., by *poco, molto, altro, diversi, vari, alcuno, nessuno, uno*, numerals, etc.). The equivalent English construction uses 'of him/her/it/them', but whereas in English the phrases 'of them', 'of it', etc., are only optional, in Italian, numerals and other quantifiers cannot stand on their own: they must be accompanied by *ne*.

Troverai diversi libri.	'You'll find several books.'
Ne troverai diversi.	'You'll find several (of them).'
Non conosco nessuno spagnolo.	'I don't know any Spaniard.'
Non ne conosco nessuno.	'I don't know any (of them).'
Ci sono tre problemi.	'There are three problems.'
Ce ne sono tre.	'There are three (of them).'
Arrivano poche lettere da Parigi.	'Few letters get here from Paris.'
Ne arrivano poche da Parigi.	'Few (of them) get here from Paris.'
Misura settanta centimetri.	'It measures 70 cm.'
Ne misura settanta.	'It measures 70.'
Vogliono costruire una capanna anche dietro la casa.	'They want to build a shed behind the house too.'

Ne vogliono costruire una anche dietro la casa.	'They want to build one behind the house too.'
Devo comprarmi una macchina ancora più spaziosa.	'I must buy an even more spacious car.'
Devo comprarmene una ancora più spaziosa.	'I must buy an even more spacious one.'

Note from the last two examples that *ne* with *uno/una* often corresponds to English pronominal 'one', or 'a . . . one'.

When quantifier + noun is preceded by a preposition (other than *di* and some uses of *da* mentioned below), *ne* cannot be used:

Ci fermavamo davanti a molti negozi.	'We stopped in front of many shops.'
Ci fermavamo davanti a molti di essi.	'We stopped in front of many of them.'
Ti puoi concentrare su alcuni problemi, ma non su tutti.	'You can concentrate on some problems, but not all of them.'
Ti puoi concentrare su alcuni, ma non su tutti.	'You can concentrate on some, but not all of them.'

We see in 4.20 that partitive noun phrases, as in *Ho dei libri vecchi* or *Ho libri vecchi*, can be substituted by *ne*. But it is also possible for *ne* to substitute the noun (e.g., *libri*) but not the adjective (in this case, *vecchi*). In effect, the adjective then modifies *ne*, and the result is a pronominal phrase usually equivalent to English 'I've got some old ones', etc. In such cases, the Italian adjective must then be preceded by *di*:

L'America ha delle spese enormi.	'America has enormous expenses.'
L'America ne ha di enormi.	'America has enormous ones.'
Non avevo mai visto degli animaletti così curiosi.	'I'd never seen such curious little animals.'
Non ne avevo mai visti di così curiosi.	'I'd never seen such curious ones.'

If the adjective is preceded by *alcuni*, then *di* may be omitted:

Ne voglio alcune belle.	'I want some beautiful ones.'

There are restrictions on the use of *ne* when this pronoun represents all or part of a *subject* noun phrase. *Ne* is acceptable when it represents a noun phrase which is the subject of a verb (in any tense) whose auxiliary is (14.20) *essere* (this includes passive verbs; for reflexives, however, see below),[2] but many speakers do not find it acceptable with a verb (in any tense) whose auxiliary is *avere*.

Subject *ne* with verbs that take auxiliary *essere*:

Verranno tre avvocati.	'Three lawyers will come.'
Ne verranno tre.	'Three [of them] will come.'
Si iscriveranno migliaia di studenti.	'Thousands of students will enrol.'
Si ne iscriveranno migliaia.	'Thousands [of them] will enrol.'
Apparvero molte cicogne.	'Many storks appeared.'
Ne apparvero molte.	'Many [of them] appeared.'
È stato ucciso il padre di Paolo.	'Ps father has been killed.'
Ne è stato ucciso il padre.	'His father has been killed.'

Non-use of subject *ne* with verbs taking auxiliary *avere*:

---

[2]It is often stated that use of *ne* is not acceptable if the subject *precedes* the verb. But many speakers are able to accept, for example, *Molti ne arriveranno* 'Many [of them] will arrive'. On this issue, see especially Lepschy (1989).

Parleranno tre avvocati.	'Three lawyers will speak.'
Parleranno tre di loro.	'Three of them will speak.'
[Not *Ne parleranno tre.*]	
Scriveranno alcuni gruppi di studenti.	'Some groups of students will write.'
Scriveranno alcuni gruppi (di loro).	'Some groups (of them) will write.'
Molte cicogne mangiarono i pesci.	'Many storks ate the fish.'
Molte di esse mangiarono i pesci.	'Many of them ate the fish.'

Although it is true that all verbs with reflexive clitic pronouns take the auxiliary *essere*, it is not the case that with all such verbs *ne* can refer to the subject of the verb. With 'true' reflexives (i.e., those verbs where the subject carries out some action on itself, so that the reflexive clitic is in effect the object of the verb), *ne* refers to the object, not the subject:

Gianni non si guarda le unghie, se ne guarda solo una.	'G is not looking at his nails, he's looking at just one of them.'

But in 'lexically reflexive' verbs (i.e., those where a clitic reflexive pronoun is an inherent part of the verb – see 6.15), *ne* refers to the subject:

Mentre gli operai sostituivano le tegole del tetto se ne sono staccate all'improvviso alcune.	'While the workmen were replacing the rooftiles some of them suddenly came loose.'
Ho riparlato del fatto ai ragazzi, ma non ho avuto l'impressione che se ne vergognassero molti.	'I mentioned the matter to the boys again, but I didn't get the impression that many of them were ashamed of it.'

Ne can also stand for *da* + noun where the subject of the verb is 'moving away from' or 'out of' something, but not where the subject is stationary:

Si avvicinò al porto e poi se ne allontanò.	'It approached the harbour and then went away from it.'
A volte le zampe delle mule sprofondano nell'argilla e non ne escono che a fatica.	'Sometimes the mules' hooves sink into the clay and have a job getting out of it.'
Ora è qui a covare l'uovo come una colomba paziente. Aspetta di vederne uscire un colombello nuovo e voglioso di vivere. [Mar.]	'Now he's here sitting on the egg like a patient dove. He is expecting to see a new little dove, keen for life, come out of it.'
Arrivò a Berlino il tre, e ne partì qualche giorno dopo.	'He got to B on the 3rd, and left [from it] a few days later.'

One could not say **Era a Copenaghen e me ne ha mandato un pacco*, since the subject was effectively stationary in Copenhagen; one might say instead *Era a Copenaghen da dove mi ha mandato un pacco* 'He was in Copenhagen from where he sent me a parcel.'

Ne also stands for *da* + noun in passive constructions (see 14.31), including 'resultative' passives expressing the mental state brought about by what the noun refers to:

I tulipani furono distrutti dal vento.	'The tulips were destroyed by the wind.'
I tulipani ne furono distrutti.	'The tulips were destroyed by it'.
Quando noto una contraddittorietà così palese, ne resto turbato.	'When I see such a glaring discrepancy, I am disturbed by it.'
Menocchio, venutone a conoscenza, ne rimase talmente scosso da esporla diffusamente.	'M, having come to learn of it, was so affected by it as to expound it far and wide.'

There are, however, some restrictions on the use of *ne*. If *di* or *da* + noun are part of a prepositional phrase (i.e., one introduced by a preposition, such as *sull'orlo della sedia* 'on the edge of the chair') then *di/da* + noun cannot easily be replaced by *ne*. Many speakers find unacceptable or awkward expressions such as **Se n'è seduto sull'orlo* for 'He sat on the rim of it', or **Ne lanciò un sasso contro la finestra* 'He threw a stone at the window of it', for *Lanciò un sasso contro la finestra della casa* 'He threw a stone at the window of the house'. Possible alternatives would be *S'è seduto sul suo orlo* and *Lanciò un sasso contro la sua finestra* or just (and rather more idiomatically) *S'è seduto sull'orlo* and *Lanciò un sasso contro la finestra*.

Ne cannot stand for a noun phrase introduced by *a*. So we cannot say, for example, **Paolo ne parlò a molti* meaning 'P spoke to many of them' (rather, one would say, *Paolo parlò a molti di loro*).

6.14 Some idioms with *ne*

Certain expressions contain the pronoun *ne* without any obvious meaning of its own. A number of these are combined with the reflexive pronoun *se*: *andarsene* 'go (away)', *starsene* 'stand still', 'remain', 'stay put', *tornarsene* 'come back', 'return':

Non le rimane che ringraziarlo ed andarsene.	'All that remains is for her to thank him and go.'
Hanno approfittato del suo starsene assorta sulla tela per squagliarsela.	'They took advantage of her standing engrossed in the canvas to run off.'

- For the type *Ne conosce di belle ragazze / Di belle ragazze ne conosce*, see 17.2.
- For agreement of the past participle with *ne*, see 14.23.

6.15 The reflexive clitic as an inherent part of some intransitive verbs: the type *alzarsi* 'to get up'

Reflexive verbs usually indicate that the subject is carrying out some action on or to itself, as in *adattarsi* 'adapt oneself', *ammazzarsi* 'kill oneself', *avvelenarsi* 'poison oneself', *esprimersi* 'express oneself', *grattarsi* 'scratch oneself', *lavarsi* 'wash oneself', *indebitarsi* 'get (oneself) into debt', *radersi* 'shave (oneself)', *spogliarsi* 'undress oneself'/'get undressed', *uccidersi* 'kill oneself', *vestirsi* 'dress oneself'/'get dressed', etc. Here the reflexive clitic could appear in the stressed form *se stesso*, etc.:

Stefano si esprime con la chitarra. =	'S expresses himself on the guitar.'
Stefano esprime se stesso con la chitarra.	'S expresses *himself* on the guitar.'

But a number of Italian intransitive verbs are 'lexically' reflexive, in the sense that a *clitic* reflexive pronoun is an inherent part of the verb. Such verbs *always* appear with a reflexive clitic (for an important exception in causative structures, see 14.29), but this reflexive clitic has no obvious reflexive meaning (the subject is not necessarily carrying out some action on itself). Moreover, the clitic reflexive pronouns of lexically reflexive verbs cannot be replaced by a stressed clitic pronoun. There is thus a contrast between 'true' reflexive verbs such as *Si critica* or *Critica sé* 'He criticizes himself', and lexical reflexives which appear as *Si alza* but never **Alza sé* 'He gets up'. Lexically reflexive verbs fall into two major groups, those which have a transitive counterpart, and those which do not. There are often slight differences in the basic meaning of the verb between the lexically reflexive form and its transitive counterpart, as some of the following examples show:

Intransitive		**Transitive**	
abbattersi	'fall down', 'lose heart'	*abbattere*	'knock down', 'fell'
alzarsi	'get up'	*alzare*	'raise', 'lift'
allontanarsi	'move away'	*allontanare*	'remove'
ammorbidirsi	'go soft'	*ammorbidire*	'make soft'
annoiarsi	'get bored'	*annoiare*	'bore'
arricchirsi	'get rich'	*arricchire*	'make rich'
avvicinarsi	'approach'	*avvicinare*	'draw [something] close'
bruciarsi	'get burned'	*bruciare*	'burn'
comportarsi	'behave'	*comportare*	'comport', 'involve'
destarsi	'awaken'	*destare*	'waken'
fermarsi	'stop'	*fermare*	'stop'
gonfiarsi	'swell up'	*gonfiare*	'inflate'
indebolirsi	'get weak'	*indebolire*	'make weak'
irritarsi	'get irritated'	*irritare*	'irritate'
offendersi	'take offence'	*offendere*	'offend'
piegarsi	'give way'	*piegare*	'fold'
raffreddarsi	'catch cold', 'cool off'	*raffreddare*	'cool'
ricordarsi	'remember'	*ricordare*	'remind'
seccarsi	'get dry' or 'get fed up'	*seccare*	'dry' or 'annoy'
scoraggiarsi	'lose heart'	*scoraggiare*	'discourage'
spaventarsi	'take fright'	*spaventare*	'frighten'
spegnersi	'go out' (of light, flame)	*spegnere*	'extinguish', 'put out'
stupirsi	'be astonished'	*stupire*	'astonish'
svegliarsi	'wake up'	*svegliare*	'awaken'
etc.			

For example:

Il carattere del vecchio gentiluomo si era ammorbidito con il passare degli anni.	'The old gentleman's character had softened with the passing of the years.'
Il passare degli anni aveva ammorbidito il carattere del vecchio gentiluomo.	'The passing of the years had softened the old gentleman's character.'
Le sue difese immunitarie si sono indebolite per lo stress.	'His immune defences weakened because of stress.'
Lo stress indebolisce le difese immunitarie.	'Stress weakens the immune defences.'
La bambina si era spaventata per un sottile rumore da dietro la porta.	'The little girl had taken fright at a slight noise from behind the door.'
Un sottile rumore da dietro la porta aveva spaventato la bambina.	'A slight noise from behind the door had frightened the little girl.'
Lucia si sveglia sempre presto.	'L always wakes up early.'
Oggi devo svegliare Lucia più presto del solito.	'Today I must wake up L earlier than usual.'

The verb *sedere* 'sit' usually means 'be seated' when used non-reflexively, and 'sit down' when used reflexively:

Alcune dame non possono neanche sedersi tanto sono elaborate e gonfie le loro gonne.	'Some ladies cannot even sit down, so elaborate and puffed out are their skirts.'
Infine Marianna aveva ottenuto che di mattina, solo a pranzo, il bambino sedesse accanto a lei.	'At last M had obtained permission for the baby to sit beside her in the morning, only at lunch.'

The transitive counterparts of the lexically reflexive verbs may, of course, appear as 'genuine' reflexive verbs. Thus one might contrast lexically reflexive *Ti alzi* 'You get up' and genuinely reflexive *Ti alzi/Alzi te* (*stesso*) *tirando sulla corda* 'You raise yourself up by pulling on the rope'.

Among lexically reflexive verbs without transitive counterparts are:

accanirsi a	'persist doggedly in'	*imbronciarsi*	'become grumpy'
accasciarsi	'collapse'	*impadronirsi di*	'take over'
accorgersi di	'realize', 'become aware'	*incamminarsi*	'set out on one's way'
addentrarsi in	'enter'		
arrabattarsi	'bestir oneself', 'muddle through'	*infischiarsi di*	'not give a damn about'
arrabbiarsi	'get angry'	*lagnarsi*	'complain'
arrendersi	'surrender'	*meravigliarsi*	'marvel', 'wonder'
astenersi	'abstain'	*ostinarsi a*	'be obstinate in'
attardarsi	'tarry'	*pentirsi di*	'repent'
avvalersi di	'avail oneself of'	*rabbuiarsi*	'get dark'
congratularsi con	'congratulate'	*ribellarsi*	'rebel'
fidarsi di	'trust'	*suicidarsi*[3]	'commit suicide'
imbattersi in	'bump into'	*vergognarsi di*	'be ashamed'

S'è pentito d'aver detto tante bugie.	'He repented of having told so many lies.'
Si vede che si vergogna.	'One can see he's ashamed.'
Quel ragazzo si infischia di quello che gli ho detto.	'That boy couldn't care less about what I said to him.'

A few intransitive verbs can be used with or without the reflexive clitic: *ammuffirsi/ammuffire* 'go mouldy', *approfittarsi/approfittare* 'take advantage of', *ricordare/ricordarsi* 'recall', 'remember':

Le patate vanno tenute al riparo della luce perché non (si) ammuffiscano.	'Potatoes should be kept out of the light so thay they don't go mouldy.'
Secondo me lui (si) approfitta della generosità di suo fratello.	'In my opinion he is taking advantage of his brother's generosity.'
Chi (si) ricorda la data di nascita di Cicerone?	'Who remembers the date of Cicero's birth?'

See also 6.14, for verbs such as *andarsene, tornarsene, starsene*.

6.16 Special use of reflexive clitics with transitive verbs: the type *leggersi un libro* 'to read a book'

With certain verbs, reflexive clitics may be used not to indicate that the subject carries out some action upon itself, but merely to indicate that the action concerns, is of interest to, or benefits, only the subject. The nuance introduced by this use of clitic reflexives is often well-nigh inexpressible in English, but one might say that while *Leggo questo libro* is a 'neutral' statement that 'I read this book', *Mi leggo questo libro* might imply that I read it because it interests me, or because I need to read it to get through an exam. Some verbs of this kind may have slightly

---

[3]One sometimes encounters a darkly ironic transitive form *suicidare*, as in *L'hanno suicidato* meaning, in effect, that what was presented as his 'suicide' was in reality a murder.

different expressions in English: *bere, mangiare* are 'to drink' and 'to eat', but *bersi* and *mangiarsi* are 'to drink up' and 'to eat up':

>*Si mangiò il formaggio e se ne andò.*   'He ate up the cheese and left.'

This usage is restricted to *clitic* reflexives, and has no stressed reflexive counterparts (you cannot say **Mangiò il formaggio a se stesso*).

6.17 Post-verbal clitics in archaic uses and set phrases: the type *Vendesi*

In old Italian, if a sentence or clause began with a verb, then the attached clitic *followed* the verb. Examples abound in medieval and renaissance texts. If the verb is a stressed monosyllable, then the consonant of the clitic is lengthened (e.g., *èvvi* for *vi è*). In the language of small advertisements, and in academic prose, remnants of this structure, with the reflexive clitic *si*, are frequently encountered to this day:

Affittasi appartamento	'Flat for rent'
Vendesi capanna	'Shed for sale'
Cercasi babysitter	'Babysitter wanted'
Comprasi	'We buy'
Offresi	'We offer'
Dicasi	'Let it be said'
Vedasi	'See'
come volevasi dimostrare	'Q.E.D.'

These structures have third person plural forms from which the final *-o* is deleted (*Cercansi, Vedansi, Dicansi*, etc.), but in advertising the singular form is now generally used with both singular and plural subjects (*Affittasi appartamenti; Comprasi francobolli*, etc.).

6.18 The non-standard type *A me mi piace*

The type *A me mi piace la carne* 'I like meat', *Gli danno un premio a Giovanni* 'They give G a prize', where the clitic redundantly occurs in the same clause alongside the noun or stressed pronoun to which it refers, is frequently encountered in casual speech (and characterizes all Italian dialects) but is generally condemned as ungrammatical and never used in formal, written Italian. It is best avoided by foreigners: one should say rather *A me piace la carne, Danno un premio a Giovanni*, etc. Note however that this construction is not to be confused with the phenomenon (discussed in 17.2, 4), whereby the indirect object noun phrase is emphasized by placing it to the right or left of the matrix sentence, often with a pause or intonation break between the moved noun and the main sentence. In such cases, the 'redundant' pronoun is acceptable in the spoken language: *A Giovanni, gli danno un premio*.

6.19 Forms of the stressed pronouns

Some stressed personal pronouns distinguish between subject forms (those used when the pronoun stands for the subject of the sentence) and 'non-subject' or 'oblique' forms (those used in every other instance, for example when the pronoun is the object of the verb, or preceded by a preposition):

	Subject	Non-subject
First person singular	*io*	*me*
First person plural	*noi*	*noi*
Second person singular	*tu*	*te*
Second person plural	*voi*	*voi*

The oblique forms are also used as stressed forms of the reflexive pronouns (often, but not necessarily, accompanied by the adjective *stesso* – see 5.18):

> *Rivedevo me (stesso), a cinque anni, che giocavo in quel giardino.*
> 'I could see myself, aged 5, playing in that garden.'

In addition to distinguishing number and case, the third person pronouns also distinguish gender, and possess a series of alternative forms, largely restricted to written, formal discourse. Some of these alternative forms refer specifically to *humans*. There is also a special third person reflexive pronoun (frequently, but not necessarily, accompanied by *stesso*):

	Subject	Non-subject
Masculine singular		
● formal	*lui*	*lui*
● formal, human	*esso*	*esso*
	egli	*lui*
Feminine singular		
● formal	*lei*	*lei*
● formal, human	*essa*	*essa*
	ella	*lei*
Masculine plural		
● formal	*loro*	*loro*
	essi	*essi*
Feminine plural		
● formal	*loro*	*loro*
	esse	*esse*
Reflexive (both genders and both numbers)		*sé*

6.20 Uses of the 'oblique' forms

The 'oblique' (non-subject) forms are used principally when they represent the stressed object of the verb, and after prepositions:

> *Lo fate per noi.* — 'You do it for us.'
> *Hanno invitato me, non te.* — 'They invited me, not you.'
> *Lo manderanno a loro.* — 'They'll send it to them.'
> *E chi ho visto? Lui con te.* — 'And who did I see? Him with you.'
> etc.

Note that *esso* and *essa* are used after prepositions, but *not* when they are the direct object of the verb, in which case *lui* and *lei* are used instead.

The oblique forms are also used in phrases comprising the pronoun modified by an adjective or noun (especially in certain exclamations):

> *beato lui!* — 'lucky him!'
> *povero me!* — 'poor me'

bravo te!	'good for you!'
me compreso	'me included'
compreso te	'you included'

The non-subject forms are also used in comparisons of equality (see 16.18) after *come* and *quanto*:

È intelligente quanto me.	'He's as intelligent as I am/as me.'
Sono italiano come te.	'I'm just as Italian as you are/as you.'

6.21 'It's me' = *Sono io*, 'It was them' = *Erano loro*, etc.

The equivalent of 'It's me', 'It's them', etc., has the verb *essere* agreeing for person and number with the pronoun, and the pronoun in its subject form. In other words one says, literally, 'I am I', 'They are they':

Sono io.	'It's me.'
Eri tu?	'Was it you?'
Saranno loro.	'It'll be them.'
Non sarò mai io a chiedere il divorzio.	'It will never be me who asks for a divorce.'
Tu sei tu e io sono io. Tutto qui.	'You're you and I'm me. Enough said.'

But a pronoun which is introduced by predicative verbs (e.g., *essere* 'be', *sembrare* 'seem', *diventare* 'become') has the oblique form:

Tu non sei me e io non sono te.	'You aren't me and I'm not you.'
Voglio essere me stesso.	'I want to be myself.'
Cerca di ridiventare te stessa.	'Try to become yourself again.'

Contrast the above with:

Voglio essere io stesso il primo a farlo.	'I myself want to be the first to do it.'
Cerca di ridiventare tu stessa la prima della classe.	'Try to become top of the class again yourself.'

6.22 Position of *io* combined with other subject pronouns: *io e lui* and *lui e io* = 'he and I'

Unlike English 'I', *io* does not have to be ordered after other nouns and pronouns with which it is coordinated: *L'abbiamo fatto io e te* (cf. 6.23) 'You and I did it', is just as acceptable as *L'abbiamo fatto tu ed io*, although *tu ed io* seems to be the preferred order in formal language.

6.23 Use of oblique *te* as subject

If the second person singular subject pronoun is *preceded* by the conjunction *e*, then the pronoun usually takes the form *te*:

Vabbene, ci andiamo insieme domani, io e te. [or *tu e io*]	'OK, we'll go there together tomorrow, you and I.'

Te is frequently used – especially in Tuscany – instead of *tu*, when the pronoun is used in isolation (for example, in response to questions), in exclamations or in imperatives:

Fallo te!	'*You* do it!'
—*Quei ricami li ho fatti io.*	'I did that embroidery'.
—*Te?*	'You did?'
Te che vuoi?	'What do *you* want?'

Me as subject pronoun does occur (particularly in northern speech), but is universally regarded as substandard.

6.24 *Noialtri* and *voialtri*

The alternative first and second person plural pronouns *noialtri, voialtri* have the advantage of distinguishing gender (cf. feminine *noialtre, voialtre*). They do not necessarily have any connotation of 'otherness'. They are common in many regional varieties of standard Italian, but are often considered substandard:

I ragazzi possono andare, ma voialtre restate qua.	'The boys can go, but you [girls] stay here.'

6.25 The type *Dicevamo con Giulio* 'Giulio and I were saying'

When a noun or pronoun is conjoined with the first person singular pronoun as the subject of a verb, one may say, as in English:

Io e Giulio studiavamo il francese insieme.	'G and I were studying French together.'
Il professore e io stavamo a chiacchierare.	'The teacher and I were chatting.'

But there is an alternative possibility, common in the spoken language, using *con* and suppressing the first person singular pronoun, so that one says, literally, 'We were studying with Giulio French', etc.:

Studiavamo con Giulio il francese.	'G and I were studying French.'
Stavamo a chiacchierare con il professore.	'The teacher and I were chatting.'

6.26 *Egli, esso, ella, essa, essi, esse* vs. *lui, lei, loro*

What *egli, esso, ella, essa, essi, esse* have in common is that in current Italian they have become restricted to written and formal registers – such as bureaucratic or academic writing, formal speeches, lectures. Their use in everyday, spontaneous discourse strikes many Italians as affected or archaic, but to differing degrees: for most native speakers the feminine singular, human, subject pronoun *ella* has a particularly recherché ring and is now probably best avoided altogether, even in formal usage (for the use of *Ella* as an especially formal address form, see 22.3), while the plurals *essi* and *esse* are fairly commonly encountered and seem to have the least elevated and archaic resonances of this series of pronouns. As a general rule, where *egli, esso* and *essa* are used, it would be an error (or a mixing of different registers) to use *lui* as a *subject* pronoun; however, the rarity of *ella* means that subject *lei* is rather more acceptable. *Egli, esso, ella, essa, essi, esse* also share a syntactic peculiarity, in that unlike other stressed pronouns they can never stand in isolation:

Egli fu subito ammesso, assieme ai colleghi.	'He was admitted immediately, together with his colleagues.'
Non lo fece egli ma lo farà essa. but	'He didn't do it but she will.'
—*Chi lo ha detto?*	'Who said so?
—*Lui/Loro.* [not **Egli/*Essi*]	'He/They (did).'

Many speakers find that *egli, esso, ella, essa, essi, esse* cannot easily be conjoined with other nouns or pronouns, and structures such as the following tend to be found very awkward:

Egli e i colleghi furono subito ammessi.	'He and his colleagues were admitted immediately.'

Egli and *ella* stand out from the other third person personal pronouns in that they are generally used as subject forms only (the use of *egli* and *ella* used as object forms is sometimes encountered, but considered incorrect), have no counterpart in the plural (where *loro* or *essi* and *esse* must be used), and refer exclusively to human beings. *Egli* and *ella* seem particularly to be used with reference to *famous* people (cf. Brunet 1985: 37). *Egli* is distinguished from *esso* in that the former refers only to humans but the latter predominantly to non-humans. Unlike *esso*, the pronouns *essa, essi* and *esse* can refer to humans and non-humans alike.

I pedoni devono circolare negli spazi per essi predisposti.	'Pedestrians must use the spaces provided for them.'
Nell'atrio dell'istituto studenti fanno la fila davanti a confessionali elettronici, sorta di bancomat della cultura ai quali essi possono chiedere nuovi piani di studi. [Rep.]	'In the hall of the institute students queue before electronic confessionals, a kind of cultural cash dispenser from which they can request new study programmes.'
Il suo intervento giova o nuoce alla causa per la quale egli si batte?	'Does his intervention help or hinder the cause for which he is fighting?'
La circostanza stessa di questo romanzo è assai significativa. Esso nasce da un'autentica collaborazione con Pinolo Scaglione.	'The very circumstances of this novel are quite significant. It is born of a genuine collaboration with PS.'
Entrò Maria dopo di lui. Essa aveva la faccia pallidissima.	'M came in after him. She had a very pale face.'
La recensione era severissima. Essa era addirittura ostile.	'The review was very severe. It was downright hostile.'

In the narration of dialogues, only *lui, lei* and *loro* (rather than *egli, lei, essi,* etc.) can appear after the verb in phrases such as *disse lui* 'said he', *rispose lei* 'she replied':

Ma io voglio fermarla, —disse lui.	'"But I want to stop her," said he.'
Se non ritornano, mica li aspetterò —rispose lei.	'"If they don't come back, I'm sure not waiting for them," she replied.'

In ordinary modern usage, *lui* and *lei* (like *loro*) function both as subject and oblique pronouns. They are principally used with reference to human beings (and sometimes animals):

Un padre e una figlia eccoli lì: lui biondo, bello, sorridente, lei goffa, lentigginosa, spaventata. [Mar.]	'There they are, a father and a daughter: he fair, handsome, smiling, she gauche, freckled, frightened.'

Quando non l'avrà più sarà come se non l'avesse rubata e il tedesco avrà un bell'andare in bestia con lui, lui lo potrà di nuovo prendere in giro. [Cal.]	'When he no longer has it it will be as if he had not stolen it and the German will be wasting his time getting cross with him, because he'll be able to pull his leg again.'
Può darsi che avesse avuto anche voglia di continuare, ma proprio lui non poteva di certo sgarrare.	'He might have wanted to go on, but he of all people couldn't afford to step out of line.'

Occasionally, *lui* and *lei* are used to refer to inanimate entities, but for many speakers such uses seem to suggest a degree of personification or anthropomorphism.

Quando si fa un film si rinuncia a qualsiasi altra cosa, è lui a occupare il primo posto, tutto il resto gli è subordinato.	'When you make a film you give up anything else, and it takes first place, with everything else subordinate to it.'
Vado nella corrente, mi ci lascio prendere e lei mi porta da sola nell'acqua alta.	'I go into the stream, I let myself be carried off, and it takes me by itself into the deep water.'

In everyday usage, the demonstratives function as third person pronouns when referring to non-humans; see 5.4.

The third person stressed subject pronouns sometimes serve to underline the identity of the subject, and are roughly equivalent to English emphatic 'himself', 'herself', etc. (They are rather less emphatic than *stesso*, which is closer in sense to 'himself, herself, etc., – and no other'.)

I ragazzi hanno portato loro il gelato.	'The boys themselves brought the ice cream.' or 'The boys brought the ice cream.'
Si è pure offerta di allevare lei il bastardo.	'She even offered to bring the bastard up herself' or 'She even offered that she would bring the bastard up.'

Note also:

È da mesi che non sembra più lui.	'He hasn't seemed himself for months.'

6.27 'Reciprocal' pronouns: 'They look at each other' *Si guardano (l'un l'altro)*

'Each other' can often be expressed in Italian simply by use of a plural clitic reflexive pronoun:

Pietro e Olivia si guardano attraverso il vetro.	'P and O look at each other through the window pane.'
Il bello e il buono si incontrano in questa osteria appena fuori da Montevarchi.	'The beautiful and the good meet each other in this inn just outside Montevarchi.'
La e-mail fa anche risparmiare: non è più necessario telefonarsi ogni giorno.	'E-mail helps you save money too: it's no longer necessary to phone each other daily.'

Note that *stressed* reflexive pronouns cannot be used in this way: *Rispettiamo noi stessi* can only mean 'We respect ourselves'.

Usually reciprocal structures involve verbs with a plural subject, but the subject may be singular if it implies a plurality, as with *gente*:

La gente si scambiava pacche sulle spalle.	'People exchanged claps on the back.'

There are other ways of indicating reciprocality (useful particularly when a reflexive structure could be ambiguous between a 'true' reflexive meaning and reciprocal meaning: e.g., *Si vedono* = either 'They see themselves' or 'They see each other'). A distinctive pronominal marker of reciprocality is the phrase *l'un l'altro* (*l'una l'altra, l'un l'altra, l'una l'altro, gli uni gli altri, le une le altre*, etc. according to gender and number). When *l'un l'altro* are functioning both as subject and object of the verb, a clitic reflexive pronoun will also be present:

Ci siamo sempre rispettati l'un l'altro.	'We have always respected each other.'
Quelle ragazze si odiano l'una l'altra.	'Those girls hate each other.'
Si mandavano lettere l'uno all'altro.	'They sent letters to each other.'

English 'each other' has become an invariable set phrase: we say 'They talked about each other' not 'They talked each about the other'. But Italian says 'They talked the one about the other', making the relation between subject *l'un* and its complement *l'altro* explicit, where appropriate, by placing a preposition in front of *l'altro*. (Note that *l'un l'altro* becomes *l'uno . . . l'altro* if the two terms are separated by a preposition or other material.)

Hanno parlato molto l'uno dell'altro.	'They talked a lot about each other.'
Unione Sovietica e America volevano lanciare missili l'una contro l'altra.	'The Soviet Union and America wanted to launch missiles at each other.' [lit. 'the one against the other']

There are signs that *l'un l'altro* is turning into a set expression in the singular, in that the preposition *a* can sometimes be omitted before *l'altro*:

Eravamo attratti l'un l'altro dai nostri reciproci interessi.	'We were attracted to each other by our mutual interests.'

The usual form of the plural is *gli uni gli altri* or *gli uni con gli altri*:

I francesi e gli italiani si sono sempre ammirati gli uni gli altri/gli uni con gli altri.	'The French and the Italians have always admired each other.'

Alternative expressions are the adverbs *a vicenda, reciprocamente, scambievolmente,* or *fra (di) loro*:

Lucia ed Elena si sono giurate a vicenda eterna amicizia.	'L and E swore to each other eternal friendship.'
Giurate di onorarvi e rispettarvi reciprocamente nella buona e nella cattiva sorte.	'Swear to honour and respect each other in good luck and in bad.'
Non sempre i fratelli si aiutano fra loro.	'Brothers don't always help each other.'

6.28 *Tra sé, tra di loro; fra me e me* 'to himself', 'amongst themselves'; 'to myself'

'Amongst themselves (ourselves, yourselves)' can be expressed either by *tra/fra* + *sé* (*noi, voi*) or *tra/fra* + *loro* (*noi, voi*):

Cominciavano a chiacchierare fra sé.	'They were starting to talk amongst themselves.'
Pregavano e bisbigliavano tra loro.	'They were praying and whispering among themselves.'

In verbs of saying or thinking 'to oneself', the pronoun is usually preceded by the preposition *fra/tra*. In what may seem a rather peculiar usage, the pronoun may appear as *sé e sé, me e me, te e te*: 'He thought to himself' = *Pensava fra sé* or *Pensava fra sé e sé*:

Riandava fra sé e sé all'accaduto di quella tragica notte.	'He went over and over in his mind what had happened on that tragic night.'
Stetti un attimo a riflettere tra me e me sul daffarsi.	'I stood for a moment reflecting to myself on what was to be done.'

But most speakers do not accept *fra noi e noi* and *fra voi e voi*.

Note that there is potential ambiguity with plural pronouns: *Bisbigliavano tra loro* could mean either 'They whispered among themselves' or 'They (each) whispered to themselves'.

6.29 Indefinite personal *si*: *Oggi si va al ristorante più spesso che in passato* 'Today people go to the restaurant more often than in the past'

A major use of the third person reflexive clitic pronoun *si* is to indicate that the subject of the verb is human, but without specifying the identity of the subject. This structure is roughly comparable to the English 'one'/'people' + verb, or generic 'you' + verb, and is conventionally (and quite misleadingly) labelled 'impersonal'. We call it here 'indefinite personal *si*'. Note that this *si* (much like English 'one') only occurs with finite verb forms; i.e., it is absent with infinitives, gerunds and past participles.

Si pensa che sia molto ricco.	'People think he is very wealthy.'
Non si potrebbe fare meglio.	'You couldn't do better.'
Oggi si continua a parlare di disoccupazione come se fossimo ancora negli anni Trenta.	'Today people still talk about unemployment as if we were still in the thirties.'
Ci sono disoccupati, a quanto si sente dire, che vanno a cercar lavoro in automobile.	'There are unemployed people, so one hears tell, who go job-hunting in their cars.'
Si può aprire il pacchetto delle patatine ma mai rovinare, spezzare, abbandonare l'involucro tra gli scaffali del supermercato.	'One may open the packet of crisps, but never destroy, tear up or discard the wrapper among the supermarket's shelves.'
Se si gira bruscamente la testa o si indossa una camicia con il collo stretto il sangue scorre con fatica e si può svenire.	'If you turn your head too sharply or you wear a shirt with a tight collar the blood flow is restricted and you may faint.'

Expressions like *si dice*,[4] *si pensa, si crede, si ritiene, si deve/può/vuole, si va*, etc. are recurrent in everyday usage (both in colloquial/informal and in formal/written Italian). For example, the indefinite personal *si* is often found in popular sayings:

---

[4]Note that in addition to *si dice* meaning 'one says' there is the colloquial *dice*:

Dice che ci sarà uno sciopero. = *Si dice che ci sarà uno sciopero.*	'They say there's going to be a strike.'

Se si ride di venerdì si piange di domenica.	'If you laugh on Friday you cry on Sunday.'
Con la pancia piena si ragiona meglio.	'You think better on a full stomach.'
Non si sputa nel piatto dove si è mangiato.	'You don't spit in the plate where you've eaten.'

Indefinite personal *si* is not used with infinitives, gerunds and past participles (for the plural agreement of the past participle in such cases, see 6.33):

Viaggiare senza fucile è pericoloso.	'To travel [i.e., that one should travel] without a rifle is dangerous.'
Viaggiando nel deserto s'incontrano moltissime situazioni pericolose.	'Travelling [i.e., as one travels] in the desert one encounters many dangerous situations.'
Una volta arrivati all'oasi, si può bere.	'Once [one has] reached the oasis, one can drink.'

6.30 The differences between indefinite personal *si* and passive *si*

We see in 14.35 that third person reflexive verbs with *si* are frequently used as passives, where the agent of the action is understood to be human. It is often difficult to draw a semantic distinction between the two types of *si*:

Si dice che sia il miglior cacciatore della zona.	'It is said/One says that he is the best hunter in the area.'
Negli USA si calcola che ogni anno da sei a otto milioni di cittadini stabiliscono relazioni sentimentali con i compagni di lavoro.	'In the USA it is calculated/one calculates that every year six to eight million citizens form emotional relationships with their workmates.'
Si può perdere anche mezza mattinata per il traffico intorno a Central Park.	'Half the morning can be wasted/One can waste half the morning because of the traffic around Central Park.'

But indefinite personal *si* has properties which distinguish it from the passive reflexive, and from other types of reflexive construction. With passive *si* the object of a transitive verb becomes its subject, and the verb agrees in number and gender with that subject. Nowadays, the construction with indefinite personal *si* usually behaves in exactly the same way, so that *Si vendono schede telefoniche* means either 'Phone cards are sold' or 'One sells phone cards'. But *occasionally* indefinite personal *si* is treated as the subject of the verb, so that the noun remains the object, and the verb agrees with subject *si* – which means that the verb has a third person singular form. Just as in English one says 'One sells phone cards', with a third person *singular* verb agreeing with the subject pronoun 'one', so one may say *Si vende schede telefoniche*:

In America si fa follie per l'aceto balsamico.	'In America people do mad things for balsamic vinegar.'
Si può perdere i sensi anche per troppa felicità.	'You can lose your senses even from excessive happiness.'
Si noleggia biciclette.	'Bicycles for hire.'

Note that in analytic tenses (i.e., those with auxiliary verb + past participle) both the auxiliary and the past participle are either in the plural (*si sono fatte follie*) or in the masculine singular (*si è fatto follie*). The latter form cannot be interpreted as passive, but only as indefinite, and absence of number and gender agreement with the noun is the hallmark of indefinite personal, as opposed to passive, structures: *Si è tagliata la torta* could mean either 'The cake was cut' or 'One cut the cake', but *Si è tagliato la torta*, without agreement, can only mean 'One cut the cake.'[5] Note, however, that to say that 'We cut the cake and served it' the second participle *must* agree with the object: *Si è tagliato la torta e si è servita ai ragazzi* 'One cut the cake and served it to the boys' or (more commonly) *Si è tagliata la torta e si è servita ai ragazzi* (identical to the passive).

When indefinite *si* is regarded as the subject of the verb, the accompanying noun remains the direct object. Like any other direct object, the noun can be replaced by a direct object clitic pronoun (*lo, la, li, le*); in such cases the verb is generally[6] singular (just as in English 'One eats them'):

La si è tagliata.	'One has cut it.'
Le si vende.	'One sells them.'
Li si mangia spesso a fine pasto.	'One often eats them at the end of a meal.'

A further difference is that the object noun phrase tends to follow the verb when *si* is indefinite personal, but that the object may come before the verb when the construction is passive:

Con il pesce non si dovrebbe usare il coltello.	'With fish you shouldn't use the knife.'
Con il pesce il coltello non si dovrebbe usare.	'With fish the knife shouldn't be used.'

Indefinite *si* is always attached to the modal verb in constructions with modal verbs (*dovere, potere, volere*, etc.) + infinitive, while passive *si* may be attached either to the infinitive or to the modal:

Cose del genere non si possono dire in pubblico.	'One cannot say things like that in public.' OR 'Things like that cannot be said in public.'
Cose del genere non si devono poter dire in pubblico.	'One should not be able to say things like that in public.' OR 'Things like that should not be able to be said in public.'
Cose del genere non possono dirsi in pubblico.	'Things like that cannot be said in public.'
Cose del genere non devono potersi dire in pubblico.	'Things like that should not be able to be said in public.'

6.31 Three peculiarities of indefinite personal *si* in combination with other clitic pronouns: the types *Si vuole farlo* 'One wants to do it', *Ci si lava* 'One washes oneself', and *Lo si prepara* 'One prepares it'

We see in 6.6 that in modal + infinitive constructions clitic pronouns behave 'as a block'. That is, that if one clitic is attached to the modal verb, then all clitics are

---

[5]Of course, *si* could also be an indirect object reflexive pronoun, in which case *Si è tagliata la torta* would mean 'She cut the cake for herself'.
[6]*Le si vendono, Li si mangiano*, etc., are also possible, but less common.

attached to the modal verb (*Te ne voglio mandare*, etc.); and if one clitic is attached to the infinitive, then all clitics are attached to the infinitive (*Voglio mandartene*). The indefinite personal clitic constitutes the sole exception to this principle, in that it *may* be attached to the modal verb even when other clitics are attached to the infinitive:

Frutta e verdura? Si dovrebbe mangiarne tutti i giorni.	'Fruit and vegetables? One should eat some every day.'
Non si voleva mandartelo.	'One didn't want to send it to you.'

Of course it would be equally possible to say *Se ne dovrebbe mangiare . . .* and *Non te lo si voleva mandare.*

It is perfectly possible for indefinite personal *si* to be combined with verbs which are independently reflexive as, for example, in 'One washes oneself'. What we might expect in such cases is a sequence of two clitic *si* pronouns, giving, say, **Si si lava*. But a sequence of two *si* pronouns is not allowed (see 6.2); instead, the first *si* must become *ci*:

Ci si lava.	'One washes oneself.' [*lavarsi*]
Ci si alza.	'One gets up.' [*alzarsi*]
Ci si trova in difficoltà.	'One finds oneself in difficulty.' [*trovarsi*]
Non ci si può permettere questo lusso.	'One can't allow oneself [*permettersi*] this luxury.'
Ci si toglie la maglia e ci si sdraia sul letto.	'One takes off [*togliersi*] one's jersey and one lies [*sdraiarsi*] on the bed.'

Si, when it is the indefinite personal pronoun 'one', but *not* when it is a reflexive pronoun, is always the last element in any sequence of clitics, apart from *ne* (6.6), which always follows it. Contrast the following:

Reflexive *si* 'to/for him/herself', etc.

Se lo era preparato prima.	'He had prepared it for himself beforehand.'
Se l'è imparata a memoria.	'He taught it to himself by heart.'
Il contadino portò il documento alla scuola, per farselo leggere dalla maestra.	'The peasant took the document to the school, to get it read to himself by the schoolmistress.'

Si meaning 'one':

Lo si era preparato prima.	'One had prepared it beforehand.'
La si è imparata a memoria.	'One learned it by heart.'
Il contadino portò il documento alla scuola, perché lo si facesse leggere dalla maestra.	'The peasant took the document to the school, so that one/somebody would get it read by the schoolmistress.'

But because *ne* follows both types of *si*, the sequence *se ne* is potentially ambiguous. The phrase *Se ne manda* could mean either 'One sends some' or 'He sends some to himself'.

Note that object clitic pronouns *lo, la, li, le* are combinable with *ci si* in the following way:

Ce le si compra.	'One buys them for oneself.'
Ce lo si prepara.	'One prepares it for oneself.'

6.32 Indefinite personal *si*, the auxiliary verb, and agreement of the past participle: *Si è viaggiato* 'One has travelled' vs. *Si è partiti* 'One has left'

A striking peculiarity of analytic forms of intransitive verbs (those with auxiliary verb + past participle) combined with indefinite *si* is that, while the auxiliary verb *essere* is always *singular*, in certain cases the past participle has (usually masculine) *plural* form. To understand when and why this happens, the following facts should be considered:

- Verbs with indefinite *si*, just like 'true' reflexive verbs, take *essere* as their auxiliary (14.20).
- When indefinite *si* is used with an intransitive verb, the verb is always singular (*Si va* 'One goes', *Si torna* 'One returns', *Si cammina* 'One walks', *Si è* 'One is', etc.).

In America si viaggia molto in aereo.	'In America one travels a great deal by plane.'
Solo in Giappone e in Italia si sta così tanto al lavoro.	'Only in Japan and Italy do people stay so long at work.'

This applies equally to the auxiliary *essere*, so that one always has the singular *si è/si era/si fu/si sarà/si sarebbe*:

Si è cantato.	'One has sung.'
Si sarà nuotato.	'One will have swum.'
etc.	

- With ordinary intransitive verbs that take *essere* as their auxiliary (14.20), the past participle agrees in number and gender with the subject (e.g., *I ragazzi sono partiti* 'The boys have left'); with those that take *avere* as their auxiliary, the past participle does not agree with the subject, and remains in the masculine singular form (e.g., *I ragazzi hanno nuotato* 'The boys have swum').
- It is a peculiarity (see 6.35) of indefinite personal verbs that introduce predicate adjectives, that the adjectives show (masculine) plural agreement: *Si è contenti* 'One is happy', *Si rimane esterrefatti* 'One ends up terrified', etc.
- While all verbs with indefinite *si* have *essere* as their auxiliary, the form of the past participle depends on whether the relevant intransitive verb *normally* takes *avere* or *essere* as the auxiliary (14.20). Where the auxiliary would normally be *avere*, the participle remains invariant and ends in *-o*; where the auxiliary would normally be *essere* there is agreement of the participle, and the agreement is masculine plural in *-i*:

In passato hanno viaggiato più in macchina che in aereo.	'In the past they travelled more by car than by plane.'
In passato si è viaggiato più in macchina che in aereo.	'In the past one travelled more by car than by plane.'
Appena saputa la notizia, hanno subito telefonato in redazione.	'As soon as the news was received, they immediately telephoned the editor's office.'
Appena saputa la notizia, si è subito telefonato in redazione.	'As soon as the news was received, one immediately telephoned the editor's office.'

Non hanno dormito bene.	'They haven't slept well.'
Non si è dormito bene.	'One hasn't slept well.'

but

Non sono mai riusciti a forzare il ritmo storico della società italiana.	'They have never succeeded in forcing the historical pace of Italian society.'
Non si è mai riusciti a forzare il ritmo storico della società italiana.	'One has never succeeded in forcing the historical pace of Italian society.'
Se sono arrivati tardi hanno perso il diritto al posto a sedere.	'If they've arrived late they've lost the right to a seat.'
Se si è arrivati tardi si è perso il diritto al posto a sedere.	'If one has arrived late one has lost the right to a seat.'
Sono giunti ormai a guardare a bocca aperta ogni sorta di fanfaronata televisiva.	'They have now reached the stage of gawping at any kind of television extravaganza.'
Si è giunti ormai a guardare a bocca aperta ogni sorta di fanfaronata televisiva.	'One has now reached the stage of gawping at any kind of televsion extravaganza.'

The principle that the past participle is plural where the verb normally takes auxiliary *essere* applies equally. If indefinite personal *si* is combined with a verb which is itself reflexive (14.20). Bear in mind that in such cases (6.31), the indefinite *si* becomes *ci*:

Si erano criticati.	'They had criticized themselves.'
Ci si era criticati.	'One had criticized oneself.'

There are two possible patterns of agreement, however, when the verb also has a direct object noun: the participle may either be masculine plural, agreeing with indefinite personal *si*, or it may agree with the object noun:

Ci si è comprati delle mele. OR *Ci si è comprate delle mele.*	'One has bought [oneself] some apples.'

A third possibility is that both the auxiliary verb and the past participle agree with the noun (cf. *Si sono comprate delle mele* 'Apples have been bought'), yielding *Ci si sono comprate delle mele*.

Note that where an object clitic pronoun *lo*, *la*, *li* or *le* is present, the participle agrees with the object clitic (cf. 14.22):

Le si è comprate.	'One has bought them.'
Lo si è visto.	'One has seen it.'

6.33 Plural predicates of verbs with indefinite personal *si*: *Si è allegri* 'One is cheerful' (or where *si* is implicit: *È meglio viaggiare armati* 'It's better to travel armed')

If a verb such as *essere*, *diventare*, *rimanere*, with indefinite *si*, is followed by a predicate adjective, that predicate adjective is plural.

Quando si è allegri, è più facile affrontare la vita.	'When you're cheerful, it's easier to face up to life.'
Se non si è dormito bene è normale sentirsi stanchi e un pò depressi.	'If you haven't slept well it's normal to feel tired and a bit depressed.'

Non si sceglie la materia della propria scrittura, casomai si è scelti.

'One does not choose the subject of one's own writing; if anything, one is chosen.'

Si rischia di intasare le casse se si è troppo lenti a raccogliere i sacchetti della spesa e a uscire.

'One risks clogging up the tills if one is too slow in picking up one's bags of shopping and leaving.'

Note the difference between:

Non c'è dubbio che se si è amati si vive più felici.

'There's no doubt that if one is loved one lives more happily.'

and

Non c'è dubbio che se si è amato si vive più felici.

'There's no doubt that if one has loved one lives more happily.'

In general, the adjective or participle takes the masculine plural form, but the feminine plural is possible where what is referred to is exclusively feminine:

In convento ci sono diciannove suore dai 25 ai 76 anni. È una piccola comunità, con i suoi alti e bassi. A volte si è più silenziose, a volte più ciarliere. In fondo anche noi siamo donne. Probabilmente se si è suore si è più generose, più aperte al prossimo, più libere di investire tempo e energie delle donne che hanno scelto di sposarsi.

'In the convent there are nineteen nuns aged 25 to 76. It's a small community, with its ups and downs. Sometimes people are more quiet, at others more chatty. In the end we are women too. Probably if you are a nun you are more generous, more open to your neighbours, freer to invest time and money than women who have chosen to marry.'

Più tempo si resta sposate con l'uomo sbagliato, più difficile sarà ricostruirsi una vita.

'The longer you stay married to the wrong man, the harder it will be to reconstruct a life for yourself.'

Nouns, too, may be plural in this context (cf. *suore* in the example above), although the singular is also possible:

Se si diventa ambasciatori/ambasciatore si acquista lo status diplomatico.

'If you become an ambassador you acquire diplomatic status.'

Solo se si è (una) mamma/mamme si capisce cosa vuol dire allevare un figlio.

'Only if you are a mother can you understand what it means to bring up a child.'

Proper names are used only in the singular when they denote a single individual:

Sembra facile scrivere un libro, ma non si è mica tutti Indro Montanelli!

'It looks easy to write a book, but we aren't all Indro Montanelli!'

Note that even where the indefinite personal pronoun is only *implicit* (e.g., with infinitives, see 6.29), the same rule of plural agreement applies. The following example is from an advertisement for an airline (*coccolati* is the past participle of *coccolare* 'to cuddle', 'make a fuss of'):

Volare è bello. Coccolati è meglio.

'Flying [i.e., for one to fly] is beautiful. [To do it while one is] being made a fuss of is better.'

Bisogna sempre viaggiare armati.

'It is always necessary to travel [i.e., that one should travel] armed.'

6.34 Other indefinite personal forms: second person forms, and third person plural forms and *uno*

In addition to the structure with *si*, which is by far the most common, there are other ways to express an indefinite subject. Just as it is possible to use 'you' in English where the sense is 'generic', but includes the person(s) addressed ('people generally – including you'), so Italian can use second person forms. There is a difference, however, between the second person singular and the plural. The former is used where the speaker/writer is included in the utterance, and something like 'in my experience', or 'I find' is implicit in the utterance. This construction occurs notably in advertisements:

Al casinò la regola è che prima vinci qualche soldo, poi ti spennano come un pollo.	'At the casino as a rule first you win a bit, then they take you to the cleaners.'
In America se ti ferma la polizia non devi scendere dalla macchina: rimani seduto e apri lentamente il finestrino.	'In America if the police stop you you must not get out of your car: stay seated and slowly open the window.'
Puoi rilassarti alle terme, dedicarti all'osservazione degli animali, immergerti nella natura.	'You can relax at the spa, spend your time observing animals, immerse yourself in nature.'

The third person address pronouns *Lei* and *Loro* (see 22.3) are never used 'generically'. In fact, 'generic' *tu*, etc. can be used even when speaking to someone one calls *Lei* – and also when addressing more than one person:

Lei avrà capito che è una cosa che ti rovina la salute.	'You must have realized that it's something that ruins your health.'

The second person *plural* is used if the speaker/writer is not included in the utterance. It is widely found, for example, when getting people to follow a set of instructions:

Dopo aver steso la crema, appoggiate gli indici e i medi agli angoli delle palpebre. Premete e tirate la pelle verso l'alto, chiudendo e aprendo gli occhi, per sei volte. Fate una pausa e riprendete.	'After applying the cream, place your forefingers and middle fingers on the corners of your eyelids. Press and pull the skin upwards, closing and opening your eyes, six times. Have a rest and repeat.'

A third person plural verb form (but not third person plural pronouns) may be used if neither the speaker nor the hearer is included, and the subject is either generic ('people generally') or indefinite (an unspecified person). 'They' + verb can be used in a similar way in English:

Dicono che domani farà bello.	'They say it'll be fine tomorrow.'
Non dimenticherò mai quando spararono a Robert Kennedy.	'I'll never forget when RK was shot/they shot RK.'
Mi hanno detto che costruiranno un garage nei locali dell'ex-supermercato Coop.	'I've been told that a garage is going to be built/they're going to build a garage on the premises of the old Coop supermarket.'

The usual equivalent to English indefinite personal 'one' is the *si* construction. However, *uno* can occasionally be used as an indefinite *subject* pronoun. *Uno* is different from *si* in that its sense is closer to 'someone', 'some people', rather than 'one' or 'people generally':

Se uno vuole, può farlo.	'If one/someone wants, they can do it.'
Uno potrebbe scandalizzarsi sentendo queste parole.	'One/some people might be shocked to hear these words.'

For the 'generic' infinitive, giving orders and instructions to whomever may be paying attention (for example, in public notices, such as *Tirare* 'Pull'), see 14.8.

6.35 An indefinite personal as object of a verb: the type *L'alcol rende tristi* 'Alcohol makes one sad'

Indefinite personal pronouns (other than second person *te/ti* – see below) can never be the *object* of a verb. The most common way of expressing a sentence such as 'Alcohol makes one sad' is simply to have no explicit direct object at all:

I capelli bianchi del vecchio stupiscono, le sue rughe incuriosiscono.	'The old man's white hair astonishes one, his wrinkles make one curious.'
Le tue osservazioni inducono a riflettere sulla natura stessa della giustizia divina.	'Your observations lead one to think about the very nature of divine justice.'
Questa barzelletta non fa ridere.	'This joke does not make one laugh.'
Il dondolio non aiuta certo a rimanere svegli.	'The rocking motion definitely doesn't help one to stay awake.'

The indefinite use of *tu* described in 6.34 does, however, allow use of *ti/te* as an object:

Se ti fissa un poliziotto, hai subito un senso di colpa.	'If a policeman looks at you, you immediately feel guilty.'

6.36 *Si* as first person plural 'we': the type *Si va* 'We go'

Indefinite *si* with a third person singular verb may be used with the value of first person plural. This usage, which was originally peculiar to Tuscany, is spreading, especially in spoken language. This structure, although in most cases identical with indefinite *si*, can be distinguished on the basis of the following features.

When the verb is intransitive, the past participle agrees in gender with the subject, e.g., it is feminine if the verb refers to women:

Appena si fu scese dal treno vedemmo Giovanni che era venuto a prenderci.	'As soon as we had got off the train we saw G who had come to pick us up.'

The verb is always third person singular, even when there is a plural object noun. However, this usage should be avoided in writing:

(Noi) non si guarda quasi mai film alla TV.	'We almost never watch films on TV.'

In Tuscan, especially in speech and at the informal/familiar/colloquial level, the personal pronoun *noi* can be used to stress that *si* is first person plural (rather than just 'indefinite'):

Si viene anche noi!	'We're coming too!'
Anche noi si è prenotato lo stesso albergo dell'anno scorso.	'We have booked the same hotel as last year as well.'

In most respects, first person plural *si* behaves just like indefinite personal *si*. For example, just as indefinite personal *si* may be combined with other uses of *si*, yielding *ci si*, so may first person plural *si*:

Si lava la camicia.	'We wash the shirt.'
Ci si lava la camicia.	'We wash our shirt.' [lit. 'We wash the shirt to ourselves.']
Si alza.	'He gets up.'
Ci si alza.	'We get up.'
etc.	

One difference is that if first person plural reflexive *ci si* is combined with an object clitic pronoun, the past participle *may* show masculine plural agreement with that pronoun. So 'We have bought them [feminine] for ourselves' might be either *Ce le si è comprati* or *Ce le si è comprate*. But in the sense 'One has bought them for oneself' only *Ce le si è comprate* is allowed. Note the order *ce* + object clitic + *si* in these cases. An alternative order is also possible when the sense is first person plural: one may also say *Ci se le è comprati*, etc.

6.37 Authorial and majestic *noi*

As in English, the first person plural may be used by an author in formal, didactic writing (or by a monarch, pope, etc.), instead of the first person singular. Accompanying adjectives are nearly always masculine plural, even where the writer is a woman:

Anche noi, pur non essendone convinti, abbiamo affermato che . . .	'We too, even though we are not convinced of it, have stated that . . .' [written by a woman]

6.38 'All of ' + pronoun: the type 'They gave it to all of us' *Ce l'hanno dato a tutti*

'All of' is simply *tutto* + pronoun:

Tutti noi lo sappiamo.	'All of us know it.'
Vennero tutti loro.	'All of them came.'

The pronoun may also be a clitic, in which case the clitic occupies its normal position in relation to the verb (see 6.3), and *tutti*, etc. follows the verb. If the clitic is an indirect object form, then *tutti* must be preceded by *a*:

Ve le manderò tutte.	'I'll send you all of them.'
Gliel'ho fatto capire a tutti.	'I explained it to all of them.'
Vi manderò una cartolina a tutti.	'I'll send you all a postcard.'

7

Relative structures

7.1 Forms of the relative pronouns

Of the relative pronouns *che*, *cui* and *il quale*, *che* and *cui* do not vary for gender or number (the distinction between them will be discussed in 7.4–10), while *il quale* (*la quale*, *i quali* and *le quali*) varies according to the gender and number of its antecedent (i.e., the noun to which it refers):

La fisica, che/la quale può considerarsi la regina delle scienze . . .	'Physics, which can be considered the queen of sciences . . .'
Queste idee, di cui/delle quali si era parlato spesso sotto il fascismo, non furono mai realizzate.	'These ideas, about which people had often spoken under fascism, were never realized.'

7.2 Impossibility of omitting relative pronouns

Unlike English, relative pronouns cannot be omitted in modern Italian:

Sono buoni gli spaghetti che mangiate adesso?	'Is the spaghetti you are eating now OK?'
L'ho portata da un medico che conosco.	'I took her to a doctor I know.'

But where the relative pronoun is the subject or object of two or more conjoined verbs, it may be omitted before the second and subsequent verbs:

Ma l'altro professore, che aveva viaggiato in Cina e conosceva bene i cinesi, si dichiarò scettico.	'But the other teacher, who had travelled in China and knew the Chinese well, said he was sceptical.'
Erano libri che leggeva e poi buttava via.	'They were books that he read and then threw away.'

7.3 The type *Il medico di cui ti avevo parlato* 'The doctor who I talked to you about'

In everyday English, a relative structure formed from 'I talked to you about the doctor' appears to involve moving the phrase 'the doctor' into a different position, but leaves the preposition 'about' stranded at the end of the sentence, and thereby separated from the noun phrase it actually governs, so we have 'the doctor [who] I talked to you about'. Formal registers of English, however, prefer 'the doctor about whom I talked to you', in which the preposition remains in front of the 'moved' noun phrase. In Italian the latter construction is not a matter of preference but an inviolable rule. Prepositions must precede the relative pronoun and can never be left 'stranded' to the right of it (see 7.8, 12 for the obligatory use of *cui* or *il quale* after a preposition):

la città nella quale ti ho portato	'the city I took you to'
il medico di cui ti avevo parlato	'the doctor who I talked to you about'
la tavola sotto la quale lasciò il pacco	'the table which he left the package under'
il palcoscenico sul quale aveva ballato da giovane	'the stage which he had danced on as a lad'

However, for the possibility of 'stranding' those prepositions which are usually followed by *a* (e.g., *davanti a*), as in *la casa alla quale ti sei fermato davanti* 'the house you stopped in front of', see 11.2.

7.4 Uses and functions of relative *che*

- *Che* can function either as the subject or as the direct object of the verb (there is no distinction between subject 'who' and object 'whom').
- It may refer either to animate or inanimate antecedents (so that it is equivalent to English relative 'who' 'which' and as well as 'that').
- It may be used both in restrictive[1] and non-restrictive relative clauses.
- It can be used with first, second or third person antecedents.
- It is usually immediately preceded by its antecedent.

È situato in quella fetta di pianura che sta fra il Po e l'Appennino.	'It's situated in that slice of plain that lies between the Po and the Apennines.'
E lì conobbi l'uomo più dolce e grande che abbia mai incontrato.	'And there I met the sweetest and greatest man I've ever encountered.'
È un fatto che ha saputo da un tale che l'aveva sentito da un tizio.	'It's something he heard from a fellow who had learned it from some bloke.'
Camminava come qualcuno che tema d'impolverarsi le scarpe.	'He walked like someone who's afraid of getting his shoes dirty.'
Io, che non ho mai detto una bugia, vi giuro che . . .	'I, who have never told a lie, swear to you that . . .'
Quella sera arrivaste voi, che tutti cercavano da tanti anni.	'That evening you arrived, [you] whom everyone had been looking for for so many years.'

Relative *che* must not be used after a preposition (*cui* or *il quale*, etc. are used instead): *Il medico di cui/del quale* [not **di che*] *ti ho parlato*, etc.

7.5 *Il che*: a relative referring to a whole clause

The invariable relative *il che* has a whole clause or proposition as its antecedent: e.g., 'which' in English 'He appeared to have been in two places at once, which was impossible'. *Il che*:

---

[1]A restrictive relative serves to *define* or *identify* the noun or noun phrase to which it refers; a non-restrictive relative simply provides additional information about that noun or noun phrase. The relative clause 'who were in the bar' is restrictive in 'The students who were in the bar were singing, while those outside kept quiet', but it is non-restrictive in 'The students, who were in the bar, were singing.' A non-restrictive relative clause can be removed ('The students were singing') without changing the basic meaning of the sentence.

- only appears at the beginning of a clause;
- may be combined with the prepositions *a, da, con* and *di* (*al che* and *col che* often correspond to the English 'whereupon' or 'and with that').

S'è già trovata in difficoltà. Il che mi preoccupa moltissimo.	'She's already found herself in difficulty. Which worries me greatly.'
Ti ho mancato di rispetto, del che ti chiedo scusa.	'I've not shown you respect, and I apologize for that.'
Fu annunciata la morte della regina. Al che la sua famiglia si mise a piangere.	'The queen's death was announced. Whereupon her family started to weep.'
Tra qualche giorno avremo pubblicato l'ultimo volume. Col che il nostro lavoro sarà terminato.	'In a few days we'll have published the last volume. With that our work will be finished.'
Lo stesso fenomeno è stato osservato ripetutatamente nei mesi successivi. Dal che deduciamo la permanenza dei cetacei in quella zona anche durante il periodo estivo.	'The same phenomenon was observed repeatedly in the following months. From which we deduce that cetaceans stay in that zone during the summer months as well.'

Exceptionally and in very formal styles, *il che* may precede the clause it refers to:

Il direttore ci disse, il che non ci dispiacque, che avremmo dovuto ripetere l'esperimento.	'The director told us, and we didn't mind this, that we would have to repeat the experiment.'

7.6 The phrase *di che*

The structure '*di che* + infinitive', meaning 'about which to ...', 'the means by which to ...', 'the wherewithal to ...', has only limited use:

Non c'è di che lamentarsi.	'There's nothing to complain about.'
Cercavano di che vivere.	'They were looking for the means to live.'
Non aveva proprio di che vantarsi.	'He certainly didn't have anything to boast about.'

Note also the expression *Non c'è di che!* = 'It really doesn't matter', 'Think nothing of it', 'Not at all!' as a polite response to expressions of apology or thanks.

7.7 *Che* as generic, 'all purpose' relative form

In popular, informal (mainly spoken) usage, *che* is often employed as an 'all purpose' relative pronoun.[2] An accompanying clitic pronoun may serve to indicate the relationship of that relative to the clause in which it appears (for example, direct object and indirect object):

Volevo dire gli studenti che gli avevi offerto un passaggio. [gli studenti a cui]	'I meant the students you'd offered a lift to.'
una ragazza che tu la conoscevi	'a girl that you knew'
Tre stronzi che sono proprio contento che non li vedo da anni.	'Three bastards I'm really happy not to have seen for years.'

---

[2]In fact there are technical reasons (cf. Cinque 1991: 465) not to regard this *che* as a 'relative pronoun' at all, but merely as a marker of subordination joining main and subordinate clauses. But for present purposes we shall classify it as a 'relative pronoun'.

While these constructions will be widely encountered in speech, they are some-what stigmatized and are probably best avoided by foreign learners.

7.8 Functions of *cui*

- *cui* is a variant of *che* which must be used after a preposition (the indirect object form corresponding to *che* is therefore *a cui*).
- *cui* without preceding preposition may be used in elevated styles instead of *a cui*:

Una sera erano state invitate al teatro Valle, il solo in cui si potesse recitare fuori del periodo di carnevale. [Mar.]	'One evening they'd been invited to the Valle theatre, the only one in which you could act outside the carnival period.'
Il luogo da cui venivi era lontano.	'The place from which you came was distant.'
Il signor marito le ha fatto venire da Firenze delle lenti da miope a cui però non riesce ad abituarsi. [Mar.]	'Her husband has had sent to her from Florence some lenses for short-sightedness which she can't get used to.'
quelle ragazze cui avevate mandato il pacco	'those girls to whom you had sent the parcel'
questa specie di sgangherato ballo in maschera cui è ridotta la politica italiana	'this kind of ungainly masked ball to which Italian politics is reduced'
L'articolo cui ti riferivi fu pubblicato nel 1893.	'The article you were referring to was published in 1893.'

7.9 *Di cui* = 'including', 'mentioned'

The phrase *di cui* (also *tra cui*) is used to mean 'among them. . .', 'among which is/are/was/were . . .', etc.:

Sono stati coinvolti nell'incidente sei ragazzi, di cui due morti.	'Six boys were involved in the accident, of whom two died.'
Hanno parlato anche vari stranieri, di cui uno spagnolo, un francese e ben quattro maltesi.	'Several foreigners spoke too, among them a Spaniard, a Frenchman, and no less than four Maltese.'

In formal and especially legal language, *di cui* + reference to a text, clause, paragraph, etc. means 'mentioned (in)', 'referred to (in)':

Gli articoli 7 e 25 del vecchio codice, di cui anche nella sezione 3.1, presentavano notevoli problemi d'interpretazione.	'Articles 7 and 25 of the old statute, mentioned also in section 3.1, created notable problems of interpretation.'
La legge di cui sopra è da considerarsi annullata.	'The above-mentioned law is to be considered annulled.'

For the use of *per cui* in non-formal discourse to mean 'and so', 'therefore' see 19.10. Note that 'the reason why' is *il motivo/la ragione per cui*.

Volevamo sapere il motivo per cui non si era presentata all'ora prevista.	'We wanted to know why she hadn't turned up at the appointed time.'

7.10 Restrictions on 'preposition + *cui*'

Certain prepositions cannot be followed by *cui*: these are *tranne, invece di, fuori, di là da, eccetto*. In such cases *il quale* is used instead:

Il vescovo, invece del quale [not *di cui*] *io avevo parlato, era stato detenuto a Siena.*	'The bishop, in whose stead I had spoken, had been detained in Siena.'

7.11 The possessive relative *il / la / i / le cui* = 'whose', 'of which'

The possessive *cui* is preceded by the definite article expressing the gender and number of the noun phrase it modifies. Unlike ordinary possessive adjectives (cf. 10.4), possessive *cui* can be preceded only by the definite (or, very rarely, the indefinite) article, and must always precede the noun.

la ragazza il cui fidanzato è morto	'the girl whose boyfriend died'
il ragazzo la cui fidanzata è morta	'the boy whose girlfriend died'
la ditta i cui direttori conosco	'the firm whose managers I know'
quegli scrittori fiorentini, le cui opere sono rinomate	'those Florentine writers, whose works are renowned'

A possessive relative structure largely confined to old-fashioned, literary, usage is the type *il/la/i/le di cui*:

una contessa fiorentina, le di cui figlie erano state presentate a corte	'a Florentine countess, the daughters of whom had been presented at court'
questo filosofo, il di cui parere era stato richiesto dal re	'this philosopher, the opinion of whom had been sought by the king'

Nowadays one would say *le figlie di cui* . . ., *il parere di cui* . . ., etc.

7.12 Functions of relative *il quale*

Il quale, etc.:

- can be used as subject or object forms, and after prepositions;
- is used especially where the relative pronoun would be ambiguous between singular and plural or masculine and feminine if the invariant *che* or *cui* were used:

la discesa in campo di Lamberto Dini, per la quale non hai nascosto la tua approvazione	'LD's entry into the fray, for which you did not disguise your approval'
Successivamente seppi che Mario e Rosanna, ai quali [not *a cui*] *avevo consigliato un periodo di riflessione, avevano litigato.*	'Later I learned that M and R, whom I had advised to take a period of reflection, had argued.'
Era venuto con la figlia del signor Rossi, senza la quale [not *cui*] *non avrebbe mai trovato la nostra casa.*	'He had come with Mr R's daughter, without whom [scil. the daughter] he would never have found our house.'

- cannot normally be used as a restrictive relative, except after a preposition or, in formal styles, when followed by a verb in the subjunctive:

I candidati i quali non dovessero presentarsi entro il 4 giugno non verranno ammessi.	'Any candidates who do not present themselves before 4 June shall not be admitted.'

- is the preferred form of relative pronoun in non-restrictive clauses when the relative is *distant* from its antecedent:

| Quante città vedemmo in quella splendida estate inglese, delle quali mi ricordo con perfetta chiarezza anche dopo cinquant'anni. | 'How many towns we saw in that splendid English summer, which [scil. the towns] I recall perfectly clearly even after 50 years.' |

- may be used only with third person antecedents (unlike *che*, *cui*):

| Avete visto me, che [not *il quale] giocavo a tennis. | [lit.] 'You saw me, who was playing tennis.' |

- is used rather than *cui* when preceded by numerals and other quantifiers + *di*:

| Ho provato sette apparati, tre dei quali funzionavano male. | 'I tried seven machines, three of which were not working properly.' |
| Questi sono gli alberi, ognuno dei quali deve essere abbattuto. | 'These are the trees, each of which must be felled.' |

Either *di cui* or *dei quali*, etc. can be used when the relative precedes the numeral or quantifier: . . . *di cui/dei quali tre funzionavano male*, etc.

- in non-restrictive clauses is usually employed as a subject relative; its use as an object (e.g., *Gli studenti, i quali hai interrogato, si sono rivelati ignoranti*, 'The students, whom you questioned, showed themselves to be ignorant') is relatively unusual.

7.13 Article + *quale* + noun = 'the said'

In elevated registers 'article + *quale*' corresponds closely to English '. . . the said . . .', '. . . and this . . .', or 'which' + noun:

| Mi rivolsi alla maestra dopo il mio soggiorno all'albergo. La quale maestra mi diede le informazioni richieste. | 'I went to the schoolmistress after my stay in the hotel. The said/And this schoolmistress gave me the required information.' |
| Erano venuti trecento insegnanti alla riunione. Il quale numero mancò di molto alle aspettative. | '300 teachers had come to the meeting. Which number fell well short of expectations.' |

7.14 *Quale* as relative adjective = 'of such a kind as'

Quale (without the article) may be used to express 'of such a kind as', 'such as', 'like':

Ci portò una conchiglia quale non si era mai vista.	'He brought us a shell such as had never been seen.'
Lì dentro era nascosto un tesoro quale non ci si può immaginare.	'Therein was hidden a treasure such as one cannot imagine.'
Sono fenomeni che non si possono esprimere attraverso una ortografia alfabetica quale è quella italiana.	'These are phenomena which cannot be expressed by a spelling system such as the Italian one is.'

Quale may also be used in the sense of 'as one who is', 'in one's capacity as':

| Vi scrivo quale rappresentante di questa ditta. | 'I write to you in my capacity as a representative of this firm.' |

7.15 The type 'What/That which you say is true', 'I believe what/that which you say', 'All [that] I do is read', 'Everything [that] you say is a lie', 'He who hesitates is lost', etc.

Relative 'what', 'that which' = *quello che* or *quel che, ciò che*. 'All [that]' = *tutto quello/ciò che*, 'Everyone who . . .' = *tutti quelli che*. (For the stylistic differences between *ciò* and *quello*, see 5.7.)

Sereni sono i proletari che sanno quel che vogliono.	'Serene are the proletarians who know what they want.'
Sapeva di latino poco più di quello che aveva imparato servendo messa.	'He knew a little more Latin than what he had learned serving at mass.'
I tratti le si sono deformati, dilatati e gli occhi le si sono infossati come se il guardare ciò che la circonda le fosse penoso.	'Her features have distorted and swollen and her eyes have sunk as if looking at what is around her were painful to her.'
Credo a tutto ciò che dici.	'I believe all/everything [that] you say.'

Note also the use of *cosa che* meaning 'which' with reference to some preceding proposition:

Disse che anziché pagare il dazio preferiva perdere la frutta rovesciandola sulla piazza, cosa che fece.	'He said that rather than pay the duty he preferred to lose his fruit by tipping it onto the square, which he did.'

7.16 *Quanto* = 'what', 'all [that]'

Quanto, literally 'as much as . . .' (see 16.18) is also widely used to express '(all) that . . .', 'what . . .', 'that which . . .'.

Rilessi quanto avevo studiato il giorno prima.	'I reread all I'd studied the previous day.'
Da quanto affermato deduco che lo conosce.	'From what [has been] stated I deduce that he knows him.'
Quanto stabilito all'inizio dell'inchiesta sarebbe bastato ad indicare chiaramente la sua colpevolezza.	'What was established at the beginning of the inquest would have sufficed clearly to indicate his guilt.'
Voglio che tu mi dica tutto quanto hai fatto.	'I want you to tell me everything you have done.'

Note that when *quanto* is the subject of a verb whose auxiliary is *essere*, the auxiliary is very commonly omitted: *quanto affermato* = *quanto è stato affermato* 'what has been stated'; *quanto successo* = *quanto era successo* 'what had happened'.

7.17 'He, she, those who . . .', 'anybody who . . .': masc. *colui che*, femin. *colei che*, pl. *coloro che*; *quello che, quella che, quelli che*; *chi*; *Chi* . . . 'if anybody . . .'

Colui che, feminine *colei che*, plural *coloro che* 'he/she/the one who . . .', 'those who . . .' are characteristic of more formal registers.

Coloro che hanno ricevuto la nostra lettera potranno entrare gratis.	'Those who have received our letter will be able to enter for free.'
Voi parlate di colei che mi ha salvato la vita.	'You're speaking of the woman who saved my life.'

Questi soldi vanno restituiti a colui che li ha persi.	'This money should be given back to the man who has lost it.'

Alternatively:

Almeno non è come tutti quelli che mi hanno usata come la diva del dolore e poi se ne sono lavate le mani.	'At least he's not like all those [men] who have used me as the "diva" of pain and then washed their hands of the matter.'
Voi parlate di quella che mi ha salvato la vita.	'You're speaking of the woman who saved my life.'
Oggi quello che molti considerano il vero «re d'Italia» va a letto a mezzanotte.	'Today the man whom many consider the real "king of Italy" goes to bed at midnight.'

Chi (always with a singular verb) can also mean 'he, she, those who', 'everybody who' or, sometimes, 'if anybody':

Alzi la mano chi non ha fatto il compito.	'Hands up those who haven't done their homework/everyone who hasn't done their homework.'
Chi ha ricevuto la nostra lettera potrà entrare gratis.	'Everyone who has received our letter will be able to enter for free.'
Non devi invitare chi non ti voglia bene.	'You mustn't invite anybody who doesn't like you.'
Sono convinto che chi ci ha seguito sin dall'inizio avrà tutto il materiale necessario.	'I'm convinced that everyone who has followed us from the beginning will have all the necessary material.'
Chi mi paga un bicchiere gli dico una cosa che poi mi dice grazie.	'If anyone'll buy me a drink I'll tell him something he'll thank me for.'
Una cosa del genere, chi se ne intendesse, sarebbe molto interessante.	'That sort of thing, for anyone who knew about it, would be very interesting.'

7.18 'No matter who', 'whoever', 'no matter what', 'whatever' *chiunque, qualunque cosa, qualsiasi cosa*

Chiunque and *qualsiasi cosa, qualunque cosa* are discussed in 9.9: in relative constructions they mean 'who-/whatever . . .', 'it doesn't matter who/what'. For the use of the subjunctive after these relatives, see 15.34:

Chiunque tu sia, non ti farò entrare.	'Whoever you are, I won't let you in.'
Caccerei via chiunque cercasse di toccarlo.	'I would drive away anyone who tried to touch him.'
Qualunque cosa tu abbia fatto, ti perdono.	'Whatever you have done, I forgive you.'

In the adjectival *quale che*, *quale* agrees with the noun; the *che* always immediately precedes the verb:

Quali che siano i tuoi progetti, dovrai venire a Roma.	'Whatever your plans may be, you will have to come to Rome.'
Quale che sia la casa che ha deciso di comprare, avrebbe dovuto dirmelo prima.	'Whichever house he has decided to buy, he should have told me first.'
Quale vino che abbiano bevuto, si sentiranno male.	'Whichever wine they've drunk, they'll feel ill.'

7.19 *Quanti* = 'all those who', 'as many as . . .'

Unlike singular *quanto* (cf. 7.16), plural *quanti* refers to humans. It is usually masculine, but feminine *quante* may be encountered where the referents are female:

Quanti lo vogliono fare lo facciano.	'Let all those who/as many people as want to do it, do it.'
Ho interrogato quanti si erano costituiti in questura.	'I questioned all those who gave themselves up at the police station.'
Si è fatto un prelievo istologico a quante avevano partorito in quel periodo.	'A smear was taken from all those who had given birth in that period.'

7.20 Relatives referring to expressions of time, space and manner ('the day when I was born'/'the day I was born', 'the place where I live'/'the place I live', 'the way that you walk'/'the way you walk', etc.)

Where 'when' is used as a relative in English; 'that' and 'on which' are also available: 'the day when I was born' = 'the day that I was born' = 'the day on which I was born'. Italian does not use *quando* at all in such cases: either *che* 'that' or preferably (especially in written and formal registers) *in cui* 'on/in which', are used instead:

il giorno che sono nato/il giorno in cui sono nato	'the day I was born'
Lo riconobbi nel momento che lo vidi./Lo riconobbi nel momento in cui lo vidi.	'I recognized him the moment I saw him.'
quegli anni che guadagnavamo soldi a tutt'andare/quegli anni in cui guadagnavamo soldi a tutt'andare	'those years when we were making money hand over fist'

Italian freely uses *dove* as a relative of place 'to/in which', 'where'. The relative *dove* may also be preceded by the prepositions *a*, *di*, *da* and *per*.

Fossi andato dove ti avevo detto io.	'I wish you'd gone where I told you.'
È questa la stanza dove lavori?	'Is this the room you work in?'
Gli occhi cercano un posto dove riposare per qualche minuto all'ombra.	'The eyes look for a place to rest in the shade for a few minutes.'
Non trovava più la stanza da dove era uscita.	'He could no longer find the room she had come out of.'

For 'the way [that] . . .' Italian has *il modo/la maniera in cui*:

Dalla maniera in cui zoppichi vedo che ti hanno operato al ginocchio.	'From the way you're limping I can see you've had the knee operation.'
Il modo in cui mi salutò mi fece capire subito che qualcosa non andava bene.	'The way he greeted me immediately told me that something was wrong.'

7.21 Italian clauses with relative pronouns equivalent to English verbs in '-ing' (*un progetto che offre molte possibilità* = 'a project offering many possibilities')

English makes extensive use of clauses containing verbs in '-ing' as an equivalent to relative pronoun + verb. Often, but not always, such cases in English might be analysed as resulting from deletion of a relative pronoun + verb 'to be': 'A man carrying a tray appeared at the door' = 'A man *who was* carrying a tray appeared at the door'. In general Italian has no equivalent to the English '-ing' type of relative, and uses instead the relative pronoun + verb. Thus the relatives in the following example would probably be rendered in English by 'necks stretching', 'mouths opening', 'standards being raised', etc.:

. . . un mare di teste ondeggianti, colli che si allungano, bocche che si aprono, stendardi che si levano, cavalli che scalpitano, un finimondo di corpi che si accalcano, si spingono, invadendo la piazza rettangolare. [Mar.]	'. . . a sea of bobbing heads, stretching necks, mouths opening, banners being raised, horses pawing the ground, an explosion of bodies pushing, shoving, as they invade the rectangular square.'
Si affacciò alla porta un uomo che portava un vassoio.	'There appeared at the door a man carrying a tray.'
All'osteria ci sono sempre gli stessi, tutt'il giorno, da anni, a gomiti sui tavoli e menti sui pugni che guardano le mosche. [Cal.]	'At the inn it's always the same people, all day long, for years, elbows on the table and chins on their fists, looking at the flies.'
Mario è lì che cerca invano di fare ordine.	'M is there trying to impose order.'

For the use of relative clauses with verbs of perception, of the type *Vede Giovanni che esce dal negozio*, see 17.28).

7.22 The type *una lettera arrivata stamattina . . . = una lettera che è arrivata stamattina . . .*

A stylistically elegant variant of the structure 'relative pronoun + *essere* + past participle' involves apparent deletion of a relative pronoun + *essere*. Such structures do not indicate the tense of the relative clause. They apply to *essere* + past participle of any verb except *essere* itself (thus you cannot say **Sono tornate le ragazze state al mare* 'The girls who have been to the sea have returned').

Gli studenti iscrittisi al corso sono tenuti a presentarsi entro il 3 aprile.	'Students who have enrolled on the course must present themselves by 3 April.'
I documenti mandatimi e che successivamente lessi spiegano tutto.	'The documents sent to me and which I subsequently read explain everything.'
Si trattava di una vecchia foto, chissà come finita lì.	'It was an old photo, and goodness knows how it had got there.'
È probabile che un elenco piu completo dei libri da lui posseduti o letti avrebbe presentato un quadro piu vario.	'It's likely that a fuller list of the books which he had owned or read would have presented a more varied picture.'
L'attore regista è stato sorpreso con Elle Macpherson, la fotomodella ora datasi al cinema.	'The actor-producer was caught with EM, the model who has now devoted herself to cinema.'
«Viva Ferdinando [. . .]» dice un altro biglietto cadutole sulla scarpa. [Mar.]	'"Long live F" says another note which has fallen on her shoe.'

7.23 The 'present participle' as relative clause: *le note riferentisi al suo caso = le note che si riferiscono al suo caso*

As explained in 3.32, relatively few Italian verbs possess a 'present participle' form in *-nte*. With those that do, and mainly in elevated, and especially bureaucratic, registers, the 'present participle' may function as a relative clause (note the similar use of '-ing' forms of verbs in English). Note that the 'present participle' does not vary for tense:

la documentazione illustrante le atrocità commesse e che tutti voi avete potuto esaminare con calma	'the documentation illustrating the atrocities committed and which all of you have been able to examine calmly'
Si era prevista una terza sezione comprendente tre o quattro paragrafi sulla Questione della Lingua.	'We had thought of a third section comprising three or four paragraphs on the *Questione della Lingua*.'
Le persone aventi diritto ad un sussidio possono rivolgersi all'ufficio centrale.	'Persons entitled to a grant can go to the central office.'
Rivendicavamo i compensi spettantici.	'We claimed the compensation due to us.'
Le note riguardantivi sono state perse.	'The notes concerning you have been lost.'

7.24 The type *un amico che non mi ricordo dove abita*

Relative structures of the type 'This is a friend of mine who I can't remember where he lives' or 'We found a slug that we really couldn't understand how it had got inside the tent', are inadmissible (although quite intelligible) in English. One would have to say 'This is a friend of mine, but/and I can't remember where he lives', etc. In Italian, however, relative structures of this kind are perfectly grammatical:

È un mio amico che non mi ricordo dove abita.	'He is a friend of mine; I can't remember where he lives.'
Trovammo una lumaca che proprio non capivamo come si fosse infilata dentro la tenda.	'We found a slug and we really couldn't understand how it had got inside the tent.'
Ma questo è un testamento che sappiamo benissimo come sia stato già aperto.	'But this will – we all know how it has already been opened.'
Decisi di scegliere una capanna che sapevo come era stata costruita.	'I decided to choose a shed whose method of construction I knew.' [lit. 'that I knew how it had been built']

7.25 The type *un libro affascinante e che solleva molti problemi*

Italian relative clauses, unlike their English counterparts, can be readily conjoined with other modifiers of a noun phrase (adjectives or prepositional phrases) by means of *e* or *ma*: thus in the following examples *affascinante, dell' unione agricoltori* are predicates conjoined, respectively, with *che solleva, che emerge, che ... farebbe*:

un libro affascinante e che solleva molti problemi	'a fascinating and highly problematic book' [lit. 'and which raises many problems']
Nei masi vivono oltre 80 mila anime, dato dell'unione agricoltori e che emerge calcolando mediamente cinque persone per maso ... [Pan.]	'In the "masi" there are more than 80 000 souls living, a fact provided by the farmers' union and arrived at [lit. 'which emerges'] by calculating 5 people per "maso" on average ...'

7.26 Repetition of the noun as a relative device

A stylistic device which serves to identify the antecedent where there is risk of ambiguity is simply to repeat the noun:

Nel 1963 scoprii la tomba di uno dei più famosi capi della tribù, tomba che a prima vista non sembrava molto interessante.	'In 1963 I discovered the tomb of one of the most famous chiefs of the tribe, which at first sight didn't seem particularly interesting.'

7.27 'Infinitival relatives': the types *Cerco un libro da leggere* 'I'm looking for a book to read'; *Non è un uomo da abbandonare i suoi amici* 'He's not a man to abandon his friends'; *Cercavo (un posto) dove mettere il libro* 'I was looking for somewhere to put the book'

English sentences such as 'I'm looking for a book to read', 'You have much work to do', can easily (if inelegantly) be paraphrased as 'I'm looking for a book <u>which I can read</u>', 'You have much work <u>which you must do</u>', etc. In other words, the infinitives 'to read', 'to do' have the status of a relative clause, express the intention or requirement that the action of the verb be carried out, and have as their (unexpressed) object a noun in the main clause ('book', 'work'). The Italian equivalent places *da* before the infinitive: *Cerco un libro da leggere*, *Hai molto lavoro da fare*, etc. Note that in this construction the infinitive may not be passivized, so that **Cerco un libro da essere letto in vacanze* is impossible. However, the passive formed with reflexive *si* (see 14.35) is possible: *Cerco un libro da leggersi in vacanza* 'I am looking for a book which can be read on holiday'.

Ho dei calcoli da fare.	'I've some calculations to do/which I must do.'
Ti darò dei pantaloni da rattoppare.	'I'll give you some trousers to patch/which you can patch.'

In many cases phrases of the *da* + infinitive type acquire a meaning roughly equivalent to 'that which is to be X-ed', or 'the wherewithal to X'. Thus the noun *il daffare* or *daffarsi* (written as one word) is 'what has to be done/the task at hand' (note also *darsi da fare* 'get busy', 'get working'), while *da mangiare* and *da bere* are 'that which is to be eaten' and 'that which is to be drunk', and *dare da mangiare*, in effect 'give that which is to be eaten'/'give the wherewithal to eat', is the usual way of saying 'to feed' (*Dà da mangiare alle galline* 'He feeds the hens'); similarly, *dare da bere* 'to give [someone] something to drink'.

The type 'He's not a man to abandon his friends' contains a different kind of relative infinitive, and means 'He's not a man of the kind that abandons his friends/who would abandon his friends'. Here too Italian may use an infinitive preceded by *da* (cf. 11.28): *Non è un uomo da abbandonare i suoi amici*.

È stata una esperienza da far venire i brividi.	'It was an experience to give you the shudders.'
Era una promessa da consolare il più nervoso dei viaggiatori.	'It was a promise to/that would console the most nervous of travellers.'

When the relative is not the direct object (or the subject) of the verb, the appropriate relative marker may be followed by the simple infinitive:

Non trovava nessuno a cui consegnare il manoscritto.	'He couldn't find anybody to whom to hand the manuscript/anybody to hand the manuscript to.'
Aveva portato un cacciavite con cui aprirli.	'He had brought a screwdriver with which to open them/to open them with.'

The place relative 'somewhere to . . .' (and its negative and interrogative counterpart 'anywhere to') is usually *un posto dove* + infinitive or just *dove* + infinitive:

Cercavo un posto dove mettere il libro.	'I was looking for somewhere to put the book.'
Non trovavo dove parcheggiare la macchina.	'I couldn't find anywhere to park the car.'

For the type *C'è da fare* 'There's [something] to be done', etc., see 17.28.

8

Interrogative structures

8.1 Forms of the interrogative pronouns, adjectives and adverbs

All the following interrogatives function both as subject and non-subject forms and, with the exception of the adjectives *quale* and *quanto*, are invariable:

TABLE 8.A

Human	*chi?*	'who?'
Non-human	*che?* *che cosa?* *cosa?*	'what?'
Reason	*perché?*	'why?'
Selection	*quale?* *che?*	'which?', 'which one?' 'which?'
Manner	*come?*	'how?', 'in what way?'
Place	*dove?*	'where?'
Quantity	*quanto?*	'how much?', 'to what degree?'

Interrogatives governed by a preposition must be preceded by that preposition (but see 11.2 for further discussion). Prepositions cannot be 'stranded' (cf. 7.3), unlike in English:

Con chi sei venuto?	'Who did you come with?'
A chi li hai dati?	'Who did you give them to?'

8.2 Chi? 'who?'

Voglio sapere chi è stato.	'I want to know who it was.'
E a chi lo farei questo saluto?	'And who am I supposed to be making this salute to?'
Di chi è questa firma?	'Whose is this signature?'

Note *chissà?* (*chi* + *sa*) is used to emphasize a question ('who knows?', 'heaven knows', etc.):

≪*È cucita a mano e sarà costata un sacco di soldi*≫, *aggiunse Mark.* ≪*Chissà a chi apparterrà?*≫	' "It's hand-sewn and must have cost a fortune," Mark added. "I wonder/who knows who it belongs to/Whoever can it belong to?" '

8.3 *Che cosa?, che?, cosa?* 'what?'

Cos'hai fatto?	'What did you do?'
Cosa sia stato è ancora da accertare.	'What it was is still to be ascertained.'
Ad Anna, però, non si sa che cosa dire.	'But they don't know what to say to A.'

There is little difference in meaning or register between these three terms. *Cosa?* is the more common form in Tuscany and northern Italy, and *che?* is used more in the south. *Che?* is syntactically different from *cosa?* and *che cosa?*, in that it must *immediately precede* a verb (except that clitic pronouns may come between it and the verb):

Che cosa farei per avere una moto così?	'What would I do to have a motorbike
OR *Cosa farei per avere una moto così?*	like that?'
OR *Che farei per avere una moto così?*	
Che cosa non farei per avere una moto così?	'What wouldn't I do to have a
OR *Cosa non farei per avere una moto così?*	motorbike like that?'

but not

*Che non farei per avere una moto così?

This rule does not apply if *che* is preceded by a preposition:

Di che non ha paura Giulio?	'Of what is G not afraid?'

Note that the final vowel of *cosa* may be optionally omitted before a following vowel, and that this is almost always the case in *Cos'è?* 'What is it?'

8.4 *Perché?* 'why?'

Ma non si sa perché lo dica visto che lui a caccia non ci va mai.	'But we don't know why he says that, since he never actually goes hunting.'
Perché non mi saluti più?	'Why don't you say hello to me any more?'

Also *per quale motivo?* = 'why?', 'for what reason?'

—Ha deciso di distruggere gli altri documenti.	'He decided to destroy the other documents.'
—Per quale motivo?	'Why?'

8.5 *Quale?* and *che?*

Quale? is a pronoun or adjective used to request *identification*: possible replies to it would contain a name, a demonstrative (*questo, quello*), or even just the act of pointing to the relevant entity. It corresponds not only to English 'which?' or 'which one?' but also, sometimes, to 'what?' In contrast, *che?*, and the pronouns *che?* or *che cosa?* request not necessarily identification (although they have this function, too) but definition, explanation. The appropriate answer to *Qual è la capitale della Polonia?* 'What is the capital of Poland?' would be *Varsavia*, 'Warsaw', but to *Che cos'è la capitale della Polonia?* 'What is the capital of Poland?' one might equally reply: *È uno dei più importanti centri commerciali dell'Europa orientale* 'It's one of the major commercial centres of eastern Europe'.

Likewise:

| —Qual è/Che cos'è la radice quadrata di 49? | 'What's the square root of 49?' |
| —È sette. | 'It's seven.' |

but

| —Che cos'è la radice quadrata di 49? | 'What's the square root of 49?' |
| —È un numero che molti considerano magico. | 'It's a number that many people consider magical.' |

Further examples:

Marianna si chiede per quale infausta alchimia i pensieri di Innocenza la raggiungano chiari e limpidi come se li potesse udire. [Mar.]	'M wonders by what unhappy alchemy I's thoughts reach her as clearly as if she could hear them.'
Quali sono state le migliori trovate?	'What were the best finds?'
—La polizia inglese non porta le armi.	'The English police don't carry guns.'
—E che polizia è?	'What kind of police force is that?'

Note that *quale* is usually abbreviated to *qual* before forms of the verb *essere* beginning with the letter *e* (*qual è?, qual era?,* etc.). The frequently encountered spelling *qual'* is an error.

8.6 Come? 'how?', 'of what kind?'

| Come giustificare l'assenza di Mariano diventato improvvisamente capofamiglia? | 'How was one to justify the absence of M, who had suddenly become the head of a family?' |

English 'what?' sometimes means 'of what kind?', 'what is it like?', or 'in what way?' In such cases Italian usually uses *come?*:

Com'è il tuo gelato?	'What is your ice cream like?'
Com'era il cacciavite che volevi comprare?	'What sort of screwdriver were you wanting to buy?'
Come sono le condizioni economiche della Romania?	'What is the economic condition of Romania?'
Come devo fare?	'What am I to do?' / 'In what way am I to act?'
Come ti chiami?	'What's your name?'

Come? = 'What (did you say)?'

| —L'ho pagato sette milioni di lire. | 'It cost me 7 million lire.' |
| —Come? Sette milioni? | 'What? 7 million?' |

8.7 Dove 'where?'

Dove is 'where to?', as well as 'where?':

| Dove vai? | 'Where are you going (to)?' |
| Dove stai? | 'Where are you?' |

also

| Da [or di] dove vieni? | 'Where do you come from?' |
| Fin dove arriverà? | 'How far will it get?' [lit. 'until where?'] |

8.8 *Quanto?* 'how much?', 'to what extent?'

Used as an adjective, *quanto* agrees with the noun; used as an adverb it is invariant:

Quanto costa?	'What/How much does it cost?'
Quanta acqua ci metto?	'How much water do I put in?'
Non so quante uova ci devo mettere.	'I don't know how many eggs to put in.'
Quanto grande è?	'How big is it?'
Quanto lentamente cammina?	'How slowly does he walk?'
Questo vino, quanto fresco va bevuto?	'How cool should this wine be drunk?'

8.9 Reinforcement of question words: '. . . on earth?', '. . . ever?', '. . . else?'

The question words may be reinforced in a variety of ways, particularly by using *mai*:

Che mai stanno facendo?	'Whatever are they up to?'
Dove mai saranno andati a finire?	'Wherever can they have got to?'

Note that *come mai?* is *not* 'however', but 'why ever?', 'why on earth?', 'how come?':

Come mai ti piace tanto?	'How come you like it so much?'

Other, more colloquial and informal, possibilities are:

Che cavolo/diamine/diavolo/stanno facendo?	'What the hell are they doing?'

'-else' is usually *altro*:

Dove altro l'avrà messa?	'Where else can he have put it?'
Come altro potevo contattarti?	'How else could I contact you?'

8.10 Interrogative *niente* 'anything?', *nessuno* 'anybody?'

These are basically negative forms meaning 'nothing' and 'nobody', but colloquially they are also used to mean 'anything', 'anybody' in questions:

Hai dimenticato niente?	'Have you forgotten anything?'
C'è nessuno lì dentro?	'Is there anybody in there?'
C'è niente da mangiare?	'Is there anything to eat?'

But *qualcuno*, *qualcosa*, etc. are used where English would use 'somebody', 'something', rather than 'anybody', 'anything':

C'era qualcuno che conoscevi alla festa?	'Was there someone you knew at the party?'
Cercavi qualcosa di particolare?	'Were you looking for something in particular?'

8.11 The type *E Mario?* 'What about Mario?'

'What about + noun?' is usually simply *E . . .?*:

E i soldi che mi dovevi dare?	'What about the money you were supposed to give me?'

'What about . . . -ing?' is usually expressed by *Che ne dici/dice/dite di* + infinitive':

Che ne dici di andare al cinema?	'What about going to the cinema?'
Che ne dite di fare due passi?	'What about going for a stroll?'

8.12 Structure of interrogative sentences

English sentence-interrogation (i.e., questions of the type expecting an answer 'yes' or 'no') generally has a different structure from affirmative sentences (e.g., 'You are coming' vs. 'Are you coming?'). But there is usually no such distinction in Italian: what distinguishes a question from a statement is the presence of the question mark (in writing), and an intonational pattern which tends to rise towards the end of the sentence (in speech).

Vieni?	'Are you coming?'
È giusto concedere la libertà a Craxi per venire a curarsi?	'Is it right to grant freedom to Craxi so that he can come and be cured?'
Non vorrai mica che ti porti in braccio?	'Are you sure you don't want me to carry you?'

In formal and literary styles, it is also possible to place the subject after the verb:

Può una donna di quarant'anni, madre e nonna, svegliarsi come una rosa ritardataria da un letargo durato decenni . . .?	'Can a 40-year-old woman, who is a mother and grandmother, awaken like a belated rose from a decades-old lethargy . . .?'

Indirect sentence-interrogation – where the question is in a subordinate clause of the type introduced in English by 'whether' – or 'if', as in 'I asked whether/if they were ready' – is introduced in Italian by *se* (for the use of the subjunctive in indirect questions, see 15.45):

Chiesi se fossero pronti.	'I asked whether they were ready.'
Non sapevamo se volessero acqua o vino.	'We didn't know whether they wanted water or wine.'
Se finiremo entro Natale nessuno lo sa.	'Whether we'll finish by Christmas nobody knows.'
Non è chiaro se farlo o no.	'It's not clear whether to do it or not.'

If a speaker repeats a question which he or she has already been asked (for example 'Am I happy? Of course I am happy', in response to the question 'Are you happy?'), Italian often places *se* in front of the repetition:

Se sono contento? Certo che sono contento!	'Am I happy? Of course I am happy.'
Se pagheremo la multa? Scherzi?	'Will we pay the fine? Are you kidding?'

Where the question does not require a 'yes/no' answer but asks 'who?', 'what?', 'why?', 'when?', 'where?', 'how?', 'how much?', etc.), the interrogative element must be followed *immediately* by the verb, so that the subject must generally follow[1] the verb:

---

[1] Of course the subject could also be placed in front of the interrogative element in certain types (cf. 17.5) of sentence structure: *I ragazzi, dove sono andati?*

Dove sono andati i ragazzi? [Not *Dove i ragazzi sono andati?*]	'Where have the boys gone?'
Quanto tempo dovettero aspettare gli altri clienti?	'How long did the other clients have to wait?'
Volevo sapere chi fosse quel signore con la moto.	'I wanted to know who that gentleman with the motorbike was.'
Cosa crede di fare quel ragazzo nel giardino?	'What does that boy in the garden think he's doing?'

The order subject + verb is possible, however, after *perché* 'why' and *per quale motivo* 'for what reason':

Perché l'ordine non è stato mandato?	'Why wasn't the order sent?'
Non capivo perché lei continuava a parlare.	'I couldn't understand why she was still talking.'

8.13 Interrogative *se* in exclamations

Se followed by the indicative is colloquially used to reinforce exclamations (the origin of this construction seems to be something like 'Are you asking me whether . . .?', 'Am I . . .?'):

Accipicchia se sono contenta!	'Boy am I happy!'
Caspita se ci vado!	'Damned if I'm going!'

9

Indefinite, quantifier and negative pronouns and adjectives

For 'indefinite personal' (so-called 'impersonal') verb constructions such as *Si canta, Uno canta*, etc., see 6.33, 34.

9.1 *Uno* 'one'; *Ne ho uno bianco* 'I have a white one'

Like its English equivalent, the pronoun *uno* can be a numeral 'one', an indefinite personal pronoun (although it is much more rarely used than *si*, see 6.34), or 'somebody':

> *È uno che non sta mai zitto.*　　　　　'He's someone/a man who's never quiet.'

Uno is also the indefinite pronoun counterpart of *quello* + adjective (see 5.9); while *quello* + adjective corresponds to English 'the + adjective + one', *uno* + adjective is 'a + adjective + one':

Ho assaggiato il vino bianco, non quello rosso.	'I tried the white wine, not the red one.'
Ho assaggiato un vino bianco, non uno rosso.	'I tried a white one, not a red one.'
Cercavo la penna rossa e ho trovato solo quella verde.	'I was looking for the red pen and only found the green one.'
Cercavo una penna rossa e ne ho trovata solo una verde.	'I was looking for a red pen and only found a green one.'

9.2 *Qualcuno* (more rarely *qualcheduno*) 'somebody', 'someone' (or 'some ones')

Qualcuno is always grammatically masculine in the sense of 'somebody'.

> *Camminava leggero come un gatto, come qualcuno che tema d'impolverarsi le scarpe.* 　'He walked as lightly as a cat, like someone afraid of getting his shoes dusty.'

Qualcuno is really *qualche* (see 9.7) + *uno*, and can combine the meaning of these two elements: 'some (ones)', 'some of them' (recall that singular forms preceded by *qualche* have plural meaning). It may refer to objects (as well as human beings), and in this case varies for gender:

> *Eppure c'è qualcuno che, più divertito che preoccupato, questa storia fatica a digerirla.* 　'Yet there are some people who, more amused than worried, have trouble swallowing this story.'

Il medico ti darà delle pastiglie, e dovrai prenderne qualcuna ogni giorno.	'The doctor will give you some pills, and you'll have to take some (of them) every day.'

Like English 'someone', *qualcuno* can also have the sense of 'a somebody', 'someone important':

Vuole diventare qualcuno.	'She wants to become somebody.'

9.3 *Un tale* 'somebody or other', and similar expressions

È un fatto che ha saputo da un tale che l'aveva sentito da un tizio.	'It's something he heard from somebody or other who'd got it from some bloke.'

The word *tizio* in the above example comes from the expression *Tizio, Caio e Sempronio* = English 'Tom, Dick and Harry', 'any old people'. *Tizio* is also a common colloquial term for 'bloke', 'guy' (with female equivalent *tizia*):

L'altro giorno mi ferma sto tizio che vuole vendermi . . .	'The other day I was stopped by this bloke trying to sell me . . .'

Note also the colloquial and non-serious *pinco pallino* 'unspecified person of no importance', 'Fred Bloggs':

Ma che 'Tiepolo'! Questo quadro può averlo fatto pinco pallino.	'What do you mean "Tiepolo"! This painting could have been done by any fool/Fred Bloggs.'

Il tal dei tali = 'so-and-so', 'such-and-such':

Vai lì e dici che sei il tal dei tali domiciliato [or la tal dei tali domiciliata] in via tal dei tali e loro ti fanno entrare.	'You go there and you say that you're so-and-so living in such-and-such a street and they'll let you in.'

The adjective *tale* is used similarly:

. . . i giudici lo sai come fanno? Vanno a sfogliare il codice, il reato tale, l'articolo tale . . . [Cas.]	'. . . do you know what the judges do? They go and flick through the legal code, such-and-such an offence, article such-and-such . . .'

9.4 *Qualcosa, qualche cosa,* and other expressions meaning 'something'

'Something' is *qualcosa* or (rather less commonly) *qualche cosa*:

Ma ci deve pur essere qualcos'altro che appartiene al mondo della saggezza e della contemplazione. Qualcosa che distolga la mente dalle sciocche pretese dei sensi. [Mar.]	'But there must also be something else which belongs to the world of wisdom and contemplation. Something to distract the mind from the foolish pretensions of the senses.'
Afferra un foglio di carta e vi scrive sopra qualcosa.	'He grabs a sheet of paper and writes something on it.'
Se alzavo gli occhi potevo vedere i cigni sempre in attesa di qualcuno che butti loro qualcosa dalle finestre. [Mar.]	'If I looked up I could see the swans always waiting for someone to throw them something from the windows.'

Qualcosa is usually masculine:

Forse qualcosa era loro sfuggito.[1]   'Perhaps something had escaped them.'

Qualcosa (but not *qualcuno*) requires *di* before a following adjective (which is always masculine):

Cerco qualcosa di più interessante.   'I'm looking for something more interesting.'

Sarà qualche cosa di nuovo.   'It'll be something new.'

But note *qualcos'altro* 'something else'.

In colloquial usage, much use is made of *una cosa*, rather than *qualcosa*, where the speaker or writer knows what 'the thing' is but chooses not to specify its identity:

Aspetta che devo fare una cosa.   'Hang on, I've got to do something.'

but

Hai detto qualcosa?   'Did you say something?'

Other expressions for 'something':

● *Un che* (or *un non so che*) 'something', 'something or other', a 'je ne sais quoi':

La sua voce aveva un (non so) che di minaccioso.   'His voice had something menacing.'

● *Alcunché* 'something or other' (rare, and usually found in negative constructions):

Qui non c'è alcunché di strano.   'There's nothing strange here.'

Also *un nonnulla*:

Mi tradireste per un nonnulla.   'You'd betray me for the merest trifle.'

● Colloquial *coso* 'thingummyjig', 'thingummybob', 'whatsit':

Devi metterci il coso, la cimice.   'You have to put a thingummyjig in it, a drawing pin.'

Coso has even spawned a verb (limited to informal and jocular language) *cosare*:

Stava in giardino a cosare.   'He was doing this and that in the garden.'

9.5 *Qualcos'altro* or *altro* 'something else', *qualcun altro* or *altri* 'somebody else', 'another [person]'

In addition to *qualcos'altro* and *qualcun altro* there is *altro* and the singular subject pronoun *altri* (the latter, which refers only to persons, belongs to more elevated registers and is rather similar to the English singular pronoun 'another' referring to persons):

---

[1] *Forse qualcosa era loro sfuggita* is also possible, however.

Ha terminato o vuole qualcos'altro?	'Have you finished or do you want something else?'
Ho ben altro in mente.	'I have something quite different in mind.'
Altri spiegherà i misteri delle stelle. Noi ci contentiamo di questi bei prati.	'Another will explain the mysteries of the stars. We are happy with these fine meadows.'

Note:

Altro è parlare altro è fare.	'It's one thing to talk, and another to act.'

'Other people' is usually plural *altri*:

Capii che altri c'erano stati molto prima di me.	'I realized that others had been there long before me.'

9.6 *Chi . . . chi . . .* 'some people . . . others . . .'

Chi rideva, chi piangeva.	'Some people laughed, others cried.'
Parlavano tutti una lingua straniera, chi il francese chi l'inglese.	'They all spoke a foreign language, some of them French, others English.'

9.7 *Qualche* 'some', 'a few'

Qualche always precedes the noun and is invariant for number and gender. The noun is always *singular*, even though the sense is usually plural (in this respect it might be compared with English 'the odd problem' = 'a few problems').

Gli occhi cercano un posto dove riposare per qualche minuto all'ombra.	'The eyes look for a place to rest a few minutes in the shade.'
Ha qualche amica a Roma.	'He has a few girlfriends in Rome.'

Qualche is sometimes used with singular sense:

Poi il W è una lettera che si sbaglia sempre. Meglio cercare qualche parola più facile. [Cal.]	'But W is a letter you always get wrong. Better to look for some easier word.'
Qualche tempo dopo Lunadro aveva scritto al vicario dell'inquisitore. [Gin.]	'Some time afterwards L had written to the inquisitor's representative.'

Un qualche + noun = 'some . . . or other'

Se ti dovessi fermare per un qualche motivo, me lo diresti.	'If you were to stop for some reason or other, you'd tell me.'

9.8 *Alcun, alcuno* 'some', 'a few', 'a certain number of', 'some (of them)', 'some people'

The singular adjective *alcun* varies exactly like the indefinite article, according to the nature of the following sound (see 4.1): *alcun giorno*, *alcuno studio*, etc. In fact the adjective *alcun* and the pronoun *alcuno* are only rarely encountered in the singular, and then usually in negative constructions where they are equivalent in meaning to *nessun, nessuno* (see 9.11) 'not any . . .':

Non ho alcuna idea.	'I have no idea.'
Non venne alcuno degli invitati.	'None of the guests came.'

In positive constructions, *qualche* is used (e.g., *Ho qualche idea* 'I have some idea' – see 9.7).

In the plural the meaning is 'some', 'a few', 'a certain number': the difference between *alcuni* and *qualche* is not always clear, but *alcuni* underscores the fact that a *certain quantity* of entities are specified, whilst *qualche* draws less attention to the quantity. Very broadly, the difference is close to that between English 'a certain number' (*alcuni*) and 'the odd' (*qualche/qualcuno*):

Alcune rane non vivono nell'acqua.	'Some/Certain frogs don't live in water.'/'There are frogs that don't live in water.'
Dove vendo le mie riviste? Alcune in America, altre qui in Italia.	'Where do I sell my magazines? Some (of them) in America, others here in Italy.'
Ho degli studenti piuttosto mediocri, ma alcuni sono proprio bravini.	'I have rather mediocre students, but some (of them)/certain ones are really smart.'

Roughly equivalent to *alcuni* is *certi* 'certain':

Certi esperti sostengono la inesistenza della vita extraterrestre.	'Certain/Some experts maintain that extraterrestrial life does not exist.'
Ha tirato fuori certi documenti sicuramente falsi.	'He pulled out some/certain documents [which were] certainly false.'

One also encounters what might be described as an 'ironic' or 'understated' use of *certo*, where the meaning is something like 'no ordinary', 'such a . . .':

Se non stai zitto ti darò certe botte!	'If you don't shut up I'll give you such a clouting!'
Era ubriaco e gridava certe parole . . .	'He was drunk and shouting some very rude words . . .'

In some cases, *certo* can be close in meaning to 'uncertain' or 'some . . . or other':

Insomma, hanno presentato certe idee, ma io non ci ho capito niente.	'Well, they presented some ideas or other, but I didn't understand any of it.'
Qui c'è un certo non so che.	'There is a certain something/something or other here.'

Note also:

una signora di un certa età	'a middle-aged lady'

Like *alcuni* but rarer and rather more formal are *taluni* and *certuni*:

Talune proposte sono risultate del tutto inaccettabili.	'Some proposals proved quite unacceptable.'

'A few' may sometimes be expressed, in effect, by negating its opposite (a kind of stylistic device of 'understatement'):[2]

I non molti abitanti che erano rimasti al paese se ne sono andati dopo il terremoto.	'The not many [i.e., the few] inhabitants left in the village went away after the earthquake.'

---

[2]Conversely, 'many' can be expressed by saying 'not a few':

Nella sua relazione abbiamo scoperto non pochi errori.	'In his report we discovered not a few [i.e. a good many] errors.'

9.9 *Chiunque* 'anybody'; *qualunque cosa, qualsiasi cosa* 'anything', 'whatever'; *qualunque, qualsiasi, quale si sia, quale che sia* 'any', 'whichever'; *tutto* 'whichever', 'any'

These correspond to English 'anybody', 'anything', 'any' in the sense of 'no matter who/what', 'who- /whatever', 'just anybody/-thing', 'no matter what /who' and 'whatever', 'whoever', 'anything who-/whatever'.

- For 'anybody', 'anything', equivalents of 'somebody', 'something' in negative or interrogative constructions, as in 'there isn't anybody/anything here', 'is there anybody/anything there?', see 9.11.
- For '-ever' in interrogatives, as in 'Whoever are you?', see 8.9.
- For '-ever' in relative constructions, as in 'Whichever one you want you can have', see 7.18.

Farei qualsiasi cosa pur di rivederlo.	'I'd do anything to see him again.'
Io sono libero di fare qualunque cosa.	'I'm free to do just anything.'
Mangia qualsiasi schifezza.	'He eats any old junk.'
Questo non è un incarico che affiderei a chiunque.	'This isn't a task I'd entrust to just anybody.'
Chiunque può assistere al dibattito.	'Anyone can be present at the debate.'

Equivalent to *qualsiasi/qualunque* is *qualsivoglia*, which is mainly restricted to written language:

Qualsivoglia richiesta verrà respinta.	'Any request will be rejected.'

Literary and archaic equivalents of *chiunque* and *qualunque cosa* are, respectively, *chicchessia, checchessia*:

Non ho paura di parlare di fronte a chicchessia.	'I'm not afraid to speak in front of anybody.'

Un + noun + *qualsiasi/qualunque/qualsivoglia* 'just any', 'any old', 'any you like to mention':

Pensa a un numero qualsiasi.	'Think of any number.'
Io non sono un agricoltore qualunque.	'I'm not just any old farmer.'

Tutto (normally 'all'), may also mean 'whichever', 'any':

Riceve gli studenti a tutte le ore.	'He receives students at any hour.'

9.10 *Da qualche parte* 'somewhere'; *da un'altra parte* or *altrove* 'somewhere else'

Credo di aver dimenticato la mia borsa da qualche parte.	'I think I've left my bag somewhere.'
Questo Manzoni l'avrà scritto altrove ma comunque non nei Promessi sposi.	'M must have written this somewhere else but anyway not in the *Promessi sposi*.'

9.11 Negative pronouns and adjectives: *nessuno* 'nobody', '(not) anybody' and *niente, nulla* 'nothing', '(not) anything', '(not) a thing'; *nessun* 'no', 'not one', '(not) any' (adjective); *niente* 'nothing', '(not) a thing'

● For the presence vs. absence of *non* before the verb when a negative adjective or pronoun occurs in the clause (*Nessuno viene* vs. *Non viene nessuno*), see 18.5. For *niente* and *nessuno* with the meaning 'anything', in questions, see 8.10.

These negative forms are used not only for 'nobody', 'nothing', 'no . . .', but also where English uses 'anybody', 'anything', 'any', 'a thing' with a negated verb. The negating element may be not only *non* but also *senza* 'without':

Non credo che nessuno lo sapesse.	'I don't think anybody knew.'
Gli uomini [. . .] si illudono di dare un corso diverso alla storia, ma non modificano un bel niente . . . [Gua.]	'Men like to think they change the course of history, but they don't change a thing . . .'
Mi trovai solo, senza niente che mi aiutasse.	'I found myself alone without anything to help me.'
Torna e vede la bottega aperta senza dentro nessuno.	'He comes back and sees the shop open without anybody in it.'
L'hanno fatto senza nessuna difficoltà.	'They did it without any difficulty.'

But in negative sentences, *alcuno* may be used in place of *nessuno* (pronoun or adjective) in formal, particularly official/bureaucratic, styles:

Non ha attualmente alcun contratto.	'He does not at present have any contract.'
Non ho visto alcuno.	'I didn't see anyone.'
senza aver visto alcuno	'without having seen anyone'
senza alcuna civetteria, senza nessuna patetica tentazione	'without any flirting, without any pathetic temptations'

When *alcuno* is used as an adjective and is postposed, the stylistic effect is even more formal, e.g., *Non ha attualmente contratto alcuno*. The invariable pronoun *chicchessia*, literary and archaic, can be used only in the singular and referring to + animate to replace *nessuno/alcuno*:

Non ho visto chicchessia.	'I saw no one.'

Note that the adjective *nessun*, etc. (which varies according to the sound at the beginning of the following words in exactly the same way as the indefinite article *un, uno, un', una* in 4.1) is always singular, even though the English equivalent may be plural:

Non ha nessuno scrupolo.	'He has no scruple(s).'
Nessun problema si presentò.	'No problem(s) came up.'

Rarely (usually in academic or technical registers), adjectival *nessun* can be used to mean (adjectival) 'zero', 'nil', 'non-existent'. In this case *nessun* may behave like any other adjective and may, for example, be preceded by an article:

Il lieve o il nessun peso del bambino lo rendeva felice.	'The slight or zero weight of the child made him happy.'

A more common adjective meaning 'nil' is *nullo*:

La somma rimasta è quasi nulla.	'The amount left is almost nil.'

Niente and *nulla* always have masculine agreement, and take *di* when followed by an adjective, except for *altro* 'else':

Nulla è cambiato.	'Nothing's changed.'
Cosa hai visto? Niente di bello.	'What did you see? Nothing nice.'
Non ha fatto nient'altro.	'He did nothing else.'

A variant of *niente/nulla*, restricted to formal styles, is *alcunché* (and also the now rare and archaic *checchessia*), which can only be used in negative sentences where the verb is preceded by *non*:

Non devi temere alcunché.	'You must fear nothing.'
Non vuole mai accettare checchessia.	'He will not accept anything whatsoever.'

Niente (but not *nulla*) can be used, in informal, colloquial, usage, as an alternative to the adjective *nessun* 'no'.[3] Unlike *nessun*, *niente* is invariant for number and gender, but the noun following may be either singular or plural:

Niente gelato per me, grazie.	'No ice cream for me, thanks.'
—*Hai molti amici?*	'Do you have many friends?'
—*No, niente amici qui, e nemmeno nel mio paese.*	'No, no friends here, and not in my village either.'

Niente is employed in informal discourse to mean 'there is/are no', 'there is/are not any':

Niente posta per me?	'(Is there) no mail for me?'
Niente luna, questa sera.	'(There is) no moon this evening.'
Niente lezione oggi?	'(Is there) no class today?'

(Il) nulla and *(il) niente* are nouns meaning 'nothingness', 'nowhere', 'nullity'. When *nulla* and *niente* are used in this way, an accompanying verb is not necessarily preceded by *non*:

Saro se lo trova sempre davanti, sbucato dal nulla, in procinto di sparire nel nulla. [Mar.]	'S is always seeing him, popping out of nowhere, and about to disappear into nowhere'.
Tu sei Dio, io sono nulla.	'You are God, I'm zero/a nobody.'

Also

fare finta di niente	'to act as if nothing were the matter'
Questo è niente!	'That's nothing!'
Si offende per niente.	'She takes offence over a trifle.'

Niente serves as an exclamation, meaning 'Never mind', 'It doesn't matter':

Niente! Torneremo domani.	'Never mind! We'll come back tomorrow.'

---

[3]Another alternative, particularly in informal speech, is *no* placed after the negated noun:

—*Vuoi del gelato?*	'Do you want some ice cream?'
—*Gelato no, fa ingrassare.*	'Not ice cream, it's fattening.'

9.12 *Ogni, ciascun/ciascuno* 'each', 'every'; *ognuno, ciascuno* (rare *ciascheduno*) 'each one', 'each person', 'everybody'

La sua invenzione è in ogni frigorifero del mondo.	'His invention is in every fridge in the world.'
Ogni anno la principessa fa fuori la bellezza di oltre un miliardo e ottocento milioni.	'Every year the princess gets through well over 1800 million.'
Ciascun fiore è stato coltivato qui vicino.	'Each flower was grown near here.'
Ognuno/Ciascuno sa perché fa il partigiano.	'Everyone knows why he is a partisan.'

The difference between *ciascun* and *ciascuno* depends on the nature of the following sound, like the indefinite article *un* and *uno* (see 4.1):

Lo danno a ciascuno studente.	'They give it to each student.'

Only *ogni* can be used with numerals:

Viene ogni dieci giorni.	'He comes every ten days.'

9.13 Distributive *ciascuno, l'uno, cadauno* 'for each one'

Hanno ricevuto diecimila lire l'uno.	'They received 10 000 lire each.'
Li ho pagati otto dollari ciascuno.	'I paid 8 dollars for each one.'

Cadauno (often abbreviated *cad.* in writing) 'each one' is nowadays mainly restricted to the quotation of prices:

magliel L.40 000 cadauna	'sweaters 40 000 lire each'

Also *a testa* 'each':

Abbiamo ordinato una birra a testa.	'We ordered a beer each.'

10

Possessives and related constructions

10.1 The types 'noun + *di* + noun': *le idee di Einstein* = 'the ideas of Einstein'/'Einstein's ideas'

The most common type of 'possessive' structure takes the form 'noun phrase + *di* + noun phrase (representing the possessor)' (cf. English 'the ideas of Einstein' = 'Einstein's ideas'). In reality, the Italian '*di* + noun' construction, like its usual English equivalents 'noun + -'s' and 'of + noun', has a very wide range of functions, many of which have little to do with what we have loosely labelled 'possession'. An account of these functions can be seen in 11.5.

la casa dello zio Salvatore	'Uncle Salvatore's house'
Di chi è quella voce che sentiamo?	'Whose [lit. 'of whom?'] is that voice we can hear?'
Un giorno questa casa sarà tutta di mio nipote.	'One day this house will all be my nephew's.'
Il Banco di Napoli, che era di Napoli dal 1539, è finito nelle mani di INA e BNL. [Rep.]	'The Bank of Naples, which had been Naples' [i.e., had belonged to Naples] since 1539, ended up in the hands of the INA and BNL.'

10.2 Non-use of the possessive adjective: the type *Ho perso l'orologio* 'I've lost my watch'

A major difference between English (like French), on the one hand, and Italian, on the other, is that the Italian possessive adjective tends to be used very sparingly – only, in fact, where the identity of the 'possessor' cannot be easily inferred from context. The possessive adjective is readily omitted, particularly with inalienable attributes of a person (such things as body parts, and thoughts, but also clothes, family members, home and employment and, indeed, the 'car'). One uses instead a noun preceded by an article (usually the definite article):

Ho dimenticato la borsa nell'aereo.	'I've left my bag on the plane.'
Non devi piangere. Dove hai messo il fazzoletto?	'You mustn't cry. Where have you put your handkerchief?'
Il presidente non sempre va in giro con la guardia del corpo.	'The president doesn't always go round with his bodyguard.'
Teneva il giornale sotto la giacca.	'She kept her paper under her jacket.'
Non mi ricordo più dove ho lasciato la macchina.	'I can't remember where I left my car.'
Non viaggia mai senza la moglie.	'He never travels without his wife.'

| *Non esiste un luogo dove sia conservata la memoria fisica di Castaneda: le ceneri sono state infatti sparse al vento nel tanto amato deserto messicano.* | 'There is no one place where C's physical record is preserved: the ashes were scattered to the winds in his much loved Mexican desert.' |

For the type of structure *Gli tocco il naso* 'I touch his nose', see 10.13.

10.3 The type 'John's eyes are green' *Giovanni ha gli occhi verdi*, etc.

What in English is generally expressed as 'possessive + noun + "to be" + predicate', such as 'John's eyes are green', 'The tree's leaves are falling' may also be paraphrased using the verb 'to have': e.g., 'John has green eyes', 'The tree has leaves that are falling', etc. In such cases, Italian regularly uses the structure '*avere* + article + noun + adjective/relative clause'. But this is only the case where the noun expressing the 'thing possessed' is a characteristic and common attribute of the subject. A phrase such as 'Her shop is very profitable' would be, much as in English, *Il suo negozio è molto redditizio*, because a 'shop' is not a characteristic, typical, attribute of a person. But with 'inalienable', typical characteristics, such as body parts, the construction with *avere* + noun, etc., is a normal way of expressing what in English would involve a possessive adjective:

Ha gli occhi verdi.	'His eyes are green.'
Aveva un occhio che gli faceva molto male.	'His eye was hurting him a lot.'
Ha la macchina tutta sporca.	'Her car is all dirty.'
Quella macchina ha il parabrezza incrinato.	'That car's windscreen is cracked.'
L'albero ha le foglie che cominciano a cadere.	'The tree's leaves are beginning to fall.'
Il televisore aveva lo schermo rotto.	'The TV set's screen was broken.'
etc.	

When the 'thing possessed' is a person, such constructions are possible, but tend to be restricted to colloquial usage:

Paola ha il marito che gioca per il Perugia.	'P's husband plays for Perugia.'
Andrea aveva una sorella infermiera.	'A's sister was a nurse.'
etc.	

10.4 Forms of the possessive adjective

| | **Singular** | | **Plural** | |
	M	F	M	F
1sg.	*mio*	*mia*	*miei*	*mie*
2sg.	*tuo*	*tua*	*tuoi*	*tue*
3sg.	*suo*	*sua*	*suoi*	*sue*
1pl.	*nostro*	*nostra*	*nostri*	*nostre*
2pl.	*vostro*	*vostra*	*vostri*	*vostre*
3pl.		*loro*		

The relative possessive (see 7.8) is *cui*.

Unlike English, the third person possessives do not indicate the sex of the possessor in the third person singular. e.g., *la sua faccia* 'his/her/its face'.

What differentiates the Italian possessive adjective from its English counterpart is that the former is really an adjective much like any other, in that:

● With the exception of *loro* and *cui*, which are invariant, the other possessives agree for gender and number with the noun they modify:

Alcune dame non possono neanche sedersi tanto sono elaborate e gonfie le loro gonne.	'Some ladies can't even sit, so elaborate and puffed out are their skirts.'
La brigata nera tornava spesso nei suoi discorsi.	'The black brigade was a recurrent theme in his speeches.'
Era andata ad assicurarsi che non fosse successo nulla alla sua vicina.	'She had gone to make sure nothing had happened to her neighbour.'
Non sopportiamo più la nostra condizione.	'We can't stand our condition any more.'
etc.	

● Just as ordinary noun phrases may begin with a determiner (article, demonstrative, etc., e.g., *il bel ragazzo* 'the handsome lad', *questo bel ragazzo* 'this handsome lad'), so a noun phrase containing a possessive adjective may begin with a determiner. In fact the possessive adjectives are *usually preceded by the appropriate definite article*, so that the normal expression for 'my cat', etc. would be *il mio gatto*, etc., but other determiners – indefinite article, partitive article (or partitive zero), demonstrative, numeral, quantifier – are all possible, and the rules for using or not using the definite, indefinite or partitive determiners with noun phrases containing possessives are exactly the same as those for any other noun phrase (see Chapter 4). Note that the indefinite article + possessive (e.g., *un amico mio/tuo*, etc.) normally corresponds to English type 'a friend of mine/yours', etc.)

Decisero di andare alla polizia e rivelare le loro scoperte.	'They decided to go to the police and reveal their discoveries.'
Non ce la faceva proprio più a sopportare la sua condizione.	'He really couldn't stand his condition any more.'
Hanno approfittato del suo starsene assorta sulla tela.	'They took advantage of her standing engrossed over the canvas.'
Pin vorrebbe fantasticare di bande di ragazzi che lo accettino come loro capo.	'P would like to fantasize about gangs of boys who accept him as their leader.' [cf. 4.14]
Mio signore, fai che io non mi perda ai miei stessi occhi.	'My lord, let me not be lost in my own eyes.'
Sono tuo amico.	'I'm your friend/a friend for you.' [cf. 4.14]
È nostro compito valutare le varie proposte.	'It is our job to assess the various proposals.' [cf. 4.14]
Ci si era posti il problema di suoi legami con la Riforma. [Gin.]	'People had been wondering about the problem of any links of his with the Reformation.' [cf. 4.20]
un mugnaio autodidatta, e un suo compaesano analfabeta [Gin.]	'a self-educated miller, and an illiterate fellow villager of his'
Questo l'hanno detto molti tuoi colleghi.	'Many colleagues of yours have said this.'
Ha respinto ogni mia proposta.	'He rejected my every proposal.'
Non mi piace per niente questa tua idea.	'I really don't like this idea of yours.'
Lo fecero dietro mio suggerimento.	'They did it at my suggestion.' [cf. 4.18]
Lo scopersi con mia grande sorpresa.	'I discovered it to my great surprise.'
Ma non c'è nulla di tuo in tutto questo.	'There's nothing of yours in all this.' [cf. 9.11]

Mio in addressing people, 'my lad', 'my friend', etc., is not preceded by the article:

Vieni qua ragazzo mio. 'Come here, my lad.'

Note certain other phrases with the preposition *a* which contain a possessive without an article: *a sua volta* 'in turn', *a suo tempo* 'in good time/'at the right moment', *in cuor suo* 'in his heart of hearts', *a suo luogo* 'at the right moment/opportunity', *a mie spese* 'at my expense', *a loro danno* 'to their detriment', *a suo confronto* 'compared with him', *a vostro agio* 'at your ease'. With the exception of *a suo luogo* and *a suo tempo*, these expressions can equally be used with the first person, second person and plural possessives (*a mia volta*, etc.).

Non vedevo l'ora di tornare a casa mia.	'I couldn't wait to get back to my home.'
Casa tua mi è sempre sembrata così accogliente.	'Your home has always seemed so welcoming to me.'
La sua casa fu distrutta durante il bombardamento.	'His house was destroyed in the bombing.'

- Like any other adjective, the possessive adjective may precede or follow the noun, although it often precedes. In certain phrases a following adjective is normal:

  Bada ai fatti tuoi. 'Mind your own business.'
  È uno che sa il fatto suo. 'He's somebody who knows what he's doing.'

- Like other adjectives, the possessive may be preceded by modifying adverbs:

  Questo è un atteggiamento molto suo. 'This is an attitude typical of him.'
  L'Italia sarà tutta tua. 'Italy shall be all yours.'

The possessive normally precedes other adjectives:

  Ha ripresentato la sua brillante idea. 'He re-presented his brilliant idea.'

However, adjectives do occasionally precede the possessive:

  Ce la siamo regalata durante l'ultima mia gravidanza. 'We gave it to ourselves as a present during my last pregnancy.'

10.5 The ambiguity of *suo* and *loro*

The Italian possessives do not distinguish the gender of the possessor, either in the plural or in the singular. Hence *il suo tetto* is ambiguous between 'his, her (*or* its) roof' and steps may need to be taken (especially in translating from English) to avoid ambiguity when the context does not make the identity of the possessor clear. One device for avoiding ambiguity involves the use of the phrases *di lui, di lei, di loro*. These normally follow the noun.

  Dovette fingere di parlargli con noncuranza per via della gente, sua madre e la madre di lui, che ascoltava. 'He had to pretend to speak to him unconcernedly because of the people, his mother and his mother [the other person's], who were listening.'

Cosa crede di fare quel pappagalletto appollaiato vicino al padre, come se lo conoscesse da sempre, come se avesse tenuto fra le sue dita le mani impazienti di lui, come se ne conoscesse a memoria i contorni, come se avesse sempre avuto da appena nato gli odori di lui nelle narici, come se fosse stato preso mille volte per la vita da due braccia robuste che lo facevano saltare da una carrozza . . .? [Mar.]	'What does that little parrot of a man perched next to her father think he's up to, as if he has always known him, as if he had held his impatient hands between his fingers, as if he knew their shape by memory, as if he had always had the smell of him in his nostrils from the moment he was born, as if he had been held around the waist a thousand times by two strong arms helping him jump down from a carriage . . .?'

Di lui, di lei, di loro usually follow the noun they modify, but in a certain deliberately archaizing style they are sometimes placed in front. The effect seems to be that of emphasizing the writer's or speaker's detachment from the text, often because what is being described is viewed as bizarre or distasteful. For example, from a newspaper report[1] of an incestuous relationship between a father-in-law and a daughter-in-law:

Una vicenda per molti versi penosa, che doveva (penosamente) risolversi nel privato, è diventata oggetto di scherno e di curiosità morbosa. Una vittima c'è già stata: il di lui figlio (e di lei marito) è uscito di testa, gridando a tutti il suo dolore di uomo doppiamente tradito.	'A story which was in many respects painful and which should have been sorted out (painfully) in private, has become a matter for derision and morbid curiosity. There has already been one victim: his son (and her husband) went out of his mind, bawling to everybody the distress he felt as a doubly betrayed man.'

In colloquial usage *suo* and *di lui/lei* are sometimes combined:

Alla fine Mara ha preso la sua macchina di lui.	'In the end M took his car.'

The possessive pronoun corresponding to *di lui*, etc., is *quello di lui*, etc.

Carlo e Maria mi hanno offerto ciascuno la propria macchina. Ho preso quella di lei, non quella di lui.	'C and M each offered me their car. I took hers not his.'

10.6 Possessive adjective + nouns denoting close relatives: 'my father' = *mio padre*

The definite article does not occur with a possessive adjective preceding *singular* nouns denoting family members: this is invariably true of *padre* 'father', *madre* 'mother', *figlio* 'son', *figlia* 'daughter', and usually the case with *sorella* 'sister', *fratello* 'brother', *nonno* 'grandfather', *nonna* 'grandmother', *nipote* 'nephew', 'grandchild', *zio* 'uncle', *zia* 'aunt', *cugino* 'cousin', *cugina* 'cousin', *moglie* 'wife', *marito* 'husband', *suocero* 'father-in-law', *suocera* 'mother-in-law', *nuora* 'daughter-in-law', *genero* 'son-in-law', *cognato* 'brother-in-law', *cognata* 'sister-in-law', etc. But the article is always present:

---

[1]Cited by Palermo (1998).

- with plural forms;
- with singular forms if they are modified by adjectives, suffixes or prefixes;
- if the possessive adjective is *loro*;
- in the (rare) cases where the possessive is placed after the noun.

Si dice che Nicoletta attenda un figlio da suo marito.	'N is said to be expecting a child by her husband.'
Fanno entrare sua sorella che lo consoli.	'They bring his sister in to console him.'
Un poco assomiglia a sua nonna.	'She is a bit like her grandmother.'
Ma non può essere nostro cugino. È nato prima di nostra zia!	'But he can't be our cousin. He was born before our aunt!'
È stato «riavvistato» assieme alla sua ex moglie.	'He has been spotted again with his ex-wife.'
Mi riferivo al suo defunto padre.	'I was referring to his late father.'
Paolo è il suo figlio minore.	'P is his younger son.'
Era anni che non vedeva il suo nipotino.	'He hadn't seen his grandson for years.'
Questo è il mio figliolo.	'This is my son.'
Tutti rispettano il loro padre.	'Everyone respects their father.'
Non ti scordare mai della madre tua.	'Never forget your mother.'

The article is commonly (but not obligatorily) used with possessive + *babbo* 'dad' and *mamma* 'mum'. It is usually employed before the possessive with *patrigno* 'stepfather', *matrigna* 'stepmother', *padrino* 'godfather' and *madrina* 'godmother' and usually with *figlioccio* 'godson' and *figlioccia* 'goddaughter'. The article is generally omitted from the possessive in the formula *Tuo Michele, Vostro Paolo,* etc., used in signing letters (but *Il tuo affezionato Michele*, etc., where the name is modified by an adjective).

10.7 Possessive pronouns: 'It's his' = *È il suo;* 'It's Maria's' = *È quello di Maria*

Adjectives can be pronominalized (see 5.9) by placing a determiner in front of them (e.g., *il bianco* or *quello bianco* 'the white one', *uno bianco* 'a white one', *tre bianchi* 'three white ones', etc.). Possessive adjectives are very similar. The possessive pronouns 'mine', 'hers', etc., are simply 'determiner (usually the definite article) + possessive adjective'. The possessive pronoun agrees in number and gender with the noun for which it stands:

Questa è una tua, non una mia.	'This is one of yours, not one of mine.'
Pare che l'onorevole Bossi [. . .] oscilli fra la ventina scarsa di deputati che avrebbe con i soli voti dei suoi e i cento che avrebbe chiesto all'Ulivo . . . [Esp.]	'It seems that Mr B is wavering between the bare score of MPs that he would have with the votes of his own [people] alone and the hundred he has reportedly asked the Olive Tree for . . .'

Italian has two equivalents to English 'one of mine/yours/his', etc. In addition to *uno mio, uno tuo, uno suo,* etc., *una mia, una tua, una sua,* one can say *uno dei miei, uno dei tuoi, uno dei suoi,* etc., *una delle mie, una delle tue, una delle sue.* There is a slight difference between them: in *Non ho bisogno di una penna, ho una tua* 'I don't need a pen, I've got one of yours', *ne ho una tua* simply states that I have one, and that it is yours, whereas *ho una delle tue* would imply not only that I have a pen that is yours, but that it is one of a larger number of pens which are yours (cf. 10.8). The same distinction can be made after numerals, *qualcuno* and *alcuno*:

Dammene qualcuno tuo /dei tuoi.	'Give me one of yours.'
Non ha bisogno della radio perché ne ha già due mie /delle mie.	'He doesn't need the radio because he already has two of mine.'
Ne sono arrivati alcuni vostri/dei vostri.	'Some of yours have arrived.'

In English 'noun + 's' can also be used as a possessive pronoun, so that 'Maria's' in the phrase 'I want Maria's' means 'I want the one belonging to Maria'. The Italian equivalent is *Voglio quello di Maria*, literally 'that of Maria', where *quello* agrees for gender and number with the noun it refers to:

Ho trovato la valigia mia ma non quella di Paolo.	'I've found my own suitcase but not Paolo's.'
Questi spaghetti sono buoni, ma quelli di mia madre sono molto più buoni.	'This spaghetti is good, but my mother's is much nicer.'

10.8 The types *Quella valigia è mia* vs. *Quella valigia è la mia*

What is the difference between the type *Quella valigia è mia* (with predicative possessive adjective) and the type *Quella valigia è la mia* (with possessive pronoun), both of which might be expressed in English by 'that suitcase is mine'? It is exactly the difference between *Quella valigia è pesante* 'That suitcase is heavy' and *Quella valigia è la pesante* 'That suitcase is the heavy one'. In other words, the type *Quella valigia è la mia* serves to *pick out* or *select* the suitcase as being 'mine' (etc.), from among a number of possibilities – i.e., 'That suitcase is [the one which is] mine'; *Quella valigia è mia* simply asserts that I am the possessor of the suitcase.

10.9 Some idioms with possessive pronouns

Ho perso tutto il mio.	'I've lost all I possess.'
Come stanno i tuoi?	'How are your folks?' (i.e., parents, family)
Ne sta facendo una delle sue.	'He's misbehaving as usual.'/'He's up to his old tricks.'
E così il nostro non fu tentato di dire la sua quando apparvero ad esempio gli ampi studi di Eino Roiha.	'And thus our man [i.e., the subject of this book] was not tempted to have his say/speak his mind when, for example, the extensive studies of ER appeared.'

10.10 What is the difference between *ne* and the possessive adjectives? *Ammira la sua intelligenza* vs. *Ne ammira l'intelligenza*

In most cases, the possessive adjectives *suo* and *loro* and the clitic *ne* (see 6.13) are interchangeable, except that *ne* cannot be used reflexively (i.e. it cannot be used to mean 'his/her/their own' or 'of him-/herself', 'of themselves'). Thus *Silvia ne fa vedere l'intelligenza* and *Silvia fa vedere la sua intelligenza* can both correspond to *Silvia fa vedere l'intelligenza di Alessandro* 'S shows A's intelligence', but only *Silvia fa vedere la sua intelligenza* is possible if the meaning is that Silvia shows her own intelligence. Likewise *Ne parla sempre* can correspond to *Parla sempre di lui* 'He always speaks about him' but not to *Parla sempre di sé* 'He always speaks about himself'.

10.11 *Proprio,* 'own'

The possessive adjective *proprio* 'own' can mean 'my own', 'your own', 'his own', 'her own', 'one's own', 'our own', 'their own'. It generally precedes the noun.

Infrangeva tanto più facilmente le regole dell'alta cucina in quanto ciò corrispondeva ai propri gusti.	'He broke the rules of haute cuisine all the more easily because that corresponded to his own tastes.'
Vale la pena di dare la propria vita per mettere fine al tradimento.	'Its worth sacrificing your [own] life to put an end to the betrayal.'
In realtà, non era dai libri che Menocchio avevo tratto la propria cosmogonia. [Gin.]	'Books were not really where M had acquired his [own] theory of the cosmos.'

Proprio may also be preceded by a possessive adjective indicating person and number of the possessor; this is *usually* the case with first and second person possessor:

Volevo il mio proprio letto.	'I wanted my own bed.'
Ma avete abbandonato il vostro proprio giardino.	'But you've abandoned your own garden.'

In indefinite constructions (cf. 6.29), there is a difference of meaning between *il proprio* and *il suo proprio*:

Ci si interroga sul proprio destino.	'One wonders about one's fate.'
Ci si interroga sul suo proprio destino.	'One wonders about his [i.e., someone else's] own fate.'

In the first of the above examples *suo* would be impossible in the sense 'one's own'; in the second *proprio* could be omitted without changing the meaning, but *suo* could not be (unless one said *sul proprio destino di Paolo* – which is marginally acceptable).

Proprio may also be used as a possessive pronoun:

Spedì la lettera di Ubaldo e la propria.	'He sent U's letter and his own.'
Poteva prendere la penna di Giulio, ma preferiva scrivere con la propria.	'He could have taken G's pen, but he preferred to write with his own.'

10.12 *Altrui* = 'someone else's', 'other people's'

The invariant *altrui* is encountered only in elevated styles. It usually follows the noun:

Non ripeteva pappagallescamente opinioni o tesi altrui.	'He did not just parrot other people's views or propositions.'
Si servì dei rottami del pensiero altrui come di pietre e mattoni.	'He used the flotsam and jetsam of other people's thought as stones and bricks.'

The pronominal form is *l'altrui* :

È impossibile difendere i propri diritti senza difendere gli altrui.	'It is impossible to defend one's own rights without defending other people's.'
L'altrui opinione deve essere sempre rispettata.	'Other people's opinion must always be respected.'

A more common structure is *quello altrui, quelli altrui,* etc., where *quello* is the pronoun and *altrui* the adjective.

10.13 The 'possessor' expressed as indirect object: *Morde la mano al professore* 'He bites the teacher's hand'; *Gli morde la mano* 'He bites his hand'

We include this construction here only because it usually corresponds to a possessive in English. But 'possession' is not, strictly speaking, quite what is involved. Rather, the Italian construction expresses that state of affairs such that by doing something to Y, we are also doing something to X, because Y is a part of X. So, if a dog 'bites the teacher's hand', it is also thereby 'biting the teacher', and if we 'shake the president's hand' we may not be exactly 'shaking the president', but we are definitely doing something which affects the president, say, 'greeting the president' (cf. also 11.18). We might think of 'Y' as the 'immediately affected' element (here, 'the hand'), and 'X' as the 'intermediately affected' element. In Italian the 'immediately affected' element usually appears as the direct object of the verb (but see below), and the 'intermediately affected' element as the indirect object (i.e., it is preceded by the preposition *a*):

Morde la mano al professore.	'He bites the teacher's hand.'
Stringiamo la mano al presidente.	'We shake the president's hand.'

Under certain circumstances the 'immediately affected' element may also be the *subject* of the verb. This is possible with all intransitive verbs which take *essere* as their auxiliary (we explain in 14.20 how the subjects of such verbs may be seen as, in certain respects, 'undergoing' or 'being affected by' the verb), but it is also possible with a few intransitive verbs which take *avere* but whose subjects may none the less be viewed as being 'affected by' the action of the verb, rather than carrying out that action (e.g., *brillare* 'to shine', *sudare* 'to sweat'). Many speakers feel that constructions of this kind are most natural when the 'intermediately affected' element takes the form of a clitic pronoun; where it is a noun or noun phrase, that noun phrase generally precedes the verb:

Gli occhi gli dolevano molto.	'Their eyes ached badly.'
Agli studenti dolevano molto gli occhi.	'The students' eyes ached badly.'
Le caddero le braccia.	[lit.] 'Her arms fell.' (= She gave up in despair.)
A Carla caddero le braccia.	'C gave up in despair.'
La pentola le scivolò tra le mani.	'The saucepan slipped through her hands.'
Alla ragazza la pentola scivolò tra le mani.	'The saucepan slipped through the girl's hands.'
Gli occhi gli brillarono per un attimo.	'His eyes shone for a moment.'
Al gatto gli occhi brillarono per un attimo.	'The cat's eyes shone for a moment.'

Only if the subject noun phrase is 'heavy' (e.g., modified by several adjectives, or by a complex adjectival phrase, or by a relative clause), is it possible to place the 'intermediately affected' element after the verb:

Dolevano molto gli occhi agli studenti stanchi dopo tante ore di studio.	'The eyes of the students, tired after so many hours of study, ached.'
Gli occhi brillarono per un attimo al gatto che ci aveva appena intravisti.	'The eyes of the cat who had just glimpsed us shone for a moment.'

Naturally, an expression of the type *Morde la mano del professore* (instead of *Morde la mano al professore*) is possible, but this would tell us nothing about whether the teacher is affected by the action, and such an utterance might even be made in the unhappy event of the hand having been amputated from the teacher. Compare also the following:

Pettinava i capelli alla sua padrona.	'She combed her mistress's hair.' [i.e., she groomed her mistress by combing her hair]
Pettinava i capelli della sua padrona.	'She combed her mistress's hair.' [i.e., perhaps where the hair has been cut off and made into a wig for somebody else]

The 'immediately affected' element is most commonly a body part:

Taglio le unghie a mia figlia.	'I cut my daughter's nails.'
Lavarono mani e piedi al bimbo.	'They washed the baby's hands and feet.'
Ruppe un braccio a suo fratello.	'He broke his brother's arm.'
Toccava la mano a te, non a me.	'He touched your hand, not mine.'
Uno strappo sul pantalone gli metteva a nudo il ginocchio. Il giovane si guardò anche lui lo strappo. [Cas.]	'A tear on his trousers left his knee bare. The youth looked at his tear as well.' [*si* is the indirect object reflexive: the tear is in his *own* trousers]
I tratti le si sono deformati, dilatati e gli occhi le si sono infossati.	'Her features have become deformed and swollen and her eyes have become sunken.'
Le parole le si confondono. Le mani le si bagnano di lacrime.	'Her words get muddled. Her hands get wet with tears.'

As the first sentence of the last example shows, the construction is also encountered with reference to entities viewed as intimately or habitually associated with the 'intermediately affected' element, even if not an inherent part of it: e.g., thoughts, clothes, the home (and its parts), family members, and even the motor car:

Hanno rubato la camicia al professore.	'They stole the teacher's shirt.'
Abbiamo offerto di lavare la macchina a Franco.	'We offered to wash Franco's car.'
una donna a cui sono stati uccisi il marito e il figlio	'a woman whose husband and son have been killed'
Camminava leggero come un gatto, come qualcuno che tema d'impolverarsi le scarpe.	'He walked as lightly as a cat, like someone afraid of getting dust on his shoes.'

There are no possessive adjectives with the 'immediately affected' element. Instead, indirect object clitic pronouns are employed:

Le stringevate la mano.	'You were shaking her hand.'

Le taglio le unghie.	'I cut her nails.'
Gli lavarono mani e piedi.	'They washed his hands and feet.'
Gli ruppe un braccio.	'He broke his arm.'
Per un attimo gli brillarono gli occhi (or *brillarono loro gli occhi*).	'For a moment their eyes shone.'
Abbiamo offerto di lavargli la macchina.	'We offered to wash his car.'
Gli è morta la moglie.	'His wife died.'
Le correvano tra i piedi.	'They were running between her feet.'
I capelli le si erano incollati al cranio.	'Her hair had stuck to the top of her head.'

'My', 'your', 'our' are expressed by the corresponding first and second person indirect object clitic pronouns.

Mi si è gonfiata la mano.	'My hand has swollen up.'
Ti ruberanno anche la camicia.	'They'll even steal your shirt.'
Ci tolgono le scarpe.	'They remove our shoes.'
State attenti che cercheranno di rubarvi la macchina.	'Careful, they'll try to steal your car.'
Mi è entrato in camera.	'He entered my room.'

Where the subject carries out some action on itself, the indirect object may of course take the form of a reflexive pronoun:

Stefano si accarezza la barba.	'S strokes his [own] beard.'
L'ultima moda delle quattordicenni?	'The latest fashion among fourteen-year-old girls? Painting their nails.'
Dipingersi le unghie.	

Note the distinction between reflexive and non-reflexive pronouns in the third person:

Gli ruppe un braccio.	'He broke his [someone else's] arm.'
Si ruppe un braccio.	'He broke his [own] arm.'
etc.	

10.14 The types *Mi lavo le mani* = 'I wash my hands' and *Chiude gli occhi* = 'He closes his eyes'

When the subject of the verb is also the 'intermediately affected' element (i.e., one is doing something to part of oneself, as in 'I wash my hands'), then an indirect object reflexive pronoun is virtually obligatory. In effect, one says 'I wash the hands to myself':

Mi lavo la faccia.	'I wash my face.'
Si mangia le unghie.	'He bites his nails.'
Vi tingete i capelli?	'Do you dye your hair?'
Mario si ruppe un braccio.	'M broke his arm.'
Toccatevi i piedi.	'Touch your feet.'

A sentence such as *Mario ruppe il suo braccio* is possible, but will be interpreted as meaning that Mario broke somebody else's arm, not that he broke his own. A sentence such as *Lavo le mie mani* is unlikely, but might be uttered where the possessive is contrastive (e.g., *Lavo le mie mani, non le tue* 'I'm washing my hands, not yours').

In the above examples, the action expressed by the verb originates *outside* the object of the verb. Thus, the washing of the face may be viewed as being done by the hands, the biting of the nails by the mouth, and so forth. But there are other cases where the action, even though ultimately caused by the subject, *appears* to originate and take place purely *within* the object of the verb. Examples might be 'He closes his eyes', 'He wrinkles his nose', 'She opens her mouth', and so forth, where the action seems to originate inside 'the eyes', 'the nose' and 'the mouth' themselves – note how easily in English these expressions are paraphrased as 'His eyes close', 'His nose wrinkles', 'Her mouth opens', etc. In such cases, where the action is viewed as originating within the object, the (reflexive) indirect object pronoun is not used and one says in Italian simply 'He closes the eyes', 'He wrinkles the nose', 'She opens the mouth', etc.:

Andrea apre gli occhi.	'A opens his eyes.'
Arriccia il naso.	'He wrinkles his nose.'
Tira fuori la lingua.	'He sticks his tongue out.'
Alzò un dito.	'She raised a finger.'
Scrolla il capo.	'He shakes his head.'

Of course it is still *possible* to say *Si apre gli occhi*, etc., but such a phrase would be most likely to be uttered in a context where an external agency (e.g., the fingers) is invoked:

È riuscita ad aprirsi gli occhi con le dita.	'She managed to open her [own] eyes with her fingers.'

10.15 A special use of the indirect object with verbs of perception and acknowledgement: *Gli sentivo la voce rauca* 'I could hear that his voice was hoarse', etc.

È la prima volta che gli vedo questa cravatta.	'It's the first time I've seen him with that tie on.'
Il medico la visitò e le scoperse un difetto al cuore.	'The doctor examined her and found [that she had] a heart defect.'
Gli sentivo la voce rauca.	'I could hear that he had a hoarse voice/that his voice was hoarse.'

In elevated registers, the same structure can be used with verbs of acknowledgement and recognition:

Gli riconosciamo molta generosità.	'We recognize that he has great generosity.'
Con tutti i pregi che riconosco al nuovo preside, non pare la persona adatta.	'For all the virtues that I acknowledge in the new headmaster, he doesn't seem the right person.'

Prepositions

11.1 Structure and syntax of prepositions: *a(d)*, *di*, etc.; *davanti alla scuola*, *verso di te*, etc.

Prepositions precede the noun or noun phrase they govern (but see 11.2), and some of the commonest prepositions comprise a single, often monosyllabic, word, such as: *a* 'to' (often *ad* before a vowel, especially where the following vowel is a stressed *a*: *ad Anna*); *da* 'from', 'by'; *dentro* 'inside'; *di* 'of' (often *d'* before a vowel, especially where the following word begins with *i*); *fra*/*tra* 'between' or 'among'; *fuori* 'outside'; *in* 'in(to)'; *lungo* 'along'; *oltre* 'beyond'; *per* 'for'; *salvo* 'save', 'apart from', 'bar'; *senza* 'without'; *sopra* 'over', 'above'; *sotto* 'under', 'beneath'; *su* 'on'; *tranne* 'except'. But there are also complex prepositions, the last element of which is *a* (or sometimes *di*, *da*, *con*), such as: (*al*) *di là di* (or *da*) 'beyond'; *al di sotto di* 'beneath'; *a causa di* 'because of'; *a confronto di* 'compared with'; *addosso a* 'onto', 'on top of'; *a fianco a* 'beside'; *al di sopra di* 'above'; *allato a* 'beside'; *davanti a* 'before', 'in front of', 'opposite' (also 'by' in expressions of motion past something); *accanto a* 'beside'; *dirimpetto a* 'opposite'; *in confronto a* 'compared with'; *incontro a* 'towards'; *insieme*/*assieme a* (or *con*) 'together with'; *intorno* (*attorno*) *a* 'around'; *invece di* 'instead of'; *per via di* 'because of'; *prima di* 'before'; *riguardo a* 'regarding'; *rispetto a* 'regarding', 'compared with'; *vicino a* 'near to'. Note the distinction between *fuori di* 'outside' (position, location) and *fuori da* 'out of' (motion out):

I cioccolatini erano fuori della scatola.	'The chocolates were out of/outside the box.'
Ha tirato i cioccolatini fuori dalla scatola.	'He pulled the chocolates out of the box.'

A number of complex prepositions (many of them indicating physical position) have the form *in* + noun + *a*: *in base a* 'on the basis of'; *in mezzo a* 'in the middle of'; *in fondo a* 'at the bottom of'; *in cima a* 'at the top of'; *in barba a* 'in the teeth of' (figuratively); *in faccia a* 'in the face of'; *in margine a* 'in the margin'/'at the edge of', etc.

In some complex prepositions the second *a* is optional: *attraverso* (*a*) 'across'; *contro* (*a*) 'against'; *dentro* (*a*) 'in', 'inside'; *dietro* (*a*) 'behind' (or 'round' a corner); *lungo* (*a*) 'along'; *presso* (*a*) 'by', 'with', 'at'; *rasente* (*a*) 'hard along'; *sopra* (*a*) 'on', 'above'; *sotto* (*a*) 'under(neath)'. *Oltre* 'beyond' must be distinguished from *oltre a* 'in addition to', and *dietro* (usually) 'behind a stationary object' from *dietro a* (usually) 'after', 'behind a moving object':

Oltre la siepe c'è un albero.	'Beyond the hedge there's a tree.'
Oltre alla siepe c'è un albero.	'In addition to the hedge there's a tree.'
Corse dietro alla macchina che si allontanava.	'He ran after the car as it drew away.'
Corse dietro la macchina parcheggiata all'ingresso.	'He ran behind the car parked at the entrance.'

Some prepositions must be followed by *di* if they govern a personal pronoun from the series *me, te, sé, lui, lei, noi, voi, loro*: *contro di* 'against'; *dietro di* 'behind'; *entro di* 'within'; *presso di* 'by', 'at'; *sopra di* 'on', 'above'; *sotto di* 'under'; *su di* 'on', 'about'; *verso di* 'towards':

Su di lei ha letto un libro stampato a Roma.	'She's read a book about her printed in Rome.'

Other prepositions are only *optionally* followed by *di*, when they govern a personal pronoun from the series *me, te, sé, lui, lei, noi, voi, loro*: e.g., *dopo* (*di*) 'after', *senza* (*di*) 'without', *tra/fra* (*di*) 'between', 'among':

È uscito dopo (di) te.	'He went out after you.'
Chiacchieravano tra (di) loro.	'They were chatting among themselves.'

But note that *di* is not usually present if the pronoun is in any way modified, or if it is conjoined with another word:

Abito presso loro due.	'I live with them both.'
Conta su se stesso.	'He counts on himself.'
Non viaggia mai senza te e mamma.	'He never travels without you and mum.'

Note the use of *di* in phrases of the form 'demonstrative + evaluative noun (expressing admiration or dislike) + noun':

quel cretino di Marco	'that idiot M'
quel genio di Nunzio	'that genius N'

11.2 'Stranding' of prepositions: *A chi ti sei seduto accanto?* 'Who did you sit next to?', etc.

In interrogative and relative structures, prepositions cannot usually be left 'stranded' to the right of the noun they govern, as they may be in spoken English; rather they must always precede the noun, noun phrase or pronoun which they govern:

A chi hai dato la chiave?	'Who(m) did you give the key to?'
Questa è la ragazza a cui ho dato la chiave.	'This is the girl that I gave the key to.'
Fu in Italia che morì, non in Spagna.	'It was Italy that he died in, not Spain.'
Di che cosa parlavate?	'What were you talking about?'

Note also

Perché hai fatto questo?	'What did you do this for?'

However, in *some* complex prepositions of the type *accanto a* (*a fianco a, davanti a, dentro a, dirimpetto a, dietro a, addosso a, insieme a/con, intorno/attorno a, sopra a, contro a, sotto a, oltre a, vicino a*) only the *a* need precede the noun phrase, while the first element *may* be left 'stranded'. The same is true of *presso a* when it means 'nearby', but not when it means 'at', 'with':

A chi ti sei seduta accanto?	'Who did you sit next to?'
la tavola alla quale s'è nascosto sotto	'the table he hid under'
la persona alla [or *con la*] *quale vivo insieme*	'the person I live together with'

Of course, the phrase *a* + noun may be replaced by an appropriate 'indirect object' pronoun (see 6.2) *ci, gli, le, loro, si*:

Gli è andato incontro tutto il battaglione.	'The whole battalion went to meet them.'
Mario se la trova sempre davanti.	'M is always finding her before him(self).'

A special case is constituted by *su* and *sopra* which can be 'stranded' only in association with the clitic pronoun *ci* (cf. 6.11):

Ci si è seduto su/sopra.	'He sat on it.'
Ci devo pensare su sopra.	'I must think about it.'

Note the possibility of deleting, in informal language, the noun or pronoun following *senza*:

È rimasto senza.	'He ran out [e.g., of money].'
Ha dovuto fare senza.	'He had to do without [e.g., wine].'

11.3 Obligatory repetition of prepositions: *Mando un libro a Paolo e a Giorgio* 'I send a book to Paolo and Giorgio'

As a general rule, conjoined nouns (nouns linked by *e, ma*, etc.) which are governed by a preposition must each be preceded by that preposition (unlike English, where the preposition need not be repeated):

Il vecchio contadino inglese [. . .] *pensava a Dio come a un «buon vecchio», a Cristo come a un «bel giovanotto», all'anima come a un «grosso osso confitto nel corpo» e all'aldilà come a un «bel prato verde.»* [Gin.]	'The old English peasant thought of God as a "nice old man", (of) Christ as (of) a "fine young man", (of) the soul as (of) a "big bone stuck in his body" and (of) the afterlife as (of) a "fine green lawn".'
Può trattarsi di un figlio, di un nipote, ma anche di un accattone, di un imbroglione, di un avversario al gioco, di una cantante, di una lavandaia, secondo il capriccio del momento. [Mar.]	'It may be about a son, (about) a nephew, but also (about) a beggar, (about) a shyster, (about) a gambling opponent, (about) a singer, (about) a washerwoman, as the fancy takes him.'

Note the distinction between *Pensava a Mario come un figlio* 'He thought of Mario like a son' (i.e., 'as a son would think of Mario') and *Pensava a Mario come a un figlio* 'He thought of Mario as a son.' If the conjoined nouns or pronouns are taken as a 'unit' or a 'set', the preposition need not be repeated:

L'ho preparato per mamma e babbo.	'I prepared it for mum and dad.'
Si recarono nelle vie solitamente frequentate da prostitute, spacciatori e drogati.	'They went into the streets usually frequented by prostitutes, drug-pushers and addicts.'

etc.

11.4 The type *un cassetto con dentro una penna/un cassetto con una penna dentro* 'a drawer with a pen in it'

English makes much use of a structure of the type 'noun + with/without + preposition + pronoun'. For example 'an envelope with your name on it', 'a dress with stripes on it', 'a drawer with/without a pen in it'. Italian never uses a pronoun in such cases and since, in English, the prepositional phrase (e.g., 'in it') is often redundant, Italian simply does not use such a phrase at all:

una busta col tuo nome	'an envelope with your name on it'
OR *una busta che porta il tuo nome*	
un vestito a righe	'a dress with stripes on it' (cf. 11.25, 29)

However, prepositions such as *a fianco, allato, attorno, davanti, dietro, dentro, fuori, intorno, sotto, sopra* – those which can also be 'stranded' (see 11.2) at the end of a clause or sentence – may appear either immediately following *con* or *senza* or after the noun:

un cassetto con dentro una penna	'a drawer with a pen in it'
un cassetto con una penna dentro	
una casa con a fianco un bar	'a house with a bar next to it'
una casa con un bar a fianco	
Trovò il negozio aperto senza dentro nessuno.	'He found the shop open without anyone in it.'
una lettera con sotto una firma illeggibile	'a letter with an illegible signature beneath it'

11.5 The multivalent preposition *di*

Some prepositions – especially the monosyllabic ones (e.g., *a, di, da, su, per*) – have multiple functions which cannot easily be defined in simple terms; many of their grammatical functions are described elsewhere in this grammar. Some are also used as adverbs. Probably the most multivalent of all the prepositions is *di*, and a detailed account of its various uses would be lengthy and complex. But in fact a number of its values happen to be exactly parallel to those of English 'of', for example:

il tramonto del sole	'the setting of the sun'/'sunset'
la presenza di Giorgio	'the presence of George [i.e., George's presence]'
le strade d'Italia	'the roads of Italy'
la città di Roma	'the city of Rome'
studente di matematica	'student of mathematics'
un venditore di libri	'a seller of books [i.e., a bookseller]'
la mancanza di soldi	'the lack of money'
una quantità di sale	'a quantity of salt'
Parlava di Giovanni.	'He was talking of/about G.'
Era accusato di omicidio.	'He stood accused of murder.'
Che gigante d'uomo![1]	'What a giant of a man!'
Si è servito della penna.	'He made use of [i.e. used] the pen.'
Hai bisogno di me.	'You have need of me [i.e., you need me].'

---

[1]See also 11.1.

Whereas constructions of the type 'seller of books' are apt to sound rather odd or stilted in English, the construction 'noun + *di* + noun' is in Italian by far the commonest way of linking one noun with another modifying it. Notice particularly that noun$_a$ + *di* + noun$_b$ corresponds to what in English are often noun$_b$ + noun$_a$ constructions, with noun$_b$ modifying noun$_a$: e.g., 'a walnut table' = 'a table of walnut' = *una tavola di noce*.

'Railways of the State'	*Ferrovie dello Stato*
'State Railways'	
'the teacher of mathematics'	*il professore di matematica*
'the mathematics teacher'	
'the book of accounts'	*il libro dei conti*
'the accounts book'	
'the selling of salt'	*la vendita del sale*
'selling salt'	
'salt selling'	
'the hunter of deer'	*il cacciatore di cervi*
'the deer hunter'	
'the growing of tomatoes'	*la coltivazione dei pomodori*
'tomato growing'	
'the love of her son'	*l'amore del figlio*[2]
'the area of the port'	*la zona del porto*
'the port area'	
'the absence of Mario'	*l'assenza di Mario*
'Mario's absence'	
'the departure of Master Tancredi'	*la partenza del signorino Tancredi*
'Master Tancredi's departure'	
'a pack of wolves'	*un branco di lupi*
'a wolf pack'	
'a watch of gold'	*un orologio d'oro*
'a gold watch'	
'a man of straw'	*un uomo di paglia*
'a straw man'	
'a smell of camphor'	*un odore di canfora*
'a photograph of me in bed'	*una fotografia di me a letto*
'the idea of building a dam'	*l'idea di costruire una diga*
'the proposal of peace'	*la proposta di pace*
'the peace proposal'	
etc.	

Many other roles of *di* (and those of other 'basic' prepositions) appear below.

11.6 Location 'at' or 'in': *in, a, dentro*

Location (both in space and time) is normally expressed by *a* where the location is viewed as a 'point', and *in* when the location is viewed as an 'area'; the distinction is usually similar to that between English 'at' and 'in':

Ci rivedremo alle sei.	'We'll meet again at six.'
A scuola non imparai niente.	'At school I learned nothing.'
Ci fermammo al pozzo.	'We stopped at the well.'

---

[2]In Italian as in English this is ambiguous between the meaning 'She loves her son' and 'Her son loves her'.

Lo trovai nell'aula.	'I found it in the classroom.'
Lo persi in mare.	'I lost it at sea.'
Non siamo mica ai tempi del tuo bisnonno.	'We really aren't [back] in the times of your great-grandfather.'
Arrivò all'ultimo momento.	'She arrived at the last moment.'
È ritornata a mezzanotte.	'She came back at midnight.'
Ci rivedremo a Natale.	'We'll meet again at Christmas.'

Note the obligatory use of *a* in expressions of 'distance away from':

Abita a dieci chilometri da Assisi.	'He lives 10 km away from Assisi.'

A is used for cities, towns, villages, etc., but also small islands (e.g., *ad Ischia*) and some larger islands (e.g., *a Cuba*); otherwise *in* is used (*a Torino* 'in Turin' but *in Piemonte* 'in Piedmont', *in Italia* 'in Italy'). The class of 'large islands' which takes *a* is the same class that does not take the definite article (see 4.7). One could also say *in Torino* where the meaning is literally 'inside/within Turin'. Also *all'estero* 'abroad', *all'interno/esterno di* 'on the outside/inside of'. *A* is used as well for 'to play (at) a game', e.g., *giocare a scacchi /a calcio* 'to play (at) chess/football'.

Another way of expressing 'within', 'inside' is *dentro*. Note that Italian uses *dentro* much more readily than English does 'inside':

L'ho trovato dentro il sacco.	'I found it in(side) the bag.'
Dentro quell'edificio si nasconde un segreto straordinario.	'In(side) that building is concealed an extraordinary secret.'

'In' in expressions such as 'blind in one eye', etc., is *da*:

Cieco da un occhio.	'Blind in one eye.'
Zoppo da un piede.	'Lame in one foot.'

Other expressions corresponding to English 'in' are:

L'ho visto per la strada.	'I saw it in the street.'
La famiglia finì in mezzo alla strada.	'The family ended up in/on the street.'
Lo leggerete sul (or nel) giornale di domani.	'You'll read it in tomorrow's newspaper.'
Al ritorno a casa passeremo da Pavia.	'On the way home we'll go through/stop off in Pavia.'

11.7 'Between', 'among' = *fra* and *tra*

Italian makes no distinction between 'among' and 'between':

Lo vidi tra i suoi amici.	'I saw him among/between his friends.'

Also:

Riconobbi uno fra i suoi amici.	'I recognized one of [i.e., from among] his friends.'

There is absolutely no difference in meaning between *fra* and *tra*, but there is a slight difference in usage, in that *fra* tends to be preferred before words beginning with *tr-* and *tra* before words beginning with *fr-*: *tra fratelli* 'between brothers' but *fra treni* 'between trains'.

Note that *tra/fra* can also mean something like 'what with ... and ...', as in:

Tra la scuola e i figli non ha mai un momento libero.	'What with school and the children she never has a free moment.'

11.8 *Da* + noun/adjective = 'at the time when **X** was . . .', 'as a . . .'

Da giovane ha condotto una vita placida, quasi anonima; da vecchio è diventato una specie di invincibile guerriero. [Ogg.]	'As a young man he led a quiet, almost anonymous, life; as an old man he became a sort of invincible warrior.'

11.9 *Da* as 'to' or 'at' the place where somebody works, lives or is (often equivalent to French *chez*)

Vado dal medico.	'I'm going to the doctor's.'
Vengo da te.	'I'm coming to your place.'
Abito da mio zio.	'I live at my uncle's place.'
Mangiamo da Franco.	'We eat 'chez' Franco/at Franco's restaurant.'
Frequentava il liceo dai francescani.	[lit. 'He went to school at the Franciscans' place'] = 'He was taught at a Franciscan school.'

11.10 'On the one side/hand' *Da un lato/una parte*; 'everywhere', *da ogni parte*

C'era oro da ogni parte.	'There was gold everywhere.'
Da una parte è difficile, dall'altra è facile.	'On the one hand it's difficult, on the other it's easy.'
Non lo trovavo da nessuna parte.	'I couldn't find it anywhere.'
Non sappiamo da che parte iniziare.	'We don't know where to begin.'

But note *d'altronde* 'on the other hand', 'besides'.

11.11 'At', 'near', 'next to', 'chez': *vicino, a fianco, presso*

'Near' is usually *vicino a*; *presso* means 'near', 'nearby', or 'with', 'at' [somebody's home/company = French *chez*]. 'Next to' is *a fianco a, accanto a, allato a*:

Abita vicino/accanto alla chiesa.	'He lives near/next to the church.'
Vivo presso i Rossi.	'I live at the Rossis' place.'
ambasciatore presso la Repubblica italiana	'ambassador to the Italian Republic'

Note that *presso* in the sense of 'chez' is limited to formal usage; the normal term is *a casa di*.

11.12 'Under', 'over'/'above', 'around', 'on', 'beyond', 'in the middle of', etc.: *sotto, sopra, intorno a, su, al di là di, in mezzo a*, etc.

È sul tavolo, sotto il giornale.	'It's on the table, under the newspaper.'
C'è una nube di gas tossico sopra la Francia.	'There is a cloud of toxic gas over France.'
Intorno al monastero c'è un giardino.	'Around the monastery there's a garden.'

Alternatives to *sotto* and *sopra* are *al di sotto di* and *al di sopra di*:

> *Al di sopra del castello volava un'aquila.*   'Above the castle flew an eagle.'

For the type *in mezzo a* 'in the middle of', *in fondo a* 'at the bottom of', etc., see 11.12. Note the distinction between *in mezzo a* 'in the middle of', 'among' and *a metà di* 'halfway through/along':

> *Sono a metà della mia carriera.*   'I'm halfway through my career.'

11.13 Motion 'to', 'towards': *a, da, verso, in, fino a*, etc.

'To' is normally *a* and 'towards' *verso*:

Vado a Roma.	'I'm going to Rome.'
Lo portò a suo padre.	'He carried it to his father.'
Andava verso Roma.	'He was going towards Rome.'
La riunione è stata rimandata a domani.	'The meeting has been put off to/until tomorrow.'
Si diresse subito alla casa dello zio Salvatore.	'He made his way immediately to uncle S's house.'
La prima cosa che fece fu di correre al telefono.	'The first thing he did was to run to the telephone.'

Because *a* is ambiguous between 'to' and 'at' it can be necessary to distinguish 'motion to' from 'location at'. In ambiguous cases, *a* will tend to be interpreted as indicating fixed location: *Prendo un taxi alla stazione* = 'I take a taxi at the station'; *Parlo alle otto* = 'I speak at 8 o'clock'; to indicate spatial or temporal destination/motion towards, an expression such as *sino a/fino a* should be used: *Prendo un taxi fino alla stazione* = 'I take a taxi to the station'; *Parlo fino alle otto* = 'I speak to /until 8 o'clock'.

With verbs of motion such as *andare* and *venire*, *da* followed by a noun referring to a person is the normal way of saying 'to' the place where the person is, or is standing. In fact, one could not use *a* in the following:

Corri dal nonno.	'Run to granddad.'
Andate da Mario, che vi sta aspettando alla fermata.	'Go to Mario; he's waiting for you at the bus stop.'

'Into' is usually *in*. *In* rather than *a* is used with locations viewed as 'areas', rather than 'points' (cf. 11.6), most notably names of countries (but not the names of cities).

Cadde nel pozzo.	'It fell into the well.'
È andato in Francia/in Italia.	'He's gone to France/to Italy.'
Piegò il foglio in quattro.	'He folded the sheet into four.'
Devo cambiare queste lire in dollari.	'I have to change these lire into dollars.'
Ti porterò in un luogo sicuro.	'I'll take you to a safe place.'

Note that 'to enter + noun' is always *entrare in*:

> *È entrato nella stanza.*   'He entered the room.'

The preposition of 'intended destination' is *per*:

l'aereo per Bucarest	'the plane for/to Bucharest'
Parto domani per Malta.	'I leave for Malta tomorrow.'

11.14 Motion 'through', 'across': *attraverso, per, lungo, rasente, da*

Motion 'across' is *attraverso* or *per* (which is also 'through' and 'along').

Camminava attraverso/per i campi:	'He walked across/through the fields.'

'Along' is *per*, or, more specifically, *lungo* 'along', or *rasente* 'hard against'.

Si muovono lentamente lungo il viottolo.	'They move slowly along the lane.'
Entrò di nascosto, rasente al muro.	'He entered secretly, keeping hard against the wall.'

Da can also mean 'through', with reference to an entrance, and 'out of', with reference to an exit:

Non si entra mai dall'ingresso principale, bensì da porticine laterali.	'One never enters through the main door, but through little side doors.'
Buttava acqua sporca dalla finestra.	'She was throwing dirty water out of/through the window.'

11.15 Motion 'from', 'source' (place, time or state from which; origin): *da, di, dentro*

Fu promosso da colonnello a generale.	'He was promoted from colonel to general.'
Nato a Lecce da padre medico e da una baronessa pugliese, conobbe la moglie nei primi anni Sessanta.	'Born in Lecce of a doctor father and a Pugliese baroness, he met his wife in the early sixties.'
Erano appena arrivati da Perugia.	'They had just arrived from Perugia.'

But 'from' is usually *di* after *essere* and before *qui/qua* and *lì/là*:

Quel ragazzo era di Madrid.	'That boy was from Madrid.'
Ma di lì a stringere una vera alleanza ce ne corre.	'But it's a long way from there to forming a real alliance.'

Note (*al*) *di là di* or *da*:

Ha una famiglia di là dal mare.	'He has a family beyond/over the sea.'

'From ... to ...' in phrases such as 'from place to place', is usually *di ... in ...*

andare di città in città	'to go from town to town'
Cambia di volta in volta.	'It changes from time to time.'
saltare di palo in frasca	[lit. 'to leap from stake to frond'] 'to beat about the bush', 'talk in a meandering way'

When 'from' means 'from within', *dentro* is often used:

L'ho preso dentro il cassetto.	'I took it out of the drawer'.

'To ask from' or 'of' somebody is *chiedere a*:

Chiese un consiglio a Mario.	'He asked for some advice from/of M.'

Note that *chiedere di* means 'ask after/about somebody'.

'To suffer from rheumatism (etc.)' is *soffrire di reumatismo* (etc.).

11.16 Spatial or temporal separation/distance from some point ('from', 'since'): *da*

Abita a dieci chilometri da Assisi.	'He lives 10 kilometres from Assisi.'
Le montagne ci dividono dal mare.	'The mountains separate us from the sea.'

11.17 Accompaniment: (*insieme*) *con*

'With' is *con*; 'together with' *insieme* (*assieme*) *con/a*:

Ballò con Giovanni.	'She danced with G.'
Proprio la settimana avanti andava al campo insieme a una zia e a un'altra donna.	'Just the week before she was going to the field together with an aunt and another woman.'

11.18 'Recipient' or 'beneficiary'(including the 'indirect object' of verbs): *a per*

As in English, the preposition *a* marks that person or thing to whom or which something is done:

Il partito ostile alla Corona e a Carlo re è pericolosamente in crescita.	'The party hostile to the Crown and to Charles as king is growing dangerously.'
Lunadro aveva scritto al vicario dell'inquisitore.	'L had written to the inquisitor's representative.'
Dico ai ragazzi che non ho soldi.	'I tell (say to) the boys that I have no money.'
Paolo dà brevi ordini ai compagni.	'P gives brief orders to his companions.'
È giusto concedere la libertà a Craxi?	'Is it right to allow [to] C his freedom?'

A can also mark the person or thing 'to whose advantage or disadvantage' something is done. *A* + noun used in this way is sometimes known as the 'dative of interest'; some of its uses shade into what is expressed in English by a possessive (e.g., *Morde la mano al professore* 'He bites the teacher's hand'), and these are examined in 10.13, 14. With the 'dative of interest', *a* + noun is in fact an indirect object of the verb, and it indicates, roughly, that through doing something to the direct object noun one is also doing something to the indirect object noun:

Ho rifatto il letto a Paolo.	'I've remade P's bed for him.'
Hanno rotto il tergicristallo alla machina.	'They broke the windscreen wiper on the car.'
Devo pulire la stanza alla signora prima di farle la spesa.	'I must clean madam's room before doing the shopping for her.'

It would be perfectly possible to use *per* in *Ho rifatto il letto per Paolo* or *Devo pulire la stanza per la signora prima di fare le spese per lei* but in this case there is no necessary implication that *Paolo* or *la signora* are in any way 'advantaged' by the action: they may simply have given orders for the bed to be made and the room to be cleaned, etc., perhaps on behalf of somebody else. If *a* is used, in contrast, there is a strong implication that it is Paolo's bed that has been remade and that he will sleep in it, and that it is the lady who will use the cleaned room, etc. Similarly, *alla machina* implies that the car is damaged by having its windscreen wiper broken, whereas *della macchina* would tell us that the wiper came from the car, but not necessarily that the car was damaged by its being broken (the car

might even no longer exist). This construction seems to be particularly characteristic of informal, colloquial usage; in more formal registers the more 'neutral'
prepositions *per*, *da*, etc., might be used.

'Disadvantage' can also include 'removal', and *a* may mark someone or something from whom or which something is taken away. In this case, use of *a* is
acceptable in any register:

Un giorno il Signore vorrà togliermi a	'One day the Lord will want to take me
questo mondo.	away from this world.'
Ho rubato il libro allo studente.	'I stole the book from the student.'
Li prendemmo a Wanda.	'We took them from W.'

Note that in the following case Italian uses *a* where English would use 'for':

Ho lasciato un messaggio a Italo.	'I left a message for I.'

11.19 Exclusion: *tranne* or *tranne che*, *meno* or *meno che*, *salvo*, *eccetto*, *fuorché*, *al di fuori di* 'except'; *a parte* 'apart from'

Ha mangiato tutto tranne (che)/a parte	'He ate everything except/apart from
la torta.	the cake.'

11.20 'Concessive' prepositions: *malgrado, nonostante* 'despite'

È un libro scritto da una bambina, o meglio	'It's a book written by a child, or rather
da una ragazzina di 12 anni. Ma malgrado	a little girl of 12. But despite that it's not
ciò non è un libro 'facile'.	an "easy" book.'
Quando muore, il poveretto è considerato	'When he dies, the poor chap is
dagli investigatori un'altra seccatura da	considered by the investigators as just
affrontare, benché tutti dovessero	another nuisance to be dealt with,
ammettere che, malgrado tutto fosse un	although everybody had to admit that
brav'uomo.	in spite of everything he was a fine
	fellow.'
Nonostante la stanchezza, si mise in viaggio.	'Despite his tiredness, he set out.'

Notice the following construction with possessive adjective + *malgrado*, e.g.,
suo malgrado 'despite him(self)':

A determinare la decisione è stato il	'The decision was determined by the
simpatico aneddoto che, tuo malgrado, ti	nice story in which, despite yourself,
ha visto protagonista nell'estate '97.	you played the main role in the summer
	of '97.'

For more on concessive constructions, see 19.14.

11.21 Cause, aim, purpose: *a causa di, per via di, grazie a, per,* etc.

A causa di is the normal phrase for 'because of'; also *per*, *per via di* and *in seguito
a* 'after [and as a result of]', *grazie a* 'thanks to', 'due to'.

È morta a causa del/per il/per via del freddo.	'She died because of/from the cold.'
È morta in seguito a un raffreddore.	'She died after a cold.'

Da, like English 'from', is also used in this sense:

È morta dalla fame.	'She died from hunger.'

One may also say *È morta di fame.*
'By', 'due to' can also be *da*:

Lo riconobbi dalla voce.	'I recognized him from/by his voice.'
Ho capito che eri triste dalla tua faccia.	'I realized you were sad from your face.'

Dietro can be used to mean 'at' in the causal sense:

Lo feci dietro suggerimento del professore.	'I did it at the teacher's suggestion.'

Il motivo di . . . 'the reason for . . .':

Voglio capire il motivo di questa rivoluzione.	'I want to understand the meaning for this revolution.'

Purpose or aim is usually signalled by *per*:

combattere per la patria	'to fight for one's country'
Studio per il'esame.	'I'm studying for the exam.'

11.22 Agency, means: *da, da parte di, di, tramite, mediante*

For the use of *da* in passive verb constructions (e.g., *Fu fatto da Marco* 'It was done by M') see 14.32. Where the action is represented by a noun rather than a verb, 'by' is *da parte di*:

L'invasione dell'Austria da parte dei tedeschi.	'The invasion of Austria by the Germans.'

'By' with books, songs and other creations is usually *di*:

un poema di Leopardi	'a poem by Leopardi'
un edificio di Lutyens	'a building by Lutyens'

Also:

La notizia mi giunse tramite l'ufficio stampa.	'The news got to me through/via the press office.'
Il meccanismo si mette in moto mediante/a mezzo di/per mezzo di una leva.	'The mechanism is set in motion by means of a lever.'

Means of transport are usually expressed by *in*:

Arrivò in bicicletta/aereo/treno/macchina.	'She arrived by bicycle/plane/train/car.'

One also encounters *con* + definite article (*Arrivò col treno*, etc.).
   A special 'agent' usage appears in: *da solo, da me, da te, da sé* = 'on one's own', 'by myself', etc.:

Non attraversare la strada da sola!	'Don't cross the road on your own!'
Non mi ha aiutata nessuno: ho fatto tutto da sola.	'Nobody helped me: I did it all on my own.'

Like English 'with', Italian *con* commonly indicates the means used to do something:

Ruppe il vetro con un martello.	'He broke the window with a hammer.'
Coprì il quadro con un lenzuolo.	'He covered the picture with a sheet.'

Note *a forza di* 'by (dint of)' (see also 17.20):

A forza di zappare tutta la giornata,	'By (dint of) hoeing all day, she earned a
guadagnò qualche soldo in più.	few pennies more.'

11.23 Content, composition, substance, smell, taste: *di*

Just as 'of' is widely used in English to express content or composition, *di* is used similarly in Italian:

un branco di giovani maschi che pare quasi composto di lupi, più che di umani.	'a gang of youths which seems almost made up of wolves, rather than humans'
Ho presentato una collezione di abbigliamento.	'I presented a collection of clothes.'
Le sue tasche erano piene di caramelle.	'His pockets were full of sweets.'
C'erano ponti di pietra e ponti di legno.	'There were bridges (made) of stones and bridges (made) of wood.'
Mi piace molto l'odore del caffè.	'I like the smell of coffee very much.'

Note that 'of gold', 'golden' is always *d'oro* never **di oro*. In expressing the substance of which something is made, *in* is also employed (e.g., *una camicia in seta* 'a silk shirt'). *Di* is also 'with' in *riempire di* 'to fill with', *circondare di* 'to surround with'.

'Smell of', 'taste of' are usually expressed as *sapere di* (for both smell and taste):

Questo vino sa d'aceto.	'This wine tastes of vinegar.'
Questa giacca sa di naftalina.	'This jacket smells of mothballs.'

Note also, with other verbs of tasting/smelling:

Questa vicenda che profuma molto [. . .] di intrighi all'italiana. [Ogg.]	'This business that has a distinct whiff of Italian-style intrigue about it.'
Puzza di sudore.	'He stinks of sweat.'

11.24 'By way of', 'as a' *in, come*; 'for' *per*

L'ha ricevuto in/come premio.	'He got it as a prize.'
Lo prendono/tengono per matto.	'They regard him as mad.'
Ho pagato sessantamila lire per l'orologio.	'I paid 60 000 lire for the watch.'

11.25 Manner, style, decoration: *a*

A may be used to indicate the *manner* or *style* in which some action is performed; by which some device or machine works; in which some object is arranged, patterned, decorated or shaped; with which some dish is made or garnished:

Lo presero a sassate.	'They stoned him [lit. 'took him by stonings'].'
una gonna a righe	'a striped skirt'
un vaso a fiori	'a flower-patterned vase'
una bomba a orologeria	'a clockwork bomb [time bomb]'
un motore a benzina	'a petrol engine'

una stufa a legna	'a wood(-burning) stove'
gli gnocchi alla romana	'dumplings Roman fashion'
Non vogliamo passare all'uninominale all'inglese.	'We don't want to go over to an English-style first-past-the-post [electoral] system.'
i tacchi a spillo	'stiletto heels'
Cammina per i campi coltivati a garofani.	'He walks through the carnation fields.' [lit. 'fields cultivated with carnations']
Dice tutto a bassa voce.	'He says everything in a whisper.'
Sfoga la sua rabbia a parole e ragionamenti, non a spari.	'He gives vent to his anger through words and arguments, not by shooting.'
La brigata nera tornava spesso nei suoi discorsi, dipinta a colori diabolici.	'He was often mentioning the black brigade, depicted in diabolical colours.'
Canta a gola spiegata.	'He sings at the top of his voice.' [lit. 'with an unfolded throat']
Fila cammina a piccoli passi titubanti.	'F walks in tiny, hesitant steps.'
Andare a piedi.	'To walk.' [lit. 'to go on/by foot']
Dispone le macchine a spina di pesce.	'He parks the cars in a chevron arrangement.' [lit. 'fish-bone fashion']

Note also *fatto a X* 'X-shaped' and the types *uno a uno* or *a uno a uno* 'one by one', *a passo a passo* (or *passo passo*) 'step by step' and *a dozzine* 'by the dozen':

Entrarono due signore fatti a pera.	'Two pear-shaped ladies came in.'
Li ho contati a uno a uno.	'I counted them one by one.'
A passo a passo ci avvicinammo alla chiesa.	'Step by step, we approached the church.'
Chiedono ai grandi partiti deputati a dozzine.	'They are asking the major parties for MPs by the dozen.'

For the use of *a, da, di, per* + infinitive, see 17.22–24.

11.26 'About', 'concerning' *su, al soggetto di*, etc.; 'according to' *secondo*

'About' can be expressed by *su*; 'with regard to', 'concerning' may be expressed by *a proposito di, riguardo a, al soggetto di*:

un discorso sui problemi dell'adolescenza	'a speech about the problems of adolescence'
Non disse niente a proposito del furto.	'He didn't say anything about the theft.'

The phrase *nei confronti di* 'concerning', 'as far as X is concerned', 'with regard to', 'towards', is used only of persons:

Ha un atteggiamento molto negativo nei confronti di Marco.	'He has a very negative attitude with regard to/towards M.'

Note *di* for 'on' or 'in' in:

esperto di cucina	'expert on cooking'
specialista di [or *in*] *reumatismo*	'specialist in rheumatism'
etc.	

11.27 'On behalf of' *dalla parte di*

Vengo dalla parte del re/da parte del re.	'I come on behalf of the king.'

Contrast this with *da parte di* (11.22).

11.28 *Da* with complements of characteristic ('typical of', 'characteristic of', 'associated with', 'characterized by'), or purpose ('intended for', 'to be -ed')

cane da caccia	'hunting dog'
I fascisti sono neri, [. . .] con le facce bluastre e i baffi da topo. [Cal.]	'The fascists are black, with bluish faces and whiskers like a mouse's.'
vaso da fiori	'vase for flowers'
Non è da lui dire queste cose.	'It's not like him to say that.'
E da ragazzino quale in parte è rimasto, non resiste alla tentazione di scherzare.	'And like the little boy which in part he still is, he can't resist the temptation to joke.'
macchina da scrivere/cucire	'typewriter'/'sewing machine'
scarpe da montagna	'mountain boots'
una ragazza dagli occhi azzurri	'a girl with blue eyes/a blue-eyed girl'
Ha le mani nelle tasche della giacca troppo da uomo per lui.	'He has his hands in the pockets of the jacket [which is] too much of a man's jacket for him.'
La signora Anna Maria è una bella donna dai capelli rossi e dai molti gioielli.	'Mrs AM is a beautiful woman with red hair and many jewels.'
Gli studenti hanno la faccia da mattina di esami.	'The students have the [kind of] expression [you associate with] the morning of an examination.'
Un salto indietro nel tempo, insomma: per lui, naturalmente, tecnico felino e quindi dalle sette³ vite. [Tut.]	'A leap backwards in time, then: for him, of course, a cat-like technician and therefore endowed with seven lives.'
un piccolo villaggio inglese dal nome impronunciabile	'a little English village with an unpronounceable name'
Spalancò i piccoli occhi da talpa.	'He opened wide his little mole-like eyes.'

Da means 'of the type characteristically intended for/associated with'. But if the meaning is 'specifically intended for/specifically associated with', then some other preposition may be used:

Pin canta bene, serio, impettito, con quella voce di bambino.	'P sings well, seriously, chestily, with that child's voice of his.' [i.e., he is a child and this is his voice]
Pin ha una voce rauca, da bambino vecchio.	'P has a hoarse voice, of the kind you associate with an older child.'
Queste sono cose da bambini.	'These are things for children/childish things.'
Questo è un ospedale per bambini.	'This is a children's hospital.' [it looks after children]

Da is also 'as' in the sense 'as if one were' or 'in the manner associated with':

Si travestiva da pirata.	'He dressed up as a pirate.'
Il marinaio parlò da gran viaggiatore.	'The sailor spoke as a great traveller.'

But if 'as' = 'in one's capacity as X' (i.e., one actually is X), then *come, in quanto* or *in qualità di* are more likely to be used:

Come/In qualità di presidente, non permetto che parliate.	'As president, I will not allow you to speak.'

---

³The longevity of Italian cats is restricted to a mere *seven* lives.

Da + noun or adjective = 'in the fashion or manner characteristic of . . .', 'as':

comportarsi da persona seria	'to behave like a serious person'
Si veste da vescovo.	'He dresses as a bishop.'
vivere da principe	'to live like a prince'
Ci trattò da ingenui.	'He treated us as if we were naive.'

11.29 An important distinction between *a, di* and *da*

Contrast the following (see 11.23, 25, 28):

un vaso di fiori	'a vase of [containing] flowers'
un vaso da fiori	'a flower vase [a vase intended for flowers]'
un vaso a fiori	'a flowery vase', 'a vase decorated with flowers'

11.30 *Da* in expressions of value

A subclass of the above usage is *da* in expressions of value:

una rapina da 200 mila lire	'a 200-thousand-lire robbery'
un giocattolo da pochi soldi	'a toy costing little money'

11.31 Adjective (or noun) + *da* = 'to such a degree that', 'to the extent that', 'such as to . . .'

This is frequent in the expressions *così . . . da . . ., tanto . . . da . . .*:

Sono tanto stanco da non reggermi più in piedi.	'I'm so tired that I can no longer stand up.'
È stato così gentile da farmi avere la chiave.	'He was kind enough to let me have the key.'
Era di una bellezza tale da incantare tutti.	'It was of such beauty as to enchant everyone.'
È abbastanza intelligente da capire quello che voglio dire.	'She's intelligent enough to understand what I mean.'
E non fare stupidaggini da farti prendere.	'And don't do the sort of stupid things that will get you caught.'

11.32 Time prepositions: duration *per, durante;* 'since' *da;* 'for as long as' *finché/fino a che;* 'in' *in, tra;* 'within', 'by' *entro;* 'before' *prima di;* 'after' *dopo*

The *duration* of a period of time, 'the time *for* which something lasts', may be expressed by the preposition *per*:

Il concerto durò per tre ore.	'The concert lasted for three hours.'

or the preposition may be omitted after verbs that are inherently durative (i.e., indicate the passage of a period of time), such as *durare* or *aspettare*:

Dovettero aspettare otto mesi.	'They had to wait 8 months.'
Può una donna di quarant'anni svegliarsi come una rosa ritardataria da un letargo durato decenni?	'Can a woman of 40 wake up like a belated rose from a drowsiness [that has] lasted decades?'

but

Per circa quindici anni Charlie Chaplin pensò di scrivere un film su Napoleone.	'For about 15 years CC thought about writing a film about Napoleon.'

English often uses 'not for . . .' in the sense 'before the end of . . .', i.e., 'the time before which something happens'. Here Italian usually uses *non . . . prima di*:

Non riuscì a recuperare i fogli persi prima di una settimana.	'He didn't manage to recover the lost pages for a week.' / 'It was a week before he managed to recover the lost pages.'

Durante has much the same sense as English 'during':

Durante il concerto si addormentò.	'During the concert he fell asleep.'

'Throughout' is *durante tutto* or *fino a tutto*:

Rimase nascosto durante tutto il bombardamento.	'He stayed hidden throughout the bombardment.'
La diffusione dell'idea continuò fino a tutto il Cinquecento.	'The spread of the idea continued right through the sixteenth century.'

English 'since' introduces the time *from* which some action or event commenced (e.g., 'I've been here <u>since</u> Monday') whereas 'for' introduces the amount of *time elapsed* since some action or event occurred ('I've been here <u>since</u> Monday, so I've been here <u>for</u> five days'). Italian uses *da* in both cases (for important differences between English and Italian in the use of tenses after *da*, see 15.10).

Sono qua da lunedì.	'I've been here since Monday.'
Sono qua da cinque giorni.	'I've been here for five days.'
Studiavo l'italiano da due anni.	'I'd been learning Italian for 2 years.'
La sorella di Marco è sempre stata pigra, fin da bambina.	'M's sister has always been lazy, ever since [she was] a child.'

As the last example above shows, *da* in the sense 'since' (but not 'for') may be reinforced by *sin* or *fin*. *Fin/Sin da* are particularly likely to be used when there is a risk that *da* may be interpreted in one of its many other functions. For example:

Ha giocato qui da bambino.	'He played here as a child.'
Ha giocato qui sin da bambino.	'He's played here since [he was] a child.'

'Until' + noun is *fino a* or *sino a* + noun:

Rimase fino alla fine.	'He stayed up to the end.'

'In' in the sense of the period of time taken for some action or event to be completed is *in*:

Raccolsero tutti i funghi in tre ore.	'They picked all the mushrooms in 3 hours.'
Riuscì a recuperare i fogli persi in una settimana.	'He managed to recover the lost pages in a week.'

If 'in' expresses time *by* which some action is completed or some event occurs, *entro* is used:

Sono sicuro che ritornerà entro tre ore.	'I'm sure he'll be back within 3 hours.'
Ti farò avere l'elenco dei nomi entro giovedì.	'I'll let you have the list of names by Thursday.'

'In' as an expression of the time 'at the end of'/'after' which some action will be completed is *tra/fra*:

Tornerà fra tre giorni.	'He'll be back in three days.'
Fra qualche minuto sapremo cosa è successo.	'In a few minutes' time we'll know what's happened.'
Voglio proprio vedere se fra tre anni il nipote che gli succederà non si recherà ogni giorno ad udienza dallo zio.	'I really want to see if in three years' time the nephew who will succeed him won't be going daily for an audience with his uncle.'

Dopo could also be used in this context (*Tornerà dopo tre giorni*, etc.). Note also the phrases *fra poco, fra breve* 'in a (short) while'.

An alternative expression is *di qui/lì a . . .* 'in . . . time':

Sapranno il risultato di qui a tre giorni.	'They'll know the result in 3 days' time [from now].'
Una volta fatto il test, sapranno il risultato di lì a tre giorni.	'Once the test has been done, they will know the result in three days' time [from then].'

'Before' + noun is *prima di* + noun; 'after' + noun is *dopo* + noun (see 11.1 for *dopo di* + pronoun):

Si erano conosciuti prima della guerra.	'They had known each other before the war.'
Dopo l'improvvida domanda, si ha l'impressione di essere cronisti appena tollerati.	'After that imprudent question, we feel like scarcely tolerated journalists.'

Prima di followed by an infinitive corresponds to English 'before . . . -ing':

Lo contattai prima di partire per New York.	'I contacted him before leaving for New York.'
Prima di uscire dovresti chiudere bene la finestra.	'Before going out you should close the window properly.'

Dopo is generally followed by the infinitive of the auxiliary verb + past participle; this construction corresponds to English 'after . . . -ing' or 'after having . . . -ed':

Dopo aver salutato i suoi genitori, si chiuse dentro il bagno.	'After saying/having said hello to his parents, he shut himself in the bathroom.'
Dopo esserci alzati così tardi, dovemmo aspettare fino alle due per mangiare.	'After getting/having got up so late, we had to wait till 2 o'clock to eat.'

Both *prima di* and *dopo* + infinitive can normally only be used when the subject of the main clause is the same as that of the subordinate clause (cf. 17.8). The phrase *in seguito a* (see 11.21) may be used for 'after' in the sense 'after and as a consequence of'.

12

Numerals and related expressions

For the obligatory use of the pronoun *ne* with numeral and other quantifier expressions, as in *Ne ho dieci* 'I have ten', see 6.13.

12.1 The cardinal numerals

0–39

0 *zero*	10 *dieci*	20 *venti*	30 *trenta*
1 *uno*	11 *undici*	21 *ventuno*	31 *trentuno*
2 *due*	12 *dodici*	22 *ventidue*	32 *trentadue*
3 *tre*	13 *tredici*	23 *ventitré*	33 *trentatré*
4 *quattro*	14 *quattordici*	24 *ventiquattro*	34 *trentaquattro*
5 *cinque*	15 *quindici*	25 *venticinque*	35 *trentacinque*
6 *sei*	16 *sedici*	26 *ventisei*	36 *trentasei*
7 *sette*	17 *diciassette*	27 *ventisette*	37 *trentasette*
8 *otto*	18 *diciotto*	28 *ventotto*	38 *trentotto*
9 *nove*	19 *diciannove*	29 *ventinove*	39 *trentanove*

40–99

40 *quaranta*	60 *sessanta*	80 *ottanta*
50 *cinquanta*	70 *settanta*	90 *novanta*

The others numerals between 40 and 99 follow the pattern given for *trenta* (i.e., *quarantuno, quarantadue, novantanove*, etc.).

100–199

100 *cento*	109 *centonove*
101 *centouno* or (rare, *centuno*)	110 *centodieci*
102 *centodue*	111 *centoundici*
103 *centotré*	112 *centododici*, etc.
104 *centoquattro*	120 *centoventi*
105 *centocinque*	121 *centoventuno*
106 *centosei*	122 *centoventidue*, etc.
107 *centosette*	180 *centoottanta* or *centottanta*, etc.
108 *centootto* or (rare) *centotto*	

200–999

200 *duecento*	400 *quattrocento*	600 *seicento*	800 *ottocento*
300 *trecento*	500 *cinquecento*	700 *settecento*	900 *novecento*

Other numbers between 200 and 999 follow the same pattern as for those between 100 and 200 (*duecentosette, seicentoquarantasei, novecentoquattro, novecentonovantanove*, etc.)

1000–999 999

1000 *mille*	2000 *duemila*
1001 *milleuno*	2001 *duemilauno*
1002 *milledue*, etc.	2002 *duemiladue*, etc.
1100 *millecento*	2100 *duemilacento*
1200 *milleduecento*	2200 *duemiladuecento*
1220 *milleduecentoventi*, etc.	2220 *duemiladuecentoventi*, etc.

The thousands above 2000 are formed in the same fashion as *duemila*, by prefixing a numeral to *-mila*. Thus:

3000 *tremila*	10 000 *diecimila*
4000 *quattromila*	90 000 *novantamila*

400 205	*quattrocentomiladuecentocinque*, etc.
999 999	*novecentonovantanovemilanovecentonovantanove*

1 000 000	*un milione*
1 300 221	*un milione e trecentomiladuecentoventuno*
3 8 425 862	*trentotto milioni e quattrocentoventicinquemilaottocentosessantadue*
999 999 999	*novecentonovantanove milioni e novecentonovantanovemilanovecentonovantanove*

etc.

1 000 000 000 ('billion' = 'one thousand million')	*un miliardo*
7 223 000 000	*sette miliardi e duecentoventitré milioni*

etc.

12.2 Variant forms of the cardinals

Common alternatives to *centouno, centodue*, etc. and *milleuno, milledue*, etc., are *cento e uno, cento e due*, etc., and *mille e uno, mille e due, tremila e sette*, etc. The *mille e uno* type is particularly used in quoting prices:

Le verrà a costare tremila e cinquecento, signora.	'That'll be three thousand five hundred (lire), madam.'

The final vowel of *otto, venti*, numerals ending in *-anta*, and *cento* is occasionally deleted before words beginning with a vowel, and particularly before *anni* and, to a lesser extent, *ore*: *diciott'anni, vent'anni, vent'ore, novant'anni, cent'anni*, etc. *Quattro* also loses its final vowel in certain set phrases:

a quattr'occhi	'face to face'
in quattro e quattr'otto	'in a trice'
le ultime ventiquattr'ore	'the last 24 hours'

12.3 General properties of the cardinals

c   They precede the noun phrase. Only in bureaucratic, official registers do we encounter structures such as *schede ventuna* 'twenty-one filing cards', *un minore di anni quindici* 'a person under fifteen years', usually in lists of items.

c   They are invariable, with the exception of *uno* (which varies for gender), and *zero* which has a plural *zeri*. See also *milione* and *miliardo* below.

c   Agreement: the type 'That two hundred pounds is too much', 'Fifteen years is a long time', is impossible in Italian, where agreement with nouns modified by numerals greater than one must always be plural:

Duecento sterline sono troppe.	'£200 is too much.'
Sarebbe riuscito a divertirsi anche senza quei duemila miliardi e questi cinquant'anni alla Fiat.	'He'd have managed to enjoy himself even without that two thousand billion [lire] and that fifty years at Fiat.'

12.4 *Uno* and numerals ending in *-uno*

The numeral *uno* modifying a noun is identical to the indefinite article (see 4.1), and varies according to the nature of the following sounds in exactly the same ways: (e.g., *un gatto, uno spazio, un amico, un'amica*). To distinguish the numeral from the indefinite article, *solo* or *unico* may be added:

Nell'un (or In un) caso ero d'accordo, nell'altro no.	'In one case I agreed, in the other I didn't.'
Un pacco è arrivato, l'altro arriverà domani.	'One parcel has arrived, the other will come tomorrow.'
Ho un unico amico.	'I have [just] one friend.'
Sarebbe bastato un solo gesto.	'[Just] one gesture would have sufficed.'

Un is used in the phrase *Un due, un due!* 'Left right, left right!', in drilling soldiers to march.

As the final element of numerals above 20, *-un(o)* is often invariant for number and gender. Feminine *-una* (e.g., *ventuna case*) is very rarely used. *-uno* optionally drops the final *-o* before the noun, especially before a vowel:

trentun(o) libri	'31 books'
quarantun anni	'41 years'
ventun(o) schede	'21 cards'
trecentonovantun anni	'391 years'
trecentoun lire	'301 lire'
ventun case	'21 houses'

In the rare cases where feminine *-una* is used, the noun is singular:

trecentouna lira	'301 lire'

In principle, a noun following *-un(o)* may be also be singular, but will always be plural if also modified by an adjective or a determiner. The best advice, however, is always to keep the noun in the plural:

Ci abbiamo passato ventun(o) giorni/giorno.	'We spent 21 days there.'
i ventun(o) giorni che abbiamo passato al mare	'the 21 days we spent by the sea'
Erano passati ventun(o) bei giorni.	'21 lovely days had gone by.'

The types *trecentoun libri* and *trecentouno libri* '301 books' seem equally acceptable. Note the appearance of final *-un* in *trecentoun scellini* (alongside *trecentouno scellini* '301 shillings'), despite the general rules for use of *un* and *uno*, given in 4.1.

In contrast, where the alternative forms of the type *cento e uno*, etc. (rather than *centouno*, etc. – see 12.2) are used, the noun must be singular: *trecento e un dollaro, trecento e una lira*, etc.

Uno also varies for number and gender when used pronominally:

Gli uni erano francesi, gli altri tedeschi.	'Some were French, the others German.'

Uno does not agree when placed after the noun and used as an ordinal number:

Dov'è la pagina uno? (= *la prima pagina*)	'Where's page 1?'
Fra poco uscirà la serie ventuno. (= *la ventunesima serie*)	'Series 21 will be out soon.'

If a numeral ends in ... *e uno* (e.g., *cento e uno* rather than *centouno*), then the following noun must be *singular*, and *uno* must agree for gender:

cento e una pagina	'101 pages'
trecento e un dollaro	'301 dollars'
Ho mille e una cosa da dirti.	'I have a thousand and one things to tell you.'

12.5 *Uno, zero, tre, mille, milione*

When *uno* and *zero* are used as nouns, their plural may be *uno* or *uni* and *zero* or *zeri*.

Millecento si scrive con due uni/uno e due zeri/zero.	'1100 is written with two ones and two zeros.'

Zero does not agree with the number or gender of the noun it modifies. Note that it normally selects a plural noun:

Ha totalizzato zero punti.	'He made a total of no points.'
Secondo i vostri calcoli sarebbero rimaste zero schede.	'By your calculations no cards are left.'

-tre as the final element of numerals above 22 (23, 33, 103, etc.) is frequently written with an accent, since it carries main word stress (cf. 2.9): *ventitré, trentatré, centotré,* etc.

Milione and *miliardo* (plurals *milioni* and *miliardi*) behave like ordinary collective nouns, rather than numerals. They are written separately from other numerals with which they are combined, and require the preposition *di* before an immediately following noun:

La città faceva sette o otto milioni di abitanti.	'The city had 7 or 8 million inhabitants.'
L'ho pagata un milione di lire.	'I paid a million lire for it.'

but

La città faceva sette milioni cinquecentomila abitanti.	'The city had 7 500 000 inhabitants.'
L'ho pagata un milione trecentomila lire.	'I paid one million three hundred thousand lire for it.'

'Odd' and 'even':

numero pari	'even number'
numero dispari	'odd number'

12.6 'Both', 'all three', 'all ten', etc.; 'another three', etc.

'Both', 'all three', etc. are expressed as *tutti/tutte* + *e* + numeral (+ definite article when used as adjectives):

Erano morti tutti e due.	'They were both dead.'
In tutti e tre i casi sembra legittimo porsi almeno la domanda.	'In all three cases it seems legitimate at least to wonder.'
Aveva perso tutte e dieci le dita.	'He'd lost all ten fingers.'

'Both' is also, principally in literary registers, *ambedue*:

Queste leggi sono ambedue assurde.	'These laws are both absurd.'

A rarer form is *ambo* (with optional variants *ambi* for masculines and *ambe* for feminines).

'Another'/'A further + numeral greater than one' is expressed as *altri/altre +* numeral (+ noun):

Ho comprato altre tre poltrone.	'I bought another three armchairs.'
Con il pieno di benzina puoi fare altri 200 chilometri.	'With a full tank you can do another 200 km.'
Quattro uomini armati seguono la carovana, altri quattro aprono la strada.	'Four armed men follow the caravan, and four more open up the way.'

12.7 Conventions for writing numerals

In ordinary written prose, numbers up to and including 10 are normally written as words; thereafter either words (*quindici*) or numerals (15) are acceptable. With numbers in the tens or hundreds of thousands, millions or billions, the prevalent usage seems to be to write *mila*, *milioni* or *miliardi* as words, even where the preceding figure is in numerals:

Se l'iniziativa del referendum raccoglierà entro il 30 settembre le 500 mila firme necessarie, la scuola potrà uscire da una situazione che scontenta tutti.	'If the referendum initiative can gather the 500 signatures needed by 30th September, schools may get out of a situation nobody is happy with.'

12.8 Ordinal numerals

The ordinals from 1st to 10th are:

1st	*primo*	6th	*sesto*
2nd	*secondo*	7th	*settimo*
3rd	*terzo*	8th	*ottavo*
4th	*quarto*	9th	*nono*
5th	*quinto*	10th	*decimo*

All ordinals above 10th are formed simply by deleting the final vowel of the cardinal numeral and adding the ending *-esimo*. But note *-treesimo* and *-seiesimo* (*-seesimo* is also possible).

11th	*undicesimo*	20th	*ventesimo*
12th	*dodicesimo*	21st	*ventunesimo*
13th	*tredicesimo*	22nd	*ventiduesimo*
14th	*quattordicesimo*	23rd	*ventitreesimo*
15th	*quindicesimo*	24th	*ventiquattresimo*
16th	*sedicesimo*	25th	*venticinquesimo*
17th	*diciassettesimo*	26th	*ventiseiesimo*
18th	*diciottesimo*	27th	*ventisettesimo*
19th	*diciannovesimo*	28th	*ventottesimo*

29th	*ventinovesimo*	1000th	*millesimo*
30th	*trentesimo*	etc.	
etc.		1234th	*milleduecentotrentaquattresimo*
100th	*centesimo*	etc.	
101st	*centunesimo*	1 000 000th	*milionesimo*
etc.		etc.	

Sono stato io il primo a farlo.	'I was the first to do it.'
Aprile è il quarto mese dell'anno.	'April is the fourth month of the year.'
È stata la milionesima cliente del Body Shop.	'She was the millionth customer of Body Shop.'

Particularly in formal, legalistic, language (*un*) *terzo* (or plural *terzi*) can mean 'someone else', 'a third party':

Il contratto deve essere firmato da un terzo.	'The contract must be signed by a third party.'
Il documento non è stato visto da terzi.	'No other parties have seen the document.'

'Last' in a series is *ultimo*:

Sono stato l'ultimo a vederlo.	'I was the last to see him.'

Note also *terzultimo* 'last but two', *quartultimo* 'last but three'.

Ennesimo,'umpteenth' literally 'nth', is used to mean an unspecified and usually large ordinal number, sometimes with a note of exasperation:

E torniamo per l'ennesima volta a parlare dei guai che avrebbe sofferto.	'Let's return for the umpteenth time to the subject of the misfortunes he has supposedly suffered.'

Ordinals agree in number and gender with the noun they modify, and usually precede their noun. With names of kings, queens, popes, etc. ordinals follow the name (and, unlike English, do not have the definite article).

Giovanni ventitreesimo	'John (the) XXIII'
Elisabetta seconda	'Elizabeth (the) II'

When an ordinal adjective is combined with a numeral (e.g., 'the first two chapters'), the numeral may precede the ordinal (e.g., *i due primi capitoli*).

12.9 Special ordinals: *undecimo, decimottavo,* etc.

Italian possesses another set of ordinals from 11 to 99 formed by conjoining the ordinal multiple of 10 (*decimo, ventesimo,* etc.) with an ordinal from *primo* to *nono*. Multiples of 10 themselves have alternative special forms up to 90:

11th	*decimoprimo* (or *undecimo*)	17th	*decimosettimo*
12th	*decimosecondo* (or *duodecimo*)	18th	*decimottavo*
13th	*decimoterzo*	19th	*decimonono*
14th	*decimoquarto*	20th	*vigesimo*
15th	*decimoquinto*	30th	*trigesimo*
16th	*decimosesto*	40th	*quadragesimo*

50th	*quinquagesimo*	80th	*ottagesimo*
60th	*sessagesimo*	90th	*nonagesimo*
70th	*settuagesimo*	etc.	

These special ordinals are restricted to literary/formal/elevated usage, and tend particularly to be used with names of centuries, numbers of chapters, monarchs, popes, etc. They are always placed after the noun:

Pio undecimo	'Pius XI'
Capitolo decimoprimo	'Chapter 11'
Qui alla stanza quadragesimasesta, il poema restò interrotto.	'Here at the 46th stanza, the poem broke off.'

12.10 Collective and approximative numerals: 'about twenty', 'scores', 'hundreds', etc.

Italian has special forms, restricted to certain numerals, indicating 'a set/group of X items', or 'approximately X items'. The meaning of English plural 'hundreds' and 'thousands' is always expressed as *centinaia, migliaia*.

2	*paio*	'pair', 'couple' (pl. *paia*, fem.)
10	*decina*[1] *(diecina)*	
12	*dozzina*	'dozen'
15	*quindicina*	
20	*ventina*	'score'
30	*trentina*	
40	*quarantina*	
50	*cinquantina*	
60	*sessantina*	
70	*settantina*	
80	*ottantina*	
90	*novantina*	
100	*centinaio*	(pl. *centinaia*, fem.)
1000	*migliaio*	(pl. *migliaia*, fem.)

The 'approximative' value is especially associated with the *-ina* forms. *Paio*, *dozzina* and the *-aio* series have this value as well, but also signify units comprising *exactly* two, twelve, one hundred, one thousand, etc., members:

Torno tra un paio di giorni.	'I'll be back in a couple of days.'
Avevamo richiesto cento paia di calzoni.	'We'd requested a hundred pairs of stockings.'
All'interno del Gaslini lavorano una quindicina di maestre d'asilo.	'Within the Gaslini there work about 15 nursery school teachers.'
Starò via una quindicina di giorni.	'I'll be away about a fortnight/two weeks.'
Quante centinaia sono contenute nel numero mille?	'How many hundreds are there in a thousand?'
Sono serviti a dar lavoro a centinaia di persone.	'They helped to give employment to hundreds of people.'
Migliaia di loro furono uccisi.	'Thousands of them were killed.'

---

[1]There is also *cinquina*, but this is limited to the sense of five numbers coming out in a lottery.

Note that while the *-ina* nouns are grammatically singular, the verbs of which they are the subject are often plural.

Other expressions of approximation:

Avrà circa sedici anni.	'He must be about 16.'
Costerà suppergiù 90 000 lire /	'It'll cost roughly/about 90 000 lire.'
circa 90 000 lire/sulle 90 000 lire.	

Note that the conjunction *o* may be omitted in expressions such as 'six or seven'; the numerals may then be linked in writing by a hyphen:

Avrà sedici diciassette anni.	'He must be 16 or 17.'
Costerà due o trecentomila lire /	'It'll cost two or three hundred thousand
due-trecentomila lire.	lire.'

The indefinite article may also be placed before a numeral to indicate approximation:

Avrà un sedici anni.	'He must be about 16.'
Disterà un trenta chilometri.	'It must be about 30 km away.'

12.11 Idiomatic *quattro* and *due* 'an indeterminate small number', *mille* 'an indeterminate large number'

C'erano quattro gatti alla riunione.	'There was scarcely a soul [lit. 'there were four cats'] at the meeting.'
Ti scrivo due/quattro righe.	'I'm writing you a few lines.'
Prendo due spaghetti.	'I'll have just a bit of spaghetti.'
Hanno già sperimentato sulla propria pelle quanto sia duro allevare contemporaneamente un nugolo di marmocchi dai mille problemi.	'They've already experienced for themselves how hard it is to bring up a gaggle of little urchins with thousands of problems all at once.'

12.12 Multiplicatives: 'double', 'triple', etc.

The multiplicative forms in common use are

single	*singolo*	double	*doppio*	triple	*triplo*

un documento in singola copia	'a document in single copy'
Prende il doppio di me.	'He gets twice what I get.'
Dieci è il doppio di cinque.	'Ten is twice five.'
un fucile a doppia canna	'a double-barrelled shotgun'
Neanche con una somma tripla lo potresti acquistare.	'You couldn't buy it even with three times that amount.'

But *un biglietto di andata* 'a single ticket'.

The remaining multiplicatives, in *-uplo*, are much less commonly used:

quadruple	*quadruplo*	octuple	*ottuplo*
quintuple	*quintuplo*	×9	*nonuplo*
sextuple	*sestuplo*	×10	*decuplo*
septuple	*settuplo*	×100	*centuplo*

Abbiamo speso il decuplo del previsto.	'We've spent ten times what we planned.'
Prendo il triplo del tuo stipendio.	'I get three times your salary.'

Note that in constructions like 'I earn three times your salary', etc., *triplo*, etc., is preceded by the masculine definite article and the term with which it is compared (cf. 16.7) is introduced by *di*:

Adjectives in *-plice* (*duplice, triplice, quadruplice, quintuplice, centuplice*, etc.) mean 'in two/three (not necessarily identical) parts or elements', 'twofold'/'threefold', etc.: e.g., *La Triplice Alleanza* 'The Triple Alliance'.

An alternative strategy for forming multiplicatives – especially instead of the *-uplo* type – uses *volte* (cf. English 'three times . . .', etc.):

È tre volte più alta di quanto mi aspettassi.	'It's 3 times higher than I expected.'
Questo vaso vale quattro volte quel che valeva venti anni fa.	'This vase is worth four times what it was worth twenty years ago.'
Porta dei carichi dieci volte superiori a quelli registrabili in orbita.	'It carries loads ten times greater than those that can be recorded in orbit.'

12.13 Percentages and other fractions

Percentages are expressed by the masculine (usually definite) determiner + numeral + *per cento*. The percentage is preceded by the masculine singular article (or demonstrative), and is always treated as *singular*:

Il 78,4 per cento degli italiani è convinto che la delinquenza sia in aumento.	'78.4 per cent of Italians believe that delinquency is on the increase.'
Quel 3 per cento che si è dichiarato contrario alla proposta non sembra aver capito che cosa abbiamo in mente.	'The 3 per cent who declared themselves against the proposal do not seem to have understood what we have in mind.'
Un tre per cento degli italiani si dichiara contento.	'About 3 per cent of Italians declare themselves content.'

Note the adverbial use of *al* in the following:

Lasciamo che prendano il potere. Così si smascherano al cento per cento.	'Let's let them take power. That way they'll reveal themselves for what they are one hundred per cent.'

Fractions other than 'half' are expressed by the masculine form of the ordinal numeral (the 'special' ordinals discussed in 12.9 are never employed) + *di* + noun:

Ho speso i tre quarti del mio stipendio.	'I've spent three quarters of my salary.'
Hanno scoperto che bastava un millesimo di quella sostanza per uccidere una persona.	'They discovered that one thousandth part of that chemical was enough to kill somebody.'

'Half' is the adjective *mezzo* which precedes the noun and agrees with it in number and gender:

Ho mangiato mezza torta.	'I ate half a cake.'

Note also the adverbial use:

Erano mezzi ubriachi.	'They were half drunk.'
La mia fidanzata è mezza spagnola.	'My girlfriend is half Spanish.'

Note that in such cases agreement of adverbially used *mezzo* is optional: one could also say *erano mezzo ubriachi*, etc.

'...and a half' may be ... *e mezzo* even where the noun is feminine:

Dopo una settimana e mezzo tornarono a casa.   'After a week and a half they came home.'

Note that, unlike English 'and a half' *e mezzo* must follow the noun (*due torte e mezzo* 'two and a half cakes').

Decimals, preceded by a comma (*virgola*), rather than a point, are expressed as follows:

10,8   *dieci virgola otto*
207,03   *duecentosette virgola zerotré*

Numbers to the right of the decimal comma are usually read as tens, hundreds, etc.

7,0678   *Sette virgola zeroseicentosettantotto*

'In', or 'out of', as in 'three out of ten', 'one in four', etc., is *su*:

Un italiano su dieci, negli ultimi dodici mesi, è stato vittima della criminalità.   'One Italian in ten, in the last twelve months, has been a victim of crime.'

—Avevano passato l'esame solo tre candidati.   'Only three candidates had passed the exam.'
—Su quanti?   'Out of how many?'

Note that whereas in English it is also possible to say 'one in ten Italians', etc., Italian allows only the type *un italiano su dieci*.

12.14 Distributives

'For each', 'for every', 'per' are often expressed as *per*:

Nei masi vivono oltre 80 mila anime, dato dell'unione agricoltori e che emerge calcolando mediamente cinque persone per maso.   'In the 'masi' there live over 80 000 souls, according to information provided by the farmers' union and arrived at by calculating on average 5 people per 'maso'.'

Si registrano una trentina di casi per milione di abitanti.   'We register about thirty cases for every million inhabitants.'
Consuma solo 7 litri per 100 chilometri.   'It uses only 7 litres per 100 kilometres.'

Speeds and prices often employ the preposition *a* or (as prescribed by more traditional grammars) simply take no preposition:

Faceva più di centocinquanta chilometri l'ora/all'ora.   'It was doing over 150 km an hour.'
Costa mille lire l'etto/all'etto.   'It costs 1000 lire a hectogram.'

'Two by two', etc.

Entrarono a due a due/ad uno ad uno.   'They came in two by two/one by one.'
Li ho contati a quattro a quattro.   'I counted them four by four.'

12.15 Groups and sets: 'There are three of them', etc.

As well as the type *Ce ne sono tre* one may say:

Sono tre.	'They number three.'
I feriti sono più di cento.	'There are more than a hundred wounded.'
I problemi che prevedo sono cinque.	'The problems I foresee number five.'

The notion 'as a group of X people' can often be expressed in Italian as '*in* + X':

Siamo in tre a lavorare su questo progetto.	'There are three of us working on this project.'
Siete andati al ristorante in otto.	'You went to the restaurant in a party of eight.'
In sette proprio non ci stiamo dentro quella macchina.	'Seven of us will never get into that car.'
Io vado in esplorazione e poi torno a prenderti. In uno è meno pericoloso che in due.	'I'm off to scout round and then I'll come back and get you. It's safer if there is just one of us rather than two.'

The same construction can be used with other types of quantifier, such as *molti, diversi, pochi*:

—*Anch'io ci andrei, fanno in diversi.*	'"I'd go too," several of them say.'

With *essere, in* may be omitted. *Sono due* is a simple enumeration: 'There are two of them', 'They number two'; *Sono in due* 'They form a group of two.'

12.16 Mathematical expressions

+	*più*
−	*meno*
×	*per/volte/moltiplicato per*
÷	*diviso*
=	*uguale / sono / fa* (or nothing)

Sette meno tre, quattro.	$7 - 3 = 4$
Sette più tre fa dieci.	$7 + 3 = 10$
Sette meno due uguale cinque.	$7 - 2 = 5$
Sette per / moltiplicato / volte tre sono / uguale / fa ventuno.	$7 \times 3 = 21$
Ventotto diviso sette uguale sette.	$28 \div 7 = 4$
OR *Sette nel 28 ci sta quattro volte.*	

'Square(d)', 'cube(d)', etc.:

tre al quadrato	3^2
tre elevato al cubo	3^3
tre alla quarantatreesima potenza	3^{43}
cento metri quadrati	100 square metres

12.17 Dimensions and measurements

Dimensions are usually expressed by adjective (*alto, largo, lontano,* etc.) + numeral + unit of measurement:

È largo due metri.	'It's 2 metres wide.'
Guareschi è alto metri uno e settanta.	'G is 1m 70 tall.'
Rita Rusic è alta almeno 15 centimetri più del marito.	'RR is at least 15 cm taller than her husband.'

Sembrano vicini ma sono lontani mille miglia.	'They seem near by but they are a thousand miles away.'
È profondo solo qualche millimetro.	'It's only a few millimetres deep.'

An alternative is *misurare/avere/fare* + unit of measurement + *di/in* + noun expressing the dimension:

Il nuovo coupé Civic è più grande del precedente: 6 centimetri in lunghezza, 1 in larghezza e 8 in altezza.	'The new Civic coupé is bigger than its predecessor: (by) 6 centimetres in length, 1 in width and 8 in height.'
Il globo terrestre misura quarantamila chilometri di circonferenza.	'The circumference of the earth is 40 000 km.'

12.18 Telephone numbers

These may be read (as in English) as a series of single numbers. Unlike English 'double one', 'treble four', etc., *doppio* and *triplo* are not used, identical successive numbers being read separately:

Devi telefonare al cinque uno uno sette cinque tre.	'You must phone five double one seven five three.'

Alternatively, they may be grouped into pairs and read as multiples of ten; if the first digit of such a pair is zero, it will be read as *zero*; if the number of digits is uneven, the first digit will be read as a multiple of 100:

Devi fare il cinquantuno diciassette cinquantatré.	'You must dial 51 17 53.'
Devi fare il novecentocinquantuno diciassette cinquantatré.	'You must dial 951 17 53.'

13

Adverbs and adverbial constructions

For 'conjoining' adverbial expressions, see Chapter 19; for adverbs of place, see 5.15, 16.

13.1 Adverbs in *-mente*

The most common type of adverb is formed by adding *-mente* to the *feminine* form of an adjective.

Adjective		Feminine	Adverb	
cieco	'blind'	*cieca*	*ciecamente*	'blindly'
corrente	'current'	[same]	*correntemente*	'currently'
cortese	'polite'	[same]	*cortesemente*	'politely'
doloroso	'painful'	*dolorosa*	*dolorosamente*	'painfully'
frequente	'frequent'	[same]	*frequentemente*	'frequently'
medio	'average'	*media*	*mediamente*	'on average'
ottimo	'excellent'	*ottima*	*ottimamente*	'excellently'
prossimo	'next'	*prossima*	*prossimamente*	'shortly'
ripetuto	'repeated'	*ripetuta*	*ripetutamente*	'repeatedly'
serio	'serious'	*seria*	*seriamente*	'seriously'
ultimo	'last'	*ultima*	*ultimamente*	'recently'
etc.				

For 'elative' adverbs, such as *lentissimamente*, see also 16.15.

Adverbs formed from adjectives that end in vowel + *-re* or *-le* remove the final *e* of the adjective before adding *-mente* (cf. also 2.8):

regolare	'regular'	*regolarmente*
particolare	'particular'	*particolarmente*
naturale	'natural'	*naturalmente*
crudele	'cruel'	*crudelmente*
incredibile	'incredible'	*incredibilmente*
stabile	'stable'	*stabilmente*
tale	'such'	*talmente*
etc.		

but *-e* is not removed in the following (because the result would be unpronounceable):

acre	'acrid', 'sharp'	*acremente*
folle	'mad'	*follemente*
molle	'soft'	*mollemente*

The following are special forms:

violento	'violent'	*violentemente*	
leggero	'light'	*leggermente*	'lightly', 'slightly'
benevolo	'benevolent'	*benevolmente*	
malevolo	'malevolent'	*malevolmente*	
pari	'like', 'equal'	*parimenti*	'likewise'
altro	'other'	*altrimenti*	'otherwise'

13.2 Adverbs may be identical to masculine singular adjectives: *parlare chiaro*, etc.

Some adverbs are identical to the (masculine) singular adjective:

Adjective		**Adverb**	
dritto or *diritto*	'straight'	*dritto* or *diritto*	'straight', 'straight ahead'
molto	'much'	*molto*	'very', 'greatly'
poco	'not much'	*poco*	'not much', 'not very'
piano	'slow'	*piano*	'slowly', 'softly'
tanto	'so much'	*tanto*	'so much', 'so', 'so very'
sodo	'firm', 'hard'	*sodo*	'hard'
storto	'twisted'	*storto*	'awry', 'wrong'
spesso	'thick'	*spesso*	'often'
troppo	'too much'	*troppo*	'too much'/'to excess'

In some cases there is a contrast in meaning between the -*mente* adverb and the 'adjective' form of the adverb:

- *Alto* 'high': *Mira alto* 'She aims high', *Vola alto* 'It flies high', vs. *altamente* 'to a high degree': *È altamente irresponsabile comportarsi in questo modo* 'It is highly irresponsible to behave like that'.
- *Basso* 'low' is used similarly to *alto* (*Vola basso*, etc.), but *bassamente* has a specifically moral sense: *Si comportò bassamente* 'He behaved basely'.
- *Certo* is 'definitely', 'for sure', 'of course', 'certainly', and may serve simply to indicate acceptance of the truth of some assertion: *Il dondolio non aiuta certo a rimanere svegli* 'The rocking motion definitely doesn't help people to stay awake', *È certo una congettura azzardata* 'It's certainly a risky conjecture', *Certo questo quadro non è autentico* 'Of course this picture isn't authentic'; *certamente* is more explictly an expression of 'certainty', and corresponds roughly to 'it is a certain/undoubted fact that': *Certamente questo quadro non è autentico* 'There's no argument that this picture is not authentic'.
- *Chiaro* 'clearly' is used in the sense 'directly', 'straightforwardly', 'without difficulty': *parlare chiaro* 'to speak clearly', 'get to the point', *Non ci vedo chiaro* 'I don't quite see what's going on', *Mi disse chiaro e tondo di andarmene* 'He told me plain and straight to go away' (note also the adverbial use of *tondo*); otherwise, *chiaramente*: *Adesso si vede chiaramente* 'Now it can be clearly seen'; *Chiaramente, io non sono responsabile* 'Clearly, I'm not responsible'.
- *Duro* is 'fast' as in *tenere duro* 'to hold fast', *dormire duro* 'to be fast asleep', vs. *duramente* 'severely', 'harshly': *Lo rimproverò duramente* 'He reprimanded him harshly'.
- *Forte* 'hard', 'loud': *Gridò molto forte* 'He shouted very loudly', *Correva forte* 'She was running hard' vs. *fortemente* 'with strength', 'intensely': *Lo critica fortemente* 'She criticizes him intensely'.
- *Giusto* is 'exactly', 'precisely', '(only) just': *È arrivato giusto in tempo* 'He

arrived (only) just in time', *Mi è costato giusto ventimila lire* 'It cost me exactly 20 000 lire', vs. *giustamente* 'rightly', 'truthfully': *Ha detto giustamente che costa troppo* 'He rightly said it costs too much'. See 13.16 for 'just' in the sense 'just now'.

- *Lontano* is the usual adverbial form (*È andato lontano* 'He's gone far/a long way'); *lontanamente* is 'remotely', as in *Non m'interessa neppur lontanamente* 'It doesn't even remotely interest me', *Me lo ricordo lontanamente* 'I can remotely/vaguely recall him'.
- *Proprio* is a general intensifier, roughly equivalent to English 'really', 'quite', 'indeed', 'actually': *È proprio stupido* 'He's really stupid', *Erano proprio state trovate tracce di eroina nel sangue* 'Traces of heroin had actually been found in the blood'. *Propriamente* is 'properly', 'accurately'.

A special case is *solo*. 'Only' is *solo* (identical to the adjective) or *soltanto*, which some Italians regard as rather more emphatic than *solo*. *Solamente* is also possible, but is less commonly used:

> *Ho solo/soltanto ottomila lire in tasca.*   'I have only 8000 lire in my pocket.'

Occasionally, *solo* may be made to agree with the noun it modifies:

> *Abbiamo voli per Venezia a partire da sole duecento sterline.*   'We have flights for Venice from only £200.'

Note that an alternative to *solo* (etc.) modifying a verb is *non* + verb + *che*:

> *Di libri italiani non ho letto che Il Gattopardo.*   'The only Italian book I've read is *The Leopard.*'
> *Non le rimane che ringraziarlo ed andarsene.*   'It remains for her only to thank him and leave.'

13.3 'Lexical adverbs': forms not predictable from the corresponding adjective (*bene, male,* etc.), or independent of adjectives (*abbastanza, sempre,* etc.)

Adjective		Adverb	
buono	'good'	*bene*	'well'
migliore	'better'	*meglio*	'better'
cattivo	'bad'	*male*	'badly'
peggiore	'worse'	*peggio*	'worse'
tardo	'late'	*tardi*	'late'

- These adverbs (except *meglio* and *peggio*) also have superlatives and other derived forms ending in -o: *benissimo, malissimo, tardissimo, benino, maluccio.* Also *benone*: *Hai giocato benone* 'You played pretty well'.
- *Bene* and *male* followed by an adjective or past participle may optionally lose their final vowel: *ben fatto* 'well made', *mal fatto* 'badly made', etc.
- Note the adverb *malamente*, formed from the old adjective *malo* 'bad', and having the sense 'seriously', 'gravely': *Era malamente indebitato quando lo conobbi* 'He was badly in debt when I met him'.
- Some lexical adverbs of time, place (see 13.3) and degree are not obviously derivable from any adjective:

abbastanza	'fairly', 'rather'	*persino/perfino*	'even'
alquanto	'rather', 'somewhat'	*piuttosto*	'rather'
anche	'also', 'even'	*poi*	'then'
assai	'very', 'extremely'	*presto*	'soon', 'early'
forse	'perhaps'	*pure*	'also', 'even', 'too'
già	'already'	*quasi*	'almost'
giù	'down'	*sempre*	'always'
intorno	'around'	*su*	'up'
mai	'never'	*subito*	'immediately'
parecchio	'very', 'a lot'	*volentieri*	'willingly', 'gladly'

Note also *come?* 'how?', *come* 'like', 'as' and *così* 'thus', 'in that way':

Come si fa a ricordarsele tutte?	'How does one manage to remember them all?'
Lasciamo che prendano il potere. Così si smascherano al cento per cento.	'Let's leave them to take power. That way they'll be revealed 100 per cent.'
Quando noto una contraddittorietà così palese, ne resto turbato.	'When I note so obvious a contradiction, I'm disturbed by it.'

13.4 Adverb-like expressions denoting physical manner/posture ending in *-oni*

Certain expressions indicating physical manner or posture are formed by adding *-oni* to a noun or verb root. Most *-oni* adverbs carry a connotation of ungainliness:

Trovò tastoni l'interruttore della luce.	'He found gropingly the light switch.' [cf. *tastare*]
Lo trovammo bocconi.	'We found him flat on his face.' [cf. *bocca*]

Also (note that *-oni* forms may sometimes be preceded by *a*):

carponi	'on all fours'	*balzelloni*	'by bounds'
striscioni	'crawling'	*saltelloni*	'by leaps'
penzoloni	'dangling'	*cavalcioni*	'on horseback', 'astride'
ginocchioni	'kneeling'	*tentoni*	'gropingly'
ciondoloni	'dangling', 'drooping'	*quattoni*	'crouchingly'
barcolloni	'swayingly'	*rovescioni*	'back to front'
coccoloni	'crouching'	*strascicioni*	'dragging along'
dondoloni	'lollingly'	*zoppiconi*	'limpingly'
sdruccioloni	'slitheringly'		

See also 11.25 for expressions such as *stare a occhi aperti* 'to be wide eyed'.

13.5 Phrasal (especially prepositional) adverbs

A very large number of adverbs and adverbial expressions comprise more than one word, frequently a preposition (usually *a, in, da, di, per*) + a noun or adjective (sometimes written as a single word). Among them are: *abbasso* 'down', 'downwards'; *adagio* 'slowly'; *a faccia a faccia* (or *faccia a faccia*) 'face to face'; *a fatica* 'with difficulty':

A volte le zampe delle mule sprofondano nell'argilla e non ne escono che a fatica. [Mar.]	'Sometimes the mules' hooves sink into the mud and can only get out with difficulty.'

all'incirca 'roughly', 'approximately'; *almeno* 'at least':

Almeno non è come tutti quelli che mi hanno usata come la diva del dolore. [Pan.]	'At least he's not like all those men who've used me as the goddess of pain.'

a momenti 'sometimes', 'at any moment' or, colloquially, 'almost':

A momenti sorride, a momenti piange.	'Sometimes he smiles, sometimes he cries.'
Se non mi avvertivi a momenti ci cascavo.	'If you hadn't warned me I would almost have fallen into it.'

a mano a mano (or *man mano*) 'little by little':

A mano a mano che scendevamo sentivamo il terribile calore della lava.	'Little by little as we climbed down, we felt the terrible heat of the lava.'

a poco a poco 'little by little':

A poco a poco cominciai a capire meglio la situazione.	'Gradually I began to understand the situation better.'

appena 'scarcely', 'just', 'barely':

Dopo l'improvvida domanda, si ha l'impressione di essere cronisti appena tollerati.	'After this imprudent question, one has the impression of being barely tolerated journalists.'

appieno 'entirely', 'completely'; *apposta* 'deliberately', 'intentionally':

Non poteva comportarsi in modo più stupido, neanche a farlo apposta.	'He couldn't have acted more stupidly, even if he'd tried.'

a stento 'with difficulty'; *a tutti i costi* 'at all costs'; *controvoglia* 'unwillingly'; *daccapo* 'from the beginning'; *dappertutto* 'everywhere'; *davvero* 'really':

Adesso si era davvero quasi arrivati.	'Now we really had almost arrived.'

di botto 'suddenly', 'abruptly'; *di certo* 'for sure':

Non verrà domani di certo.	'He won't come tomorrow for sure.'

di continuo 'continually'; *di fresco* 'recently'; *di mezzo* 'in the way'; *di nascosto* 'secretly'; *di notte* 'by night'; *di nuovo* 'again':

Lui lo potrà di nuovo prendere in giro.	'He'll be able to pull his leg again.'

di rado 'seldom', 'rarely'; *di recente* 'recently'; *di sicuro* 'certainly'; *di solito* 'usually'; *in alto* 'up', 'upwards'; *in cambio* 'in exchange', 'on the other hand'; *in basso* 'down', 'downwards'; *in breve* 'briefly', 'in brief'; *in fretta* 'in haste', 'hastily'; *oltre modo/oltremisura* 'excessively'; *sul serio* 'seriously', 'not jokingly':

All'inizio pensavo scherzasse, ma dopo capii che diceva sul serio.	'At first I thought he was joking, but later I realized he was saying it seriously.'

su per giù 'roughly', 'approximately':

La stanza misura cinque metri per quattro, su per giù.	'The room measures 5 m by 4 m, approximately.'

per caso 'by chance', 'accidentally':

Io ero venuto a chiedere se, per caso, avesse denunciato il furto. etc.	'I had come to ask if, by any chance, he had reported the theft.'

Other adverbial phrases are *un po'* 'a bit':

Le cose diventano un po' antipatiche.	'Things are getting a bit unpleasant.'

and in colloquial usage *un sacco, un mondo, un mucchio, un fottio* 'lots', 'a whole load':

Sei un sacco carino.	'You're really cute.'
Mi diverto un mondo.	'I'm having a whale of a time.'

13.6 Other ways of forming adverbial expressions

Adverbial expressions of manner can be created from the structures *in maniera* + feminine adjective (or *in modo* + masculine adjective):

Mi guardò in maniera scandalizzata.	'She looked at me with outrage.'
Domandò in maniera brusca . . .	'He asked brusquely . . .'
Gli fu risposto in maniera gentile.	'He was answered kindly.'
Annuì in modo espressivo.	'He nodded expressively.'
Ha reagito in maniera contraria alle proprie idee.	'He reacted in a manner contrary to his ideas.'

In some cases, uses of the *in maniera* type serve particularly to emphasize physical manner, whereas a *-mente* adverb might have a different interpretation:

Mangiò in maniera molto rapida.	'He ate very rapidly.' [e.g., with hasty gestures, unceremoniously, impatiently]
Mangiò molto rapidamente.	'He ate very rapidly.' [i.e., 'It didn't take him long to eat.']

Adverbial expressions with *alla* + feminine adjectives are really elliptical forms of *alla maniera* + adjective. Some of these may have rather idiosyncratic, and sometimes slightly derogatory, meanings.

vestire alla francese	'to dress in the French fashion'
pagare alla romana	lit. 'to pay Roman fashion', i.e. 'each person to pay their own share'

Note also:

Faremo alla meglio.	'We'll do as best we can.' / 'We'll muddle through.'

A further possibility for adverbs of manner is *con* + noun. Similar structures are available in English, but Italian makes notably more use of them than English does.

Rispose con entusiasmo.	'He answered with enthusiasm/ enthusiastically.'
Lesse la lettera con indifferenza.	'He read the letter with indifference/ indifferently.'
etc.	

13.7 Interrogative and exclamative forms of adverbs ('How well does he sing?', 'How well he sings!', etc.)

Interrogatives of adverbs are formed by placing *quanto* before the adverb:

Quanto lentamente ha camminato?	'How slowly did he walk?'
Quanto tardi arrivarono?	'How late did they arrive?'
Quanto frequentemente partono?	'How frequently do they leave?'
etc.	

For exclamations, the most general structure involves placing *come* at the beginning of the clause, while the adverb remains in its usual position:

Come canta male!	'How badly he sings!'
Come cammina piano!	'How slowly he walks!'
Come scrive in fretta!	'How hastily he writes!'
etc.	

With lexical adverbs (*bene*, *male*, *piano*, etc.) an alternative, colloquial and idiomatic expression is *Che* + adverb + *che* + verb or, rather less idiomatically, *Quanto* + adverb + (*che*) + verb:

Che male che canta!	'How badly he sings!'
Che piano che cammina!	'How slowly he walks!'
Quanto male gioca!	'How badly he plays!'

13.8 Meaning and function of adverbs

It will be obvious from much of the foregoing that the meaning or function of an adverb is not necessarily 'transparent'. In the case of adverbs in *-mente*, their meaning generally corresponds closely to the adjectives from which they are derived. But note:

prossimo 'next'	*prossimamente* 'shortly', 'in a while from now'
successivo 'next'	*successivamente* 'next', 'after that'
ultimo 'last'	*ultimamente* 'recently', 'latterly' ('lastly' is *per ultimo*)
diverso 'different'	*diversamente* 'differently', but also 'otherwise'

Deve essersene andata in fretta;	'She must have left in a hurry; otherwise
diversamente avrebbe lasciato un messaggio.	she'd have left a message.'

The meaning of other adverbial expressions is often much less transparent; see for example *giusto*, *proprio*, *spesso* in 13.2.

In English the adverbial ending '-ly' cannot be attached to adjectives of origin or nationality (we cannot say 'Luxemburgishly', 'Finnishly', 'Italianly', etc.). The same is generally true of Italian *-mente* (one would not say **lussemburghesemente*, **finnicamente*, etc.), but it is sometimes possible to form *-mente* adverbs from what may be loosely termed 'familiar and common' adjectives of origin, such those referring to Italy, regions of Italy, and Italy's close associates (whether geographical or political). Adverbs such as *italianamente*, *milanesemente*, even *americanamente*, generally mean 'as is typical of Italians/Italy, the Milanese/Milan, Americans/America', etc.

13.9 Adverbs immediately precede any adjective or other adverb they modify: *Canta troppo poco* 'He sings too little' etc.

una giornata molto lunga	'a very long day'
delle idee piuttosto assurde	'some rather absurd ideas'
Si dimostrava straordinariamente lento nel capire.	'He proved extraordinarily slow on the uptake.'
I miei studenti sembrano proprio intelligenti.	'My students seem really intelligent.'
Ha studiato molto attentamente tutti i documenti.	'He studied all the documents very attentively.'
Parla particolarmente bene l'italiano.	'He speaks Italian particularly well.'
Si capiva ben facilmente il discorso che faceva.	'One understood very easily what he was saying.'
Ci sono ben troppi e troppo inattendibili ostacoli.	'There are really too many and too unforeseeable obstacles.'
etc.	

13.10 *-mente* adverbs cannot be combined with each other

One *-mente* adverb cannot modify another one. Thus one can say *Canta molto bene* 'He sings very well', but to say 'He acted entirely correctly' we may have *Ha agito del tutto correttamente, Ha agito in maniera interamente corretta*, etc., but not **Ha agito interamente correttamente*. Likewise *Suonava magistralmente bene* 'He played masterfully well', but not **Suonava magistralmente chiaramente*.

13.11 Adverbs follow verbs

When adverbs modify a verb, they generally follow that verb. But this still leaves three possibilities. An adverb may appear:

(1) Immediately after the verb:

Esamina attentamente i libri.	'He attentively examines the books.'
Perde spesso il portafoglio.	'He often loses his wallet.'

(2) Following the complement (e.g., the object – cf. 17.1) of the verb:

Esamina i libri attentamente.	'He examines the books attentively.'
Si rivolgono alla maestra timidamente.	'They turn to the schoolmistress shyly.'

(3) Between an auxiliary or a modal verb and the following participle, gerund or infinitive:

Ha attentamente esaminato i libri.	'He attentively examined the books.'
Sta attentamente esaminando i libri.	'He is attentively examining the books.'
Voleva attentamente esaminare i libri.	'He wanted attentively to examine the books.'

Certain adverbs only occur in position **(1)** (i.e., immediately after the verb) when they modify the verb: this applies to time adverbs that are 'indefinite' (e.g., *spesso, a volte*) rather than 'definite' like *ieri, domani*:

Criticava spesso la politica estera tedesca.
not *Criticava la politica estera tedesca
spesso.*
etc.

'He often criticized German foreign
policy.'

Otherwise, agent-oriented adverbs (i.e., those focusing on the manner in
which the agent carries out the action expressed by the verb) usually occur in
position **(1)** (immediately following the verb), particularly if the verb has a
lengthy complement following it:

*Legge attentamente tutti i libri scritti
durante quel periodo.*
etc.

'He reads attentively all the books
written in that period.'

But agent-oriented adverbs may also occupy position **(2)** (after the complement of the verb) and, much less commonly, position **(3)**:

Legge tutti i libri attentamente.
Ha letto tutti i libri attentamente.
Ha attentamente letto tutti i libri.
etc.

'He reads attentively all the books.'
'He read attentively all the books.'
'He attentively read all the books.'

Bene 'well', *meglio* 'better' and *male* 'badly', *peggio* 'worse' never occur in
position **(3)**:

Ha tagliato la torta male.
Ha tagliato male la torta.
not *Ha male tagliato la torta.*

'She has cut the cake badly.'

Result-oriented adverbs (those focusing on the extent or degree to which the
action expressed by the verb is carried out, such as *completamente, pesantemente,
molto, poco*) also usually occur in position **(1)**, immediately following the verb.
They may occasionally appear in position **(3)** (between modal/auxiliary and
main verb), but not in position **(2)** (after the complement):

Canta continuamente la stessa canzone.
*Ha cantato continuamente la stessa
canzone.*
*Ha continuamente cantato la stessa
canzone.*
not *Canta la stessa canzone continuamente.*
Apprezza molto i tuoi commenti.
Ha apprezzato molto i tuoi commenti.
Ha molto apprezzato i tuoi commenti.
not *Apprezza i tuoi commenti molto.*

'She continually sings the same song.'
'She has continually sung the same
song.'

'He much appreciates your comments.'
'He has appreciated your comments
very much.'
'He appreciates your comments very
much.'

*Da lontano fanno pensare a tre grosse
tartarughe che si muovano lentamente
lungo il viottolo.*
not *Da lontano fanno pensare a tre grosse
tartarughe che si muovano lungo il viottolo
lentamente.*

'From a distance they bring to mind
three large tortoises slowly moving
along the lane.'

Not all result-oriented adverbial expressions can be introduced in position **(3)**,
between the auxiliary and the verb; among those that tend not to be are: *in/a
tempo* 'in time'; *al volo* 'instantly'; *a vicenda* 'mutually' (cf. 6.27); *alla rinfusa*

'higgledy-piggledy'; *di sbieco* 'slanting', 'askew'; *a male* 'the wrong way' (e.g., *Se l'è avuta a male* 'He took it badly/the wrong way').

Focusing adverbs (those which serve to restrict or draw attention to, or re-inforce, the verb, such as *esclusivamente, unicamente, anche, solo, soltanto, solamente, perfino, proprio, davvero, quasi, affatto*), also occupy position **(1)** (immediately after the verb), except that they *must* take position **(3)** whenever there is an auxiliary + verb:

Si pettina anche.	'She combs herself too.'
Si è anche pettinata.	'She has even/also combed herself.'
not *Si è pettinata anche.*	
Ha persino cantato!	'He's even sung!'
L'ha proprio ucciso.	'He's really killed him.'
Adesso si era davvero quasi arrivati.	'Now we really had almost arrived.'
L'ha fatto soltanto cantare.	'He only made him sing.'
Ti faremo anche ridere.	'We'll make you laugh too.'
etc.	

What happens to focusing adverbs when there are *two* auxiliaries (for example, in the *passato prossimo*, pluperfect, etc., of the passive)? Most of these adverbs may either follow the first auxiliary or the second one:

Non gli era proprio stato detto.	'It hadn't actually been said to him.'
Non gli era stato proprio detto.	

It is generally rare[1] for any adverb to be positioned in front of the verb, except that this is obligatory when a focusing adverb modifies an infinitive:

Solo criticare è antipatico.	'Just to criticize is unpleasant.'
etc.	

13.12 Sentence adverbial expressions

Sentence adverbs (those which modify whole sentences or clauses, such as *chiaramente* 'clearly', 'of course', *personalmente* 'personally', *verosimilmente* 'in all likelihood') usually appear at the beginning of a sentence or clause. Less commonly, they may occur within a sentence or clause or at the end of it: in these cases they tend to be separated by an audible pause, and in writing by commas:

Purtroppo/Ironicamente/Naturalmente/ Probabilmente non è riuscito a raggiungerlo.	'Unfortunately/Ironically/Naturally/ Probably he didn't manage to reach him.'
Non è riuscito a raggiungerlo, purtroppo/ ironicamente/naturalmente/probabilmente.	'He didn't manage to reach him, unfortunately/ironically/naturally/ probably.'

---

[1] It is also possible with some adverbs indicating volition, e.g.,

Intenzionalmente contaminare la carne è imperdonabile.	'Intentionally to contaminate the meat is unforgivable.'

But the order *contaminare la carne intenzionalmente* is much more natural.

Non è riuscito, purtroppo/ironicamente/ *naturalmente/probabilmente, a raggiungerlo.*	'He didn't manage, unfortunately/ ironically/naturally/probably, to reach him.'
Normalmente/Di solito/Finalmente/ *Diversamente vado in vacanza con* *Giovanna.*	'Normally/Usually/At last/Otherwise I go on holiday with G.'
Vado in vacanza con Giovanna, *normalmente/di solito/finalmente/* *diversamente.*	'I go on holiday with G, normally/ usually/at last/otherwise.'
Vado in vacanza, normalmente/di solito/ *finalmente/diversamente, con Giovanna.* etc.	'I go on holiday, normally/usually/at last/otherwise, with G.'

'Otherwise', is *altrimenti*. An alternative in colloquial usage, when 'otherwise' modifies a whole sentence or clause, is *se no* (often written *sennò*).

Stai attento a non giocare in cucina. *Altrimenti/Sennò sono guai.*	'Mind you don't play in the kitchen. Otherwise there'll be trouble.'

13.13 Adverbial uses of adjectives

It is possible to use adjectives, agreeing in number and gender with the subject of the verb, as adverbs. In such cases, the adjective not only modifies the verb but can also be viewed as being predicated on the subject of the sentence. That is to say that a phrase like *Marco e Carlo si fermarono allibiti*, literally 'M and C stopped astonished' or 'M and C stopped in astonishment', is equivalent to 'M and C were astonished and (therefore) stopped', and *Sorrideva affettuosa* 'She smiled affectionately' is roughly 'She smiled and she looked affectionate (as she did so)', etc. Other examples are:

I raggi del sole devono scendere diritti.	'The sun's rays must shine down straight.'
Camminava leggero come un gatto.	'He walked as lightly as a cat.'
Gli uccelli volano bassi.	'The birds fly low.'
Le mani di Fila si muovono goffe e rapide.	'F's hands move clumsily and rapidly.'
etc.	

A particularly important adverbial use of the adjective is *tutto* meaning 'all', 'completely', 'quite' before another adjective:

Maria era tutta sconvolta.	'M was entirely/quite/all upset.'
Erano tutte contente.	'They were really happy.'

The second example above is potentially ambiguous: it might mean either 'They were really happy' or just 'They were all happy'. But to express the latter sense Italian tends to add a quantifier expression after *tutti/e*: e.g., *Erano tutte quante contente* 'They were happy each and every one', *Erano tutti quanti stupidi* 'They were stupid to a man'; or *Erano tutte e due* (*tutte e tre*, etc.) *contente, erano tutti e quattro* (etc.) *stupidi*.

A particular adverbial use of an adjective involves *bello* which, in informal usage, can be used to modify an adjective and is roughly equivalent to English 'nice . . .', 'nice and . . .' or 'well and truly . . .'. It may take the form *bell'e* + adjective, or *bello* + adjective, where *bello* agrees in number and gender with the noun:

Cercavo una corda bella spessa.	'I was looking for a nice thick rope.'
Ecco tre pizze bell'e fatte.	'Here are three pizzas nice and ready.'

Adesso sei bello pulito.	'Now you're nice and clean.'
Quel gatto è bell'e morto.	'That cat is well and truly dead.'

13.14 Adverbial phrases using imperative forms (*corri corri* 'at a run', etc.)

A repeated second person singular imperative form can have a special, adverbial, function, roughly equivalent to 'by dint/force of -ing', 'by gradually -ing', 'by -ing away', etc. This is particularly commonly encountered in the expressions *cammina cammina* and *corri corri*:

Cammina cammina, raggiunse il pozzo.	'He walked and walked until he reached the well.'
Corri corri, il prete arrivò a casa prima che scoppiasse la tempesta.	'By running hard, the priest got home before the storm broke.'

also

Scava scava, la talpa sbucò nella cantina di Mario.	'By digging away, the mole popped out in M's cellar.'
Rifletti rifletti, riuscì a trovare la soluzione.	'He thought and thought till he found the solution.'

etc.

13.15 Phrasal verbs with adverbs of place: *andare via* 'to go away', *venire fuori* 'to come out', etc.

Italian makes considerably less use of phrasal verbs of the 'go away' type than does English, but rather more use than many of its sister languages (for example, French). The Italian forms are largely limited to place adverbs *giù* 'down', *su* 'up', *fuori* 'out', *dentro* 'inside', *avanti* 'forward', *via* 'off', 'away', *indietro* 'back' which are most commonly combined with 'basic' verbs of motion, carrying and placing, such as *andare, venire, portare, tirare, mettere*. Note that while *andare fuori* 'to go out', *andare giù* 'to go down', *venire su* 'to come up', etc., are possible in Italian, one could equally use simple verbs such as *uscire, scendere, salire*, where they are available:

Forse era tempo di prepararsi ad andare via.	'Perhaps it was time to prepare to go away.'
Portiamo giù questo barile.	'Let's carry this barrel down.'
Tre autocarri venivano su per la carrozzabile.	'Three vans were coming up [along] the track.'
Quando [. . .] lo ebbero poi portato via (e, sì, lo avevano trascinato per le spalle sino alla carretta cosicché la stoppa del pupazzo era venuta fuori di nuovo) [. . .] [Lam.]	'When they had taken it away (and yes, they'd dragged it by the shoulders up to the cart so that the doll's stuffing had come out again) . . .'
Non si sa mai cosa va a tirar fuori.	'You never know what he is going to pull out.'
Frugando fra i vecchi bauli e le damigiane d'olio è saltata fuori una vecchia tela scurita e impolverata. Marianna la tira su . . . [Mar.]	'As she rummaged among the old trunks and the demijohns of oil, out jumped an old, darkened and dusty canvas. M pulls it up . . .'

It is very frequently the case that where English can express a wide variety of meanings by using a common phrasal verb + different adverbs of place, Italian tends to use a distinct verb or verb phrase for each meaning. Illustration of this fact belongs in a dictionary, rather than a grammar, but we illustrate below some possible Italian equivalents of the verb 'look' and 'stand' + adverb (bear in mind that some of the English expressions have more than one meaning, and that these may be expressed in different ways in Italian):

'look down'	*abbassare lo sguardo*
'look up'	*alzare lo sguardo*
'look away'	*distogliere lo sguardo*
'look back'	*guardarsi dietro le spalle/riandare con la mente*
'look round'	*guardarsi intorno* [lit. 'look about oneself']
'look out'	*stare attento* [in the sense 'be careful']
'stand up'	*alzarsi* (*in piedi*)
'stand out'	*fare spicco/essere prominente*
'stand down'	*ritirarsi/dimettersi*
'stand away'	*stare al largo*

13.16 Time adverbs

Ora and *adesso* ('now') are synonymous, although *ora* is principally characteristic of Tuscany (also Liguria and Sicily). Both can mean 'just now' and 'in a moment':

La lettera à arrivata ora.	'The letter arrived just now.'
Adesso arrivo, aspetta un attimo!	'I'm just coming, wait a moment!'

'Just', 'only just' is also *appena*:

Ero appena tornato dal lavoro quando lo vidi.	'I had just got back from work when I saw him.'
Girava per le stanze sistemando gli asciugamani appena stirati.	'She was wandering through the rooms sorting out the just [freshly] ironed towels.'
Li avevano appena visti quando decisero di arrendersi.	'They had just seen them when they decided to surrender.'

A colloquial way of expressing 'recentness' is *bell'e*:

È bell'e smesso di piovere.	'It's just this minute stopped raining.'
È inutile che tu chiami le ragazze, sono bell'e andate via.	'There's no point you calling the girls, they've just gone.'

Ormai (or *oramai*) is 'now' in the sense 'by now':

Ormai è troppo tardi.	'(By) now it's too late.'
Questi problemi sono ormai risolti.	'These problems are now sorted out.'

Allora is 'then', 'at that time'; *poi* 'then', 'subsequently':

Allora non esistevano automobili.	'Then cars did not exist.'
Un giorno risolverò il problema da solo. Allora capirete perché non vi ho aiutati.	'One day I'll solve the problem on my own. Then you'll see why I didn't help you.'

Note that whereas *allora* is 'then', '<u>at</u> that time', *poi* is 'then', '<u>after</u> that time'. In other words, *poi* emphasizes temporal succession. *Allora* also often carries connotations of causality, introducing an event which follows from some situation obtaining at a particular time. Consider the following:

Gli diremo che suo figlio è ammalato. *Allora tornerà a casa.* *Gli diremo che suo figlio è ammalato. Poi* *tornerà a casa.*	'We'll tell him his son is ill. Then he'll come home.' 'We'll tell him his son is ill. Then he'll come home.'

In the first example, *allora* implies 'at that time', 'in the circumstances of/because of his knowing that his son is ill'. In the second, *poi* can simply mean 'subsequently', 'the next thing he'll do': there is not *necessarily* any causal relationship between our telling him his son is ill and his returning home.

Note that *allora* can be preceded by a preposition (as can 'then' in English):

La scrittrice americana ha esordito nel 1950. *Da allora ha scritto oltre venti romanzi.*	'The American writer started out in 1950. Since then she has written over twenty novels.'
Fino ad allora non avevo mai sentito parlare *del tronco cerebrale.*	'Until then I'd never heard of the cerebral trunk.'

'Still' *ancora; non ancora* 'not yet':

Eri ancora in giro?	'Were you still about?'
È possibile che non abbiano ancora riaperto?	'Can they possibly not have reopened yet?'

Sempre, in addition to meaning 'always', is also 'still':

Ho vissuto sempre a Roma.	'I've always lived in Rome.'
Il fatto che da Piacenza in su sia sempre lo *stesso fiume non significa niente.* [Gua.]	'That above Piacenza it is still the same river means nothing.'
È sempre lì che ci aspetta.	'He's still there waiting for us.'

'Already' is *già*:

Alzati che sono già le nove!	'Get up. It's already nine o'clock!'
So già che non c'è più speranza.	'I already know there's no hope left.'

Note also the use of *già in/a* 'as early as', 'already in', *già prima di* 'even before':

Già nel 1938 si guardava la televisione.	'People were watching television as early as 1938.'
Già prima di Colombo avevano avuto *contatti con l'Europa.*	'Even before Columbus they'd had contact with Europe.'

'Never' or 'not ever' is *mai*:

Non glielo darò mai. Mai e poi mai! *Mai nessun ragazzo ha saputo di ragni che* *facciano il nido, tranne Pin.*	'I'll never give it to him. Never, ever!' 'Never has any boy heard of spiders making nests, except for P.'

'Ever' is *mai*:

Hai mai letto I promessi sposi?	'Have you ever read *The Betrothed*?'
E lì conobbi l'uomo più dolce e più grande *che abbia mai incontrato.*	'And there I met the sweetest and greatest man I have ever encountered.'

'Sometimes' *talvolta, a volte, qualche volta*:

A volte le zampe delle mule sprofondano *nell'argilla.*	'Sometimes the mules' feet sink into the clay.'
Sono ostacoli che talvolta possono sembrare *insuperabili.*	'These are problems that may sometimes seem insurmountable.'

'Every so often', 'from time to time' *ognitanto/ogni tanto, di quando in quando*:

Di quando in quando si sente qualche piccolo terremoto.	'From time to time we feel some small earthquake.'
Ognitanto bisogna dimenticare il lavoro.	'Every so often one must forget work.'

Also *quando ... quando* or *ora ... ora ...* 'sometimes ... sometimes':

Girava ora a sinistra ora a destra.	'He was turning sometimes left sometimes right.'
Quando chiacchiera, quando legge il giornale: insomma non combina nulla.	'Sometimes he chats, sometimes he reads the paper: he doesn't get up to anything, in other words.'

'Often' is *spesso*:

Quando ero a New York lo vedevo spesso.	'When I was in New York, I saw him often.'

'Before(hand)' or 'first' is *prima*; 'after(wards)' or 'later' is *dopo* (or *più tardi* 'later'):

È doveroso, però, che chi effettua queste denunce accerti prima, bene ed esattamente come stiano le cose.	'But whoever lodges these denunciations should first ascertain fully and accurately how things stand.'
Qualche tempo dopo, ricevemmo una lettera dal preside.	'Some time after, we received a letter from the headmaster.'

'First(ly)', 'first of all' *prima, dapprima*; 'last(ly)' *alla fine, finalmente*:

Dapprima non lo avevo visto.	'First of all I didn't see him.'
Finalmente posso dire che la faccenda è andata molto bene.	'Lastly I can say that the matter went very well.'

Per primo is 'first', and *per ultimo* 'last', in the sense of 'as the first one', 'as the last one':

Mario entrò per primo ed io per ultimo.	'M came in first and me last.'
Hanno firmato loro per primi.	'They signed first.'

'Henceforth', 'from now on' may be expressed as *d'ora in poi*. 'Thereafter', 'from then on' as *d'allora in poi'*.

'Ago' is *fa*, placed like English 'ago' *after* the time expression:

È morto qualche anno fa.	'He died a few years ago.'
Ma l'ho visto solo due minuti fa!	'But I saw him only two minutes ago!'
Ce ne siamo accorti poco fa.	'We realized it a short while ago/just now.'

Like English 'ago' (and unlike French *il y a*, which has a past form *il y avait*), *fa* is invariable and can only be used in relation to now, the time of speaking. To say 'before', or 'earlier' one uses *prima*:

Era morto qualche anno prima.	'He'd died a few years earlier.'
Ma l'avevo visto solo due minuti prima!	'But I'd seen him only two minutes before!'
Ce n'eravamo accorti poco prima.	'We'd realized it shortly before.'

Alternative ways of expressing 'ago' are:

c *or è* and *or sono* (with plural time periods), both restricted to literary and formal styles:

Duecento anni or sono nasceva a Padova il più famoso dei miei antenati.	'Two hundred years ago the most famous of my ancestors was born in Padua.'

- *è/sono* + time expression + *che* + verb:

  È un mese che mi ha scritto l'ultima volta.   'He last wrote to me a month ago.'

  Sono tre anni che l'ho visto.   'I saw him three years ago.'

- *sarà* + time expression 'about . . . ago' (in informal registers):

  Ho consegnato il compito sarà un mese.   'I handed in the assignment about a month ago.'

  Ho smesso di fumare saranno quindici anni.   'I gave up smoking about 15 years ago.'

Among the meanings of *già* is 'formerly':

Piazza Matteotti (già Piazza Nuova)   'Piazza Matteotti (formerly Piazza Nuova)'

Gianni De Michelis, già ministro degli esteri, ha fatto sapere ieri che . . .   'GDM, the former foreign minister, announced yesterday that . . .'

13.17 Position and function of negative adverbs and adverbial phrases: *mai* 'never'; *mica* '(certainly) not' (colloquial); *neanche, nemmeno, neppure* '(not) even' (also 'and nor', 'and not')

For the presence vs. absence of *non* before the verb in these cases, see 8.5.

The rules for the positioning of negative adverbs in relation to the verb are essentially those applying to other adverbs, as described in 13.11. They may appear:

- in front of the verb, where they serve emphatically to negate the whole sentence: e.g., *Mai l'ho fatto.*
- after the verb: e.g., *Non l'ho fatto mai.*
- between an auxiliary and a following past participle, infinitive or gerund: e.g., *Non l'ho mai fatto, Non glielo farò mai fare* 'I'll never make him do it'.
- between a modal verb and the following infinitive if the sentence contains *non*: *Non lo devi mai fare.*

Contini non indica mai nelle sue missive l'anno.   'C never gives the date in his letters.'

Mai l'ho visto senza cappello.   'Never have I seen him hatless.'
Mai Gianni direbbe cose del genere!   'Never would G says things like that!'
Ma io mica rido per quello che ha detto!   'But I'm certainly not laughing at what he said!'

—Ma quello non è il maresciallo Caputo?   'Isn't that Marshal C?'
—No, Caputo mica è così alto!   'No, C sure isn't that tall.'
All'epoca neanche sapevamo che cosa fosse l'editoria.   'At the time we didn't even know what publishing was.'
Quell'uomo non sa neanche il proprio indirizzo.   'That man doesn't even know his own address.'
Non capisco perché non gli faccia mai guardare [or *guardare mai*] *la TV.*   'I don't understand why he never lets him watch TV.'
Cerca suo figlio? Lo faccio subito chiamare [or *chiamare subito*].   'Are you looking for your son? I'll have him called for immediately.'

Mai, neanche, nemmeno, neppure can also stand for whole sentences or for verb phrases which they modify. There is not always an exact equivalent in English ('not even' cannot stand for a whole sentence), and the English equivalent is often 'never' + a substitute verb such as 'is', 'was', 'does', 'did', etc. or 'not even that', 'he hasn't even done that', etc.:

—*Eri già stato a Parigi?*	'Have you been to Paris before?'
—*Mai.*	'Never.'
Paolo è stato spesso in carcere, Franco mai.	'P has often been in prison, F never has.'
—*Allora ha fatto spese?*	'Has he done the shopping then?'
—*Neppure.*	'Not even that.'
Al padre non piace il vino rosso. Al figlio nemmeno.	'The father doesn't like red wine. 'Nor does the son.'
No, Prodi non si è fatto vivo, e neppure Scalfaro.	'No, P didn't turn up, and neither did S.'
Sono ammesse solo opere mai pubblicate neppure parzialmente.	'Only works [which have] never [been] published, even partially, are accepted.'

When *mica* stands for a verb in this way, it must always be followed by a subject, an object and adjective or an adverb (for more on *mica*, see 18.3.):

mica vero [=*Non è mica vero.*]	'not true'
Mica male [=*Non è mica male*], *per un esordiente!*	'Not bad, for a beginner!'
Lorena si alzava sempre alle cinque per studiare, mica il fratello.	'L always got up at 5 o'clock to study, but her brother sure didn't.'

In addition to negating verbs, *nemmeno, neppure, neanche* can also negate an element immediately following them (much as in English):

Neanche due lire mi sono rimaste.	'I don't even have two lire left.'
Nemmeno il matrimonio l'ha resa felice.	'Not even marriage has made her happy.'
Nemmeno Montaigne avrebbe potuto dire meglio.	'Not even M could have said it better.'
Neppure domani lo avremo.	'We won't have it even tomorrow.'
Non aveva neppure le autorizzazioni in ordine.	'He didn't have even his authorizations in order.'
Vent'anni fa non c'erano editori specializzati in libri-gioco, neanche all'estero.	'Twenty years ago there no publishers specializing in toy-books, not even abroad.'
Neanche/nemmeno/neppure se mi dai un milione farò quello che vuoi!	'Not even if you give me a million will I do what you want!'

Note the idiom *neanche per sogno*:

Pentirmi? Neanche per sogno.	'Me repent? No way./You must be joking./No chance.'

Particularly in the spoken language, there is a strong tendency to use adverbs (e.g., *affatto, assolutamente* 'not at all') or adverbial phrases (*per niente/niente* '(not) at all', *in nessun caso* 'in no case', *mai e poi mai* 'never ever'). *Affatto* and *assolutamente* mean 'altogether', 'quite', 'entirely', 'absolutely', and may be used in non-negative sentences (although use of *affatto* in this way is restricted to very formal, literary usage):

Affatto bello gli sembrò lo spettacolo.	'The show seemed quite beautiful to him.'

Certe coincidenze sono assolutamente inspiegabili.	'Some coincidences are absolutely inexplicable.'
In quel giardino c'è un pino assolutamente straordinario.	'In that garden there is a quite extraordinary pine tree.'

However, while *assolutamente* is widely employed in non-negative sentences, it is also used to reinforce negatives, and *affatto* tends nowadays to be employed only in negative sentences introduced by *non*. Although they usually occur after the verb, they can also be placed between the auxiliary and the past participle or between a modal verb and the infinitive:

Non sono affatto sparito.	'I haven't disappeared at all.'
E io vi dico che Carlo non era affatto un fascista.	'And I'm telling you that C was not a fascist at all.'
Mio padre di fronte alla sua dotta moglie non si scompone assolutamente.	'My father is not in the least troubled in the presence of his learned wife.'
Questo documento non prova assolutamente la sua innocenza.	'This document in no way proves his innocence.'
Non siamo affatto preparati a questo radicale mutamento del mondo.	'We are not at all ready for this radical transformation of the world.'
Non dovete affatto preoccuparvi di pulire, ci penseranno i ragazzi.	'You simply mustn't bother about cleaning, the kids will do it.'
Non indicare assolutamente il mittente sulla busta.	'Under no circumstances indicate the sender on the envelope.'
Naturalmente quest'opera non vuole assolutamente sostituirsi al testo.	'Of course this work is not in any way intended to replace the text.'

Assolutamente, affatto and *niente affatto* are frequently used, in answering questions, to mean 'absolutely not':

—*È stata colpa tua!*	'It was your fault!'
—*Affatto/Niente affatto!/Assolutamente/ Assolutamente no!*	'Not at all!'/'No way!'

To express English 'Absolutely!' in this context one might also say: *Senz'altro!/ Certo!/Sicuramente!* To express 'It is not absolutely true' one might say *Non è del tutto vero, Non è completamente vero.*

Common alternatives to *affatto/assolutamente* are *per niente/per nulla.* They can be replaced by the adverb *niente* at a very informal level:

Quella ragazza non mi piace per niente/nulla.	'I don't like that girl at all.'
Questo gelato non è niente buono.	'This ice-cream is no good at all.'
Non ha niente fortuna.	'He gets no luck.'

Note also phrases such as *non entrarci niente/nulla* 'to have nothing to do with (it)', *non avere nulla/niente a che vedere con* 'to have no connection with':

Tu non c'entri niente.	'You've got nothing to do with it.'
Questa pratica non c'entra nulla con i principi di corretta gestione aziendale.	'This practice has got nothing to do with the principles of proper company management.'
Queste clinichette non hanno nulla a che vedere con gli istituti privati.	'These little clinics have no connection with/have nothing to do with private institutes.'

The adverbial phrases *in nessun caso, mai e poi mai* are employed in main clauses only when the verb is in the future, future-in-the-past, present and past conditional, imperative, present subjunctive, to say that something was not or will not ever be the case:

Non venire in nessun caso prima delle cinque.	'In no case come before 5.'
Non ti confiderei mai e poi mai i miei progetti.	'I would never ever reveal to you my plans.'

Mai e poi mai and *in nessun caso* can also occur in sentence initial position without *non* to emphasize the negation: *Mai e poi mai ti confiderei i miei progetti*, etc.

Like English 'never!', *mai!* can be used as a particularly emphatic form of *no!*:

—*Ti arrendi?*	'Will you surrender?'
—*Mai!*	'Never!'

Negatives can also be reinforced by the following superlative expressions:

Non ho la più pallida idea di chi sia quell'uomo.	'I haven't the foggiest idea who that man is.'
Non fa il minimo sforzo per aiutarla.	'He doesn't make the slightest effort to help her.'
Non ha fatto il minimo accenno all'accaduto.	'I made not the slightest allusion to what had happened.'

Un cavolo, un accidenti can replace the negative expressions listed above (*affatto, assolutamente, per niente,* etc.) to emphasize the negation, in familiar, colloquial style. They are frequently combined with *Non me ne importa ...,* etc. (of which much more vulgar variants are *Non me ne frega ...,* etc.) to mean 'I couldn't care less':

Michele rispose che non gliene importava/ fregava un cavolo/un accidenti di quello che era successo.	'M answered that he couldn't give a damn about what had happened.'
C'era una nebbia che non si vedeva un cavolo/accidenti.	'There was such a fog that you couldn't see a bloody thing.'

14

Forms of the verb

14.1 Some descriptive terms

Most verb forms have the following basic structure:

root (+ thematic vowel) + grammatical desinence(s)

The 'root' is the part of the verb expressing the lexical meaning of the verb (e.g., 'sing', 'sleep', 'do'); the thematic vowels, *a*, *e* and *i*, have no meaning of their own, but are systematically present in certain parts of the verb (for example, the second person plural present indicative, the imperfect tense) and help to identify the *conjugation* (see below) to which a verb belongs; the grammatical desinences carry most of the information about the grammatical category of the verb (e.g., 'infinitive', 'second person plural'). Thus:

cantare	*cant* (root 'sing') + *a* (thematic vowel) + *re* (infinitive desinence)
cantate	*cant* (root 'sing') + *a* (thematic vowel) + *te* (second person plural desinence)
cantavamo	*cant* (root 'sing') + *a* (thematic vowel) + *va* (imperfect indicative desinence) + *mo* (first person plural desinence)
dormire	*dorm* (root 'sleep') + *i* (thematic vowel) + *re* (infinitive desinence)
dormite	*dorm* (root 'sleep') + *i* (thematic vowel) + *te* (second person plural desinence)
dormivamo	*dorm* (root 'sleep') + *i* (thematic vowel) + *va* (imperfect indicative desinence) + *mo* (first person plural desinence)

Roots may either be *stressed* (as in first person singular *canto*) or *unstressed* (as in first person plural *cantiamo*). This stress distinction plays a major role in the structure of certain verbs.

Verb forms are further divided into 'synthetic' and 'analytic': briefly, synthetic forms constitute a single word, comprising a root, a thematic vowel (where present) and a grammatical desinence (e.g., *canto* 'I sing', *vengo* 'I come'); analytic forms comprise two (occasionally more) words, one – the 'auxiliary' – expressing mainly grammatical information, such as person, mood number, and the other expressing principally the lexical meaning of the verb (e.g., *Ho cantato* 'I have sung', *Sono venuto* 'I have come').

14.2 Conjugations

The conjugations are conventionally defined as follows:

- First conjugation: thematic vowel *a* in the infinitive (*cantare, parlare, amare,* etc.) For *fare*, classified in the second conjugation, see below.

- Second conjugation: these verbs have thematic *e* in the infinitive. In the overwhelming majority of second conjugation verbs this *e* is unstressed, and the stress falls on the root of the infinitive: *ric<u>e</u>vere* 'receive', *p<u>e</u>rdere* 'lose', *es<u>i</u>stere* 'exist', *sc<u>e</u>ndere* 'go down', etc. In a small minority of about twenty basic verbs, many of which happen, none the less, to be extremely frequently used, stress does fall on thematic *e* in the infinitive: *tem<u>e</u>re* 'fear', *vol<u>e</u>re* 'want', *sap<u>e</u>re* 'know', *av<u>e</u>re* 'have', *cad<u>e</u>re* 'fall', *piac<u>e</u>re* 'please', *giac<u>e</u>re* 'lie', *god<u>e</u>re* 'enjoy', *par<u>e</u>re* 'seem', *dov<u>e</u>re* 'must', *persuad<u>e</u>re* 'persuade', *pot<u>e</u>re* 'can', *riman<u>e</u>re* 'stay', *sed<u>e</u>re* 'sit', *tac<u>e</u>re* 'be silent', *ten<u>e</u>re* 'hold', *val<u>e</u>re* 'be worth', *ved<u>e</u>re* 'see', etc. Included in the second conjugation are some other verbs with root-stressed infinitives: *fare* 'do' and infinitives in *-rre* (e.g., *produrre* 'produce', *trarre* 'draw', *porre* 'put'). Note that *most* second conjugation verbs have additional irregularities (especially in the root), not present in the sample conjugations given immediately below.
- Third conjugation: thematic vowel *i* in the infinitive (*dormire* 'sleep', *finire* 'finish', *sentire* 'feel', etc.).

The following illustrate the major conjugational classes:

First conjugation

Infinitive	Gerund	Past participle
cantare	*cantando*	*cantato*

	Present indicative	Subjunctive	Passato remoto
1sg.	*canto*	*canti*	*cantai*
2sg.	*canti*	*canti*	*cantasti*
3sg.	*canta*	*canti*	*cantò*
1pl.	*cantiamo*	*cantiamo*	*cantammo*
2pl.	*cantate*	*cantiate*	*cantaste*
3pl.	*cantano*	*cantino*	*cantarono*

	Future	Conditional	Imperf. indicative	Imperf. subjunctive
1sg.	*canterò*	*canterei*	*cantavo*	*cantassi*
2sg.	*canterai*	*canteresti*	*cantavi*	*cantassi*
3sg.	*canterà*	*canterebbe*	*cantava*	*cantasse*
1pl.	*canteremo*	*canteremmo*	*cantavamo*	*cantassimo*
2pl.	*canterete*	*cantereste*	*cantavate*	*cantaste*
3pl.	*canteranno*	*canterebbero*	*cantavano*	*cantassero*

Second conjugation

Infinitive	Gerund	Past participle
temere	*temendo*	*temuto*
ric<u>e</u>vere	*ricevendo*	*ricevuto*

	Present indicative	Subjunctive	Passato remoto
1sg.	*temo*	*tema*	*temei/temetti*
	ricevo	*riceva*	*ricevei/ricevetti*
2sg.	*temi*	*tema*	*temesti*
	ricevi	*riceva*	*ricevesti*
3sg.	*teme*	*tema*	*temé/temette*
	riceve	*riceva*	*ricevé/ricevette*

	Present indicative	Subjunctive	Passato remoto
1pl.	temiamo	temiamo	tememmo
	riceviamo	riceviamo	ricevemmo
2pl.	temete	temiate	temeste
	ricevete	riceviate	riceveste
3pl.	temono	temano	temerono/temettero
	ricevono	ricevano	riceverono/ricevettero

	Future	Conditional	Imperf. indicative	Imperf. subjunctive
1sg.	temerò	temerei	temevo	temessi
	riceverò	riceverei	ricevevo	ricevessi
2sg.	temerai	temeresti	temevi	temessi
	riceverai	riceveresti	ricevevi	ricevessi
3sg.	temerà	temerebbe	temeva	temesse
	riceverà	riceverebbe	riceveva	ricevesse
1pl.	temeremo	temeremmo	temevamo	temessimo
	riceveremo	riceveremmo	ricevevamo	ricevessimo
2pl.	temerete	temereste	temevate	temeste
	riceverete	ricevereste	ricevevate	riceveste
3pl.	temerenno	temerebbero	temevano	temessero
	riceverenno	riceverebbero	ricevevano	ricevessero

Third conjugation

	Infinitive	Gerund	Past participle
	dormire	dormendo	dormito
	finire	finendo	finito

	Present indicative	Subjunctive	Passato remoto
1sg.	dormo	dorma	dormii
	finisco	finisca	finii
2sg.	dormi	dorma	dormisti
	finisci	finisca	finisti
3sg.	dorme	dorma	dormì
	finisce	finisca	finì
1pl.	dormiamo	dormiamo	dormimmo
	finiamo	finiamo	finimmo
2pl.	dormite	dormiate	dormiste
	finite	finiate	finiste
3pl.	dormono	dormano	dormirono
	finiscono	finiscano	finirono

	Future	Conditional	Imperf. indicative	Imperf. subjunctive
1sg.	dormirò	dormirei	dormivo	dormissi
	finirò	finirei	finivo	finissi
2sg.	dormirai	dormiresti	dormivi	dormissi
	finirai	finiresti	finivi	finissi
3sg.	dormirà	dormirebbe	dormiva	dormisse
	finirà	finirebbe	finiva	finisse
1pl.	dormiremo	dormiremmo	dormivamo	dormissimo
	finiremo	finiremmo	finivamo	finissimo
2pl.	dormirete	dormireste	dormivate	dormiste
	finirete	finireste	finivate	finiste
3pl.	dormiranno	dormirebbero	dormivano	dormissero
	finiranno	finirebbero	finivano	finissero

14.3 Major irregular verbs

The following illustrate the major patterns of irregularity encountered in the conjugations of Italian verbs (listed in alphabetical order). Section 14.4 will indicate how the formation of other verbs can be inferred on the basis of these verbs.

affigere 'affix'

	Infinitive	Gerund	Past participle
	affiggere	*affiggendo*	*affisso*

	Present indicative	Subjunctive	Passato remoto
1sg.	*affiggo*	*affigga*	*affissi*
2sg.	*affiggi*	*affigga*	*affiggesti*
3sg.	*affigge*	*affigga*	*affisse*
	etc.	etc.	etc.

andare 'go'

	Infinitive	Gerund	Past participle
	andare	*andando*	*andato*

	Present indicative	Subjunctive	Passato remoto
1sg.	*vado*	*vada*	*andai*
2sg.	*vai* **Imper.** *vai, va'*	*vada*	*andasti*
3sg.	*va*	*vada*	*andò*
1pl.	*andiamo*	*andiamo*	*andammo*
2pl.	*andate*	*andiate*	*andaste*
3pl.	*vanno*	*vadano*	*andarono*

	Future	Conditional	Imperf. indicative	Imperf. subjunctive
1sg.	*andrò*	*andrei*	*andavo*	*andassi*
	etc.	etc.	etc.	etc.

annettere 'annex'

	Infinitive	Gerund	Past participle
	annettere	*annettendo*	*annesso*

	Present indicative	Subjunctive	Passato remoto
1sg.	*annetto*	*annetta*	*annettei* (or *annessi*)
2sg.	*annetti*	*annetta*	*annettesti*
3sg.	*annette*	*annetta*	*annetté* (or *annesse*)
	etc.	etc.	etc.

apparire 'appear'[1]

	Infinitive	Gerund	Past participle
	apparire	*apparendo*	*apparso*

---

[1]Alternatively, this verb may be conjugated like *finire* (*apparisco, apparii*, etc.)

	Present indicative	Subjunctive	Passato remoto
1sg.	*appaio*	*appaia*	*apparvi*
2sg.	*appari*	*appaia*	*apparisti*
3sg.	*appare*	*appaia*	*apparve*
1pl.	*appariamo*	*appariamo*	*apparimmo*
2pl.	*apparite*	*appariate*	*appariste*
3pl.	*appaiono*	*appaiano*	*apparvero*

	Future	Conditional	Imperf. indicative	Imperf. subjunctive
1sg.	*apparirò*	*apparirei*	*apparivo*	*apparissi*
	etc.	etc.	etc.	etc.

assumere 'assume'

Infinitive	Gerund	Past participle
assumere	*assumendo*	*assunto*

	Present indicative	Subjunctive	Passato remoto
1sg.	*assumo*	*assuma*	*assunsi*
2sg.	*assumi*	*assuma*	*assumesti*
3sg.	*assume*	*assuma*	*assunse*
	etc.	etc.	etc.

avere 'have'

Infinitive	Gerund	Past participle
avere	*avendo*	*avuto*

	Present indicative	Subjunctive	Passato remoto
1sg.	*ho*	*abbia*	*ebbi*
2sg.	*hai* **Imper.** *abbi*	*abbia*	*avesti*
3sg.	*ha*	*abbia*	*ebbe*
1pl.	*abbiamo*	*abbiamo*	*avemmo*
2pl.	*avete* **Imper.** *abbiate* *abbiate*		*aveste*
3pl.	*hanno*	*abbiano*	*ebbero*

	Future	Conditional	Imperf. indicative	Imperf. subjunctive
1sg.	*avrò*	*avrei*	*avevo*	*avessi*
	etc.	etc.	etc.	etc.

bere 'drink'

Infinitive	Gerund	Past participle
bere	*bevendo*	*bevuto*

	Present indicative	Subjunctive	Passato remoto
1sg.	*bevo*	*beva*	*bevvi*
2sg.	*bevi*	*beva*	*bevesti*
3sg.	*beve*	*beva*	*bevve*
	etc.	etc.	etc.

	Future	Conditional	Imperf. indicative	Imperf. subjunctive
1sg.	*berrò*	*berrei*	*bevevo*	*bevessi*
	etc.	etc.	etc.	etc.

cadere 'fall'

	Infinitive	Gerund	Past participle
	cadere	cadendo	caduto

	Present indicative	Subjunctive	Passato remoto
1sg.	cado	cada	caddi
2sg.	cadi	cada	cadesti
3sg.	cade	cada	cadde
	etc.	etc.	etc.

	Future	Conditional	Imperf. indicative	Imperf. subjunctive
1sg.	cadrò	cadrei	cadevo	cadessi
	etc.	etc.	etc.	etc.

chiedere 'ask'

	Infinitive	Gerund	Past participle
	chiedere	chiedendo	chiesto

	Present indicative	Subjunctive	Passato remoto
1sg.	chiedo	chieda	chiesi
2sg.	chiedi	chieda	chiedesti
3sg.	chiede	chieda	chiese
	etc.	etc.	etc.

chiudere 'close'

	Infinitive	Gerund	Past participle
	chiudere	chiudendo	chiuso

	Present indicative	Subjunctive	Passato remoto
1sg.	chiudo	chiuda	chiusi
2sg.	chiudi	chiuda	chiudesti
3sg.	chiude	chiuda	chiuse
	etc.	etc.	etc.

cogliere 'gather', 'pick'

	Infinitive	Gerund	Past participle
	cogliere	cogliendo	colto

	Present indicative	Subjunctive	Passato remoto
1sg.	colgo	colga	colsi
2sg.	cogli	colga	cogliesti
3sg.	coglie	colga	colse
1pl.	cogliamo	cogliamo	cogliemmo
2pl.	cogliete	cogliate	coglieste
3pl.	colgono	colgano	colsero

concedere 'concede'

Infinitive	Gerund	Past participle
concedere	*concedendo*	*concesso*

	Present indicative	Subjunctive	Passato remoto
1sg.	*concedo*	*conceda*	*concessi* or *concedei*
2sg.	*concedi*	*conceda*	*concedesti*
3sg.	*concede*	*conceda*	*concesse* or *concedette*
	etc.	etc.	etc.

condurre 'lead'

Infinitive	Gerund	Past participle
condurre	*conducendo*	*condotto*

	Present indicative	Subjunctive	Passato remoto
1sg.	*conduco*	*conduca*	*condussi*
2sg.	*conduci*	*conduca*	*conducesti*
3sg.	*conduce*	*conduca*	*condusse*
	etc.	etc.	etc.

	Future	Conditional	Imperf. indicative	Imperf. subjunctive
1sg.	*condurrò*	*condurrei*	*conducevo*	*conducessi*
	etc.	etc.	etc.	etc.

conoscere 'know'

Infinitive	Gerund	Past participle
conoscere	*conoscendo*	*conosciuto*

	Present indicative	Subjunctive	Passato remoto
1sg.	*conosco*	*conosca*	*conobbi*
2sg.	*conosci*	*conosca*	*conoscesti*
3sg.	*conosce*	*conosca*	*conobbe*
	etc.	etc.	etc.

correre 'run'

Infinitive	Gerund	Past participle
correre	*correndo*	*corso*

	Present indicative	Subjunctive	Passato remoto
1sg.	*corro*	*corra*	*corsi*
2sg.	*corri*	*corra*	*corresti*
3sg.	*corre*	*corra*	*corse*
	etc.	etc.	etc.

cuocere 'cook'

Infinitive	Gerund	Past participle
cuocere	*cuocendo* (*cocendo*)	*cotto*

	Present indicative	Subjunctive	Passato remoto
1sg.	*cuocio*	*cuocia*	*cossi*
2sg.	*cuoci*	*cuocia*	*cuocesti (cocesti)*
3sg.	*cuoce*	*cuocia*	*cosse*
1pl.	*cuociamo (cociamo)*	*cuociamo (cociamo)*	*cuocemmo (cocemmo)*
2pl.	*cuocete (cocete)*	*cuociate (cociate)*	*cuoceste (coceste)*
3pl.	*cuociono*	*cuociano*	*cossero*

	Future	Conditional	Imperf. indicative	Imperf. subjunctive
1sg.	*cuocerò (cocerò)*	*cuocerei (cocerei)*	*cuocevo (cocevo)*	*cuocessi (cocessi)*
	etc.	etc.	etc.	etc.

dare 'give'

	Infinitive	Gerund	Past participle
	dare	*dando*	*dato*

	Present indicative	Subjunctive	Passato remoto
1sg.	*do*	*dia*	*diedi/detti*
2sg.	*dai* **Imper.** *da', dai*	*dia*	*desti*
3sg.	*dà*	*dia*	*diede/dette*
1pl.	*diamo*	*diamo*	*demmo*
2pl.	*date*	*diate*	*deste*
3pl.	*danno*	*diano*	*diedero/dettero*

	Future	Conditional	Imperf. indicative	Imperf. subjunctive
1sg.	*darò*	*darei*	*davo*	*dessi*
	etc.	etc.	etc.	etc.

devolvere 'devolve'

	Infinitive	Gerund	Past participle
	devolvere	*devolvendo*	*devoluto*

	Present indicative	Subjunctive	Passato remoto
1sg.	*devolvo*	*devolva*	*devolvei*
2sg.	*devolvi*	*devolva*	*devolvesti*
3sg.	*devolve*	*devolva*	*devolvé*
	etc.	etc.	etc.

dire 'say'

	Infinitive	Gerund	Past participle
	dire	*dicendo*	*detto*

	Present indicative	Subjunctive	Passato remoto
1sg.	*dico*	*dica*	*dissi*
2sg.	*dici* **Imper.** *di'*	*dica*	*dicesti*
3sg.	*dice*	*dica*	*disse*
1pl.	*diciamo*	*diciamo*	*dicemmo*
2pl.	*dite*	*diciate*	*diceste*
3pl.	*dicono*	*dicano*	*dissero*

	Future	Conditional	Imperf. indicative	Imperf. subjunctive
1sg.	*dirò*	*direi*	*dicevo*	*dicessi*
	etc.	etc.	etc.	etc.

dirigere 'direct'

	Infinitive	Gerund	Past participle
	dirigere	*dirigendo*	*diretto*

	Present indicative	Subjunctive	Passato remoto
1sg.	*dirigo*	*diriga*	*diressi*
2sg.	*dirigi*	*diriga*	*dirigesti*
3sg.	*dirige*	*diriga*	*diresse*
	etc.	etc.	etc.

dolersi 'complain'

	Infinitive	Gerund	Past participle
	dolersi	*dolendosi*	*dolutosi*

	Present indicative	Subjunctive	Passato remoto
1sg.	*mi dolgo*	*mi dolga*	*mi dolsi*
2sg.	*ti duoli*	*ti dolga*	*ti dolesti*
3sg.	*si duole*	*si dolga*	*si dolse*
1pl.	*ci doliamo* (*dogliamo*)	*ci doliamo* (*dogliamo*)	*ci dolemmo*
2pl.	*vi dolete*	*vi doliate* (*dogliate*)	*vi doleste*
3pl.	*si dolgono*	*si dolgano*	*si dolsero*

	Future	Conditional	Imperf. indicative	Imperf. subjunctive
1sg.	*mi dorrò*	*mi dorrei*	*mi dolevo*	*mi dolessi*
	etc.	etc.	etc.	etc.

dovere 'have to'

	Infinitive	Gerund	Past participle
	dovere	*dovendo*	*dovuto*

	Present indicative	Subjunctive	Passato remoto
1sg.	*devo/debbo*	*debba* (*deva*)	*dovei/dovetti*
2sg.	*devi*	*debba* (*deva*)	*dovesti*
3sg.	*deve*[2]	*debba* (*deva*)	*dové/dovette*
1pl.	*dobbiamo*	*dobbiamo*	*dovemmo*
2pl.	*dovete*	*dobbiate*	*doveste*
3pl.	*devono/debbono*	*debbano* (*devano*)	*doverono/dovettero*

	Future	Conditional	Imperf. indicative	Imperf. subjunctive
1sg.	*dovrò*	*dovrei*	*dovevo*	*dovessi*
	etc.	etc.	etc.	etc.

[2]When followed by *essere*, the final *-e* is usually removed: *dev'essere*.

eccellere 'excel'

	Infinitive	Gerund	Past participle
	eccellere	eccellendo	eccelso[3]

	Present indicative	Subjunctive	Passato remoto
1sg.	eccello	eccella	eccelsi
2sg.	eccelli	eccella	eccellesti
3sg.	eccelle	eccella	eccelse
	etc.	etc.	etc.

empire 'fill'

	Infinitive	Gerund	Past participle
	empire	empiendo	empito

	Present indicative	Subjunctive	Passato remoto
1sg.	empio	empia	empii
2sg.	empi	empia	empisti
3sg.	empie	empia	empì
1pl.	empiamo	empiamo	empimmo
2pl.	empite	empiate	empiste
3pl.	empiono	empiano	empirono

	Future	Conditional	Imperf. indicative	Imperf. subjunctive
1sg.	empirò	empirei	empivo	empissi
	etc.	etc.	etc.	etc.

esprimere 'express'

	Infinitive	Gerund	Past participle
	esprimere	esprimendo	espresso

	Present indicative	Subjunctive	Passato remoto
1sg.	esprimo	esprima	espressi
2sg.	esprimi	esprima	esprimesti
3sg.	esprime	esprima	espresse
	etc.	etc.	etc.

essere 'be'

	Infinitive	Gerund	Past participle
	essere	essendo	stato

	Present indicative	Subjunctive	Passato remoto
1sg.	sono	sia	fui
2sg.	sei **Imper.** sii	sia	fosti
3sg.	è	sia	fu
1pl.	siamo	siamo	fummo
2pl.	siete **Imper.** siate	siate	foste
3pl.	sono	siano	furono

---

[3]But forms of this verb with auxiliary + past participle are very rare.

	Future	Conditional	Imperf. indicative	Imperf. subjunctive
1sg.	*sarò*	*sarei*	*ero*	*fossi*
2sg.	*sarai*	*saresti*	*eri*	*fossi*
3sg.	*sarà*	*sarebbe*	*era*	*fosse*
1pl.	*saremo*	*saremmo*	*eravamo*	*fossimo*
2pl.	*sarete*	*sareste*	*eravate*	*foste*
3pl.	*saranno*	*sarebbero*	*erano*	*fossero*

estinguere 'extinguish'

Infinitive	Gerund	Past participle
estinguere	*estinguendo*	*estinto*

	Present indicative	Subjunctive	Passato remoto
1sg.	*estinguo*	*estingua*	*estinsi*
2sg.	*estingui*	*estingua*	*estinguesti*
3sg.	*estingue*	*estingua*	*estinse*
	etc.	etc.	etc.

fare 'do'

Infinitive	Gerund	Past participle
fare	*facendo*	*fatto*

	Present indicative	Subjunctive	Passato remoto
1sg.	*faccio*	*faccia*	*feci*
2sg.	*fai* **Imper.** *fa'*, *fai*	*faccia*	*facesti*
3sg.	*fa*	*faccia*	*fece*
1pl.	*facciamo*	*facciamo*	*facemmo*
2pl.	*fate*	*facciate*	*faceste*
3pl.	*fanno*	*facciano*	*fecero*

	Future	Conditional	Imperf. indicative	Imperf. subjunctive
1sg.	*farò*	*farei*	*facevo*	*facessi*
	etc.	etc.	etc.	etc.

fondere 'melt'

Infinitive	Gerund	Past participle
fondere	*fondendo*	*fuso*

	Present indicative	Subjunctive	Passato remoto
1sg.	*fondo*	*fonda*	*fusi*
2sg.	*fondi*	*fonda*	*fondesti*
3sg.	*fonde*	*fonda*	*fuse*
	etc.	etc.	etc.

leggere 'read'

Infinitive	Gerund	Past participle
leggere	*leggendo*	*letto*

	Present indicative	Subjunctive	Passato remoto
1sg.	*leggo*	*legga*	*lessi*
2sg.	*leggi*	*legga*	*leggesti*
3sg.	*legge*	*legga*	*lesse*
	etc.	etc.	etc.

mettere 'put'

	Infinitive	Gerund	Past participle
	mettere	*mettendo*	*messo*

	Present indicative	Subjunctive	Passato remoto
1sg.	*metto*	*metta*	*misi*
2sg.	*metti*	*metta*	*mettesti*
3sg.	*mette*	*metta*	*mise*
	etc.	etc.	etc.

morire 'die'

	Infinitive	Gerund	Past participle
	morire	*morendo*	*morto*

	Present indicative	Subjunctive	Passato remoto
1sg.	*muoio*	*muoia*	*morii*
2sg.	*muori*	*muoia*	*moristi*
3sg.	*muore*	*muoia*	*morì*
1pl.	*moriamo*	*moriamo*	*morimmo*
2pl.	*morite*	*moriate*	*moriste*
3pl.	*muoiono*	*muoiano*	*morirono*

	Future	Conditional	Imperf. indicative	Imperf. subjunctive
1sg.	*morirò* (rare *morrò*)	*morirei*	*morivo*	*morissi*
	etc.	etc.	etc.	etc.

muovere 'move'

	Infinitive	Gerund	Past participle
	muovere	*muovendo* (*movendo*)	*mosso*

	Present indicative	Subjunctive	Passato remoto
1sg.	*muovo*	*muova*	*mossi*
2sg.	*muovi*	*muova*	*muovesti* (*movesti*)
3sg.	*muove*	*muova*	*mosse*
1pl.	*muoviamo* (*moviamo*)	*muoviamo* (*moviamo*)	*muovemmo* (*movemmo*)
2pl.	*muovete* (*movete*)	*muoviate* (*moviate*)	*muoveste* (*moveste*)
3pl.	*muovono*	*muovano*	*mossero*

	Future	Conditional	Imperf. indicative	Imperf. subjunctive
1sg.	*muoverò* (*moverò*)	*muoverei* (*moverei*)	*muovevo* (*movevo*)	*muovessi* (*movessi*)
	etc.	etc.	etc.	etc.

nascere 'be born'

Infinitive	Gerund	Past participle
nascere	nascendo	nato

	Present indicative	Subjunctive	Passato remoto
1sg.	nasco	nasca	nacqui
2sg.	nasci	nasca	nascesti
3sg.	nasce	nasca	nacque
1pl.	nasciamo	nasciamo	nascemmo
2pl.	nascete	nasciate	nasceste
3pl.	nascono	nascano	nacquero

	Future	Conditional	Imperf. indicative	Imperf. subjunctive
1sg.	nascerò	nascerei	nascevo	nascessi
	etc.	etc.	etc.	etc.

nascondere 'hide'

Infinitive	Gerund	Past participle
nascondere	nascondendo	nascosto

	Present indicative	Subjunctive	Passato remoto
1sg.	nascondo	nasconda	nascosi
2sg.	nascondi	nasconda	nascondesti
3sg.	nasconde	nasconda	nascose
	etc.	etc.	etc.

nuocere 'harm'

Infinitive	Gerund	Past participle
nuocere	nuocendo (nocendo)	nuociuto (nociuto)

	Present indicative	Subjunctive	Passato remoto
1sg.	nuocio (noccio)	noccia	nocqui
2sg.	nuoci	noccia	nocesti
3sg.	nuoce	noccia	nocque
1pl.	nuociamo (nociamo)	nuociamo (nociamo)	nuocemmo (nocemmo)
2pl.	nuocete (nocete)	nuociate (nociate)	nuoceste (noceste)
3pl.	nocciono	nocciano	nocquero

	Future	Conditional	Imperf. indicative	Imperf. subjunctive
1sg.	nuocerò (nocerò)	nuocerei (nocerei)	nuocevo (nocevo)	nuocessi (nocessi)
	etc.	etc.	etc.	etc.

parere 'seem'

Infinitive	Gerund	Past participle
parere	parendo	parso

	Present indicative	Subjunctive	Passato remoto
1sg.	paio	paia	parvi
2sg.	pari	paie	paresti

	Present indicative	Subjunctive	Passato remoto
3sg.	*pare*	*paia*	*parve*
1pl.	*pariamo (paiamo)*	*pariamo (paiamo)*	*paremmo*
2pl.	*parete*	*pariate (paiate)*	*pareste*
3pl.	*paiono*	*paiano*	*parvero*

	Future	Conditional	Imperf. indicative	Imperf. subjunctive
1sg.	*parrò*	*parrei*	*parevo*	*paressi*
	etc.	etc.	etc.	etc.

piacere 'please'

	Infinitive	Gerund	Past participle
	piacere	*piacendo*	*piaciuto*

	Present indicative	Subjunctive	Passato remoto
1sg.	*piaccio*	*piaccia*	*piacqui*
2sg.	*piaci*	*piaccia*	*piacesti*
3sg.	*piace*	*piaccia*	*piacque*
1pl.	*piacciamo*	*piacciamo*	*piacemmo*
2pl.	*piacete*	*piacciate*	*piaceste*
3pl.	*piacciono*	*piacciano*	*piacquero*

	Future	Conditional	Imperf. indicative	Imperf. subjunctive
1sg.	*piacerò*	*piacerei*	*piacevo*	*piacessi*
	etc.	etc.	etc.	etc.

piangere 'weep'

	Infinitive	Gerund	Past participle
	piangere	*piangendo*	*pianto*

	Present indicative	Subjunctive	Passato remoto
1sg.	*piango*	*pianga*	*piansi*
2sg.	*piangi*	*pianga*	*piangesti*
3sg.	*piange*	*pianga*	*pianse*
1pl.	*piangiamo*	*piangiamo*	*piangemmo*
2pl.	*piangete*	*piangiate*	*piangeste*
3pl.	*piangono*	*piangano*	*piansero*

	Future	Conditional	Imperf. indicative	Imperf. subjunctive
1sg.	*piangerò*	*piangerei*	*piangevo*	*piangessi*
	etc.	etc.	etc.	etc.

porre 'put'

	Infinitive	Gerund	Past participle
	porre	*ponendo*	*posto*

	Present indicative	Subjunctive	Passato remoto
1sg.	*pongo*	*ponga*	*posi*
2sg.	*poni*	*ponga*	*ponesti*
3sg.	*pone*	*ponga*	*pose*

	Present indicative	Subjunctive	Passato remoto
1pl.	*poniamo*	*poniamo*	*ponemmo*
2pl.	*ponete*	*poniate*	*poneste*
3pl.	*pongono*	*pongano*	*posero*

	Future	Conditional	Imperf. indicative	Imperf. subjunctive
1sg.	*porrò*	*porrei*	*ponevo*	*ponessi*
	etc.	etc.	etc.	etc.

potere 'be able'

Infinitive	Gerund	Past participle
potere	*potendo*	*potuto*

	Present indicative	Subjunctive	Passato remoto
1sg.	*posso*	*possa*	*potei*
2sg.	*puoi*	*possa*	*potesti*
3sg.	*può*	*possa*	*poté*
1pl.	*possiamo*	*possiamo*	*potemmo*
2pl.	*potete*	*possiate*	*poteste*
3pl.	*possono*	*possano*	*poterono*

	Future	Conditional	Imperf. indicative	Imperf. subjunctive
1sg.	*potrò*	*potrei*	*potevo*	*potessi*
	etc.	etc.	etc.	etc.

redigere 'edit'

Infinitive	Gerund	Past participle
redigere	*redigendo*	*redatto*

	Present indicative	Subjunctive	Passato remoto
1sg.	*redigo*	*rediga*	*redassi*
2sg.	*redigi*	*rediga*	*redigesti*
3sg.	*redige*	*rediga*	*redasse*
	etc.	etc.	etc.

rimanere 'stay'

Infinitive	Gerund	Past participle
rimanere	*rimanendo*	*rimasto*

	Present indicative	Subjunctive	Passato remoto
1sg.	*rimango*	*rimanga*	*rimasi*
2sg.	*rimani*	*rimanga*	*rimanesti*
3sg.	*rimane*	*rimanga*	*rimase*
1pl.	*rimaniamo*	*rimaniamo*	*rimanemmo*
2pl.	*rimanete*	*rimaniate*	*rimaneste*
3pl.	*rimangono*	*rimangano*	*rimasero*

	Future	Conditional	Imperf. indicative	Imperf. subjunctive
1sg.	*rimarrò*	*rimarrei*	*rimanevo*	*rimanessi*
	etc.	etc.	etc.	etc.

rompere 'break'

Infinitive	Gerund	Past participle
rompere	rompendo	rotto

	Present indicative	Subjunctive	Passato remoto
1sg.	rompo	rompa	ruppi
2sg.	rompi	rompa	rompesti
3sg.	rompe	rompa	ruppe
	etc.	etc.	etc.

salire 'go up'

Infinitive	Gerund	Past participle
salire	salendo	salito

	Present indicative	Subjunctive	Passato remoto
1sg.	salgo	salga	salii
2sg.	sali	salga	salisti
3sg.	sale	salga	salì
1pl.	saliamo	saliamo	salimmo
2pl.	salite	saliate	saliste
3pl.	salgono	salgano	salirono

	Future	Conditional	Imperf. indicative	Imperf. subjunctive
1sg.	salirò	salirei	salivo	salissi
	etc.	etc.	etc.	etc.

sapere 'know'

Infinitive	Gerund	Past participle
sapere	sapendo	saputo

	Present indicative	Subjunctive	Passato remoto
1sg.	so	sappia	seppi
2sg.	sai **Imper.** sappi	sappia	sapesti
3sg.	sa	sappia	seppe
1pl.	sappiamo	sappiamo	sapemmo
2pl.	sapete **Imper.** sappiate	sappiate	sapeste
3pl.	sanno	sappiano	seppero

	Future	Conditional	Imperf. indicative	Imperf. subjunctive
1sg.	saprò	saprei	sapevo	sapessi
	etc.	etc.	etc.	etc.

scindere 'cleave'

Infinitive	Gerund	Past participle
scindere	scindendo	scisso

	Present indicative	Subjunctive	Passato remoto
1sg.	*scindo*	*scinda*	*scissi*
2sg.	*scindi*	*scinda*	*scindesti*
3sg.	*scinde*	*scinda*	*scisse*
	etc.	etc.	etc.

scuotere 'shake'

Infinitive	Gerund	Past participle
scuotere	*scuotendo (scotendo)*	*scosso*

	Present indicative	Subjunctive	Passato remoto
1sg.	*scuoto*	*scuota*	*scossi*
2sg.	*scuoti*	*scuota*	*scuotesti (scotesti)*
3sg.	*scuote*	*scuota*	*scosse*
1pl.	*scuotiamo (scotiamo)*	*scuotiamo (scotiamo)*	*scuotemmo (scotemmo)*
2pl.	*scuotete (scotete)*	*scuotiate (scotiate)*	*scuoteste (scoteste)*
3pl.	*scuotono*	*scuotano*	*scossero*

	Future	Conditional	Imperf. indicative	Imperf. subjunctive
1sg.	*scuoterò (scoterò)*	*scuoterei (scoterei)*	*scuotevo (scotevo)*	*scuotessi (scotessi)*
	etc.	etc.	etc.	etc.

sedere 'sit'

Infinitive	Gerund	Past participle
sedere	*sedendo*	*seduto*

	Present indicative	Subjunctive	Passato remoto
1sg.	*siedo* (rare *seggo*)	*sieda* (rare *segga*)	*sedei*
2sg.	*siedi*	*sieda* (rare *segga*)	*sedesti*
3sg.	*siede*	*sieda* (rare *segga*)	*sedé*
1pl.	*sediamo*	*sediamo*	*sedemmo*
2pl.	*sedete*	*sediate*	*sedeste*
3pl.	*siedono* (rare *seggono*)	*siedano* (rare *seggano*)	*sederono*

	Future	Conditional	Imperf. indicative	Imperf. subjunctive
1sg.	*siederò*	*siederei*	*sedevo*	*sedessi*
	etc.	etc.	etc.	etc.

solere 'be wont'

Infinitive	Gerund	Past participle
solere	*solendo*	*solito* ['sɔlito]

	Present indicative	Subjunctive	Passato remoto
1sg.	*soglio*	*soglia*	[none]
2sg.	*suoli*	*soglia*	
3sg.	*suole*	*soglia*	
1pl.	*sogliamo*	*sogliamo*	
2pl.	*solete*	*sogliate*	
3pl.	*sogliono*	*sogliano*	

	Future	Conditional	Imperf. indicative	Imperf. subjunctive
	[none]	[none]	*solevo*	*solessi*

sorgere 'rise'

	Infinitive	Gerund	Past participle
	sorgere	*sorgendo*	*sorto*

	Present indicative	Subjunctive	Passato remoto
1sg.	*sorgo*	*sorga*	*sorsi*
2sg.	*sorgi*	*sorga*	*sorgesti*
3sg.	*sorge*	*sorga*	*sorse*
1pl.	*sorgiamo*	*sorgiamo*	*sorgemmo*
2pl.	*sorgete*	*sorgiate*	*sorgeste*
3pl.	*sorgono*	*sorgano*	*sorsero*

	Future	Conditional	Imperf. indicative	Imperf. subjunctive
1sg.	*sorgerò*	*sorgerei*	*sorgevo*	*sorgessi*
	etc.	etc.	etc.	etc.

spegnere 'extinguish'

	Infinitive	Gerund	Past participle
	spegnere	*spegnendo*	*spento*

	Present indicative	Subjunctive	Passato remoto
1sg.	*spengo*	*spenga*	*spensi*
2sg.	*spegni*	*spenga*	*spegnesti*
3sg.	*spegne*	*spenga*	*spense*
1pl.	*spegniamo*	*spegniamo*	*spegnemmo*
2pl.	*spegnete*	*spegniate*	*spegneste*
3pl.	*spengono*	*spengano*	*spensero*

	Future	Conditional	Imperf. indicative	Imperf. subjunctive
1sg.	*spegnerò*	*spegnerei*	*spegnevo*	*spegnevi*
	etc.	etc.	etc.	etc.

stare 'stand', 'be'

	Infinitive	Gerund	Past participle
	stare	*stando*	*stato*

	Present indicative	Subjunctive	Passato remoto
1sg.	*sto*	*stia*	*stetti*
2sg.	*stai* **Imper.** *stai, sta'*	*stia*	*stesti*
3sg.	*sta*	*stia*	*stette*
1pl.	*stiamo*	*stiamo*	*stemmo*
2pl.	*state*	*stiate*	*steste*
3pl.	*stanno*	*stiano*	*stettero*

	Future	Conditional	Imperf. indicative	Imperf. subjunctive
1sg.	*starò*	*starei*	*stavo*	*stessi*
	etc.	etc.	etc.	etc.

stringere 'squeeze'

Infinitive	Gerund	Past participle
stringere	stringendo	stretto

	Present indicative	Subjunctive	Passato remoto
1sg.	stringo	stringa	strinsi
2sg.	stringi	stringa	stringesti
3sg.	stringe	stringa	strinse
1pl.	stringiamo	stringiamo	stringemmo
2pl.	stringete	stringiate	stringeste
3pl.	stringono	stringano	strinsero

	Future	Conditional	Imperf. indicative	Imperf. subjunctive
1sg.	stringerò	stringerei	stringevo	stringessi
	etc.	etc.	etc.	etc.

svellere 'pluck out'

Infinitive	Gerund	Past participle
svellere	svellendo	svelto

	Present indicative	Subjunctive	Passato remoto
1sg.	svello (rare *svelgo*)	svella (rare *svelga*)	svelsi
2sg.	svelli	svella (rare *svelga*)	svellesti
3sg.	svelle	svella (rare *svelga*)	svelse
1pl.	svelliamo	svelliamo	svellemmo
2pl.	svellete	svelliate	svelleste
3pl.	svellono (rare *svelgono*)	svellano (rare *svelgano*)	svelsero

tenere 'hold'

Infinitive	Gerund	Past participle
tenere	tenendo	tenuto

	Present indicative	Subjunctive	Passato remoto
1sg.	tengo	tenga	tenni
2sg.	tieni	tenga	tenesti
3sg.	tiene	tenga	tenne
1pl.	teniamo	teniamo	tenemmo
2pl.	tenete	teniate	teneste
3pl.	tengono	tengano	tennero

	Future	Conditional	Imperf. indicative	Imperf. subjunctive
1sg.	terrò	terrei	tenevo	tenessi
	etc.	etc.	etc.	etc.

tergere 'wipe'

Infinitive	Gerund	Past participle
tergere	tergendo	terso

	Present indicative	Subjunctive	Passato remoto
1sg.	*tergo*	*terga*	*tersi*
2sg.	*tergi*	*terga*	*tergesti*
3sg.	*terge*	*terga*	*terse*
1pl.	*tergiamo*	*tergiamo*	*tergemmo*
2pl.	*tergete*	*tergiate*	*tergeste*
3pl.	*tergono*	*tergano*	*tersero*

	Future	Conditional	Imperf. indicative	Imperf. subjunctive
1sg.	*tergerò*	*tergerei*	*tergevo*	*tergessi*
	etc.	etc.	etc.	etc.

trarre 'draw'

	Infinitive	Gerund	Past participle
	trarre	*traendo*	*tratto*

	Present indicative	Subjunctive	Passato remoto
1sg.	*traggo*	*tragga*	*trassi*
2sg.	*trai*	*tragga*	*traesti*
3sg.	*trae*	*tragga*	*trasse*
1pl.	*traiamo*	*traiamo*	*traemmo*
2pl.	*traete*	*traiate*	*traeste*
3pl.	*traggono*	*traggano*	*trassero*

	Future	Conditional	Imperf. indicative	Imperf. subjunctive
1sg.	*trarrò*	*trarrei*	*traevo*	*traessi*
	etc.	etc.	etc.	etc.

udire 'hear'

	Infinitive	Gerund	Past participle
	udire	*udendo*	*udito*

	Present indicative	Subjunctive	Passato remoto
1sg.	*odo*	*oda*	*udii*
2sg.	*odi*	*oda*	*udisti*
3sg.	*ode*	*oda*	*udì*
1pl.	*udiamo*	*udiamo*	*udimmo*
2pl.	*udite*	*udiate*	*udiste*
3pl.	*odono*	*odano*	*udirono*

	Future	Conditional	Imperf. indicative	Imperf. subjunctive
1sg.	*udirò* (rare *udrò*)	*udirei* (rare *udrei*)	*udivo*	*udissi*
	etc.	etc.	etc.	etc.

uscire 'go out'

	Infinitive	Gerund	Past participle
	uscire	*uscendo*	*uscito*

	Present Indicative	**Subjunctive**	**Passato remoto**
1sg.	*esco*	*esca*	*uscii*
2sg.	*esci*	*esca*	*uscisti*
3sg.	*esce*	*esca*	*uscì*
1pl.	*usciamo*	*usciamo*	*uscimmo*
2pl.	*uscite*	*usciate*	*usciste*
3pl.	*escono*	*escano*	*uscirono*

	Future	**Conditional**	**Imperf. indicative**	**Imperf. subjunctive**
1sg.	*uscirò*	*uscirei*	*uscivo*	*uscissi*
	etc.	etc.	etc.	etc.

valere 'be worth'

Infinitive	**Gerund**	**Past participle**
valere	*valendo*	*valso*

	Present indicative	**Subjunctive**	**Passato remoto**
1sg.	*valgo*	*valga*	*valsi*
2sg.	*vali*	*valga*	*valesti*
3sg.	*vale*	*valga*	*valse*
1pl.	*valiamo*	*valiamo*	*valemmo*
2pl.	*valete*	*valiate*	*valeste*
3pl.	*valgono*	*valgano*	*valsero*

	Future	**Conditional**	**Imperf. indicative**	**Imperf. subjunctive**
1sg.	*varrò*	*varrei*	*valevo*	*valessi*
	etc.	etc.	etc.	etc.

vedere 'see'

Infinitive	**Gerund**	**Past participle**
vedere	*vedendo*	*visto/veduto*

	Present indicative	**Subjunctive**	**Passato remoto**
1sg.	*vedo*	*veda*	*vidi*
2sg.	*vedi*	*veda*	*vedesti*
3sg.	*vede*	*veda*	*vide*
1pl.	*vediamo*	*vediamo*	*vedemmo*
2pl.	*vedete*	*vediate*	*vedeste*
3pl.	*vedono*	*vedano*	*videro*

	Future	**Conditional**	**Imperf. indicative**	**Imperf. subjunctive**
1sg.	*vedrò*	*vedrei*	*vedevo*	*vedessi*
	etc.	etc.	etc.	etc.

venire 'come'

Infinitive	**Gerund**	**Past participle**
venire	*venendo*	*venuto*

	Present indicative	Subjunctive	Passato remoto	
1sg.	*vengo*	*venga*	*venni*	
2sg.	*vieni*	*venga*	*venisti*	
3sg.	*viene*	*venga*	*venne*	
1pl.	*veniamo*	*veniamo*	*venimmo*	
2pl.	*venite*	*veniate*	*veniste*	
3pl.	*vengono*	*vengano*	*vennero*	

	Future	Conditional	Imperf. indicative	Imperf. subjunctive
1sg.	*verrò*	*verrei*	*venivo*	*venissi*
	etc.	etc.	etc.	etc.

vincere 'win'

Infinitive	Gerund	Past participle
vincere	*vincendo*	*vinto*

	Present indicative	Subjunctive	Passato remoto
1sg.	*vinco*	*vinca*	*vinsi*
2sg.	*vinci*	*vinca*	*vincesti*
3sg.	*vince*	*vinca*	*vinse*
1pl.	*vinciamo*	*vinciamo*	*vincemmo*
2pl.	*vincete*	*vinciate*	*vinceste*
3pl.	*vincono*	*vincano*	*vinsero*

	Future	Conditional	Imperf. indicative	Imperf. subjunctive
1sg.	*vincerò*	*vincerei*	*vincevo*	*vincessi*
	etc.	etc.	etc.	etc.

volere 'want'

Infinitive	Gerund	Past participle
volere	*volendo*	*voluto*

	Present indicative	Subjunctive	Passato remoto
1sg.	*voglio*	*voglia*	*volli*
2sg.	*vuoi* **Imper.** *vogli*	*voglia*	*volesti*
3sg.	*vuole*	*voglia*	*volle*
1pl.	*vogliamo*	*volete*	*volemmo*
2pl.	*volete* **Imper.** *vogliate*	*vogliate*	*voleste*
3pl.	*vogliono*	*vogliano*	*vollero*

	Future	Conditional	Imperf. indicative	Imperf. subjunctive
1sg.	*vorrò*	*vorrei*	*volevo*	*volessi*
	etc.	etc.	etc.	etc.

14.4 How to deduce the conjugation of other irregular verbs from their infinitives

All irregular verbs not discussed above conjugate according to one of the patterns illustrated here (or in 14.5):

TABLE 14.A

Infinitive ends in	Conjugate like	Example verbs
-acere	piacere	tacere giacere spiacere sottacere
-cadere	cadere	accadere scadere
-cere	vincere	torcere convincere
-chiedere	chiedere	richiedere
-correre	correre	occorrere concorrere soccorrere
-cuotere	scuotere	percuotere riscuotere
-dere (other than verbs in -ndere, and -cadere, chiedere, richiedere)	chiudere	ridere esplodere uccidere perdere
-dire (if -dire = dire 'to say')	dire	benedire maledire contraddire (but see 14.11)
-durre	condurre	addurre sedurre tradurre produrre
-empire	empire	riempire
-ergere (but ergere follows piangere)	tergere	emergere spargere aspergere
-escere	conoscere	crescere decrescere increscere
-ettere	annettere	sconnettere connettere riflettere deflettere
-figgere	affiggere	infiggere sconfiggere
-fondere	fondere	diffondere confondere
-gere (except stringere and verbs in -ergere)	piangere	giungere porgere svolgere accorgersi
-ggere (but see -figgere)	leggere	correggere affliggere
-gliere	cogliere	sciogliere scegliere togliere
-inguere	estinguere	distinguere
-manere	rimanere	permanere
-mettere	mettere	promettere smettere ammettere scommettere
-muovere	muovere	commuovere promuovere (but see 14.7)
-ndere (but see -fondere, -ondere)	prendere	scendere rendere contundere
-ondere (but see -fondere)	nascondere	rispondere corrispondere
-oscere	conoscere	riconoscere
-porre	porre	comporre supporre imporre
-primere	esprimere	comprimere imprimere deprimere
-rigere or -ligere	dirigere	erigere negligere
-rompere	rompere	corrompere irrompere interrompere
-scindere	scindere	proscindere
-scrivere	scrivere	trascrivere iscrivere
-sedere	sedere	possedere

TABLE 14.A – *cont*

Infinitive ends in	Conjugate like	Example verbs
-stare (if *-stare* clearly = 'stand')	*stare*	*ristare sottostare sovrastare*
-stringere	*stringere*	*costringere astringere*
-sumere	*presumere*	*assumere*
-tenere	*tenere*	*ottenere sostenere appartenere*
-trarre	*trarre*	*contrarre distrarre ritrarre contrarre*
-valere	*valere*	*prevalere equivalere invalere*[4]
-venire	*venire*	*avvenire convenire*
-vivere	*vivere*	*convivere sopravvivere*

14.5 'Mixed' conjugation verbs: *compiere* and verbs in *-fare*

The verb *compiere* 'carry out', 'complete' appears to conflate two conjugations: its infinitive, gerund, past participle, the singular and third person plural forms of the present tense, belong to the second conjugation. The remaining parts of the verb (second person plural of the present, the imperfect tense, past historic, future and conditional) belong to the third conjugation. In fact there exists a variant of *compiere*, namely *compire*, which is an entirely regular third conjugation verb (*compisco*, *compisci*, etc.):

	Infinitive	Gerund	Past participle
	compiere	*compiendo*	*compiuto*

	Present indicative	Subjunctive	Passato remoto
1sg.	*compio*	*compia*	*compii*
2sg.	*compi*	*compia*	*compisti*
3sg.	*compie*	*compia*	*compì*
1pl.	*compiamo*	*compiamo*	*compimmo*
2pl.	*compite*	*compiate*	*compiste*
3pl.	*compiono*	*compiano*	*compirono*

	Future	Conditional	Imperf. indicative	Imperf. subjunctive
1sg.	*compirò*	*compirei*	*compivo*	*compissi*
	etc.	etc.	etc.	etc.

Adempiere, 'fulfil', conjugates like *compiere*.

The formation of *soddisfare* 'satisfy', and a number of other verbs derived from *fare*, is often described as 'uncertain' by grammar books, and shows considerable variation in actual usage. *Soddisfare* tends to behave partly like *fare* and partly like first conjugation verbs: past participle, past historic, imperfect, and second person plural present indicative follow *fare* (in the first person singular one

---

[4]Used only in the third person singular and plural, and in the past participle.

sometimes finds the ending *-fò* – cf. *fo* an archaic and regional variant of *faccio*). The remaining forms of the verb may also follow *fare*, but in modern usage normally follow a first conjugation pattern:

Infinitive	Gerund	Past participle
soddisfare	*soddisfacendo* (*soddisfando*)	*soddisfatto*

	Present indicative	Subjunctive	Passato remoto
1sg.	*soddisfo* (*soddisfò, soddisfaccio*)	*soddisfi* (*soddisfaccia*)	*soddisfeci*
2sg.	*soddisfi* (*soddisfai*)	*soddisfi* (*soddisfaccia*)	*soddisfacesti*
3sg.	*soddisfa* (*soddisfà*)	*soddisfi* (*soddisfaccia*)	*soddisfece*
1pl.	*soddisfiamo* (*soddisfacciamo*)	*soddisfiamo* (*soddisfacciamo*)	*soddisfacemmo*
2pl.	*soddisfate*	*soddisfiate* (*soddisfacciate*)	*soddisfaceste*
3pl.	*soddisfano* (*soddisfanno*)	*soddisfino* (*soddisfacciano*)	*soddisfecero*

	Future	Conditional	Imperf. indicative	Imperf. subjunctive
1sg.	*soddisferò* (*soddisfarò*) etc.	*soddisferei* (*soddisfarei*) etc.	*soddisfacevo* etc.	*soddisfacessi* etc.

The verbs *disfare* 'undo', *liquefare* 'liquefy', *assuefarsi* 'become accustomed', *rarefarsi* 'become rarefied', usually follow *fare*, but are like *soddisfare* in the present indicative; their preferred first person singular form is usually in *-fò* (*liquefò*, etc.), although there is a preference for *disfo*.

14.6 The desinences of the present tense

The present tense is characterized by the following desinences attached to the root of the verb.[5]

TABLE 14.B

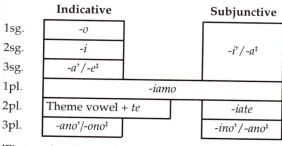

	Indicative	Subjunctive
1sg.	*-o*	
2sg.	*-i*	*-i*[†] / *-a*[‡]
3sg.	*-a*[†] / *-e*[‡]	
1pl.	*-iamo*	
2pl.	Theme vowel + *te*	*-iate*
3pl.	*-ano*[†] / *-ono*[‡]	*-ino*[†] / *-ano*[‡]

[†]First conjugation verbs
[‡]Non-first conjugation verbs

---

[5]For cases in which the *i* of the desinences *-iamo* and *-iate* are not pronounced, see 2.2.

The conjugation of the present tense of *andare, fare, avere, dare, sapere, stare* is given in 14.3. Note particularly the monosyllabic forms in the first person singular (except *andare* and *fare*), pronounced [ɔ], [dɔ], [sɔ], [stɔ], and that their third person plural forms are formed by adding *-nno* to the third person singular.

It will be seen from 14.2 that there are two kinds of present tense form of third conjugation verbs (*dire* and *compire* are special cases, see 14.3 and 14.5): one, like *dormire*, forming its present in the manner indicated above, and another, like *finire*, for which the element *-isc-* appears between the root and the desinence in all singular forms, and in the third person plural (but not in the first and second persons plural). The majority of third conjugation verbs follow *finire*, but there is a relatively small group (many of which are, however, in very frequent use), whose present *desinences* – but not necessarily their roots – follow the pattern of *dormire*. These verbs need to be learned as a list. They are:

> *aprire* 'open'; *coprire* 'cover'; *cucire* 'sew'; *fuggire* 'flee'; *morire* 'die'; *offrire* 'offer'; *partire* 'leave'; *pentirsi* 'repent'; *sentire* 'feel'; *salire* 'go up'; *soffrire* 'suffer'; *uscire* 'go out'; *udire* 'hear'; *venire* 'come'

Derivatives of these verbs (e.g., *assalire* 'assail'; *scoprire* 'discover'; *sfuggire* 'escape'; *risentire* 'be sensitive'; *riuscire* 'succeed'; *svenire* 'faint') usually follow the same pattern. Note that *partire* follows *finire* when it means to 'divide up' (like its derivatives *spartire* 'divide up', *scompartire* 'share'): e.g., *Partiscono i beni* 'They divide up the goods'. The verb *riempire* 'fill' (and *empire* 'fill', conjugated like it) needs special attention, for the present tense, where an *i* appears at the end of the root. The verb *cucire* 'sew' (and its derivative *scucire* 'unpick') has a minor complication in spelling, in that an *i* is written after the root wherever the desinence begins with *-a* or *-o*: The reason for this is to indicate that the root is pronounced [kutʃ] not [kuk] (see 2.2):

	Present indicative	**Subjunctive**
1sg.	*cucio*	*cucia*
2sg.	*cuci*	*cucia*
3sg.	*cuce*	*cucia*
1pl.	*cuciamo*	*cuciamo*
2pl.	*cucite*	*cuciate*
3pl.	*cuciono*	*cuciano*

All other *-ire* verbs (i.e., the vast majority) behave like *finire*. Hence *capire* 'understand': *capisco*, etc., *usufruire* 'enjoy the use of': *usufruisco*, etc.

Seven verbs follow *either* pattern (e.g., *mentire*: either *mento*, etc. or *mentisco*, etc.):

> *aborrire* 'abhor'; *applaudire* 'applaud'; *assorbire* 'absorb'; *inghiottire* 'swallow'; *mentire* 'lie'; *nutrire* 'nourish'; *tossire* 'cough'

The verbs *muggire* 'low' (like cattle) and *ruggire* 'roar' are either *mugge* – *muggono, rugge* – *ruggono* or *muggisce* – *muggiscono, ruggisce* – *ruggiscono*, in the third person indicative, but the *-isc-* form is preferred in other parts of the present (e.g., subjunctive *muggisca* – *muggiscano, ruggisca* – *ruggiscano*).

14.7 The present tense root (vowel alternations; mobile verbs in -gere, -cere, -scere, -gliere, etc.)

The root of the present tense, especially in non-first conjugation verbs, is apt to show variation according to person and number. In general, these variations have to be learned separately for each individual verb, but certain recurrent patterns can be recognized, most importantly:

Root pattern 1
(The root of the 1sg., 2sg., 3sg. and 3pl. is different from the root of the 1pl. and 2pl.)[6]

1sg.
2sg.
3sg.
1pl.
2pl.
3pl.

A number of types of root variation follow this pattern:

(i) Root stress.
With the exception of verbs like *finire*, stress always falls on the *root* of the 1sg., 2sg., 3sg. and 3pl. root, but on the *desinences* of the 1pl. and 2pl. Note, however, that the very presence or absence of the *-isc-* element in verbs like *finire* follows Pattern 1.

(ii) 'Mobile diphthongs'.
Certain verbs have root variation between a diphthong *ie* or *uo* and a monophthong *e* or *o*. These so-called 'mobile diphthongs' usually follow Pattern 1, the diphthong occurring in the 1sg., 2sg., 3sg. and 3pl. present tense root, but not elsewhere. See *morire, cuocere, muovere, sedere, scuotere* above. The 'mobility' of the diphthong is in fact optional in *cuocere, scuotere* and *muovere* (but not in its derivative *promuovere*); in these verbs the diphthong may – and nowadays usually does – appear everywhere in the verb (*muoviamo – muovevo – muoverò – muovessi,* etc.), except for the past participles (*mosso, cotto, scosso*) and the forms in *moss-, coss-* and *scoss-* in the *passato remoto* (*mossi – mosse – mossero,* etc.). *Nuocere* (whose diphthong was originally limited to the 2sg. and 3sg. present) frequently extends the diphthong to the whole of the verb (e.g., *nuocio – nuociuto,* etc.). Some first conjugation verbs (e.g., *tonare* 'thunder') have mobile diphthongs, but the diphthong may – and usually does in modern Italian – appear throughout the whole verb: e.g.:

---

[6]For the *absence* of this pattern in verbs such as *sciare* and *spiare*, see 2.2.

Infinitive	Gerund	Past participle
suonare/sonare	suonando/sonando	suonato/sonato

	Present indicative	Subjunctive	Imperfect indicative	Imperfect subjunctive
1sg.	suono	suoni	suonavo/sonavo	suonassi/sonassi
2sg.	suoni	suoni	suonavi/sonavi	suonassi/sonassi
3sg.	suona	suoni	suonava/sonava	suonasse/sonasse
1pl.	suoniamo/soniamo	suoniamo/soniate	suonavamo/sonavamo	suonassimo/sonassimo
2pl.	suonate/sonate	suoniate/soniate	suonavate/sonavate	suonaste/sonaste
3pl.	suonano	suonino	suonavano/sonavano	suonassero/sonassero

(iii) Other alternations following Pattern 1.

It will be noted that the root vowel changes of *dovere, udire, uscire,* and the some of the variation in the present indicative of *andare, avere,* also follow Pattern 1.

Root Pattern 2

(The root of the 1sg. and 3sg. present indicative and subjunctive and the 2sg. and 3sg. subjunctive is different from the rest of the present tense.)

Indicative	Subjunctive
1sg.	1sg.
2sg.	2sg.
3sg.	3sg.
1pl.	1pl
2pl.	2pl.
3pl.	3pl.

Prominent among verbs of this kind are verbs in *-gliere* like *cogliere* (e.g., *sciogliere* 'loosen', *togliere* 'remove', *scegliere* 'choose'), those in *-cere, -(g)gere* and *-scere* like *vincere, leggere, sorgere, nascere* (likewise *accorgersi* 'realize', *affiggere, cingere* 'gird', *conoscere, crescere, emergere* 'emerge', *fingere* 'feign', *giungere* 'join', *indulgere* 'indulge', *mungere* 'milk', *pascere* 'graze', *piangere* 'weep', *proteggere* 'protect', *spingere* 'push', *stringere* 'grasp', *struggere* 'melt down', *tingere* 'dye', *ungere* 'smear', *volgere* 'turn', etc.)

Other consonantal alternations showing the same patterning are found in *apparire, cogliere, dolere, dovere, morire, nuocere, piacere, porre, rimanere, salire, scegliere, solere, spegnere, tenere, valere, venire.*

14.8 Regular imperatives

Second person singular imperative

In first conjugation verbs, the second person singular imperative form is identical to the third person singular present indicative:

3sg. pres. ind.	2sg. imperative
canta	*canta* 'sing'
parla	*parla* 'speak'
si ferma	*fermati* 'stop'
lo mangia	*mangialo* 'eat it'
etc.	

In other conjugations, the second person singular imperative is usually identical to the second person singular present indicative:

2sg. pres. ind.	2sg. imperative
temi	*temi* 'fear'
metti	*metti* 'put'
dormi	*dormi* 'sleep'
lo finisci	*finiscilo* 'finish it'
etc.	

Second person singular negative imperative

It is a peculiarity of all second person *singular* imperatives that their *negative* uses the *infinitive* of the verb:

Infinitive	2sg. negative imperative
cantare	*non cantare*
parlare	*non parlare*
fermarsi	*non fermarti/non ti fermare*
mangiarlo	*non mangiarlo/non lo mangiare*
temere	*non temere*
dormire	*non dormire*
finirlo	*non lo finire/non finirlo*
etc.	

First person plural imperative

The first person plural imperative ('let's sing', etc.) is always identical to the first person plural present indicative:

1pl. pres. ind.	1pl. imperative
cantiamo	*cantiamo* 'let's sing'
ci fermiamo	*fermiamoci* 'let's stop'
facciamo	*facciamo* 'let's do'
leggiamo	*leggiamo* 'let's read'
serviamo	*serviamo* 'let's serve'
lo finiamo	*finiamolo* 'let's finish it'
etc.	

The first person plural negative imperative is formed in the same way: *Non facciamo così* 'Let's not do that', etc.

Second person plural imperative

The second person plural imperative is usually identical to the second person plural present indicative:

2pl. pres. ind.	2pl. imperative
cantate	*cantate* 'sing'
vi fermate	*fermatevi* 'stop'
fate	*fate* 'do'
leggete	*leggete* 'read'

2pl. pres. ind.	2pl. imperative
servite	*servite* 'serve'
lo finite	*finitelo* 'finish it'

The negative imperative is formed in the same way: *Non fate così* 'Don't do that', etc.

Note that the negative second person plural imperative of *credere* is frequently the subjunctive *crediate*:

Non crediate, cari amici, che sia finita	'Do not think, dear friends, that this
questa triste storia.	sorry tale is over.'

The third person imperative: the imperative with *Lei* and *Loro*

With third person address forms (see 22.3), the third person *subjunctive* serves as the imperative:

3sg.pres. sub.	3sg. imperative	3pl. pres. sub.	3pl. imperative
canti	*canti*	*cantino*	*cantino*
si fermi	*si fermi*	*si fermino*	*si fermino*
faccia	*faccia*	*facciano*	*facciano*
legga	*legga*	*leggano*	*leggano*
dorma	*dorma*	*dormano*	*dormano*
lo finisca	*lo finisca*	*lo finiscano*	*lo finiscano*

The negative imperative is formed in the same way: *Non faccia così*, etc.

The infinitive is extensively used as an imperative in what might be termed 'generic instructions' – those directed at anyone who might happen to read or hear them. This construction is especially common in public notices and announcements, and in recipes sets of instructions for the use of machines, etc.

Spingere [sign on a door]	'Push'
Tirare [sign on a door]	'Pull'
Non scendere prima che il treno sia fermo.	'Do not get out until the train stops.'
Non disperdere nell'ambiente. [instruction	'Do not throw away in the
on plastic bottle]	environment.'
Lavare prima di tagliare.	'Wash before cutting.'

Note that the reflexive pronoun used in this construction is always third person:

Mettersi nella corsia di destra. [road sign]	'Get in right hand lane.'

14.9 Special imperative forms

The verbs *andare, dare, dire, stare, fare* have special imperative forms in the second person singular:

andare	*vai* or *va'*
dare	*dai* or *da'*
dire	*di'*
fare	*fai* or *fa'*
stare	*stai* or *sta'*

But derivatives of *dire* have regular imperatives: *benedici* 'bless', *maledici* 'curse', *contraddici* 'contradict'.

In general these alternative possibilities are interchangeable; for many speakers, neither produces *rafforzamento fonosintattico* (2.6). The spellings *va, da*, etc., without apostrophe are sometimes also used. However when the imperative is followed by a clitic pronoun (6.1), the form used is *va, da, fa, sta* and the consonant of the immediately following clitic is doubled:

Fai come ti dice la nonna!	'Do as grandmother tells you!'
Dai una penna alla zia.	'Give a pen to your aunt.'
Vai a casa.	'Go home.'
Dammene quaranta.	'Give me 40.'
Fatti vedere domani alle cinque.	'Show up tomorrow at 5.'
Vallo a sotterrare!	'Go and bury him.'

As an interjection expressing encouragement or surprise, only *dai* is used:

Ma dai, non piangere!	'Come on, don't cry.'
Dai, dai, tira più forte.	'Go on, go on, pull harder.'

The verbs *avere, essere, sapere, volere* have special imperative forms in the second person singular and plural. Notice that these special second person singular imperatives are identical to the present subjunctive, except that the final *-a* of the subjunctive is missing in the singular:

	avere	*sapere*	*volere*	*essere*
2sg.	*abbi*	*sappi*	*vogli*	*sii*
2pl.	*abbiate*	*sappiate*	*vogliate*	*siate*

The imperative of *sapere* usually means 'be aware that', and that of *volere* 'be so good as to . . .', 'kindly . . .'. The latter is also found with expressions such as *vogli bene* 'love', 'care for':

Sappiate che verranno fucilati.	'Know that they will be shot.'
Vogliate restituire il foglio entro la data indicata.	'Be so good as to return the sheet by the date indicated.'

Another special imperative is *to'*. Originally an imperative of *togliere* (today meaning 'remove' but in older Italian also meaning 'take'), *to'* is now restricted to very informal discourse and used when passing some object to a person. Its nearest English equivalent might be 'Here you are'.

Vuoi il sale? To'!	'Do you want the salt? Here it is!'

To' can also express surprise:

To'! Guarda chi si vede!	'Well! Look who's here!'

14.10 Future and conditional

The major characteristics of the future and conditional are:[7]

(i) They each have a set of desinences which are always stressed (on the first vowel) and are the same for all verbs, regardless of conjugation:

---

[7]For the *spelling* of some future and conditional tense forms of the first conjugation, such as *mangerò*, see 2.2.

	Future		**Conditional**	
1sg.	*-ò*	-['ɔ]	*-ei*	-['ɛi̠]
2sg.	*-ai*	-['ai̠]	*-esti*	-['esti̠]
3sg.	*-à*	-['a]	*-ebbe*	-['ɛbbe]
1pl.	*-emo*	-['emo]	*-emmo*	-['emmo]
2pl.	*-ete*	-['ete]	*-este*	-['este]
3pl.	*-anno*	-['anno]	*-ebbero*	-['ɛbbero]

(ii) They share a common verb stem to which the desinences are attached. This future/conditional verb stem is often identical to the infinitive (minus the final *-e*):

Infinitive	**Future**	**Conditional**
vendere 'sell'	*venderò*, etc.	*venderei*, etc.
fare 'do'	*farò*, etc.	*farei*, etc
produrre 'produce'	*produrrò*, etc.	*produrrei*, etc.
porre 'put'	*porrò*, etc.	*porrei*, etc.
dormire 'sleep'	*dormirò*, etc.	*dormirei*, etc.
dire 'say'	*dirò*, etc.	*direi*, etc.

(iii) The future-conditional verb stem is, none the less, distinct from the infinitive in the first and second conjugations:

● In first conjugation verbs, the thematic vowel *a* of the infinitive is replaced by *e*:

Infinitive	**Future**	**Conditional**
cantare 'sing'	*canterò*, etc.	*canterei*, etc.
parlare 'speak'	*parlerò*, etc.	*parlerei*, etc.
comprare 'buy'	*comprerò*, etc.	*comprerei*, etc.

The sole exceptions are:

dare 'give'	*darò*, etc.	*darei*, etc.
andare 'go'	*andrò*, etc.	*andrei*, etc.
stare 'stand'	*starò*, etc.	*starei*, etc.

● In many second conjugation verbs (those with stressed thematic *e* in the infinitive) the thematic vowel *e* of the infinitive is removed:

Infinitive	**Future**	**Conditional**
avere 'have'	*avrò*, etc.	*avrei*, etc.
dovere 'have to'	*dovrò*, etc.	*dovrei*, etc.
sapere 'know'	*saprò*, etc.	*saprei*, etc.
potere 'be able'	*potrò*, etc.	*potrei*, etc.
parere 'seem'	*parrò*, etc.	*parrei*, etc.
cadere 'fall'	*cadrò*, etc.	*cadrei*, etc.
godere 'enjoy'	*godrò*, etc.	*godrei*, etc.
vedere 'see'	*vedrò*, etc.	*vedrei*, etc.
avvedersi 'realize'	*mi avvedrò*, etc.	*mi avvedrei*, etc.

Among these second conjugation verbs, in those whose roots end in *l* or *n*, not only is the thematic vowel removed, but the *l* and *n* are replaced by *r*:

volere 'want'	*vorrò*, etc.	*vorrei*, etc.
dolere 'ache'	*dorrà*, etc.	*dorrebbe*, etc.
rimanere 'stay'	*rimarrò*, etc.	*rimarrei*, etc.
tenere 'hold'	*terrò*, etc.	*terrei*, etc.
valere 'be worth'	*varrò*, etc.	*varrei*, etc.

Other second conjugation verbs do not remove the thematic vowel in future and conditional:

intravedere 'glimpse'	*intravederò, intravederei*
persuadere 'persuade'	*persuaderò, persuaderei*
piacere 'please'	*piacerò, piacerei*
possedere 'own'	*possiederò, possiederei*
prevedere 'foresee'	*prevederò, prevederei*
provvedere 'plan'	*provvederò, provvederei*
sedere 'sit'	*siederò, siederei*
soprassedere 'postpone'	*soprassiederò, soprassiederei*
stravedere 'misjudge'	*stravederò, stravederei*
tacere 'be silent'	*tacerò, tacerei*
temere 'fear'	*temerò, temerei*
travedere 'misjudge'	*travederò, travederei*

● Other irregular future/conditional stems appear in *venire, essere, bere* and *vivere*:

venire 'come'	*verrò*, etc.	*verrei*, etc.
essere 'be'	*sarò*, etc.	*sarei*, etc.
bere 'drink'	*berrò*, etc.	*berrei*, etc.
vivere 'live'	*vivrò*, etc.	*vivrei*, etc.

Udire and *morire* have both *udirò/ morirò*, etc. and *udrò, morrò*, etc., but the latter types are now old-fashioned.

14.11 Imperfect tense forms

The characteristics of the imperfect indicative and subjunctive are:

(i) All verbs (except the indicative of *essere*) have the same desinences for indicative and subjunctive, respectively. These desinences are unstressed, except for the 1pl. and 2pl. indicative *-vamo* (-['vamo]) and *-vate* (-['vate]). They are:

	Imperfect indicative	Imperfect subjunctive
1sg.	*-vo*	*-ssi*
2sg.	*-vi*	*-ssi*
3sg.	*-va*	*-sse*
1pl.	*-vamo*	*-ssimo*
2pl.	*-vate*	*-ste*
3pl.	*-vano*	*-ssero*

(ii) These desinences are attached to a stem which, in most cases, comprises the root + the thematic vowel. The thematic vowel is stressed (except in the 1pl. and 2pl. indicative):

cantavo	*cantassi*	*sapevo*	*sapessi*
cantavi	*cantassi*	*sapevi*	*sapessi*
cantava	*cantasse*	*sapeva*	*sapesse*
cantavamo	*cantassimo*	*sapevamo*	*sapessimo*
cantavate	*cantaste*	*sapevate*	*sapeste*
cantavano	*cantassero*	*sapevano*	*sapessero*

vendevo	*vendessi*	*dormivo*	*dormissi*
vendevi	*vendessi*	*dormivi*	*dormissi*
vendeva	*vendesse*	*dormiva*	*dormisse*
vendevamo	*vendessimo*	*dormivamo*	*dormissimo*
vendevate	*vendeste*	*dormivate*	*dormiste*
vendevano	*vendessero*	*dormivano*	*dormissero*

As a rule of thumb, this stem is identical to that found in the second person plural present indicative. Thus:

Infinitive	2pl. pres. ind.		Imperfect indicative	Subjunctive
produrre 'produce'	*producete*		*producevo*	*producessi*
trarre 'draw'	*traete*		*traevo*	*traessi*
porre 'put'	*ponete*		*ponevo*	*ponessi*

Note, however, that *fare* and derivatives have imperfect *facevo, facessi,* and *dire* has *dicevo, dicessi*. Derivatives of *dire*, such as *benedire* 'bless', *maledire* 'curse', occasionally show imperfect *benedivo, maledivo*, etc., but these forms are considered substandard.

(iii) The verb *essere* and the subjunctive of *dare* and *stare* have irregular imperfect forms:

Imp. ind.	Imp. subj.	Imp. ind.	Imp. subj.	Imp. ind.	Imp. subj.
ero	*fossi*	*davo*	*dessi*	*stavo*	*stessi*
eri	*fossi*	*davi*	*dessi*	*stavi*	*stessi*
era	*fosse*	*dava*	*desse*	*stava*	*stesse*
eravamo	*fossimo*	*davamo*	*dessimo*	*stavamo*	*stessimo*
eravate	*foste*	*davate*	*deste*	*stavate*	*steste*
erano	*fossero*	*davano*	*dessero*	*stavano*	*stessero*

14.12 Forms of the *passato remoto*

The *passato remoto* has the following general characteristics:

(i) All verbs have the same first and second person desinences:

1sg.	*-i*	2sg.	*-sti*	1pl.	*-mmo*	2pl.	*-ste*

(ii) All 2sg., 1pl. and 2pl. desinences are attached to a verb stem which (with one exception) is identical to that found in the imperfect subjunctive; indeed the 2pl. *passato remoto* and the 2pl. imperfect subjunctive are always *wholly identical*. In every case, stress falls on the last vowel of the stem:

Imperfect subjunctive	Passato remoto	Imperfect subjunctive	Passato remoto	Imperfect subjunctive	Passato remoto
canta-ssi	*canta-sti*	*vende-ssi*	*vende-sti*	*dormi-ssi*	*dormi-sti*
canta-ssimo	*canta-mmo*	*vende-ssimo*	*vende-mmo*	*dormi-ssimo*	*dormi-mmo*
canta-ste	*canta-ste*	*vende-ste*	*vende-ste*	*dormi-ste*	*dormi-ste*

Imperfect subjunctive	Passato remoto	Imperfect subjunctive	Passato remoto	Imperfect subjunctive	Passato remoto
pone-ssi	*pone-sti*	*riduce-ssi*	*riduce-sti*	*trae-ssi*	*trae-sti*
pone-ssimo	*pone-mmo*	*riduce-ssimo*	*riduce-mmo*	*trae-ssimo*	*trae-mmo*
pone-ste	*pone-ste*	*riduce-ste*	*riduce-ste*	*trae-ste*	*trae-ste*

Imperfect subjunctive	Passato remoto	Imperfect subjunctive	Passato remoto	Imperfect subjunctive	Passato remoto
de-ssi	de-sti	ste-ssi	ste-sti	fo-ssi	fo-sti
de-ssimo	de-mmo	ste-ssimo	ste-mmo	fo-ssimo	fu-mmo
de-ste	de-ste	ste-ste	ste-ste	fo-ste	fo-ste

The sole exception is the 1pl. *passato remoto* of *essere*, which is *fummo*.

Root-stressed vs. non-root-stressed *passato remoto*

In order to discuss the remainder of the *passato remoto*, a fundamental distinction must be made between those verbs which in the first person singular, third person singular and third person plural are stressed on the root, and those which are not so stressed. The former have many highly unpredictable features, the latter are formed in a regular and predictable fashion.

Non-root-stressed *passato remoto*

Virtually all first and third conjugation verbs, and a minority of second conjugation verbs, are not root-stressed in any part of the *passato remoto*. They form their *passato remoto* by attaching the relevant person desinences to the stem of the imperfect subjunctive, which carries stress on the thematic vowel. The third person *plural* desinence is always *-rono*. The third person *singular* desinence is slightly more complex: in second and third conjugation verbs it is simply zero (or, to put it another way, the third person singular simply ends in the stressed thematic vowel). In the first conjugation the desinence *-ò* is attached directly to the root (the thematic vowel is not present):

First conjugation	**Second conjugation**	**Third conjugation**
canta-i	teme-i	dormi-i
canta-sti	teme-sti	dormi-sti
cant-ò	tem-é	dorm-ì
canta-mmo	teme-mmo	dormi-mmo
canta-ste	teme-ste	dormi-ste
canta-rono	teme-rono	dormi-rono

Of second conjugation verbs, the following is a comprehensive list of those having a non-root-stressed *passato remoto*:

> *accedere* 'enter', *battere* 'beat', *cedere* 'yield', *credere* 'believe', *decedere* 'decease', *dovere* 'have to', *esigere* 'demand', *fendere* (rare) 'split', *incedere* 'walk in procession', *mescere* (rare) 'pour', *mietere* 'reap', *pascere* 'graze', *potere* 'be able', *premere* 'press', *prescindere* 'do without', *procedere* 'proceed', *(ri)splendere* 'shine', *temere* 'fear', *vendere* 'sell'.

For *concedere* 'yield' and *succedere* 'happen', see below.

These verbs have an alternative set of desinences in the 1sg. (*-etti*), 3sg. (*-ette*) and 3pl. (*-ettero*), which can be used interchangeably with the desinences listed above, but tend to be avoided where the root ends in *-(t)t* (i.e., *battetti*, *potetti*, etc., are not used).

vendetti	vendemmo	temetti	tememmo
vendesti	vendeste	temesti	temeste
vendette	vendettero	temette	temettero

The verbs *dare*, *stare* and *venire* belong to the class of root-stressed verbs, discussed below.

Root-stressed *passato remoto*

Most second conjugation verbs, together with *dare*, *stare*, *venire*, have root-stressed forms. Optionally (see below) *aprire*, *coprire*, *offrire*, *scoprire*, *soffrire*, *apparire*, *comparire* also have root-stressed forms. The third person singular desinence is always *-e*; that of the third person plural is always *-ero*. There is always a difference between the vowels and/or the consonants of the stressed roots and those of the unstressed roots. For example:

1sg.	seppi	volli	ebbi	feci	venni	
	sapesti	volesti	avesti	facesti	venisti	2sg.
3sg.	seppe	volle	ebbe	fece	venne	
	sapemmo	volemmo	avemmo	facemmo	venimmo	1pl.
	sapeste	voleste	aveste	faceste	veniste	2pl.
3pl.	seppero	vollero	ebbero	fecero	vennero	

The nature of these differences is highly idiosyncratic. There is no way of predicting which second conjugation verbs have a root-stressed *passato remoto*, and no wholly reliable way of predicting the nature of the stressed root. Some patterns are unique to a single verb, or are limited to just two or three. Others are recurrent, notably:

chiudere – chiusi	*mordere – morsi*, etc.
cogliere – colsi	*scegliere – scelsi*, etc.
leggere – lessi	*sconfiggere – sconfissi*, etc.
piangere – piansi	*porgere – porsi*, etc.
prendere – presi	*rispondere – risposi*, etc.

The following lists all the distinct types of root-stressed *passato remoto* verbs.

Infinitive	1sg.	2sg.	3sg.	1pl.	2pl.	3pl.
apparire	*apparvi*[8]	*apparisti*	*apparve*	*apparimmo*	*appariste*	*apparvero*
aprire	*apersi*[9]	*apristi*	*aperse*	*aprimmo*	*apriste*	*apersero*
assumere	*assunsi*	*assumesti*	*assunse*	*assumemmo*	*assumeste*	*assunsero*
avere	*ebbi*	*avesti*	*ebbe*	*avemmo*	*aveste*	*ebbero*
bere	*bevvi*	*bevesti*	*bevve*	*bevemmo*	*beveste*	*bevvero*
cadere	*caddi*	*cadesti*	*cadde*	*cademmo*	*cadeste*	*caddero*
dirigere	*diressi*	*dirigesti*	*diresse*	*dirigemmo*	*dirigeste*	*diressero*
chiudere	*chiusi*	*chiudesti*	*chiuse*	*chiudemmo*	*chiudeste*	*chiusero*
cogliere	*colsi*	*cogliesti*	*colse*	*cogliemmo*	*coglieste*	*colsero*
concedere	*concessi*[10]	*concedesti*	*concesse*	*concedemmo*	*concedeste*	*concessero*
conoscere	*conobbi*	*conoscesti*	*conobbe*	*conoscemmo*	*conosceste*	*conobbero*
correre	*corsi*	*corresti*	*corse*	*corremmo*	*correste*	*corsero*
cuocere	*cossi*	*c(u)ocesti*	*cosse*	*c(u)ocemmo*	*c(u)oceste*	*cossero*

---

[8]The stressed root is much less common than *apparii*, etc.
[9]The stressed root is much less common than *aprii*, etc.
[10]*Concedere* more frequently has the non-root-stressed pattern *concedei*, etc.

Infinitive	1sg.	2sg.	3sg.	1pl.	2pl.	3pl.
dare	diedi or detti	desti	diede or dette	demmo	deste	diedero or dettero
dire	dissi	dicesti	disse	dicemmo	diceste	dissero
discutere	discussi	discutesti	discusse	discutemmo	discuteste	discussero
eccellere	eccelsi	eccellesti	eccelse	eccellemmo	eccelleste	eccelsero
espellere	espulsi	espulse	espulse	espellemmo	espelleste	espulsero
esprimere	espressi	esprimesti	espresse	esprimemmo	esprimeste	espressero
essere	fui	fosti	fu	fummo	foste	furono
estinguere	estinsi	estinguesti	estinse	estinguemmo	estingueste	estinsero
fare	feci	facesti	fece	facemmo	faceste	fecero
fondere	fusi	fondesti	fuse	fondemmo	fondeste	fusero
leggere	lessi	leggesti	lesse	leggemmo	leggeste	lessero
mettere	mise	mettesti	mise	mettemmo	metteste	misero
muovere	mossi	muovesti	mosse	muovemmo	muoveste	mossero
nascere	nacqui	nascesti	nacque	nascemmo	nasceste	nacquero
nuocere	nocqui	nocesti	nocque	nocemmo	noceste	nocquero
parere	parvi	paresti	parve	paremmo	pareste	parvero
piacere	piacqui	piacesti	piacque	piacemmo	piaceste	piacquero
piangere	piansi	piangesti	pianse	piangemmo	piangeste	piansero
piovere	–	–	piovve	–	–	piovvero
porre	posi	ponesti	pose	ponemmo	poneste	posero
prendere	presi	prendesti	prese	prendemmo	prendeste	presero
ridurre	ridussi	riducesti	ridusse	riducemmo	riduceste	ridussero
riflettere†	riflessi†	riflettesti	riflesse	riflettemmo	rifletteste	riflessero
redigere	redassi	redigesti	redasse	redigemmo	redigeste	redassero
redimere	redensi	redimesti	redense	redimemmo	redimeste	redensero
rimanere	rimasi	rimanesti	rimase	rimanemmo	rimaneste	rimasero
risolvere	risolsi	risolvesti	risolse	risolvemmo	risolveste	risolsero
rompere	ruppi	rompesti	ruppe	rompemmo	rompeste	ruppero
sapere	seppe	sapesti	seppe	sapemmo	sapeste	seppero
scindere	scissi	scindesti	scisse	scindemmo	scindeste	scissero
scrivere	scrissi	scrivesti	scrisse	scrivemmo	scriveste	scrissero
scuotere	scossi	scuotesti	scosse	scuotemmo	scuoteste	scossero
spegnere	spensi	spegnesti	spense	spegnemmo	spegneste	spensero
stare	stetti	stesti	stette	stemmo	steste	stettero
tenere	tenni	tenesti	tenne	tenemmo	teneste	tennero
trarre	trassi	traesti	trasse	traemmo	traeste	trassero
valere	valsi	valesti	valse	valemmo	valeste	valsero
vedere	vidi	vedesti	vide	vedemmo	vedeste	videro
venire	venni	venisti	venne	venimmo	veniste	vennero
vincere	vinsi	vincesti	vinse	vincemmo	vinceste	vinsero
vivere	vissi	vivesti	visse	vivemmo	viveste	vissero
volere	volli	volesti	volle	volemmo	voleste	vollero

†The verb *succedere* is root-stressed when it means 'happen' (e.g., *successe* 'it happened'), but not root-stressed (*succedei*, etc.) when it means 'to take the place of', 'succeed' (to a throne). *Riflettere* is root-stressed in the sense 'to reflect light', but non-root-stressed (*riflettei*, etc.) in the sense 'to ponder'.

14.13 Verbs that lack a *passato remoto*

These are almost exactly the same verbs that lack a past participle, for which see 14.16. *Solere* has no *passato remoto* but does have a past participle (*solito* ['sɔlito]).

14.14 The past participle of first and third conjugation verbs: *-ato* and *-ito*

'Past participle' is a misnomer, since the relevant verb form has no necessary connection with the 'past', even though it plays a major role in, among other things, the construction of a number of past tense forms (for which see 14.19).

The past participles of virtually all first and third conjugation verbs (represented here by *parlare, finire*) are characterized, respectively, by the (masculine singular) ending *-ato* (feminine singular *-ata*, masculine plural *-ati*, feminine plural *-ate*) and *-ito* (feminine singular *-ita*, masculine plural *-iti*, feminine plural *-ite*). This ending is attached to the same root that appears in the infinitive:

parlare	*parlato*	*dare*	*dato*	*andare*	*andato*
finire	*finito*	*dormire*	*dormito*	*servire*	*servito*

Exceptions in the third conjugation are:

venire	*venuto*	*morire*	*morto*	*apparire*	*apparso*
aprire	*aperto*	*coprire*	*coperto*	*comparire*	*comparso*
offrire	*offerto*	*soffrire*	*sofferto*	*seppellire*	*sepolto*

Derivatives of these exceptional verbs form their past participle in the same way (*avvenire, avvenuto*, etc.; *scoprire, scoperto*, etc.). The form *sepolto* coexists with regular *seppellito*, but *sepolto* is the form normally employed in adjectival uses of the participle: *il tesoro sepolto*, 'the buried treasure', etc.

14.15 The past participle of second conjugation verbs

It is impossible to generalize about the past participle of second conjugation verbs, except to say that the form of the participle is not systematically predictable on the basis of any other part of the verb. The participles fall into two classes, root-stressed and non-root-stressed.

(i) Non-root-stressed second conjugation past participles in *-uto*:

Most non-root-stressed past participles consist of the root + *-uto*.

accedere	*acceduto*	*pascere*	*pasciuto*
battere	*battuto*	*piacere*	*piaciuto*
bere	*bevuto*	*piovere*	*piovuto*
cadere	*caduto*	*potere*	*potuto*
cedere	*ceduto*	*premere*	*premuto*
conoscere	*conosciuto*	*procedere*	*proceduto*
credere	*creduto*	*sapere*	*saputo*
crescere	*cresciuto*	*sedere*	*seduto*
dovere	*dovuto*	*tacere*	*taciuto*
giacere	*giaciuto*	*temere*	*temuto*
godere	*goduto*	*tenere*	*tenuto*
mescere	*mesciuto* (rare)	*tessere*	*tessuto*
mietere	*mietuto*	*vendere*	*venduto*
nuocere	*nociuto*	*volere*	*voluto*

Note that verbs in *-cere* have a non-root-stressed past participle in *-ciuto* (likewise *giacere – giaciuto, (di)spiacere – (di)spiaciuto, tacere – taciuto*).

Certain verbs display a different root in the past participle, in addition to the -*uto* desinence:

bere	*bevuto*	*devolvere*	*devoluto*	*vivere*	*vissuto*

(ii) Verbs with root-stressed and non-root-stressed past participles:

Certain verbs possess two past participles. *Vedere* has *visto* or *veduto*. The former is more commonly used, and is the only one possible in expressions such as *Cose mai viste!* 'Things such as have never been seen before!' In contrast, two derivatives of *vedere*, *avvedersi* and *ravvedersi*, have only the past participle in -*uto*; *provvedere* has only *provveduto* when used intransitively (*Ha provveduto a tutto* 'She's thought of everything in advance'), but either *provvisto* or *provveduto* in the sense 'provide', 'furnish'. *Perdere* 'lose' has *perso* or *perduto*. In addition to *successo* 'happened', *succedere* has *succeduto* when the verb has the sense of 'to take the place of', 'succeed' (to a throne, etc.).

(iii) The type *esistere – esistito*:

Verbs whose infinitives end in -*sistere* all form their past participle in -*ito*. Thus *esistere*, – *esistito*, and likewise, *assistere* 'be present', *consistere* 'consist', *desistere* 'desist', *insistere* 'insist', *persistere* 'persist', *resistere* 'resist', *sussistere* 'subsist'.

(iv) Root-stressed past participles:

The overwhelming majority of verbs with root-stressed past participles belong to the second conjugation. The stressed roots are all characterized by idiosyncratic features (cf. *passato remoto*, 14.12) affecting the root-final consonant and often also the stressed vowel. As a rule, verbs which have root-stressed past participles are the same verbs that have root-stressed *passati remoti*, although the form of the past participle cannot necessarily be inferred from the *passato remoto*, or vice versa. A few verbs which have 'regular' *passato remoto* have root-stressed past participles (e.g., *esigere*). The following illustrates the fifty types of past participle. Some are limited to just one or two verbs; others represent major classes with many members:

affiggere	*affisso*	*fare*	*fatto*
assumere	*assunto*	*fondere*	*fuso*
chiedere	*chiesto*	*leggere*	*letto*
chiudere	*chiuso*	*mettere*	*messo*
cogliere	*colto*	*muovere*	*mosso*
condurre	*condotto*	*nascere*	*nato*
correre	*corso*	*parere*	*parso*
cuocere	*cotto*	*perdere*	*perso*
dire	*detto*	*piangere*	*pianto*
dirigere	*diretto*	*porgere*	*porto*
discutere	*discusso*	*porre*	*posto*
eccellere	*eccelso*	*prendere*	*preso*
esigere	*esatto*	*redigere*	*redatto*
espellere	*espulso*	*redimere*	*redento*
esprimere	*espresso*	*rimanere*	*rimasto*
essere	*stato*	*risolvere*	*risolto*
estinguere	*estinto*	*rispondere*	*risposto*
estollere	*estolto*	*scindere*	*scisso*

scrivere	*scritto*	*tergere*	*terso*
scuotere	*scosso*	*trarre*	*tratto*
spegnere	*spento*	*valere*	*valso*
stringere	*stretto*	*vedere*	*visto*
succedere	*successo*	*vincere*	*vinto*
svellere	*svelto*	*volgere*	*volto*

Note the different prefix in *restringere* 'shrink', 'restrict', past participle *ristretto*.

14.16 Verbs that lack a past participle

A few – mainly rare – verbs lack a past participle. Where there is a readily available alternative expression, this is suggested below (in the *passato prossimo* form) in brackets:

> *competere* 'be someone's concern/business' (*è stato di competenza di . . .*), *concernere* 'concern', 'regard' (*ha riguardato*), *discernere* 'discern' (*ha scorto*), *distare* 'be distant/ away' (*è stato distante*), *divergere* 'diverge' (*è stato divergente*), *esimere* 'exempt' (*è stato esente*), *fendere* 'split', *fulgere* 'shine', *incombere* 'be incumbent' (*è stato incombente*), *mescere* 'pour' (*ha versato*), *mingere* 'urinate' (*ha orinato*), *procombere* 'fall forward' (*è caduto in avanti*), *prudere* 'itch' (*ha cominciato a prudere*), *serpere* 'snake', 'meander' (*ha serpeggiato*), *splendere* and *risplendere* 'shine' (*ha brillato*), *stridere* 'yell' (*ha strillato*), *urgere* 'be urgent' (*è stato urgente*), *vertere* 'turn/depend [on]'.

14.17 The gerund

The gerund is invariant (i.e., it never varies for gender or number). The first conjugation gerund is formed from the root + -*ando*:

Infinitive	Gerund
rappresentare 'represent'	*rappresentando*
dare 'give'	*dando*
parlare 'speak'	*parlando*
saltare 'jump'	*saltando*
etc.	

In the remaining conjugations, the gerund is formed from the root + -*endo*.

Infinitive	Gerund
sapere 'know'	*sapendo*
finire 'finish'	*finendo*
volere 'want'	*volendo*
morire 'die'	*morendo*
etc.	

In verbs where the root of the infinitive is different from that of the imperfect (see 14.11), it is the *imperfect* root which forms the basis of the gerund:

Infinitive	Imperfect	Gerund
fare 'do'	*facevo*	*facendo*
produrre 'produce'	*producevo*	*producendo*
dire 'say'	*dicevo*	*dicendo*
etc.		

The exception is *essere*:

Infinitive	Imperfect	Gerund
essere	*ero*	*essendo*

14.18 Agreement of the verb with its subject: *La gente canta* 'People sing'; *Io e Giulio andavamo a scuola* 'Giulio and I went to school'; *Tu ed io lo faremo* 'You and I will do it'

With third person subjects, the verb is in the third person singular form if the subject is singular and third person plural if the subject is plural. This rule is observed far more rigidly in Italian than in English. For example, *gente* 'people' and *maggioranza* 'majority' take singular verbs because they are singular (see also 3.8):

La gente canta.	'People sing.'
La maggioranza degli italiani è convinta che la criminalità sia in aumento.	'The majority of Italians are convinced that crime is on the increase.'

Use of plural nouns in such cases (e.g., *La gente cantano* and even *La maggioranza degli italiani sono convinti . . .*) is often encountered in informal, colloquial speech but is not admissible in formal registers. The optional use of plural verbs with singular subjects where the subject is viewed as a collection of individuals, characteristic, for example, of British English (e.g., 'The government are incompetent', 'Italy have won the championship', etc.), is not found in Italian (*Il governo è incompetente, L'Italia ha vinto il campionato*, etc.). Italian *nessuno* 'none', 'not one', is also strictly singular:

Nessuno di loro è venuto.	'None of them have come.'

Speakers of English (which lacks distinct person endings in the plural of verbs) need to pay careful attention to agreement where the verb has two, co-ordinated, subjects one or more of which is not third person ('You and I . . .', 'He and you . . . .', etc.). If a third person subject is conjoined with a first person pronoun (*io* or *noi*), the first person plural of the verb must be used:

Io e Giulio andavamo a scuola insieme.	'G and I went to school together.'
Noi e i nostri amici siamo un po' matti.	'We and our friends are a bit mad.'

If a third person subject is conjoined with a second person pronoun, a second person plural verb is required:

Che fate tu e i tuoi amichetti?	'What are you and your little friends up to?'
Verrete voi e Giulio.	'You and G will come.'

Where first and second person pronouns are conjoined, the verb will be first person plural:

Tu ed io andremo insieme a parlare col sindaco.	'You and I will go and talk to the mayor together.'

There is a tendency in spoken English to use a third person form in relative clauses of the type 'It's me that does this', 'It's you who believes these things', etc., regardless of the person of the antecedent of the relative pronoun. This is never true in Italian (*Sono io che faccio questo, Sei tu che credi queste cose*). See also 6.21.

14.19 Analytic verb forms comprising 'auxiliary *avere* or *essere* + past participle': the forms of the perfective infinitive, perfective gerund, *passato prossimo* indicative and subjunctive, pluperfect (*trapassato*) indicative and subjunctive, past anterior (*trapassato remoto*), future perfect

All verbs (but see 14.16) have a set of forms comprising an auxiliary verb *avere* or *essere* + the past participle. In modern Italian, the auxiliary always precedes the past participle; the only words which can be introduced between auxiliary and past participle are focusing adverbs (for examples see 13.11), and certain temporal adverbs (see 13.16).

The verb forms consisting of *avere/essere* + past participle are:

● Perfective infinitive – infinitive of the auxiliary + past participle:

avere cantato 'to have sung', *essere venuto* 'to have come', *avere deciso* 'to have decided', *essere sceso* 'to have gone down', etc.

● Perfective gerund – gerund of the auxiliary + past participle:

avendo cantato 'having sung', *essendo venuto* 'having come', *avendo ricevuto* 'having decided', *essendo sceso* 'having gone down', etc.

● *Passato prossimo* indicative – present indicative of auxiliary + past participle:

1sg.	*ho cantato*	*sono venuto/-a*	*ho ricevuto*	*sono sceso/-a*
2sg.	*hai cantato*	*sei venuto/-a*	*hai ricevuto*	*sei sceso/-a*
3sg.	*ha cantato*	*è venuto/-a*	*ha ricevuto*	*è sceso/-a*
1pl.	*abbiamo cantato*	*siamo venuti/-e*	*abbiamo ricevuto*	*siamo scesi/-e*
2pl.	*avete cantato*	*siete venuti/-e*	*avete ricevuto*	*siete scesi/-e*
3pl.	*hanno cantato*	*sono venuti /-e*	*hanno ricevuto*	*sono scesi/-e*

● *Passato prossimo* subjunctive – present subjunctive of auxiliary + past participle:

1sg.	*abbia cantato*	*sia venuto/-a*	*abbia ricevuto*	*sia sceso/-a*
2sg.	*abbia cantato*	*sia venuto/-a*	*abbia ricevuto*	*sia sceso/-a*
3sg.	*abbia cantato*	*sia venuto/-a*	*abbia ricevuto*	*sia sceso/-a*
1pl.	*abbiamo cantato*	*siamo venuti/-e*	*abbiamo ricevuto*	*siamo scesi/-e*
2pl.	*abbiate cantato*	*siate venuti/-e*	*abbiate ricevuto*	*siate scesi/-e*
3pl.	*abbiano cantato*	*siano venuti/-e*	*abbiano ricevuto*	*siano scesi/-e*

● Pluperfect indicative – imperfect indicative of auxiliary + past participle:

1sg.	*avevo cantato*	*ero venuto/-a*	*avevo ricevuto*	*ero sceso/-a*
2sg.	*avevi cantato*	*eri venuto/-a*	*avevi ricevuto*	*eri sceso/-a*
3sg.	*aveva cantato*	*eri venuto/-a*	*aveva ricevuto*	*era sceso/-a*
1pl.	*avevamo cantato*	*eravamo venuti/-e*	*avevamo ricevuto*	*eravamo scesi/-e*
2pl.	*avevate cantato*	*eravate venuti/-e*	*avevate ricevuto*	*eravate scesi/-e*
3pl.	*avevano cantato*	*erano venuti/-e*	*avevano ricevuto*	*erano scesi/-e*

● Past anterior (or *trapassato remoto*) – *passato remoto* of auxiliary + past participle:

1sg.	*ebbi cantato*	*fui venuto/-a*	*ebbi ricevuto*	*fui sceso/-a*
2sg.	*avesti cantato*	*fosti venuto/-a*	*avesti ricevuto*	*fosti sceso/-a*
3sg.	*ebbe cantato*	*fu venuto/-a*	*ebbe ricevuto*	*fu sceso/-a*
1pl.	*avemmo cantato*	*fummo venuti/-e*	*avemmo ricevuto*	*fummo scesi/-e*

2pl.	*aveste cantato*	*foste venuti/-e*	*aveste ricevuto*	*foste scesi/-e*
3pl.	*ebbero cantato*	*furono venuti/-e*	*ebbero ricevuto*	*furono scesi/-e*

● Pluperfect subjunctive – imperfect subjunctive of auxiliary + past participle:

1sg.	*avessi cantato*	*fossi venuto/-a*	*avessi ricevuto*	*fossi sceso/-a*
2sg.	*avessi cantato*	*fossi venuto/-a*	*avessi ricevuto*	*fossi sceso/-a*
3sg.	*avesse cantato*	*fosse venuto/-a*	*avesse ricevuto*	*fosse sceso/-a*
1pl.	*avessimo cantato*	*fossimo venuti/-e*	*avessimo ricevuto*	*fossimo scesi/-e*
2pl.	*aveste cantato*	*foste venuti/-e*	*aveste ricevuto*	*foste scesi/-e*
3pl.	*avessero cantato*	*fossero venuti/-e*	*avessero ricevuto*	*fossero scesi/-e*

● Future perfect – future of auxiliary + past participle:

1sg.	*avrò cantato*	*sarò venuto/-a*	*avrò ricevuto*	*sarò sceso/-a*
2sg.	*avrai cantato*	*sarai venuto/-a*	*avrai ricevuto*	*sarai sceso/-a*
3sg.	*avrà cantato*	*sarà venuto/-a*	*avrà ricevuto*	*sarà sceso/-a*
1pl.	*avremo cantato*	*saremo venuti/-e*	*avremo ricevuto*	*saremo scesi/-e*
2pl.	*avrete cantato*	*sarete venuti/-e*	*avrete ricevuto*	*sarete scesi /-e*
3pl.	*avranno cantato*	*saranno venuti/-e*	*avranno ricevuto*	*saranno scesi/-e*

14.20 Which auxiliary: *avere* or *essere*? Auxiliary selection in transitive, reflexive and intransitive verbs

Verbs form their *passato prossimo*, future perfect, pluperfect and *trapassato remoto* by combining the appropriate form of the auxiliary *avere* or *essere* with the past participle. On what basis does a verb take *avere* or *essere* as its auxiliary? The answer is in part very simple (where transitive and reflexive verbs are concerned) and in part rather complex (where intransitive verbs are concerned).

Avere is the auxiliary of all transitive verbs (that is, verbs which have a subject, and an object noun phrase – where the 'object' is, normally, the noun phrase that 'undergoes' the action expressed by the verb).

Hanno visto Mario a Parigi.	'They saw M in Paris.'
Il vino aveva rovinato la sua vita.	'Wine had ruined his life.'
Avendo pagato il conto, non ho più debiti.	'Having paid the bill, I have no more debts.'

etc.

For the type *È valso ottomila lire* 'It was worth 8000 lire', with auxiliary *essere*, see below.

Reflexive verbs take auxiliary *essere*. But this statement needs a little modification: in fact, '*clitic* reflexive verbs take *essere*' – that is to say any verb which is formed using one of the clitic reflexive pronouns (see 6.1, 2) *mi, ti, si, ci, vi*. But reflexive verb forms formed with *stressed* pronouns always take *avere*:

Ha disprezzato se stessa.	'She despised herself.'
Avevano criticato se stessi.	'They had criticized themselves.'
Il giovane ha sparato prima alla moglie e poi a se stesso.	'The young man shot first at his wife then at himself.'

etc.

Clitic reflexive verbs function not only as 'true' reflexives but also as 'reciprocals', 'indefinite personal' and 'passive' constructions (6.29–33; 14.35): in all of these cases, the auxiliary is *essere*:

Si è tagliata.	'She cut herself.'
Si erano criticati.	'They had criticized themselves.'
Dopo essersi lavata, fece colazione.	'After having washed she had breakfast.'
Ci si sarà alzati prima dell'alba.	'People will have got up before dawn.'
L'articolo s'era pubblicato a Parigi.	'The article had been published in Paris.'

etc.

Which auxiliary do *intransitive* verbs take? A great many of them take *avere*; about 300 take *essere*; roughly 150 can take either auxiliary, usually with a subtle distinction of meaning. The task of learning which intransitives take which auxiliary can be simplified if certain basic principles are grasped. It should be stressed, though, that there is no foolproof 'magic formula' for predicting auxiliaries, and not every case neatly and unambiguously conforms to the general principles.

Consider the relationship between the subject *acqua* and the (feminine) past participle *cambiata* in the following sentences:

(a) *L'acqua è forse più scura, comunque molto cambiata da come la ricordo.*
'The water is perhaps darker, at any rate very different from the way I remember it.'

(b) *L'acqua è sempre fresca: è cambiata ogni giorno.*
'The water is always fresh: it is changed every day.'

Cambiata in **(a)** (*L'acqua è ... cambiata ...*) is interpretable as an adjective (we have translated it, in fact, with 'different') which asserts a state or condition affecting the subject noun (*l'acqua*); in **(b)**, *l'acqua ... è cambiata* is a passive[11] construction, in which the subject, 'water', is viewed as undergoing or being affected by the action expressed by the verb. In both cases the subject of the sentence, *l'acqua*, does not instigate, cause or control the 'change' expressed by *cambiata*: the water is, literally, 'passive': 'something has happened to it'. Now it is no accident that *è cambiato, -a* is also the *passato prossimo* of *cambiare*:

Ho messo un po' di zolfo e l'acqua è subito cambiata.	'I put in a bit of sulphur and the water immediately changed.'

As a general rule:

- *Essere* tends to be the auxiliary used with intransitive verbs (like *cambiare*) whose subjects play little or no role in effecting or controlling the action or state expressed by the verb.
- *Essere* tends also to be the auxiliary used with verbs which emphasize resultant states, rather than actions leading to those states.

In contrast:

- *Avere* tends to be the auxiliary used with intransitive verbs whose subjects play a major role in effecting or controlling the action or state expressed by the verb.

---

[11]*L'acqua è cambiata* is a possible passive in Italian although in fact, for reasons explained in 14.33, a more natural way to say this might be *L'acqua viene cambiata*.

- *Avere* tends also to be the auxiliary used with intransitive verbs which emphasize actions rather than resultant states.

A major class of verbs taking *essere* expresses 'states' (including *permanence in a state* and *changes of state*). For example:

> *affondare* 'sink'; *ammalare* 'fall ill'; *annegare* 'drown'; *appassire* 'wilt'; *arrossire* 'blush'; *arrugginire* 'go rusty'; *aumentare* 'increase'; *cambiare* 'change'; *crescere* 'grow'; *decrescere* 'ebb'; *dimagrire* 'lose weight', 'get thin'; *diminuire* 'diminish'; *dipendere* 'depend', 'be dependent'; *divampare* 'flare up'; *divenire* 'become'; *diventare* 'become'; *esistere* 'exist'; *esplodere* 'explode'; *fiorire* 'flower', 'bloom'; *imputridire* 'go rotten'; *ingrassare* 'put on weight', 'get fat'; *invecchiare* 'grow old'; *marcire* 'get overripe', 'go off'; *migliorare* 'get better', 'improve'; *morire* 'die'; *nascere* 'be born'; *peggiorare* 'get worse'; *restare* 'stay'; *rimanere* 'remain'; *scadere* 'fall due', 'expire'; *scoppiare* 'burst', 'explode'; *sfumare* 'shade off', 'merge into'; *sopravvivere* 'survive'; *svenire* 'faint'

Ma come sei cresciuta!	'My, how you've grown!'
Le mani le sono diventate robuste per il tanto impastare.	'Her hands became sturdy through so much kneading.'
Le gemelle erano nate il 6 maggio.	'The twin girls had been born on 6 May.'
Marco è rimasto a Palermo con la moglie.	'M has stayed in Palermo with his wife.'
Il suo passaporto era scaduto.	'His passport had expired.'
Era scoppiata una bomba.	'A bomb had exploded.'

The verbs *essere* itself, and *esistere*, also have *essere* as auxiliary:

Sono stati sessantanove i colpi partiti.	'Sixty-nine shots were fired.'
Erano state invitate a pranzo.	'They had been invited to lunch.'
Fosse stato vivo mio padre!	'If only my father had been alive!'
Non sono mai esistiti draghi fuori dalle favole!	'Dragons have never existed outside fairy tales!'

Closely related to 'state' and 'change of state' verbs are those which emphasize spatial position, or change of spatial position. Verbs of immobility, such as 'stand', 'stay put', 'lie', and the basic verbs of motion, indicating movement 'in', 'out', 'up', 'down', 'away', 'back', take *essere* (but we see below that some, less basic, verbs of motion, whose subjects intrinsically have a very high degree of 'input' and 'control' in the verb, take *avere*). Among these *essere* verbs are:

> *andare* 'go'; *arrivare* 'arrive'; *cadere* 'fall'; *crollare* 'collapse'; *entrare* 'enter', 'come in'; *fuggire* 'flee'; *giacere* 'lie'; *giungere* 'arrive'; *irrompere* 'burst in'; *partire* 'leave'; *salire* 'go/come up'; *sbucare* 'pop out'; *scappare* 'escape'; *scendere* 'go/come down'; *scivolare* 'slip'; *sfuggire* 'escape'; *stare* 'stand'; *tornare* 'return'; *uscire* 'go out'; *venire* 'come'

Fossi andato dove so io il giorno che t'ho conosciuta!	'I wish I had gone to a certain place I know the day I met you!'
Gianni capisce che sono arrivati nei pressi di Matera.	'G realizes they've arrived near Matera.'
A gennaio sarà già entrata in vigore la legge sulla vendita di bibite alcoliche.	'In January the law on the sale of alcoholic drinks will already have come into force.'
Il cadavere del cavaliere è giaciuto trecento anni dentro questa tomba.	'The knight's body has lain for 300 years in this tomb.'
Forse qualcosa era loro sfuggito.	'Maybe something had escaped them.'
La statua era stata solo tre anni in Piazza Navona.	'The statue had stood only three years in Piazza Navona.'

Io ero venuto a chiedere se avesse denunciato il furto.	'I had come to ask whether he had reported the theft.'

Riuscire 'to succeed', derived from *uscire*, also always takes *essere*:

La levatrice è riuscita a fermare l'emorragia.	'The midwife managed to staunch the haemorrhage.'

Verbs of 'seeming'/'appearing', and 'occurring'/'happening'/'befalling' are characterized by a very low, or nil, input from the subject. Consequently, they take auxiliary *essere*:

> *accadere* 'happen'; *apparire* 'appear', 'show up'; *avvenire* 'come about'; *capitare* 'happen', 'turn out'; *parere* 'seem'; *risultare* 'turn out'; *scomparire* 'disappear'; *sembrare* 'seem'; *sorgere* 'arise', 'crop up'; *sparire* 'disappear'; *succedere* 'happen'; *svanire* 'vanish'; *toccare (a)* 'befall', 'fall' (to somebody), 'be somebody's turn', etc.

A volte mi è capitato di avere più di venti alunni.	'Occasionally it has happened to me that I've had/I've turned out to have more than 20 pupils.'
Il suo progetto era risultato impossibile.	'His plan had turned out (to be) impossible.'
Piazza San Pietro le era sembrata un regno incantato.	'St Peter's Square had seemed to her an enchanted kingdom.'
Sono sorti diversi problemi.	'Various problems have cropped up.'
Era andata ad assicurarsi che non fosse successo nulla alla sua vicina.	'She had gone to make sure that nothing had happened to her neighbour.'
È toccato a me comunicargli la triste notizia.	'It fell to me to give him the sad news.'

Another class of verbs typically taking *essere* are verbs whose English equivalents frequently consist of *to be* + adjective. Prominent are expressions of:

- (in)adequacy: *mancare* 'be missing/lacking'; *bastare* 'be sufficient/enough'; *valere (a)* 'be good enough (to)';
- value: *valere* 'be worth'; *costare* 'cost';
- evaluation of quality: *piacere* 'be pleasing'; *dispiacere* 'be displeasing'; *rincrescere* 'be regrettable' (to someone);
- necessity, urgency: *bisognare* 'must', 'be necessary'; *occorrere* 'be necessary'; *volerci* 'be required', 'be necessary'; *premere* 'be urgent'; *spettare* 'be due' (to someone), 'be up to' (someone), 'be someone's responsibility to'.

Quei tre fucili non erano bastati a difenderci.	'Those 3 rifles had not been enough to defend us.'
Mi era occorso anche l'aiuto dei miei studenti.	'I had need of my students' help too.'/'My students' help was necessary to me too.'
Mi sei tanto mancata.	'I've missed you so much.' [lit. 'You have been lacking to me so much.']
Quanti chiodi ti ci sono voluti?	'How many nails did you need?'
È spettato a noi pulire la stanza.	'It fell to us to clean the room.'
Ci sono piaciute le tue poesie.	'Your poems were pleasing to us.'/'We liked your poems.'
Questa cosa gli era dispiaciuta.	'This thing had been displeasing to him.'/'He hadn't liked this.'
Mi è rincresciuto offenderlo.	'I was sorry to offend him.'
Le tue proteste non sono valse a farlo pentire.	'Your protests were not enough to make him repent.'

Verbs expressing value such as *valere* and *costare* are often followed by a noun phrase expressing the *amount* of the value: this is known as a 'measure complement', and should not be confused with the direct object of a transitive verb[12]. The verbs still take *essere* as auxiliary:

La vendita dell'appartamento è valsa un centinaio di milioni.	'The sale of the flat was worth about a hundred million.'
Quella macchina mi è costata un occhio dalla testa.	'That car cost me an arm and a leg.'

The intransitive verbs that always take *avere* are basically complementary to those that take *essere*: they are verbs whose subjects typically or necessarily play an active role in, or have a high degree of control over, what is expressed by the verb. Among them are:

abbaiare 'bark'; *acconsentire* 'agree'; *agire* 'act'; *allunare* 'land on the moon'; *ansimare* 'pant'; *aspettare* 'wait'; *assistere* 'attend'; *attecchire* 'put down roots'; *attendere* 'wait'; *ballare* 'dance'; *camminare* 'walk'; *cantare* 'sing'; *cavalcare* 'ride' (horse); *credere* 'believe'; *decollare* 'take off' (aircraft); *esitare* 'hesitate'; *galoppare* 'gallop'; *girare* 'go around', 'wander about'; *girovagare* 'wander'; *giurare* 'swear'; *lavorare* 'work'; *marciare* 'march'; *mentire* 'lie'; *navigare* 'navigate'; *nuotare* 'swim'; *osare* 'dare'; *parlare* 'talk'; *passeggiare* 'go for a stroll'; *pensare* 'think'; *posteggiare*[13] 'park'; *puttaneggiare* 'play the whore'; *rantolare* 'moan', 'give death rattle'; *riflettere* 'reflect'; *rimuginare* 'ponder'; *sbagliare* 'make a mistake'; *sciare* 'ski'; *soffiare* 'blow'; *soggiornare* 'stay', 'spend time'; *spiare* 'spy'; *tambureggiare* 'drum'; *tardare* 'delay', 'be slow in'; *temporeggiare* 'temporize'; *trotterellare* 'trot'; *ubbidire* 'obey'; *urlare* 'scream'; *viaggiare* 'travel'

Come vorrebbe non essere mai salita su quel tetto, non avere mai spiato dentro la stanza di Innocenza, non avere mai respirato quell'aria chiara, velenosa. [Mar.]	'How she wishes she had never gone up on that roof, she had never spied in I's room, had never breathed that clear, poisonous air.'
Ci aveva rimuginato su per anni.	'He'd been pondering over it for years.'
Avevano parlato della villa.	'They'd spoken of the villa.'
Ho capito che se avessi avuto paura, che se avessi urlato, anche io ero finita.	'I realized that if I'd been afraid, if I'd screamed, I'd have been finished too.'
Mi avevi giurato che non le parlavi più, ad Anna.	'You had sworn to me that you would never speak to A again.'

Some of the intransitives taking *avere* do not fit very easily into the categorization given above. Among them are verbs expressing bodily motions and reactions, where the degree of 'control' by the subject may be low or nil, although the subject may still be viewed as an 'active participant': in a sense it *produces* the action expressed by the verb:

ansimare 'pant'; *dormire* 'sleep'; *ruttare* 'belch'; *squillare* 'ring (of telephone)'; *starnutire* 'sneeze'; *sudare* 'sweat'; *tossire* 'cough', etc.

---

[12]A direct object can be made into the subject of a passive sentence:

Ha pagato mille lire.	*Sono state pagate mille lire.*

But a measure complement cannot behave in this way:

È valso mille lire.	**Sono state valse mille lire.*

[13]In general, verbs in *-eggiare*, which tend to indicate the performance of some activity by the subject, take *avere*.

Non ho dormito bene. Ho tossito tutta la notte.	'I didn't sleep well. I coughed all night.'

Verbs of motion which emphasize not 'change of place', but the *manner* in which the subject moves also generally take *avere*:

deviare 'deviate', 'swerve'; *galleggiare* 'float'; *gocciolare* 'drip'; *ondulare* 'undulate'; *oscillare* 'oscillate'; *serpeggiare* 'meander'; *sventolare* 'flutter' (flag); *tremare* 'tremble', etc.

All'ultimo momento il proiettile aveva deviato, salvandogli la vita.	'At the last moment the bullet had swerved, saving his life.'

A certain number of intransitives take either auxiliary, but the auxiliaries are not freely interchangeable: the selection of *avere* or *essere* is usually sensitive to the principles outlined above. With certain verbs, *avere* is used when the emphasis is on the execution/performance of the activity, especially where the subject can be viewed as actively controlling the activity; *essere* is used when what is in the foreground is a state, change of state or change of position which the subject undergoes. Among verbs that behave in this way are:

appartenere 'belong'; *correre* 'run'; *circolare* 'circulate'; *approdare* 'come ashore'; *cominciare* 'begin'; *durare* 'last'; *emigrare* 'emigrate'; *espatriare* 'leave one's country'; *finire* 'stop', 'end'; *incrudelire* 'be cruel'; *progredire* 'progress'; *volare* 'fly'; *seguire* 'follow'; *slittare* 'slide'; *sfociare* 'emerge', 'debouch'; *saltare* 'jump'; *vivere* 'live'

The distinction can be rather clearly seen by comparing the following sentences:

È corso al campo sportivo in un'ora.	'He ran to the sports ground in an hour.'
Ha corso al campo sportivo per un'ora.	'He ran at the sports ground for an hour.'

The sentence with *essere* emphasizes his having got to the sports ground, and the fact of his having *run* there is rather in the background; significantly, time expressions with the preposition *in* (*in una ora*) are typically associated with the time taken to reach some *resultant state*. The sentence with *avere*, in contrast, emphasizes the activity: what he did was *run*; we are also told that this was the activity he performed at the sports ground and the *duration* of his doing it; time expressions emphasizing the duration of an action are, by the way, typically introduced by the preposition *per*. Other, similar, examples are:

Aveva messo il piede su una mina ed era saltata in aria.	'She'd stepped on a mine and it had blown up.' [lit. 'It had jumped in the air.']
Aveva saltato più alto che poteva per farsi notare.	'She had jumped as high as she could to get herself noticed.'
Ho spiegato la lezione e lui ha seguito molto attentamente.	'I explained the lesson and he followed very carefully.'
È seguita una lezione sull'opera di Leonardo.	'A lesson on Leonardo's works followed/came next.'
I miei figli sono emigrati all'estero.	'My children have emigrated.' /'... are abroad.'
I miei figli hanno emigrato a causa della disoccupazione.	'My children have emigrated because of the unemployment.'
Il Banco di Napoli è finito nelle mani di INA e BNL.	'The Bank of Naples has ended up in the hands of the INA and the BNL.'

I muratori hanno cominciato alle otto e finito alle tre.	'The bricklayers started at 8 and finished at 3.'
La linguistica è progredita molto negli ultimi cinquant'anni.	'Linguistics has progressed a lot/come a long way over the past 50 years.'
Ho progredito molto nei miei studi.	'I've made a lot of headway in my studies.'/'I've got a lot done in my studies.'
L'anello era appartenuto alla regina Vittoria.	'The ring had belonged to Queen Victoria.'
Non ho mai appartenuto al PCI.	'I've never belonged to the Communist Party.'
L'imperatore ha incrudelito per quindici anni.	'The emperor behaved cruelly for 15 years.'
L'imperatore è incrudelito.	'The emperor has become cruel.'

In certain other cases, *avere* tends to be used when the subject might be seen as having some *potential* control over the verb. This shows up rather nicely with a verb such as *traboccare* 'overflow': *essere* is regularly used where the subject is the substance overflowing:

Il tè è traboccato dalla tazza.	'The tea overflowed from the cup.'

But if the subject is the *container*, i.e., the thing which might, potentially, restrain the overflowing, *avere* is used:

La tazza ha traboccato.	'The cup overflowed.'

Other verbs which behave similarly are: *straripare* 'to overflow' (of river), *abbondare* 'to abound in', *sgocciolare* 'to drip':

Le selve cretacee avevano sempre abbondato di mammiferi.	'The Cretaceous forests had always had abundant mammals.'
I mammiferi erano sempre abbondati nelle selve cretacee.	'Mammals had always been abundant in the Cretaceous forests.'

With the verb *vivere*, the distinction is between 'to be alive', 'to be living' (*essere*) and 'to lead one's life' (*avere*). Intransitive *vivere* with auxiliary *avere* is very close in meaning to transitive *vivere* meaning 'to live through' (e.g., *Ha vissuto tante brutte esperienze* 'He's been through so many nasty experiences').

Non era vissuto durante la guerra.	'He hadn't lived/been alive during the war.'
Aveva vissuto davvero durante la guerra.	'He had really lived/He'd led a real life during the war.'

Verbs expressing meteorological and other atmospheric conditions (e.g., *nevicare* 'snow', *piovere* 'rain', *gelare* 'freeze', *lampeggiare* 'lighten', *balenare* 'lighten', *tuonare* 'thunder', *abbuiare* 'turn dark', *imbrunire* 'to fall (dusk)', *spiovere* 'stop raining', may take either auxiliary. In this case it is far from clear that there is any real nuance distinguishing forms with auxiliary *essere* and those with *avere*, although for some speakers it seems that use of *essere* is associated with the *state resultant* from some atmospheric event, whilst *avere* focuses on the action expressed by the verb:

—*Che tempo ha fatto stanotte?*	'What was the weather like last night?'
—*Ha piovuto.*	'It rained.'

Il rumore attutito delle gomme indicava che era nevicato durante la notte.	'The dull sound of the tyres indicated that it had snowed overnight.'
Pareva che avrebbe piovuto sempre.	'It seemed it would go on raining for ever.'

Note that *piovere*, used colloquially to mean 'turn up', takes *essere*, while *fulminare* 'fulminate' and *tuonare* 'sound off', take *avere*:

Ad un tratto ci è piovuto in mezzo Carlo.	'All of a sudden C turned up in our midst.'
Ha tuonato per ore contro i suoi nemici.	'He sounded off against his enemies for hours.'

Many of the verbs that take *essere* when intransitive can also be used transitively, in which case they necessarily take *avere*. For example:

Hanno cambiato il sistema.	'They've changed the system.'
Non hanno servito la torta.	'They haven't served the cake.'
Hanno migliorato la rete ferroviaria.	'They've improved the railway network.'
Mi hanno aumentato lo stipendio.	'They've increased my salary.'
Ha salito la scala.	'He went up/ascended the ladder.'

14.21 *Ho voluto partire* or *Sono voluto partire*? Selection of auxiliaries with modal verbs (*volere, sapere, potere, dovere*) and aspectual verbs (*cominciare a, continuare a, finire di*) followed by an infinitive

Which auxiliary is employed with modal verbs (*volere, potere, sapere, dovere*) or aspectual verbs (*cominciare a, continuare a, finire di*) followed by an infinitive? Normally, the auxiliary is *avere*:

Ho dovuto lavorare tutta la notte.	'I had to work all night.'
Hanno voluto aprire la scatola.	'They tried to open the box.'
Avevi potuto prenderlo?	'Had you been able to get it?'
Hai cominciato a russare.	'You started to snore.'
Aveva finito di mangiare.	'She'd stopped eating.'
etc.	

However, if the auxiliary of the verb appearing in the infinitive is *essere*, then *essere* usually becomes the auxiliary of the modal/aspectual verb:

Si è dovuta alzare.	'She had to get up.'	(cf. *Si è alzata.*)
Noi saremmo dovuti rimanere nella caserma.	'We would have had to stay in the barracks.'	(cf. *Saremmo rimasti.*)
Non sarebbero potuti esistere.	'They would not have been able to exist.'	(cf. *Sarebbero esistiti.*)
Il fiore è cominciato a appassire.	'The flower started to wilt.'	(cf. *È appassito.*)
etc.		

But the requirement that the modal/aspectual take *essere* if the infinitive is that of a verb taking *essere* is not absolute. Where the modal takes *essere* the whole structure 'modal + infinitive' is analysed, so to speak, as a *single unit*, in which the modal/aspectual verb is demoted to a mere subordinate adjunct of the main verb and consequently carries the auxiliary associated with the main verb. But it is also possible to view 'modal + infinitive' as consisting of *two* independent verbs, in which the modal is not 'subordinate'. This is likely to be the case where the intention is to emphasize the meaning of the modal verb; for example:

—*Non voglio sapere che ha fatto, voglio sapere cosa ha voluto.*	'I don't want to know what he did, I want to know what he wanted.'
—*Ha voluto entrare senza pagare.*	'What he wanted was to get in without paying.'
—*Perché non sei sceso?*	'Why didn't you come down?'
—*Perché non ho potuto scendere.*	'Because I just couldn't (get down).'

The distinction between the 'single unit' analysis and the 'two verb' analysis is important in another respect, namely the placement of clitic pronouns. If the modal/aspectual + infinitive is analysed as a single unit, then any clitic pronouns must be attached to the modal verb; if they are analysed as two verbs, the clitic pronouns must be attached to the infinitive. It follows from this that, where the main verb takes auxiliary *essere*, attachment of the clitic to the modal/aspectual implies selection of auxiliary *essere* for the modal/aspectual, and vice versa, and attachment of the clitic to the infinitive implies selection of auxiliary *avere* for the modal, and vice versa:

Si è potuta alzare. or *Ha potuto alzarsi.*	'She was able to get up.'
Ci siamo voluti tornare. or *Abbiamo voluto tornarci.*	'We wanted to go back there.'
Ve ne siete dovuti andare. or *Avete dovuto andarvene.*	'You had to go away.'
C'è saputo entrare.	'He managed to get in there.'
Ha saputo entrarci.	'He knew how to get in there.' etc.

Avere is required where the main verb is *essere, diventare, risultare, sembrare, restare* (all of which normally take auxiliary *essere*) followed by a noun phrase, an adjective or a past participle:

Ha dovuto essere molto difficile.	'It must have been very difficult.'
Non abbiamo voluto sembrare scortesi.	'We didn't mean to seem rude.'
A quell'ora avrebbe potuto già essere partita.	'At that time she might already have left.'

Avere is also required with modal verbs in passive constructions:

Ha fatto tutto da sola. Non ha voluto essere aiutata.	'She did everything on her own. She wouldn't be helped.'
Tutte queste cose hanno potuto essere vendute a buon prezzo.	'All these things were able to be sold at a good price.'

14.22 Agreement of the past participle: *Le ragazze sono arrivate ma non le ho viste*, etc.

Past participles never agree for gender and number with the subject, if the auxiliary is *avere*:

Le ragazze hanno cantato.	'The girls have sung.'
Avrete ballato molto.	'You [pl.] must have danced a lot.'

But wherever the auxiliary is *essere* (in passives, reflexives and many intransitives) the past participle agrees (but see 14.23, 24 below) in number and gender with the subject:

Sono state bevute due birre.	'Two beers were drunk.'
Sono scoppiate delle bombe.	'Bombs have exploded.'
Erano tornati alle sette.	'They had come back at 7.'
Patrizia se ne sarebbe pentita più tardi.	'P would regret it later.'
A che ora vi siete alzate, ragazze?	'When did you get up, girls?'
I ragazzi? Si sono bevuti otto birre.	'The boys? They drank down 8 beers.'
Si sono bevute otto birre.	'Eight beers were drunk.'

For an explanation of the past participle with the indefinite subject pronoun *si* (e.g., *Si è partiti*, *Si è ballato*), where agreement is *plural*, but occurs only when the auxiliary verb would *normally* be *essere* (cf. *È partito* vs. *Ha ballato*), see 14.20.

14.23 Agreement of the past participle with object pronouns

In old Italian (and occasionally to this day, especially in the usage of some southern Italians), the past participle frequently agreed in number and gender with the direct object of the verb. This is no longer generally the case in the modern language:[14] in deliberately archaizing, literary usage one may sometimes encounter a structure such as *Quando i figli ebbero delusa ogni sua aspettativa, egli si rassegnò alla sua triste sorte* 'When his children had disappointed his every expectation, he resigned himself to his sad fate', but *deluso*, without agreement, would now be normal.[15] The sole case in the modern language in which the participle must agree with an object noun arises with 'clausal' uses of the participle of a transitive verb (described in 15.22):

Interrogati gli studenti, il poliziotto riuscì subito a rintracciare il colpevole.	'Having interrogated the students, the policeman immediately managed to track down the culprit.'

Agreement remains common, and in certain important cases obligatory, where the object is a clitic pronoun:

- The past participle *must* agree in number and gender with the third person direct object clitic pronouns *lo, la, le, li*.

Quanto l'hai aspettata?	'How long did you wait for her?'
Li hanno avvistati stamattina.	'They spotted them this morning.'

---

[14]The complications in agreement patterns which can occur when the past participle agrees with object nouns will not be considered here, since agreement with object nouns is never obligatory in modern Italian, and largely restricted to regional varieties. For an account, see Salvi in Renzi and Salvi (1991: 238–44).

[15]The types *Aveva depositati i soldi in banca* and *Aveva i soldi depositati in banca* 'He had the money deposited in the bank', are perfectly normal in modern Italian, but here *avere* is not an auxiliary but the full verb 'to have', 'possess', 'keep' and its object is *i soldi*. *Depositati* is a past participle used adjectivally and modifying the object *i soldi*. The first example, with the adjective preceding the object, is roughly 'He had the money at the bank, where he had deposited it'; the second is 'He had the money which had been deposited at the bank'.

E, dopo, gliele avrebbe anche date.	'And, then, she'd even give them to him.'
Avvisatala, non avevano altro da fare.	'Once they'd warned her, they had nothing else to do.'

- The past participle generally agrees in number and gender with the noun to which the partitive object clitic *ne* refers:

Scartata quest'ipotesi, l'esame della sua ecclesiologia ne aveva suscitata un'altra. [Gin.]	'With this hypothesis out of the way, the examination of his ecclesiology had raised another one.'
In dodici incontri disputati Rossi ne aveva vinti undici e perduto uno.	'In 12 matches played R had won 11 and lost 1.'
Volevano sapere quanti ne avesse consumati e quanti ne avesse rimandati.	'They wanted to know how many he had consumed and how many he had sent back.'

There is no agreement if *ne* stands for a phrase introduced by *di* or *da*:

Abbiamo parlato di lei.	*Ne abbiamo parlato.*	'We talked about her.'
Ho allontanato i libri dalle fiamme.	*Ne ho allontanato i libri.*	'I pulled the books away from them.'

Partitive constructions with *di* (see 4.20) are an exception: *Ne ho letti = Ho letto dei libri.*

There are two[16] possible agreement patterns with *ne* where the verb has both a partitive object *and* a quantifier object. The participle can either agree with the partitive (*mele*), or with the quantifier (*due chili*):

Di mele, ne avrà mangiati due chili.	'He must have eaten 2 kilos of apples.'
Di mele, ne avrà mangiate due chili.	'He must have eaten 2 kilos of apples.'

- The past participle may, *optionally*, agree in number and gender with first and second person direct object pronouns *mi, ti, ci, vi*. There is no discernible difference of function or meaning between agreement and non-agreement in these cases:

Mi avrebbe voluto contenta.	'He would have wanted me happy.'
Sei sicuro di non avermi vista?	'Are you sure you didn't see me?'
Sei Silvia? Scusa, non ti avevo riconosciuto.	'Are you S? Sorry, I didn't recognize you.'
Quasi non credevo ai miei occhi quando ti ho vista.	'I could scarcely believe my eyes when I saw you.'

The following is a particularly striking example of the lack of difference between agreement and non-agreement:

È venuto a trovarci quasi ogni giorno, ci ha abbracciato piangendo, ci ha confortati. Ci ha quasi commosso. E invece ci ha traditi fino all'ultimo.	'He came to see us daily, he embraced us with tears, he comforted us. He almost moved us. And yet he betrayed us to the last.'

---

[16]In styles which allow agreement with an object noun phrase, there is of course a third possibility:

Di mele, ne avrà mangiati due chili.	'He must have eaten 2 kilos of apples.'

● The past participle nowadays only very rarely agrees in number and gender with object relative forms *che, il quale*, etc. The following example is from Lampedusa's *Il Gattopardo*:

> *Lo aveva fatto imballare in due ceste che* 'He had had it packed in two baskets
> *aveva poi lasciate in cortile.* which he had then left in the yard.'

The best advice is *not* to make agreement in such cases:

> *la mantellina che gli ha tolto di dosso* 'the cape she removed from him'
> *Dopo tutte le spese che ho fatto . . .!* 'After all the expense I've been to . . .'

In reciprocal reflexive constructions (see 6.27), agreement is generally with the subject, but if the reflexive pronoun is an indirect object form, and there is also a direct object (as in 'They gave presents to each other'), then it is possible in more formal styles to have the participle agree in gender and number with the object:

> *Gli sposi si sono scambiati/scambiate le* 'The bride and groom exchanged
> *fedi nuziali.* wedding rings.'
> *Finalmente dopo tanti litigi i miei* 'After so much argument my brothers
> *fratelli si sono dati/data la mano.* have made it up.' [lit. 'given to each
>   other the hand']

14.24 A special case of past participle agreement: the type *I ragazzi se le sono prese*

If the verb *both* has auxiliary *essere and* has a third person direct object clitic, does the participle agree with the subject or the direct object pronoun? This situation can arise with reflexive verbs in which the reflexive pronoun is an indirect object, and in such cases agreement with the third person direct object clitic *always over-rides* agreement with the subject:

> *I ragazzi se le sono prese.* 'The boys took them (for themselves).'
> *Se lo erano trovato davanti.* 'They found it in front of themselves.'
> *Questa febbre ce la saremo beccata in India.* 'We must have caught this fever in
>   India.'

Agreement is also usually (but not obligatorily) made in such cases with *ne*, overriding agreement with the subject:

> *Me ne sono preparati/preparato tre.* 'I prepared three of them for myself.'
> *Di mele, la nonna se n'è potute/potuta* 'Apples grandmother managed to eat
> *mangiare solo due.* up only two of.'

14.25 Causative structures: *Faccio cantare Gianni* 'I make G sing', *Faccio cantare la canzone a Gianni* 'I make G sing the song', *Faccio cantare la canzone* 'I have the song sung', etc.

Causative structures express the notion of 'making/getting/causing/having somebody/something (to) do something' or 'making/getting/causing/having something (to be) done'.[17] The basic Italian causative structure (see also Robustelli 1995) is *fare* + infinitive:

> *Faccio cantare Gianni.*   'I make G sing.'

What Italian expresses by *fare*, however, covers a range of functions which in English tend to be expressed by different verbs: while English 'make' + infinitive has connotations of coercion, *fare* also means 'let', 'allow':

> *Lo faccio entrare.*   'I make him come in.' or
>   'I let him (come) in.'
> *Ti faccio avere le chiavi.*   'I'll let you have the keys.'

Note that *fare* + infinitive also corresponds to 'have' or 'get' + past participle:

> *Ho fatto pulire la stanza.*   'I had the room cleaned.'
> *Fece costruire un palazzo.*   'He had a palace built.'

14.26 The infinitive in causative structures

The form of the infinitive following *fare* in the causative construction cannot be modified in any way:

- The 'analytic' (see 6.4) infinitive (e.g., *aver cantato, esser partito*, etc.) can never be used (only *cantare, partire*, etc.).
- The infinitive cannot be passivized, even if the sense is passive (*Faccio cantare la canzone* 'I cause the song to be sung', never **Faccio essere cantata la canzone*).

> *L'associazione Noi-Rom combatte da sempre per far integrare gli zingari nelle scuole pubbliche.*   'The Noi-Rom association has always fought to get gypsies integrated into state schools.'
> *Per fortuna RAI Tre ha fatto trasmettere in diretta la splendida interpretazione di Vanessa Redgrave nel ruolo di Eleonora Fonseca Pimentel.*   'Luckily RAI 3 had VR's splendid performance as EFP broadcast live.'

- No clitic pronoun (see 6.1, 2) can ever be attached to this infinitive (either after it or before it). The causative construction behaves, in fact, just like 'analytic' forms of the verb in respect of the placement of clitic pronouns: the clitic always attaches to the *auxiliary* (in this case *fare*) – according to the normal rules of clitic placement – never to the infinitive.

> *Facendola entrare, si accorse di aver sbagliato porta.*   'While letting her in, he realized he'd got the wrong door.'
> *Era così a corto di quattrini che se li faceva prestare perfino dai poveracci.*   'He was so short of money that he got it lent to himself even from the poor.'

---

[17]Related to causative structures are what we may term 'transformatives', i.e., sentences of the type 'He made his shed into a studio'. A possible (but relatively unusual and archaic) way of expressing this in English is to say 'He made of the shed a studio', and this latter construction is the normal way of expressing such notions in Italian (using *fare di*):

> *Aveva fatto della capanna uno studio.*   'He'd made the shed into a studio.'
> *A fare del Polo una forza di trasformazione culturale può contribuire la presenza attiva di uomini di cultura liberale.*   'The active presence of men of liberal culture may contribute to making the Polo a force for cultural transformation.'

Vuoi una presa per il telefono vicino alla tua scrivania? Va bene, ti ce la farò mettere appena possibile.	'Do you want a telephone point by your desk? OK, I'll get one put in for you there as soon as possible.'

The third person plural pronoun *loro* may precede or follow the infinitive (see also 6.7), but when *loro* is the indirect object of the infinitive, it follows. In the following examples, therefore, *loro* must follow the infinitive when the meaning is 'the truth is told to them' (*la verità viene detta loro*):

Ha fatto dire loro la verità.	'He made them tell the truth.' OR 'He had the truth told to them'.

14.27 The subject and object of the infinitive in causatives: *Faccio cantare Gianni* 'I make G sing', and *Faccio cantare la canzone a Gianni* 'I make G sing the song'

The infinitive following *fare* in causative constructions may be viewed as having a subject and an object. In *Faccio cantare Gianni* and *Faccio cantare la canzone a Gianni*, the phrases *cantare Gianni* and *cantare la canzone a Gianni* might be viewed as corresponding, respectively, to the sentences *Gianni canta* 'G sings' and *Gianni canta la canzone* 'G sings the song', in which *Gianni* is the *subject* of the verb, and *la canzone* the *object*. So, in the causative structure, we may say that *Gianni* is the subject of the infinitive and *la canzone* the object. We have seen that the infinitive can also have passive value, so that *Faccio cantare la canzone* means 'I have the song sung'; in this case, *la canzone* is the subject of a corresponding passive sentence (*La canzone è cantata*).

A property of the subject of the infinitive in causatives is that it can never be placed between *fare* and the infinitive; the subject generally follows the infinitive:

Maria fa correre Gianni.	'M makes G run.'
Faccio scrivere Gianni.	'I make G write.'
Una calzamaglia nera e un maglione sopra il ginocchio faranno sembrare più snella anche una ragazza grassottella.	'A black knitted stocking with a pullover over the knees will make even a chubby girl look slimmer.'
Alessandro Magno fece marciare le sue truppe per giorni e giorni.	'Alexander the Great made his troops march for days and days.'
Oggi nessun professore fa alzare in piedi i ragazzi quando entra in classe.	'Nowadays no teacher makes the children stand up when he enters the classroom.'

If the infinitive also has an object,[18] then its subject must be preceded by the preposition *a* (the corresponding clitic pronouns are the indirect object forms *gli*, *le*, *loro*, etc.) – as in *Faccio cantare la canzone a Gianni* 'I make G sing the song' or *Gliela faccio cantare* 'I make him sing it'. The subject of the infinitive preceded by *a* as a rule immediately follows the infinitive, unless the object of that infinitive is emphasized, or the infinitive is part of an idiomatic expression (such as *far perdere la testa* (figuratively) 'make (someone) lose their head', *far girare le scatole*[19] 'get up (someone's) nose' / 'be a pain in the neck to somebody', etc.):

---

[18]The object can in principle be direct or indirect (e.g., *Gli faccio parlare al professore* 'I make him speak to the teacher').
[19]A colloquial expression best not used in polite company.

Lucio fece leggere alla sorella l'ultima lettera spedita da Giorgio prima di essere ucciso.	'L made his sister read the last letter sent by G before he was killed.'
I poliziotti fanno annusare ai cani le vesti del ragazzo.	'The police let the dogs sniff the boy's clothes.'
Quando entrai trovai Giovanni che faceva bere a Maria un bicchiere di vino.	'When I came in I found G making M drink a glass of wine.'
Averti incontrato ha fatto cambiare totalmente rotta alla mia vita.	'Meeting you made my life completely change course.'
Con un movimento continuo, fate compiere alle braccia dei cerchi in su, e in giù.	'With a continuous movement, make your arms describe circles up and down.'
Quella donna da giovane ha fatto perdere la testa a dozzine di uomini!	'When that woman was young she made dozens of men lose their heads!'
Fai sputare la caramella al bambino, è troppo grossa e potrebbe soffocarlo.	'Make the child spit the sweet out; it's too big and could choke him.'
I nove anni che seguirono, li dedicò a far sudare sangue ai venditori.	'He dedicated the following nine years to making the traders sweat blood.'
Quello studente fa girare le scatole a tutti i suoi professori.	'That student is a pain in the neck to all his teachers.'

Note that among the things that count as the 'object' of the infinitive are subordinate clauses (cf. *Ha capito il loro desiderio di partire* 'He understands their wish to leave', where *il loro desiderio* is the object, and *Ha capito che desiderano partire* 'He understands that they wish to leave', where *che desiderano partire* is equivalent to the object). The object subordinate clause can also appear as an infinitive (cf. *Ha imparato il francese* 'He learned French', *Ha imparato a parlare il francese* 'He learned to speak French'). Accordingly, in causative structures where the 'object' of the infinitive is a subordinate clause, the subject of the infinitive is preceded by *a*:

Le multe devono essere molto salate per far capire agli automobilisti che bisogna cambiar regime.	'Fines have to be very stiff to make motorists understand that they have to change their ways.'
A chi volevano far credere che si trattava di una bombola di gas?	'[lit. 'Whom did they want to make believe that it was about a gas canister?']
Mia madre fece notare a mio padre che ero un buon cantante.	'My mother made my father notice [i.e., pointed out] that I was a good singer.'
La maestra Alfredina Cesari ha fatto imparare a leggere e a scrivere a mezza Pescia.	'The teacher AC got half Pescia to learn to read and write.'

We have seen that the infinitive can also have passive value. In this case, the agent of the action can be expressed by *da* + noun (which usually immediately follows the infinitive):

Il marito fa seguire e fotografare i due amanti da un detective.	'The husband has the two lovers followed and photographed by a detective.'
Nei primi voli farò affiancare i piloti da un istruttore anziano.	'In the early flights I'll have the pilots accompanied by an older instructor.'
Fai avvertire il direttore dal portiere, e vieni subito con i documenti.	'Have the director warned by the doorman, and come immediately with the documents.'
Non vorrai far avvelenare i tuoi clienti da cibo avariato!	'You surely don't want to have your clients poisoned by tainted food!'

Perché la domanda sia valida, è necessario far autenticare la firma da un notaio.	'For the request to be valid, you have to get the signature authenticated by a lawyer.'

The difference between the subject of the infinitive preceded by *a*, and that preceded by *da*, is fairly obvious, in that *a* corresponds to an 'underlying' transitive sentence, and *da* to an 'underlying' passive:

Farò lavare la tovaglia alla Bruna.	'I'll get B to wash the tablecloth.' [cf. 'B washes the tablecloth']
Farò lavare la tovaglia (dalla Bruna).	'I'll get the tablecloth washed (by B).' [cf. 'The tablecloth is washed by B']

In the first example, I am causing Bruna to do something, in the second, the focus is on the tablecloth, and I am causing something to be done to the tablecloth (by Bruna).

Often *da* is preferred to *a* if the subject of the infinitive is a human being:

Sono una coppia di disgraziati, sfornano bambini e poi li fanno adottare da coppie danarose senza figli.	'They are a pathetic couple; they breed children and then get them adopted by childless couples with money.'
L'Alitalia fa adottare ai suoi aerei tutte le tecnologie più sofisticate.	[lit. 'Alitalia is having its planes adopt all the most sophisticated technology.']

Occasionally, the difference of meaning between *a* + noun and *da* + noun is rather greater as, for example, in the following pair:

La mamma fa prendere la medicina al bambino.	'The mother makes the child take the medicine.'
La mamma fa prendere la medicina dal bambino.	'The mother makes the child take hold of the medicine/has the medicine taken hold of by the child.'

The subject of the infinitive is followed by *da* when the causative verb *fare* is reflexive:

Piega il foglio e lo caccia in una tasca del grembiule di Innocenza, perché se lo faccia leggere da Raffaele Cuffa o da Geraci. [Mar.]	'He folds the paper and shoves it into a pocket in I's apron, so that she can get it read to her by RC or by G.'
Poppea si faceva lavare dalle schiave nel latte d'asina.	'P had herself washed by her slavegirls in ass's milk.'
È così gentile che si fa amare da tutti.	'He's so nice that he makes himself loved by everyone.'
Troppi disperati si sono fatti abbagliare dall'idea dell'America.	'Too many desperate people have let themselves be dazzled by the idea of America.'

The subject of the infinitive is introduced by *da* if the infinitive already has an indirect object introduced by *a*:

Ho fatto telefonare dalla mia segretaria a tutti i clienti che avevano ordinato il modello difettoso.	'I had my secretary call all the customers who had ordered the faulty model.'
Ho fatto spedire da Marco il telegramma ai nonni.	'I had the telegram sent by M to his grandparents.'

But if the subject of the infinitive appears as an indirect object clitic pronoun, the use of *a* for the indirect object of the infinitive is fully acceptable:

Le ho fatto telefonare a tutti i clienti che avevano ordinato il modello difettoso.
Gli ho fatto spedire il telegramma ai nonni.

'I had her call all the customers who had ordered the faulty model.'
'I made him send the telegram to his grandparents.'

Da is also preferred where *a* might make the sentence ambiguous (for example where *a* + noun could be either the subject of the infinitive or its indirect object):

Ho fatto distribuire il pane dai ragazzi.
Ho fatto distribuire il pane ai ragazzi.

'I had the children distribute the bread.'
'I had the bread distributed to the children.'
OR 'I had the children distribute the bread.'

14.28 Causatives with *lasciare*

Lasciare 'let', 'allow', behaves just like *fare*, except that the subject of the infinitive can take a direct object form even when the infinitive has another object, and can be placed between *lasciare* and the infinitive:

Non lascerei mai mio marito aprire la mia corrispondenza.
Non lo lascerei mai aprire la mia corrispondenza.

'I would never let my husband open my mail.'
'I'd never let him open my mail.'

14.29 Reflexive verbs and causatives

We see in 14.26 that the infinitive in causative structures cannot carry a clitic pronoun, and of course this includes reflexive clitics. This fact means that a sentence such as 'Gianni makes Marco criticize himself' could not be expressed as **Gianni fa criticarsi Marco*. In cases of this kind reflexive verbs are simply avoided altogether, and some other construction is used, normally *fare sì che* + subjunctive (meaning roughly 'to bring it about that . . .'). So 'Gianni makes Marco criticize himself' would be *Gianni fa sì che Marco si critichi*. This avoidance of the reflexive is found where *true* reflexives are concerned, i.e., where the verb expresses some action which the subject carries out on or to itself, and the reflexive clitic is actually the direct or indirect object of the verb. But many Italian verbs with reflexive clitics are not 'true' reflexives, in that the reflexive clitic does not represent a 'real' direct or indirect object of the verb. In many such 'lexically reflexive' verbs (see 6.15), the reflexive clitic is simply an inherent part of the verb, and the verb cannot normally appear without the clitic: among such verbs are *pentirsi* 'repent', *accorgersi* 'realize', *vergognarsi* 'be ashamed', *arrabbiarsi* 'get angry'; in others the reflexive clitic is an inherent part of intransitive uses of the verb (even though the verb may also be used transitively: e.g., *annoiarsi* 'get bored', *aprirsi* 'open', *alzarsi* 'get up' *svegliarsi* 'wake up', *arricchirsi* 'get rich', *gonfiarsi* 'swell up'). 'Lexically reflexive' (see 6.16) verbs *can* be used in the infinitive in causative constructions, but they always appear stripped of their otherwise obligatory reflexive clitic pronoun:

La coscienza di quello che aveva fatto lo fece vergognare di se stesso.
Charlie Chaplin ha fatto divertire generazioni di spettatori.

'Realization of what he had done made him [be] ashamed of himself.'
'CC made generations of film-goers enjoy themselves.'

Al mattino faccio alzare mio figlio alle sette.	'In the morning I make my son get up at 7.'
Quanto m'ha fatto annoiare quel signore!	'How that man made me get bored!'

It is impossible to 'embed' any other type of reflexive verb as an infinitive in a causative construction. To say 'Make the child wash himself', neither **Fai lavarsi il bambino* nor even **Fai lavarsi il bambino* are possible. Rather, the verb 'wash' has to appear in the subjunctive, usually preceded by an expression such as *fare sì che* ('cause/bring it about that . . .'): *Fai sì che il bambino si lavi.* Of course *Fai lavare il bambino* is a possible sentence, but its meaning is not reflexive, and it would normally be interpreted as 'Get the child washed' – one might add *da qualcuno* 'by someone'. A sentence such as *Fai svegliare il bambino* is however ambiguous: it could either mean 'Get the child woken up (by someone)' or it could mean 'Get the child to wake up', because *svegliare* can be both a transitive verb taking a direct object ('wake somebody up') and a lexically reflexive intransitive verb *svegliarsi* meaning 'become awake'.

14.30 The passive

Passive structures serve to focus on the person or thing undergoing an action, while putting the agent or causer of that action into the background, or removing it altogether. In terms of grammatical structure, it might be helpful to imagine that the passive is 'derived' from a basic sentence with a subject and a direct object. In 'passivization', that direct object becomes the subject of the verb, while the original subject (usually the agent or causer of the action) is either relegated to a prepositional phrase (English 'by', Italian *da*), or simply not expressed at all. Thus, if we take a sentence like *Negli ultimi tempi i terroristi hanno compiuto numerosi attentati* 'Recently terrorists [subject] have carried out numerous attacks [object]', the corresponding passive will be *Negli ultimi tempi numerosi attentati sono stati compiuti (dai terroristi)* 'Recently numerous attacks [subject] have been carried out (by terrorists).' In fact there are two major types of passive in Italian: one of them involves a third person reflexive verb (e.g., *La carne si mangia* 'Meat is eaten') and will be discussed in 14.35; but as the examples above illustrate, the most basic type of passive comprises an auxiliary verb + past participle:

> auxiliary verb (*essere* but also *venire* and *andare*) + past participle (agreeing for gender and number with the subject) (+ *da* + noun)

Some further examples:

Il conflitto balcanico è stato vissuto dall'opinione pubblica come un evento lontano.	'The Balkan conflict was experienced by public opinion as a remote event.'
Quasi l'intero dibattito è stato occupato da questo fondamentale argomento: ma gli uomini preferiscono ancora le bionde?	'Virtually the whole debate was taken up with one fundamental issue: do gentlemen still prefer blondes?'
Il primo servizio completo da tavola commissionato dalla zarina Elisabetta Petrovna nel 1756 è conservato nelle sale dell'Ermitage.	'The first complete table service commissioned by the tsarina EP in 1756 is conserved in the halls of the Hermitage.'
Quante altre fosse comuni dovranno essere scoperte prima che ci si decida ad intervenire?	'How many more common graves will have to be discovered before people decide to intervene?'

La gestione dell'ordine e della sicurezza internazionale non può essere delegata a un solo paese.	'The oversight of order and international security cannot be delegated to just one country.'
Decine di migliaia di morti avrebbero potuto essere evitate se l'intervento fosse stato più tempestivo.	'Tens of thousands of deaths could have been avoided had the intervention been quicker.'
Il dottor Maffei è stato nominato Primario Ortopedico dell'Ospedale di Pescia.	'Dr M was named Head Orthopaedist of Pescia Hospital.'
Anche quest'anno in Italia sono state vendute più bottiglie di champagne che di spumante italiano.	'In Italy more bottles of champagne than of Italian spumante have been sold again this year.'
All'atto dell'acquisto il pesce deve avere un lieve sentore di alghe marine, ma è importante capire se è stato bagnato o lavato con acqua per camuffarne l'odore.	'At the moment of purchase fish must have a faint smell of seaweed, but it is important to find out whether it has been washed or rinsed with water to hide the smell.'

The subject and the auxiliary need not be repeated in conjoined sentences having the same subject:

Nell'ultimo decennio Sarajevo è stata martoriata dall'artiglieria serba, snaturata nella sua vita quotidiana da continui bombardamenti, tagliata fuori dal mondo da un assedio implacabile.	'In the last ten years Sarajevo has been tormented by Serb artillery, distorted in its daily life by continual bombardments, cut off from the world by a ruthless siege.'

The auxiliary need not be repeated when the subject of the conjoined sentences is different:

In un battibaleno l'uomo fu imbavagliato, la donna legata alla sedia, e i ragazzi chiusi nel baule dell'auto che partì piano piano, cercando di non dare nell'occhio, come se nulla fosse accaduto.	'In a flash the man was gagged, the woman tied to the seat, and the children locked in the boot of the car which slowly drove off, trying to be unobtrusive, as if nothing had happened.'

In causative constructions, (see 14.28) the *causative* verb is passivized, but the following infinitive never is (unlike English):

Nel '65 fu fatta approvare dal Parlamento la legge di riforma.	'In 1965 the reform law was caused to be approved by Parliament.'
Vedendo il suo enorme successo in Francia, viene spontaneo domandarsi come faccia Paolo Conte a farsi amare, dunque capire da un pubblico che ne ignora la lingua.	'In light of his enormous success in France, one inevitably wonders how PC manages to make himself loved, understood, by an audience who don't know his language.'

14.31 *Da* and *da parte di* expressing the agent in passives

The agent of the action is introduced by the preposition *da*, while *con* indicates what the agent uses to perform the action:

Il pescespada fu issato a bordo con lunghi uncini dai pescatori.	'The swordfish was hoisted on board with large hooks by the fishermen.'

The agent can be introduced by *da parte di* when it is somehow 'in contrast' to someone else, either expressed in the same sentence (the subject, a complement, another agent) or not:

> *Da parte del Preside è stato adottato un atteggiamento rigido che ha fatto infuriare i docenti.*
> 'As for the Headmaster, a rigid attitude was adopted by him which infuriated all the teachers.'
> *Da parte dei suoi genitori è stato fatto tutto il possibile per non fargli pesare la situazione.*
> 'As for his parents, everything possible was done by them not to make his situation worse.'

14.32 Only direct objects can be passivized in Italian: why a passive of the type 'The student was promised a book' is impossible in Italian (and other ways in which one might say it)

In Italian, unlike English, only the *direct object* of a verb can be made into the subject of a passive sentence. No noun preceded by a preposition (including indirect objects preceded by *a*) can ever become the subject of a passive sentence. What matters is whether the noun is preceded by *a* or some other preposition *in Italian*, regardless of its status in English. Thus in English 'obey' takes a direct object ('The boys obeyed the teacher'), but in Italian *ubbidire* is followed by *a* (*I ragazzi hanno ubbidito al professore*) and consequently its object cannot be made the subject of a passive verb (you *cannot* say **Il professore è stato ubbidito dai ragazzi* 'The teacher was obeyed by the boys'). We can see how the direct, but never the indirect, object can be passivized in the following examples:

> *Promisero il libro allo studente.*
> 'They promised the student the book.'
> *Il libro fu promesso allo studente.*
> 'The book was promised to the student.'
> not **Lo studente fu promesso il libro.*
> 'The student was promised the book.'
> *La figlia del sindaco ha offerto un mazzo di fiori alla soprano.*
> 'The mayor's daughter offered a bouquet of flowers to the soprano.'
> *Un mazzo di fiori è stato offerto alla soprano (dalla figlia del sindaco).*
> 'A bouquet of flowers was offered to the soprano (by the mayor's daughter).'
> not **La soprano è stata offerta un mazzo di fiori (dalla figlia del sindaco).*
> 'The soprano was offered a bouquet of flowers (by the mayor's daughter).'

All this raises the question of how one *could* say in Italian 'The student was promised a book', etc. One effect of the passive is to throw into relief an object of the verb, and another way of picking out or focusing on some element of a sentence is (as we see in 17.2) simply to move it to the beginning of the sentence. So the indirect object *allo studente* could be placed at the beginning of the sentence, while the agent or causer could be put into the background by passiving the *direct* object of the verb. Thus *I ragazzi* [subject] *promisero il libro* [direct object] *allo studente* [indirect object] would become *Allo studente* [indirect object] *fu promesso il libro* [subject] (*dai ragazzi*) – literally 'To the student was promised a book (by the boys)'. 'The student' could also be thrown into relief within the sentence simply by eliminating any mention of the agent, an effect which might be achieved either with the third person passive *si* (see 14.35), or by using an 'indefinite' third person plural verb (see 6.34): *Allo studente si promise un libro* or *Allo studente promisero un libro*.

14.33 The passive auxiliaries *essere*, *andare* and *venire*

Essere, which is the most common passive auxiliary, can be used to form the passive in all tenses except the *trapassato remoto* (see 14.19):

Dopo che i bambini furono [never **furono stati*] *visti uscire, i poliziotti fecero irruzione nell'appartamento.*	'After the children had been seen coming out, the police burst into the apartment.'

Andare as passive auxiliary can normally only be used with third person subjects, and has different connotations according to the verb with which it occurs. With past participles of verbs indicating loss, destruction or disappearance, like *perso* 'lost', *disperso* 'dispersed', *smarrito* 'lost', *distrutto* 'destroyed', *dimenticato* 'forgotten', 'abandoned', *deluso* 'disappointed', *speso* 'spent', etc. *andare* is commonly used as a passive auxiliary, and retains some of its basic sense of 'going (away)'; the English equivalent is often 'get (lost, destroyed, etc.)'. In this use of *andare*, the agent is never expressed:

Nascondi l'assegno, potrebbe andare perso in tutta questa confusione.	'Hide the cheque, it could get lost in all this mess.'
Nel 1966 a Firenze andarono distrutti capolavori inestimabili.	'In 1966 priceless masterpieces were/got destroyed in Florence.'

With other verbs, *andare* expresses obligation – that which should or ought to be done[20] – and the structure *andare* + participle can be seen as synonymous with *dover essere* + participle. This construction is most frequently used in informal language, although not exclusively so. Note that it *cannot* be used in the 'analytic' tense forms comprising auxiliary *essere* + *andato*, or with the *passato remoto*: so *È andato fatto*, *Andò fatto* are impossible in the sense 'It had to be done'. The grammatical subject is usually inanimate (not a person), and it *is* possible to express the agent (introduced by *da*), although expression of the agent is unusual. In the rare cases where the subject is animate, the agent is never expressed:

I bambini non vanno mai spaventati con racconti paurosi, o con la minaccia che orchi o streghe possano portarli via dalle loro case.	'Children should never be frightened with scary stories, or with the threat that ogres or witches might carry them away from their houses.'
Col tempo imparerai che tuo marito non va contraddetto quando si arrabbia.	'In time you'll learn that your husband should not be contradicted when he gets angry.'
Il prezzemolo non va/andava/andrà (but not **è andato/*era andato/*fu andato*) *mai aggiunto alle altre verdure prima dell'ebollizione, perché potrebbe risultare dannoso.*	'Parsley should never be/should never have been/will never have to be added to other vegetables before boiling, because it could be harmful.'
Dopo aver inserito i propri dati e quelli della vettura che si vuole acquistare, va selezionata la formula di acquisto preferita.	'Having entered your own data and those of the vehicle you intend to purchase, the preferred method of purchase should be chosen.'

---

[20]In fact, both *va fatto* and *andrebbe fatto* could express 'should be ...' or 'ought to be ...' in English. The form in the conditional simply attenuates slightly the force of the utterance, and often implies a conditional clause of the type 'if such-and-such should be the case', or 'if I might say so'.

I cavi elettrici vanno maneggiati solo da chi è munito di adeguati guanti isolanti.	'Electric cables should be handled only by those wearing appropriate insulated gloves.'
Le fragole vanno lavate accuratamente, una a una, capovolgendole a testa in giù con il picciolo attaccato. Al momento di servirle, vanno disposte in coppette singole, condite con il loro sugo di marinatura e coperte con la panna montata appena zuccherata.	'Strawberries should be washed carefully, one by one, turning them upside down with the stalk still attached. On serving them, they should be arranged in individual little cups, dressed with their own marinated juice and covered with lightly sweetened whipped cream.'
Perché sia valida la domanda va spedita entro il sessantesimo giorno di pubblicazione sulla Gazzetta Ufficiale. *Contrariamente a quanto si crede, la farina non va setacciata per evitare la formazione di grumi, ma semplicemente per aumentarne il volume.*	'For the application to be valid it should be sent within sixty days of publication in the *Gazzetta Ufficiale.'* 'Contrary to common belief, flour should not be sieved to stop lumps forming, but simply to increase its volume.'

In colloquial usage, the imperfect of *andare* + past participle expresses 'should have been ...':

Queste cose andavano dette subito, ora è troppo tardi.	'These things should have been said immediately, now it's too late.'

Venire + past participle is different from *essere* in that it is explicitly 'dynamic', expressing 'entry into some state', 'undergoing a process' or 'subjection to regular/repeated action'. Contrast *La porta è aperta* 'The door is open(ed)', which is ambiguous between a 'stative' interpretation ('the door is open') and dynamic ('the door is/gets opened'), with *La porta viene aperta*, which unambiguously states that the door 'gets opened', that some action has been carried out on the door. Indeed, *venire* in this construction often corresponds to English 'get'. Some of the following examples show however that, unlike *andare*, *venire* readily permits expression of the agent with *da*:

Il nonno venne rallegrato dall'arrivo inaspettato dei nipotini.	'The grandfather was cheered up by the unexpected arrival of his grandchildren.'
Era chiaro che i ragazzi venivano maltrattati.	'It was obvious the children were being ill-treated.'
I traghettatori non hanno scrupoli, sulle loro barche non vengono osservate neanche le più elementari norme igieniche.	'The ferry operators have no scruples; on their boats not even the most basic hygienic standards get observed.'
I clandestini vennero gettati a mare senza alcun riguardo nemmeno per i bambini o le donne incinte.	'The illegal immigrants got thrown into the sea without any regard even for children or pregnant women.'
Nel nostro albergo le lenzuola e gli asciugamani vengono cambiati quotidianamente.	'In our hotel sheets and towels get changed daily.'
Se non specificate di volere la mezza porzione, vi verrà servita automaticamente quella intera.	'If you don't specify that you want a half portion, you'll get served a whole portion automatically.'
Il retrogusto di cioccolata di questa appassionata miscela di caffé viene esaltato dall'incontro con la panna.	'The chocolaty aftertaste of this fantastic blend of coffees is further enhanced by the addition of cream.'

I nostri prodotti vengono sottoposti ai test più rigorosi e severi, per questo superano l'esame degli intenditori più raffinati.	'Our products are subjected to the most rigorous and strict testing, so they pass muster with the most discerning connoisseurs.'
Il caffé viene servito in salotto insieme con i liquori.	'Coffee is being served in the lounge with the liqueurs.'
Il pompelmo viene servito tagliato a metà e gli spicchi, già staccati dalla buccia, verranno portati alla bocca con il cucchiaio.	'Grapefruit gets served cut in two and the portions, already separated from the skin, will be brought to the mouth with the spoon.'
All'improvviso venne sparato un colpo, e il cervo si accasciò sull'erba.	'Suddenly a shot was fired, and the deer collapsed on the grass.'
All'inizio del XVIII secolo a San Pietroburgo venne aperta la prima fabbrica di porcellane, chiamata fabbrica imperiale.	'At the beginning of the 18th century in St Petersburg the first porcelain factory was opened, called the imperial factory.'

If the tense is present/imperfect/future, a passive sentence with auxiliary *venire*, like *Sui muri attorno al negozio vengono/venivano/verranno affissi gli annunci* indicates a dynamic action 'On the walls around the shop the notices are/were being /will be put up'. The corresponding sentence with *essere* as passive auxiliary *Sui muri attorno al negozio sono/erano/saranno affissi gli annunci* may have the same interpretation, but *tends* to be interpreted as stative: in fact one could even translate this sentence as: 'On the walls around the shop the notices are/were/will be on display.' Passive *venire* cannot be used in its 'analytic forms' (so one cannot say **Queste cose sono/erano/saranno venute fatte*), but it *can* be used in the *passato remoto*. The question then arises of what the difference is between *Sui muri attorno al negozio furono affissi gli annunci* and *Sui muri attorno al negozio vennero affissi gli annunci*. If there is a difference, it is that *essere* emphasizes the *fact* of the notices being but up, while *venire* focuses on the action. Similarly, in the following example:

Subito dopo la Rivoluzione, l'arte della porcellana fu usata con sapienza per la propaganda del nuovo regime.	'Immediately after the Revolution, the art of porcelain was skilfully used for the propaganda of the new regime.'

fu merely asserts a historical fact; *venne* in this context might be translated as 'began to be used', emphasizing the action.

Venire + past participle can also be used with causative *fare*:

Prima della seconda guerra mondiale l'olio di fegato di merluzzo veniva fatto dare dai medici ai bambini con scrupolosa regolarità.	[lit. 'Before the Second World War cod liver oil was caused to be given by doctors to children with scrupulous regularity.'] 'Before the Second World War doctors made people give cod liver oil to children with scrupulous regularity.'
Il buono è valido soltanto se viene fatto timbrare da uno dei negozianti che aderiscono all'iniziativa promozionale.	[lit. 'The voucher is valid only if it gets caused to be stamped by one of the traders participating in the promotional scheme.'] 'The voucher is valid only if one gets it stamped by one of the traders participating in the promotional scheme.'

14.34 *Venire* + past participle signalling involuntary occurrence to somebody: *Mi venne fatto di . . .* 'I chanced to . . .'

Remnants of an Old Italian use of *venire* + past participle accompanied by an indirect object, expressing involuntary or fortuitous occurrence to somebody, can be seen in *Mi viene detto/fatto/scritto*:

Per fortuna mi venne fatto di girarmi, e vidi che il bambino stava armeggiando alla presa della corrente.	'Luckily I happened to turn round, and I saw that the child was playing around at the power point.'

14.35 Third person reflexives as passives: the type *Si legge il giornale* 'The newspaper is read'

Another way of forming the passive is to use a third person reflexive verb form with the reflexive clitic *si*. This structure, often called '*si* passivante', is used only when the agent of the action (often only implicit) is human: *Si distrusse Dresda* 'Dresden was destroyed' implies a human agent, not, for example, 'an earthquake' – whereas *Dresda fu distrutta* could equally imply a human or non-human agent. As with ordinary passives, the subject of the verb is the entity which undergoes the action of the verb, and the verb agrees in number and gender with the subject; as with any other reflexive verb, the auxiliary is always *essere*.

In Occidente ogni giorno si sprecano enormi quantità di cibo.	'In the West every day vast quantities of food are wasted.'
Si vedono in giro ragazzi vestiti in modo stranissimo.	'Very strangely dressed kids are seen about.'
Si sono pubblicate foto che avrebbero dovuto restare nascoste.	'Photos that should have remained hidden have been published.'
Anche in Nuova Zelanda si conosce il cibo italiano.	'Even in New Zealand Italian food is known.'
Attenzione a quando si acquistano capi di abbigliamento alle svendite!	'Be careful when items of clothing are bought in sales!'
È un libro sul come riemergono, come si interpretano, come si superano le violenze sessuali.	'It's a book on how rape is reappearing, how it is interpreted, how it is got over.'
Dalla grande cura delle illustrazioni si possono desumere tante informazioni sulla vita e sulle abitudini degli animali.	'From the great care taken with the illustrations so much information about the life and habits of the animals can be deduced.'
La Fondazione fra un anno sarà completamente aperta al pubblico, ma già da oggi si possono richiedere testi e documenti.	'In a year the Foundation will be completely open to the public, but from today texts and documents can be requested.'
Gli uomini non sposati si dicono celibi, le donne non sposate . . . zitelle!	'Unmarried men are called bachelors, unmarried women . . . spinsters!'
Gli esperimenti si dividono in innocui e pericolosi. È ovvio che quando se ne compiono di pericolosi, si dovrebbero adottare misure di sicurezza adeguate.	'Experiments are divided into harmless and dangerous ones. It is obvious that when dangerous ones are performed, adequate safety measures should be adopted.'

The *si*-passivante construction can, of course, also be used with gerunds, infinitives and past participles:

Non vedendosi nessuno in giro, nè sentendosi rumore di sorta, il ragazzo decise di uscire dal suo nascondiglio.

'Since nobody could be seen about, and no noise of any kind being heard, the boy decided to emerge from his hiding place.'

Finalmente, sentitosi l'ite missa est, la cerimonia finì e gli invitati furono liberi di lanciarsi sul buffet.

'At last, the "Ite missa est" having been heard, the ceremony ended and the guests were free to fall upon the buffet.'

Questo non è un vestito da mettersi la sera, tuttalpiù puoi portarlo il pomeriggio.

'This is not a dress to be put on in the evening, at most you can wear it in the afternoon.'

The subject generally follows the verb, but if the meaning is 'must/may/can be (done)', then the subject may come before the verb:

La carne davvero tenera si trova solo in macelleria.

'Really tender meat may be found only at the butcher's.'

Solo in macelleria si trova la carne veramente tenera.

Il pesce non si taglia mai con il coltello.

'Fish must/can never be cut with the knife.'

Non si taglia mai il pesce con il coltello.

The agent may be introduced by *da parte di* (or *da parte* + adjective) but as a rule the agent is not expressed with *si* passivante:

Da parte degli adulti non si dovrebbero mai usare espressioni volgari davanti ai bambini.

'Coarse language should never be used by adults in front of children.'

Da parte panamense si afferma che niente cambierà nella gestione del canale dopo lo smantellamento delle basi USA.

'It is stated by the Panamanians that nothing will change in the management of the canal after the dismantling of the US bases.'

15

Uses of the verb forms

15.1 Future tense to express future time

Future tense forms may be used, as in English, to express future time (i.e., time later than the time of speaking/writing):

Desidero salvare i nostri 35 anni di matrimonio e non sarò mai io a chiedere il divorzio.	'I want to save our 35 years of marriage and I shall never be the one to ask for a divorce.'
Fra poco gli salterò in groppa.	'In a moment I'll jump on his back.'
—E poi che cosa farai?	'And then what will you do?'
—Come, che cosa farò?	'What do you mean, what will I do?'
Più staremo divisi più ci capiremo.	'The longer we shall remain divided the better we shall understand each other.'
Non si sa se riuscirà a sopravvivere.	'We don't know whether he'll manage to survive.'

The so-called 'future perfect', comprising future auxiliary and past participle, expresses (as it normally does in English) a point in time later than the present but *before* some reference point in the future:

Avremo raccolto tutti i dati fra qualche ora.	'We will have gathered all the data in a few hours' time.'
Nel 2000 avrò vissuto quarant'anni in Italia.	'In 2000 I'll have lived 40 years in Italy.'
Sono sicura che saranno ritornati prima dell'alba.	'I'm sure they'll have come back by dawn.'

15.2 The future-in-the-past and the (past) conditional: 'She said he would come' = *Disse che sarebbe venuto*

The 'future-in-the-past' expresses futurity viewed from the standpoint of some point of time in the past, rather than from the standpoint of the time of speaking. Thus:

Future (relative to time of speaking)	**Future-in-the-past**
Now I realize that <u>he will come</u> soon.	Then I realized that <u>he would come</u> soon.
It is already 11 o'clock and it's clear <u>I won't finish</u> before 12.	It was already 11 o'clock and it was clear I <u>wouldn't finish</u> before 12.
The bell indicates that the train <u>will arrive</u> in 10 minutes.	The bell indicated that the train <u>would arrive</u> in 10 minutes.

In English (as in many Romance languages such as French, Spanish or Portuguese), the 'future-in-the-past' is usually signalled by the 'present conditional'. What is remarkable about Italian is that, in order to express the 'future-in-the-past', the present conditional (e.g., *verrebbe*, *sarebbe*, *finirei*) is not used.[1] Instead, a 'past conditional' (i.e., a verb form consisting of the conditional of the auxiliary + past participle: *Sarebbe venuto* 'He would have come', *Sarebbe stata* 'She would have been', *Avrebbe finito* 'He would have finished', etc.) must be used. So what one says, literally, is not 'I realized he <u>would come</u>', but 'I realized he <u>would have come</u>', etc.:

Poi mi resi conto che sarebbe venuto poco dopo.	'Then I realized that he would come soon.'
Erano già le undici ed era chiaro che non avrei finito prima delle dodici.	'It was already 11 and it was clear I wouldn't finish before 12.'
Il campanello indicava che il treno sarebbe arrivato fra dieci minuti.	'The bell indicated that the train would arrive in 10 minutes.'
Avevo l'impressione che si sarebbe alzata da un momento all'altro e mi avrebbe parlato.	'I had the impression that she would get up at any moment and speak to me.'
Hanno approfittato del suo starsene assorta sulla tela per squagliarsela, contando sul fatto che non li avrebbe sentiti sghignazzare e correre. [Mar.]	'They took advantage of her being engrossed in the canvas to run off, counting on the fact that she wouldn't hear them sneering and running.'

The Italian past conditional can also, of course, occur in 'past counterfactuals' (17.31), so that a number of the above examples, taken out of context, could just as easily be interpreted as ordinary past conditionals (e.g., 'I had the impression that she would have got up at any moment and would have spoken to me').

15.3 Future after *quando* 'when', *finché (non)* 'until', *(non) appena* 'as soon as', *dopo che* 'after', *una/ogni volta che* 'once', *subito che* 'immediately', *mentre* 'while'

English does not allow future tense forms after time conjunctions 'when', 'until', 'as soon as', 'after', 'once', 'immediately (that)', 'while', but Italian requires future or future-in-the-past forms in these circumstances:

Quando sarò partito, allora comincerai a sentire la mia mancanza.	'When I've left, then you'll begin to miss me.'
. . . e finché non lo farete e non lo avrete dimostrato a me resterete in peccato mortale, che io conosca le vostre azioni, o no. [Lam.]	'and until you do it and have demonstrated it to me, you shall remain in mortal sin, whether I know your actions or not.'
Continuerai ad avere questo problema finché non avrai cambiato l'interruttore.	'You'll go on having this problem until you've changed the switch.'
Te lo dirò appena lo saprò.	'I'll tell you as soon as I know.'
Io canterò mentre tu suonerai.	'I'll sing while you play.'

---

[1]So that the 'present conditional' is restricted in current usage to expressing the outcome of some 'counterfactual' situation (see 17.31): *Se fosse possibile, rimarrei a casa* 'If it were possible, I'd stay at home.' Just occasionally one may encounter the present conditional used as a future-in-the-past, but this is now very rare and restricted to old-fashioned, literary usage.

A complication arises when the verb following *quando, finché (non), dopo che, appena, subito che, una volta che* is a 'future-in-the-past' (i.e., expresses future time from the perspective of a point of time in the past). In formal and particularly written language, the form taken by the verb in these circumstances is *not* the past conditional usually employed to express the 'future-in-the-past'; instead, what is used is a pluperfect subjunctive (i.e., imperfect subjunctive of the auxiliary + past participle):

Perché finché fosse stato comandante, noi saremmo dovuti rimanere nella caserma.	'Because as long as he was [i.e., 'he would be'] commandant, we would have to stay in the barracks.'
Furono avvisati che quando avessero ricevuto l'ordine avrebbero dovuto rispondere immediatamente.	'They were informed that when they received [i.e., they would receive] the order they would have to respond immediately.'

For the future-in-the-past type *Sapeva che se fosse venuto, lo avrebbe visto*, see 17.35.

15.4 The present and imperfect tenses as expression of future time

It is characteristic of informal and spoken Italian that future time is indicated not by 'future', 'future perfect' and 'future-in-the-past' tense forms, but by the present, *passato prossimo* and imperfect indicative tense forms, respectively. Indeed, in ordinary, informal, discourse, expressions such as *Te lo manderò quando l'avrò finito* 'I'll send you it when I've finished it', or *Seppi che sarebbe arrivato dopo qualche giorno* 'I learned he'd arrive in a few days' time', sound unduly elaborate. The more spontaneous expressions would be *Te lo mando quando l'ho finito* and *Seppi che arrivava dopo qualche giorno*.

Poi, quando se n'è andato, gli si possono fare gli sberleffi dietro.	'Then, when he's gone, we'll be able to make faces at him behind his back.'
Lasciamoli che prendano il potere. Così si smascherano al cento per cento.	'Let's let them take power. In that way they will be completely unmasked.'
Mi avevi giurato che non le parlavi più.	'You had sworn to me that you would never speak to her again.'
Quando mi ha detto che quei soldi me li restituiva il mese dopo, ci ho creduto.	'When he told me he would give me the money back the next month, I believed it.'

In fact, in informal discourse the present tends to be used to express future time, while the future tense forms tend to be restricted to the 'conjectural' value (see 15.5). This, by the way, is the situation that obtains in many dialects of central and southern Italy, where the future tense form – when it exists at all – is principally 'conjectural'.

15.5 The 'conjectural' use of future tense forms: *Saranno le otto* 'It must be 8', 'It's probably 8', etc.

Future tense forms frequently have a different function, essentially unconnected with future time, which might be described as 'conjectural' or 'speculative'. Such

:nglish: 'You'll be wanting your supper
)er now', 'He'll have gone home by now'
me by now'. Italian makes extensive use
can often provide a simple and elegant
ght be introduced by phrases such as
oubt', 'I dare say', 'I suppose', 'I should
it or perfect tense; the conjectural future
lish 'must' as in 'You must be tired after
.e fact that you've been on the journey
respond to 'I wonder . . .'. Note that the
it in such constructions, and the future

	'I can imagine how annoyed Your Excellency must be about master T's departure.'
È cucita a mano e sarà costata un sacco di soldi! Chissà a chi apparterrà?	'"What can have/I wonder what's happened: is the ammunition used up? . . . Or maybe the gunner has died . . ." says G apprehensively.'
	'It's hand sewn and must have/I bet it cost a fortune! I wonder who it belongs to?'
. . . mentre nel secolo scorso sarà stato inimmaginabile usare l'aggettivo elettrico in modo connotativo, noi possiamo oggi benissimo parlare di un'elettrica atmosfera.	'. . . while during the last century it must have been/I suppose it was/it was presumably inconceivable to use the adjective 'electric' connotatively, today we can easily speak of an "electric atmosphere".'
Non crederai mica che noi litigassimo sul serio: si scherzava.	'Surely you don't think we were really arguing: we were joking.'

The conjectural future may also have a 'concessive' sense:

Avrai anche ragione ma io non lo voglio.	'You may well be right/Maybe you're right/I dare say you're right, but I don't want it.'
Sarà, ma mi pare difficile.	'That may be/Perhaps so/I dare say, but I think it's unlikely.'

Note also *non sarà/non sarà che* + subjunctive which usually introduce rhetorical questions: for the sake of politeness speakers present as a conjectural possibility what they believe to be true:

Non sarà che abbia sbagliato giorno?	'Surely he hasn't got the wrong day?'
Non sarà che non si siano svegliati?	'Surely they haven't failed to wake up?'

15.6 The 'historic future'

Especially in historical and biographical narratives, a third person *future* tense form is sometimes used to indicate an unambiguously *past* event. The stylistic effect is often 'synoptic', that is to say that it is rather akin to *listing* the contents or chapter headings at the beginning of a book, in that the historic future usually serves to present an overview of a succession of key events in the past. Its use is never obligatory:

Cosa sia stato quel trauma lo espresse poeticamente un altro giovane, meno che ventenne, Ugo Foscolo, nell'ode "Bonaparte liberatore" [. . .]. Lo descriverà nuovamente, in prosa questa volta, due anni dopo, in una dedica a Bonaparte. [Esp.]

'What that trauma was was poetically expressed by another young man, still under twenty, UF, in the ode "Bonaparte liberatore" [. . .]. He described it again, this time in prose, two years later, in a dedication to B.'

15.7 Equivalents of the English types 'I'm going to do it (next week)' and 'I'm doing it (next week)'

English has an alternative future form consisting of 'be going to + verb' (e.g., 'I'm going to stay here in bed'). No exact equivalent exists in Italian (unlike, for example, French *Je vais rester ici au lit* and Spanish *Voy a quedarme aquí en la cama*). An Italian sentence such as *Vado a restare qui a letto* is practically nonsense, since *vado*, a verb of motion, is incompatible with the immobility of 'staying in bed'. Where *andare a* + infinitive is used, it indicates actual motion: *Vado a comprare il giornale* 'I'm on my way to buy a paper.' The normal equivalent of English 'be going to' is either a future tense or a present tense: *Resterò/Resto qui a letto.*

But English 'be going to' + infinitive, and also 'be + . . .-ing', can also be used to denote future events whose occurrence is viewed as already fixed, arranged, planned, necessary, determined: 'We're going to arrive in London in six weeks' time', 'We're arriving in London in six weeks' time' are approximately equivalent to 'It is settled/arranged/fixed/definite that we shall arrive in London in six weeks' time' or 'We are to arrive in London in six weeks' time'. Often the Italian equivalent is simply to use a present or future form:

Arriviamo/Arriveremo a Londra fra sei settimane.
'We're arriving/We're to arrive in London in six weeks' time.'

Crispi, che sarebbe diventato poi primo ministro, era allora un rivoluzionario.
'C, who was later to become prime minister, was then a revolutionary.'

A more explicit way of showing that the future event is fixed or necessary is to use the present of *dovere* + infinitive:

Dobbiamo arrivare a Londra fra sei settimane.
'We're arriving in London in six weeks' time.'

Devo scendere alla prossima fermata.
'I'm getting out at the next stop.'

Le cose che dovevano verificarsi di lì a poco ci lasciarono col fiato sospeso.
'The things that were to happen shortly afterwards took our breath away.'

15.8 *Stare per* + infinitive = 'to be about to . . .'

Sto per comperare una giacca di pelle.
'I'm about to buy a leather jacket.'

Stavamo per entrare quando vedemmo Giorgio all'ingresso.
'We were about to go in when we saw G at the entrance.'

Sta per piovere.
'It's about to rain.'

Note also *essere/stare lì lì per* 'to be on the very edge of'/'just about to'.

Other expressions meaning 'to be about to . . .', 'to be on the point of . . .' are *essere sul punto di, accingersi a, essere in procinto di*:

Era sul punto di partire.	'He was about to leave.'
Si accingeva a ritirarsi.	'He was on the point of withdrawing/ getting ready to withdraw.'
Mentre era in procinto di controllare i documenti, l'ufficiale fu colpito a un braccio da un proiettile.	'As he was about to check the documents, the officer was struck in the arm by a bullet.'

What principally differentiates these constructions from (the much more common) *stare per*, is that they always presuppose that the subject of the verb is an agent who intends to carry out the action. Therefore one could not say **Era in procinto di piovere* for 'It was about to rain'. *Essere in procinto di* and *accingersi a* are characteristic of more elevated, formal styles; *stare per* has no such association.

15.9 The future vs. the subjunctive: *Non credo che venga* 'I don't think he's coming' vs. 'I don't think he'll come'

Italian does not have a 'future of the subjunctive'; consequently, *Non credo che venga* can be ambiguous between 'I don't think he's coming' and 'I don't think he'll come', and *Non credevo che venisse* between 'I didn't think he was coming' and 'I didn't think he'd come'. Likewise:

Anche lei era alla ricerca di una figura maschile che la compensasse della mancanza di quella paterna.	'She too was searching for a male figure who would compensate her for the lack of a father figure.'
Voleva essere certo che non avessero ripensamenti all'ultimo momento.	'He wanted to be certain they wouldn't have second thoughts at the last moment.'

If this ambiguity is undesirable (for example, if the 'futurity' of the verb cannot be inferred from context, but needs to be communicated), the present subjunctive can usually be replaced by a verb in the future, and the imperfect subjunctive by a future-in-the-past:

Non credevo che venisse OR *che sarebbe venuto.*	'I didn't think he'd come.'
Io ritengo che scenda OR *che scenderà. Prima o poi.*	'I reckon he'll come down. Sooner or later.'
Era possibile che lo eliminasse OR *che lo avrebbe eliminato.*	'It was possible he'd eliminate it.'
Non sappiamo se ci riesca OR *se ci riuscirà.*	'We don't know whether he'll manage.'
È difficile che lo legga OR *che lo leggerà.*	'He's unlikely to read it.'

However, replacement of the subjunctive by the future indicative is not possible after *senza che* and *benché* (but see 15.43 for circumstances in which *benché* may be followed by an indicative).

15.10 Present and imperfect tenses after *da* (*Canta/Cantava da tre ore* 'He has/had sung for three hours')

English sentences such as 'He has sung/has been singing for three hours' and 'He has sung/has been singing since four o'clock' express the fact not only that the subject 'has sung' in a period of the immediate past, commencing three hours ago/at four o'clock, but also that the subject *is still singing* in the present. In Italian (as in many other European languages), the form of the verb used expresses the fact that the action 'overlaps' a point of time in the present, that it is *still going on*. In other words, in such constructions Italian uses a *present* tense form:

Luigi canta ormai da tre ore.	'L has been singing now for 3 hours.'
Sono in pensione dall'anno scorso.	'I've been retired since last year.'
Vive a Parigi da anni.	'He's lived in Paris for years.'

Verb forms that are not labelled as 'present tense', but can refer none the less to present (or non-past) time, can also be used in this context (see 15.5, 48; 17.31 for the 'present' values of these examples):

Dovrebbero essere in pensione già da un bel pezzo.	'They ought to have been retired for a good while now.'
Luigi canterà da tre ore.	'L has probably been singing for 3 hours.'

An exactly parallel situation occurs in the past and future. English 'He had sung/had been singing for three hours' or 'He had sung/had been singing since four o'clock' means not only that he *had* sung in the past, but that, at some subsequent reference point in the past, he *was* (still) *singing*. In such cases, Italian uses an *imperfect* tense form:

Luigi cantava allora da tre ore.	'L had been singing at that point for 3 hours.'
Ero in pensione da due anni, quando decisi di tornare al lavoro.	'I'd been retired for two years when I decided to go back to work.'
Gli Azzurri perdevano da mezz'ora quando Rossi segnò di nuovo.	'The Azzurri had been losing for half an hour when R scored again.'

And 'He will have sung/will have been singing for three hours' or 'He will have sung/will have been singing since four o'clock' will be expressed by a future tense form:

Luigi canterà allora da tre ore.	'L will have been singing at that point for 3 hours.'
Sarò in pensione da due anni, quando comincerò ad avere voglia di tornare al lavoro.	'I'll have been retired for two years when I start wanting to go back to work.'

It is perfectly possible for the *passato prossimo* (*ha cantato*, etc.), *passato remoto* (*cantò*, etc.), *trapassato* (*aveva cantato*, etc.) and future tense to be used with *da*, but in such cases there is implicitly no 'overlap' with any reference point in the present, past or future. In such cases, Italian *da* often corresponds to English 'from', rather than 'since' or 'for':

Anche Mike, che aveva perso suo padre da poco quando ci innamorammo, continuava a ripetermi che mi mandava Dio per colmare quel vuoto. [Ogg.]	'M too, who had lost his father only recently [lit. 'since little'] when we fell in love, was always telling me that God sent me to fill the void.'
Da allora il suo errore è stato fatto proprio da ogni generazione di francesi.	'From that time his error was inherited by each generation of Frenchmen.'
Rimase a Parigi dalla fine della guerra sino alla sua morte.	'He stayed in Paris from the end of the war until his death.'

15.11 The use of the pluperfect (*trapassato prossimo*) and the *trapassato remoto*

The pluperfect (and its variant the *trapassato remoto* – see below) corresponds generally to English verb forms in 'had + past participle', and expresses the occurrence of an event at a point in time prior to some reference point in the past:

Mi avevi giurato che non le parlavi più, ad Annita.	'You had sworn to me that you would never speak to A again.'
Aveva messo il piede su una mina ed era saltata in aria.	'She'd stepped on a mine and it had blown up.'
Erano tutti ritornati entro mezzanotte.	'They had all returned by midnight.'
etc.	

For uses of the pluperfect in past counterfactual sentences, see 17.31.

A difference between Italian and English is that there are cases where English may use a 'perfect' tense ('have' + past participle), whilst Italian uses a pluperfect. These are typically negative or interrogative sentences in which the English perfect is, or might be, followed by the word 'before', and the difference arises because in Italian the *passato prossimo* is very strongly associated with 'relevance to the present' (see 15.16). Thus in sentences such as 'She has never (before) seen the book that you are showing her now', 'Have you been in this room (before)?' a *passato prossimo* would be inappropriate, because at the *present* moment it is obviously true that the subject has seen the book (for she is now looking at it), and has been in the room (for you are now in it). The likely Italian equivalents are therefore *Non aveva mai visto il libro che le fai vedere adesso* and *Eri già stata in questa stanza?*

In general, the pluperfect seems to be much more readily used in Italian than in English to present events which are in some sense the 'prelude' to the central event in a narrative. The following Italian pluperfects would sound unnatural if translated as pluperfects into English (the example is taken from an article in which readers are asked to judge the likely legal outcome of the circumstances described):[2]

La Casa editrice XYZ aveva preso in affitto alcuni locali nello scantinato d'un vasto edificio e vi aveva depositato libri di sua proprietà. Un giorno, per il cattivo funzionamento di una pompa sistemata nel vano caldaia del fabbricato, si verificò l'allagamento dei locali di cui la Casa editrice era conduttrice e la maggior parte dei libri subì notevoli danni. Dopo avere invano richiesto il risarcimento del condominio, essa si decise ad intraprendere una azione legale contro quest'ultimo.	'The XYZ publishing house rented some premises in the basement of a large building and deposited books belonging to it there. One day, a malfunctioning pump in the building's boiler space caused the premises run by the publishing house to flood, and most of the books were seriously damaged. After unsuccessfully seeking compensation by the condominium, the publishing house decided to sue them.'

This usage is particularly observable with the verb *nascere*. A past time narrative will tend to use the pluperfect *era nato*, etc., when stating when persons in the narrative were born (an event perforce prior to their actions in the narrative):

---

[2]For further discussion of this example, and of the 'preludial' use of the pluperfect, see Miklić (1998).

Si sono conosciuti nel gennaio 1998. Lui era nato nel 1957, lei nel 1962.	'They met in January 1998. He was born in 1957, she in 1962.'

The *trapassato remoto* comprises the *passato remoto* of the auxiliary verb and the past participle. The *trapassato remoto* is simply a variant of the pluperfect which must be used in the following combination of circumstances:

- the verb expresses a single event, completed immediately before the event expressed by the main verb *and also*:
- the verb is preceded by temporal expressions part of whose meaning is 'as soon as', 'immediately after': these are *dopo che, (non) appena, subito che, una volta che, quando, allorquando, finché (non)*.

Appena lo ebbe riconosciuto, andò ad abbracciarlo.	'As soon as she had recognized him, she went to embrace him.'
Non fu contenta finché non ebbero finito.	'She was not happy until after they had finished.'
Quando finalmente ebbe saputo della tragedia, si mise a piangere. etc.	'When at last she had heard about the tragedy, she started to cry.'

There is no *trapassato remoto* of *essere* (and no *trapassato remoto* of passive verbs). Occasionally, other time expressions may also select the *trapassato prossimo*:

In due o tre giorni Nino ebbe fatto amicizia con loro e si parlavano a risatine e gomitate.	'In [i.e., after] two or three days, N had made friends with them and they were exchanging giggles and nudges.'

Note that when *quando* and the other temporal expressions do not contain the meaning 'as soon as', 'immediately after', or the verb does not express a single and completed event, the ordinary pluperfect is used:

Quando aveva completato un pezzo, alzava il lavoro per guardarlo.	'Whenever/Every time she had completed a piece, she would lift up her work to look at it.'
Mi ricordo che una volta che aveva sbagliato mi ero messo a ridere.	'I recall that on one occasion when/at a time when he had made a mistake, I had started to laugh.' [Here the laughter is presented as roughly simultaneous with the mistake, rather then coming 'after' it.]
Quella casa con i campi intorno era mia proprietà da quindici anni, da quando un nonno molto vecchio ne aveva fatto donazione al nipote.	'That house with the fields around it had been my property, ever since/from the moment when a very elderly grandparent had made a gift of it to his grandson.'
Quando l'aveva ormai lasciato fuori da qualche ora, andò a controllarlo.	'After she had left it out for some hours, she went to check it.'

Literary usage also possesses a construction meaning 'as soon as . . .', which inverts the order of past participle and auxiliary and inserts *che* between them (i.e., past participle + *che* + *passato remoto* of the auxiliary):

Partiti che furono i poliziotti, le ragazze ripresero a ballare.	'As soon as the policemen had left, the girls started to dance again.'
Raggiunto che ebbi il pianerottolo, sostai un poco.	'As soon as I had reached the landing, I paused a moment.'

15.12 Imperfect vs. *passato remoto* and *passato prossimo*

For the use of the imperfect to refer to the 'future-in-the-past', see 15.4; for its use in past conditional sentences, see 17.35.

In the use of indicative past tenses in Italian there is a contrast between the imperfect on the one hand, and the *passato prossimo* and *passato remoto* on the other (we deal with the nature of the difference between the *passato remoto* and the *passato prossimo* in 15.16). Broadly speaking, the principle underlying this contrast is that the imperfect expresses an action or event in the past relative to the moment of speaking and *viewed without regard for its temporal limits*. To put it another way, the action or event is viewed 'from within', and the beginning and conclusion of the event (assuming the past event in question even has a beginning and a conclusion) are simply 'out of sight' or 'in the background', not the focus of our attention. In contrast, the *passato remoto* and the *passato prossimo* view the past event 'from outside', focusing on its 'external', temporal limits. Metaphors are liable to be highly misleading in linguistic description, but it may be helpful, up to a point, to regard the perspective on the past event expressed by the imperfect as being like the perspective that someone swimming underwater in a lake has of that lake: i.e., an internal perspective in which the edges of the lake and its surface are at best out of focus, and possibly invisible. In contrast, the *passato remoto* and the *passato prossimo* are equivalent to viewing the lake 'from outside', from a perspective, say, of someone flying over it in an aeroplane, for whom its shores and its surface are clearly delineated, but not its inner substance.

It is worth stressing that the choice of imperfect vs. *passato remoto/prossimo* is not dictated by the nature of the past event itself, but simply by the way the speaker or writer chooses to view that event. In principle, *any* past event can be expressed using either possibility. For example, a sentence such as 'He died yesterday morning at 3.25' is *unlikely* to be used in the imperfect tense, not least because the context specifies a completed segment of past time – but the imperfect is, none the less, not actually impossible (see 15.13).

The imperfect typically expresses 'background information', the prevailing state of affairs or event 'within which' some other event which is the central focus of attention occurred. This focal event which is, so to speak, in the 'foreground' is usually a completed occurrence, expressed by the *passato remoto* or the *passato prossimo*. Contexts such as *per*, *in* or precise times or dates, which specify the temporal limits or completedness of a past event, virtually always select the *passato remoto/prossimo*; others, such as *mentre*, which typically present background information about prevailing situations, are accompanied by imperfects:

Mentre guidava gli venne in mente un'idea.	'As he drove an idea came to him.'
Guidò per due ore e poi fece una pausa.	'He drove for two hours and then had a break.'
Risolse il problema in otto secondi.	'He solved the problem in 8 seconds.'
Per molti anni Maria ha preso il treno ogni giorno per andare al lavoro.	'For many years M took the train daily to go to work.'
È morto ieri alle 15,35, mentre veniva trasportato in ospedale.	'He died yesterday at 15.35, while he was being taken to hospital.'
In meno di un anno ingrassò di venticinque chili, e l'aumento portò a una maggiore infelicità.	'In under a year he put on 20 kilos, and the increased weight led to greater unhappiness.'

> *Elvira Sellerio amministrò la RAI tra il '93*   'ES ran the RAI between '93 and '94.'
> *e il '94.*

The contrast between the imperfect expressing 'background information' and the *passato remoto/prossimo* expressing a completed past event which is placed in the foreground appears in the following. The focal *passato prossimo/remoto* is frequently introduced by expressions such as *quando, poi, allorché*:

> *Guardavo tranquillamente la televisione*   'I was happily watching TV when
> *quando all'improvviso le immagini divennero* suddenly the images became confused
> *confuse e poi il quadro sparì del tutto.*   and then the picture disappeared
>   altogether.'
>
> *Sembrava che volesse solo uomini più vecchi* 'She seemed to want only men older
> *di lei. Poi ha incontrato Giuseppe,*   than herself. Then she met G, 14 years
> *quattordici anni di meno, e i ruoli si sono*   her junior, and the roles were
> *ribaltati.*   reversed.'

Note that because the *passato remoto/prossimo* is, so to speak, 'inside' the event or state denoted by the imperfect, the imperfect can indicate events simultaneous with the other verb. In contrast, two or more *passati remoti/prossimi*, precisely because they express an event viewed from 'outside', will be interpreted normally as expressing successive, not simultaneous or overlapping events. The first example below suggests that Andrea's drinking coffee was *interrupted* by the exploding bomb; the second that *after* the bomb exploded Andrea quietly had a coffee (maybe showing thereby his *sang froid*).

> *Quando scoppiò la bomba, Andrea beveva*   'When the bomb exploded, A was
> *tranquillamente un caffè.*   quietly drinking a coffee.'
> *Quando scoppiò la bomba, Andrea bevve*   'When the bomb exploded, A quietly
> *tranquillamente un caffè.*   had a coffee.'

While the imperfect usually expresses background information, in narrative the *passato prossimo* and the past historic often serve to 'make the story go on', to convey the succession of events of which the narrative is made up:

> *Sul tavolo c'era il libro che mi aveva regalato* 'On the table was the book A had
> *Anna. Era Prìncipe delle nuvole, l'ultimo*   given me. It was *Prìncipe delle nuvole,*
> *romanzo di Gianni Riotta. Il titolo sembrava* GR's latest novel. The title seemed
> *invitante. Ho preso in mano il volume, e ho*   inviting. I picked up the volume, and
> *cominciato a leggere la prima pagina.*   began to read the first page.'

We illustrate below some typical uses of the imperfect. Some common English counterparts of Italian imperfect forms are 'was . . .-ing', or expressions of habitual activity such as 'used to . . .' or 'would . . .' (see 15.49). Note that it is very important, if translating from English into Italian, to distinguish conditional 'would' (e.g., 'She would come if . . .' = *Verrebbe se . . .*) from habitual 'would' (e.g., 'She would come every day' = *Veniva ogni giorno*):

● The imperfect expressing prevailing past states, conditions and situations:

> *Era piccolo, gobbo, odiava la bellezza*   'He was small, hunchbacked and
> *femminile. Eppure le donne gli cedevano,* hated feminine beauty. Yet women
> *attratte dal fascino intellettuale.*   yielded to him, attracted by his
>   intellectual charm.'
>
> *Aveva i capelli lisci, e gli occhi verdi*   'He had straight hair, and his green
> *erano marcati da ciglia lunghe, scure e* eyes were set off by long, dark silky
> *setose.*   lashes.'

C'era una volta una regina bellissima che desiderava tanto una figlia . . .

'Once upon a time there was a very beautiful queen who so desired to have a daughter . . .'

In quel tempo l'Italia era in fase di organizzazione, e le sue classi politiche non potevano certo avere a disposizione una tradizione efficiente di comando e di efficienza amministrativi.

'At that time Italy was in a phase of organization, and its political classes certainly could not have available to them an effective tradition of command and administrative efficiency.'

Alla metà del secolo XIX il 70–80% della popolazione non sapeva nè leggere nè scrivere.

'In the mid-19th century 70 to 80% of the population could neither read nor write.'

Quello che mi diventava sempre più chiaro, mentre mi ingozzavo come un'oca di Strasburgo, era che il mio pane, il mio burro, i miei disturbi psicosomatici erano proprietà che non bastavano a zavorrarmi convenientemente. Dovevo poter dire 'mio' riferendomi a qualcos'altro. Mi sembrava che su di me ci fosse un buco al posto dell'anima, e dentro a quel buco, niente. [Dur1.]

'What was becoming increasingly clear to me, as I stuffed myself like a Strasbourg goose, was that my bread, my butter, my psychosomatic ailments were factors which were not sufficient to provide me with the appropriate ballast. I had to be able to say that something else was "mine". It seemed to me that I had a hole in place of a soul, and that in that hole there was nothing.'

- The imperfect expressing habitual activity (= 'used to . . .', 'would . . .'):

Giovanni e Giacomo a una certa ora se ne andavano: avevano una famiglia.

'G and G would always leave at a certain time: they had families.'

Saltava le lezioni e trascurava i compiti, preferendo passare la giornata a casa delle amiche.

'She would skip classes and neglect her homework, preferring to spend the day at her friends' homes.'

Dopo il divorzio tutto era diverso. L'unico conforto? Al mattino mi svegliavo e sapevo dov'ero. Per esempio, il letto era lo stesso dove avevo dormito dieci anni con Riccardo, mangiavo allo stesso tavolo, facevo la spesa allo stesso supermarket. Solo, non dovevo più comprare il formaggio. Io il formaggio lo odio. [Dur1.]

'After the divorce everything was different. The sole consolation was that in the morning I would wake up and know where I was. For example, the bed was the same bed in which I had slept for 10 years with R, I ate at the same table, I shopped at the same supermarket. Except that I no longer had to buy the cheese. Cheese I can't stand.'

La sera, quando rientrava dal lavoro, stava dieci minuti sotto la doccia, poi si sedeva davanti alla toelette ricoperta di tulle rosa, e mentre si massaggiava le mani con la crema mi faceva ripetere le tabelline. Mio padre tornava la sera, e lei gli andava incontro tutta trepida e profumata. Lui commentava le notizie del telegiornale, e lei gli dava sempre ragione, e girava intorno al tavolo con la zuppiera riempiendo il piatto prima a lui, poi alla nonna, poi a me. Lei si serviva sempre per ultima. [Dur1.]

'In the evening, when she got back from work, she would spend 10 minutes in the shower, then would sit at her makeup table covered in pink tulle, and as she massaged her hands with cream she would make me repeat my tables. My father would come home in the evening, and she would go up to him all trembling and sweet-smelling. He would comment on the TV news, and she would always agree with him, and would go round the table with the tureen filling his dish first, then grandmother's, then mine. She would always serve herself last.'

Durante l'assedio di Leningrado la gente pensava solo al cibo, e i bambini imploravano di morire.

'During the siege of Leningrad people used to think only of food, and the children would beg to die.'

Quando eravamo appena sposati facevamo colazione a letto la domenica mattina: io preparavo il cappuccino e scaldavo le sfogliatelle, lui mi aspettava sotto le coperte e ogni volta accoglieva il vassoio come se fosse una sorpresa.	'When we were just married we used to have breakfast in bed on Sunday mornings: I would make the cappuccino and heat the sfogliatelle, he would wait for me under the blankets and would always receive the tray as if it were a surprise.'
Maria prendeva il treno ogni giorno alle 7.45.	'M used to take the train daily at 7.45.'

15.13 The 'narrative imperfect': uses of the imperfect where the *passato remoto/prossimo* would be expected

The following example describes a fantasy or daydream; the imperfect tenses in this context convey the effect of experiencing the events as they unfold:

Sotto le sue carezze lei chiuse gli occhi e cominciò a sognare. Ecco, loro due partivano per la vacanza che sognavano da anni. Un volo in aereo e arrivavano all'albergo, quello vecchiotto che già conoscevano. Ordinavano una cena leggera, e si portavano in camera una bottiglia di champagne. Cominciavano i giorni più belli della sua vita. Ma sarebbe successo davvero?	'Under his caresses she closed her eyes and began to dream. There they were, the two of them were leaving on the holiday they'd dreamed of for years. A plane trip and they were arriving at the hotel, the little old one they already knew. They ordered a light dinner, and took a bottle of champagne back to their room. The loveliest days of her life began. But would it really happen?'

In this case the use of the imperfect is unexceptional, but it helps to explain the kind of stylistic effect which can be achieved in those cases called 'narrative imperfects', where – despite the fact that one would normally expect a *passato remoto/prossimo* – an imperfect form is used instead. Such usage achieves the effect of projecting the reader/hearer 'inside' the past event, focusing on the unfolding of the event rather than its completion. It occurs, for example, in newspaper reports (especially headlines) but also in historical narrative as a way of lending vividness to a reported past event (notably births and deaths of famous people):

Il ragazzo affermava che lui e l'ex-fidanzata si vedevano anche dopo essersi lasciati.	'The boy stated that he and his ex-girlfriend saw each other even after separating.'
La guerra, scoppiata nel 1914, durava circa cinque anni, e si concludeva col trattato di Versailles.	'The war, which broke out in 1914, lasted about four years and ended with the Treaty of Versailles.'
Due secoli fa nasceva, a Bonn, Ludwig van Beethoven.	'Two centuries ago LvB was born in Bonn.'

A related effect of the 'narrative imperfect', particularly noticeable in journalistic reports of sporting events, is to cancel the effect of 'successiveness' (see 15.12) associated with sequences of verbs in the *passato remoto/prossimo*, so that events may be presented as partially overlapping in time:

Al ventitreesimo Zeman cambiava volto al suo gruppo: mandava negli spogliatoi Tommasi sostituendolo con Fabio Junior. La Roma si faceva più aggressiva, si svegliava finalmente dal lungo letargo e cominciava a impensierire gli avversari.	'In the 23rd minute Z changed the turn out of his group: he sent T off to the changing rooms substituting him with FJ. Rome became more aggressive, woke up at last from their long slumber and began to give their opponents something to worry about.'

15.14 The 'polite' imperfect

The imperfect tense can be used instead of a present indicative or conditional to soften the tone of questions, or answers containing a statement of desire:

Pronto, mi scusi, volevo sapere quando aprirà la mostra a Palazzo Reale.	'Hello, excuse me, I wanted to know when the exhibition at Palazzo Reale will open.'
Scusa se ti disturbo, venivo solo a vedere se c'eri.	'Sorry to bother you, I was only coming to see whether you were in.'

15.15 The 'ludic imperfect'

A curious use of the imperfect tense occurs in children's language in the preparatory stages of role-playing games, in which roles are being assigned. The English equivalent would normally be a future tense:

Io ero il dottore e tu venivi per farti visitare.	'I'll be the doctor and you'll be coming for a check-up.'
Va bene, però poi il dottore ero io e tu mi facevi vedere dove ti fa male.	'OK, but then I'll be the doctor and you'll show me where it hurts.'

15.16 The *passato remoto* vs. the *passato prossimo*

There is an important geographical dimension to the distinction between these two tense forms. In northern Italian *dialects* the *passato prossimo* largely supplanted the past historic, and in dialects of the extreme south the *passato remoto* is extensively used instead of the *passato prossimo*. These dialectal differences have, to some extent, been carried over into regional varieties of the standard language, so that the spoken Italian even of educated northern Italians tends to lack the *passato remoto*, whilst speakers from the far south may show a greater propensity to use the *passato remoto* than the rest of their compatriots. A difference in the use of the two tense forms still exists in spoken Tuscan and in most dialects and the spoken Italian of central and southern Italy, as well as in literary language, journalistic language and high-register spoken Italian. The main difference between these two past forms is that the *passato prossimo* expresses an action that is felt to be linked to the present, while the past historic expresses an action that is no longer felt to be related to the present. The terms *prossimo* and *remoto* are rather misleading, for what is relevant in choosing between these two tenses is not 'nearness/remoteness' in time, but the degree of 'psychological involvement': if the event, whenever it occurred – one/a hundred/ten thousand year(s) ago – is felt by the speaker/writer to be linked to his/her present time, even for a merely psychological reason (the speaker/writer is still feeling the consequences of what happened, he/she vividly remembers the fact, he/she is somehow still involved in it, etc.), the *passato prossimo* will be used. On the other hand, if the action is felt as unrelated to the present time, the *passato remoto* will be chosen. One might, rather loosely speaking, say that the *passato remoto* indicates that the event is felt as 'over and done with', while the *passato prossimo* indicates that the event is over but not 'done with':

Ieri ho dato mille lire a un lavavetri, mi ha fatto pena.	'Yesterday I gave a window cleaner 1000 lire; I felt sorry about it.' [and, implicitly, I still do]
Ieri detti mille lire a un lavavetri perché mi fece pena, ma ho deciso di non farlo più.	'Yesterday I gave a window cleaner 1000 lire because I felt sorry about it, but I have decided not to do it again.'

The *passato prossimo* is often used for recent events simply because recent events by their very nature tend to be felt as relevant to the present:

Stamattina i ragazzi hanno marinato la scuola per andare al mare.	'This morning the boys played truant to go to the seaside.'
Il Presidente della Repubblica ha annunciato oggi la sua disponibilità a ricandidarsi.	'The President of the Republic announced today that he is prepared to stand for re-election.'
Nel pomeriggio l'autostrada è stata riaperta al traffico.	'This afternoon the motorway was reopened to traffic.'
Sono rientrato a casa mezz'ora fa.	'I got home half an hour ago.'

In the following passage, taken from a newspaper report, the *passato remoto* is used for events that are felt as no longer directly relevant to what the journalist wants to describe (the parents' distress). The *passato prossimo* is used for events that are felt to be 'connected' to the present situation, because they are the cause of the distress:

'Voglio sapere chi è stato' fu la prima cosa che disse Nicola agli amici quando lo avvertirono del ritrovamento del corpo di sua figlia. Le ultime parole in pubblico invece le pronunciò in cattedrale: 'Noi tutti e i tuoi amici, quelli veri, ti abbiamo sempre voluto bene'. E calcò la voce su 'quelli veri'. Un particolare che non sfuggì a nessuno. E fu proprio in quel giorno che i genitori vennero assaliti da un tremendo sospetto. 'Glielo feci notare proprio io quello strano necrologio a firma del fidanzato', afferma lo zio. E oggi che non ci sono dubbi sulla colpevolezza del giovane, la madre racconta disperata, 'È venuto a trovarci quasi ogni giorno, ci ha abbracciato piangendo, ci ha confortati, ha detto che era pronto a fare qualsiasi cosa per aiutarci. Gli abbiamo creduto tutti. Ci ha quasi commosso. E invece ci ha traditi fino all'ultimo.'	'"I want to know who it was," was the first thing N said to his friends when they informed him of the discovery of his daughter's body. But his last public words he uttered in the cathedral: "All of us and your friends, your real ones, have always loved you." And he stressed the words "your real ones". A detail which escaped nobody. And it was that very day that her parents were assailed by a tremendous suspicion. "It was me who pointed out to him that strange obituary signed by her boyfriend," states her uncle. And today, when there is no doubt about the young man's guilt, the mother states in despair: "He came to see us almost daily, he embraced us in tears, he consoled us, told us he was prepared to do anything to help us. We all believed him. He almost moved us. Yet he betrayed us to the end."'

The difference in the use of the past tenses shows how psychological, not temporal, distance is relevant in choosing between the two. Here what Nicola said, i.e. that he was informed by his friends that the body of his daughter had been discovered and that he and his wife started to suspect her boyfriend of murder, is seen as psychologically distant. What is important and deeply felt, is that the two parents have been betrayed again and again by their daughter's boyfriend, and they still suffer from it.

Further examples of the 'psychological connection with the present' associated with the *passato prossimo* are:

—*Cos'hai al braccio?*
—*Mi fa male perché ieri ho giocato troppo a tennis.*

'What's wrong with your arm?'
'It's hurting me because I played too much tennis yesterday.'

—*Guarda come è ridotta la spiaggia, le mareggiate l'hanno dimezzata.*

'Look what a state the beach is in; the tides have swept it half away.'

In the following the speaker/writer feels still involved, or simply interested, in the action described:

Sai che non sopporto i telefonini. Bene, l'altra sera sono andato a una cena, è venuto fuori il discorso e io ho fatto una tirata pazzesca su quanto li odio. Mentre stavo ancora parlando, ne squilla uno. È calato il silenzio e nessuno ha avuto il coraggio di rispondere. Nessuno! Quello ha continuato a squillare per mezz'ora!

'You know I can't abide mobile phones. Right, the other evening I went out to dinner and they came up in conversation, so I launched into a terrible tirade about how much I loathe them. While I was still talking, one of them rings. Silence fell and nobody had the guts to answer it. Nobody! The thing rang non-stop for half an hour!'

Especially in journalistic language, the *passato prossimo* may be used to present fresh information:

È nato in Toscana il figlio di Sting.
È uscita la nuova Ford.
11 miliardi a Peschici: ha giocato tutto il paese.

'Sting's son has been born in Tuscany.'
'The new Ford has appeared.'
'Eleven billions [won] in Peschici: the whole village played.'

The *passato prossimo* can also be used for completed actions which are still being repeated into the present (or where there is an implication that they are still being repeated in the present). The English equivalent is almost always 'have + past participle' or 'have been + . . .-ing' and, correspondingly, these structures in English will almost always be expressed by the *passato prossimo* (but for the type 'He has done it/been doing it since . . .', see 15.10). The *passato prossimo* has this sort of value particularly when used in connection with expressions like *in questa settimana* 'this week', *quest'anno* 'this year', *nell'ultimo mese* 'this month', etc., *recentemente, di recente, ultimamente* 'recently', *finora* 'hitherto':

Sono andato molte volte in Inghilterra.
Da giovane andai molte volte in Inghilterra.

'I've often been to England.'
'As a youngster I often went to England.'

Nell'ultimo mese l'indice della borsa di Milano ha presentato oscillazioni preoccupanti.
Per duemilacinquecento anni l'Occidente ha costruito la sua civiltà sullo slancio verso il domani, sulla speranza.
Fino a oggi ho vissuto felicemente da scapolo.

'Over the last month the Milan stock exchange has been showing worrying oscillations.'
'For 2500 years the West has constructed its civilization on the thrust towards tomorrow, on hope.'
'Until today I have lived happily as a bachelor.'

Time expressions with *fa/scorso*, such as *un anno fa* 'a year ago', *l'anno scorso* 'last year', etc. at the end of the sentence, and time expressions within 24 hours, tend to favour the *passato prossimo*:

Ho visto [rather than *vidi*] *mio marito l'ultima volta un anno fa/l'anno scorso.*	'I last saw my husband a year ago/last year.'
Un anno fa ho visto/vidi per l'ultima volta mio marito.	'A year ago I saw my husband for the last time.'
È partita [rather than *Partì*] *stamattina alle sette.*	'She left this morning at 7.'

The *passato prossimo* can focus on a condition arising from a momentaneous event or action:

I ragazzi si sono dimenticati la buona educazione.	'The boys have forgotten their manners.'
Ho capito cosa intendi.	'I understand what you mean.'[3]
Ho finito di mangiare.	'I've finished eating.'
Gli spaghetti si sono raffreddati.	'The spaghetti's got cold.'
Bruna e Vittorio si sono comprati una casa nuova.	'B and V have bought a new house.'

Talking of people who are dead, the past historic tends to be used. In the following example the use of the *passato prossimo* may imply that they are still alive, that of the *passato remoto* that they are dead:

I miei nonni ebbero/hanno avuto otto figli, mio padre è il più giovane.	'My grandparents had 8 children, and my father is the youngest.'

But the *passato prossimo* is used in obituaries. Phrases such as *Si è spento X; Ci ha lasciato X; È morto/deceduto/scomparso X; È tornato alla Casa del Padre X; È mancato X; Ha concluso la sua vita terrena X* are all common formulae for saying 'X has died.'

15.17 The 'progressive': *Sta leggendo, Va leggendo, Viene leggendo* 'She's reading'

These constructions serve to present the verb as a progressive, sustained, developing action. They cannot be used with the gerund of verbs such as *essere* 'be',[4] *stare* 'be (standing)', *sedere* 'be seated', *rimanere/restare* 'remain', 'stay', *avere* 'have', *possedere* 'possess', *giacere* 'be lying', *capire* 'understand', *sapere* 'know', 'be aware', *volere* 'want', *potere* 'be able' which indicate (physical or mental) states of the subject, rather than sustained incremental activity. However, some of these verbs may be used to denote an *action* rather than a *state*, in which case they may appear in the progressive (e.g., *Sta avendo molto successo* 'She's having a lot of success', where *avere* means not 'possess' but 'obtain', 'acquire', or *Il computer sta capendo le istruzioni che abbiamo digitato* 'The computer is in the process of understanding/working out the instructions we've keyed in').

---

[3]It is noticeable that where English tends to say 'I understand', etc. and 'I understood', etc., Italian prefers respectively the *passato prossimo* and the pluperfect: *Scusi, non ho capito* 'Sorry I don't understand', *Gli dissi che non avevo capito* 'I told him I didn't understand.'
[4]The English progressive of 'to be' often has the meaning of 'to behave/act': cf. 'He's stupid' and 'He's being stupid', 'She's kind' and 'She's being kind'. Italian equivalents might be *Si sta comportando in modo stupido* (or *Sta facendo lo stupido*) and *Si sta comportando in modo simpatico.*

In old Italian, the *Sta leggendo* type was simply a combination of *stare* 'stand', 'be immobile' and a gerund, and meant something like 'He stands and reads', 'He stands reading'. In literary usage as late as the early twentieth century *stare* could not easily combine with verbs of motion or 'weather verbs' (e.g., one did not say *sta andando, sta cadendo, sta piovendo*), because of the original implausibility of combining a verb of immobility with such verbs suggesting mobility (one cannot 'stand' and at the same time 'go' or 'fall', and 'it stands and rains' would be a nonsense). Extension of this construction to verbs implying movement or meteorological activity is a rather recent development, which may still tend to be avoided in particularly formal and conservative styles.

There exist a number of constraints on the *sta leggendo* type. It cannot be used if the event is curtailed by specification of any time limit (so one cannot say **Stava mangiando solo per cinque minuti* 'She was eating only for five minutes'), and cannot be used if the action is not continuous (one cannot say **Stava pulendo la stanza ogni tre giorni* 'She was cleaning the room every three days', because the action was regularly interrupted). It is not normally possible to use the *sta leggendo* type after verbs such as *volere, potere* and *dovere*: one would not normally[5] say *Può/Deve/Vuole starlo leggendo* 'She can/must/wants to be reading it'.

The difference between, say, *Legge il giornale* and *Sta leggendo il giornale* is not necessarily that between English 'She reads the newspaper' and 'She's reading the newspaper'. In modern colloquial English, if the event described is simultaneous with the time of speaking there is no simple alternative to saying 'She's reading the newspaper';[6] but Italian allows either *Legge il giornale* or *Sta leggendo il giornale*, using the latter only to underline the progressive, developing nature of the activity. Similarly, in the past, 'She was reading' corresponds both to *Leggeva il giornale* and to *Stava leggendo il giornale*.

Stare in this construction can only be used in the infinitive, the future, the present or the imperfect tense forms (so one cannot say, for example, **Era stato leggendo*); it does not occur in the passive (you cannot say **Sta essendo letto*):

Saputo che si sta parlando con Daniela di quanto gli assomigli Leonardo, sparisce in uno dei corridoi.	'Having learned that we are talking to D about how much L looks like him, he disappears into one of the corridors.'
Che si stia trasformando in uno di quei cani che popolavano i sogni della signora madre? [Mar.]	'Can she really be turning into one of those dogs who inhabited her mother's dreams?'
Non sto dicendo che gli avversari politici non vadano combattuti anche con queste armi.	'I'm not saying that political opponents should not be fought with these weapons too.'
Ora è giorno, e l'omone sta pisciando sulle ceneri spente. [Cal.]	'Now it's daybreak, and the big man is peeing on the dead ashes.'
I contadini stavano discutendo su chi dovesse pagare il dazio sulla frutta.	'The peasants were arguing about who was to pay the duty on fruit.'

---

[5]But *Può starlo leggendo* and *Deve starlo leggendo* are in principle possible (if a little awkward) where the sense is 'epistemic', i.e., 'It may be that she is reading it', 'It must be that she is reading it'.

[6]'She reads the newspaper' expresses a general or habitual occurrence; the phrase can truthfully be uttered even at a time when she is not reading the newspaper.

Nulla poteva placare l'ondata di rabbia e risentimento che gli stava montando dentro.	'Nothing could placate the wave of rage and resentment which was building up within him.'
Sembrava che l'albero stesse crescendo davanti ai miei occhi.	'It seemed the tree was growing before my eyes.'

Note that where English uses the progressive present form as a kind of 'definite future', Italian uses a different kind of structure (see 15.7): 'I'm going to Rome next Friday' *Devo andare/Vado a Roma venerdì prossimo*.

The types *va leggendo* and *viene leggendo* are mainly characteristic of elevated styles and can be used, unlike *sta leggendo*, in any tense form (one can say *andò leggendo*, *è venuto leggendo*, etc.). They can also retain their original meaning, literally, 'she goes/comes and reads' or 'she reads as she goes/comes'), e.g., *Andavano leggendo tutti i cartelli* 'They went round reading all the notices'. But in modern usage they normally have meanings similar to the *sta leggendo* type, except that *andare* and *venire* are more 'incremental' or 'cumulative', emphasizing a gradual increase (or decrease):

Le foglie vanno cadendo sempre più numerose; si avvicina l'autunno.	'The leaves are falling in ever greater numbers; autumn is drawing on.'
Erano decenni che sentiva come il fluido vitale [. . .] andasse uscendo da lui lentamente ma continuamente.	'For decades he'd felt as if the vital fluid was going out of him slowly but continually.'
Andava leggendo il libro di Cassola con crescente entusiasmo.	'He was reading C's book with growing enthusiasm.'
Un poco va assomigliando alla madre.	'She's getting a bit like her mother.'
Già a metà settimana si andavano delineando i protagonisti e i progetti principali della rivolta.	'Already halfway through the week the protagonists and main aims of the revolt were becoming clearly defined.'

The *va leggendo* type is also particularly common with verbs which indicate very rapid successions of repeated actions; English equivalents frequently employ the adverbial 'away':

Andava tamburellando con le dita sulla scrivania mentre scriveva.	'He was drumming away with his fingers on the desk as he wrote.'
Va mangiando la torta senza riguardo alle buone maniere.	'He is eating away at the cake, heedless of good manners.'
Andavano bussando alle porte, ma invano.	'They were knocking away at the doors, but in vain.'

This last example could also mean 'They went round knocking at the doors, but in vain'.

The *viene leggendo* type is similar to *va leggendo*, except that some of the basic meaning of 'coming' remains, in that the construction is strongly associated with 'coming towards someone or something' (either figuratively or literally): whereas *Il tesoriere si accorge che la sterlina va aumentando di valore* is 'neutral' (the treasurer simply realizes that the pound is increasing in value), *Il tesoriere si accorge che la sterlina viene aumentando di valore* implies that value of the pound is approaching some point particularly of interest to the treasurer; and as an outside observer, one might say *Questa biblioteca è andata acquistando una serie di volumi sulla storia del protestantesimo* 'This library has been acquiring a series of volumes on the history of Protestantism', but as the librarian, or a user of the library with a particular interest in the subject, one might say (although this construction is becoming increasingly rare) *Questa biblioteca è venuta acquistando una serie di volumi sulla storia del protestantesimo.*

15.18 The type *stare a fare* 'to be doing','to be engaged in doing', *trovarsi a fare* 'to find oneself doing', etc.

The *stare a fare* structure is similar to *stare facendo*, but different in certain respects. First, it is very common in colloquial, informal Italian but tends to be rare in written and formal usage. Second, there are no restrictions on the tense forms in which *stare* can occur (except that it cannot be used in the *trapassato remoto*), so that one can say *È stato un'ora a preparare da mangiare* 'He was busy preparing some food for an hour', *Stettero tutta la giornata a pescare* 'They were busy fishing all day.' Third, as the preceding examples show, this construction is possible even when the time span is delimited. Fourth, the action need not be uninterrupted: *Stava a pulire la stanza ogni tre giorni* 'She was busy cleaning the room every three days'. The most fundamental difference, however, is that in this construction *stare* has connotations of 'immobility', so that it cannot be combined with verbs of motion: one may say *Stava andando* 'She was going', but not **Stava ad andare.*

In fact, the *a* + infinitive structure may be preceded by other verb expressions indicating location or position (see also 17.28 for *a* + infinitive after verbs of perception, such as *Lo vidi a giocare al calcio* 'I saw him playing football'):

Un bel giorno mi trovai a Foligno a cercare la casa di mio nonno.	'One fine day I found myself in Foligno looking for my grandfather's house.'
Che sia in giardino a leggere un libro, che sia nel salone giallo a fare i conti con Raffaele Cuffa, che sia in biblioteca a studiare l'inglese, Saro se lo trova sempre davanti. [Mar.]	'Whether he is in the garden reading a book, or in the yellow drawing room doing the accounts with RC, or in the library learning English, S is always coming across him.'

The expression often has the sense of 'spend one's time . . .-ing':

Lui sta tutto il giorno a guardare la TV.	'He spends all day watching TV.'
I ragazzi stanno a ciondolare tutto il giorno nei bar.	'The boys spend all day hanging round in bars.'

A colloquial equivalent of *senti!* 'listen!', is *stai a sentire!*:

Stammi a sentire un attimo.	'Listen to me for a moment.'

15.19 Verbal expressions of physical stance: *essere seduto, essere in piedi* 'to be sitting, standing', etc.

English has a number of expressions indicating physical position or attitude, of the type 'be . . .-ing'. Italian does not have equivalents using *stare/andare/venire* + gerund. Rather, *essere* + past participle (or other expressions) tend to be used:

essere seduto	'to be sitting'
essere in piedi	'to be standing'
essere sdraiato	'to be lying down'
etc.	

15.20 Meaning of the gerund

Gerunds are forms of the verb which generally provide 'background information' (such as means, manner, cause, circumstance) to the main verb of a sentence.
They are inherently 'imperfective' (cf. 15.13) and the action or state they express
is not, therefore, viewed as necessarily completed before the action expressed by
the main verb occurs.[7] The main functions of the gerund are the following:

- Means by which or manner in which the action of the main verb is carried out
  (= 'by . . .-ing'):

Chiese qualcosa a una bimbetta, e questa gli rispose indicando proprio in direzione della loro casa.	'He asked a little girl something, and she replied by pointing right in the direction of their house.'
Voltando la testa fa in tempo a scorgere un pezzo della gonnella di Agata.	'By turning her head she is in time to make out a piece of A's petticoat.'
Mi consolo stringendolo tra le braccia e girandogli la chiavetta del carillon.	'I console myself by hugging him in my arms and turning the key of the musical box for him.'
Abbonatevi oggi telefonando al 70 80 70.	'Subscribe today by phoning 708070.'
Poi abbiamo reso l'ambiente più caldo sostituendo i mobili moderni con quelli antichi.	'Then we made the atmosphere warmer by replacing the modern furniture with antiques.'
. . . il famoso dieci o dodici per cento del vecchio PSI era arrivato in vista del venti solo comprando le tessere e creando una enorme clientela pronta a tradire.	'. . . the famous 10 or 12% of the old PSI had got within sight of 20% only by buying up party cards and creating an enormous clientele prepared to betray it.'

- The attitude with which something is uttered

Parlando francamente, mi pare assurdo.	'To speak frankly/Frankly speaking, I think it's absurd.'
Giudicando da quanto mi dici, devono essere romani.	'Judging by what you tell me, they must be Roman.'

- The *circumstances* of the action expressed in the main clause (reasons, causes,
  what was happening or was the case at the time):

Sapeva di latino poco più di quello che aveva imparato servendo messa.	'He knew little more Latin than he had learned (due to) serving at mass.'
È certo una congettura arrischiata, trattandosi di un testo molto complesso.	'It's certainly a hazardous conjecture, since it's a very complex text.'
Essendo a servizio da molto, aveva acquistato un'aria cittadina.	'Having been in service for a long time, she had acquired a city air.'
Le mani di Fila si muovono goffe e rapide districando la matassa dei capelli di Marianna.	'F's hands move clumsily and rapidly as they pick apart the tangled mass of M's hair.'

  The gerund can also have the value of a hypothetical clause (i.e., 'if such-and-
  such were the case . . .')

Dovendo pernottare a Gubbio, vi telefonerò senz'altro.	'Should I have to spend the night in Gubbio, of course I'll phone you.'

---

[7]Thus there is a contrast between the gerund and the (rare) so-called 'absolute' uses (see
15.22) of the past participle: *Aperta la porta entrò* 'When he had opened the door he came
in' vs. *Aprendo la porta entrò* 'As he opened the door he came in'.

Essendo la signora Tozzi d'accordo, procederemo direttamente alla vendita del materiale.	'If Mrs T agrees, we shall proceed to sell the material straight away.'

Notice the concessive use of the gerund preceded by *pur* = 'even though . . .':

Non è possibile confidare in chi, pur amandoti ciecamente, alla fine resterà incomprensibile e lontano.	'You can't confide in someone who, although he loves you blindly, will in the end remain incomprehensible and distant.'
Sono diplomata maestra d'asilo, ma pur avendo bussato a tante porte nessuno mi ha dato un lavoro.	'I'm a qualified nursery teacher, but although I've knocked on so many doors, nobody has given me a job.'

The 'circumstantial' use also includes a 'coordinative' value, that which 'also happened at the same time': this type of gerund can also be paraphrased by 'and' or 'but' + verb. In the following examples the verbs preceded by 'and' could equally be rendered in English by '. . .-ing':

Lavorò tutta la notte, consegnando il manoscritto all'alba.	'He worked all night, and handed the manuscript in/handing the manuscript in/to hand the manuscript in at dawn.'
D'altronde era difficile che restassero soli di giorno perché c'era sempre una serva che girava per le stanze accendendo un lume, rifacendo il letto, riponendo la biancheria pulita negli armadi, lucidando le maniglie delle porte, sistemando gli asciugamani appena stirati nel 'cantaranu' accanto alla bacinella dell'acqua. [Mar.]	'Anyway it was difficult for them to be together by day because there was always a maid who went round the rooms and lit a candle, remade the bed, put clean laundry back in the cupboards, polished the doorhandles, placed the freshly ironed towels in the "cantaranu" by the water basin.'
Il PDS avrebbe fatto osservare l'enormità della cifra, dicendosi però disposto a trattare.	'The PDS has apparently remarked on the vastness of the amount, yet still declares that it is ready to negotiate.'

The 'circumstantial' use of the gerund includes a number of fixed expressions:

Strada facendo, s'imbattè in uno spaventapasseri.	'On his way/As he went along, he bumped into a scarecrow.'
Stando così le cose, non possiamo proseguire.	'This being so, we can go no further.'
Mangiando e bevendo si fece tardi.	'They ate and drank till it got late.'

In the negative, Italian makes a distinction between what would be expressed in English as 'by not . . .-ing' and 'without . . .-ing': in the latter case, *senza* + infinitive must be used:

Sono riuscita a convincerlo non facendo vedere quanto ero incerta io stessa.	'I managed to convince him by not showing how uncertain I myself was.'
Sono riuscita a convincerlo senza far vedere quanto ero incerta io stessa.	'I managed to convince him without showing how uncertain I myself was.'

There is a perfective form of the gerund, formed from the auxiliary *avendo* or *essendo* + past participle. This is used fairly similarly to English 'having + past participle'. But this perfective gerund means only 'because', 'given that', 'since . . .', never 'after', which is *dopo* + infinitive or *dopo che* + finite verb or *quando* + trapassato remoto:

Essendo partito prima dell'alba, fu a Roma entro mezzogiorno.	'Having left before dawn, he was in Rome by midday.'

Avendo Paolo studiato a lungo, non si prevedono problemi per gli esami.	'P having studied at length, no problems are expected for the examinations.'
Dopo aver chiuso le porte, andò a dormire.	'Having closed the doors, he went to bed.'
Quando furono tornati, chiesero da mangiare.	'Having returned, they asked for something to eat.'

15.21 Syntax of the gerund: why *Vidi il ragazzo uscendo dalla chiesa* does NOT mean 'I saw the boy as he left the church', etc.

The subject of an Italian gerund is generally interpreted as identical to that of the main verb of the sentence in which it occurs. One effect of this is that sentences like *Vidi il ragazzo uscendo dalla chiesa, Abbiamo incontrato mio nonno passeggiando, Lasciarono la madre sventolando il fazzoletto* can *only* be interpreted as 'I saw the boy as I came out of the church', 'We met my grandfather as <u>we</u> went for a walk', 'They left their mother waving <u>their</u> handkerchiefs' and never as 'I saw the boy as <u>he</u> came out of the church', 'We met my grandfather as <u>he</u> went for a walk', 'They left their mother waving <u>her</u> handkerchief', for here the subject of the gerund is different from that of the verbs 'I saw', 'We met', 'They left'. The most natural way to express the latter meanings involves using the 'pseudo-relative' construction (i.e., *che* + verb), as described in 7.21 and 17.29 (for the type *Vidi il ragazzo uscire dalla chiesa* see 17.28):

Vidi il ragazzo che usciva dalla chiesa.	'I saw the boy coming out of the church.'
Abbiamo incontrato mio nonno che passeggiava.	'We met my grandfather going for a walk.'
Lasciarono la madre che sventolava il fazzoletto.	'They left their mother waving her handkerchief.'

The requirement that the subject of the gerund be the same as the subject of the main verb does not apply where the gerund constitutes a separate clause with its own, explicit, subject. In such cases, the subject always follows the gerund (see further examples in 15.20):

Uscendo il ragazzo dalla chiesa, lo vidi.	'As the boy was coming out of the church, I saw him.'
Avendo il professore viaggiato moltissimo nel Messico, lo invitiamo a tenere una conferenza sui popoli indigeni messicani.	'The professor having travelled a good deal in Mexico, we are inviting him to give a lecture on Mexican indigenous peoples.'

Constructions of this kind, with the subject of the gerund made explicit (and placed after the gerund), are, in fact, restricted to elevated and formal language. But there are other (more common) constructions in which the gerund has no explicit subject of its own, yet is not the same as the subject of the main verb. A notable case arises where the subject of the gerund is interpretable as 'indefinite personal' 'one', 'people generally' (see 6.29):

Il cameriere è stato ricompensato, offrendogli centomila lire.	'The waiter was compensated by [someone] offering him 100 000 lire.'

Le lacune verranno colmate usando tecniche ultramoderne.	'The gaps will be filled in by [someone] using ultramodern techniques.'
L'appetito viene mangiando.	'Appetite comes as one eats.'
La febbre scenderà somministrando l'antibiotico.	'The fever will go down by [someone] administering the antibiotic.'
Il suo caro Nord, stando ai sondaggi, sembra abbandonarla.	'Your beloved North, judging by [if one judges by] the opinion polls, seems to be abandoning you.'

The subject of the gerund may also be interpreted as the 'psychological sub-ject' (rather than the grammatical subject) of the main verb. The 'psychological subject' may be defined, loosely, as the principal agent or experiencer of the main clause, even though that agent or experiencer may not be the grammatical sub-ject of the main verb. Consider the following examples:

Frugando fra i vecchi bauli è saltata fuori una bambola impolverata. Le ragazze la guardano incuriosite.	'As they rummage among the old trunks a dust-covered doll has come to light. The girls look at it curiously.'
Scavando la tomba capitò all'archeologo di vedere uno scorpione.	'Excavating the tomb, the archaeologist happened to see a scorpion.'

Le ragazze is interpretable as the subject of *frugando* because the girls are the 'agent' whose rummaging causes the doll to come to light, even though the grammatical subject of *è saltata* is the *bambola* and not *le ragazze*. Similarly, *l'arche-ologo* is, grammatically, the indirect object and not the subject of *capitò*, which means 'it happened', but he is the 'psychological subject', the one who sees the scorpion, and is therefore interpreted as the subject of *scavando*.

15.22 'Clausal' uses of the past participle: the types *Arrivati andarono a mangiare* 'Having arrived they went to eat', *Conclusa l'inchiesta, andarono a mangiare* 'Having concluded the inquiry they went to eat' and *Fattolo andarono a mangiare* 'Having done it they went to eat'

Characteristic of written and formal registers is the use of the past participle as a clause, providing 'background information' to the main verb of the sentence (such as the conditions or circumstances preceding the action of the main verb). Phrases such as *Arrivati i colleghi andarono a mangiare* and *Conclusa l'inchiesta, andarono a mangiare* and *Fattolo andarono a mangiare* mean, respectively, 'The col-leagues having arrived/Once the colleagues had arrived/Since the colleagues had arrived/With the colleagues' arrival they went to eat', 'The inquiry having been concluded/Once the inquiry had been concluded/Since the inquiry had been concluded/With the inquiry concluded they went to eat', and 'Having done it/Once they had done it/Since they had done it/With it done they went to eat'. The clausal use of the past participle is most common with those verbs that take auxiliary *essere* (14.20): i.e., passives and *most* intransitive verbs (see below).

In all cases clitic pronouns are attached to the end of the participle, and sub-ject nouns usually follow the participle.

Allontanatisi alquanto gli uomini di Marco, riuscimmo a prenderli di mira.	'M's men having moved away a little, we managed to aim at them.'
Invitata a intervenire, Giulia ebbe paura.	'Having been invited to intervene, G felt frightened.'
Costretto giorno e notte a sorvegliare sua figlia, finì per avere un esaurimento nervoso.	'Being obliged night and day to keep an eye on his daughter, he ended up having a nervous breakdown.'
Date le condizioni ormai impossibili, hanno pernottato a Susa.	'Given/In view of the now impossible conditions, they spent the night in Susa.'
Scartata quest'ipotesi, l'esame della sua ecclesiologia ne aveva suscitata un'altra.	'This hypothesis having been laid aside, the examination of his ecclesiology had raised another one.'
L'odore di polvere non le dava più fastidio come appena arrivata.	'The smell of dust no longer annoyed her as it had when she had first arrived.'

The participles in such constructions may be preceded by temporal, conditional, and other conjunctions:

Appena nata la figlia di Bernardo, tutti accorsero a congratularsi col padre.	'As soon as B's daughter was born, everyone came to congratulate the father.'
La temperatura, se scesa sotto un certo livello, veniva aumentata automaticamente.	'The temperature, if it had dropped below a certain level, was automatically raised.'
Lavoravano solo se pagati in anticipo.	'They would work only if they had been paid in advance.'

There is one class of intransitive verbs with which this construction is not possible, namely those that indicate an ongoing (durative) action or state but do not imply the completion or termination of that action or state, such as *lavorare*, *nuotare*, *camminare*: you cannot say **Nuotato due ore, tornò a casa* 'Having swum for two hours, he went home' (one might say instead *Avendo nuotato due ore . . .*).

The use of this construction with verbs taking auxiliary *avere* is relatively rare (but note the commonly used phrase *dopo mangiato* (as in *Dopo mangiato andremo a Perugia* 'After we've eaten, we'll go to Perugia'). In the (especially rare) cases where the participle is accompanied both by a subject and an object, the order is participle + subject + object (e.g., *Fatto l'ispettore l'inchiesta, andò a mangiare* 'The inspector having conducted the inquiry, he went to eat').

Di solito, appena finito di lavare i piatti scappava fuori.	'Usually, as soon as she'd finished washing up he went out.'
Trovatili assenti, si recò subito in municipio.	'Having found them absent, he immediately went to the town hall.'
Corrette le bozze, Patrizia decise di fare una passeggiata.	'Having corrected the proofs, P decided to go for a walk.'
Saputo che si sta parlando con Daniela di quanto gli assomigli Leonardo, sparisce in uno dei corridoi.	'Having learned that we are talking to D about how much L looks like him, he disappears into one of the corridors.'

15.23 The type *Ti credevo già partita = Credevo che fossi già partita*

Note the following, stylistically elegant, alternative to constructions of the type *pensare/credere/sapere/dire che* + verb:

Credevo che fossi già partita.	*Ti credevo già partita.*	'I thought you'd already left.'
Sapevo che era entrato prima di me.	*Lo sapevo entrato prima di me.*	'I knew he'd gone in before me.'
Direbbero che siete nati negli anni sessanta.	*Vi direbbero nati negli anni sessanta.*	'They'd say you were born in the 60s.'

This construction – in which the subject of the subordinate clause becomes the object of the main verb, and the subordinate verb appears in the past participle – is possible when the main verb is one of believing or asserting, and the verb in the subordinate clause would normally take the form 'auxiliary *essere* + past participle'. Note also, with *volere*:

Una vecchia tradizione lo voleva morto in una sparatoria.	'An old tradition would have it that he'd died in a shoot-out.'

15.24 The infinitive as noun: the type *Il partire è sempre triste* 'Leaving is always sad'

Any infinitive may be used as a noun, whose meaning is, roughly, 'the fact or action of X-ing'; the English equivalent is often just the '-ing' form of the verb.

A volte il fare uno scherzo cattivo lascia un gusto amaro.	'Sometimes making a bad joke leaves a bitter taste.'
Hanno approfittato del suo starsene assorta sulla tela.	'They took advantage of her standing engrossed over the canvas.'
Quest'amicizia però mi rende ancora più libero nel criticarli, nel dir loro: ma siete matti.	'But this friendship makes me even freer in criticizing them, in saying to them: you're mad.'
E costui ebbe per due o tre giorni un bel da fare nel seguirli di ristorante in ristorante.	'And for 2 or 3 days he had a pointless time following them from restaurant to restaurant.'
Non poté trattenersi dal farglielo notare.	'He couldn't refrain from pointing it out to him.'
I tratti le si sono deformati come se il guardare ciò che la circonda le fosse penoso.	'Her features have become deformed, as if looking at her surroundings were painful to her.'
Le mani le sono diventate robuste per il tanto impastare.	'Her hands have become sturdy through so much kneading.'
Si è dimostrato molto generoso nel ritirarsi per preparare loro la strada.	'He proved very generous in withdrawing to prepare the way for them.'
Mark, nell'aggrapparsi ai ciuffi d'erba, si trovò in mano uno strano ciondolo d'oro.	'M, in the act of grabbing at the tufts of grass, found a strange gold pendant in his hand.'
quel suo avermi appoggiato durante tante tragedie	'the fact that he had supported me [lit. 'that his having supported me'] through so many tragedies'
Al sentirla svenne.	'Upon hearing her he fainted.'

The infinitive-nouns, as the above examples show, behave like any other noun: they may be modified by articles (indefinite as well as definite), demonstratives (e.g., *quel cantare* 'that singing'), adjectives (e.g., *Il bellissimo cantare mi incantò* 'The beautiful singing enchanted me') and prepositions. But the infinitive remains verb-like in that it may be accompanied by a subject as well as an object noun; the subject generally follows the infinitive:

L'avergli Carlo prontamente mandato una risposta ci ha molto sorpreso.	'C's having promptly sent him a reply greatly surprised us.'
Il cantare i sardi queste ballate mi scandalizzò.	'The Sardinians singing these ballads shocked me.'/'The fact that the Sardinians sang these ballads shocked me.'
Il criticarti non mi piace affatto.	'I don't like criticizing you at all.'

Note that the direct object of the infinitive in such constructions is never preceded by *di* (unlike English 'of'): *il cantare ballate sarde* '(the) singing (of) Sardinian ballads', etc. But the subject of the infinitive may be preceded by *di*: *Il cantare dei sardi è molto armonioso* 'The Sardinians' singing is very harmonious'. There is, however, a difference of meaning between the types *il cantare i sardi . . .* and *il cantare dei sardi . . .*, in that the former means 'the fact that the Sardinians sing' 'or 'that the Sardinians should sing', whilst *il cantare dei sardi* is simply 'the Sardinians' singing' or 'the singing of the Sardinians', etc.

The infinitives may also be modified by adverbs: *Il correre freneticamente avanti e indietro non serve a niente* 'Running frantically back and forth is pointless.'

In general, the rules for the use of the article with these infinitives are the same as for any other abstract/generic noun (see 4.4). Just as an abstract noun such as *azione* would appear with an article in, say, *con l'azione, dall'azione, per l'azione* so one says *col fare, dal fare, nel fare*, etc. Whenever an infinitive used as a noun is preceded by *con, da* or *in* it must take an article: e.g., *finire col fare* 'to end up doing', *cominciare col fare* 'to begin by doing', *cessare dal fare* 'to cease doing', *trattenersi dal fare* 'refrain from doing', *essere lungi dal fare* 'to be far from doing', *consistere nel fare* 'to consist of doing', *stare nel fare* 'to be/lie in doing', *esitare nel fare* 'to hesitate in doing', etc. Note particularly the use of *nel* + infinitive to mean 'while . . .-ing', and *al* + infinitive to mean 'on/upon . . .-ing'.

In fact, the infinitive may also appear unaccompanied by an article (and also unaccompanied by prepositions or adjectives or any of the other accoutrements of nounhood):

Nessuno gli ha mai detto che costruire è meglio di distruggere.	'No one has ever told him that to build is better than to destroy/that it is better that one should build than that one should destroy.'

but in this case the sense is somewhat closer to 'the idea or notion of building/destroying', whereas the form with the article is more 'the fact/action of building/destroying' (cf. also 4.20).

Nessuno gli ha mai detto che il costruire è meglio del distruggere.	'No one has ever told him that construction is better than destruction/that the action of building is better than the action of destroying.'

As the example below shows, the corresponding English forms may often look like imperatives, but Italian tends to use an infinitive where what is foremost is the basic notion expressed by the verb, rather than a specific instruction to anybody:

Semplificare, semplificare e ancora   '"Simplify, simplify and simplify
semplificare: ripete ossessivamente lo slogan. again," the slogan repeats obsessively.'

The 'infinitive nouns' are not normally listed separately in dictionaries, simply because their meaning is wholly predictable from that of the relevant verb. But there are a few cases where the infinitive has acquired other, more idiosyncratic senses, for example *il dovere* 'duty' (corresponding to one sense of *dovere*, but cf. *debito* 'debt'); *il piacere* 'pleasure'; *il potere* 'power' (but cf. *la potenza* 'potency' or 'power' in the sense of 'powerful nation', etc., as in *le potenze alleate* 'the allied powers'); *il parlare* 'dialect', 'speech variety', *l'essere* (*umano*) '(human) being', *il succedersi* 'succession' (e.g., *Fu un succedersi di guai* 'It was a succession of misfortunes'), etc.

The infinitive may also appear with a subject noun or pronoun, often in exclamations, where the sense is close to 'the very idea of . . .'. In this sense it is very similar to the use of *che* + subjunctive, illustrated in 15.32.

Io cantare! Ma scherzi!   'Me sing! You must be joking.'
Mario insegnare matematica! Mai e poi mai! 'M teach maths! Never, ever!'

15.25 What is the subjunctive?

Learners sometimes ask 'What does the subjunctive mean?' A better question, in fact, might be 'What does the indicative mean?', for the subjunctive arguably means rather *less* than the indicative, and this is part of the key to its usage. It may be helpful to view the subjunctive as being similar to the infinitive, which expresses the 'dictionary definition', 'what the verb basically means' ('sleep', 'dance', etc.). The difference is that, while the infinitive carries no information about person, number or tense,[8] the subjunctive does express person, number and some limited information about tense (past and non-past). The indicative, in contrast, signals not only lexical meaning, person and number, but also a rich array of tenses (for example future and *passato remoto*, wholly lacking in the subjunctive) and, above all and most importantly, asserts a 'realization', 'an actual occurrence', of the notion expressed by the verb. The subjunctive, then, expresses the 'basic notion', the 'dictionary definition', 'what the verb means', plus person and number of the subject and some information about tense – but, unlike the indicative, is simply 'neutral' when it comes to asserting whether or not what is expressed by the verb is (was/will be) actually 'realized'.

15.26 Contexts selecting the subjunctive

It follows from the above that the subjunctive, rather than the indicative, will tend to occur *in contexts which assert or imply that the verb is not 'realized'*. But what

---

[8]It is significant that in many respects the subjunctive acts like a variant of the infinitive (as a kind of infinitive which also indicates person and tense): e.g., *Voglio ballare* 'I want to dance', *È bello ballare* 'It's nice to dance', correspond to *Voglio che balliate* 'I want you to dance', *È bello che ballino* 'It's nice that they're dancing'. The claim that the infinitive 'does not express tense' is not undermined, by the way, by the distinction between, say, *cantare* and *aver cantato*, which is a difference of aspect (the latter indicates the completedness of the action), rather than of tense.

are these 'contexts'? It must be said first of all that it is not the case that all occurrences of the Italian subjunctive can be explained in terms of such contexts. Some cases (for example in subordinate clauses after verbs of wanting or ordering) are clearly so determined; in others the role played by context may be far less transparent; yet in others it is very hard indeed to ascribe selection of the subjunctive to the meaning of the context in which it occurs, and criteria that are purely lexical (e.g., the subjunctive must appear after certain conjunctions and not others), or even stylistic (the subjunctive tends to be preferred in more elevated styles) may have to be invoked. There is, then, no point in trying to pretend that there is a magic formula that can predict every occurrence of the subjunctive. But an understanding of the general principles determining selection of the subjunctive none the less helps to make sense of many of its uses.

In the great majority of cases, the subjunctive occurs in a subordinate clause (usually, a clause introduced by *che ...*) and the context is provided by a main clause which does not assert the actual occurrence, or 'realization' of the verb of the subordinate clause. In *Vogliamo che balliate*, *Vogliamo* is the main clause, and *che balliate* is the subordinate clause. Note that while the English equivalent of the Italian subordinate clause often begins with 'that', it may also take the form of an infinitive ('We want you to dance'), or even a gerund ('We want you dancing').

Main clause structures which select a subjunctive in the subordinate clause fall into two kinds. There are those which *automatically require* a subordinate clause with a subjunctive verb, such as *volere che ...* 'to want that ...', *desiderare che ...* 'to wish that ...', *non vedere l'ora che ...* 'not to be able to wait for ...', *ordinare che ...* 'to order that', *aspettare che ...* 'to wait for (someone) to ...', and *occorrere che ...*, *bisognare che ...* 'to be necessary that ...', which necessarily introduce a notion rather than a realized event (after all we could not, under normal circumstances, 'want you to dance' or 'order you to dance', and it could not be 'necessary that you should dance', from a perspective in which it was a fact that you were already actually dancing, or would subsequently dance).

Other main clauses *may*, but do not necessarily, constitute a context in which the verb in the subordinate clause is presented as unrealized. Contrast *Diciamo che balliate* 'We tell [i.e., say that you should/order that] you to dance' with *Diciamo che ballate* 'We say [i.e., assert the fact/reality that] you're dancing'.

15.27 English structures equivalent to the Italian subjunctive

There is no reliable correspondence between an Italian subjunctive and any particular English grammatical structure. What is most important is an understanding of the circumstances *within Italian* which lead to selection of the subjunctive. But among the English expressions which *sometimes* correspond to an Italian subjunctive, we find:

- 'let + (pro)noun + verb' ('Let him come' [*Che*] *venga*);
- 'may + (pro)noun + verb' ('May he come!' [*Che*] *venga*);
- 'object of main verb + infinitive' ('I want him to come' *Voglio che venga*);
- 'for + (pro)noun + infinitive' ('It's important for him to come' *È importante che venga*);

- '(pro)noun + . . .-ing' ('without him/his coming' *senza che lui venga*);
- 'should + verb' ('It's important that he should come' *È importante che venga*);
- '(pro)noun + subjunctive verb' ('It's important that he come' *È importante che venga*);
- '(pro)noun + not + subjunctive verb' (mostly characteristic of US English) ('It's important that he not come' *È importante che non venga*),

etc.

Note that most of these English constructions also correspond to other structures, with different meanings, in Italian (e.g., *Lasciatelo venire* 'Let/Allow him to come'; *Può venire?* 'May he come?'; *È importante per lui venire* 'For him [i.e., he thinks] it's important to come'; *Se venisse* 'Should he come/were he to come', etc.).

15.28 The subjunctive as 'notion'/'idea': in subordinate clauses introduced by expressions of wanting, requiring, intending, ordering, fearing, permitting, preventing, hoping, etc.

The subjunctive expresses the notion/concept/idea of the verb, but not the realization or actual occurrence of the verb. Subordinate clauses introduced by expressions of wanting, requiring, intending, ordering, stipulating sufficient conditions, fearing, preventing, etc., have a subjunctive verb because the subordinate clause necessarily expresses an 'unrealized' occurrence, a *notion* whose fulfilment is (or is not) desired. The following main clause verbs require a subjunctive in the subordinate clause:

augurarsi che	'to wish that'
avere paura che	'to fear that'
bastare che	'to be enough/sufficient that'
bisognare che	'to be necessary that'
chiedere che	'to ask that'
desiderare che	'to desire/wish that'
esigere che	'to demand that'
essere necessario che	'to be necessary that'
evitare che	'to avoid something/body . . .-ing'
impedire che	'to prevent that/from . . .-ing'
importare che	'to be important that/matter that'
occorrere che	'to be necessary that'
ordinare che	'to order that'
permettere che	'to permit that/allow to'
sperare che	'to hope that'
temere che	'to fear that'
volere che	'to want that'

For example:

Vuoi che ti porti in braccio?	'Do you want me to carry you?'
Impedì che venissero distribuiti i volantini.	'He prevented the leaflets from being distributed.'
Hanno paura che l'edificio gli caschi addosso.	'They are afraid that the building will fall on top of them.'

Ordinò che l'esercito si ritirasse.	'He ordered that the army should retreat.'
Eviterà che si sentano rumori.	'That will avoid noises being heard.'
Occorreva che si demolissero tutte le case costruite prima della guerra.	'It was necessary that all the houses built before the war be destroyed.'
Bastava che me lo dicessero prima.	'It was sufficient/All that was necessary was that they told me first.'
Il suo solo scopo è che la gente lo ammiri.	'His only aim is for people to admire him.'
Importa che tu ci sia durante il congresso.	'It's important that you should be there during the congress.'
Proprio non permetto che mi diano del tu.	'I simply won't allow them to call me "tu".'
Speriamo che tu ci riesca. etc.	'Let's hope you manage it.'

Sperare che is often followed by a present indicative in informal usage. But if the following verb is in the imperfect, the subjunctive is normally found.

Many other expressions do not necessarily or inherently express wishing, ordering, intending, fearing, etc., but *may* do so. If they do, the verb in the subordinate clause after *che* will appear in the subjunctive; if they do not, the subordinate verb will appear in the indicative. Compare the following pairs of examples, and the differences between their suggested English translations:

Lo sconosciuto ha fatto loro cenno che camminino più lentamente.	'The stranger has signalled to them that they should walk more slowly.'
Lo sconosciuto ha fatto loro cenno che camminano più lentamente.	'The stranger has signalled to them that they are walking more slowly.'
È previsto che i docenti si dedichino al recupero.	'It is intended/planned that the teachers should dedicate themselves to remedial teaching.'
È previsto che i docenti si dedicheranno al recupero.	'It is foreseen/predicted that the teachers will dedicate themselves to remedial teaching.'
Sa cosa le sta dicendo: che si sbrighi a salutare la madre.	'She knows what she's saying to her [telling her she should do]: that she should hurry up and greet her mother.'
Sa cosa le sta dicendo: che si sbriga a salutare la madre.	'She knows what she's saying to her: that she is hurrying up to greet her mother.'
Evidentemente, il senso è quello che non si dicano le cose segrete ad alta voce.	'Clearly the intention is that secret things should not be said out loud.'
Evidentemente, il senso è quello che non si dicono le cose segrete ad alta voce.	'Clearly the sense is that secret things are not said out loud.'
Risposi che andassero a dormire.	'I answered that they should go to bed.'
Risposi che andavano a dormire.	'I answered that they were going to bed.'
Ha deciso che vengano sterminate le formiche.	'She has decided that [i.e., has made up her mind to give the order that] the ants should be exterminated.'
Ha deciso che vengono sterminate le formiche.	'She has decided [i.e., reached the conclusion] that the ants are being exterminated.'

The exclamation *chissà che . . .*, largely restricted to informal spoken language, is close to 'if only . . .', or 'let's hope that . . .', and is followed therefore by a subjunctive:

Chissà che guarisca.	'Let's hope he gets better.'
Chissà che il Perugia vinca il campionato.	'Let's hope Perugia win the championship.'

15.29 The subjunctive after conjunctions expressing purpose, intention

The conjunctions, *affinché, acciocché,* expressing 'purpose, intention (that something be realized)' (see 19.13) are followed by a subjunctive, as is *perché* when it means 'in order to' (not when it means 'because'; but see 15.42). The phrases *in maniera che, in modo che, così che* 'so that' followed by a subjunctive express that something is done *in order that* the notion expressed by the verb should come about; but if the following verb is in the indicative, it simply indicates a *result*, without any necessary connotation of intention:

Aprì le finestre affinché / acciocché / perché respirassero meglio.	'He opened the windows so that they could breathe better.'
Accesero un fuoco in modo che / in maniera che / così che li vedessero subito.	'They lit a fire so that [i.e., in order that / with the intention that] they should see them immediately.'

but

Aprì le finestre perché respiravano meglio.[9]	'He opened the windows because they were breathing better.'
Accesero un fuoco in modo che / in maniera che / così che li videro subito.	'They lit a fire so that [i.e., with the result/outcome that] they saw them immediately.'

Further examples:

Il volume descrive sommariamente il percorso di un manoscritto nella redazione delineando le diverse operazioni che devono essere compiute affinché esso si trasformi in un libro.	'The volume summarizes a manuscript's progress through editing, sketching the various operations which have to be carried out for it to become a book.'
Acciocché non si creassero equivoci, tutti i consiglieri sono stati invitati personalmente a partecipare alla prossima assemblea.	'That no misunderstandings should arise, all advisors were personally invited to attend the next assembly.'

Note however that the causative constructions (cf. 14.29) *fare che* and *fare sì che* are generally followed by a subjunctive, regardless of whether what is caused is 'intentional' or merely an 'accidental result':

Il sole ha fatto sì che muoiano tutti gli alberi.	'The sun made all the trees die.'
Mio signore, fai che io non mi perda ai miei stessi occhi, fai che sappia mantenere l'integrità del cuore. [Mar.]	'Lord, make sure that I do not become lost to my own eyes, make sure that I can know how to maintain the integrity of my heart.'

---

[9]One could also say *Aprì le finestre perché così respiravano meglio* 'He opened the windows because that way they breathed/could breathe more easily', and it might be felt that here *respiravano meglio* expresses an intention, even though it is in the indicative. True, intention is implicit, but the indicative expresses primarily *the fact which led him to open the window* – he knew that they definitely would be able to breathe more easily if he opened the window.

15.30 The subjunctive after expressions such as *purché* 'provided that', *a meno che* 'unless', and other constructions introducing hypotheses (e.g., *mettiamo che* 'let's suppose')

The subjunctive is used after conjunctions which specify some condition or ideal which is to be fulfilled (e.g., 'provided that/on condition that/as long as …' – see also 19.11): *purché, a condizione che, sempre che, a patto che, ammesso che*; also *in caso* and *per il caso che* 'just in case'. For uses of *se* … which also belong here, see 17.31.

Le ammetteremo purché la somma richiesta non superi le cinquantamila lire.	'We'll allow them on condition that the sum requested is not greater than 50 000 lire.'
La corsa avrà luogo sempre che non piova.	'The race will take place as long as it doesn't rain.'
Ammesso che possano bastargli per avviare un simile programma. E, soprattutto, che gli elettori decidano di mandarcelo davvero, a Palazzo Chigi.	'Provided that he can have enough of them to launch such a plan. And, above all, that the electorate really does decide to put him into Palazzo Chigi.'
Hanno acconsentito a patto che venissero tolti gli altri gravami finanziari.	'They agreed on condition that the other financial burdens be removed.'
Presi un ombrello in caso piovesse.	'I took an umbrella in case it rained.'

Similarly, *a meno che* 'unless' (which we may think of as meaning 'on condition that not …') is always followed by a verb in the subjunctive; note that the verb following *a meno che* is generally preceded by *non*:

Penso che abbiamo finito, a meno che Andreina non voglia intervenire ancora.	'I think we've finished, unless A wants to say something further.'

This idiosyncrasy of the *a meno che* construction is not quite as unfamiliar as it looks: English *unless* contains an originally negative prefix *un-* (similarly, <u>un</u>til in Italian is often *fino a che non*).

Verbs which serve to formulate a hypothesis (*mettere che, porre che, assumere che, ipotizzare che*) are also followed by a subjunctive:

Mettiamo che l'esercito si debba ritirare; che cosa ne conseguirebbe?	'Let's assume that the army has to retreat; what would be the consequence?'
Ipotizzando che l'America fosse stata scoperta dai portoghesi, prima di Colombo, riuscì a risolvere il problema.	'By hypothesizing that America had been discovered by the Portuguese, before Columbus, he managed to solve the problem.'

15.31 The subjunctive in an apparent main clause: the types *Venga domani, Magari venisse domani*, etc.

The main clause 'context' for the selection of the subjunctive may be 'implicit' but absent. In such cases the subjunctive appears to occur in a main clause, rather than a subordinate clause. But, significantly, the 'main clause' subjunctives are often (optionally) preceded by the subordination marker *che* (or by *se*). Typically, such subjunctives have meanings corresponding to English 'may …', 'let …'

when they contain a present subjunctive, and 'if only . . .', 'would that . . .', when they contain a past subjunctive.

(*Che*) *Non sia detto!*	'Let it not be said!'
(*Che*) *Lo facciano subito.*	'May they do it immediately'.
(*Se*) *Fosse vero!*	'If only it were true!'/'Would it were true!'
(*Che*) *Muoia il nemico!*	'Death to the enemy!'/'May the enemy die.'
(*Se*) *Sapessi quanto sono felice.*	'If only you knew how happy I am.'
O del distaccamento non si fidano e allora lo sciolgano. O ci credono partigiani come gli altri e allora ci mandino in azione. [Cal.]	'Either they don't trust the detachment and in that case let them dissolve it. Or they believe we are ordinary partisans and in that case let them send us into action.'
Ti si seccasse la voce in gola, una buona volta!	'[I wish] your voice would dry up in your throat, for once.'
(*Che*) *Nessuno dica una parola.*	'[Let] nobody say a word.'
E poi i cani, che siano grandi o piccoli, che stia alla larga dai cani.	'And then dogs, whether they are large or small, [we require that/let her] steer clear of dogs.'

Compare also the famous operatic phrase *Nessun dorma*, a poetic variant of *Nessuno dorma*, 'Let nobody sleep'.

What is unexpressed in the above examples could easily be expressed as, say:

Voglio/Ordino che/È necessario che non sia detto!
Voglio/Ordino che/Bisogna che lo facciano subito.
Vorrei che fosse vero!
Vogliamo che muoia il nemico!

and so forth.

Main clauses introduced by *magari*, in the sense 'if only . . .', 'would that . . .' also contain a verb in the subjunctive:

Magari avessimo qualche soldo in più!	'If only we had a little bit more money!'
Magari tu fossi qui!	'If only you were here!'

15.32 The type *L'idea che non lo sappia è assurda* or *Che non lo sappia è assurdo*

The subjunctive is used in clauses that express not assertions of fact but merely the 'idea', 'notion', 'concept'. Thus a subjunctive is generally required after *l'idea che* and similar expressions:

L'idea/L'ipotesi che Luigi non sappia l'italiano è davvero assurda.	'The idea that L doesn't know Italian is really absurd.'

Often 'the idea/notion/proposition that' is expressed simply by *che* at the beginning of the clause:

Che Luigi non sappia l'italiano è assurdo.	'[The idea/notion/proposition] that L doesn't know Italian is absurd.'

15.33 The subjunctive in relative clauses: *Cercava uno studente che sapesse il giapponese* 'He was looking for a student who knew Japanese', etc.

The distinction between the subjunctive expressing an idea or notion which is not realized (but whose realization or non-realization is desired/intended), and the indicative expressing an actual realization of the notion expressed by the verb, is particularly clear in relative clauses. A sentence such as

Paolo cercava uno studente che sapesse il giapponese.	'P was looking for a student who knew Japanese.'

means, roughly, that 'he was looking for any student who could meet the ideal/desired condition of knowing Japanese [but a student meeting this condition might, or might not, exist]'. In contrast:

Paolo cercava uno studente che sapeva il giapponese.	'P was looking for a student who knew Japanese.'

can mean that there actually was a student who knew Japanese (i.e., that the notion of a student knowing Japanese was actually realized), and that that was the student Paolo was looking for. However, in informal usage the indicative tends to be used for both cases.

In the following examples, the use of the subjunctive is consistent with the relative clause expressing an ideal rather than an event or fact. If we were to replace the verbs in the subjunctive by verbs in the indicative, we would be indicating that there actually *is* 'a gang of boys who accept him', and that big boys really *are* 'forced to admire him', that there actually *was* someone 'sharing his loneliness', and that there really was a specific male figure who would 'compensate for the lack of a father figure':

Pin vorrebbe sdraiarsi nella sua cuccetta e stare a occhi aperti e fantasticare, [. . .] fantasticare di bande di ragazzi che lo accettino come loro capo [. . .] e tutti insieme andare contro i grandi e picchiarli e fare cose meravigliose, cose per cui anche i grandi siano costretti a ammirarlo. [Cal.]	'P would like to stretch out in his bunk and lie with his eyes open daydreaming, daydreaming about gangs of boys who accept him as their chief and all taking on the big boys together and beating them up and doing wonderful things, things such that even big boys are forced to admire him.'
Vedovo, senza figli, sperava di trovare [. . .] una giovane donna che dividesse la sua solitudine. Anche Eva [. . .] era confusamente alla ricerca [. . .] di una figura maschile che la compensasse della mancanza di quella paterna. [Ogg.]	'As a childless widower, he hoped to find a young woman who would share his loneliness. E too was groping for a male figure who would compensate for the lack of a father figure.'
Cercava una capanna dove potessero lasciare gli arnesi.	'He was looking for a shed where they could leave their tools.'

Consider also the following examples, where the presence of the subjunctive in the relative clause emphasizes the potentially realizable, but not necessarily realized, condition, concept, notion, idea of 'any Germans who spoke/happened to speak our language', and 'anyone who possesses/happens to possess the most sacred of rights'. If an indicative verb were used in these examples, then *i tedeschi che parlavano la nostra lingua* might be taken to refer to a specific set of Germans who actually could speak our language and *chi possedeva il più sacro dei diritti* to an individual who indeed possessed such rights.

Gamper bollava come nemici da sopprimere non solo gli italiani, ma perfino i tedeschi che parlassero la nostra lingua. [Pan.]	'G branded as enemies to be wiped out not only the Italians, but even the [*or* 'any'] Germans who spoke our language' [*or* 'whichever Germans spoke our language'].
L'ingresso in un convento di clausura non è cosa breve, anche per chi possegga il più sacro dei diritti.	'Entry into a closed convent is not a rapid matter, even for whoever possesses the most sacred of rights.'

The subjunctive can also occur in relative clauses where the main clause indicates a desire or intention:

Aveva preso degli appunti che li aiutassero ad orientarsi.	'He'd taken some notes that would help them find their way about.' [i.e., he'd taken some notes in order to help them find their way about]
Attacca il manifesto bene in alto, dove tutti possano vederlo e leggerlo facilmente.	'Attach the poster nice and high up, where everyone can see it and read it easily.'

15.34 The subjunctive after indefinite relatives: *chiunque venga* 'whoever comes', etc.

It follows from what has been said about the subjunctive in relative clauses that pronouns whose meaning is inherently 'anyone who', 'anything that', 'any . . . that/who', 'anywhere that', 'in whatever way that' (cf. 7.19) will be followed by the subjunctive:

Qualunque cosa tu faccia, non ti scriverò mai.	'Whatever you do, I'll never write to you.'
Dovunque voi andiate, loro vi seguiranno.	'Wherever you go, they'll follow you.'
Chiunque fosse, non m'interessava conoscerlo.	'Whoever he was, I wasn't interested in meeting him.'
Qualsiasi cosa fosse necessaria è stata fatta.	'Whatever was necessary was done.'
Quale che sia stata la loro decisione, sono sicuro che hanno ragione.	'Whatever their decision was, I'm sure they're right.'

However, in more informal registers one often encounters an indicative in such contexts: *Qualunque cosa fai, non ti scriverò mai*, etc.

15.35 The set phrase *Che io sappia* 'As far as I know'

Che io sappia, Marco non è mai stato in Inghilterra.	'As far as I know, M has never been to England.'
—*È tornato il professor Franchi?* —*Che io sappia, no.*	'Is Professor F back?' 'Not as far as I know.'

15.36 The subjunctive with negated relatives

If the main clause is negative, the effect is usually to negate the reality of what is asserted in the relative clause, and so a subjunctive tends to be employed in the relative clause, at least in more elevated registers:

Ci sono dei giorni dell'anno in cui non c'è rete, non c'è velo, non c'è essenza che possa tenere lontane le zanzare. [Mar.]	'There are some days of the year when there is no net, there's no veil, there's no essence which can keep off the mosquitoes.'
Non c'erano studenti che sapessero il giapponese.	'There weren't any students who knew Japanese.'

Likewise *nessuno che . . ., niente che . . .*:

Non c'è niente che possiate fare.	'There's nothing you can do.'
Nessuno che avesse vissuto in Africa avrebbe detto una cosa simile.	'Nobody who'd lived in Africa would have said something like that.'

15.37 The subjunctive in relative clauses after superlatives and other 'exclusive' structures: *Era la più bella/la prima città che avesse mai visto* 'It was the most beautiful/the first city he had ever seen'

This use of the subjunctive after superlatives (*il più . . . che, il meno . . . che*) and similar 'exclusive' expressions such as *l'unico . . . che, il solo . . . che, il primo . . . che, l'ultimo . . . che, uno dei pochi . . . che, il massimo . . . che, il minimo . . . che*) is limited to formal discourse and is less commonly encountered in informal language. It is difficult to account for it in terms of the general principles mentioned hitherto, and the distinction is often more one of register than of meaning. But there is some resemblance with the structures illustrated in 15.33, in that the subjunctive tends to be used where the relative pronoun denotes an indefinite, unspecified entity:

Cercava il primo/l'ultimo che era entrato.	'He was looking for the first/last one who had come in.'
Cercava il primo/l'ultimo che fosse entrato.	'He was looking for whoever had come in first/last.'

Broadly speaking, the use of the subjunctive after superlatives, etc., seems to add emphasis to the superlative (something like 'absolutely the most/least/only/first, etc.', or 'the most/least/only/first, etc., of any you could mention'), whereas the indicative does not have such force. And in general, the subjunctive after superlative relatives is particularly apt to occur in the context of expressions which serve to underscore 'superlativeness' or 'uniqueness', such as *mai* 'ever', *al mondo* 'in the world' or *in vita mia* 'in my life'.

Sei l'unico che abbia visto.	'You're the only one he saw [at all].'
Sei l'unico che ha visto.	'You're the only one he saw.'
Era una delle poche donne che fossero state elette alla presidenza.	'She was one of the very few women who had been elected president.' [Exceptionally for a woman, she had been elected president.]

Era una delle poche donne che erano state elette alla presidenza.	'She was one of the few women who had ever been elected president.' [A few women had been elected president. She was one of them.]
Paolo è la persona meno arrogante che ho/abbia conosciuto durante la riunione di Venezia.	'P is the least arrogant person I met at the Venice meeting.'
Paolo è la persona meno arrogante che io abbia mai conosciuto in vita mia.	'P is the least arrogant person I've ever met in my life.'
Venezia è la città più splendida che c'è/ci sia.	'Venice is the most splendid city there is.'
Venezia è la città più splendida che ci sia al mondo.	'Venice is the most splendid city there is in the world.'
Era il tavolino più piccolo che avevano/ avessero avuto nel negozio.	'It was the smallest bedside table they had had in the shop.' [The smallest bedside table in the shop was that one.]
Era il tavolino più piccolo che avessero mai avuto nel negozio.	'It was the smallest bedside table they had ever had in the shop.'

15.38 The subjunctive (vs. indicative) after adjective + *che*. The types *È ridicolo che lo dica* and *Che lo dica è ridicolo*

In general, subordinate clauses introduced by 'adjective + *che*' specify notions or concepts, rather than assert factual occurrences. Subjunctives almost always occur when the subordinate is introduced by adjective + *che*:

È probabile che siano tutti morti.	'It's likely they've all died.'
Era possibile che saltasse tutta in aria.	'It was possible that it would all blow up.'
È incredibile che abbiano rinunciato ai loro diritti.	'It's incredible that they have given up their rights.'
È doveroso, però, che chi effettua queste denunce accerti prima come stiano le cose.	'But it is proper that the person making these allegations should first ascertain how things stand.'
Diventava essenziale che facessero vedere la patente ogni volta che entravano.	'It was becoming essential that they showed their driving licences every time they came in.'
È normale che i ragazzi facciano baldoria dopo gli esami.	'It's normal for kids to live it up after the exams.'
È logico che lo abbia scritto in spagnolo.	'It's logical that he should have written it in Spanish.'

etc.

Note also the type, where *che* + subjunctive in the interrogative seems roughly equivalent to 'Do you really think that . . .?', 'Is it believable that . . .?':

Che sia lui?	'Can it really be him?'
Che si stia trasformando in uno di quei cani che popolavano i sogni della signora madre? [Mar.]	'Can she be turning into one of those dogs who filled her mother's dreams?'

The indicative is however usually employed where the adjective explicitly asserts that what follows in the subordinate clause is a fact: e.g., *certo che* 'certain that', *incontestabile che* 'incontestable that', *indiscutibile che* 'indisputable that', *indubbio che* 'beyond doubt that', *innegabile che* 'undeniable that', *noto che* 'well known that', *ovvio che* 'obvious that', *sicuro che* 'sure that', *vero che* 'true that', etc.

È vero che gli Azzurri non giocano più come una volta.	'It's true/a fact that the Azzurri no longer play the way they used to.'
Era ovvio che gli faceva male la ferita.	'It was obvious that the wound was hurting him.'
Ero certa che avevi raccolto tutti i fogli.	'I was certain you'd gathered all the sheets.'
È incontestabile che il fumo nuoce alla salute.	'It's indisputable that smoking damages your health.'
etc.	

In the following example:

Voleva essere certo che non avessero ripensamenti all'ultimo momento.	'He wanted to be certain that they wouldn't have second thoughts at the last moment.'

the subjunctive expresses an *intention*: 'he wanted to make sure/see to it that . . .'. And if phrases such as *certo che*, usually selecting the indicative, are negated, or appear in the interrogative, then a subjunctive normally follows in the subordinate clause.

Non è affatto certo che il congiuntivo sia usato in italiano moderno in misura significativamente maggiore oppure minore che non nelle prime fasi della storia della lingua.	'[The notion] that the subjunctive is used in modern Italian to a significantly greater or smaller degree than in the earliest phases of the history of the language is not certain at all.'
Sei certo che la cintura sia allacciata?	'Are you sure the belt's fastened?'

If the subordinate clause beginning with *che* . . . is placed *in front of* the main verb, then a subjunctive is normal, precisely because in such constructions the *notion* or *idea* expressed by the verb is presented first, and only subsequently confirmed as being fact by an expression such as *è vero*, etc.

Che gli Azzurri non giochino più come una volta è vero.	'[The notion] that the Azzurri no longer play the way they used to is true.'
Che gli facesse male la ferita era ovvio.	'That the wound was hurting him was obvious.'
Che il fumo nuocia alla salute è incontestabile.	'[The notion] that smoking damages your health is indisputable.'

A rather similar principle accounts for the fact that with the expression *Certo è che*, only an *indicative* may follow; for in such constructions movement of the adjective to the beginning of the sentence serves particularly to underline the factual reality of what is asserted in the subordinate clause:

Certo è che gli Azzurri non giocano più come una volta.	'What is certain is that the Azzurri no longer play the way they used to.'

When the certainty or factuality of what is asserted in the subordinate clause is negated, or questioned, then a subjunctive is almost always used:

Non è vero che gli Azzurri non giochino più come una volta.	'It's not true that the Azzurri no longer play the way they used to.'

Non era ovvio che gli facesse male la ferita.	'It was not obvious that the wound was hurting him.'
Eri certa che avessi raccolto tutti i fogli?	'Were you sure I'd gathered all the sheets?'
È davvero incontestabile che il fumo nuoccia alla salute?	'Is it really indisputable that smoking damages your health?'

Also:

L'idea che Giovanni avesse lasciato aperte tutte le porte la preoccupava molto.[10]	'The idea [i.e., the suspicion] that G had left all the doors open worried her greatly.'
Che piova non ne dubito, ma ciò non ti autorizza ad arrivare con tre ore di ritardo.	'[The claim] that it's raining I don't doubt, but that doesn't mean you're entitled to arrive 3 hours late.'
Che fosse uno studente non lo negava, ma non voleva farlo entrare.	'That he was a student she didn't deny, but she wouldn't let him in.'
Che si trattasse di una bambina l'aveva saputo dal primo mese di gravidanza.	'That it was to be a little girl she had known from the first month of her pregnancy.'

15.39 The subjunctive after *può darsi che*

The subjunctive is always used after *può darsi che*, 'maybe . . .', 'perhaps . . .', 'it's possible that . . .':

Può darsi che avesse avuto anche voglia di continuare, ma proprio lui non poteva di certo sgarrare.	'It's possible that/Maybe he had even wanted to go on, but he of all people could certainly not afford to put a foot wrong.'

15.40 The subjunctive after expressions of 'belief/opinion/ mental impression/seeming/doubting that . . .': *Credo che venga; la convinzione che debbano essere fatti . . .; Mi pare che sia vero; l'opinione che possa esistere*'; *Dubito che sia vero*, etc.

A rule which must be observed in formal registers of Italian – but is less consistently observed in informal usage – is that the verb of a subordinate clause appears in the subjunctive if it is introduced by a main clause expressing a belief/opinion/mental impression that . . . (e.g., *credere che, pensare che, sembrare che, supporre che, dubitare che*):[11]

Io ho sempre pensato/creduto che si dovesse risolvere la questione comunista.	'I've always thought that one should resolve the communist question.'

---

[10]Compare this with *L'idea che Giovanni aveva chiuso a chiave tutte le porte la rassicurava molto.* 'The idea [i.e., the knowledge] that G had closed all the doors reassured her greatly.'
[11]Note that a statement that happens to constitute in itself an expression of opinion or belief does not of itself require the subjunctive. If we say *Esistono le fate* we are simply *stating as a fact* that 'fairies exist' (that it is only our belief is immaterial); but if we say 'We believe that fairies exist', *Crediamo che esistano le fate*, we are explicitly stating that we *believe* in their existence, and a subjunctive is required.

Non credo che fosse il suo obiettivo.	'I don't think it was his aim.'
Mi era passato per la testa che potesse essere già arrivato.	'It went through my mind that he might already have arrived.'
Immagino che tu sia stanco.	'I imagine you're tired.'
Pare che il lavoro sia tutto da rifare.	'It seems to me that the work will have to be done all over again.'
Mi sembrò che tu mi volessi uccidere.	'It seemed to me that you were trying to kill me.'
Io sono favorevole alla presenza dell'esercito in Sicilia e trovo criminale che la sinistra l'abbia voluto eliminare dalla Calabria e dalla Campania.	'I'm in favour of the presence of the army in Sicily and I think it's criminal that the left should have tried to eliminate it from Calabria and Campania.'
Suppongo che lo leggiate anche voi.	'I suppose you're reading it too.'
Dubitava che i francobolli potessero essere falsi.	'She doubted that the stamps could be fakes.'
Ritenevano che l'Italia dovesse vincere.	'They reckoned Italy would win.'
Sospettano che il ladro sia Mario.	'They suspect the thief is M.'
Ebbi la sensazione che qualcuno mi stesse sorvegliando.	'I had the sensation someone was watching me.'
Ho l'impressione che tu non mi voglia accompagnare.	'I have the impression you don't want to come with me.'

This principle applies even with firmly held beliefs:

Il 78,4 per cento degli italiani è convinto che la delinquenza sia in aumento.	'78.4% of Italians are convinced that delinquency is on the increase.'
Cresce ogni giorno la convinzione che la disoccupazione vada diminuendo.	'The conviction is growing daily that unemployment is falling.'
Ha la certezza che Mario l'abbia fatto.	'He's certain [in his own mind]/It's his firm belief that M has done it.'

If a verb of saying or asserting is equivalent to 'express the opinion/view that . . .' , then a subjunctive is also possible in the subordinate:

I maligni dicono che il nonno Ignazio Sebastiano riscuotesse fino alla sua morte [. . .] una gabella 'sul coito'. [Mar.]	'Wicked people say [would have us believe] that grandfather IS until his death levied a tax "on copulation".'
Si racconta che spesso i due litighino.	'It's claimed the pair often have rows.'
Trovo che cucinino molto male in Inghilterra.	'I find that they cook very badly in England.'

After verbs such as *pretendere che* 'to claim that', which generally introduce an expression of opinion rather than a factual assertion, the subjunctive is normal:

Adesso pretendono che anche tu sia stato coinvolto.	'Now they're claiming you were involved too.'

However, with verbs of belief and opinion an indicative may also appear in the subordinate clause, in which case the sense of the subordinate clause is 'the fact that':

Non crede che io ho smesso di fumare.	'He doesn't believe [the fact that] I've given up smoking.'

The negative of *dubitare che* is usually also followed by a subjunctive, but an indicative is possible (because if one 'does not doubt' something, one accepts its truth):

> *Non dubitava che i francobolli potessero/* 'She did not doubt that the stamps
> *potevano essere falsi.*   could be fakes.'

The indicative is obligatory after the negative imperative 'don't doubt' (e.g., *non mettere in dubbio che, non mettete in dubbio che, non metta in dubbio che, non mettano in dubbio che*), and positive imperative 'believe', e.g., *credi, crediate* (see 14.9), *creda, credano*:

> *Credi che non sono bugiardi.*   'Believe that they aren't liars.'
> *Non mettere in dubbio che ti conoscono.* 'Have no doubt that they know you.'

Capire che may also be followed by a subjunctive when it means 'to get the idea that' (i.e., where someone has in fact *mis*understood something): ̄

> *Avevo capito che aspettassero il documento* 'I'd understood/got the idea that they
> *oggi. Ma invece andava consegnato ieri.*   were expecting the document today.
>   But it should have been handed in
>   yesterday.'

15.41 The subjunctive after expressions of 'mental reaction': *Temo che venga; la paura che possa soffrire; Sono contento che l'abbia fatto*, etc.

A further rule observed in formal registers of Italian, but rather less strictly in informal usage, is that the subjunctive occurs in subordinate clauses introduced by main clauses expressing mental or emotional reaction (e.g., 'joy, sadness, pleasure, displeasure, anger, fear, surprise, sympathy, incomprehension that . . .'):

> *Mi stupisce che tu gli dia da mangiare.*   'I'm astonished you feed him.'
> *Sono contento che siano arrivati, finalmente.*   'I'm pleased they've arrived, at last.'
> *il terrore che suo figlio potesse essere*   'the terror that her son might be
> *morto*   dead'
> *È sorpreso/Lo sorprende che ti abbia riso*   'He's surprised/It surprises him that
> *in faccia.*   she laughed in your face.'
> *Sono commosso che siano tutti venuti a*   'I'm moved that they've all come to see
> *trovarmi.*   me.'
> *Io non ho nulla in contrario che bari al gioco.* 'I've no objection to him cheating.'/'I
>   don't mind him cheating.'
> *Mi fa pena che manchiate tanto di rispetto*   'It's pitiful that you are so lacking in
> *nei suoi confronti.*   respect towards him.'
> etc.

Notice that *capire che, non capire che, non spiegarsi che*, expressions which would normally select an indicative, require a subjunctive when they mean, respectively, 'not to be surprised that', and 'to be surprised that':

> *Capisco che tu non voglia parlare con i tuoi*   'I understand/I'm not surprised/I can
> *nemici, ma uno sforzo bisogna comunque*   see that you don't want to talk to your
> *farlo.*   enemies, but you must make an effort.'
> *Proprio non mi spiego che mi abbia piantato*   'I can't work out why/I can't see
> *in asso così.*   why/I'm baffled that he should have
>   ditched me like that.'

15.42 The subjunctive in contexts where the main clause 'does not assert as a fact': *Non dice che sia vero; Nega che sia vero; Sono uscita senza che mi vedessero; Non che mi abbiano visto*, etc.

A main clause which *asserts or implies that the content of the subordinate clause is not a fact*, usually selects a subjunctive in the subordinate.[12] This is particularly apparent in those cases where a main clause that would normally be followed by an indicative is negated:

Diceva che i gioielli non erano falsi.	'He was saying that the jewels were not false.'
Non diceva che i gioielli fossero falsi.	'He wasn't saying that the jewels were false.'

Also:

Non è scritto da nessuna parte che questo vecchio dai capelli gialli appartenga agli Ucrìa. [Mar.]	'It's not written anywhere that this old man with the white hair belongs to the Ucrìas.'
Questo non vuol dire che siano stati liberati.	'This doesn't mean that they've been freed.'

Verbs of denying are generally followed by a subjunctive (but an indicative is also possible in less formal usage):

Negava che fosse uno studente, e non voleva farlo entrare.	'She denied he was a student, and she wouldn't let him in.'

If the denial is negated, the following verb should be indicative: *Non negava che era uno studente, ma non voleva farlo entrare.* 'She didn't deny he was a student, but she wouldn't let him in.' But it is increasingly common to encounter a subjunctive even after *non negare che*, and in general one may say that *negare che* (positive or negative) tends to be followed by a subjunctive whether affirmative or negative.

The phrase *senza che* 'without' by its very meaning excludes the factual reality of what follows and therefore requires a subjunctive:

Sono uscita senza che mi vedessero.	'I got out without them seeing me.'
Partorì di nascosto, senza che suo padre lo sapesse.	'She gave birth secretly, without her father knowing about it.'

Similar are *non che* 'not that . . .', *non è che* 'it's not that . . .' (also, in very informal usage, *mica che*) and *non perché* 'not because . . .', when their function is to exclude the factual reality of what follows:

Mi piace prendere un grappino dopo mangiato; non che io sia un grande bevitore, s'intende.	'I like a drop of grappa after a meal; not that I'm a great drinker, of course.'
Non l'ha fatto perché ti detesti, ma perché non ha riflettuto.	'He did it not because he hates you, but because he didn't think.'

---

[12]It is important, in this regard, to distinguish 'not asserting that something is the case' from 'asserting that something is not the case'; in the former, Italian uses a subjunctive in the subordinate clause, in the latter, an indicative.

Non è che sia proprio stupido, ma lo trovo un po' lento nel capire.	'It's not that he's really stupid, but I find him a bit slow on the uptake.'
Vado spesso a cena fuori non perché mi diverta, ma per lavoro.	'I often dine out not because I enjoy it, but for my job.'

15.43 The subjunctive after expressions that imply that factual reality is 'immaterial': *Benché sia un ladro, lo ammiro* 'Although he's a thief, I admire him'; *Che venga o no, non lo aspetterò* 'Whether he's coming or not, I won't wait for him', etc. The type *per bello che fosse* . . . 'however beautiful it was . . .'

The 'concessive' conjunctions (see also 19.14) *benché*, *sebbene* (and the now archaic *ancorché*), *per quanto*, *nonostante (che)*, *quantunque*, *malgrado (che)* all with the meaning 'although', 'despite the fact that', are generally followed by a verb in the subjunctive:

L'area dei Laghi, delle Prealpi e delle Alpi centrali, benché sia meno decentrata del 'Nord Est', rappresenta una regione estremamente vitale dell'economia italiana.	'The area of the lakes, the Prealpi and the central Alps, although it's less decentralized than the "North East", represents an extremely vital region in the Italian economy.'
A considerarne lo sguardo, quantunque sia più giovane di lui, la fanciulla sembra incommensurabilmente più anziana.	'If one considers her look, although she is younger than him, the girl seems immeasurably older.'

In contrast, 'even though' (*anche se*) always takes an indicative (as does the now archaic *con tutto che* 'although'):

Mi accusò di aver detto il falso, anche se io non avevo mai aperto bocca.	'He accused me of lying, even though I had never said a word.'

Compare this with *Mi avrebbe accusato di aver detto il falso, anche se io non avessi mai aperto bocca* 'He would have accused me of lying even if I'd never said a word'.

Note also that *benché* may be followed by an indicative when it means 'but', 'yet', 'on the other hand': *Lui mi accusò di aver detto il falso, benché il suo amico non ha aperto bocca* 'He accused me of lying, but/yet his friend didn't say a word.'

Subordinate clauses which in English are introduced by 'whether' (in the sense 'it doesn't matter that . . .') are expressed as *che* + subjunctive. Sometimes *che* meaning 'whether' can be omitted at the beginning of a clause:

Che sia in giardino a leggere un libro, che sia nel salone giallo a fare i conti con Raffaele Cuffa, che sia in biblioteca a studiare l'inglese, Saro se lo trova sempre davanti. [Mar.]	'Whether he is in the garden reading a book, or whether he is in the yellow drawing room doing the accounts with RC, or whether he's in the library learning English, S is always finding him in front of him.'
E poi i cani, grandi o piccoli che siano, che stia alla larga dai cani. [Mar.]	'And dogs, whether they be large or small, let her steer clear of dogs.'
La sua era una vita randagia, senza donne né amici, tedeschi o italiani che fossero. [Ogg.]	'His was the life of a stray, without women or friends, whether they were German or Italian.'
Venga o non venga, non m'importa.	'Whether he comes or not, I don't care.'

Another type of concessive construction which also requires a subjunctive verb is *per* + adjective + *che* + verb, equivalent to English 'however + adjective + verb':

Per bello che fosse, non lo avrei mai pagato due milioni.	'However beautiful it was, I would never have paid 2 million for it.'
Per famoso che sia diventato Andrea Bocelli è rimasto attaccato alla sua Lajatico.	'However famous he may have become, AB stayed attached to his Lajatico.'

Note also the (rare!) construction *per* + infinitive + *che* + subjunctive of *fare*:

Per cercare che facesse non riusciva a trovare una soluzione.	'Search as he might he couldn't find a solution.'

15.44 The subjunctive after 'noun + *che*': *è una vergogna che, il fatto che,* etc.

Where the subordinate clause is introduced by a noun + *che*, the selection of indicative or subjunctive in the subordinate does not always fit very easily with the principles outlined so far (for a more detailed account, see Wandruszka in Renzi and Salvi 1991: 477–81). As a rule, nouns that express opinions, hypotheses, mental impressions or emotional reactions are followed by a subjunctive:

È una crudeltà che gli uomini siano costretti a lavorare tutta la vita.	'It is cruel that men should be forced to work their whole life.'
Era una vergogna che non avessero nemmeno dell'acqua da bere.	'It was disgraceful that they didn't even have some water to drink.'

The phrase *Fortuna che* 'luckily' always takes the indicative, whilst *Peccato che* 'It's a pity' may take either subjunctive or indicative:

Fortuna che c'era dell'acqua da bere.	'Luckily there was water to drink.'
Peccato che non c'era / non ci fosse acqua da bere.	'It's a pity there was no water to drink.'

With phrases equivalent to English 'the good/bad thing is that', the subordinate clause tends to contain an indicative:

Il guaio è che non hanno tempo.	'The trouble/bad thing is they've no time.'
Il bello era che avevano i soldi.	'The nice thing was that they had the money.'

Phrases such as *il fatto che* 'the fact that', *la notizia che* 'the news that', *la circostanza che* 'the circumstance that', can easily take either the subjunctive or the indicative, with a decided preference for the indicative in more informal and colloquial usage:

Il fatto che lo abbia / ha respinto non significa niente.	'The fact that he rejected it means nothing.'

But the phrases *sta il fatto che* or *fatto sta che* 'the fact remains that', and *essere un fatto che* 'to be a fact that' are always followed by the indicative.

15.45 The subjunctive in 'indirect questions': the type *Non so se siano qua, Chiedeva chi fosse*, etc.

In sentences such as 'I don't know whether they're here', 'He asked who she was' the subordinate clauses 'whether they're here', 'who she was' constitute 'indirect questions', corresponding to the 'direct' questions 'Are they here?', 'Who is she?' When indirect questions are introduced by expressions of 'knowing whether/if/ who/what/why/how . . .' or 'asking/wondering whether/if/who/what/why/ how . . .', the indirect question tends to contain a subjunctive:

un testamento che non si sa come sia stato già aperto	'a will of which no one knows how it could already have been opened'
Marianna si chiede per quale infausta alchimia i pensieri di Innocenza la raggiungano chiari e limpidi come se li potesse udire. [Mar.]	'M wonders by what unhappy alchemy I's thoughts are reaching her as clearly and limpidly as if she could hear them.'
I contadini stavano discutendo su chi dovesse pagare il dazio sulla frutta.	'The peasants were arguing about who was to pay the duty on fruit.'

The use of the subjunctive, rather than the indicative, tends to occur after verbs of knowing in main clauses that have *interrogative* ('does he know . . .?') or *negative* ('he doesn't know . . .') force. The force of the subjunctive in such cases is to downplay the importance of the actual 'answer' to the indirect question, either because the speaker/writer does not know what the 'answer' is, or because the intent is to underscore the mental state of 'not knowing' implicit in the main clause:

Dovrò dargli la mia carta d'identità, perché non sa come mi chiamo.	'I will have to give him my identity card, because he doesn't know what my name is.' [but of course the writer does]
Dovranno dargli le loro carte d'identità perché non sa come si chiamino.	'They will have to give him their identity cards, because he doesn't know what their names are.' [and, implicitly, the writer doesn't know either]
Questi bambini sanno cosa significhi soffrire?	'Do these children know what suffering means?' [the focus is on the children's lack of understanding of the true nature of suffering]
Questi bambini sanno cosa significa soffrire?	'Do these children know what suffering means? [a simple enquiry as to whether the meaning of the word is known to the children]
Ma non sanno perché lo dica visto che lui a caccia non ci va mai.	'But they don't know/can't work out why he says it, given that hunting is something he never does.'
Ma non sanno ancora perché lo dice, perché non hanno potuto chiedergli il motivo.	'But they don't yet know the reason why he says it, because they haven't been able to ask him the reason.'
Ignorano chi sia stato il ladro.	'They don't know who the thief was.'

But when *sapere* is neither interrogative nor negated (i.e., when it is affirmative) the indirect question is almost always in the indicative, although the picture is complicated by the fact that where the emphasis is on *awareness* of the fact contained in the subordinate clause, rather than on what the subordinate clause asserts, a subjunctive is at least possible, and this especially when the verb of knowing is in a past tense form:

Sanno bene chi è/sia il ladro.	'They know who the thief was.'
Sapeva benissimo chi era/fosse.	'She knew very well who he was.'

If the indirect question is placed at the beginning of the sentence a subjunctive is normal, at least in formal registers:

Cosa sia stato quel trauma lo espresse *poeticamente un altro giovane.*	'What that trauma was, was poetically expressed by another young man.'
Dove fossero andati rimane un mistero.	'Where they had gone is still a mystery.'

When *come* is used as an alternative to *che*, meaning 'that', the subordinate verb is generally in the subjunctive, at least in careful and formal language:

Hanno spiegato come il loro padre avesse *viaggiato per tutto il mondo.*	'They explained that/how their father had travelled all over the world.'

The subjunctive is generally used in indirect questions introduced by *quanto*:

Hanno già sperimentato sulla propria pelle *quanto sia duro allevare contemporaneamente* *un nugolo di marmocchi dai mille problemi.* *[Ogg.]*	'They have already found out for themselves how hard it is to bring up a flock of kids with a thousand problems.'
Saputo che si sta parlando con Daniela di *quanto gli assomigli Leonardo, sparisce in* *uno dei corridoi.*	'Having learned that we are speaking to Daniela about how much Leonardo looks like him, he disappears into one of the corridors.'

15.46 The subjunctive after time conjunctions: *quando, prima che, finché*, etc.

Prima che 'before', always requires a subjunctive:

Te lo daranno prima che tu parta.	'They'll give it to you before you leave.'
Morì prima che arrivasse l'ambulanza.	'He died before the ambulance arrived.'

Fino a che and *finché*, 'until', take a verb in the subjunctive (optionally preceded by *non*) where the sense is 'until such time as', but tend to take the indicative where the duration is known and definite ('until that time when'). It follows that the subjunctive tends to be used where the reference is oriented towards the future, and the indicative where it looks back towards the past:

Dice che resterà/resta a letto finché non si *senta meglio.*	'He says he'll stay in bed until [i.e., until such time as] he feels better.'
Disse che sarebbe restato a letto finché non *si fosse sentito meglio.*	'He said he'd stay in bed until [i.e., until such time as] he felt better.'
Disse che restò a letto finché non si sentì *meglio.*	'He said he'd stayed in bed until [i.e., until that time when] he felt better.'

Finché can also mean 'for as long as' in which case it is never followed by *non*); again, the indicative tends to be used with reference to past time (or the present), but the subjunctive with reference to the future:

Finché fece bel tempo non portò l'ombrello.	'As long as the weather was fine he didn't take an umbrella.'
Finché sei giovane, goditi la vita.	'While you're [still] young, enjoy life.'

Farò come voglio, finché mi bastino i soldi.   'I'll do what I want as long as I have
enough money.'

For *quando* + subjunctive, in the sense 'if', see 17.36; for *quando* + pluperfect subjunctive as a 'future-in-the-past', see 15.3.

15.47 The subjunctive after verbs of happening: *Succede/Capita/Avviene/Accade che venga*, etc.

Verbs meaning 'to happen that' are followed by a subjunctive when they are
close in meaning to 'it's possible that', 'it may happen that'; usually, in such
cases, the 'happening' verb is in the present, imperfect or future tense. When the
'happening' verb can be roughly paraphrased as 'what happened was that . . .',
an indicative is used:

Capitava spesso che avesse qualche amico   'He was often liable to have a few
a casa.   friends at home.'
Se succede che lui non ci sia, noi andremo   'If he turns out not to be there, we'll go
a casa.   home.'
Capitò che c'erano due cavalli già pronti.   'What happened was that there were
                                                two horses there ready.'
È successo che ho perso il portafoglio.   'What happened was that I lost my
                                                wallet.'

15.48 Tense and the subjunctive: *Voglio che venga; Vorrei che venisse; Volevo che venisse*, etc.

The so-called 'present' subjunctive is really better labelled 'non-past', because it
is actually used with reference both to present and to future time: *Non credo che
venga* = 'I don't think he's coming' or 'I don't think he'll come'. For the possibility of using the future tense, rather than the present subjunctive, when it is cru-
cial to distinguish future from present time (e.g., *Credo che verrà*), see 15.9.

If the main clause contains a verb in the present or future tense (or the *passato
prossimo* used with reference to the present, see 15.16) then any appropriate tense
of the subjunctive can, in principle, occur in the subordinate (e.g., *Non credo che
venga* 'I don't think he's coming/will come', *Non credo che venisse* 'I don't think
he was coming', *Non credo che sia venuto* 'I don't think he's come', *Non credo che
fosse venuto* 'I don't think he had come').

If the main clause contains a past-tense verb (imperfect, *passato remoto*, pluperfect, or *passato prossimo* with past reference [see 15.16], past conditional), then
a past-tense form of the subjunctive (imperfect subjunctive or pluperfect subjunctive) is employed: e.g., *Non credevo/avevo creduto/credetti/avrei creduto che
venisse; Non credevo/avevo creduto/credetti/avrei creduto che fosse venuto*.

If the main clause contains a present conditional, only a past (imperfect or pluperfect) subjunctive is usually possible in the subordinate, even though the reference may actually be to present time: *Non crederei che venisse* 'I wouldn't think
he is/was coming', *Non crederei che fosse venuto* 'I wouldn't think he had come',
Vorrei che venisse/fosse venuto 'I'd like him to come/ to have come'.

15.49 Equivalents of English 'will', 'would', 'shall', 'should'

These verb forms can pose problems. Of course 'will + verb' and 'would + verb' often correspond to Italian future and conditional verb forms (see 14.10):

'He will come tomorrow.'	*Verrà domani.*
'If you told him, he would come tomorrow.'	*Se glielo dicessi, verrebbe domani.*
'He said he would come later.' etc.	*Disse che sarebbe venuto dopo.*

But we see in 15.12 that 'would' in the sense 'was in the habit of', 'used to' can correspond to an imperfect tense form:

'G would/used to go to school every day with his teddy bear.'	*Gianni andava a scuola ogni giorno con l'orsacchiotto.*

Another, rather more formal, way of expressing this habitual 'would' is to use the imperfect of the verb *solere* or of the phrase *essere solito* 'be wont'/'be accustomed':

Gianni soleva/era solito andare a scuola ogni giorno con l'orsacchiotto.	'G would/was wont to go to school every day with his teddy bear.'

But many English uses of 'will' and 'would' do not correspond to any of the above Italian structures. 'Will' (and its original past form 'would') was at one time a verb meaning 'want', and in some cases it retains something of this original meaning. Sentences like 'Paul just won't learn French', 'The car won't start' are not necessarily future but may indicate 'unwillingness', 'refusal', 'obstinacy', in which case an Italian expression of 'unwillingness' or 'resistance' could be appropriate. These sentences could be translated as *Paolo proprio non vuole imparare il francese* or *Paolo proprio si rifiuta d'imparare il francese, La macchina proprio non vuole partire* or *La macchina proprio si rifiuta di partire*. Similarly, the past tense form 'Paul just wouldn't learn French' would correspond to *Paolo proprio non voleva imparare il francese*, etc.

'Will' and its past tense form 'would' can also be used in English to express (often undesirable) 'wilful persistence/insistence', rather than futurity; in such cases, 'will' and 'would' are always stressed: e.g., 'Paul <u>will</u>/<u>would</u> keep interrupting while I am/was studying', 'I tried to turn it off, but that blasted radio <u>will</u>/<u>would</u> turn on automatically at 5.30'. In such cases, appropriate Italian expressions of 'wilful insistence' need to be sought, such as *Paolo si ostina/si ostinava ad interrompere mentre studio/studiavo*, and *Ho cercato di spegnerla, ma quella maledetta radio continua/continuava ad accendersi automaticamente alle 5,30*, etc.

There is a further use of (stressed) 'would' in English which indicates that the activity expressed by the verb is somehow characteristic, or to be expected, of the subject of the verb (often with overtones of scepticism or world-weary familiarity with such a characteristic). An example in British English which has become something of a set phrase is 'Well they would, wouldn't they', i.e. 'This is just the kind of behaviour one would expect of them./This is just what you'd expect', used sceptically of people who deny involvement with some event which would damage their reputation if they were to admit being associated with it. Also 'He <u>would</u> lose his key', meaning 'It's typical of him to lose his key', 'If anybody were going to lose his key, you can bet it was him.' There is no simple formula for expressing this function in Italian. For the first examples one might say *C'era da aspettarselo* 'That was to be expected' or *Ma cosa volete che dicano!* 'Well what do you expect them to say!' (note the use of *volere* to mean 'expect').[13] For the second one might say *Ma certo che la chiave l'ha persa lui. Chi altro volete che sia stato?* 'Of course he's lost the key. Who else do you expect it to have been?', or *È proprio da lui perdere la chiave* 'It's just typical of him to lose the key' (for this use of *da*, see 11.28).

English 'shall' (and 'should') is also used (at least in formal and literary usage) in future and conditional constructions ('We shall arrive tomorrow', 'We knew we should be there before midnight'), but it has various other functions, more or less closely linked with the original meaning of the verb which was one of 'duty', 'obligation', 'having to'. These functions are particularly clear in questions: 'Shall I clear the table?' need not be a future interrogative but an enquiry about our duties, in which case the Italian equivalent might be *Devo sparecchiare?* In modern English 'should', although originally a past tense form of 'shall', is principally used as a kind of conditional of 'shall', so 'Should I clear the table' would be *Dovrei sparecchiare?*

English 'shall' in first person plural interrogatives is often a kind of imperative, a way of making a proposal about action to be taken: 'Shall we clear the table?', 'Shall we go home now?', etc. The Italian equivalent generally uses *vogliamo*: *Vogliamo sparecchiare?*, *Vogliamo tornare a casa ora?*, etc.

15.50 Equivalents of 'must', 'must have'; 'should', 'should have'; 'ought to', 'ought to have', etc.

'Must' is usually *dovere*:

Devi essere stanca.	'You must be tired.'
Dobbiamo toglierci le scarpe prima di entrare.	'We must take our shoes off before entering.'
Devono essere già le nove.	'It must already be nine o'clock.'

Use of 'must' as a past tense form is now relatively unusual in English ('had to' being more normal): the Italian equivalent is usually the imperfect of *dovere*:

Sapevo che dovevo rispondere subito.	'I knew I must/had to answer immediately.'
Ero sicuro che doveva essere molto stanca.	'I was sure she must be very tired.'

Note that if a perfective form of *dovere* is used, it suggests the *completion* of the action expressed by the infinitive (cf. 15.12 on the distinction between perfective and imperfective forms). *Doveva rispondere subito* tells us merely that he had to answer immediately, but says nothing about whether he actually did so; *Ha dovuto rispondere subito* suggests that he had to answer and did so.

'Should' is also a slightly less emphatic version of 'must' used, like 'must', to mean either moral obligation or logical necessity in the present. A near synonym

---

[13]The use of *volere* to mean 'expect' results in its use in contexts where 'want' would be unlikely in English: *Come vuole che io finisca prima di gennaio?* 'How does he expect me to finish before January?' or *Perché volete che il governo ci aumenti le tasse prima di gennaio?* 'Why do you expect the government to increase our taxes before January?'

of 'should' in these functions is 'ought to': ('You should/ought to always wash your hands before eating', 'If this object is really made of lead, it should/ought to be very heavy'). The usual Italian equivalent is the conditional of *dovere*: *Dovresti sempre lavarti le mani prima di mangiare, Se questo oggetto è davvero di piombo, dovrebbe essere molto pesante*, etc. For the use of *andare* as an auxiliary verb meaning 'should be', 'ought to be' in passive constructions (e.g., *Questo vino andrebbe servito fresco* 'This wine should be served chilled'), see 14.33.

'Must have ...' is generally expressed by the *passato prossimo* of *dovere* (i.e., auxiliary verb + *dovuto*):

Ha dovuto lavorare molto.	'He must have worked a lot.'
Sono dovuti tornare prima dell'alba.	'They must have got back before dawn.'

But it is also possible to say *Deve aver lavorato molto* and *Devono essere tornati prima dell'alba*, which emphasizes the fact that we can deduce from evidence which we *now* have that he worked hard or that they returned before dawn.

'Should have' and 'ought to have' + past participle are expressed as *avrei dovuto*, etc. or *sarei dovuto*, etc. + infinitive (for the selection of the auxiliary verb, see 14.21):

Ci saremmo dovuti lavare le mani prima di mangiare.	'We should have washed our hands before eating.'
Avreste dovuto controllare l'olio.	'You ought to have checked the oil.'
La reazione avrebbe dovuto aver luogo dopo alcuni momenti.	'The reaction should have taken place after a few moments.'
Avrebbe dovuto parlartene ieri.	'He ought to have talked to you about it yesterday.'
Sarebbe dovuto tornare prima delle nove.	'He ought to have come back before nine o'clock.'

15.51 Equivalents of 'can'/'could', 'may'/'might'

The principal difficulty for English speakers lies in using the correct equivalents of 'could', 'could have', 'might', 'might have' each of which has a range of meanings which have to be differentiated in Italian (see 15.49–52). However, the rather subtle and complex distinctions in English between 'can'/'could' on the one hand and 'may'/'might', on the other, are not usually made in Italian, which tends to use *potere* for both.

Può tornare domani.	'He may come back tomorrow.' OR 'He can come back tomorrow. '
Non so se qualcuno di voi possa avere in mente di chi si tratta.	'I don't know if any of you may have an idea of who we're talking about.'

But where 'can' or 'may' mean 'It is possible that ...', Italian frequently uses *Può darsi che* + subjunctive:

Può darsi che torni domani.	'He may come back tomorrow.' [i.e., 'It is possible that he will come back tomorrow.']
Può darsi che avesse avuto anche voglia di continuare, ma proprio lui non poteva di certo sgarrare.	'It may even be that he had wanted to go on, but he of all people could not slip up.'

In contrast, *Può tornare domani,* etc. could mean not only 'It is possible that he'll come back tomorrow', but also 'He is able to come back tomorrow', 'He is allowed to come back tomorrow'. *Può darsi* can also be used to mean 'maybe', 'perhaps':

—*Tornerà domani?*　　　　　　　　　　'Will he be back tomorrow?'
—*Può darsi.*　　　　　　　　　　　　　'Maybe.'

15.52　'May not', 'might not' and 'cannot'

English 'He may do it' and 'He might do it' can be expressed as *Può farlo* and *Potrebbe farlo.* In Italian as in English these sentences are ambiguous between 'He is/would be able to do it' and 'It may/might be the case that he will do it'. In the negative, however, Italian makes a distinction: *Non può farlo* is 'He is not able to do it' and *Non potrebbe farlo* is 'He would not be able to do it', but *Può non farlo* and *Potrebbe non farlo,* with the negative marker following *potere,* are 'It may be that he won't do it', 'It might be that he won't do it' – i.e., 'He may not do it', 'He might not do it'.

'May not' is ambiguous in a further respect: it can mean both 'is not able' and 'is not permitted'. The latter meaning is virtually identical to 'must not', and *dovere* is frequently used rather than *potere*:

I negozi non devono aprire prima delle 8.	'The shops may not open until 8.' [i.e., 'it is not permitted']
I negozi possono non aprire prima delle 8.	'The shops may not open until 8.' [i.e., 'It may be that they won't' or 'They are allowed not to.']

In English 'cannot' can function as a negative of 'must'. Here, again, *dovere* tends to be used in Italian:

Dev'essere facile cucinare per due persone.	'It must be easy to cook for two people.'
Non dev'essere facile cucinare per trenta persone.	'It can't be easy to cook for 30 people.'

15.53　The tense ambiguity of 'could' and 'might'

English 'could' and 'might' may be present conditional or future-in-the-past (see 15.2) (e.g., 'If he were here now we could/might tell him', 'He said he could/might be there in three minutes'), or past tense (e.g., 'Yesterday he couldn't leave the office'), of 'can'. An easy diagnostic for the function of 'could' or 'might' in English is to replace them by 'be able' or 'be possible for': e.g., 'If he were here now we would be able/it would be possible for us to tell him', 'He said he would be able/it would be possible for him to be there in three minutes', 'Yesterday he was not able/it was not possible for him to leave the office'. In Italian these various functions of 'could' and 'might' are always distinguished by using the appropriate tense form of *potere* (or where appropriate *sapere* – 15.52):

Negli anni Quaranta non potevano attraversare la frontiera perché era chiusa.	'In the 40s they couldn't cross the frontier because it was closed.'
Quel giorno non ho potuto prendere l'autobus a causa dello sciopero.	'I couldn't catch the bus that day because of the strike.'

Mi promise che avrei potuto farlo il mese seguente.	'He promised me I could [would be able to] do it the following month.'
Quel taxi che arriva potrebbe essere il nostro.	'That taxi that's coming could be ours.'
Se fosse qui ora glielo potremmo dare.	'If he were here now we might/could give it to him.'
Potrebbe essere difficile.	'That might/could be difficult.'
Capii che avrebbe potuto farlo.	'I realized he might do it.' [i.e., 'It was possible that he would do it.']
Poteva fare quel che voleva.	'He could[14] [was able to] do what he wished.'

15.54 Different functions of 'might have', 'could have' and 'may have', 'can have'

English 'might have' and 'could have' are usually expressed by the past conditional of *potere* (*avrebbe potuto/sarebbe potuto*, etc.):

Con gli occhiali, avrebbe potuto vederlo.	'With his glasses, he might have seen it.'
Mi dissero che sarebbe potuta morire prima che tornassimo.	'They told me she might have died before we returned.' [it would have been possible for her to die]

In such cases, and especially in informal discourse (see 15.4), the imperfect of *potere* may also be used:

Con gli occhiali, poteva vederlo.	'With his glasses, he might have seen it.'
Mi dissero che poteva morire prima che tornassimo.	'They told me she might have died before we returned.'

But 'might have' and 'could have' can have another function, which is to indicate that it was possible at a given time in the past that some event had occurred earlier than that time. A sentence like 'He couldn't find his wallet; he might/could have left it on the train' could be paraphrased as 'He couldn't find his wallet and it was possible that he had left it on the train'. Here Italian would be likely to use an imperfect tense form of *potere* + infinitive of auxiliary verb + past participle:

Questo quadro poteva averlo fatto Miró.	'M might/could have made this picture.' [i.e., it was possible that M had made it]
Il poliziotto sospettava che potesse essere caduta.	The policeman suspected she might/could have fallen.' [that it was possible that she had fallen]
Non trovava il portafoglio; poteva averlo dimenticato sul treno.	'He couldn't find his wallet; he might/could have lost it on the train.'

The present form 'may have' usually means 'it is possible that some event has occurred' (the negative of 'may have' in this sense is often 'can't have'). For example, 'He can't find his wallet; he may have left it on the train', is paraphrasable as 'He can't find his wallet; it is possible that he has left it on the train'.

---

[14]In old-fashioned English 'might' could be used here too, but it is now very unusual in the sense 'was able to'.

Here Italian is likely to use a present[15] form of *potere* + infinitive of auxiliary + past participle:

Questo quadro può averlo fatto Miró.	'M may have done this picture.' [i.e., it is possible that M has done it]
Il poliziotto sospetta che possa essere caduta.	'The policeman suspects she may have fallen.' [that it is possible that she has fallen]
Non trova il portafoglio; può averlo dimenticato sul treno.	'He can't find his wallet; he may have left it on the train.'
Il treno non può essere già partito.	'The train can't already have left.'

When 'might have' is equivalent to 'ought to have', the past conditional of *dovere* is likely to be used:

Avresti dovuto dirmi che non avevi le chiavi. Ora come facciamo a entrare?	'You might have told me you didn't have the keys. Now how do we get in?'

15.55 'Can', 'could' ambiguous between 'be possible', *potere*, and 'know how', *sapere*

'Can', 'could' can mean both 'be able to' in the sense 'be possible/permitted for someone to do something' and 'know how to'. In Italian this distinction is usually made explicit, *potere* being used for 'possibility' and *sapere* for 'know how':

Uno strumento come il violino poteva agevolmente accompagnarlo nelle sue solitarie passeggiate in campagna.	'An instrument like the violin could easily accompany him on his solitary country walks.'
Ma non si può far finta che non sia successo nulla.	'But we can't [it's not possible for us to] pretend nothing's happened.'
Il problema è che Carlo di tasca sua non può accontentarla.	'The problem is that Charles cannot [it is impossible for him to] keep her happy out of his own pocket.'
Non abbandonare mai i poveri: sono gli unici che sanno essere fedeli.	'Never abandon the poor: they are the only ones who can [know how to] be faithful.'
Ecco un altro dei giochi che sa fare solo Lupo Rosso.	'Here's another of the tricks that only LR can [knows how to] do.'

15.56 'Can' in verbs of perception, understanding, finding: *Non lo vedo* 'I can't see it'

English verbs of perception and understanding are commonly preceded by 'can'/'could': 'I can see/hear/feel it', 'I can understand it'. In Italian, the verb of perception, unaccompanied by *potere* or *sapere*, is normally used. The same applies to verbs of 'finding'.

Non ti vedo nemmeno.	'I can't even see you.'
È inutile che parliate a bassa voce. Vi sento lo stesso.	'It's no good whispering. I can hear you anyway.'

---

[15]In principle, a future of *potere* can be used as well: *Potrà averlo fatto* 'It will be possible that he has done it'.

Non trovo il mio impermeabile.	'I can't find my raincoat.'
Capisco che tu sia triste.	'I can understand that you're sad.'
Non capiva l'orario.	'He couldn't understand the timetable.'

If *potere* is used with verbs of perception, etc., emphasis is usually being placed on the fact that it is possible to see, etc.:

Se alzavo gli occhi potevo vedere [. . .] i cigni sempre in attesa di qualcuno che butti loro qualcosa. [Mar.]	'Whenever I looked up, I got to see the swans still waiting for somebody to throw them something.'

Note that 'I can see', etc. used with reference to a particular place or situation (e.g., because it is too dark in a room), rather than to a permanent condition, is usually *Ci vedo*, etc. The use of *ci* in this case is largely restricted to intransitive uses of the verb, but also commonly occurs with *niente* and *qualcosa*.

Qui è tutto buio. Non ci vedo (niente).	'It's all dark here. I can't see (a thing).'
Ci vedi (qualcosa)? Posso anche accendere la luce.	'Can you see (anything)? I can turn the light on if you want.'

15.57 'Can' = 'succeed in', 'manage to'

'Can' often has the sense 'succeed in', 'manage to' – in other words it can mean something like 'be able as a result of trying'. In such cases Italian often uses *riuscire a*: *Non riesce ad aprire la porta*, *Se riesce a caricare il fucile spara* mean 'He can't open the door', 'If he can load the rifle he'll shoot', with the implication that he is attempting to open the door or load the rifle. *Non può aprire la porta*, *Se può caricare il fucile . . .*, in contrast, are less specific and could mean any of: 'He's failing to open the door' / 'It is not possible for him to open the door' / 'He's not allowed to open the door'; 'If he manages to load the rifle . . .' / 'If it is possible for him to load the rifle . . .' / 'If he is allowed to load the rifle . . .', etc.

Note that *passato prossimo* and *passato remoto* forms of *potere* and *sapere*, precisely because they indicate 'completion of an action', are often better expressed in English as 'managed to', rather than simply 'could'. Correspondingly, 'managed to' in the past tense can often be expressed just by the *passato remoto* or *passato prossimo* of these verbs (as well as by *riuscire a*):

È potuto entrare senza problemi.	'He managed to get in without difficulty.'
Seppe esprimere la sua riconoscenza in un italiano più che accettabile.	'He managed to express his gratitude in a more than acceptable Italian.'

A colloquial expression meaning 'manage (to)', 'make it' is *farcela (a)* (see 6.9):

Ce la fai ad aprire la finestra?	'Can you [manage to] open the window?'
Finalmente ce l'ho fatta!	'At last I've done it/managed to do it/made it!'

16

Comparative, superlative and related constructions

16.1 Forming the comparative and superlative of adjectives and adverbs: 'more', 'most' = *più*, 'less', 'least' = *meno*

Both the comparatives and the superlatives of adjectives and adverbs are usually formed by placing *più* ('more', 'most') or *meno* ('less', 'least') in front of the adjective or adverb:

Cercava il libro più leggero.	'He was looking for the lighter/lightest book.'
Questa vernice è meno liquida.	'This paint is less liquid.'
Questa vernice è la meno liquida.	'This paint is the less/least liquid one.'
I ragazzi camminano più lentamente di me, ma la loro sorella cammina più lentamente di tutti noi.	'The boys walk more slowly than me, but their sister walks (the) most slowly of all of us.'

Unlike English ('the lighter book' vs. 'the lightest book'), or French (*le livre plus léger* vs. *le livre le plus léger*), Italian does not usually distinguish comparative and superlative forms.[1]

The use of the (masculine singular) definite article with the superlative of adverbs (e.g., *La loro sorella cammina il più lentamente di tutti noi*) is possible, but unusual. A special case, limited to particularly elevated registers, occurs when a noun *not* preceded by a definite article is followed by a superlative adjective + another qualifying adjective, such as *possibile* or *concepibile*. In these cases, the superlative adjective must be preceded by the definite article (agreeing with the noun):

Occorre un meccanismo il più sensibile possibile.	'We need the most sensitive possible mechanism/a mechanism which is the most sensitive possible.'
Contemplavano situazioni le più orrende concepibili.	'They were contemplating the most horrible situations conceivable/ situations which were the most horrible that could be conceived.'

---

[1]Constructions such as *Cercava il libro il più leggero* – where, as in French, the superlative adjective is preceded by the definite article – may occasionally be encountered in literary writing, but are best not imitated.

16.2 Special forms of comparatives and superlatives: *migliore, meglio* 'better'/'best', *peggiore, peggio* 'worse'/'worst', etc.

Six adjectives and adverbs have special ('lexical') comparative forms instead of, or as well as, *più* + adjective/adverb.

buono	*migliore* [sometimes *più buono*]	'better'/'best'
bene	*meglio*	'better'/'best'
cattivo	*peggiore* [sometimes *più cattivo*]	'worse'/'worst'
male	*peggio*	'worse'/'worst'
grande	*maggiore* or *più grande*	'bigger'/'greater'
piccolo	*minore* or *più piccolo*	'smaller'/'lesser'

Più cattivo and *più buono* tend to be used – rather than *peggiore* and *migliore* – when the sense is 'more ill-natured', 'more unpleasant' and 'more good-natured', 'nicer', 'more agreeable':

La nuova proposta è molto migliore della mia.	'The new proposal is much better than mine.'
È una delle migliori insegnanti d'italiano che conosciamo	'She's one of the best teachers of Italian' that we know
Mia nonna era molto più buona di mia madre.	'My grandmother was much nicer/kinder than my mother.'

Maggiore and *minore* tend to be used rather than *più grande* and *più piccolo* where the sense is 'greater/lesser in degree, age or importance': e.g., *fratello maggiore/minore* 'older/younger brother', *la maggior parte* 'the majority', *un autore minore* 'a minor author', *un'area minore* 'a lesser (smaller or less important) area'. In contrast, *fratello più grande* could mean either 'older' or, simply, 'bigger'/'taller'; *la parte più grande* 'the bigger'/'larger part', *un autore più piccolo* 'a (physically) smaller author', *un'area più piccola* 'a smaller area'. The rather learned and elevated connotations of *maggiore* and *minore* also tend to mean that these forms are avoided in informal registers: *Sei il più grande* (rather than *il maggiore*) *ladro che conosco!* 'You're the biggest thief I know!'

Just as one uses the adverbs *bene* and *male* to mean 'good', 'fine', 'OK' and 'bad' (*È bene che tu non studi troppo* 'It's good that you don't overstudy'), so the corresponding comparatives are the adverbs *meglio* and *peggio*: e.g., *È meglio che tu non studi troppo; Ancora peggio: abbiamo perso anche la macchina* 'Even worse, we've lost the car too'. Use of *meglio* and *peggio* as (invariant) adjectives (e.g., *Questa è la meglio macchina*) is considered substandard.

Comparatives meaning 'less' have no 'special forms': one says simply *meno bene, meno buono*, etc. Note *meno male* is an idiomatic expression meaning 'It's just as well', 'Thank goodness', 'That's a relief':

—*Abbiamo ritrovato la vostra macchina.*	'We've found your car again.'
—*Ah, meno male.*	'Ah, just as well.'

In very erudite registers (scholarly writing, etc.) there is a further series of *-ore* comparatives introduced into Italian from Classical Latin: *viciniore* 'closer', *seriore* 'later', *esteriore* 'outer', *interiore* 'inner'. In much more common usage are the adjectives *superiore* 'upper' or 'superior', *inferiore* 'lower' or 'inferior' and *ulteriore* 'further', 'additional' (e.g., *Ho chiesto ulteriori informazioni* 'I asked for further information'). 'Further'/'farther' as comparative of 'far' is *più lontano*.

16.3 Comparative quantifiers: *più/meno mele* 'more/fewer apples', etc.; *Le mele costano (di) più/(di) meno* 'Apples cost more/less', etc.

Più and *meno* also function as quantifiers, immediately followed by the noun. *Più* is equivalent to English 'more', and *meno* to 'less' (with mass nouns) or 'fewer' (with quantifiable nouns). Note that they are invariable for number and gender:

Nella mia classe ci sono più ragazze che ragazzi.	'In my class there are more girls than boys.'
In questa minestra ci voleva meno olio e più sale.	'This soup needed less oil and more salt.'
Vogliamo meno leggi e meno tasse.	'We want fewer laws and fewer taxes.'

The phrase *un po' più* and *un po' meno* are optionally followed by *di* before the noun:

Ci ho messo un po' più (di) benzina.	'I put a bit more petrol in.'

Più and *meno* also function as adverbs modifying verbs, with the sense 'to a greater/lesser degree'. In such cases, *più* and *meno* are normally preceded by *di*, and this especially when they occur at the end of a clause or sentence:

Se avessimo riflettuto di più, forse non saremmo partiti.	'If we'd reflected more/longer, perhaps we would not have left.'
Negli ultimi mesi ha studiato molto di meno.	'In recent months he's been studying a lot less.'
A Giovanni scrivo sempre di più.	'I am writing to G more and more.'

16.4 The type *ottocento lire in più* '800 lire more'/'an extra 800 lire'

The usual counterpart of English phrases of the kind 'quantifier + noun + more/less' is 'quantifier + noun + *in più/in meno*'.

Il pacchetto arrivava sempre con qualche bottiglia in meno.	'The packet always arrived with a few bottles less.'
Gli lasciammo sei uova in più.	'We left him six extra eggs.'
C'erano due capre in più.	'There were an extra two goats.'
Ogni punto di tassazione in meno equivale a un risparmio di 20 mila miliardi.	'Every point of taxation less is equivalent to a saving of 20 thousand billions.'

16.5 The type *cambiare in meglio/peggio* 'to change for the better/worse'

Negli ultimi quarant'anni, la situazione è cambiata in meglio/in peggio.	'In the last 40 years, the situation has changed for the better/for the worse.'

16.6 How to say 'I had better . . .', etc.

The English phrase 'I (etc.) had better . . .', meaning 'I ought to', 'it would be to my advantage to', but usually with a strong overtone of urgency or immediate necessity, has no simple equivalent in Italian. *Convenire a* 'to be advantageous to' is one expression, perhaps further modified by some element expressing urgency or insistence:

> *Ti conviene proprio farlo domani.*　　'You'd (really) better do it tomorrow.'

Other possible expressions are simply the conditional of *dovere*, or *bisogna che* . . .

> *Dovreste telefonargli.*　　'You'd better phone him.'
> *Bisogna che tu lo faccia domani.*　　'You'd better do it tomorrow.'

The Italian equivalent of 'you'd better' may often be reinforced by some phrase underscoring the speaker's insistence, such as *mi raccomando* 'I entreat', 'mind you do':

> *Vi conviene consegnare il compito oggi,*　　'You'd better hand in the assignment
> *mi raccomando.*　　today [mind you do].'

16.7 'Than' in comparatives: the comparators *che* and *di* before nouns, adjectives, adverbs and prepositions

Italian has two comparators corresponding to English 'than', *che* and *di*. It is difficult to give a simple general account of the distinction between them, and there is some variation in usage (cf. Brunet 1984: 123–93 for an extensively illustrated overview of the problem). However, it is useful to bear in mind that one of the major functions of *che* in Italian is to introduce a verb in subordinate clauses. And as a rule, the comparator *che* indicates what we might term the 'virtual presence' of a verb or a verb phrase following it. Specifically, *che* is used where the verb of the main clause (that preceding the comparator) could potentially be repeated after the comparator; a second, but slightly less strictly applied, condition for use of *che*, is that the subject of this 'virtual' verb should be identical to the subject of the main verb. In other cases, *di* is used.

Same verb, same subject 'virtually present' after the comparator:

> *Maria mangia più mele che pere.*　　'Maria eats more apples than [she eats] pears.'

Same verb virtually present after comparator, but different subject (so *di* preferred):

> *Maria mangia più mele di Marco.*　　'Maria eats more apples than Marco [eats apples]'.

No verb possible after comparative (so *di* obligatory):

> *Maria ne ha mangiate più di otto.*　　'Maria has eaten more than eight of them.'

Some further observations (which in fact follow from the above principles) are that:

- *Che* is always used when two adjectives modifying the same noun phrase or pronoun are compared:

> *Paolo è più furbo che intelligente.*　　'P is more sly than [P is] intelligent.'

● *Che* is always used when the comparator is immediately followed by a preposition:

Ha parlato più con Francesco che con Maria.	'She talked to F more than [she talked] to M.'

● *Che* is *generally* used when the main verb, and the 'understood' verb to the right of the comparator, share the same subject:

Conosco la sposa meglio che lo sposo.	'I know the bride better than [I know] the groom.'

as opposed to

Conosco la sposa meglio dello sposo.	'I know the bride better than the groom [knows the bride].'

Also:

L'artrite reumatoide colpisce le donne più che gli uomini.	'Rheumatoid arthritis affects women more than [it affects] men'.
un branco di giovani maschi che pare quasi composto di lupi, più che di umani [Pan.]	'a pack of young males which seems almost [to be] made up of wolves rather than [to be] made up of humans'
Quel film parla più di amore che di guerra.	'That film deals more with love than [it deals] with war.'
È meglio mangiare la pasta che la carne.	'It's better to eat pasta than [to eat] meat.'

An example in which the clause introduced by the comparator *precedes* the main clause is:

I temi della lotta contro l'olocausto nucleare ben più che nei corridoi felpati di Montecitorio camminano fra la gente comune.	'Issues about the struggle against nuclear holocaust are far more afoot among ordinary people than [they are afoot] in the plush corridors of Montecitorio.'

When a comparison is made between two infinitives, the subjects are always identical, and *che* is therefore normally used. In many cases, the subject of the infinitive is the indefinite personal (see 6.29) 'one', 'people generally':

È certo assai più difficile perdere una guerra che vincerla.	'It's certainly much more difficult to lose a war than [it is difficult] to win it. [i.e., that one should lose a war than that one should win it].

Some examples in which, for the reasons described above, *di* is the comparator, are:

Ne ha più di quaranta.	'He has more than 40 of them.'
Meno del 10% dei romeni possono permettersi vacanze all'estero.	'Less than 10% of Romanians can afford holidays abroad.'
Più stupidi di così non si può essere.	'One can't be more stupid than that.'
C'era molta meno gente del solito.	'There were a lot fewer people than [what was] usual.'
E questi fatti piacevano parecchio alla gente, perché erano molto più verosimili di quelli veri.	'And people really liked these facts, because they were much more plausible than the real ones [were].'
Il nuovo coupé Civic è più grande del precedente.	'The new Civic coupé is bigger than the earlier model [was].'

Gianni ha mangiato più caramelle di te.	'G has eaten more sweets than you [have eaten].'
Ricordo che aveva una manica più lunga dell'altra.	'I remember he had one sleeve [which was] longer than the other one [was].'
Aurora era cresciuta più presto delle altre.	'A had grown up faster than the others [had grown up].'
Eroina e cocaina uccidono molto più del terrorismo.	'Heroin and cocaine kill much more than terrorism [kills].'

Di is obligatory where the subject of the 'virtual' verb is different and is a pronoun, but in other cases where the subject is different, *che* is also possible, especially where the subject of the main verb occurs *after* the main verb:

La domestica era molto più furba di me [not *che io*].	'The servant was much more sly than me.'
Sembrava che giocasse con tutti e sulle barche ci stava più lui che i clienti.	'He seemed to play with everyone and *he* spent more time on the boats than his clients [spent].'
Canta molto meglio mia sorella che mio fratello.	'My sister sings much better than my brother [sings].'
Era più brava lei, che veniva dalla campagna, che i ragazzi di paese.	'She, who came from the countryside, was better than the village boys [were].'

Note the idiomatic fixed expressions *più che altro* 'most of all', 'if anything', and *più che mai* 'more than ever':

Più che altro aveva paura.	'If anything/Most of all he was frightened.'
Piove più che mai.	'It rains more than ever.'

16.8 Comparatives where the second element is a verb phrase (1): 'New York is bigger <u>than I thought</u>' = *New York è più grande <u>di quanto pensassi</u>*, etc.

Where the second element of the comparison is a verb phrase, certain complications arise. The strategy most commonly adopted by Italian is, in effect, to turn that verb phrase into a noun phrase introduced by a relativizer ('what . . .', 'that which . . .'). So a sentence such as 'New York is bigger than <u>I thought</u>' becomes 'New York is bigger than <u>what I thought</u>'. 'What' is here generally rendered by the relativizer *quanto* (cf. 7.16) + indicative or subjunctive verb or, slightly less commonly, *quel(lo) che* + indicative verb or *come* + indicative verb. The comparator (see 16.7) in such constructions is always *di*.

Mario è più intelligente di quanto credevo/credessi.	'M is more intelligent than I believed.'
Il problema era più complesso di quel che sembrava.	'The problem was more complex than it seemed.'
Piazzato di fronte alla realtà di un evento molto speciale pare persino più giovane e garrulo di quanto la sua carta di identità possa indicare.	'Faced with the reality of a very special development he seems even younger and more talkative than his identity card might proclaim.'

For the use of redundant *non* in such constructions, see 16.9, 10, 11.

16.9 Comparatives where the second element is a verb phrase (2): 'New York is bigger <u>than I thought</u>' = New York è più grande <u>che non pensassi</u>, etc.

It is also possible to express 'than + verb' simply as *che* + verb. But in this case the verb is almost always in the subjunctive and, most remarkably, it is nearly always preceded by the word *non*. This *non* is a part of the comparative construction which carries absolutely no connotation of negativity:

Hanno molte più armi che non ne abbiano i francesi.	'They have many more weapons than the French have.'
Si rivelò assai più fanatico che non ci fossimo aspettati.	'He turned out to be much more fanatical than we had expected.'
Quel ragazzo è molto più sveglio che tu non creda.	'That boy is a lot brighter than you think.'

16.10 More about redundant *non* in comparative constructions: *Era più alto di quanto non credessi* 'He was taller than I thought', *È più rosso che (non) marrone* 'It's more red than brown'

The use of redundant *non* is not restricted to the type described above. It is also *optionally* (but frequently) used after *di quanto* (cf. 7.16). Where *non* is used, the following verb is generally in the subjunctive:

Mario è più intelligente di quanto non credessi.	'M is more intelligent than I believed.'
Il problema era più complesso di quel che non sembrasse.	'The problem was more complex than it seemed.'

Moreover, in comparative constructions introduced by *che* the redundant *non* can be optionally used not only before verbs but also before nouns, adjectives, adverbs and prepositional phrases:

Hanno molte più armi che non i francesi.	'They have many more weapons than the French.'
Era più depresso che non arrabbiato.	'He was more depressed than angry.'
Lavorava più con un senso di dovere che non con entusiasmo.	'He worked more with a sense of duty than with enthusiasm.'
Non è affatto certo che il congiuntivo sia usato in italiano moderno in misura significativamente maggiore oppure minore che non nelle prime fasi della storia della lingua.	'That the subjunctive is used in modern Italian to a significantly greater or smaller degree than in the earliest phases of the history of the language is not certain at all.'

16.11 'Rather than' = più che (non) or piuttosto che (non)

Voleva la panna piuttosto che (non) il latte.	'He wanted the cream rather than the milk.'
Voleva più la panna che (non) il latte.	
Voleva la panna più che (non) il latte.	

In general, *piuttosto che* is used rather than *piuttosto di*, but the latter is sometimes encountered in contexts where the comparator *di* is possible (see 16.7).

16.12 How to say 'I'd rather', etc.

'Would/'d rather' is usually the present conditional of *preferire*, and 'rather have' the past conditional:

Preferirei tornare a casa.	'I'd rather go home.'
Preferireste rimanere qua?	'Would you rather stay here?'
Avremmo preferito leggere il giornale.	'We would rather have read the paper.'

16.13 The expression of 'in' in superlative structures: *l'edificio più alto del mondo* = 'the tallest building in the world', etc.

In general, Italian uses *di* where English has 'in' or 'of' in superlative constructions. A less common alternative, corresponding to English 'of' + plural noun, is *tra* or *fra*:

Non più di tre anni fa [. . .] Sean Connery è stato riconosciuto come il divo più sexy del mondo. [Ogg.]	'No more than three years ago SC was recognized as the sexiest film star in the world.'
Simona era sempre la meno intelligente dei (or tra i) miei studenti.	'S was always the least intelligent of my students.'

16.14 The type *un edificio dei più splendidi* = 'a most splendid building'

An alternative way of expressing the elative ('most . . .') is to place *dei/delle più* or *fra i/le più* + plural adjective after the noun:

Ha raccolto dei fiori dei/fra i più belli.	'He picked some most beautiful flowers.'
Disse una parola delle più brutte.	'He said a most ugly word.'

16.15 Adjectives with the 'elative' ending *-issimo*: 'very', 'extremely', 'highly', 'most . . .'; and *pessimo* 'very bad', *ottimo* 'very good', *minimo* 'minimal', 'very small'; *massimo* 'maximum'

Italian makes great use of a suffix *-issimo* which can be added to most adjectives after deleting the final vowel of the adjective: e.g., *intelligente* – *intelligentissimo* 'most intelligent', *alto* – *altissimo* 'extremely high'. Note that adjectives in *-co*, *-go* and *-io* use their masculine plural stems when adding the *-issimo* ending: this means that if their masculine plural (see 3.2, 6) is *-chi* and *-ghi*, then the *h* also appears before *-issimo* (*ricco* – pl. *ricchi* – *ricchissimo* 'very rich', *largo* – pl. *larghi* – *larghissimo* 'very wide'); but if the plural is *-ci* (or *-gi*), then no *h* is present (*simpatico* – pl. *simpatici* – *simpaticissimo* 'very nice', 'likeable', *greco* – pl. *greci* – *grecissimo* 'extremely Greek'). *Adjectives* in plural *-gi* are almost unknown, although one could, in principle, have *belgissimo* 'extremely Belgian', following *belgi* plural of *belga*. By the same principle, *serio* – plural *seri* – *serissimo* 'very serious', but *pio* – *pii* – *piissimo* 'most pious'.

The *-issimo* ending was originally introduced into Italian from Classical Latin, where -ISSIMUS could also have superlative value (i.e., 'the most ...'), but in Italian its meaning is not 'superlative' but 'elative', i.e., 'very ...', 'highly ...', 'extremely ...', or 'most ...' (but not 'the most ...'). Thus:

Queste idee mi sembrano interessantissime.	'These ideas seem to me most interesting.'
Queste idee mi sembrano le più interessanti.	'These ideas seem to me the most interesting ones.'

Also

La Regina d'Inghilterra è ricchissima.	'The Queen of England is extremely rich.'
Ha due braccia lunghissime.	'He has extremely long arms.'
Ucciderebbe anche la propria madre, che è un reato gravissimo.	'He'd kill his own mother, which is a most serious crime.'
Anche se non si è più giovanissime, si può cominciare da capo.	'Even if we are no longer very young, we can start all over again.'

Just as *cattivo, buono, piccolo* and *grande* may have special 'lexical' comparative-superlative forms (cf. 16.2), so they may have special elative forms:

cattivo	*cattivissimo* or *pessimo*
buono	*buonissimo* or *ottimo*
piccolo	*piccolissimo* or *minimo*
grande	*grandissimo* or *massimo*

Cattivissimo and *buonissimo* are generally used when the sense is 'extremely (un)pleasant', '(dis)agreeable'. *Pessimo* and *ottimo* express rather more detached judgements of the quality or value of some object, activity or person. *Pessimo* is broadly 'of poor quality', 'highly undesirable', 'useless', 'unacceptable', and *ottimo* is 'excellent', 'first rate', 'of very high quality'.

Questi spaghetti sono buonissimi.	'This spaghetti is lovely.'
Questi spaghetti sono ottimi.	'This spaghetti is first class.'
È un cuoco cattivissimo.	'He's a very ill-natured chef.'
È un cuoco pessimo.	'He's a very bad chef.' / 'He cooks very badly.'
È di cattivissimo umore.	'She's in an appalling/very nasty mood.'
È in pessima salute.	'She's in terrible/extremely bad health.'

Piccolissimo and *grandissimo* tend to express the more 'basic' meanings of these two adjectives ('tiny', 'minute' and 'very large', 'enormous'), and sometimes carry overtones of close emotional involvement absent from the more detached *minimo* and *massimo*. These latter are closer in meaning, respectively, to 'minimum', 'minimal', 'slightest', 'least' and 'maximum', 'maximal', 'greatest', 'highest', 'supreme', 'ultimate'. But the distinction between these forms is by no means always clear-cut. Note that *grandissimo* is used when the sense is '(morally) very great', and also corresponds to *grande* in phrases such as *un grande bevitore* 'a great drinker', 'someone who drinks a lot' – *un grandissimo bevitore* 'a huge drinker', 'someone who drinks hugely'.

La somma che mi offrono è piccolissima.	'The amount they are offering me is minute/extremely small.'

La somma che mi offrono è minima.	'The amount they are offering me is minimal.'
Ho un piccolissimo dolore al dito.	'I have a very tiny pain in my finger.'
Non ho la minima idea.	'I haven't the slightest idea.'

Certain other adjectives also have 'special' elative forms:

acre	*acerrimo*	'most sharp', 'bitter'
celebre	*celeberrimo*	'most famous'
celere	*celerrimo*	'most swift'
integro	*integerrimo*	'utterly whole/pure'
misero	*miserrimo*	'quite wretched'
salubre	*saluberrimo*	'most salubrious'

All five of these forms are restricted to learned, literary usage, and the 'regular' type *miserissimo*, etc., is perfectly possible (although *acerrimo* and *integerrimo* commonly occur in phrases such as *un acerrimo nemico* 'an implacable enemy', *una vita integerrima* 'an utterly blameless life'). Similarly restricted to learned registers are:

benefico	*beneficentissimo*	'most beneficent'
maledico	*maledicentissimo*	'most evil-speaking'
munifico	*munificentissimo*	'most munificent'
benevolo	*benevolentissimo*	'most benevolent'
malevolo	*malevolentissimo*	'most malevolent'

In everyday usage, the *-issimo* forms of these adjectives tend not to be used, *molto/assai/estremamente benefico*, etc., being preferred.

16.16 Adverbs with *-issimo: benissimo*, etc.

The *-issimo* ending can also be attached to adverbs, except for those ending in *-mente* (see 13.1):

bene	*benissimo*	'extremely well'
male	*malissimo*	'very badly'
piano	*pianissimo*	'very softly/slowly'
lontano	*lontanissimo*	'very far'
vicino	*vicinissimo*	'very close'
etc.		

Parla benissimo l'italiano.	'He speaks Italian extremely well.'
Si è sentito malissimo.	'He felt awful.'
Andrai lontanissimo.	'You'll go an extremely long way.'
Abbiamo litigato spessissimo.	'We argued extremely often.'

The form *assaissimo* 'utterly', 'absolutely', from *assai*, is restricted to jocular usage. It is in principle possible to combine *-issimo* and the adverb ending *-mente* by adding *-mente* to a feminine adjective in *-issima*: *simpaticissima – simpaticissimamente*, *integerrima – integerrimamente*, etc., but such forms tend to be avoided, and it is preferable to say, for example, *in modo simpaticissimo/integerrimo*.

16.17 Nouns with *-issimo: la finalissima*, etc.

It is marginally possible to add *-issimo* (*-issima* for feminines) to nouns. The meaning can be equivalent to 'the ultimate ...', 'the last word in ...', 'the ... to end all ...', 'the top ...', but the effect may often be jocular and modish, and such forms are probably best avoided in formal and serious discourse. Some examples now accepted in common usage are:

finale – finalissima	'grand finale of sporting competition, etc.'
poltrona – poltronissima	'front seat at theatre'
ultima – ultimissima	'final edition of newspaper', 'latest piece of news', 'gossip'
veglione – veglionissimo	'New Year's Eve celebrations'
generale – generalissimo	'generalissimo', 'supreme commander'

16.18 Comparisons of equality ('as ... as'; 'as much ... as'; 'as many ... as')

Comparisons of equality are usually expressed by *tanto ... quanto; altrettanto ... quanto; tanto ... come; così ... come*. As quantifying adjectives 'as much ... as ...', 'as many ... as ...', *(altret)tanto* and *quanto* agree in number and gender with the nouns they qualify. *Così ... come* is *not* used to express 'as much/many ... as'.[2]

La tavola è tanto larga quanto alta.	'The table is as wide as (it is) high.'
La tavola è altrettanto larga quanto alta.	
La tavola è così larga come alta.	
Mangia tanto quanto può.	'He eats as much as he can.'
Ha mangiato tante mele quante pere.	'He's eaten as many apples as pears.'
Sono a metà della mia carriera e ho deciso di interpretare tanti 'nonni' e 'vecchi zii' quanti 'giovani' ho già portato sullo schermo. [Ogg.]	'I'm in mid career and I've decided to act as many "grandfathers" and "elderly uncles" as I have already presented "youngsters" on screen.'
Mussolini era odiato in Italia come in Inghilterra.	'M was hated as much in Italy as in England'.
Maria è bella quanto me.	'M is as beautiful as me/I am.'
È tanto bella quanto distratta.	'She is as beautiful as (she is) absent-minded.'
un computer grande quanto una macchina fotografica da portare a tracolla	'a computer as big as a camera you can sling over your shoulder'

Only an oblique (see 6.2) form of the pronouns (*me, te,* etc.) can be used after *quanto* or *come*.

Note expressions such as *quanto prima* 'as soon as possible', *quanto mai* 'as much as can be', *quanto possibile* 'as much as possible':

Ti prego di farmi avere le chiavi quanto prima.	'Please let me have the keys as soon as possible.'
È una parola quanto possibile evitata.	'It's a word that's avoided as much as possible.'
È una ragazza noiosa quanto mai.	'She is a girl [who is] as boring as could be.'

The order *(altret)tanto ... quanto* can, occasionally, be reversed:

---

[2]The adverbs *tanto, altrettanto, così* may be omitted in these constructions (e.g., *La tavola è larga come alta*), but such omission is unusual.

Sono due razze speciali: quanto i tedeschi sono rossicci, carnosi, imberbi, tanto i fascisti sono neri, ossuti, con le facce bluastre e i baffi da topo. [Cal.]	'They are two special breeds: as the Germans are ruddy, fleshy and beardless, so the fascists are dark, bony, blue-faced and rat-whiskered.'

Note that *altrettanto* can also mean 'the same', 'likewise' or, as a quantifier, 'the same number/amount':

Abbandonarono la loro macchina e noi fummo costretti a fare altrettanto.	'They abandoned their car and we were forced to do likewise.'
Aveva sette fucili e altrettante bombe a mano.	'He had seven rifles and the same number of hand grenades.'

Note also the use of *altrettanto* in returning thanks of good wishes:

—*Buon appetito!*	'Bon appétit!'
—*Altrettanto!*	'The same to you!'
—*Buona fortuna!*	'Good luck!'
—*Altrettanto!*	'Thank you!'

16.19 'The same as . . .' = *lo stesso di/che*

Aveva la stessa macchina di/che Mario.	'He had the same car as Mario.'
Faremo lo stesso dell'/che l'altra volta.	'We'll do the same as last time.'

16.20 'The more . . ., the more'; 'the less . . ., the less'

In comparisons of this type Italian does not use the definite article. Usually *più . . . più, meno . . . meno; quanto più . . . tanto più; quanto meno . . . tanto meno*:

Più puzzolenti e pidocchiosi eravamo, più erano contente. [Cal.]	'The more stinking and louse-ridden we were, the happier they were.'
Meno staremo divisi più ci capiremo.	'The less divided we stand, the better we'll understand each other.'
Sono sicuro che chi ci ascolta e ha bambini a casa sarà molto contento di questa invenzione perché più si consuma più si vede l'oggetto che c'è dentro e più chiaramente i bambini sono contenti di consumarlo.	'I'm sure our listeners who have kids at home will be delighted with this invention because the more you use it the more you see the object inside and the more obviously happy the kids are to use it.'

The second *meno* or *più* in such constructions may be preceded by *e*:

Meno studi e meno impari.	'The less you study the less you learn.'

16.21 'More and more . . ./less and less . . .' = *sempre più/meno . . .*

Marco diventava sempre meno cordiale e sempre più depresso.	'M was getting less and less cordial and more and more depressed.'
Col passare dei giorni la situazione sembra sempre peggiore.	'As the days go by the situation seems worse and worse.'

16.22 Repetition (reduplication) of adjective or adverb as an intensifier: the type *rosso rosso* 'very very/really/ever so/extremely red'

Repetition (reduplication) of an adjective or an adverb is a possible way of intensifying or underscoring what the adjective or adverb expresses. Reduplication is characteristic of informal registers only, and often carries a nuance of playfulness or non-seriousness. Both in its meaning and in the registers in which it can be used, it has something in common with English 'ever so + adjective/adverb'. There is no pause between the repeated adjectives or adverbs and, as a general rule, there are no more than two unstressed syllables between the stressed vowels of the reduplicated forms; to put it another way, reduplication tends not to occur with adjectives or adverbs of more than three syllables (including adverbs in -*mente*), so that *Fatelo subito subito* 'Do it straight away' seems much more acceptable than *Fatelo immediatamente immediatamente*.

Rimasero zitti zitti.	'They kept dead quite/ever so quiet.'
Camminano adagio adagio.	'They walk very slowly.'
Mi raccomando, fatelo presto presto.	'Please make sure you do it as soon as you can.'
Era un topo piccolo piccolo.	'It was a tiny little mouse.'/'It was ever such a little mouse.'

Note *pian piano* 'very slowly' as well as *piano piano*.

Reduplication is sometimes encountered even in nouns, as in *Questo è caffè caffè* 'This is real/genuine coffee'.

17

Aspects of sentence structure

17.1 Basic organization of declarative sentences: *Paolo mangia la carne* 'P eats the meat', *È arrivato Paolo* 'P has arrived', etc.

An important principle in the organization of sentence structure is the distinction between the 'theme' – 'that which the sentence is about' and the 'rheme', that part of the sentence which communicates information about the theme. The theme generally precedes the rheme: in a sentence such as *Paolo mangia la carne* 'Paolo eats the meat', *Paolo* is the theme, that which the sentence is about, and *mangia la carne* conveys information about the theme. Another important distinction is that between 'old' or 'given' information (that which is already known, either explicitly, because it has already been mentioned, or implicitly, from the general context) and 'new' information; the 'new' information always contains the most prominent stress in a sentence. In the context of the question *Cosa fa Paolo?*, the sentence *Paolo mangia la carne* has as its 'given' element *Paolo* and as its 'new' element *mangia la carne* (within which the main stress may fall either on *mangia* or *carne*). Very commonly, the theme, the old information, and the grammatical subject of the verb all coincide, as in the preceding example. The result is that the subject *normally* precedes the verb (because the theme must precede the rheme), and generally conveys old information.

The normal word order in an Italian sentence is thus to have the subject (S) preceding the verb (V). In turn, the verb precedes its complement[1] (C); within the complement, the object (O), precedes all other kinds of complement (giving 'SVOC' word order):

Il gergo utilizza la grammatica e la fonetica del dialetto locale.	'The jargon uses the grammar and the phonetics of the local dialect.'
Mio marito aveva un negozietto di alimentari in Trastevere.	'My husband had a little grocery shop in Trastevere.'
L'acqua aveva formato una pozza sul pavimento.	'The water had formed a puddle on the floor.'
Il cancello di ferro con lo stemma degli Alliata Valguarnera era chiuso.	'The iron gate with the AV coat of arms was closed.'

---

[1]The 'complement' may be defined here as any element, other than the subject, which 'completes' the verb phrase, such as the object of the verb ('Bill sees <u>the dog</u>'), a prepositional phrase ('Bill lives <u>in Italy</u>') or a clause ('Bill sees <u>that the dog is here</u>').

Bear in mind that the situation is different where clitic (unstressed) object pronouns are concerned, because they precede or follow the verb according to the special rules given in 6.3. Also, Italian does not normally express *subject* pronouns (cf. 6.1), with the result that sentences often begin with a verb where English has a subject pronoun before the verb (cf. *Gianni parla francese* 'G speaks French' but *Parla francese* 'He speaks French').

Consider also:

Aprirà la serie il simpaticissimo Braccobaldo, con la storia di Braccobaldo pompiere. Seguiranno poi altri popolari personaggi.	'The series will be opened by the lovable Braccobaldo, with the story of Braccobaldo the fireman. Other popular characters will follow.'

The themes of these sentences are really 'opening the series', and 'what follows'; the subjects of the verb constitute the new information about who it is that will 'open the series' and 'follow'.

There is a class of verbs in which the subject and the theme do not normally coincide, in which the subject is characteristically part of the rheme and where, consequently, the subject normally follows the verb. The relevant verbs are ones in which the theme can be understood as a 'place' or 'scene', and the subject provides the information about what happens there. The English equivalents are often expressible (if only in elevated registers) as 'there + verb + subject'. Among these verbs are those expressing 'arriving',[2] 'appearing', 'entering onto the scene', 'happening', 'occurring', 'being lacking', also 'being sufficient/enough', etc.:

Nel frattempo arrivarono i risultati dell'autopsia: erano proprio state trovate tracce di eroina nel sangue.	'Meanwhile the results of the autopsy came through/there arrived the results of the autopsy: traces of heroin had been found in the blood.'
Apparvero due strane forme.	'Two strange shapes appeared.'/'There appeared two strange shapes.'
Passarono ancora circa due mesi senza nessuna notizia di Nino.	'About another two months went by/ There went by another two months without any news of N.'
Entrarono Nino e un altro.	'There came in N and somebody else.'
Scoppiò una bomba in Piazza Navona.	'A bomb exploded/There exploded a bomb in Piazza Navona.'
Vanno sui giornali nomi del genere e noi due, con le nostre belle facce, nemmeno in TV.	'Names like that get in the papers/ There appear in the papers names like that and we two with our pretty faces don't even get on TV.'
È successo un incidente gravissimo.	'An extremely serious accident has occurred.'/'There has occurred an extremely serious accident.'
Non si può far finta che non sia successo nulla.	'We can't pretend nothing has happened.'

---

[2] Contrast *arrivare* with *partire* 'leave'. Most Italians feel that the subject most naturally precedes *partire* (e.g., *Mario è partito* 'M has left'). It is significant that it is correspondingly difficult (but not impossible) to use 'there' in English. Compare 'There arrived a friend of mine' with 'There left a friend of mine.'

È accaduto quello che più temevo.	'What I was most afraid of has occurred.'
Mancano ancora settemila lire.	'7000 lire is still missing.' / 'There is still 7000 lire missing.'
Basteranno tre litri di latte.	'Three litres of milk will be enough.'
Basta nominare la donazione di organi per suscitare discussioni.	'It's enough to mention organ donation to arouse debate.'

Most verbs of this kind belong to the class which also takes *essere* as auxiliary (see 14.20). But a few, such as *telefonare* 'telephone', *suonare* 'ring', 'call', which take *avere*, commonly behave in a similar way:

—*Ci sono notizie?*	'Any news?'
—*Ah, sì, ha telefonato il sindaco.*	'Oh, yes, the mayor phoned.'

Verbs such as *mancare* 'be lacking (to someone)', *servire* in the sense 'be of use (to someone)', *piacere* 'be pleasing (to someone)', *dispiacere* 'be displeasing (to someone)' tend to have as their in-built 'theme' the person or thing who experiences the lack, usefulness, (dis)pleasure, etc.; here again the grammatical subject usually follows:

A Giorgio manca il passaporto.	lit. 'G lacks his passport.'
A me servono le sue impressioni.	'His impressions are of use to me.'
A Carla piacevano moltissimo le mele.	'C liked apples a lot.'

But the position of the subject is very dependent on context. Even in verbs where the subject normally follows the verb, the subject may constitute the 'theme', by virtue of having previously been mentioned:

—*Che ha fatto Nino?*	'What did N do?'
—*Nino è entrato.*	'N came in.'

Here *Nino è entrato* is a reply to a question *about Nino*, and *è entrato* is the rheme, the new information *about Nino*. Note the impossibility, in English, of using 'there' to translate the above example ('What did Nino do? *There came in Nino'). Further examples are:

Ci dissero di aspettare ancora due mesi. Ma i due mesi passarono senza nessuna notizia di Nino.	'They told us to wait another two months. But the two months went by without any news of N.'
Tutti temevano una esplosione, e infatti dopo qualche giorno la bomba è scoppiata.	'Everyone was afraid of an explosion, and after a few days the bomb did go off.'
Lui denuncia le 'manovre dall'esterno'. Ma i kamikaze arrivano dai campi profughi di Gaza . . . [Pan.]	'He denounces "manoeuvres from outside". But the suicide bombers are coming from the refugee camps of Gaza . . .'

The last example shows that a 'theme' need not have been *explicitly* mentioned before. The example appears in an article concerning, among other things, 'suicide bombings', but the word *kamikaze* ('suicide bomber') has not been explicitly mentioned before.

17.2 Left-marked word order: *Un caffè lo prenderei proprio volentieri!* 'A coffee I'd just love', etc.

When an element of the sentence other than the grammatical subject is the theme, that element is moved, or 'dislocated', to the 'left' of the sentence. It needs to be said, however, that Italian makes relatively little use of one 'left-moving' structure much favoured by English, namely passive constructions where the object of the verb is moved to subject position and becomes the subject of the verb. For example, to emphasize the object *la mia macchina* in a sentence like *Un sasso ha colpito la mia macchina* 'A stone hit my car', Italian could have, as we shall see, *La mia macchina l'ha colpita un sasso*, lit. 'My car hit it a stone', or *La mia macchina, un sasso l'ha colpita*, lit. 'My car, a stone hit it.' A sentence like *La mia macchina è stata colpita da un sasso*, corresponding to English 'My car was hit by a stone', would be a relatively unlikely option (see further 14.32 for restrictions on what can undergo passivization in Italian).

A sentence with 'normal' word order is:

> *Dario ha conosciuto Francesca Duranti a New York lo scorso aprile.* 'D met FD in New York last April.'

Here the 'theme' is Dario, and the rest of the sentence tells us something about Dario. But in the following, phrases expressing place and time are moved to the beginning of the sentence, making them the theme. What follows tells us something *about* what happened in New York last April:

> *A New York lo scorso aprile Dario ha conosciuto Francesca Duranti.* 'In New York last April D met FD.'

while the following makes 'last April' the theme, and tells us *about* last April:

> *Lo scorso aprile Dario ha conosciuto Francesca Duranti a New York.* 'Last April D met FD in New York.'

Left-dislocation mostly affects direct and indirect objects, prepositional complements, and whole clauses. If a direct object is dislocated, what we may term a 'trace'[3] of it is normally 'left behind' in the form of a clitic pronoun accompanying the verb from which the direct object has been removed:

> *Quelle lacrime lei le piangeva per Rosario.* 'She was shedding those tears for R.'
> *Questa cedevolezza credo proprio di averla presa tutta dalla parte Alliata.* 'I really think I got all of this yielding quality from the Alliata side.'
> *Tutte le sue giornate, essa le cominciava al risveglio delle sei.* 'All her days she started with the six o'clock alarm call.'
> *Un appello al buon senso glielo ha lanciato anche Berlusconi.* 'B too sent out to him an appeal for common sense.'
> *Che il Parlamento difficilmente avrebbe approvato la legge, lo sapevano tutti.* 'That Parliament was unlikely to pass the law, everybody knew.'

---

[3]'Trace' is a transparent and appropriate term. It is important to stress, however, that we are *not* using it here in the technical sense which it has in generative linguistic theory, of a phonetically null element supposedly occupying the place from which a syntactic element has been moved.

Dislocating the direct object without leaving behind a clitic 'trace' implies a contrast between the direct object and something else, which may even be unexpressed:

Minori meditazioni, ma altrettante *emozioni, provoca la vista di Alberobello.*	'The sight of A provokes lesser meditations, but just as many emotions.'

Compare also the following examples, where the first implies a contrast (say, 'I knew granddad Enrico but not my other granddad'), and the second merely suggests that *il nonno Enrico* has already been mentioned, that it is *il nonno Enrico* we are talking about:

Il nonno Enrico sono riuscita a conoscere *prima che morisse.*	'Granddad E I did get to know before he died.'
Il nonno Enrico sono riuscita a conoscerlo *prima che morisse.*	'I got to know granddad E before he died.'

The pronoun *ne* is used as the 'trace' if the object of the verb is a 'partitive' plural (cf. 4.20), or if it is a singular 'mass' noun (in these constructions, the partitive or mass nouns may be preceded by *di*). As some of the examples below show, 'pronominalized adjectives' (i.e., adjectives used as pronouns, with meanings like 'red ones', 'yellow ones'), are frequently found in such constructions:

Ma (di) città, ne avete vedute?	'But cities you've seen some of?'
(Di) pasta ne mangio poca.	'Pasta I don't eat much of.'
(Di) riso ne vorrei un chilo.	'Rice I'd like a kilo of.'
—*Ha delle rose rosse?*	'Do you have red roses?'
—*(Di) rosse non ne ho,*	'Red ones I don't have, but there are
ma ce ne sono di gialle bellissime.	some lovely yellow ones.'

But the trace is *lo, la,* etc. if the noun is a 'countable' singular noun:

—*Ha una rosa rossa?*	'Do you have a red rose?'
—*Rossa non l' ho, ma ce ne sono di gialle* *bellissime.*	'A red one I don't have, but there are some lovely yellow ones.'

and the trace is *li, le* when a plural noun is 'restricted' by an adverbial expression:

Caramelle buone come queste, le troverete *solo da Guglielmo.*	'Sweets this good you'll only get at G's.'

Pronominal quantifiers ('none', 'nobody', 'nothing', 'all', etc.) never have a trace clitic:

Nessuno ho visto fuori.	'Nobody did I see outside.'
Niente ti ho portato.	'Nothing have I brought you.'
Tutto ho capito.	'Everything I have understood.'

If the dislocated element is a direct object first or second person singular pronoun, in colloquial speech it tends (in central and southern Italy) to be preceded by the preposition *a*, even though it is the direct object:

A me non mi toccano.	'Me they won't touch.'
A te hanno invitato?	'Did they invite you?'

If the left-dislocated element is an indirect object pronoun, the use of the clitic trace is limited to the informal level, and usually to spoken language:

'A me', dichiarò Nonna Dinda, 'mi piace *di più Rossella.'*	'"I like R better," declared Granny D.'

Such structures may be more acceptable where the indirect object is a noun:

A Mario queste cose non gli piacciono.   'M doesn't like these things.'

The indirect object tends to appear in sentence-initial position with so-called 'psychological' verbs such as *piacere* 'be pleasing', *interessare* 'interest', *sembrare* 'seem', *soddisfare* 'satisfy', *importare* 'matter', and with *mancare* 'be lacking':

A Ninnarieddu poco importava, in realtà, che crollasse la casa.   'N didn't really much care about the house collapsing.'

A lui non piaceva affatto trovarsi in laguna.   'He did not at all like being in the lagoon.'

A Satori mancava l'ultima falange del mignolo sinistro.   'S was missing the last segment of his left little finger.'

Complements preceded by prepositions can be dislocated:

Anche con Michele, però, Rosetta andava d'accordo fino a un certo punto.   'With M too, though, R got along up to a point.'

Di Camilla Cederna leggevo tutto.   'I read everything by CC.'

Sulla bomba di Roma Fini ha parlato da leader.   'About the Rome bomb F spoke like a leader.'

Con le bombe non si scherza.   'You don't mess around with bombs.'

Noi a un pastrocchio così non parteciperemo mai!   'We'll never take part in a mess like that!'

E, su quella brutta storia che l'ha portata per più di due mesi in carcere, nell'estate scorsa, quale presunta protagonista di un traffico internazionale di droga, Gioia Maria Tibiletti, attrice e produttrice cinematografica, oggi va all'attacco.   'And over that nasty episode that brought her more than two months in jail, last year, for having a supposed leading role, for once, in an international drug-trafficking operation, GMT, a film actress and film producer, is today going onto the attack.'

Complements preceded by prepositions take clitic 'trace' pronouns according to the following scheme:

● *Di* and *da* + noun = *ne*:

Di Marco non mi importa/non me ne importa niente.   'About M I care not a bit.'

Della presenza di Ida, rimasta un poco indietro al limite della rampa, non s'interessava [or non se ne interessava] nessuno.   'Nobody was yet concerned about the presence of I, who had remained a little behind at the edge of the ramp.'

Da Roma non posso/non ne posso certo tornare in serata.   'Rome I certainly can't get back from during the evening.'

● *In* and *su* have trace *ci* (rarely *vi*):

Nel salotto ho messo/ci ho messo il sofà del nonno.   'In the living room I've put grandfather's sofa.'

Su questo argomento non trovo/ci trovo niente da dire.   'On this matter I find nothing to say.'

● *Con* + noun has trace *ci* (never *vi*):

Con Chiara andrei/ci andrei volentieri al cinema.   'With C I'd gladly go to the cinema.'

Per + noun never has a trace clitic:

Per i suoi amici lei darebbe l'anima.   'For her friends she'd give her life.'

Time expressions, adverbs and whole adverbial expressions tend to be in initial position and never take a trace clitic pronoun:

Il giorno seguente, io mi svegliai alle prime luci.	'The next day I woke up at the crack of dawn.'
D'estate è bello restare fuori fino a tardi.	'In the summer it's nice to stay out till late.'

Left-dislocation can also apply to adjectives. In the following example, the adjective *sereno*, once mentioned, becomes the theme:

Ma non è un uomo sereno. Sereni erano i suoi padri, i grandi padri borghesi che creavano la ricchezza. Sereni sono i proletari che sanno quel che vogliono [. . .] Sereni sono i sovietici, che hanno deciso tutto e ora fanno la guerra con accanimento e metodo . . . [Cal.]	'But he is not a serene man. His forefathers were serene, his great bourgeois forefathers who created wealth. The proletarians who know what they want are serene. The Soviets, who have decided everything and are now doggedly and methodically waging war, are serene . . .'

More than one element of a sentence can be left-dislocated. For example:

Al medico quel piede glielo dovresti far vedere.	'You ought to show that foot to the doctor.'
Il pacco a Roma ce lo manderanno domani.	'They'll send the parcel to Rome tomorrow.'

To take the first example, it is implicit that both the doctor, and the foot, have already been mentioned, or are obvious from the general context. For example, the conversation may have been about the doctor, and the speaker may have noticed (even without it being mentioned) that the addressee has a wounded foot. So 'doctor' and 'foot' constitute 'givens', and are also the themes. The 'rheme', what is being said about the doctor and the foot, is then that the addressee should have it examined by him.

17.3 Cleft sentences: *È a Roma che andrei proprio volentieri!* 'It's Rome I'd really like to go to!'; *È stato Paolo a dirlo* 'It was Paul who said it', etc.

The theme of a sentence is not necessarily 'old' information. A common device, where the theme actually constitutes something 'new', in contrast with what may be expected from context, is the 'cleft' structure:

Stamattina è arrivato Paolo. Ma era Lucia che aspettavamo, non Paolo.	'This morning Paolo came. But it was Lucia we were expecting, not Paolo.'

In cleft structures the sentence or clause commences with *essere* followed by a noun or pronoun (with which *essere* agrees for number and person) and by either *che* + verb or an infinitive. A 'cleft' variant of a sentence such as *L'emozione mi aveva chiuso la gola* 'The excitement had choked me' would be *Era l'emozione che mi aveva chiuso la gola* 'It was the excitement that had choked me'. Some other examples are:

Era il vento che faceva suonare il campanello a tutte le ore.	'The wind was what was making the bell ring at all hours.'

Era lui che mi raccontava di Fila che si era fatta mettere gravida a quindici anni dal cognato.	'It was he who was telling me about F getting pregnant by her brother-in-law at fifteen.'
È con Bertinotti che si è verificata la scissione di Rifondazione.	'It was with B that the split-up of Rifondazione occurred.'
È per i suoi figli che sopporta ancora il marito.	'It's for her children that she still puts up with her husband.' / 'Her children are why she still puts up with her husband.'
Sono gli italiani che si opporranno alla proposta.	'It's the Italians who will oppose the proposal.'
Siete voi che l'avete detto.	'It's you who said it.'
È te⁴ che cerchiamo.	'It's you we're looking for.'
È domani che dobbiamo partire.	'It's tomorrow we have to leave.'

As the translations above show, equivalent structures exist in English, although clefting seems to be a more frequently and naturally used device in Italian than in English.

In the cleft structures, *essere* is most commonly[5] in the present, imperfect or future tense forms, while the verb following *che* expresses most of the information about the tense, etc., of the event. The alternative type of cleft structure is *essere* + subject noun/pronoun + *a* + infinitive. *Essere* is placed at the beginning of the sentence and the subject noun or pronoun is followed by an infinitive, usually of the 'simple' kind (in other words, 'analytic' infinitives of the type *aver detto, essere venuto* are rare).[6] This construction is particularly preferred where the action expressed by the verb is voluntary or intentional on the part of the subject (so that *È stato Mario a morire* 'It was M who died', or *È stato l'albero a cadere* 'It was the tree that fell', both sound odd: *È Mario che è morto* and *È l'albero che è caduto* would be preferred):

Sarà il comitato a decidere.	'It'll be the committee that decides.'
Sarebbe stata Carla a intervenire.	'It would have been C that intervened.'
Non venga a dirci che è il buon Dio a infilargli la carta falsa nel polsino.	'Let him not try and tell us that the good Lord is slipping the false card up his sleeve.'
Era stato Russo [. . .] a rinvenire quella cosa [. . .], a rivoltarla, a nascondere il volto col suo fazzolettone rosso, a ricacciare con un rametto le viscere dentro lo squarcio del ventre, a coprire poi la ferita con le falde verdi del cappottone. [Lam.]	'It was R who had found the thing, turned it over, hid its face with his big red handkerchief, pushed its innards back into the gash in its stomach with a stick, covered the wound with the green skirts of his greatcoat.'

Note that it is also possible, in the infinitival cleft construction, to have the infinitival clause as the theme, with the main verb and subject as the rheme:

---

[4]Note that when non-subject *me* and *te* are focused in cleft constructions, the verb is third person singular *è*. But in the plural, even where the pronoun is the object, the verb agrees with it in person and number: *Siete voi che cerchiamo*, etc.

[5]But other tenses are not impossible: *È stato lui che si è rifiutato di venire* 'It was he who refused to come'.

[6]But a sentence such as *È stato Gianni a aver detto che non c'era bisogno di portare la tenda!* 'It was G who had said that we didn't need to bring the tent' is possible.

A innestargli nella parete addominale quella pompa, e a collegarla con due tubi al ventricolo sinistro, è stata l'équipe diretta da Adalberto Grossi.	'The pump was grafted onto his abdominal wall, and connected by two tubes to the left ventricle, by the team directed by AG.'

17.4 The 'hanging theme' (*Il nostro professore, gli dobbiamo moltissimo* '[As for] our teacher, we owe him a lot')

An important device for creating something 'new' as the theme, restricted largely to spoken (but not necessarily colloquial) language, is what is sometimes called the 'hanging theme' – where (usually) a noun or noun phrase is mentioned, then followed by a sentence commenting on it. It can sometimes be difficult to distinguish this from 'dislocation' to the left of the sentence, but hanging themes are different from left-dislocated elements in that they have not been 'extracted' from the sentences with which they occur. Rather, the 'hanging theme' is mentioned, and is then followed by a complete, free-standing, sentence commenting on the theme. For example, one could not say **Il nostro professore, dobbiamo moltissimo* because **dobbiamo moltissimo* is not a well-formed sentence in its own right (*dobbiamo moltissimo* requires an indirect object complement). Likewise, in *Al nostro professore gli abbiamo parlato molto* 'We have spoken a lot to our teacher', we have a clear left-dislocation. But with the hanging theme the theme need not bear any of the markers (such as prepositions) of the role which it plays inside the sentence; so *Il nostro professore, gli abbiamo parlato molto* is clearly a 'hanging theme' structure, there being no indirect object preposition before *il professore*. And as long as the following sentence is grammatically correct, it need not contain any clitic trace of the hanging theme. So one could say any of:

Il nostro professore, gli dobbiamo moltissimo.	'[As for] Our teacher, we owe him a great deal.'
Il nostro professore, dobbiamo moltissimo a lui.	'[As for] Our teacher, we owe him a great deal.'
Il nostro professore, dobbiamo moltissimo a questo splendido uomo.	'[As for] Our teacher, we owe that splendid man a great deal.'

Some more examples are:

Roma, non ci vado mai.	'[As for] Rome, I never go there.'
Roma, non vado mai in questa città.	'[As for] Rome, I never go to that city.'
La chiesa, ne sono uscite solo due persone.	'[As for] The church, only two people came out of it.'
Il professor Santangelo, la nostra università gli deve molto.	'[As for] Professor S, our university owes a lot to him.'
Mia madre, queste cose non le piacciono.	'[As for] My mother, she doesn't like these things.'

The subject of a sentence can also become a hanging theme:

Michele, lui non ci parlava affatto con gli sfollati perché, come ci disse, non voleva farsi cattivo sangue.	'Michele never ever spoke to mad people because, as he told us, he didn't want to incur ill-feeling.'

Note that the hanging theme is always followed by a comma in writing.

17.5 The type *Dormire, dormo poco*

Characteristic of spoken language is a construction, rather similar to the 'hanging theme' construction, in which the main verb of a clause or sentence is first given in the infinitive form before that clause or sentence. It is difficult to find any natural-sounding equivalent for this in English, but the force of *Dormire, dormo poco* is something like 'As for sleeping, I don't sleep much'. Some examples are:

Mangiare, ha deciso di non mangiare più.	'As for eating, he's decided not to any more.'
Chiacchierare, in chiesa la gente non ci chiacchiera più.	'As for chattering, people don't chatter in church any more.'

17.6 Right-marked word order: *Lo prenderei proprio volentieri, un caffè* 'I'd really like to have a coffee'

The subject, the direct object, most complements and whole clauses can also be dislocated to the right of the sentence. Right-dislocation tends to have the function of 'echoing' or recalling to attention something regarded as 'given' or 'understood' in the preceding part of the sentence. The complements of the verb are usually also marked by an appropriate clitic trace, in the same way as for left-dislocation:

Ha mangiato tutto, il cane.	'He's eaten everything, the dog has.'
Mi ha amato molto, mia madre.	'She loved me a lot, my mother.'
Ora sono contenta di averla visitata l'ultima volta poco prima che morisse, la zia Saretta.	'Now I'm pleased to have visited her for the last time not long before she died, aunt S.'
L'hanno chiamato al telefono, il magistrato.	'They called the magistrate to the phone.'
Oggi non potrei più entrarci, nella vecchia villa di famiglia.	'Today I could no longer enter the old family villa.'
E, dopo, gliele avrebbe anche date, a Vinicio.	'And, then, she'd even give V them.'

The last two examples show that the *order* of elements in a right-dislocated sentence may be the same as that of a normal sentence. The dislocation is apparent, rather, in the fact that right-dislocated structures always consist of *two* 'tone groups'. In *Oggi non potrei più entrarci, nella vecchia villa di famiglia*, the phrases *Oggi non potrei più entrarci* and *nella vecchia villa di famiglia* each have the same intonation patterns as if they were uttered separately, in isolation; there may even be a slight pause between them.[7]

17.7 Subordinate clauses: the subordination marker *che*. So *che viene* 'I know that he's coming', etc.

Che is the word which usually corresponds to English 'that' in introducing subordinate clauses:

---

[7]Rather similar is the intonation pattern of an English sentence such as 'He's very happy, isn't he' where both parts normally have the same intonation as the independent utterances 'He's very happy' and 'Isn't he?'

Dico che è vero.	'I say (that) it's true.'
Sapevo che avevi paura.	'I knew (that) you were afraid.'
Credo che lo abbia.	'I think (that) he has it.'
Temo che non venga.	'I fear (that) he won't come.'

As these examples show, while in English is often possible to omit 'that', the presence of *che* is virtually obligatory in Italian (you cannot say **Dico è vero*). In late medieval Italian, however, omission of *che* was common, and could apply even more extensively than omission of 'that' in modern English. A few remnants of this older situation survive (optionally) into the modern language. Italian occasionally allows omission of *che* particularly in clauses introduced by verbs of opining, seeming, requesting, hoping and fearing, notably *parere* 'seem', *volere* 'want', *pregare* 'pray' and *credere* 'believe', *sperare* 'hope' (note that these verbs are characteristically followed by a subordinate clause in the subjunctive, see 15.40–2):

Pare lo facciano apposta.	'It seems they're doing it deliberately.'
Soggiunse che avrebbe preferito non si fosse mai parlato tra noi, di questo.	'He added that he preferred that we had never discussed this.'
Non credo sia distante più di un centinaio di chilometri.	'I don't think it's more than a hundred kilometres away.'
Si spera lo facciano in tempo.	'It is hoped they'll do it in time.'
Telefonò al suo capo pregandolo gli confermasse l'incarico.	'He phoned his boss asking him to confirm his appointment.'

The scope for possible omission of *che* seems to be rather wider in contexts where there is another *che* preceding the subordinate clause:

un albero che aveva dato ordine fosse serbato	'a tree which he had ordered should be preserved'

Omission of *che* tends to be restricted to formal (e.g., bureaucratic or literary usage), and the best advice is always to insert *che* unless one is very confident about the contexts in which it is possible to omit it.

17.8 Infinitives in subordinate clauses: *Voglio partire* 'I want to leave', *Gli ordino di partire* 'I order him to leave'

As in English, the verb of an Italian subordinate clause often appears in the infinitive, sometimes preceded by a preposition (*a*, *di*, etc.).[8] Note that *che* + finite verb, rather than the infinitive, is normally used where the subject of the main verb and that of the subordinate are not the same (i.e., not 'coreferent'). In a sentence such as 'John wanted Philip to go home', the subject of 'go home' – i.e. Philip, the person who will 'go home' – is not the same as the subject of 'want', which is 'John'. But in 'John wanted to go home', the subject of both 'want' and 'go home' is the same, namely 'John', and so we have coreferentiality.

Giovanni voleva tornare subito a casa.	'G wanted to go straight home.'
Credo di essere stato sciocco a dire di no.	'I believe that I have been silly to say no.'

---

[8] For use of the past participle as a virtual subordinate clause, see 15.22.

Penso di essere stato uno stupido a darti retta.	'I think that I was a fool to take notice of you.'
Aldo sapeva di aver lasciato il passaporto a casa.	'A knew he'd left his [A's] passport at home.'
Giovanni voleva che sua moglie tornasse subito a casa.	'G wanted his wife to come straight home.'
Credo che tu sia stato sciocco a dire di no.	'I think you were silly to say no.'
Penso che Luigi sia stato uno stupido a darti retta.	'I think that L was a fool to take notice of you.'
Aldo sapeva che Luigi aveva lasciato il passaporto a casa.	'A knew L had left his [L's] passport at home.'

We suggested in 15.25 that one of the similarities between the infinitive and the subjunctive was that they both tended to express the 'notion' of the verb, rather than any realization of what the verb expresses. Accordingly, in subordinate clauses where an infinitive might normally be expected (because the two subjects are coreferent) an ordinary indicative verb form introduced by *che* can sometimes be employed where the subordinate clause expresses a fact (that one thinks, believes, etc.):

Penso che sono stato uno stupido a darti retta.	'I think/recognize that I was a fool to take notice of you.'

17.9 Verbs taking the infinitive without a preposition: *Devo farlo* 'I must do it', etc.

Modal verbs *dovere* 'have to', *potere* 'be able', *sapere* 'know how to', *volere* 'want', and *osare* 'dare', take the infinitive without a preposition (for the behaviour of auxiliaries and clitics in such constructions, see 6.4, 14.21):

Ho dovuto studiare fino a notte fonda per l'esame di anatomia.	'I had to study into the depths of the night for my anatomy exam.'
Sono potuta andare all'Università per iscrivermi alla Facoltà di Lettere.	'I was able to go to the University to enrol in the Faculty of Letters.'

Verbs expressing liking, preferring, wishing – *volere* 'want', *adorare* 'adore', *amare* 'love', *bramare* 'yearn', 'long', *desiderare* 'desire', *preferire* 'prefer' – are followed by the bare infinitive in the subordinate clause when the subject of the main verb is coreferent with the subject of the subordinate verb. Otherwise they take *che* + subjunctive. Note that the English counterparts of the Italian infinitive are sometimes an infinitive, sometimes the form in '-ing':

La donna voleva soltanto essere lasciata in pace.	'The woman only wanted to be left in peace.'
Come vorrebbe non essere mai salita su quel tetto, non avere mai spiato dentro la stanza di Innocenza, non avere mai respirato quell'aria chiara, velenosa. [Mar.]	'How she would like never to have climbed onto that roof, never to have spied into I's room, never to have breathed that clear, poisonous air.'
Adoro bere il prosecco con gli stuzzichini prima di cena.	'I adore drinking prosecco with appetizers before dinner.'

Nei piccoli paesi, dove si ama mantenere le vecchie tradizioni, tutto il paese partecipa alla festa del patrono.	'In little villages, where people like to keep up the old traditions, everyone takes part in the saint's-day celebrations.'
Nessun attore desidera diventare popolare nel luogo delle vacanze dove cerca solo la tranquillità.	'No actor wishes to become popular in the holiday spot where all he wants is peace and quiet.'

Many 'impersonal' constructions corresponding to English 'it is . . . that . . .', or 'it + verb + that', like *basta* 'it's sufficient', *bisogna* 'it's necessary', *conviene* 'it's appropriate/advantageous', *dispiace* 'it causes regret', *importa* 'it's important', 'it matters' *occorre* 'it's necessary', *piace* 'it's pleasing', *duole* 'it causes grief', *sorprende* 'it's surprising', *è una fortuna/uno scandalo/una vergogna* 'it's good luck/a scandal/a shame'), generally take *che* + subjunctive (see 15.44, 47). But if the subject of the verb in the subordinate clause is 'indefinite personal', i.e., 'one', 'people', (generic) 'you', then an infinitive will be used:

Basta dire che il personaggio centrale, Paula, è una rockstar.	'It is enough to say [that people should say] that the main character, P, is a rock star.'
Nella vita importa essere onesti.	'In life it is important [for people] to be honest.'
Per partecipare al concorso occorre inviare un testo di 30 parole.	'To take part in the competition you [generic] have to send in a 30-word text.'

The bare infinitive[9] is also used after *essere/risultare/sembrare/diventare* + adjective (e.g., *È bello/brutto/divertente/noioso/importante* 'It is fine/nasty/amusing/boring/important'):

È molto importante tornare prima delle nove.	'It's very important to come back before 9.'
Diventava sempre più divertente vederlo ballare.	'It was getting funnier and funnier to see him dance.'
Sembra impossibile immaginarsi una tale situazione.	'It seems impossible to imagine such a situation.'
Era assai deprimente leggere l'elenco dei morti.	'It was extremely depressing to read the list of the dead.'

The infinitive can be used if the person or thing which is the subject of the subordinate clause appears also in the main clause as an indirect object of the main verb:

Gli basta non essere visto.	'It is enough for him that he shouldn't be seen.'
Al direttore non importa guadagnare molti soldi.	'It is not important to the director that he should earn lots of money.'

Similarly, *piacere* 'be pleasing to' takes the bare infinitive if the subject of the infinitive is coreferent with the indirect object of *piacere*, otherwise it takes *che* + subjunctive verb:

---

[9]Note that this fact is often a source of error to those familiar with French. French would normally use *de* before the infinitive. The equivalent of *Il est important de le faire* is *È importante farlo* and not **di farlo*. That said, the . . . *di farlo* type is sometimes encountered in the usage of non-Tuscans (e.g., in the writing of Svevo).

Ad Alberto Sordi è sempre piaciuto farsi una pennichella dopo pranzo.	'AS has always liked to have a snooze after lunch.'

This use of the infinitive is possible even where the person or thing that is the subject of the infinitive is an *implicit* indirect object of the main verb. In the following example, it is implicit that the people for whom 'it is fitting/advantageous' (*conviene*) are 'us' (the subject of the infinitive):

Conviene metterci d'accordo.	'We ought to come to an agreement.'
È divertente essere qui con voi.	'It's fun [for us] to be here with you.'
È stata una fortuna arrivare in tempo.	'It was lucky [for us] we arrived in time.'

Note that the infinitive can never be used in the subordinate clause if the subject is actually present in the subordinate clause:

È bello poter giocare senza pericoli.	'It's nice [for people] to be able to play without danger.'
È una vergogna permettere a tutti l'accesso a siti osceni.	'It's a disgrace to allow [that people allow] everyone access to obscene sites.'

but

È bello che la gente possa giocare senza pericoli.	'It's nice for people to be able to play without danger.'
È una vergogna che Internet permetta a tutti l'accesso a siti osceni.	'It's a disgrace that the Internet allows everyone access to obscene sites.'

17.10 Verbs which take *di* + infinitive in the subordinate clause, when the subject of main verb and subordinate verb are the same. The type *Dice di essere stanco* 'He says he's tired' vs. *Dice che è stanca* 'She says she's tired'

● Declarative verbs (asserting, saying, denying that, etc.):

> *affermare* 'state', *aggiungere* 'add', *annunciare* 'announce', *asserire* 'assert', *comunicare* 'communicate', *confessare* 'confess', *dar segno* 'indicate', *dichiarare* 'declare', *dire* 'say that' or 'say/give order to', *far cenno* 'make a sign that', *giurare* 'swear', *informare* 'inform', *narrare* 'narrate', *negare* 'deny', *persuadere* 'persuade', *promettere* 'promise', *raccontare* 'recount', *riferire* 'report', *rifiutarsi* 'refuse to', *ripetere* 'repeat', *rispondere* 'answer', *rivelare* 'reveal', *sapere* 'know', *scrivere* 'write', *spiegare* 'explain', *urlare* 'yell' (and also *dare notizia* 'give notice', *dare comunicazione* 'announce'), etc.:

Carlo De Benedetti afferma di non aver autorizzato nessuno a fare dichiarazioni a suo nome.	'CDB states that he did not allow anyone to make statements in his name.'
Il comandante USA ha affermato che il suo paese rispetterà gli obblighi conseguenti al trattato con Panama.	'The US commander has stated that his country will respect its obligations arising from its treaty with Panama.'
La curatrice del 'Diario postumo' annuncia di voler rendere pubblici i documenti a Lugano.	'The editor of the "Posthumous Diary" announces that she wants to make the documents public in Lugano.'
La casa editrice, nata nel 1997, ha annunciato che il piano editoriale è ancora in corso di stesura.	'The publishing house, formed in 1997, has announced that the editorial programme is still being drawn up.'

Enrico Micheli dichiara di essere per prima cosa scrittore.	'EM declares that he is first and foremost a writer.'
Umberto Eco dichiara che certi problemi etici sono per lui diventati più chiari dalla riflessione su alcuni problemi semantici.	'UE declares that certain ethical problems have become clearer to him through thinking about some semantic problems.'
Santo giurò di fargliela pagare.	'S swore he'd make him pay for it.'
Sei libri giurano che Diana si convertì all'Islam.	'Six books swear that D converted to Islam.'
Freddamente il capufficio informò il povero Fantozzi di averlo licenziato.	'Coldly the head of the office told poor F that he'd sacked him.'
Il preside informa che la scuola riaprirà il 1 settembre.	'The headmaster announces that the school will reopen on 1 September.'
La scrittrice Laura Restrepo narra nel suo romanzo di avere incontrato un angelo a Bogotà.	'The writer LR narrates in her novel that she met an angel in Bogotá.'
Johnson, medico infettato da HIV, narra a Roma che la battaglia contro il suo AIDS è appena iniziata.	'J, an HIV-positive doctor, states in Rome that the battle against his AIDS has just begun.'
Il ministero ha negato di aver dato finanziamenti alla rivista.	'The ministry denied having given funds to the magazine.'
Maria ha negato che i manoscritti fossero autentici.	'M denied that the manuscripts were genuine.'
Internet Bookshop promette di portare agli italiani un servizio simile a quello della mitica Amazon.com.	'Internet Bookshop promises to bring Italians a service like that of the mythical Amazon.com.'
Veltroni promette che i libri avranno un prezzo fisso.	'V promises that the books will have a fixed price.'
Yasser Arafat, sorvegliato da guardie del corpo armate di mitra, sa di rischiare ogni giorno la vita.	'YA, watched over by machine-gun-carrying bodyguards, knows he risks his life daily.'
Il Narratore sa che Silvia ha paura, pudore di certe sensazioni forti e nuove che prova.	'The Narrator knows that S is afraid, ashamed of certain powerful new sensations she is experiencing.'

- Verbs of believing, doubting, judging, hoping, thinking, suspecting, such as *credere* 'believe', *dubitare* 'doubt', *giudicare* 'judge', *immaginare* 'imagine', *ipotizzare* 'surmise', 'hypothesize', *pensare* 'think', *reputare* 'reckon', *riconoscere* 'acknowledge', *ritenere* 'reckon', *sospettare* 'suspect', *sostenere* 'reckon', *sperare* 'hope', *stimare* 'reckon', *supporre* 'suppose' (also *essere dell'idea/consapevole/ conscio / convinto* 'to have the idea', 'be aware', 'be conscious', 'be convinced', *rendersi conto* 'realize', *avere il dubbio, avere il sospetto* 'have the suspicion'):

Maria Candela è una ragazzina cubana che non ha mai visto il mare ma crede di averne un pezzetto dentro di sé.	'MC is a little Cuban girl who has never seen the sea but who believes she has a piece of it inside her.'
Nella situazione di marginalità del ghetto che lei descrive nel suo libro crede che sia la donna a soffrire di più?	'In the alienation of the ghetto which she describes in her book does she thinks it's women who suffer most?'
Il ragazzo era convinto di avere fatto colpo sulla bella ragazza che lo fissava dalla macchina accanto.	'The boy was convinced he'd scored a hit with the pretty girl staring at him from the car alongside.'
Era un uomo burbero e solitario ed era convinto che ci fosse nell'aria una rivoluzione rurale di grande portata.	'He was a rough, lonely man and was convinced that there was a far-reaching rural revolution in the air.'

Penso di essere stata molto influenzata dai miei genitori almeno fino a quando non mi sono sposata.	'I think I was greatly influenced by my parents at least until I got married.'
Penso che sia difficile sopportare la realtà della vecchiaia, ma anche che sia necessario accettare questo corso naturale delle cose.	'I think it's difficulty to bear the reality of old age, but also that we have to accept this natural course of events.'

- Verbs of feeling, emotion, etc.:

accontentarsi 'to be happy', 'make do with', *arrabbiarsi* 'be angry', *avere paura* 'be afraid', *avere vergogna* 'be ashamed', *avere la sensazione/l'impressione* 'have the sensation/impression', *compiacersi* 'be pleased', *dolersi* 'complain', *fingere* 'pretend', *godere* 'enjoy', *indignarsi* 'be indignant', *lamentarsi* 'complain', *lodarsi* 'be proud', *meravigliarsi* 'be amazed', *minacciare* 'threaten', *onorarsi* 'be honoured', *rallegrarsi* 'rejoice', *rammaricarsi* 'regret', *stupirsi* 'be astonished', *temere* 'fear' (also *provare meraviglia* 'feel amazed', *essere compiaciuto* 'be pleased'):

La donna si accontentò di guardarlo senza dire nulla.	'The woman was content to look at it without saying anything.'
Il prigioniero si accontentò che gli levassero le manette.	'The prisoner was satisfied that they took off his handcuffs.'
Ci si dovrebbe vergognare di aver taciuto per anni.	'One should be ashamed of having been silent for years.'
Angelica si vergognò che il padre l'avesse vista seminuda.	'A was ashamed that her father had seen her half-naked.'
Il padre di Beatrice, seduto sul letto, fingeva malamente di guardare la televisione.	'B's father, sitting on the bed, pretended unconvincingly to be watching TV.'
Michele Serveto finse che la pistola non fosse sua.	'MS pretended that the gun was not his.'
Elia è un uomo che conosce la paura e la sofferenza, e teme di cedere ai sentimenti.	'E is a man who knows fear and suffering, and fears giving in to his feelings.'
I vecchi parlano in fretta perchè temono che l'interlocutore si annoi e se ne vada.	'Old people talk fast because they are afraid that their interlocutor will get bored and go away.'

- Verbs expressing permission, agreement, acceptance, decision, choice: *accettare* 'accept', 'agree', *concordare* 'agree', *convenire* 'agree', *decidere* 'decide', *risolvere* 'resolve', *scegliere* 'choose':

Il mio libro racconta l'esperienza di un senatore che accetta di fare il senatore come una sorta di 'servizio civile' in nome della collettività.	'My book is about the experience of a senator who agrees to be a senator as a kind of "civic duty" in the name of the community at large.'
Jared non accetta che i figli, al ritorno da scuola, continuino ad usare la lingua francese o a vestire con abiti occidentali.	'J cannot accept that his children, on coming back from school, continue to use French or dress in Western clothes.'
Giorgio scandalizzò la famiglia quando decise di lasciare le scuole superiori e di arruolarsi nell'esercito.	'G shocked his family when he decided to leave higher education and enlist in the army.'
Ma la giustizia dei bianchi decide che non può accettare di lasciare fuori un nero, anche se non ci sono prove certe contro di lui.	'But white justice decides that it cannot agree to leave out a black person, even if there is no evidence against him.'

- Verbs of realizing, forgetting, remembering: *accorgersi* 'realize', *capire* 'understand', *dimenticare* 'forget', *rendersi conto* 'realize', *ricordare* 'forget', *trascurare* 'neglect':

Con immensa rabbia Andrea capì di essere stato escluso.	'To his utter fury A realized he'd been left out.'
Si capisce che era una rivoluzionaria, non come tanti altri giovani che ballavano fino all'alba.	'We understand that she was a revolutionary, not like so many other young people who danced till dawn.'
Quando recita Fo fa il pazzo e il buffone, non dimentica mai d'essere su un palcoscenico.	'When he acts F plays the madman and the buffoon, and never forgets he's on a stage.'
Abbiamo forse dimenticato che Buzzati, amato dai lettori, fu snobbato dall'accademia?	'Maybe we've forgotten that B, beloved of his readers, was snubbed by academics?'
Joakim guarda fuori dalla finestra: a un tratto si accorge che c'è un bambino appeso per i calzoni e a testa in giù a un albero del giardino. E poi si accorge di avere soltanto sognato. [www]	'J looks out of the window: suddenly he realizes there's a child hanging head down by his trousers from a tree in the garden. And then he realizes he's only been dreaming.'

17.11 Verbs of asking, permitting, ordering, forbidding, preventing with *di* + infinitive: the type *Chiedo di entrare* 'I ask to come in' vs. *Chiedo che entri* 'I ask him to come in'

With verbs of asking, permitting, ordering, forbidding, preventing, *di* + infinitive occurs in the subordinate clause not only in (the rare) cases where the subject of the subordinate verb is coreferential with the 'that' of the main verb but also where the subject of the subordinate verb is coreferential with the direct or indirect object of the main verb. However, in these latter cases it is equally possible to have *che* + subjunctive verb (e.g., *Preghiamo il Signore di concederci la sua pace* or *Preghiamo il Signore che ci conceda la sua pace* 'We pray the Lord to grant us his peace'). Once again, *di* + infinitive is not possible if the subject noun of the subordinate clause is actually present in the subordinate clause.

- Verbs taking a direct object, and *di* + infinitive: *implorare* 'implore', *pregare* 'pray', 'ask', *supplicare* 'beg', 'beseech':

Beatrice lo aveva implorato a lungo di non abbandonarla.	'B had long implored him not to abandon her.'
Il cieco implorava che gli venisse restituita la vista.	'The blind man begged that his sight be restored.'
Ti prego di venire puntuale alla riunione perchè comincerà alle tre precise.	'I beg you to be on time for the meeting because it'll start at three on the dot.'
Preghiamo che il Signore ci conceda la sua pace.	'We pray that the Lord give us his peace.'
I due vecchietti avevano supplicato il padrone di casa di rimandare lo sfratto.	'The two old folk had begged their landlord to postpone their eviction.'
I prigionieri supplicavano che qualcuno desse loro da bere.	'The prisoners begged someone to give them a drink.'

- Verbs taking an indirect object, and *di* + infinitive: *chiedere* 'ask', *comandare* 'order', *concedere* 'grant', *consigliare*[10] 'advise', *dire* 'tell' [someone to do something], *impedire* 'prevent', *ordinare* 'order', *permettere* 'allow', *proibire* 'forbid', *proporre* 'propose', *raccomandare* 'recommend', *vietare* 'forbid':

A un certo punto il gioco chiede al giocatore di infilare un floppy nel computer.	'At one point the game asks the player to insert a floppy disk into the computer.'
Tutta la comunità europea chiede che le vittime dell'Olocausto vengano risarcite.	'The whole European community asks for the victims of the Holocaust to be recompensed.'
Disse al contadino di aspettare.	'He told/ordered the peasant to wait.'
Disse che il contadino aspettasse.	'He said that the peasant should wait.'
Il sergente comandava al reparto di portare rifornimenti alla prima linea, e di fermarsi solo lo stretto necessario.	'The sergeant ordered the detachment to take supplies to the front line and to stop only as long as absolutely necessary.'
Il merito va tutto al generale Lorenzini, lui per primo comandò che i soldati attraversassero il fiume anziché costeggiarlo.	'All the credit goes to general L, who was the first to order that the soldiers cross the river rather than go along the bank.'
La timidezza gli impedisce di suonare il campanello della porta della ragazza.	'Shyness stops him ringing the girl's doorbell.'
Impedirò ad ogni costo che si porti a termine un'impresa così scellerata.	'I'll do my utmost to stop such a wicked plan being carried through.'
La direttrice del collegio aveva vietato alle educande di affacciarsi alla finestra.	'The college head had forbidden her pupils to lean out of the window.'
La commissione sanitaria aveva vietato che i rifugiati fossero ospitati in case private per paura del contagio.	'The health board had forbidden refugees to be taken into private houses from fear of infection.'
Preso dalle vertigini, lo scalatore si vietò di guardare giù.	'Feeling giddy, the climber would not allow himself to look down.'

Evitare is also followed by *di* + infinitive:

Evita di far perdere tempo alla gente.	'He avoids wasting people's time.'
Evita che la gente perda tempo.	'He avoids people wasting time.'

- If the object of the main verb is 'indefinite personal', i.e., 'one', 'people generally', 'you' (generic), (cf. 6.29, 35) it is usually not expressed at all: e.g., *La sua musica ispira* 'His music inspires [one/people/you]'. If this 'implicit' object is also the subject of the subordinate verb, then *di* + infinitive is used:

Consigliava di non telefonare dopo le nove.	'He advised [people] not to phone after 9.'
Si prega di non entrare nel bar in costume da bagno.	'Please do not enter [lit. 'One begs (people) not to enter'] the bar in bathing costumes.'
Si raccomanda di comporre il prefisso telefonico prima del numero selezionato.	'One advises ['people are advised'] to dial the code before the number selected.'

---

[10]*Consigliare* as well as *ammonire* 'warn', *avvertire* 'warn', *occuparsi* 'be busy', *premurarsi* 'make haste to', *raccomandare* 'recommend', *ricusarsi* 'refuse', *rifiutarsi* 'refuse', *scongiurare* 'beseech', *sforzarsi* 'strive', *supplicare* 'beg', can also take (albeit rarely) *a* + infinitive.

Si raccomanda vivamente di portare con sé tutta la documentazione medica.	'One strongly recommends [people] to bring all their medical documentation with them.'

- When verbs of forbidding and allowing are used in the (third person) passive they are followed by the bare infinitive:

A me ormai adolescente era proibito, ad esempio, sedermi sul divano con le scarpe.	'Even when I was an adolescent I was forbidden [lit. 'it was forbidden to me'], for example, to sit on the sofa with my shoes on.'
Ai ragazzi era stato proibito leggere testi latini in traduzione.	'The boys had been forbidden [lit. 'to the boys it had been forbidden'] to read Latin texts in translation.'

The verb *essere* is often omitted in, for example, official notices expressing prohibition:

Proibito fumare	'No smoking'
Vietato utilizzare, senza permesso, i dati personali dei cittadini.	'Personal data on citizens must not be used without permission.'

- Verbs of 'happening' (*succedere/accadere/avvenire/capitare*) preferably take *di* + infinitive when the subject of the infinitive also appears as the indirect object of the main verb. In other cases, such verbs take *che* + finite verb (for the use of the subjunctive here, see 15.47):

Le accade spesso di svenire.	'It often happens to her that she faints.'
Accade spesso che svenga.	'It often happens that she faints.'
A Maurizio Bettini capita sempre più spesso di vedersi citato nelle pagine culturali dei più importanti quotidiani italiani.	'It often happens to MB that he sees himself quoted on the cultural pages of Italy's major dailies.'
Ti è mai capitato di esserti dovuto vergognare di quello che avevi detto?	'Has it ever happened that you had to be ashamed of what you'd said?'

Here, too, where the indirect object of the verb is 'indefinite personal' ('one', 'people', 'us', etc.), it is left unexpressed, but the *di* + infinitive construction may still be used:

Succede spesso di essere coinvolti in cose più grandi di noi.	'It often happens [to people/us] that they/we are involved in things greater than ourselves.'

17.12 Verbs of stopping/ceasing some activity usually take *di* + infinitive: *Smette di fumare* 'He stops smoking', etc.

Non è mai riuscito a smettere di fumare.	'He's never managed to give up smoking.'
Ho finito di lavorare.	'I've stopped working.'

Finire a exists but means 'to end up . . .-ing': *È finito a vendere giornali* 'He ended up selling papers.'

17.13 Verbs taking *a* + infinitive: the type *Continua a fumare* 'He continues to smoke', etc.

● Verbs indicating beginning, continuing, starting, movement, continuation in a state, succeeding, are followed by *a* + infinitive in the subordinate clause:

accorrere 'come running', *affacciarsi* 'appear at door/window', *affrettarsi* 'hurry', *alzarsi* 'get up', *andare* 'go', *arrivare* 'arrive', *attaccare* 'start', 'set about', *buttarsi* 'throw oneself', *chinarsi* 'bend down', *continuare* 'continue', *correre* 'run', *entrare* 'enter', *fermarsi* 'stop', *giungere* 'reach', *mettersi* 'start', *passare* 'pass', *persistere* 'persist', *precipitarsi* 'plunge', *prendere* 'begin', *proseguire* 'carry on', *recarsi* 'make one's way', *restare* 'stay', *rimanere* 'stay', *ritirarsi* 'withdraw', *ritornare* 'return', *riuscire* 'succeed', *salire* 'go up', *scendere* 'go down', *sedere* 'sit', *seguitare* 'continue', *sostare* 'stay', *spingersi* 'thrust oneself', *stare* 'stand', *tornare* 'return', *trattenersi* 'delay', *venire* 'come', *voltarsi* 'turn':

Tutte le volte che andavo a trovarle attaccavano a chiedermi le ultime novità.	'Whenever I went to see them they started asking me the latest news.'
Annoiato da tutte quelle chiacchiere, Riccardo si mise a guardare fuori.	'Feeling bored with all the talk, R started to look outside.'
Eccitati alla vista dei grandi, i bambini presero a ballare anche loro.	'Excited at the sight of the grown ups, the children started to dance too.'
L'unica ragione per la quale Santo proseguiva a studiare era la paura di deludere i genitori.	'The only reason S went on studying was fear of disappointing his parents.'
Si passa tutta la vita con un'altra persona e non si riesce mai a capire cos'ha nella testa quell'altro.	'One spends all one's life with somebody and never manages to understand what the other person's thinking.'
Tutto il paese era accorso a vedere la scena.	'The whole village had come running to see the scene.'
Affacciati a vedere chi è.	'Come to the door and see who it is.'
La seguiamo in cucina, e lei si affretta a richiudere la porta dietro di noi.	'We follow her into the kitchen, and she rushes to close the door behind us.'
Le donne di casa alla fine del pranzo si alzarono tutte insieme a sparecchiare.	'The maids all got up together after lunch to clear the table.'
Invece di spaventarsi, la bimba si buttò a ridere come una matta.	'Instead of being frightened, the little girl started laughing like mad.'
Emma scese a assicurarsi che il portone fosse ben chiuso.	'E came down to make sure the front door was properly closed.'
È ancora presto, siediti a fare due chiacchiere.	'It's still early, sit down for a bit of a chat.'
Per vincere la tristezza che l'aveva preso all'improvviso, il giovane controvoglia si spinse a uscire.	'To overcome the sadness that had suddenly come over him, the young man forced himself against his will to go out.'
Non stare a perdere tempo!	'Don't stand around wasting time!'
Torniamo a vivere insieme, non sopporto più la tua mancanza.	'Let's live together again, I can't stand you're being away any longer.'
Stupita, Mara si voltò a guardarlo con aria interrogativa.	'M was astonished and turned to look at him quizzically.'

With *condurre* 'lead', *mandare* 'send', *portare* 'bring', *spedire* 'send', *trascinare* 'drag', the subject of the infinitive usually appears as the direct object of the main verb:

Ho mandato Mario a ritirare il pacco alla posta.	'I sent M to get the parcel from the post office.'

Quando saremo fidanzati ufficialmente ti porterò a conoscere la mia famiglia.	'When we're officially engaged I'll take you to meet my family.'
Fosse per me, ti spedirei a zappare la terra, altro che scuola!	'If I had anything to do with it, I'd send you to till the soil, forget school!'
Furibonda la donna l'afferrò per un braccio e la trascinò a vedere quello che aveva fatto.	'In her fury the woman grabbed her arm and dragged her to see what she'd done.'

In the following, the direct object of the main verb is 'indefinite personal' (cf. 6.29, 35), and therefore not expressed:

Il riflettere se esistano 'universali semantici' conduce ad identificare una nozione che appare comune a tutte le culture.	'Reflecting on the existence of "semantic universals" leads us/people to identify a notion which appears common to all cultures.'

- Verbs expressing attitude or striving towards:

abbandonarsi 'abandon oneself', *abituarsi* 'get used to', *accanirsi* 'be dogged in', *adattarsi* 'adapt oneself', *adoperarsi* 'strive', *ambire* 'aim', *aspirare* 'aspire', *attendere* 'wait', *azzardarsi* 'venture', *decidersi* 'make up one's mind to', *esitare* 'hesitate', *far bene/male/presto/tardi/in tempo* 'be good/bad/early/late/in time', *faticare* 'toil', *godere* 'enjoy', *imparare* 'learn', *impegnarsi* 'commit oneself', *indugiare* 'dwell', 'tarry', *insistere* 'insist', *mirare* 'aim', *penare* 'toil', *perdersi* 'lose oneself', *prepararsi* 'prepare', *provare* 'attempt', *rinunciare* 'give up', *risolversi* 'resolve', *riuscire* 'succeed', *sbagliare* 'be wrong', *stancarsi* 'get tired', *tendere* 'tend':

Per Dina è difficile abituarsi a dormire sola la notte.	'For D it is difficult to get used to sleeping alone at night.'
Orribili le immagini degli invasori che si accanivano a torturare gli indigeni.	'How horrible are the images of invaders who were relentless in torturing the natives.'
Mi adatto facilmente a dividere la cucina con i miei ospiti.	'I can easily get used to sharing my kitchen with my guests.'
Lara ambisce a diventare critico d'arte, ma non sa bene di cosa si tratti.	'L aims to become an art critic, but he doesn't really know what it's about.'
Il Bettazzi aspirava davvero ad essere eletto senatore.	'B really aspired to being elected senator.'
Non ti azzardare a venirmi ancora tra i piedi!	'Don't dare get under my feet again.'
Eleonora esitava a dire di sì.	'E hesitated to say yes.'
Fai bene ad andare in palestra, il fisico va curato.	'You're right to go to the gym, you should look after your physique.'
Per l'età ormai faticava ad andare nei campi.	'Due to his age he now found it hard to go to the fields.'
Per imparare a sciare bene non basta il maestro una volta l'anno, ci vuole una pratica costante.	'To learn to ski properly it's no good taking a class once a year, you need constant practice.'
Se ci impegnamo a dare un'ora la settimana del nostro tempo ai malati, ne guadagneremo anche noi.	'If we commit ourselves to giving an hour a week of our time to the sick, we'll gain by it too.'
Non capisco perchè tu debba penare così a fare cose che non ti piacciono.	'I don't understand why you should struggle to do things you don't like.'
Non perderti a fare i giochini al computer, devi lavorare.	'Don't waste time doing computer games, you must work.'
La commissione si prepara ad esaminare il nuovo bilancio.	'The commission is preparing to examine the new balance.'

Berlinguer prova a rialzare il morale degli insegnanti italiani con una circolare di auguri.	'B is trying to raise the morale of Italian teachers with a greetings circular.'
Eltsin rinuncia a chiedere il proseguimento della discussione.	'Yeltsin is giving up asking for the discussion to continue.'
Una nuova indagine riuscirà a chiarire i punti oscuri della faccenda.	'A new investigation will manage to throw light on the obscure points of this matter.'
Il papa ormai si stanca troppo a compiere viaggi intercontinentali.	'The Pope is now getting too tired in making international journeys.'
La letteratura pulp tende ad assumere tinte troppo fosche.	'Pulp literature is tending to take on excessively sinister shades.'

Note however *tentare di* 'attempt to' and *cercare di* 'try to':

Ho cercato di dirtelo.	'I tried to tell you.'

● The following verbs also take *a* + infinitive: *aiutare* 'help', *autorizzare* 'permit', *chiamare* 'summon', *condannare* 'condemn', *convincere* 'convince', *esortare* 'exhort', *incitare* 'incite', *incoraggiare* 'encourage', *indurre* 'induce', 'make [someone do something]', *invitare* 'invite', *obbligare* 'oblige', *persuadere* 'persuade to', *sollecitare* 'entreat'; in these cases the subject of the infinitive appears as the object of the main verb:

Primo ha aiutato Stefano a ripulire la cucina.	'P helped S clean the kitchen again.'
Nessuno ti ha autorizzato a usare il mio telefono senza chiedermelo.	'No one said you could use my telephone without asking me.'
Il giudice chiamò il fratello della vittima a deporre.	'The judge summoned the victim's brother to make a deposition.'
La giuria ha condannato Stevanin a rimanere in carcere.	'The jury condemned S to remain in prison.'

Notice that *insegnare* 'teach' takes an indirect object:

Se la scuola insegnasse ai ragazzi a rispettare la natura, l'ambiente ne guadagnerebbe.	'If schools taught children to respect nature, the environment would be the better for it.'

Some verbs can select a different preposition before the infinitive without altering the meaning. *Vergognarsi* 'be ashamed' can be followed by *a* + infinitive or *di* + infinitive with no substantial difference in meaning:

Mi vergogno di/a uscire malvestito.	'I'm ashamed to go out badly dressed.'

and *avere diritto a* 'have the right to' coexists with *avere il diritto di*:

I mutilati di guerra hanno diritto a entrare senza biglietto.	'The war wounded have the right to enter without a ticket.'
Gli anziani hanno il diritto di usufruire dello sconto ferroviario.	'Old people have the right to take advantage of a discount on the railways.'

Esitare 'hesitate', *perdersi* 'lose oneself', *insistere* 'insist', *sbagliare* 'be wrong' can take *in* or *a* + infinitive with no substantial difference in meaning:

Forse sbaglio a/nel dirti queste cose.	'Perhaps I'm wrong to tell you these things.'

With a few verbs there is a slight difference of meaning:

accennare a + infinitive = 'show signs of'
accennare di + infinitive = 'make a sign', 'signal'

È vero, la crisi del mercato non accenna a regredire, le case editrici continuano a ridurre l'organico.	'It's true, the market crisis shows no sign of retreating; publishing houses are still downsizing their staff.'
Con un rapido movimento degli occhi, l'uomo le accennò di nascondersi.	'With a rapid movement of his eyes, the man signalled to her to hide.'

aspettare a + infinitive = 'wait before doing something'
aspettare di + infinitive = 'expect'

Aspetta ad andartene, non ho ancora finito il discorso.	'Wait before you go, I still haven't finish speaking.'
Cosa si aspetta di ricevere e dare in questa nuova esperienza di docente in una scuola di scrittura?	'What is he expecting to receive and give in the new experience as a teacher in a writing school?'

struggersi a + infinitive = 'do one's utmost to'
struggersi di + infinitive = 'ache to'

È inutile struggersi a lisciarsi i capelli, se sono ricci non c'è niente da fare.	'There's no point in killing yourself trying to get your hair straight; if it's curly there's nothing to be done.'
Caterina si struggeva di vederlo dopo mesi di lontananza.	'C was aching to see him after so many months' separation.'

pensare a + infinitive = 'think about', 'have in mind'
pensare di + infinitive = 'think', 'believe that'

Faceva freddo, ma Carla pensava a entrare in qualche bar, e prendere una bella cioccolata calda.	'It was cold, but C was thinking of going into some bar and having a nice hot chocolate.'
E l'occidente sbaglia se pensa di poterlo esorcizzare con l'universalismo rigido.	'And the west is wrong if it thinks that it can exorcize it with rigid universalism.'

compiacersi a + infinitive = 'do with pleasure'
compiacersi di + infinitive = 'condescend/deign/be pleased to do something'
compiacersi in + infinitive = 'feel pleasure in'

I neoeletti si compiacciono molto ad essere intervistati e leggersi poi sui giornali.	'The newly elected love to be interviewed and then read about themselves in the papers.'
Se tu ti compiacessi di alzare i piedi, potrei spazzare sotto la tavola.	'If you would be so good as to lift your feet, I could sweep under the table.'
La signora Maria si compiacque nel vedere la nipote così ben vestita.	'Madam M felt pleasure in seeing her niece so well dressed.'

17.14 A special use of *a* + infinitive: the type *e Mario a cantare* 'and then Mario started singing'

This is the so-called 'narrative infinitive', comprising subject noun or pronoun + the preposition *a* + infinitive and usually preceded by *a*. Fundamentally, this seems to be an elliptical construction, especially used in the narration of past events, which is roughly equivalent to *e poi cominciò a* . . . 'and then/and immediately he started to . . .':

Lo videro uscire di corsa, e tutti a gridare 'Al ladro!'	'They saw him run out, and everybody shouted "Stop thief!"'
Si sentì sparare, e mia sorella a nascondersi sotto il letto.	'Shooting was heard, and my sister immediately hid under the bed.'

17.15 Verbs taking *dal* or *nel* + infinitive: *Lo scoraggia dal farlo* 'He discourages him from doing it', *Il problema sta nel trovarlo* 'The problem lies in finding him', etc.

Certain verbs take *dal* or *nel* + infinitive (cf. also 15.24). Very often, the corresponding English verbs are followed by 'from', 'off', or by 'in'. Among verbs taking *dal* are: *astenersi* 'abstain from', *cessare* 'cease from', *cominciare* 'begin with/by', *desistere* 'desist from', *guardarsi* 'steer clear of', *tornare* 'come back from', *scoraggiare* 'discourage from':

Lo voleva scoraggiare dall'affacciarsi alla finestra.	'She wanted to discourage him from showing his face at the window.'

Among verbs taking *nel* (which also normally admit *a*) are *consistere* 'consist of', *esitare* 'hesitate in', *perdersi* 'lose oneself in', *sbagliare* 'be wrong in', *stare* 'be', 'lie in'. Many expressions comprising nouns or adjectives are followed by *nel* + infinitive (much like English 'in . . . ing'):

Il problema sta nell'identificare i veri colpevoli.	'The problem lies in identifying the real culprits.'
Forse ho sbagliato nell'accettarlo.	'Maybe I made a mistake in accepting it.'
Provammo molta gioia nel vederli giocare.	'We had great joy in seeing them play.'

17.16 Purpose and consecutive clauses introduced by *per* and *da*: the types *L'ha fatto per avvertirti* 'He did it (in order) to warn you', *Bevve tanto da ubriacarsi* 'He drank so much that he got drunk'

Subordinate clauses expressing purpose or goal, such as are introduced in English by 'in order to', 'so that' or 'to', are discussed in 15.29 (dealing with the appearance of subjunctives in such clauses). However, when the subject of these clauses is coreferential with that of the main clause, the subordinate clause is usually introduced by *per* or *in modo da* followed by an infinitive.

Bisogna credersi davvero belle per partecipare a Miss Italia.	'You have to think you're really beautiful (in order) to participate in Miss Italy.'
Per arrivare in fondo al vicolo, i raggi del sole devono scendere diritti rasente le pareti fredde.	'(In order) to reach the end of the lane, the sun's rays have to come hard down the sides of the cold walls.'
Si è dimostrato molto generoso nel ritirarsi per preparare loro la strada.	'He showed himself to be very generous in withdrawing (in order) to prepare the way for them.'
Lo si distrae dai suoi dipinti bellicosi per chiedergli se è quella la stanza dove fa l'alba per guardarsi i programmi televisivi di tutto il mondo. [Ogg.]	'One distracts him from his warlike paintings (in order) to ask him if that is the room where he stays up till dawn (in order) to watch TV programmes from all over the world.'

In fact, the subject of main and subordinate clause need not be strictly coreferential, for the subject of the subordinate often appears as a direct or indirect object of the main clause:

È giusto concedere la libertà a Craxi per venire a curarsi?	'Is it right to give C his liberty so that he can come and be cured?'
Gli americani [. . .] mi misero subito davanti a un microfono per raccontare quello che avevo passato. [Ogg.]	'The Americans immediately put me in front of a microphone to tell what I'd been through.'

Note the expression *fare per* 'to make (as if) to':

Il duca fa per bussare ma la porta gli viene spalancata.	'The duke makes to knock/is about to knock, but the door is thrown open before him.'

Consecutive clauses introduced by degree phrases of the type 'so much that', 'enough to', 'such as to' take *che* + finite (usually indicative) verb if the subjects are not coreferential:

Ti sono così fedele [. . .], che se il Signore volesse togliermi al mondo dei viventi e portarmi via, continuerei ad esserlo anche dal Cielo. [Ogg.]	'I'm so faithful to you that if the Lord wanted to remove me from the world of the living and carry me away, I'd still be faithful even from heaven.'
Si è talmente/tanto/così arrabbiato che gli abbiamo sparato addosso.	'He got so angry that we shot at him.'

But if the subjects are coreferential, they take *da* + infinitive (cf. also 11.28):

Si è talmente arrabbiato da spararci addosso.	'He got angry enough to shoot at us.'
Non era così alto da poterci vedere.	'He wasn't so tall as to be able to see us.'
Qua c'è tanto oro da accontentare tutti.	'Here there's enough gold to satisfy everyone.'
Era una minaccia tale da far venire i brividi.	'It was a threat to send shivers down your spine.'

Occasionally, the degree expression can be omitted, for example:

Qua c'è oro da accontentare tutti.	'Here there's enough gold to satisfy everyone.'

Troppo, however, is usually followed by *per*:

Fa troppo caldo per uscire.	'It's too hot to go out.'

17.17 Subordination with verbs of seeming and appearing: *Sembra che cada, Sembra cadere, Gli sembra di cadere*, etc.

Verbs of seeming and appearing, *sembrare* 'seem', *parere* 'seem', 'appear', *risultare* 'turn out', 'prove to be', display all of the following subordination patterns:

(i) *Sembra che Giovanna cada.* 'It seems that G's falling.'
(ii) *Gli sembra che Giovanna cada.* 'It seems to him that G's falling.'
(iii) *Giovanna sembra cadere.* 'G seems to be falling.'
(iv) *Giovanna gli sembra cadere.* 'G seems to him to be falling.'

(v) *A Giovanna sembra di cadere.*   'It seems to G that she [i.e., Giovanna] is falling.'

(vi) *Sembra di cadere.*   'It seems to one that one is falling.'

These different possibilities are less complicated than they may appear. Types (i) to (iv) are in fact pretty straightforward. The difference between (i) with *che* + subjunctive and (iii) with the bare infinitive is more or less that between English 'It seems that Giovanna is falling', and 'Giovanna seems to be falling.' There is very little difference in meaning, and the two types are often interchangeable. Types (ii) and (iv) are merely variants of types (i) and (iii), in which the person to whom it seems that Giovanna is falling (here expressed as the indirect object *gli*) is specified. Type (v), where the subordinate infinitive is introduced by *di*, is in fact very similar to (iv), except that in this case the subject of the subordinate verb is coreferential with the indirect object of the main verb (so the 'faller' is also the person to whom it seems that she is falling). As we see in 17.8, where the subject of the subordinate verb is coreferential with the indirect object of the main verb, *di* + infinitive is normally used. Type (v) is especially common with first person subjects, even though the corresponding English structure is often 'I/We seem + infinitive':

> *Mi sembra di essere in difficoltà.*   'I seem to be in difficulty.'
> *Ci sembrava di avere un problema.*   'We seemed to have a problem.'

Alternatives such as *Sembra che io sia in difficoltà* or *Sembro essere in difficoltà* would indicate simply that this appears to be the case to others, but not (necessarily) to me. So one might say:

> *Sembra che io sia in difficoltà, lo so, ma vi*   'It seems I'm in difficulty, I know, but I
> *giuro che non è vero.*   swear to you it's not true.'

Type (vi) is actually a variant of type (v), except that in this case the indirect object of the main verb (which is coreferential with the subject of the subordinate) is an 'indefinite personal' form ('one', 'people', etc.), and is therefore unexpressed (cf. 6.29). So the sense of, say, *Sembra di essere in difficoltà* is 'It seems [to one] that one is in difficulty'. This tends to be more naturally expressed in English as 'One seems to be in difficulty.'

17.18 The bare infinitive with subject noun after verbs of asserting and believing: *Crede essere il Barolo superiore a tutti gli altri vini* 'He believes Barolo to be superior to all other wines', etc.

In Italian, rather as in English, there is a construction with verbs of asserting and believing in which the subject of a subordinate infinitive also appears to be the direct object of the main verb (cf. English 'He believes Barolo to be superior to all other wines', etc. = 'He believes that Barolo is superior . . .'). Note that the subject of the infinitive generally follows the infinitive and that, if it is a pronoun, it takes a subject form.

> *Afferma esser stata io la colpevole.*   'He asserts me to have been the guilty one.'

Si ritenne essere la figlia colpevole.	'One held the daughter to be guilty.'
Dichiarava essere invalidi tutti i documenti rilasciati prima del 30.	'He declared all documents issued before the 30th to be invalid.'

In any case, this construction is largely limited to formal, elevated, registers, and the type *Crede che il Barolo sia superiore a tutti gli altri vini* would be much more likely in ordinary discourse.

The infinitive is not used where the main verb is passive. Such expressions as 'He is believed to be honest' or 'She is known to be a liar' would be expressed in Italian by using an 'indefinite personal' construction in the main clause: *Si crede che sia onesto*, *Si sa che è una bugiarda*.

17.19 Adjectives as subordinate clauses: the type 'I believed him innocent' *Lo credevo innocente*

A characteristic of formal and literary discourse (with parallels in English), occurring after main verbs of believing, knowing and asserting, is the type *Credevo Mario innocente* or *Lo credevo innocente* meaning 'I believed M [to be] innocent', 'I believed him [to be] innocent'. Similarly:

Non li aveva chiamati perché li sapeva già morti.	'She hadn't called them because she knew them [to be] already dead.'
Riteneva invalide tutte le sue obiezioni.[11]	'He held all his objections [to be] invalid.'
Dichiarò aperta la sessione.	'He declared the session [to be] open.'

17.20 Adjectives as subordinate clauses: the type 'He made the document public' *Ha reso pubblico il documento* and 'He dyed the sheet red' *Ha tinto il lenzuolo di rosso*, etc.

The structure 'verb + noun phrase + adjective' occurs in English in a causative structure such as 'He made the text intelligible'. In such cases, Italian usually employs not *fare* but *rendere*:

La curatrice del 'Diario postumo' annuncia di voler rendere pubblici i documenti a Lugano.	'The editor of the "Posthumous Diary" announces that she wants to make the documents public in Lugano.'
Poi abbiamo reso l'ambiente più caldo sostituendo i mobili moderni con quelli antichi.	'Then we made the ambience warmer by replacing modern furniture with older.'
Quest'amicizia però mi rende ancora più libero nel criticarli.	'But this friendship makes me even freer in criticizing them.'

But English has a wide range of similar-looking constructions in which the main verb expresses an activity carried out on the noun, and the adjective expresses a state of the noun resulting from that action, such as 'He dyed the sheet red', 'He sucked the orange dry', etc. Not only can such structures not be

---

[11]For the position of the adjective in this and the next example, see 3.31. *Riteneva tutte le sue obiezioni invalide* is a possible alternative, but would be liable to be interpreted as 'He retained all his invalid objections.'

translated literally into Italian (you would not say *Ha tinto il lenzuolo rosso*, etc., for this would simply mean 'He dyed the red sheet'), but there is just no simple equivalent structure in Italian. Here are some possibilities:

'He dyed the sheet red.'	*Ha tinto il lenzuolo di rosso.*
'He sucked the orange dry.'	*Ha succhiato l'arancio fino in fondo.* [lit. 'He sucked the orange down to the end.']
'She hammered the nail flat.'	*Ha battuto il chiodo fino a renderlo piatto/fino ad appiattirlo.* [lit. 'She beat the nail until she made it flat/until she flattened it.']
'She beat her brother unconscious.'	*Ha picchiato suo fratello fino a fargli perdere i sensi.* [lit. 'She beat her brother until she made him lose his senses.']
'She licked the spoon clean.'	*Ha leccato il cucchiaio fino a pulirlo completamente./Ha pulito il cucchiaio con la lingua.* [lit. 'She licked the spoon until she cleaned it completely.'/'She cleaned the spoon with her tongue.']
'They shot him dead.'	*Lo uccisero a colpi di pistola.* [lit. 'They killed him by blows of pistol.']
'He shouted himself hoarse.'	*Ha gridato fino a perdere la voce.* [lit. 'He shouted until he lost his voice.'] or *Si è sgolato.*

It is clear from the suggested translations of the English that there is a variety of equivalent Italian structures. Verbs of dyeing, colouring, perfuming, etc., are usually followed by *di* + a *noun* indicating colour, etc.; while *rosso* in the example given above may look like an adjective, it is in fact a noun derived from the (masculine) adjective (cf. *Mi piace il rosso* 'I like [the colour] red' – cf. 3.15; 20.1) and therefore does not vary for gender:

Hanno dipinto la loro barca di bianco.	'They painted their boat white.'

In other cases, a common device involves *fino* ('up to', 'until') + *a* + a verb (in the infinitive) which expresses the change of state undergone by the noun (*pulire* 'clean', *appiattire* 'flatten', *far perdere i sensi* 'cause to lose [someone's] senses', etc.). The example with *fino in fondo* shows the use of a prepositional phrase *in fondo* 'to the bottom', 'to the end', to capture the notion of sucking the orange dry. At other times it may be possible to find a single verb which captures the whole notion, like *sgolarsi* 'to shout oneself hoarse' or *denudare* 'to strip naked'. Phrases such as *a forza di* (cf. 11.22) 'by dint of' or *a colpi di*, lit. 'by blows of', can often be made good use of in these contexts:

A forza di martellare, riuscì a raddrizzare il chiodo.	'He hammered the nail straight.' [lit. 'By dint of hammering, he managed to straighten the nail.']

17.21 Adjective + preposition + infinitive: the type *Sono felice di vederti* 'I'm happy to see you', *Sono fortunata a incontrarti* 'I'm lucky to meet you', etc.

An adjective in the main clause may introduce a subordinate clause whose verb is in the infinitive and preceded by a preposition. Although the corresponding

English structure is often an infinitive, many of the examples below will show that the English equivalent sometimes consists of preposition + '...-ing' (or even 'that' + verb). A point to bear in mind is that where English has preposition + '...-ing', Italian normally has preposition + infinitive.[12] In Italian an infinitive regularly appears where the subject of the main clause and that of the subordinate are coreferential (17.8). Adjectives can be roughly divided into two groups: those taking *di* + infinitive, and those taking *a/in/per/da* + infinitive; some can belong to both groups.

17.22 Adjectives taking *di* + infinitive in the subordinate clause

Adjectives of feeling, emotion and capability take *di* + infinitive when the subject of the main and subordinate clauses is coreferential (i.e., represent the *same* person or thing), e.g.:

Gianni è felice di essere a casa.	'G is happy to be at home.'
Ho visto Gianni felice di essere a casa.	'I've seen G happy to be at home.'

The underlined adjectives below may also take *per* + 'analytic' infinitive (i.e., infinitive *avere* or *essere* + past participle) when the reason which has 'caused' the feeling/emotion is emphasized, as in:

addolorato 'sorry', 'regretful', *ansioso* 'anxious', *avido* 'avid', *bisognoso* 'needful', *bramoso* 'yearning', *capace* 'capable', *certo* 'certain', *colpevole* 'guilty', *compiaciuto* 'pleased', *consapevole* 'aware', *contento* 'happy', *convinto* 'convinced', *cosciente* 'aware', *curioso* 'curious', *degno* 'worthy', *desideroso* 'desirous', 'wishing', *disperato* 'desperate', *dispiaciuto* 'displeased', *entusiasta* 'enthusiastic', *felice* 'happy', *fiducioso* 'confident', *fiero* 'proud', *grato* 'pleased', *immemore* 'unmindful', *impaziente*, 'impatient', *incapace* 'incapable', *irritato* 'irritated', *libero* 'free', *lieto* 'happy', *memore* 'mindful', *mortificato* 'mortified', *onorato* 'honoured', *orgoglioso* 'proud', *rammaricato* 'regretful', *responsabile* 'responsible', *riconoscente*, 'grateful', *sicuro* 'sure', *smanioso* 'eager', *soddisfatto* 'satisfied', *sorpreso* 'surprised', *sospetto* 'suspected', *stanco* 'tired', *stufo* 'fed up', *superbo* 'proud', *suscettibile* 'susceptible', *timoroso* 'fearful'

Sono veramente addolorato di non vederlo più.	'I'm truly sorry not to see him again.'
Sono veramente addolorato di/per non averlo potuto salutare prima che partisse.	'I'm truly sorry not to have been able to say goodbye to him before he left.'
Era sempre teso, avido di primeggiare, gli si leggeva in volto l'ambizione.	'He was always tense, avid to be top, ambition was written in his face.'
I Fenici, poiché non erano politicamente forti, furono capaci di sviluppare una invidiabile rete di commerci.	'The Phoenicians, not being politically strong, were able to develop an enviable trading network.'
Annalisa era certa che nessuno riuscisse a capire i suoi pensieri più nascosti, ma la sua amica migliore era sicura di averne letto almeno qualcuno.	A was sure that nobody could divine her innermost thoughts, but her best friend was sure that she had read at least one of them.'
All'improvviso si sentì colpevole di/per averla coinvolta in un problema più grande di lei.	'He suddenly felt guilty of having involved her in a problem greater than her.'
Il commissario Montalbano non fu contento di essere svegliato in piena notte.	'Commissioner M was not pleased at being woken in the middle of the night.'

---

[12]An exception is 'by + ...-ing', which is normally a gerund (see 15.20).

Deborah Compagnoni, convinta di avere ormai la vittoria in tasca, si concesse finalmente un sorriso.

'DC, convinced she now had victory in her pocket, at last allowed herself a smile.'

La psicoterapia non può funzionare se il paziente non è cosciente di essere al centro di un processo lungo e doloroso.

'Psychotherapy won't work if the patient is not aware that they are the centre of a long and painful process.'

Visto quello che era successo, l'uomo non si sentiva degno di rivolgerle la parola.

'In view of what had happened, the man did not feel worthy to speak to her.'

Sono dispiaciuta di/per avere avuto un atteggiamento freddo verso di te.

'I'm sorry for having had a cold attitude towards you.'

Felice, grata per/di essere stata invitata, la ragazza prese posto al tavolo d'onore.

'Happy, grateful for having been invited, the girl took her place at the head table.'

I giudici considerarono il vecchio scrittore inabile, ma non incapace di intendere e volere.

'The judges held the old writer to be incapacitated, but not incapable of understanding and exercising his will.'

È un compagno di lavoro difficile, sembra sempre irritato di essere qui.

'He's a difficult workmate, he always seems annoyed at being here.'

Se ti sei stufato sei libero di andartene anche subito.

'If you've had enough you're free to leave straight away even.'

I vecchi, memori di aver avuto un peso determinante nella costruzione del paese, non sanno rassegnarsi a questo sfacelo.

'Old people, mindful of having had a determining influence in the construction of the country, cannot resign themselves to this debacle.'

Sono onorato di/per aver avuto la possibilità di conoscerla.

'I'm honoured to have had the chance to meet you.'

Tengo molto ad essere presentata come una scrittrice russa e sono doppiamente orgogliosa di portare un pezzettino del mio paese in Italia.

'I'm very keen on being presented as a Russian writer and I'm doubly proud to be bringing a little piece of my country to Italy.'

Venne via in furia, rammaricata di/per averle detto delle sciocchezze.

'She came away in fury, remorseful at having said foolish things to her.'

I criminali nazisti sono giudicati ormai da tutti responsabili di aver perpetrato i più infami delitti.

'Nazi criminals are now universally judged responsible for having perpetrated the most wicked crimes.'

Occorre sempre presentarci all'appuntamento sicuri di convincere il nostro esaminatore che sappiamo.

'We must always turn up for the appointment certain that we'll convince our examiner that we know our stuff.'

I rappresentanti devono essere convincenti ma controllati, non mostrarsi maniosi di convincere il cliente della bontà dei loro prodotti.

'Representatives must be convincing but restrained, and not show themselves over eager to convince their clients of the goodness of their products.'

Soddisfatto per avergli detto finalmente quello che pensava, Luca uscì sbattendo la porta.

'Feeling satisfied at finally having told him what he thought, L went out slamming the door.'

Sono sorpresa di sentirti dire queste cose.

'I'm surprised to hear you say these things.'

With *certo, consapevole, convinto, cosciente, sicuro*, an indicative verb form introduced by *che* can sometimes be employed when *di* + infinitive would be expected, to express the factual realization of the event instead of just the 'notion' of the verb:

Sono sicuro che sono stato uno stupido a darti retta.

'I'm sure I was a fool to take notice of you.'

The use of *che* + indicative instead of *di* + infinitive is growing in informal registers, but it is advisable to avoid it:

Sono disperato che non posso venire.	'I'm desperate at not being able to come.'
Sono preoccupato che non ho un lavoro.	'I'm worried that I haven't a job.'

The following set phrases are used when one is introduced to people for the first time:

Lieto/felice/onorato di conoscerla.	'Pleased to meet you.'

17.23 Adjectives taking *a/in/per/da* + infinitive

Adjectives belonging to this group can sometimes take more than one preposition. Most take *a*, but they can also take *in* or *per* according to the characteristics of the action expressed by the infinitive. A few adjectives can even exhibit the full range of prepositions with little substantial difference in meaning:

Gianni è bravo a scrivere romanzi.	'G is good at writing novels.'
Gianni è bravo nello scrivere romanzi.	'G is good in/at writing novels.'
Gianni è bravo per scrivere romanzi.	'G is good for writing novels.'

The preposition *a* often denotes destination or goal (e.g., *Vado a Roma* 'I'm going to Rome', *Lo do ai ragazzi* 'I give it to the boys'). So where an adjective takes the preposition *a* + infinitive, it is often (but not always) the case that the action expressed by the infinitive represents an end point, a goal, a purpose; adjectives of attitude, aptitude, or striving towards are commonly followed by *a* + infinitive. The English equivalent is often 'to', 'at', 'on' or 'for' + '. . .-ing'.

abile 'able(to)', 'clever (at)', *abituato* 'accustomed (to)', *adatto* 'suitable (for)', *affaccendato* 'busy (at)', *assorto* 'absorbed (in)', *attento* 'intent (on)', *atto* 'apt (for)', *avvezzo* 'accustomed/wont (to)', *bravo* 'good (at)', *costretto* 'obliged/forced (to)', *deciso* 'decided/resolved (to)', *dedito* 'dedicated (to)', *destinato* 'destined (for)', *diretto* 'directed/aimed (at)', *disadatto* 'unsuitable (for)', *disponibile* 'available (for)', *disposto* 'prepared/ready (for)', *esitante* 'hesitant (to)', *fortunato* 'lucky (in)', *idoneo* 'suitable (for)', *impegnato* 'busy (at)', 'committed (to)', *impotente* 'powerless (to)', *inabile* 'incapable (of)', *inadatto* 'unsuited (for)', *incline* 'inclined (to)', *insufficiente* 'insufficient', 'inadequate (for)', *intento* 'intent (on)', *intenzionato* 'intending (to)', *interessato* 'interested (in)', *lesto* 'quick (to)', *necessario* 'necessary (for)', *occupato* 'busy (at)', *preparato* 'ready (for)', *pronto* 'ready (for)', *propenso* 'inclined (to)', *prossimo* 'near to', 'on the point of', *recalcitrante* 'recalcitrant (to)', *restio* 'resistant/reluctant (to)', *riluttante* 'reluctant (to)', *rivolto* 'directed (to)', *soggetto* 'subject (to)', *sollecito* 'solicitous (in)', *sordo* 'deaf (to)', *sufficiente* 'sufficient (for)', *teso* 'directed (at)', *valido* 'valid (for)', *veloce* 'quick (to)', etc.

I reparti speciali devono essere abili a intervenire al momento giusto.	'The special units must be capable of intervening at the right moment.'
I veri potenti non si confondono con il popolino, loro sono abituati a cenare in stanze private.	'Really powerful people are not to be confused with the common people, they are accustomed to dining in private rooms.'
Non lo vedo adatto a ricoprire quell'incarico.	'I cannot see he is suitable for undertaking that duty.'
L'espressione del suo viso sembrava assorta a contemplare qualcosa che noi non potevamo vedere.	'The expression on his face seemed engrossed in contemplating something which we could not see.'
Stiamo attenti a non esagerare.	'We are careful not to exaggerate.'

Scrivevo in modo talmente veloce che dopo mezz'ora ero costretto a fermarmi per un crampo alla mano.	'I wrote so fast that after half an hour I was being forced to stop by writer's cramp.'
Annalisa è stata decisa fin dall'inizio a diventare medico.	'A has been determined to become a doctor from the start.'
Donne che amano altre donne stanno uscendo allo scoperto e sono molto meno disposte a tacere la propria verità.	'Women who love other women are coming out and are much less inclined to keep the truth about themselves quiet.'
Non sono mai stata disposta a fare compromessi sui sentimenti.	'I've never been ready to make compromises about my feelings.'
Insomma è stato solo molto fortunato a cavarsela senza un graffio.	'So he was very lucky to get off without a scratch.'

Ordinal numbers, and *solo*, *unico* 'sole', 'only' and *ultimo* 'last', also take *a* + infinitive:

Ma la speranza è l'ultima a morire, in Corso Sempione.	'But hope is the last thing to die, in Corso Sempione.'
La terza a parlare fu Giovanna.	'The third woman to speak was G.'
Il primo viaggiatore a fermarsi a Cannara avrà una brutta sorpresa.	'The first traveller to stop at C will have a nasty surprise.'

A + infinitive is often used, as we have seen, when the verb of the subordinate clause is viewed, broadly, as a goal or purpose. The combination 'adjective + *nel*[13] + infinitive', in contrast, tends to express the state or manner of the subject *in* carrying out the action expressed by the infinitive. Among adjectives that may take *nel* + infinitive are those indicating attitude or capability in doing something: *abile* 'able', *affaccendato* 'busy', *amareggiato* 'bitter', *assorto* 'engrossed', *bravo* 'good', *competente* 'competent', *coraggioso* 'brave', *deciso* 'determined', *efficace* 'effective', *esitante* 'hesitant', *forte* 'strong', *impegnato* 'committed', *lesto* 'quick', *occupato* 'busy', *sollecito* 'solicitous', *veloce* 'fast'. *Concorde* 'agreed' always takes *nel* + infinitive:

Tutti furono concordi nel giudicare un successo il convegno sul Gattopardo *organizzato a New York da Gioacchino Lanza Tomasi.*	'They were all agreed in judging the conference on *The Leopard* which GLT organized in New York a success.'
Riccardo Chiaberge è abilissimo nello scegliere i personaggi più interessanti da intervistare.	'RC is very able in choosing the most interesting personalities to interview.'
Corrado Stajano è stato un grande scrittore civile della Prima e della Seconda Repubblica, forte e coraggioso nel denunciare i mali della Prima, amareggiato e deluso nel guardare quelli della Seconda.	'CS was a great civic writer of the First and Second Republic, strong and brave in denouncing the ills of the First, bitter and disenchanted in considering those of the Second.'

Contrast also:

Erano tutti d'accordo nel respingerlo.	'They all agreed in rejecting it.'
Erano tutti d'accordo a/per respingerlo.	'They all agreed to reject/on rejecting it.' [goal]

---

[13]*In* followed by an infinitive is always combined with the definite article, see 15.24.

È bravissima a nascondere quel che pensa.	'She's very good at hiding what she thinks.' [goal]
È bravissima nel nascondere quel che pensa.	'She is very good in hiding what she thinks.'

Per is used to emphasize the idea of 'purpose' with adjectives indicating 'to be appropriate/ready/suitable for' like *adatto, appropriato, efficace, necessario, preparato, sufficiente, valido,* etc. The distinction between *a* and *per* is here sometimes akin to that in English between simple 'to' and 'in order to':

Scopo dell'associazione è promuovere e tutelare le condizioni necessarie ad/per assicurare un efficiente servizio di biblioteche.	'The aim of the association is to promote and foster the conditions necessary to/in order to ensure an efficient library service.'
Netscape è pronta a/per lanciare sul mercato nuovi programmi di navigazione.	'Netscape is geared to launch onto the market new navigation programmes.'
Un periodo di tempo così breve non è sufficiente a/per formulare un giudizio sull'attività della ditta in questione.	'Such a short period of time is not enough to/in order to form a judgement on the activity of the firm in question.'

Note that *essere pronto a* can be used for 'be prepared to', 'be ready to', 'be quick to':

Francesca era pronta ad ammettere di avere sbagliato.	'F was quick to admit she'd been wrong.'
Tullio era pronto a svolgere una relazione.	'T was prepared to give a talk.'

Sufficiente 'sufficient' can be followed either by *a* or *da*, with no substantial difference in meaning:

Ho scritto romanzi e racconti in numero sufficiente a/da riempire un intero scaffale.	'I have written novels and stories in sufficient quantity to fill a whole shelf.'

Dal + infinitive (note the presence of the definite article) is used after adjectives like *alieno* literally 'alien', *lontano* 'far', to express 'from ...-ing', an attitude of moral distance from something:

Non preoccuparti, sono lontanissima dal pensar male di te!	'Don't worry, I'm a long way/far from thinking ill of you.'
È un ragazzo timido, alieno dal misurarsi con gli altri, insomma un po' strano.	'He is a shy boy, averse from measuring himself against others, a bit odd really.'

Note also *esser lungi dal* 'be far from' (i.e., 'be uncharacteristic', 'unlikely'):

Era lungi dal dichiararsi colpevole.	'He was far from declaring himself guilty.'

17.24 The type *bello da vedere/a vedersi/a vedere* 'beautiful to see', *facile da dire/a dirsi/a dire* 'easy to say'

Adjectives such as *adatto* 'suitable', *bello* 'beautiful', *buono* 'good', *brutto* 'ugly', *commovente* 'moving', *delizioso* 'delicious', *difficile* 'difficult', *duro* 'hard', *facile* 'easy', *faticoso* 'wearisome', *impossibile* 'impossible', *indecente* 'indecent', *inusuale* 'unusual', *pronto* 'ready', *raro* 'rare', *strano* 'strange', *utile* 'useful', etc., take *da* + infinitive when the action expressed by the infinitive is seen as something that has to be, or will be, 'undergone' by the noun to which the adjective refers:

latte pronto da bere senza farlo bollire	'milk ready to drink without boiling it'
È un sentiero agevole da seguire anche per chi non conosce il luogo.	'It's an easy path to follow even for people who don't know the locality.'
Il gelato di Vivoli è delizioso da gustare in ogni stagione.	'Vivoli ice cream is delicious to taste at any time of year.'
Questa bistecca è dura da masticare.	'This steak is tough to chew.'
Alcuni francobolli sono facili da trovare, altri sono ormai esauriti.	'Some stamps are easy to find, others are now out of print.'
Un temperino è un oggetto utilissimo da tenere in borsa.	'A penknife is a most useful object to keep in your pocket.'

In the above examples the noun which the adjective modifies *undergoes* the action expressed by an infinitive. There is, then, a close similarity between such constructions and passives – cf. *Il latte è bevuto senza farlo bollire* 'The milk is drunk without boiling it', etc. Note, however, that in the *da* + infinitive construction a passive infinitive cannot be used (i.e., one can say *pronto da bere* but never **pronto da essere bevuto*). The passive meaning associated with *da* + infinitive can also be expressed by a passive -*si* (cf. 14.35) attached to the infinitive:

Sono cose difficili da confessarsi a un marito.	'They are difficult things to confess to a husband.'
Le calze elastiche sono indicate da portarsi se si hanno problemi di circolazione.	'Elastic stockings are recommended to be worn if one has circulation problems.'
È difficile da credersi, ma il nuovo Scottex casa è veramente più assorbente.	'It's hard to believe, but new household Scottex really is more absorbent.'

A may be used instead of *da* in *strano a dirsi* 'strange to relate', *terribile a vedersi* 'terrible to see', *brutto a guardarsi* 'ugly to look at', *facile a farsi* 'difficult to do', *difficile a dirsi* 'difficult to say', etc. Here the construction with *a* implies a sort of durativity which is absent in the corresponding sentences with *da*: *strano da dire*, etc. The distinction is not easy to capture in English, but one might (rather awkwardly) paraphrase the *strano a dirsi* type as something like 'strange in the telling', 'difficult in the saying', etc. Note that *facile a* and *difficile a* may readily be used in place of *facile da* and *difficile da*: *È molto facile/difficile a dire* 'It's very easy/hard to say.'

Buono a (or *per*) and *buono da* correspond respectively to 'able to' and 'suitable for':

Non è buono ad allacciarsi le scarpe.	'He's no good at tying his shoelaces.'
Quando si accorse che non era più buono a lavorare come prima, il padrone lo chiamò nel suo ufficio e gli propose di andare in pensione.	'When he realized he was no longer good for work as before, the boss called him into his office, and proposed to him that he should retire.'
È buona da bere quest'acqua?	'Is this water drinkable?'
I cantuccini sono buoni da inzuppare nel vinsanto.	'"Cantuccini" are good for dunking in "vinsanto".'

17.25 Other expressions with *da* + infinitive: *avere da*, *esserci da*

Avere da + infinitive means 'to have to [do something]':

Ho da fare le valigie.	'I have to pack the suitcases.'
Aveva da sbucciare le patate.	'He had to peel the potatoes.'
Hai da fare stamani?	'Have you [something] to do this morning?' / 'Are you busy this morning?'

Esserci da + infinitive is a very common expression meaning roughly 'There is something to be X-ed' or 'One ought to X':

C'è da dire che non ha lavato tutti i piatti.	'It must be said that he hasn't washed all the dishes.'
Qui c'è da riflettere.	'Here we'll have to think.' / 'We ought to think about this.' / 'There's food for thought here.'

For structures of the type *Cerco un libro da leggere* 'I'm looking for a book [which] to read', see 7.27.

17.26 *Di sì* and *di no* as subordinate clauses: *Penso di sì* 'I think so' and *Penso di no* 'I don't think so'

After verbs of asserting and believing, English frequently uses 'so'. The Italian equivalent is *di sì* where the main verb is positive, and *di no* where it is negative (*di no* also corresponds to English 'not', or in some cases 'not to'):

—*Non ci sono dei tratti autobiografici nel suo personaggio?*	'Aren't there autobiographical traits in his character?'
—*Sì, credo proprio di sì.*	'Yes, I do believe so.'
—*Non ci sono dei tratti autobiografici nel suo personaggio?*	'Aren't there autobiographical traits in his character?'
—*No, credo proprio di no.*	'No, I really don't believe so.'

Note also the following, where *di no* stands for *non uscire*:

Non so se uscire o no. Forse è meglio di no.	'I don't know whether to go out or not. Perhaps it's better not to.'

17.27 Forms of the infinitive in subordinate clauses: *Credo di farlo* vs. *Credo di averlo fatto*

Where the main clause expresses belief, knowing, assertion, seeming (e.g., *credere, dire, sembrare*), an infinitive in the subordinate clause may either be the ordinary 'synthetic' infinitive (e.g., *fare, arrivare*) or the 'analytic' form, consisting of auxiliary verb + past participle (e.g. *aver fatto, essere arrivato*). If the infinitive of the subordinate clause expresses an event *prior* to that of the verb of the main clause, then the analytic type is used; if the verb of the subordinate clause expresses an event not prior to that of the main clause, the ordinary infinitive is used. Generally, the analytic infinitive in a subordinate clause corresponds to the *passato prossimo*, *passato remoto* or pluperfect:

So che l'ho fatto.	'I know I've done it.'
So di averlo fatto.	'I know I've done it.'
So che lo feci.	'I know I did it.'
So di averlo fatto.	'I know I did it.'
So che lo avevo fatto.	'I know I'd done it.'
So di averlo fatto.	'I know I'd done it.'

If the verb of the main clause is in a past tense form, then the analytic infinitive corresponds to a pluperfect verb form:

Sapevo che lo avevo fatto.	'I knew I'd done it.'

Sapevo di averlo fatto.	'I knew I'd done it.'
Seppi/Ho saputo che lo avevo fatto.	'I learned I'd done it.'
Seppi/Ho saputo di averlo fatto.	'I learned I'd done it.'

but, where the verb of the subordinate clause is not prior to that of the main clause, the ordinary infinitive will be used:

Sapevo che lo facevo/avrei fatto.	'I knew I was doing/would do it.'
Sapevo di farlo.	'I knew I was doing/would do it.'

If the verb in the subordinate clause is a future perfect, only the *che* + verb construction is possible:

So che lo avrò fatto prima di domenica.	'I know I'll have done it by Sunday.'

Other examples:

Sento di aver dimenticato qualcosa.	'I feel I've forgotten something.'
Mi accorgo di essere stato ingannato.	'I'm realizing I've been deceived.'
Dopo aver ammesso di aver detto in passato di essere 'nato cristiano' . . . [Gin.]	'After admitting saying in the past that he had been "born a Christian" . . .'
Attorno però sembrava essersi costruito un nuovo rispetto.	'But all around he seemed to have constructed for himself a new respect.'

For the use of the 'analytic' infinitive after modal verbs such as *dovere* and *potere* see 15.50, 54.

Where the subordinate clause is introduced by an adjective, the analytic infinitive (preceded by *di* or *per*) is also used to emphasize the cause or origin of the state expressed by the adjective. See 17.23 for examples.

17.28 Perceptual structures: the types *Vedo Gianni scendere dal treno* 'I see G get off the train', *Sento Chiara chiamare Riccardo* 'I hear C call R', *Guardo aprire il regalo a Maria* 'I watch M open the parcel', *Sento criticare il professore* 'I hear the teacher criticized', *Sento Gianni a cantare* 'I hear G singing', etc.

Verbs of perception (e.g., *ascoltare* 'listen', *avvertire* 'notice', *guardare* 'watch', *notare* 'note', *osservare* 'observe', *scorgere* 'make out', *spiare* 'spy', *percepire* 'perceive', *sentire* 'hear', 'feel', *udire* 'hear', *vedere* 'see') and some other verbs which are not, strictly speaking, perception verbs but contain a perceptual element, such as *immaginare* 'imagine', *cogliere (con l'udito)* 'catch (the sound of)', *ricordare* 'remember', *seguire (con gli occhi)* 'follow (with one's gaze)', and also *ecco* (see 17.30 below), may be followed by a subordinate clause whose main verb is in the infinitive:

Sento cantare Gianni OR *Sento Gianni cantare.*	'I hear G sing(ing)'.

or by a subordinate clause containing a finite verb (i.e., a verb form that indicates person and tense); here two types of structure are possible:

Sento Gianni che canta.	'I hear G singing.' [lit. 'I hear G who is singing.']
Or *Sento che Gianni canta.*	'I hear that G is singing.'

We examine first the constructions using the bare infinitive: *Sento Gianni cantare* and *Sento cantare Gianni* (the type *Sento Gianni a cantare* and *Sento Gianni che canta* will be discussed later). It should be noted at the outset that the Italian infinitive in these constructions may correspond to three different verb forms in English (in ways that will become clear below); namely, the bare verb (*Sento cantare Gianni* can mean 'I hear G sing'), the '. . .-ing'[14] form of the verb (*Sento cantare Gianni* can mean 'I hear G singing') or a past participle where the sense of the infinitive is passive (*Sento cantare la canzone* 'I hear the song sung').

There are two types of perception structure involving the bare infinitive, distinguished not only by structural differences, but also by a nuance of meaning. In what we shall call 'Type 1', what is perceived is a *complete event*; in 'Type 2', what is perceived is primarily an *entity*, and that 'entity' is the person or thing that is the subject of the infinitive. In Type 2 it is not *necessarily* the case that the complete event or action in which that person or thing is involved is perceived as well: it may not be perceived at all, or it may just be in the background.[15]

Type 1 constructions strikingly share properties with causative structures (see 14.25–7). What applies to *fare* + infinitive in causative structures applies equally to perception verb + infinitive:

(i) In Type 1 the subject of the infinitive in the subordinate must always follow the infinitive and cannot intervene between main verb and infinitive:

Causative	Perception structure
Faccio cantare Gianni. 'I make G sing.'	*Sento cantare Gianni.* 'I hear G singing.'

(ii) In Type 1, if the verb in the infinitive also has its own direct object, then the subject of that infinitive must be preceded by the preposition *a*:

Causative	Perception structure
Faccio cantare la canzone a Gianni. 'I make G sing the song.'	*Sento cantare la canzone a Gianni.* 'I hear G sing the song.'
Feci sventolare un fazzoletto a Riccardo. 'I made R wave a handkerchief.'	*Vidi sventolare un fazzoletto a Riccardo.* 'I saw R wave a handkerchief.'

(iii) In Type 1, the verb in the infinitive is *invariant*. It cannot be passivized (you cannot say **Sento essere cantata la canzone* any more than you can say **Faccio essere*

---

[14]For the non-use of the Italian gerund in such constructions, see 15.21.

[15]Such distinctions also exist in English. Contrast the sentences 'I saw John leave the church' and 'I saw John leaving the church'. For most native speakers of English it seems to be the case that what is perceived in 'John leave the church' is a whole event comprising John, an act of leaving and a church; it implies that I saw the church, and John leaving it, just as much as I saw John. In 'I saw John leaving the church' what is perceived is *John*, but the act of his leaving the church was not *necessarily* directly seen as well. Rather, 'leaving the church' constitutes additional information about what John was doing when I saw him (one could quite easily say 'I did see John leaving the church, but I didn't actually see the church').

cantata la canzone), nor can it appear in an analytic (see 14.19) form (you cannot say **Sento aver cantato la canzone a Gianni* any more than you can say **Faccio aver cantato la canzone a Gianni*). Clitic pronouns must always be attached to the perception verb, not to the infinitive:

Causative	**Perception structure**
Gli faccio cantare la canzone. 'I make him sing the song.'	*Gli sento cantare la canzone.* 'I hear him sing the song.'
Glielo feci aprire. 'I made her open it.'	*Glielo vidi aprire.* 'I saw her open it.'
Lo si farà aprire. 'One will cause it to be opened.'	*Lo si vedrà aprire.* 'One will see it (being) opened.'
L'ho fatta scrivere. 'I had it written.'	*L'ho vista scrivere.* 'I saw it written.'

(iv) In Type 1, if the infinitive is passive in meaning it remains unchanged (as observed above), but the agent of the action may still be indicated by *da* + noun:

Causative	**Perception structure**
Faccio cantare la canzone (da Gianni). 'I have the song sung (by G).'	*Sento cantare la canzone (da Gianni).* 'I hear the song sung (by G).'
Feci sventolare un fazzoletto da Riccardo. 'I caused a handkerchief to be waved by R.'	*Vidi sventolare un fazzoletto da Riccardo.* 'I saw a handkerchief (being) waved by R.'

A very important point to note here is that in such passive constructions, Italian has an infinitive where English may have a past participle. Compare also:

Vedo abbattere gli alberi.	'I see the trees felled.'
Sento criticare il professore.	'I hear the teacher criticized.'

(v) In Type 1, as in causatives, the infinitive cannot be negated (you cannot say **Vedo non cantare la canzone a Gianni* just as you cannot say **Faccio non cantare la canzone a Gianni*).

(vi) In Type 1 a reflexive infinitive is simply not allowed: you cannot say **Ho visto lavarsi Mario* just as you cannot say **Ho fatto lavarsi Mario*. However (and unlike causatives – see 6.15 and 14.26), a 'lexically reflexive' verb, such as *pentirsi* 'repent', always retains its reflexive pronoun:

Causative	**Perception structure**
Faccio pentire Gianni dei suoi peccati. 'I make G repent his sins.'	*Vedo pentirsi Gianni dei suoi peccati.* 'I see G repent his sins.'

Some further examples of Type 1 are:

Nel negozio Maurizio Serretti di Pisa guarda lavorare Adriana: nessuno taglia i capelli come lei!	'In the shop MS from Pisa watches A work: nobody cuts hair like she does.'
Gli spettatori rimasero seduti in silenzio a veder scorrere lentamente le ultime immagini del film.	'The audience remained seated in silence watching the final images of the film slowly go by.'
Mi fa star male veder dare uno schiaffo a un bambino.	'It pains me to see a slap given to a child.'
Ho sentito aprire il portone da qualcuno che non riusciva a trovare la chiave giusta.	'I heard the door being opened by somebody who couldn't find the right key.'

> *Sai che Lucia aspetta un bambino? L'ho sentito dire l'altra sera a casa di Irene.*
>
> 'Do you know L's expecting a baby? I heard about it [lit. 'I heard it said'] the other night at Irene's.'

The main difference in Type 2 structures is that while in Type 1 the perception verb and the infinitive behave rather like an inseparable 'block', in Type 2 the perception verb and the verb in the infinitive behave, in most respects, straightforwardly like two 'normal' and separate verbs. This means that nouns and pronouns (including clitics) which are objects of the perception verb are placed according to the normal rules of object (see 17.1) and clitic placement (see 6.3, 4) in relation to the perception verb. And nouns and pronouns (including clitics) which are objects of the infinitive are placed according to the normal rules of object and clitic placement in relation to the infinitive. The subject of the infinitive may appear either to the left or to the right of the infinitive, according to the normal rules of ordering of verb and subject, and the subject is not preceded by *a* when the infinitive also has a direct object. In a sentence of the type 'I hear Gianni singing the song', 'Gianni' is the object of the verb 'to hear' (as well as being the subject of 'sing the song'), and can therefore appear in the normal object position immediately after the perception verb: *Sento Gianni cantare la canzone* (compare this with Type 1 *Sento cantare la canzone a Gianni*). In Type 2, unlike Type 1, the infinitive can be negated. And, finally, reflexive infinitives are perfectly possible in Type 2.

Some examples of Type 2, with object nouns and clitics in the 'normal' position for the verbs to which they logically belong, possible negation of the infinitive, etc., are:

> *Ho visto Gianni uscirne* OR *Ho visto uscirne Gianni.*
>
> 'I saw G come out of it.'
>
> *Nel negozio Maurizio Serretti di Pisa guarda Adriana lavorare: nessuno taglia i capelli come lei!*
>
> 'In the shop MS from Pisa watches A working [*or* 'as she works']: nobody cuts hair like she does.'
>
> *Vidi Riccardo sventolare un fazzoletto.*
>
> 'I saw R waving a handkerchief.'
>
> *Gli spettatori rimasero seduti in silenzio a vedere le ultime immagini del film scorrere lentamente.*
>
> 'The audience remained seated in silence watching the last images of the film slowly going by.'
>
> *Lo vidi ascoltarla.*
>
> 'I saw him listening to it.'
>
> *Lo sento cantare la canzone.*
>
> 'I hear him sing the song.'
>
> *Tutti i pomeriggi alle 4 vedo i bambini quasi gettare il loro zaino pesante tra le braccia delle madri che li aspettano pazienti.*
>
> 'Every afternoon at 4 I see the children practically fling their heavy backpacks into the arms of their mothers who are patiently waiting for them.'
>
> *Le fiamme erano già alte quando vidi la donna non esitare un momento a gettarsi nel fuoco per cercare di salvare il suo cane.*
>
> 'The flames were already high when I saw the woman not hesitate for a moment before throwing herself into the fire to try and save her dog.'
>
> *Sai che Lucia aspetta un bambino? Ho sentito dirlo l'altra sera a casa di Irene.*
>
> 'Do you know L's expecting a baby?' 'I heard about it [lit. 'I heard it said'] the other night at Irene's.'
>
> *Ho visto molte persone pentirsi troppo tardi di ciò che avevano fatto.*
>
> 'I've seen a lot of people repent too late of what they had done.'
>
> *Ho sentito chiudersi la porta.*
>
> 'I heard the door close [itself].'
>
> *Ho sentito chiudere la porta.*
>
> 'I heard [someone] close the door.'
>
> *Ho visto scriverla.*
>
> 'I saw it written / saw [someone] write it.'

Type 2 shares with Type 1 the inadmissibility of the analytic infinitive (i.e., the infinitive of the auxiliary *avere* or *essere* + past participle), although Type 2 does allow the analytic infinitive in very elevated registers, such as bureaucratic language, but in such cases the perception verb is closer in meaning to 'realize', 'understand', 'learn', and does not involve direct perception of an event or of somebody participating in an event:

Con soddisfazione abbiamo visto le regioni aver acquistato sempre più autonomia.	'We have been pleased to see/learn that the regions have acquired ever greater autonomy.'

The passive of the infinitive (*essere* + past participle) is also not usually found with Type 2. Instead (as with Type 1 and causative verbs) the ordinary infinitive is used – and the passive subject must *follow* the infinitive:

Siamo rimasti sulla banchina finché è stato possibile vedere agitare i fazzoletti.	'We remained on the platform for as long as we could see the handkerchiefs being waved.'
Ma ogni volta che sentiva pronunciare il nome: Cappellini Arturo, Mara trasaliva.	'But whenever she heard the name Arturo Cappellini uttered, M was startled.'

However, Type 2 does allow passivization of the infinitive, preferably by using auxiliary *venire* rather than *essere* + past participle (cf. 14.34):

Guardavo le piante venire abbattute a una a una per far spazio alla piscina, e mi piangeva il cuore.	'I watched the trees being felled one by one to make way for the swimming pool, and my heart wept.'

A variant on Type 1, especially common in informal usage, is perception verb + *a* + infinitive (cf. also 15.21 and 17.29 above). This is equivalent to English 'See [etc.] someone . . .-ing'. Often, the English equivalent may be followed by 'away':

Vedo sempre Carlo a lavare la macchina. È proprio fissato!	'I always see C washing away at his car. He's obsessed!'

17.29 Perception verbs + finite structure: the 'pseudo-relative' type *Vedo Gianni che gioca a tennis* 'I see G playing tennis' (vs. *Vedo che Gianni gioca a tennis* 'I see that G is playing tennis')

Perception verbs may be followed by two kinds of finite structure. One is called the 'pseudo-relative', and in it the object of the perception verb is followed by the relative marker *che* (never by the relative pronouns *il/la quale* – cf. 7.12) + finite verb (cf. 7.21 for a similar structure). The English equivalent is usually of the kind 'perception verb + noun + . . .-ing':[16]

Ho visto Gianni che giocava a tennis.	'I saw G playing tennis.'

---

[16]For the non-use of the Italian gerund in such constructions, see 15.21.

As with the 'Type 2' construction described above, in the pseudo-relative the thing directly perceived is primarily an *entity*, namely the subject of the verb in the subordinate clause, while the *event* in which that subject is involved is not *necessarily* perceived directly. The relative marker *che*, which represents the subject of the finite clause (*Gianni legge*), is coreferent (see 17.8) with the object of the perception verb (*Ho visto Gianni*). Two important respects in which the 'pseudo-relative' is unlike an ordinary (non-restrictive, see 7.4, footnote) relative clause are (i) the fact that in the pseudo-relative there is never any pause or intonation break between the noun and *che* (*Ho visto Gianni* [pause] *che leggeva il giornale* would mean only 'I saw G, who was reading the paper') and (ii), quite unlike ordinary relatives, the noun which is the object of the perception verb can be replaced by a clitic pronoun. The sentence *L'ho visto che leggeva il giornale* can mean only 'I saw him reading the paper' (not 'I saw him who was reading the paper'). Another feature of the pseudo-relative is that the verb in the subordinate clause cannot be negated: one can say *Ho visto Gianni che leggeva il giornale*, but not * *Ho visto Gianni che non leggeva il giornale*. Some further examples of the pseudo-relative construction are:

Dovettero ascoltare il sindaco che ripeteva come sempre le solite stupidaggini.	'They had to listen to the mayor repeating the usual stupidities as ever.'
Improvvisamente sentii Bruno che parlava in diretta da Napoli.	'All of a sudden I heard B speaking live from Naples.'

The type *Ho visto che Gianni leggeva il giornale* should also be mentioned, but it is unproblematic. Its meaning is simply 'I saw that G was reading the paper', rather than 'I saw G read/reading the paper': here the subordinate clause itself is the object of the perception verb, and the construction is much the same as what one finds with *credere che*, *dire che*, etc. (see 17.7, 8). In this case, the perception verb tends to be more akin to 'understand' or 'realize', and does not necessarily express direct perception of an event or of any participant in the event. The pseudo-relative (like Type 1 and Type 2 perception structures, illustrated above) involves *direct* perception of someone or something who is carrying out some action, whereas the type *Ho visto che Gianni giocava a tennis* does not necessarily entail seeing Gianni, let alone seeing anyone actually play tennis (cf. English 'I saw that G was playing tennis – because he left a note telling me that that was what he was doing').

Because the pseudo-relative (like other perception constructions) expresses *direct* perception, the tense of the verb following *che* must always be capable of expressing an action simultaneous with the act of perception (see also 15.12 on past tenses). So after present tense *Vedo* (or *Ho visto* with present time reference – see 15.16), we expect *che* + present tense (*Vedo/Ho visto Gianni che legge il giornale*); after future tense *vedrò*, we expect *che* + future or present tense (for the future value of present tense forms, cf. 15.4) (*Vedrò Gianni che leggerà/legge il giornale*); after past tense *vidi*, *vedevo*, *avevo visto* we expect *che* + imperfect tense (*Vidi/Vedevo/Avevo visto Gianni che leggeva il giornale*).

17.30 The type *Ecco arrivare Gianni* or *Ecco Gianni che arriva* 'Here's G arriving'

A subordinate clause can also be introduced by *ecco*, 'here's', 'there's', or 'and so', followed either by an infinitive or by *che* + indicative verb, according to principles described in 17.7, 8 above:

Ecco D'Alema instaurare un incontro settimanale con i giornalisti.	'There's D'A setting up a weekly meeting with journalists.'
Ecco i miei studenti che giocano a calcio.	'There are my students playing football.'
Si avvicina alla finestra per vederlo attraversare il cortile col suo passo leggero. Infatti eccolo lì che esce dalla porta delle scale.	'She goes up to the window to watch him cross the courtyard with his light step. And there he is coming out of the stairway door.'
Ecco a Trieste cadere accoltellato, per una rapina da 200 mila lire, l'oste Libero Laganis.	'And here we see the landlord LL knifed [lit. 'falling knifed'] in Trieste for a 200 000 lire robbery.'

17.31 The major types of 'conditional' sentences: *Se viene lo vedrai* 'If he comes you'll see him', *Se fosse venuto lo avresti visto* 'If he had come you would have seen him', etc.

Italian 'if'-constructions fall into three main types, according to the kind of verb that occurs in the 'protasis' (the clause that contains the 'if'-element) and the 'apodosis' (the clause that expresses what will happen if the hypothesis expressed in the protasis is fulfilled):

TABLE 17.A

Type 1

Protasis	Apodosis
Se + present indicative	present (or future) indicative
Se ti trova a casa,	*(allora) ti picchia (ti picchierà).*
'If he finds you at home,	(then) he'll beat you.'

TABLE 17.B

Type 2

Protasis	Apodosis
Se + imperfect subjunctive	present conditional
Se ti trovasse a casa,	*(allora) ti picchierebbe.*
'If he found you at home,	(then) he'd beat you.'

TABLE 17.C

Type 3

Protasis	Apodosis
Se + pluperfect subjunctive	past conditional
Se ti avesse trovato a casa,	*(allora) ti avrebbe picchiato.*
'If he had found you at home,	(then) he would have beaten you.'

Type 1, much like its English counterpart, expresses a hypothesis about a present state of affairs which may, or may not, eventually be fulfilled. The result of its fulfilment (in the apodosis) is usually in the *present* tense, especially where the apodosis expresses something which must already be the case, given the fulfilment of the protasis. But a future tense in the apodosis is also possible, particularly when the protasis contains some explicit indication of futurity, such as *domani* or *fra qualche giorno*:

Se volete togliere le rughe dalla fronte, costerà tre o quattro milioni.	'If you want to remove the wrinkles from your forehead, it'll cost 3 or 4 million.'
Se domani fa bel tempo, forse usciremo.	'If the weather's nice tomorrow, maybe we'll go out.'

When *se* means 'if', 'whenever', or 'even though', the apodosis usually contains a present indicative:

Se fa bel tempo, vado al mare.	'If/Whenever the weather's nice, I go to the seaside.'
Se Giulio ha gravi problemi di salute, non è così ammalato come Paolo.	'Even though G has serious health problems, he's not as sick as P.' 'G may have serious health problems, but he's not as sick as P.'
Anche se non si è più giovanissimi, si può cominciare da capo.	'Even if we aren't very young any more, we can start all over again.'

Rather as in English, Type 1 can also have a *passato prossimo* either in the protasis or in the apodosis (or both):

Se hai mangiato troppo, ti senti / ti sentirai male.	'If you've overeaten, you feel/you'll feel ill.'
Se gliel'hai consegnato, hai fatto tutto quello che ti chiede.	'If you've handed it to him, you've done all that he asks of you.'

A variant on Type 1, largely restricted to formal usage, has a future (or future perfect) in the protasis as well. The *se* + future indicates, roughly, that the fulfilment of the hypothesis, if it comes about, is not expected until some later time:

Se l'iniziativa del referendum raccoglierà entro il 30 settembre le 500 mila firme necessarie, la scuola potrà uscire da una situazione che scontenta tutti.	'If the referendum initiative should manage to gather the 500 thousand signatures necessary by 30 September, schools will be able to escape a situation nobody likes.'
Se non si sarà costituito entro il 4 luglio, verrà arrestato.	'If he hasn't turned himself in by 4 July, he'll be arrested.'

Types 2 and 3 both introduce hypotheses that are *counterfactual* (i.e., contrary to fact):

c   Type 2 has an imperfect subjunctive in the protasis and a present conditional in the apodosis: the protasis, despite the presence of an *imperfect* subjunctive, does not refer to past time but implies that the hypothesis is definitely not fulfilled at present, the apodosis stating what would happen were that hypothesis to be fulfilled (e.g., 'If it were here we would be able to see it').

c   Type 3 has a pluperfect subjunctive in the protasis, and a past conditional (cf. 14.10) in the apodosis; it indicates that the hypothesis was never fulfilled, and the apodosis states what would have happened had that hypothesis been fulfilled (e.g., 'If it had been here we would have been able to see it'). Some variants on Type 3 will be discussed later.

Se io fossi ricco, ti comprerei una macchina.	'If I were rich [but I'm not] I'd buy you a car'.
Ti sono così fedele, che se il Signore volesse togliermi al mondo dei viventi e portarmi via, continuerei a esserlo anche dal Cielo.	'I am so faithful to you that if the Lord wanted to take me away from this world [but He doesn't] I'd go on being faithful even from Heaven.'
Se io fossi stato ricco, ti avrei comprato una macchina.	'If I had been rich [but I wasn't] I'd have bought you a car'.
Se me l'avessero detto, sarei venuta subito.	'If they'd told me [but they never did], I'd have come immediately.'
Se ci fossi stato io, non lo avrebbero fatto.	'If I'd been there [but I wasn't], they wouldn't have done it.'

An alternative to Type 3 has a *present* conditional in the apodosis. This is possible where the emphasis is on what the consequence would be *now*, had the unfulfilled condition in the past actually been fulfilled:

Se avessimo preso il treno delle otto, saremmo già a Napoli.	'If we'd taken the 8 o'clock train, we'd already be in Naples.'

Similarly, a Type 2 imperfect subjunctive protasis may be accompanied by a past conditional, when the apodosis expresses what would already have happened if the condition were fulfilled:

Se fosse in Italia, ci avrebbe già contattato.	'If he were in Italy, he would already have contacted us.'

Note that as in English it is possible to coordinate two or more protases without repetition of the se[17]: *Se fa bel tempo e tu sei libero, potremo andare al mare* 'If the weather's nice and you're free, we can go to the seaside.'

17.32 Come se 'as if'

The phrase *come se* 'as if' is always followed either by an imperfect subjunctive (the condition is not realized now and isn't likely to be – see 17.31, Type 2), or a pluperfect subjunctive (the condition was definitely never realized – Type 3):

Cosa crede di fare quel pappagalletto appollaiato vicino al padre, come se lo conoscesse da sempre, come se avesse tenuto fra le sue dita le mani impazienti di lui, come se ne conoscesse a memoria i contorni, come se avesse sempre avuto da appena nato gli odori di lui nelle narici, come se fosse stato preso mille volte per la vita da due braccia robuste che lo facevano saltare da una carrozza. [Mar.]	'What does that little parrot of a man perched next to her father think he's up to, as if he had[18] always known him, as if he had held his impatient hands between his fingers, as if he knew their shape by memory, as if he had always had the smell of him in his nostrils from the moment he was born, as if he had been held around the waist a thousand times by two strong arms helping him jump down from a carriage?'

---

[17]And without special complications of the kind which apply in French.
[18]The use of an imperfect subjunctive in the Italian reflects the fact that the phrase 'He has always known him' would be *Lo conosce da sempre*, with a present tense form (see 15.10).

17.33 The type *Se venivi lo vedevi* 'If you had come, you would have seen him', *Bastava dirlo* 'It would have been enough to say so'

Type 3 (17.31) has a major rival in colloquial, informal usage, which contains an *imperfect indicative* both in the protasis and the apodosis. In fact, in everyday, informal speech, use of the 'pluperfect subjunctive + past conditional type' is generally considered clumsy and stilted, and the imperfect indicative is preferred:

Era meglio se lo lasciavi libero di giocare con gli amici.	'It would have been better if you had left him free to play with his friends.'
= Sarebbe stato meglio se lo avessi lasciato libero di giocare con gli amici.	
Se riuscivamo a metterli a posto, però, Mussolini la guerra non la faceva!	'If we had succeeded in sorting them out, though, Mussolini would never have made war!'
= Se fossimo riusciti a metterli a posto, però, Mussolini la guerra non l'avrebbe fatta!	

The two structures are sometimes combined:

Se lo sapevo, lo avrei fatto.	'If I'd known, I'd have done it.'
Se lo avessi saputo, lo facevo.	

Note that imperfect indicatives are frequently used in verbs like *dovere, potere, occorrere, convenire, bastare, essere sufficiente/possibile,* etc. instead of the past conditional:

Bastava che tu fossi stato un po' più attento!	'It would have been enough for you to be a bit more careful!'
Potevi arrivare prima.	'You could have arrived earlier.'
Conveniva farlo in anticipo.	'It would have been appropriate to do it in advance.'
Era sufficiente dirlo.	'It would have been enough to say so.'

17.34 *Se* = 'despite the fact that', 'even though', 'whenever': the type *Se lo vide, non me l'ha detto* 'If he saw him, he never told me', etc.

It is perfectly possible for *se* to be followed by any past indicative verb form, in cases where *se* introduces not a counterfactual hypothesis but a fact, and its meaning is closer to 'even though', 'despite the fact that', 'given that', or also 'whenever', 'every time that':

Se perfino le levatrice la dava per morta forse era tempo di prepararsi ad andare via con la bambina chiusa nella pancia. [Mar.]	'If/Given/In view of the fact that even the midwife was giving her up for dead perhaps it was time to prepare to leave with the baby still inside her belly.'
Se alzavo gli occhi potevo vedere i cigni.	'If/Whenever I looked up I could see the swans.'
Ma se si era abituata al carcere, non le avrebbe fatto impressione nemmeno il tribunale.	'But if/in view of the fact that she had got used to prison, not even the tribunal would overawe her.'

17.35 The type *Se fosse venuto, lo avrebbe visto* as a 'future-in-the-past: *Sapevo che se fosse venuto, lo avrebbe visto* 'I knew that if he came, he would see it'

The Type 3 construction has a further meaning which is rather different from that of a counterfactual hypothesis in the past. It may simply function as the 'future-in-the-past' structure corresponding to Type 1 (see also 15.2 for the 'future-in-the-past'). Thus a sentence such as *So che se ti trova a casa ti picchia/picchierà* 'I know that if he finds you at home he'll beat you', can be transposed into the past as *Sapevo che se ti avesse trovato a casa ti avrebbe picchiato* 'I knew that if he found you at home he'd beat you'. The following phrases could therefore be interpreted, according to context, either as a 'past counterfactual' or as a 'future-in-the-past':

Si mise le mani sotto i capelli, per vedere come sarebbe stata se li avesse avuti gonfi. [Cas.]	'She put her hands under her hair, to see what she would look like if she wore it bouffant.' OR 'She put her hands under her hair, to see what she would have looked like if she had worn it bouffant.'
Poi conobbi una ragazza, e allora passavo le giornate pensando a come si sarebbe comportata quella ragazza se io fossi diventato imperatore del Messico o se fossi morto. [Gua.]	'Then I met a girl, and I spent my days thinking how that girl would behave if I became emperor of Mexico or if I died.' OR 'Then I met a girl, and I spent my days thinking how that girl would have behaved if I had become emperor of Mexico or if I had died.'

17.36 Other ways of expressing 'if': *Venisse domani, Qualora venisse domani*, etc.

'Counterfactual' hypotheses can also be expressed by the bare imperfect or pluperfect subjunctive forms, without *se*:

Avessi avuto i soldi, non avresti avuto questi problemi.	'Had you had the money, you wouldn't have had these problems.'
Mi dovessero anche torturare, non rivelerei mai il segreto.	'Even if they were to torture me, I'd never reveal the secret.'

This construction can also have an 'optative' force, expressing a wish or a desire:

Fosse vero!	'If only it were true.'
Me l'avessi detto prima!	'If only you'd told me before!'

Alternatives to *se* are *qualora*, *ove*, *laddove* (all restricted to formal styles), and *quando* (which, unlike 'ordinary' *quando*, has the sense 'if and when', 'should it turn out to be the case that' when followed by the subjunctive), and *nel caso (che)*; there is also *casomai*, largely restricted to informal usage. In all these cases the verb of the protasis will be in the subjunctive. The distinction between present and past subjunctives remains as explained above:

Qualora i lettori ritengano l'opera inviata interessante, verranno contattate le case editrici più importanti sollecitando la pubblicazione dell'opera stessa.	'If readers find the work sent interesting, major publishing houses will be contacted requesting that the work itself be published.'
La patente di guida le sarebbe ritirata qualora lei commettesse un'altra infrazione.	'Your driving licence would be withdrawn if you committed a further offence.'
È prevista la chiusura immediata dell'esercizio quando non si compiano le condizioni suesposte.	'It is expected that the business will close immediately if the above mentioned conditions are not met.'
Nel caso senta questi dolori, avvisi subito il medico.	'If you do feel these pains, tell the doctor immediately.'
Nel caso il testo non riuscisse chiaro, mi potresti telefonare.	'If the text were not to be clear, you could call me.'
Casomai succedesse qualcos'altro, mi devi telefonare.	'If anything else should happen, you must phone me.'

17.37 The type *a pensarci* 'if you think about it'

An occasional alternative to *se* + verb is simply *a* followed by the infinitive:

In fondo alle pozze dormono le anguille che a togliere l'acqua si possono acchiappare con le mani.	'At the bottom of the shafts sleep eels, which, if you remove the water, can be caught with your hands.'
A pensarci più a lungo non gli avresti scritto.	'If you'd thought about it longer, you wouldn't have written to him.'
A considerarne lo sguardo, quantunque sia più giovane di lui, la fanciulla sembra incommensurabilmente più anziana.	'If one considers her look, although she is younger than him, the girl seems immeasurably older.'

17.38 Conditional sentences using the imperative + e or o: the type *Stai zitto o ti picchio* 'Shut up or I'll hit you'

As in English, a type of conditional sentence can be formed from an imperative + *e* or *o* + verb:

Leggi questa lettera e ti convincerai che ho detto la verità.	'Read this letter and you'll be convinced that I've been telling the truth.'
Vieni stasera a cena o mi offendo davvero!	'Come this evening or I'll really be offended.'
Alza le mani o sparo.	'Hands up or I shoot.'

18

Negative constructions

For negative pronouns, see 9.11; for negative adverbs and adverbial phrases, 13.17.

18.1 Simple negation with *non*

The usual way of negating a verb is to place *non* immediately in front of it (e.g., *Non parla* 'She does not speak'). In constructions comprising auxiliary verb + participle/gerund, *non* precedes the auxiliary (e.g., *Non ha parlato* 'She has not spoken', *Non sta parlando* 'She isn't speaking'); the only thing that can intervene between *non* and the verb is one or more clitic pronouns: (e.g., *Non me ne parlare* 'Don't speak to me about it'), etc.

The negator normally negates the verb immediately following it, so that there is a clear difference of meaning between the following:

Ho cercato di non correre.	'I tried not to run.'
Non ho cercato di correre.	'I did not try to run.'

But, as in English, Italian has sentences in which placing the negator in front of the main verb, rather than in front of the infinitive, does not necessarily express a different meaning. In other words, negation may be understood as applying to the infinitive, even though the *non* precedes the main verb. This is possible mainly with verbs of seeming or opinion (*credere* 'believe', *pensare* 'think', *aspettarsi* 'expect', *parere*, *sembrare* 'seem', etc.), and verbs of wishing and intending (*intendere* 'intend', *volere* 'want', *desiderare* 'wish', etc.):

Sembra che Alberto non arrivi in tempo.	'It seems that A will not arrive in time.'
Credeva che tu non fossi italiana.	'He thought you weren't Italian.'
Voglio che tu non parta.	'I want you not to leave.'

The effect of placing *non* in front of the main verb is ambiguous, for *non* may be understood as negating either the main verb or the infinitive:[1]

Non sembra che Alberto arrivi in tempo.	'It doesn't seem that A will arrive in time.'/'It seems that A won't arrive in time.'

---

[1] The reading in which *non* negates the first verb is more natural in a context where there is an implicit contrast with another verb; in such cases the verbs may carry particularly strong emphatic stress. For example *Non credeva che tu fossi italiana, lo sapeva* 'He didn't <u>think</u> you were Italian, he <u>knew</u> you were.'

Non credeva che tu fossi italiana.	'He didn't think you were Italian.'/'He thought you weren't Italian.'
Non voglio che tu parta.	'I don't want you to leave.'/'I want you not to leave.'

Not only verbs, but also nouns, adjectives, pronouns, adverbs, prepositional phrases, and quantifiers can be negated by placing *non* in front of them. Quite often this is simply a more emphatic alternative to negating the verb. For example, *non* not only negates but also singles out a constituent when it is contrasted with a following one by the conjunction *ma*:

Vogliono comprare non un appartamento, ma una villa!	'They want to buy not a flat but a villa!'
Alberto mi è sembrato non allegro come al solito, ma quasi triste.	'A seemed to me not cheerful as usual, but almost sad.'
Vado non con la bicicletta, ma in auto, perché fa troppo freddo.	'I'm going not by bike, but by car, because it's too cold.'
Ritengo quest'impresa non impossibile, ma lenta e laboriosa.	'I consider this undertaking not impossible, but slow and laborious.'

Non before an adjective (or past participle) also corresponds to English 'non-' or 'un-' (or to a relative clause of the type 'which/who is not . . .'), as well as 'not':

Scegli i bocci non aperti, durano di più.	'Pick the unopened blooms/the blooms that are not open, they last longer.'
Il medico mi ha ordinato di mangiare cibi non grassi.	'The doctor has ordered me to eat non-fat foods.'
Una vera signora veste abiti non appariscenti.	'A real lady wears unobtrusive clothes/clothes that are not loud.'
Tutti i passaporti non italiani verranno esaminati.	'All non-Italian passports/passports that are not Italian will be examined.'
Vestiti nuovi e non nuovi si ammucchiavano alla rinfusa nella stanza.	'New and not new clothes were jumbled in a heap in the room.'

As in English, there a clear difference in meaning between:

Non molti sono venuti.	'Not many came.'
and	
Molti non sono venuti.	'Many didn't come.'

Non before a noun also corresponds to English 'non-':

Studenti e non studenti hanno riempito le strade.	'Students and non-students filled the streets.'

Negation of adverbs which stand for whole sentences or clauses and of preposition + noun phrases is relatively unusual, and sometimes a little awkward stylistically, but it is an increasing trend in modern Italian:

—*Ho ragione?*	'Am I right?'
—*Non esattamente* [i.e. *Non ha esattamente ragione*], *ma lei ha capito abbastanza.*	'Not exactly, but you've understood well enough.'
L'ho visto non in gran forma.	'I saw him not in the best of form.'

18.2 The types *Vieni o no?* 'Are you coming or not?', *Studenti o no/non* 'Students or non-students', etc.

In English, a negated verb preceded by 'or' or 'and' may be replaced by 'not'; the Italian equivalent is *no* (never *non*):

Gli telefono per sapere se verrà o no.	'I'm phoning him to find out whether he'll come or not.'
Non ha ancora deciso se sposarsi o no!	'He still hasn't decided whether to marry or not.'

But, unlike English, negated nouns and adjectives can also be replaced in this way, and in this case *non* is also possible (but unusual):

Studenti e no (non) hanno riempito le strade.	'Students and non-students filled the streets.'
Vestiti nuovi e no (non) si ammucchiavano alla rinfusa nella stanza.	'New and not new clothes were jumbled in a heap in the room.'

In addition to *non/no* standing for negated nouns, adjectives and verbs, *meno* may also be used:

Non ha ancora deciso se sposarsi o meno!	'He still hasn't decided whether to marry or not!'
Gli telefono per sapere se verrà o meno.	'I'm phoning him to find out whether he'll come or not.'
Non m'interessa la natura misteriosa o meno della chiamata.	'I'm not interested in the mysterious or non-mysterious nature of the call.'
Si potrebbe discutere a lungo sulla costituzionalità o meno del progetto.	'One could talk for a long time about the constitutionality or non-constitutionality of the project.'

18.3 The uses and position of the colloquial negator *mica* (and *punto*)

The negator *mica* is characteristic of colloquial, informal, registers. It is certainly an oversimplification to state, as some grammars do, that *mica* is just an emphatic variant of *non* and equivalent, say, to *affatto*. Briefly, we may say here[2] that *mica* is a negator which serves to highlight the *presuppositions* of assertions, questions and orders: a negative assertion such as *Non è freddo qua dentro* 'It's not cold in here' *presupposes* that somebody or something has led us to understand that it *is* cold – otherwise there would be no reason to make the utterance; one is unlikely to ask a question such as *Non hai fatto colazione?* 'Haven't you had breakfast?' except where one has reason to presuppose that the addressee probably has not had breakfast – the question *expects* the answer 'no'. And a negative imperative, such as *Non andare di là!* 'Don't go over there!' presupposes that the addressee actually is 'going over there' (or may do so) – otherwise there would be no reason to give the negative order.

Mica in assertions serves emphatically to negate presuppositions or expectations on the part of the speaker or addressee, so that its meaning is something like 'contrary to expectation'. (British) English 'actually' seems to capture *some* of the force of *mica*:

---

[2]A particularly penetrating survey of the use and syntax of *mica* may be found in Cinque (1991: 311–23).

Non è mica freddo qua dentro!	'It's not cold in here actually!' [even though I/you expected it would be]
Mica sei il primo a dirmelo!	'You aren't the first person to tell me that, actually!' [even though you may think you are]

Note that it is only possible to place *mica* in front of the verb when the expectation being negated is that of the person addressed. Thus *Mica è freddo qua dentro* could only be uttered where the addressee, by words or behaviour, had indicated that he or she expected it to be cold; if this expectation is only on the part of the speaker, we have *Non è mica freddo qua dentro*, etc.

In interrogative sentences, *mica* underlines that the questioner 'expects not'; English equivalents often contain 'I suppose ... not', or 'by any chance'. The effect is often one of 'politeness', in that the speaker avoids placing an obligation on the addressee by making it understood that he or she anticipates a negative answer or refusal:

Ciao, sono Laura, sai mica a che ora è la cena stasera?	'Hi, I'm L, I suppose you wouldn't know what time dinner is tonight?'
(Non) Ha mica qualcosa sul blu cobalto?	'You wouldn't have anything cobalt bluish by any chance?'

Note that in interrogatives where *mica* follows the verb, the presence of *non* in front of the verb is only optional. The effect of placing *mica* in front of the verb in interrogatives is particularly to emphasize the fact that the questioner expects a negative answer.

Mica with imperatives would imply the expectation that the addressee *is doing*, or is likely to do, that which is being forbidden. A sentence such as *Non toccare mica i documenti* 'Don't you touch the documents' would carry the suggestion that the addressee is in the habit of touching the documents, or acting in a way likely to lead him to touch the documents. In other words, *mica* highlights the circumstances which led to the utterance of the negative imperative *Non toccare i documenti*, in contrast, is rather more polite.

As a general rule,[3] *mica* is not used in most subordinate clauses – one cannot say **Ha finto di non essere mica stanca* 'She pretended not to be tired', **Ti ordino di non uscire mica* 'I order you not to go out'. Nor is it possible in restrictive relatives: (i.e., relative clauses which serve to *define* or *identify* a noun) one cannot say **La ragazza che non era mica timida li conosceva tutti* 'The girl who wasn't shy knew them all' (restrictive relative), but one can say *La ragazza, che non era mica timida, li conosceva tutti* 'The girl, who certainly wasn't shy, knew them all' (an appositive relative, where the relative clause describes, rather than defines or identifies, *la ragazza*).[4] *Mica* can, however, appear where the subordinate clause constitutes the main assertion being made, introduced by verbs of knowing, believing or asserting:

---

[3] But see Cinque (1991: 318).

[4] In Tuscany, one often finds *punto*, rather than *mica*, used either as an adverb (both as sentential negation and in conjunction with *non*), or meaning 'not any' in negative sentences (in which case it agrees in number and gender with the noun it modifies):

Punto mi piace quella ragazza.	'I really don't like that girl.'
Non mi piace punto quella ragazza.	'I don't like that girl at all.'
Non c'è rimasta punta marmellata.	'There's no jam left.'
Non ho mangiato punto bene in quel ristorante.	'I didn't eat at all well in that restaurant.'

Mi giurò che non era mica vero.	'He swore to me it wasn't true.'
Devi sapere che non sono mica contento di lei.	'You have to know that I'm not happy with her.'
Credo che Lucio non venga mica, stasera.	'I don't think L's coming this evening.'

18.4 *Non* as a reinforcing element in exclamations and questions

As in English, negation may be used to lend emphasis to an assertion, notably in exclamations:

Cosa non ha comprato!	'What didn't he buy!'/'What he bought!'
Quello che non è uscito dalla sua bocca!	'What didn't come out of his mouth!'/'The things that came out of his mouth!'

In questions, negation of the verb can have an effect equivalent to English 'isn't it?', 'don't they?', 'wasn't it?', and so forth. In other words, it invites a confirmatory answer to the question:

E non giocava così anche l'Inter?	'And didn't Inter play like that too?'
Ma non dovevi parlare anche tu?	'But you were supposed to speak too, weren't you?'
Non sono stati loro i primi ad iscriversi, allora?	'They were the first to sign up, weren't they?'

A similar effect can be achieved by the tag-phrase *non è vero?* (in northern Italy *nevvero?*) (cf. French *n'est-ce pas?*):

Ma il sisma dell'80 distrusse il paese intero, non è vero?	'But the 1980 earthquake destroyed the whole village, didn't it?'
Viene anche tua moglie, nevvero?	'Your wife's coming too, isn't she?'

18.5 The type *Nessuno viene* vs. *Non viene nessuno*, etc. Negative pronouns, adjectives, adverbs and conjunctions *before* the verb vs. negative pronouns, adjectives, adverbs and conjunctions *after* the verb

Italian differs in an important way from English with regard to the relation between negative pronouns, adjectives, adverbs and conjunctions and the *verb* of the clause in which they appear:

- If a negative pronoun (subject or object), adjective, adverb or conjunction *follows* the verb, then the verb *must* be preceded by *non*:

Non è arrivato nessuno puntuale.	'Nobody arrived on time.'
Non ho amato nessuno più di lui.	'I loved nobody more than him.'
Non trovo nessun collega disposto ad aiutarmi.	'I can't find any colleague prepared to help me.'
Non vidi niente e non voglio saperne niente.	'I didn't see anything and I don't want to know anything about it.'
Non l'ho mai visto senza cappello.	'I've never seen him hatless.'
Non si comporta bene neanche a scuola.	'He doesn't behave well even at school.'

Tu mi sembri uno che nemmeno in sogno farebbe gol.	'You strike me as someone who couldn't score a goal even in his dreams.'
Aldo non parla né tedesco né francese.	'A speaks neither German nor French.'

- If a negative pronoun (subject or object), adjective, adverb or conjunction *precedes* the verb (cf. 17.2), then the verb is not[5] preceded by *non*:

Nessuno è arrivato puntuale.	'Nobody arrived on time.'
Nessuno ho amato più di lui.	'Nobody did I love more than him.'
Nessun collega trovo disposto a aiutarmi.	'No colleague can I find ready to help me.'
Niente vidi e niente voglio saperne.	'I didn't see anything and I don't want to know anything about it.'
Mai l'ho visto senza cappello.	'I've never seen him hatless.'
Neanche a scuola si comporta bene.	'Not even at school does he behave well.'
Tu mi sembri uno che nemmeno in sogno farebbe gol.	'You strike me as someone who couldn't score a goal even in his dreams.'
Aldo né parla tedesco né parla francese.[6]	'A neither speaks German nor does he speak French.'

This principle applies equally where the verb is both preceded and followed by a negative pronoun (subject or object), adjective, adverb or conjunction (*Nessuno è mai arrivato puntuale* 'Nobody has ever arrived on time', etc.).

As a rule, negative pronouns, adjectives, adverbs or conjunctions *follow* the verb (so that the verb is preceded by *non*). This is true even of subject negative pronouns *niente* and *nulla*, although subject *nessuno* is also commonly found in front of the verb. As in other cases (cf. 17.2), the effect of placing the negative element towards the beginning of the sentence and before the verb is to lend particular emphasis to that element.

Niente potrà fermare la scienza.	'Nothing will be able to stop science.'
Neppure Arianna è venuta alla festa.	'Not even A came to the party.'

Placing object negative pronouns, and subject negative pronouns of intransitive verbs taking auxiliary *essere* (see 14.20) in front of the verb is particularly characteristic of literary styles:

Nessuno ho amato più di lui.	'Nobody did I love more than him.'
Nulla ci sfugge e tutto si scheda.	'Nothing escapes us and everything is filed.'

- The negative time adverbs *mai* 'never', (*non*) *più* 'no longer', and the 'focusing' negative adverbs *neanche*, *nemmeno*, *neppure* 'not even', occupy the same positions in relation to the verb as other time adverbs and focusing adverbs (see 13.9, 12, 16, 17).

18.6 'No longer' *non . . . più*

'No longer . . .' or 'not . . . again' is *non . . . più*:

---

[5]In informal spoken language the type *Nessuno non viene* is sometimes encountered.
[6]This structure with *né* is rather unusual. The more natural structure would be *Aldo non parla né tedesco né francese*.

Non ti far più vedere.
Quando non l'avrà più sarà come se non
l'avesse rubata.
I libri? Non ci sarà neanche più bisogno
di bruciarli, tanto la gente non li legge.

'Don't show yourself again.'
'When he no longer has it, it will be as if
he hadn't stolen it.'
'Books? It won't even be necessary any
longer to burn them, after all people
don't read them.'

19

Conjunctions and discourse markers

19.1 'And' e

Much like English 'and', *e* (or *ed*)[1] can conjoin elements of any kind (including whole clauses):

Sono gialli e verdi.	'They are yellow and green.'
Arrivarono Gianni e Marco.	'G and M arrived.'
Dopo la guerra, e anche durante la guerra, si era dichiarato pacifista.	'After the war, and even during the war, he had declared himself a pacifist.'
Paola gioca a scacchi e Mario pulisce la stanza.	'P is playing chess and M is cleaning the room.'
Ci sono professori e professori.	'There are teachers and teachers.' [i.e., 'Some are good and some bad', OR 'There are lots of teachers.']
Andava su e giù in ascensore.	'He was going up and down in the lift.'

Usually in speech, but more and more in narrative and in journalistic language, *e* can introduce a new sentence with a force close to 'in addition', 'moreover', 'also', 'and so', 'and then':

E poi, a parte il rischio di avere fatto un viaggio a vuoto, non finirò per mettermi nei guai? E, per ultimo, è vero che hanno messo dei microfoni nascosti in camera mia?	'And then, apart from the risk of having been on a pointless journey, won't I end up getting in trouble? And, finally, is it true they've put hidden microphones in my room?'
E se fosse tutto un inganno? Se lui mi prendesse in giro?	'And suppose it was all a trick? Suppose he was fooling with me?'

E can also be used to emphasize repetition or duration:

Pannella ha parlato per ore e ore.	'P spoke for hours and hours.'

and, introducing a clause, to mean 'but', 'however':

Ha novantacinque anni e legge senza occhiali.	'He's 95 but he can read without glasses.'

As in English, in lists of several items *e* need only be inserted before the last element:

---

[1] *E* has a variant *ed* which may be used optionally when a vowel immediately follows. But *ed* is preferred before those forms of *essere* which begin with *e-*: *Ed era lui* 'And it was him', *Voleva vedere ed essere visto* 'He wanted to see and be seen', etc.

Ho preso il formaggio, i pomodori, le uova e qualche bottiglia di birra.	'I took the cheese, the tomatoes, the eggs and some bottles of beer.'

19.2 'Both ... and' e ... e, etc.

'Both ... and ...' is usually *e ... e ...* :

Apprezzano e il vino e la birra.	'They like both wine and beer.'
Hanno amici e a Milano e a Roma.	'They have friends both in Milan and Rome.'

There can be more then two coordinated terms:

Hanno amici e a Milano e a Roma e a Venezia. Un po' dappertutto, insomma.	'They have friends in Milan and in Rome and in Venice. Just about everywhere, really.'

An alternative to *e ... e* is *sia ... sia* or *sia ... che*:

L'ho e/sia sentito dire da mia cugina, e/sia visto con i miei occhi.	'I've both heard it said by my cousin, and seen it with my own eyes.'
L'ho sentito e/sia dire da mia cugina, e/sia sussurrare da certe malelingue.	'I've heard it both said by my cousin, and whispered by certain gossips.'
Lo troverai sia nel mio libro che nel libro di Marco.	'You'll find it both in my book and in M's book.'

As with *e ... e*, *sia ... sia/che* can be used with more than two terms:

Hanno amici sia a Milano sia/che a Roma sia/che a Venezia.	'They have friends in Milan and in Rome and in Venice.'

Other possible ways of expressing 'both ... and' are *tanto ... quanto* or *tanto ... che*:

Tanto Paolo quanto/che Marco sono felici.	'Both P and M are happy.'

Yet another possibility is *vuoi ... vuoi*, which generally conjoins expressions of cause or purpose:

Vuoi per pigrizia, vuoi per reale stanchezza, Riccardo quella domenica decise di non uscire.	'Either from laziness or from real tiredness, R decided not to go out that Sunday.'

Similar to *vuoi ... vuoi* are *vuoi che ... o che, o che ... o che, che ... o* + subjunctive verb:

Vuoi che/o che/che fosse pigro o che/o fosse davvero stanco, Riccardo quella domenica decise di non uscire.	'Either because he was lazy or because he was really tired, R decided not to go out that Sunday.'

Note that the various 'both ... and' constructions do not normally conjoin *verbs* in Italian. A sentence such as 'He both speaks and writes Japanese' might simply be *Parla e scrive il giapponese* while 'It's both raining and snowing' could be *Piove e nevica allo stesso tempo* or *Piove e nevica insieme*.

19.3 'Also', 'too', 'as well', 'even' *anche* and *pure*

Era stanco ed anche un po' arrabbiato.	'He was tired and a bit angry too.'
È venuta anche Maria.	'M came too.'

Non sto dicendo che gli avversari politici non vadano combattuti anche con queste armi.	'I'm not saying that political opponents should not also be fought with these weapons.'
Anche Mike, che aveva perso suo padre da poco quando ci innamorammo, continuava a ripetermi che mi mandava Dio per colmare quel vuoto.	'M too, who had lost his father when we fell in love, was always telling me that God was sending me to fill that empty space.'
Bisognerà pure che rifacciano il lastricato.	'They'll also need to re-lay the paving stones.'
Lei è di Roma. Il marito pure.	'She's from Rome. Her husband too.'
Si è pure offerta di allevare lei il bastardo.	'She even offered to bring the bastard up herself.'

Note that, following an imperative, *pure* can have a force similar to that of English 'do . . .', making the imperative rather more polite:

Venga pure, signore. Il pranzo è servito.	'Do come over, sir. Dinner's ready.'

19.4 'Not to mention' *nonché*

In formal language, the last member of a list can be preceded by *nonché*:

Difficile condensare in poche righe la produzione leopardiana. Saggi, poesie, dissertazioni, nonché un diario enciclopedico sono solo alcuni dei suoi lavori.	'Leopardi's output is hard to condense into a few lines. Essays, poems, dissertations, as well as an encyclopaedic diary are but a few of his works.'

19.5 'Neither . . . nor' *né . . . né (neppure)*

Two negative sentences can be conjoined by *e non* 'and not' or by *né* 'nor'. Note the following examples and their English equivalents (*né . . . né* is 'neither . . . nor'):

Gianni non beve alcool e non fuma prima di una gara.	'G doesn't drink alcohol and doesn't smoke before a contest.'
Gianni non beve alcool né fuma prima di una gara.	'G doesn't drink alcohol nor does he smoke before a contest.'
Gianni né beve alcool né fuma prima di una gara.	'G neither drinks alcohol nor smokes before a contest.'

Né . . . né can also conjoin noun phrases, pronouns, adjectives and adverbs:

Né il padrone né il garzone hanno mai amato molto il lavoro.	'Neither the master nor the lad have ever much liked work.'
Non canta né bene né male.	'He sings neither well nor badly.'
Mara non gli sembrava né bella né brutta.	'M seemed neither beautiful nor ugly to him.'
Non ci sono finestre, né alte né basse.	'There are no windows, neither high nor low.'

Note that when *né . . . né* conjoins two subjects of a verb, at least one of which is singular (as in the first example above), the verb normally agrees with both, and is plural. But if the verb *precedes* the conjoined subjects, it may be either singular or plural:

Non l'ha/l'hanno fatto né Paolo né Mario.	'Neither P nor M did it.'

But when answering interrogative questions with singular verbs, such as *Chi l'ha fatto?* 'Who did it?', one tends to reply using the singular verb even if two subjects are conjoined by *né . . . né*: *Non l'ha fatto né Paolo né Mario*.

If the first of two conjoined elements is negated, and that negation also applies to the second element, Italian uses *né* in cases where English may admit *or*: This is particularly true after *senza* 'without', where English could only have 'or':

La sua era una vita randagia, senza donne né amici . . .	'His was a roaming life, without women or friends . . .'
Non l'ho detto né scritto.	'I didn't say or write it.'

Where *né* is a phrasal conjunction (usually preceded by a comma) meaning 'and neither . . ., nor', agreement is only with the first subject:

Non ha aperto la finestra Marco, né Giulia.	'M did not open the window, nor did G.'

19.6 'Or' o, oppure, ovvero, etc.

Prendo una birra o/oppure un'aranciata.	'I'll have a beer, or an orangeade.'
Quando la sera torno a casa mi preparo qualcosa da mangiare o/oppure, se ne ho voglia, telefono a un amico e usciamo per una pizza.	'When I get home in the evening I prepare something to eat or, if I feel like it, I phone a friend and we go out for a pizza.'
Nei sogni veniva spesso inghiottito da un orrendo pescione che oltretutto puzzava tremendamente. Oppure gli capitava di essere su uno scivolo che non finiva mai. [www]	'In his dreams he was often swallowed up by a horrible great fish which above all stank terribly. Or he would find himself on a never-ending slide.'

Ovvero may be simply 'or', but also functions to introduce a paraphrase of what has been already said (like *ossia* below), and is mainly used in formal registers:

Fu questo il momento in cui la mente di Zeus fu 'accecata da Ate'; ovvero, come diremmo noi [. . .] fu allora che Zeus commise il suo terribile errore. [www]	'That was when Z's mind was "blinded by Atis"; or, as we would say [. . .] that was when Z committed his terrible mistake.'
Ecco il 'Manifesto della sinistra nella società della comunicazione'. Ovvero un documento della Quercia per colmare gli antichi ritardi della sinistra italiana nel definire un progetto per il futuro in un mondo dominato dalle telecomunicazioni.	'Here is the "Manifesto of the left in the communication society". Or a document from the Oak to make up for the old delays of the Italian left in defining a project for the future in a world dominated by telecommunications.'

An equivalent expression is *ossia*, also mainly used in writing and in formal registers:

Il medium indicherebbe al tempo stesso il luogo dell'evento e ciò che sta in mezzo, ossia si 'intromette' fra l'evento e la ricezione dell'evento.	'The medium would indicate at the same time the event and what is in between, or it "puts itself between" the event and reception of the event.'

When *o* conjoins two nouns which are the subject of the sentence, the verb agreement can be either in the singular or in the plural. The verb tends to be in the plural if the subject is postponed:

Mio fratello o mio zio verrà/verranno certamente domani.	'My brother or my uncle will certainly come tomorrow.'
Domani verranno certamente mio fratello o mio zio.	

19.7 'Either . . . or' o . . . o

O . . . o 'either . . . or' can conjoin two, or more than two, terms:

Sarà stato o Mario, o Paolo, o Franca.	'It must have been either M, or P, or F.'

O . . . oppure is also possible.

19.8 Adversative conjunctions: *ma* 'but', *eppure* 'yet', *mentre* 'while' *bensì* 'but', *invece* 'however', *nondimeno* 'none the less', *peraltro* 'however', *piuttosto* 'rather', *se(n)nonché* 'except that', *tuttavia* 'however', *anzi* 'rather', *però* 'but'/'however'

Ma 'but'

Ha preso non la valigia ma la borsa.	'He took not the suitcase but the bag.'
Non sono italiani ma francesi.	'They're not Italian but French.'
Serveto voleva morire sorridendo, ma i muscoli della faccia gli erano rimasti contratti.	'S wanted to die smiling, but the muscles of his face had contracted.'
Paolo è simpatico ma un po' timido.	'P is nice but a bit shy.'
Da dieci anni la nostra ditta recupera le eccedenze per ridistribuirle a chi ha troppo poco da mangiare. Ma quest'anno vorremmo fare qualcosa di più.	'For 10 years our firm has been taking the glut and redistributing it to those who have too little to eat. But this year we'd like to do something more.'

Rather as in English, *ma* can be used to intensify what follows it, by introducing a note of insistence:

Mio marito fa un lavoro stressante, ma così stressante che a volte mi preoccupo per la sua salute.	'My husband does a stressful job, so stressful that I sometimes worry about his health.'
Al concerto non mancava nessuno, ma proprio nessuno.	'Everybody was at the concert, but absolutely everybody.'

Ma at the beginning of an utterance often serves to express a nuance of surprise or impatience:

Ma ti danno solo due settimane di vacanze?	'[Do you mean to say] you only get two weeks' holiday?'
Quest'amicizia però mi rende ancora più libero nel criticarli, nel dir loro: ma siete matti.	'Yet this friendship makes me even freer in criticizing them, in saying to them: "You must be mad".'
Ma la vuoi smettere di fumare!	'Will you stop smoking!'
Ma non ne posso più!	'Oh I can't stand any more!'

Like English 'but', *ma* can have the force of 'however', 'none the less', 'on the other hand', not only within a sentence, but also at the beginning of a sentence or paragraph; in this use it is often preceded by a pause in spoken language and by a semicolon or full stop in writing.[2]

---

[2] A detailed discussion of this and other uses of *ma* is to be found in Sabatini (1997).

Eppure 'and yet'

La Wehrmacht non aveva fatto niente per nascondere i preparativi, eppure proprio la mancanza di segretezza sembrava confermare l'idea escogitata da Stalin che tutto questo dovesse far parte di un piano.
È passato ormai un anno da quando un incidente ha chiuso tragicamente l'esistenza di Diana Spencer. Eppure la polemica sulla sua dinamica e la mitizzazione del personaggio sono tutt'altro che in declino.
Eppur si muove.[3]

'The Wehrmacht had done nothing to hide its preparations, and yet the very lack of secrecy seemed to confirm the idea thought up by S that all this must be part of a plan.'
'A year has now gone by since DS met her tragic end in an accident. And yet the argument about how it happened and the creation of myths around her are anything but in decline.'
'And yet it moves.'

Bensì 'but'

Questo progetto era stato varato senza l'ambizione di fornire certezze e conclusioni, bensì con la sola preoccupazione di stimolare un confronto tra le varie ricerche e posizioni.
Non è essenziale conoscere personaggi ricchi e potenti, bensì è importante poterci arrivare in caso di bisogno ...

'This project had been launched without any aim of providing certainties and conclusions, but just out of a concern to stimulate comparison between the various types of research and positions.'
'It isn't essential to know rich and powerful people, but it is important to be able to get to them if you need to ...'

Unlike conjunctions such as *eppure* or *anzi*, *bensì* cannot introduce a new sentence although (as the last example above shows), it can introduce a clause within a sentence. Its meaning is best captured as 'but in fact': it must be preceded by a clause containing a negative, and serves to introduce a statement of what is actually the case, given that a preceding proposition has been negated.[4]

Invece 'however', 'instead'

La sua biografia ci aveva un po' intimorito, invece l'incontro ci propone una donna bella e intelligente ...
Quando Claudia mi diede il primo bacio pensai che finalmente sarei stato felice sempre. Invece cominciai a essere infelice sempre.

'Her biography had rather scared us, but meeting her reveals a beautiful and intelligent woman ...'
'When C gave me the first kiss I thought that at last I'd be happy for ever. But instead I started to be unhappy for ever.'

Italian makes far more extensive use of *invece* than English does of 'however' or 'instead'. It is an extremely common marker of any proposition which contradicts an expectation created in a previous sentence or clause. Often, an equivalent English utterance might contain no conjunction at all:

È doveroso, però, che chi effettua queste denunce accerti prima, bene ed esattamente come stiano le cose, onde evitare di gettare fango su persone che invece non hanno colpa alcuna e nulla hanno da rimproverarsi.

'It is right, however, that some making such denunciations first ascertain, properly and exactly how things stand, so as to avoid throwing mud on people who are blameless and have nothing to reproach themselves for.'

---

[3]The words supposedly uttered by Galileo Galilei after he had been obliged formally to recant his claim that the earth moved around the sun.
[4]It is equivalent, therefore, to Spanish *sino* and German *sondern*. But its use instead of *ma* is not obligatory in Italian.

Mentre 'while', 'and'

As in English, *mentre* may sometimes mean little more than 'and':

Paolo giocava a calcio, suo fratello lavava i piatti, mentre Gigi preparava gli spaghetti.	'P played football, his brother washed up, while G cooked the spaghetti.'

Piuttosto 'rather'

Mi asterrò dal lanciare accuse contro altre persone; piuttosto, racconterò semplicemente quel che accadde.	'I shall refrain from making accusations against others; rather, I shall simply state what happened.'
Piuttosto d'incontrarlo, cambierà strada.	'Rather than meet him, she'll change her route.'
Preferisco che mi critichi, piuttosto che m'ignori.	'I prefer him to criticize me, rather than ignore me.'
Non è ricco, piuttosto felice.	'He's not rich, rather he's happy.'

Particularly in spoken language, *piuttosto* (like English 'rather') may follow the second element it conjoins:

Non mangiare il gelato: una mela, piuttosto.	'Don't eat the ice cream: an apple, rather.'

Tuttavia 'however', 'yet'

Chet Baker con la sua tromba dominò la scena del jazz negli anni '50, tuttavia nel decennio successivo si trovò risucchiato in una spirale sempre crescente di eroina, cocaina e droghe chimiche. [www]	'CB with his trumpet dominated the jazz scene in the 50s, yet in the following decade he was sucked into an ever widening spiral of heroin, cocaine and chemical drugs.'
Pisa è nota nel mondo per la Piazza dei Miracoli. Tuttavia ci sono tante altre cose interessanti da vedere oltre al Duomo e alla Torre Pendente.	'Pisa is famous for Piazza dei Miracoli. However there are so many other interesting things to see besides the Duomo and the Leaning Tower.'

Anzi

Anzi is 'in fact', but serves to introduce additional, *unexpected* information after a preceding statement. It is similar to 'on the contrary' or 'not just that', 'but . . .' or even the old-fashioned 'nay, rather . . .':

Non è buono, anzi è cattivo.	'It's not good, rather it's bad.'
Non è buono, anzi è buonissimo.	'It's not (just) good, it's first rate.'
Pietro non sopportava più l'idea di riprendere la pratica della professione medica, anzi non sopportava più nemmeno la vista del sangue.	'P could no longer bear the idea of going back into medicine, in fact he could no longer even bear the sight of blood.'
L'Italia però non è in una situazione di vera inferiorità, anzi detiene addirittura il primato in alcuni settori.	'But Italy is not in a really inferior position, rather it is actually leader in some areas.'
Sarà per me un piacere accompagnarvi e assistervi nelle vostre prime esperienze Web. Sono qui per questo. Anzi, è tutta la mia vita.	'It will be a pleasure for me to come with you and assist you in your first Web experiences. That's what I'm here for. In actual fact it's my whole life.'

Anzi can also be used in isolation, to mean 'far from it', 'quite the contrary':

Non mi dispiace affatto. Anzi!	'I don't mind at all. On the contrary!/Far from it!'

Però 'however', 'yet', 'but'

> *Mi fa piacere che tu ti sia ricordata del mio* 'I'm glad you've remembered my
> *compleanno. Però era la settimana scorsa.* birthday. It was last week, though.'
> OR *Era la settimana scorsa, però.*

Unlike *ma*, *però* does not have to appear at the beginning of a clause. *Però* can also be used in isolation in speech, usually with lengthening of the final vowel, to imply that there may be reasons to qualify or disagree with what has just been said ('but even so . . .', etc.):

> *Non è che mi dia proprio fastidio. Però . . .* 'It's not that I really mind it. But all the
> same . . .'

Però pronounced at the beginning of a sentence and followed by a pause, may also express surprise or disappointment:

> *Però, che coraggio hai avuto!* 'My, how brave you were!'

19.9 Declarative conjunctions: *cioè, vale a dire, infatti, invero*

Declarative conjunctions introduce material which confirms, explains or emphasizes what has been already said.

Cioè 'that is', 'i.e.', 'I mean'

> *Dato che io non sono in realtà un uomo* 'Given that I'm not really a free man,
> *libero, cioè ho una storia politica e un* that is I have a political history and a
> *pubblico che è sempre stato da me* public that I have always
> *incoraggiato . . .* encouraged . . .'
> *Il Mondo dell'Arcobaleno è caratterizzato* 'The World of the Rainbow is
> *da una particolare realtà sociale: i Regni* characterized by a particular social
> *Uniti. Cioè tre regni che hanno trovato un* reality: the United Kingdoms. That is,
> *accordo ed una convivenza comune . . .* three kingdoms, which have come to an
> agreement and managed to live
> together . . .'
> *Quando dico suspense tutto il resto, sto* 'When I say suspense and so forth I'm
> *parlando di tecnica. Della capacità, cioè, di* talking of technique. Of the ability, I
> *mettere assieme parole raggiungendo un* mean, to put together words and attain
> *effetto voluto . . .* a desired effect . . .'
> *I brevi saggi del volumetto di Eco malgrado* 'The brief essays in E's little volume,
> *la varietà dei temi, sono di carattere etico,* despite their varied themes, have an
> *e cioè riguardano quello che sarebbe bene* ethical nature, and that is to say that
> *fare . . .* they deal with what it would be right to
> do . . .'
> *Invece adesso vivendo in una fase di* 'Although now it lives in a phase of
> *disperazione, di infelicità, l'umanità ritorna* desperation, of unhappiness, humanity
> *alle proprie radici originarie, cioè ritorna al* is getting back to its own roots, in other
> *passato.* words it's getting back to its past.'

Cioè is the most used declarative. In informal speech, it is often used rather vacuously, simply as a 'filler' – a way of giving the speaker time to think of what he or she is going to say next. In this use, it is rather like 'I mean' in English:

> *Non sono tutti scemi. Cioè . . . c'è qualcuno* 'They're not all stupid. I mean . . . one or
> *bravino, cioè accettabile.* two are quite good, I mean acceptable.'

Vale a dire 'that is to say', 'in other words', 'i.e.'

Questo è un alimento naturale, sano, fresco, di bell'aspetto, leggero e saporito, vale a dire è adatto a tutti.	'This is a natural foodstuff, healthy, fresh, attractive, light and tasty, in other words it's suitable for everybody.'
Per quanto se ne sa, la stoffa di cui erano fatti i dinosauri non era diversa da quella di una qualunque altra creatura vivente. Ciò che conta è come tutta questa roba era messa insieme. Vale a dire che ciò che davvero vi serve è un manuale di istruzioni per fare un dinosauro. [www]	'As far as we know, the stuff of which dinosaurs were made was no different from that of any other living creature. What matters was how all this was put together. In other words what you really need is an instruction manual for making a dinosaur.'

The last example shows that when *vale a dire* introduces a new sentence, it is followed by *che*.

Infatti 'indeed'

Infatti looks rather like English 'in fact'; in fact it is quite different. For while 'in fact' *contradicts* some expectation created in a previous sentence or clause, *infatti* serves to *confirm* that an expectation already created is actually the case. 'Indeed' is perhaps the nearest English counterpart to *infatti*, but *infatti* is not as stylistically marked as 'indeed', and it (together with its variant form *difatti*) is extensively used to make *explicit* a confirmation which English often tends to leave *implicit*.

Non esiste un luogo dove sia conservata la memoria fisica di Castaneda: le ceneri sono state infatti sparse al vento nel tanto amato deserto messicano. [www]	'There is no one place where C's physical record is preserved: his ashes were scattered to the wind in his much loved Mexican desert.'
Se qualcuno si aspetta da questo libro un manuale di scrittura, non è quello che troverà. Non si tratta infatti di un manuale tecnico, strutturato in capitoli, indici e voci di riferimento . . .	'If anyone's expecting a writing manual from this book, that's not what he'll find. It's not a technical manual, organized into chapters, indexes and reference words . . .'
Non c'è niente di più interessante che conoscere i santi, i ladri e i pazzi; infatti sono gli unici capaci di una conversazione sensata.	'There's nothing more interesting than getting to know saints, thieves and madmen; they are the only ones up to a sensible conversation.'
È sempre più difficile usare il giornale come mezzo per comunicare le proprie idee. Infatti il sistema giornalistico non è interessato a capire che cosa penso io . . .	'It's getting more and more difficult to use a newspaper as a means of communicating one's own ideas. The journalistic system is not concerned to know what I think . . .'
Molte sono le situazioni traumatiche di cui i bambini sono vittime: l'abuso sessuale, l'anoressia mentale, l'attaccamento eccessivo a una figura parentale. Infatti i disegni dei bambini vittime di incesto, o le raffigurazioni fatte dalle anoressiche durante la psicoterapia parlano chiaro. [Ven.]	'Many are the traumatic situations of which children are victims: sexual abuse, mental anorexia, over-attachment to a parent figure. The drawings of children who have been the victims of incest, or the representations created by anorexics during psychotherapy speak clearly for themselves.'

Infatti may also be used in isolation to mean 'indeed', 'just so':

—*Ma sono tutti bugiardi!*	'They're all liars!'
—*Infatti!*	'Indeed so!'

How, then, does one say 'in fact' in Italian? Among the possibilites are *invece* (see above) or *in realtà*:

Petra parla così bene l'inglese che qualcuno la crede inglese. In realtà è tedesca.

'P speaks English so well that some people think she's English. In fact she's German.'

Invero 'indeed'

Invero is restricted to elevated registers, and sounds old-fashioned or affected in speech:

L'universalità delle conoscenze scientifiche è un mito smentito dalla pratica stessa della scienza, invero gli sbandierati valori oggettivi sono al contrario un ostacolo al progredire della ricerca scientifica.

'The universality of scientific knowledge is a myth belied by scientific practice itself, indeed the much-vaunted objective values are in fact an obstacle to the progress of scientific research.'

19.10 Conclusive conjunctions: *dunque, quindi, perciò, pertanto, per cui,* 'therefore'; *ebbene* 'so'; *ora* 'now'; *allora* 'then'; *ecco che* 'and so'

Conclusive conjunctions such as *dunque, quindi, perciò, pertanto, ebbene, ora, allora,* etc.,[5] mark sentences that express the consequence/result of what has been said before, and are often used to introduce the next step in a narrative:

Dunque 'so', 'therefore'

Quanti di voi sanno cos'è la 'creatina'? Pochi? Va bene, cominciamo dall'inizio. Dunque sull'uso e abuso di questa sostanza farmaceutica da parte dei giocatori di calcio è esplosa una delle interminabili polemiche tormentone dell'estate 1998. [Ven.]

'How many of you know what "creatine" is? Few of you? OK, let's start at the beginning. It was over the use and abuse of this pharmaceutical substance by football players that one of the interminable polemical storms of summer 1998 blew up.'

Hugo Claus è un autore colpevolmente poco conosciuto in Italia, che invece ha internazionalmente una notevole fama. Dunque è un autore da leggere con grande attenzione. [www]

'HC is an author lamentably little known in Italy, who is actually internationally famous. So he's an author to be read with close attention.'

L'uomo come tale deve soffrire, è questo il prezzo che deve pagare per il peccato originale. Perché alleviarlo? E dunque non è difendibile una scienza che intenda aiutare l'uomo nel suo cammino terreno se, ancora nel XIX secolo, la Chiesa si oppone alla vaccinazione antivaiolosa? [www]

'Man as such must suffer, this is the price he must pay for original sin. Why alleviate it? So isn't a science which aims to help man along his earthly path defensible if, still in the nineteenth century, the Church is opposed to smallpox vaccination?'

---

[5]*Dunque, quindi, ebbene, ora, perciò, pertanto, allora* can be used also as sentence modifiers in connection with a copulative/disjunctive/adversative conjunction:

Aspettavo il dottor Sergi per le sette ma sono ormai le otto e, quindi, me ne vado. Abbiamo aperto ieri sera una bottiglia di vino, e penso quindi che ce ne sia rimasto un po'.

'I was expecting Dr S at 7 but it's already 8, so I'm off.'
'We opened a bottle of wine yesterday evening, so I think there's a drop left.'

> *Notevole narratore di avventure e viaggi, Francisco Coloane compirà 90 anni nel 2000. Un grande vecchio della narrativa, dunque, che solo recentemente gli italiani hanno conosciuto.* [www]

'A noteworthy narrator of adventures and travel, FC will be 90 in 2000. So he is a grand old man of narrative, whom the Italians have only recently got to know.'

Quindi 'so', 'therefore'

> *Le e-mail che giungono in redazione ad Alice.it sono numerose. Quindi siamo costretti a selezionarle in base a criteri rigidi.*

'A great many e-mails reach the editor's office at Alice.it. Therefore we are obliged to select them by rigid criteria.'

> *Grazie alla rete, per la prima volta il rivenditore sa che cosa sta per ricevere e che cosa non riceverà dall'editore. Può quindi informare i suoi clienti di conseguenza ed offrire così un servizio migliore.*

'Thanks to the net, for the first time the retailer knows what he's going to receive and what he won't receive from the publisher. Therefore he can inform his clients as a result and thereby offer a better service.'

> *La prima bozza di ipotesi che io ho proposto ha molto interessato la Colorado film e Salvatores si è dimostrato entusiasta, quindi è diventata qualcosa di più che un gioco.*

'The first outline proposal I made greatly interested Colorado film and S was keen, so it became rather more than a game.'

Ebbene

Ebbene is 'well then, . . .', or 'well, . . .'

> *Consideriamo soprattutto quei quotidiani che sono stati esaminati nel decennio 80–89. Ebbene, l'elemento che emerge con più evidenza è l'incremento del numero delle segnalazioni.*

'Let's consider particularly the dailies examined in the decade 80–89. Well, the most salient fact is the increase in the number of mentions.'

> *Polemiche. Calvino contro Pasolini? Ebbene sì, però bisogna scandagliare di più.*

'Polemics. C against P? Well yes, but we need to dig a little deeper.'

Ora

Ora is 'now', or 'now then', used to introduce the next stage in a narrative:

> *Francisco Coloane è un grande vecchio della narrativa che solo recentemente gli italiani hanno conosciuto. Ora, l'opera di quest'uomo incanutito ma non meno brillante di un tempo è lentamente tradotta anche nel nostro paese.*

'FC is a grand old man of narrative whom Italians have got to know only recently. Now, the works of this white-haired but still just as brilliant man, are slowly being translated in our country.'

> *Ora, devo dirti una cosa spiacevole.*

'Now, I have something unpleasant to tell you.'

Ora che . . . is 'now (that) . . .' in the sense of 'given that . . .', 'since . . .':

> *Ora che sei in pensione avrai finalmente tempo di venirmi a trovare.*

'Now you've retired at last you'll have time to come and see me.'

> *Ora che è estate la sera in genere ceniamo in terrazza.*

'Now that it's summer we usually dine out on the balcony.'

Perciò 'therefore', 'thereby', '(and) so'

A Città del Capo, che è la mia città, c'è una colonia molto importante di italiani, anche influenti, perciò ho avuto modo di conoscere lo spirito italiano già nel passato.	'In Cape Town, my city, there's a very substantial colony of Italians, some of them influential, and in that way I was able to get to know the Italian spirit in the past as well.'
Ciò che mi interessava era capire quale idea dell'audience avessero i professionisti dell'industria televisiva, e perciò parlammo delle ricerche a cui stava partecipando insieme ai suoi colleghi.	'I was interested to know what idea of the audience television industry professionals had, and therefore we talked about the research he was involved in with his colleagues.'
Ho insegnato ad Harlem, ma vi ho anche vissuto e vi sono andata a scuola io stessa, e perciò ho visto tutte le sfaccettature dell'insegnamento e della vita di Harlem.	'I taught in Harlem, but I lived there and went to school there too, and so I saw all facets of teaching and living in Harlem.'

Allora (frequently *e allora*) 'then', 'so' (in the sense 'and as a result')

Ad esempio che cosa significa essere uno scrittore gay? Non si parla mai di uno scrittore definendolo 'eterosessuale', e allora perché c'è bisogno di farlo per chi è omosessuale?	'For example what does it mean to be a gay writer? We never speak of a writer as "heterosexual", so why must we do so for homosexuals?'
E allora, se la mia testimonianza, il mio racconto di sopravvissuta ai campi di sterminio, la mia presenza nel cuore di chi comprende la pietà, serve a far crescere, parlerò.	'So, if my witness, my story as a death camp survivor, my presence in the heart of those who understand compassion, will help people grow, I'll speak.'
Virginia era troppo bassa, allora ogni notte si addormentava pregando perché durante il sonno, il suo corpo si allungasse.	'V was too short, so every night she would go to sleep praying that her body would lengthen as she slept.'

Pertanto 'therefore'

Le buone qualità mentali, una volta sviluppate in modo adeguato, si accrescono all'infinito. Pertanto la pratica spirituale ci dà sia la felicità a lungo termine sia una maggiore forza interiore giorno dopo giorno. [www]	'Good mental qualities, once adequately developed, grow infinitely. Therefore spiritual exercise gives us both long-term happiness and a greater inner strength from day to day.'
Da tempo, però, si sentiva la necessità di un sostanziale aggiornamento che tenesse conto dell'evoluzione delle conoscenze. Si è pertanto proceduto a un lavoro che ha portato prima alla lista di aggiornamento. [www]	'For some time, however, they had felt the need for a substantial update which took into account the development of their knowledge. Therefore we set about the task which first led to the list of updates.'

A number of conclusive conjunctions are also used to introduce a sentence, and sometimes in speech are used (usually followed by a slight pause) to start a conversation or 'to break the ice'. *Dunque* often has a force like 'Right, then, here is what I have to say . . .', while *allora* is 'So . . .':

Dunque, oggi studieremo le cause della Seconda Guerra Mondiale.	'Right then, today we'll look at the causes of the Second World War.'
—*Cosa voleva Lei?*	'What did you want?'
—*Dunque, volevo una borsa di pelle.*	'Right, I wanted a leather bag.'

> *Allora professore, posso chiederle qualche*   'So professor, may I ask you for some
> *chiarimento?*   clarification?'

Quindi and *perció* used in this way mean 'so', 'in view of that':

> *Quindi che cos'hai fatto?*   'So what did you do?'
> *Penso, perció esisto.*   'I think, therefore I am.'

Per cui 'so therefore . . .'

The frequently used phrase *per cui* is widely used in colloquial non-formal discourse to connect two propositions the second of which expresses the outcome or result of what is expressed in the first. *Per cui* can only occur at the beginning of a sentence or clause:

> *Ho ancora qualche pagina da correggere,*   'I still have some pages to correct, which
> *per cui non credo di poter uscire con te*   is why I don't think I'll be able to come
> *stasera.*   out with you this evening.'
> *Nessuno ci aveva avvertiti, per cui ci*   'No one had warned us, so we set out.'
> *mettemmo in viaggio.*

Ecco che . . .

The phrase *ecco che* . . . is sometimes used in informal styles to mean 'and so', 'as a result', often with an overtone of 'no great surprise then that . . .':

> *Raggiungere lo scalo è troppo difficile e*   'Reaching the airport is too difficult and
> *costoso. Ecco che gli uomini d'affari*   expensive. And so businessmen prefer
> *preferiscono evitare Malpensa 2000.*   to avoid Malpensa 2000.'

19.11 Conditional conjunctions: *purché* 'provided', *a condizione che*, *a patto che*, 'on condition that', *sempre che* 'always assuming'

One of the major conditional conjunctions, *se* 'if', and its equivalents, is dealt with in 17.31–8, where the structure of conditional sentences in general is explained. We deal here with conjunctions with the meaning 'on condition/provided that'.[6] These are always followed by verbs in the subjunctive (15.30). With the exception of *purché*, clauses introduced by these expressions always follow the main clause.

Purché tends to express a *minimal* condition necessary for something else to be the case, 'just so long as':

> *Sono tuttavia sovvenzionabili le spese*   'However grants may be made for
> *relative a monografie, collezioni, riviste,*   expenses regarding monographs,
> *dischi, CD, purché siano parte integrante*   collections, disks, CDs so long as they
> *del progetto.*   are an integral part of the project.'
> *Purché tu me li consegni domani, lo*   'As long as you give them to me
> *autorizzo.*   tomorrow, I'll allow it.'

A condizione che and *a patto che* tend to be stronger than *purché* and mean 'strictly on the condition that some other requirement be fulfilled first'; they may only *follow* the main clause:

---

[6]On conditional conjunctions, see for example Visconti (1996).

Dica pure a Sacracorona che son pronto a servirlo [. . .] a patto che in cambio mi dia una delle sue figlie in moglie . . . [www] *Dice, in sostanza, che bisogna prendere tempo, che la situazione si può risolvere solo a condizione che quella casa [. . .] sia venduta.* [www]	'Do tell S that I'm ready to serve him on condition that he gives me in exchange one of his daughters to be my wife . . .' 'In effect he says that we need to take our time, that the situation can be sorted out only on condition that the house is sold.'

Sempre che . . . states a presupposition – something that must be the case if something else is to happen. Its meaning is akin to 'always assuming':

I fisici scossero la testa: i nuclei degli elementi dell'organismo erano pressoché eterni, ma forse si poteva ottenere qualche informazione dagli isotopi radioattivi, sempre che ce ne fossero.	'The physicists shook their heads: the nuclei of the elements of the organism were practically eternal, but perhaps some information could be gleaned from the radioactive isotopes, always assuming there were any.'

19.12 Causal conjunctions: *perché, poiché, giacché, siccome, in quanto, che, considerato/visto/dato/dal momento che, per il fatto/motivo/la ragione che*, etc.

These introduce a clause explaining the reason for an action/event. When the subjects of the main and the causal clause are coreferential (i.e., refer to the same person or thing) *per* + infinitive (present/past) can be used, otherwise we find *perché* 'because', *poiché, giacché, siccome* 'since', 'as', *in quanto* 'in as much as', 'in that', *considerato/visto che* 'bearing in mind/seeing that', *dato/dal momento che* 'since', *per il fatto che, per il motivo che, per la ragione che* 'because', etc.:

Per essere stato pigro e non essersi alzato a chiudere la finestra, Carlo aveva passato una notte agitata.	'Because of having/Because he had been lazy and not got up to close the window, C had spent a restless night.'
Quando spuntò l'alba, siccome di giorno non poteva circolare, il piccolo marziano si rimpiattò nell'ombra della soffitta di un secolare palazzo nobiliare.	'At daybreak, as he could not go about by day, the little Martian hid away in the shade of the attic of an ancient stately home.'
Eleonora si vestì con un abito a fiori che aveva trovato in un mercatino dell'usato. Siccome in quella stagione al mattino poteva far freddo, indossò un maglione.	'E put on a flower-patterned dress she'd found in a second-hand market. Since at that time of year it could get cold in the morning, she wore a jumper.'
Poiché il Senato aveva decretato che i libri di Cassio fossero dati alle fiamme, a nulla valse la sua ferma difesa della libertà di parola.	'Since the Senate had decreed that C's books should be consigned to the flames, his stout defence of freedom of speech was in vain.'
Questa è una stesura che non ritengo definitiva ma continuamente perfettibile, poiché poche sono le cose che ogni giorno si riescono a trasmettere, molte quelle nuove che si imparano.	'This is a draft which I do not hold to be definitive but continually perfectible, since there are few things which one can manage to transmit daily, and the new things one learns are many.'
Il diritto d'autore è un concetto relativamente nuovo per la Repubblica Popolare Cinese, giacché la prima legge in materia è stata promulgata nel settembre 1990.	'Author's rights are a relatively new concept for the People's Republic of China, since the first law was passed in September 1990.'

Su un lato del municipio c'è un grande orologio vegliato dalla morte in persona: o almeno così sembra, dato che si tratta di uno scheletro . . .	'On one side of the town hall there is a clock watched over by death in person: or so it seems, given that it is in fact a skeleton . . .'

Poiché and *giacché* are mainly used in writing, while *siccome, in quanto, considerato che, visto che, dato che, dal momento che,* and also *per il fatto che, per il motivo che, per la ragione che* are equally used in writing and in spoken Italian.

We see in the above examples that, much as in English, clauses introduced by conjunctions meaning 'since', 'given that', etc. (*dal momento che, dato che, giacché, siccome, visto che, poiché*) usually *precede* the main clause, but those introduced by 'because' *perché* virtually always follow the main clause. If we need to move a '*perché* clause' to the beginning of the sentence, we must use *poiché*:

Torino è in lutto perché è scomparso Giulio Einaudi.	'Turin is in mourning because GE is dead'.
Poiché è scomparso Giulio Einaudi, Torino è in lutto.	'Because GE is dead, Turin is in mourning.'

All causal clauses can appear as parenthetic clauses between commas after the subject of the main clause:

Il fax, giacché non è partito, deve essere rispedito al più presto.	'The fax, since it didn't go through, must be sent again as soon as possible.'

Causal clauses are frequently left-dislocated (cf. 17.2) in informal speech:

Il fax, giacché non è partito, lo devi rispedire al più presto.

Like English 'because', *perché* can be modified by focusing (cf. 13.9) adverbs, and can be focused in a cleft (cf. 17.3) sentence; this is not the case, as in English, with expressions meaning 'since', 'given that', etc.

L'ha detto semplicemente perché [not *poiché,* etc.] *voleva farsi sentire.*	'He said it simply because he wanted to be heard.'
È proprio perché [not *poiché,* etc.] *si dice che vi soggiornò il Barbarossa che il nome completo di questo paese è San Miniato al Tedesco.*	'It is precisely because B is said to have stayed here that this village's full name is San Miniato al Tedesco.'

Causal 'for' in constructions like 'He thanked me for doing it', 'He apologized for being late' is usually expressed by *per* or *di* + infinitive auxiliary verb + past participle:

Ti ringrazio di/per avermi fatto questo favore.	'Thank you for doing me this favour.'
Almeno scusati di/per aver fatto tardi!	'At least apologize for being late!'

But in spoken and informal registers, we find also *che* + finite verb:

Ti ringrazio che mi hai fatto questo favore.
Almeno scusati che hai fatto tardi!

Che 'because' in informal spoken language

In informal spoken language *perché* is replaced by *che* after imperatives. The English equivalents tend to lack any conjunction at all (but *che* could not be omitted from the eqivalent expressions in Italian):

Stai attento che qui si scivola.	'Mind out: it's slippery here.'
Prendi l'ombrello che piove.	'Take the umbrella: it's raining.'
Entra dentro che fa freddo.	'Come in: it's cold.'

19.13 Purpose conjunctions: *perché, acciocché, affinché* (*per* or *a* + infinitive)

These introduce a clause explaining the intention or the purpose of the action/event expressed in the main clause, and usually follow it. The commonest purpose conjunctions are *per* or *a* + infinitive, *perché* or *affinché* + subjunctive. Examples of the use of the subjunctive after *perché, acciocché, affinché* may be seen in 15.29:

Aprì le finestre affinché/acciocché/perché respirassero meglio.	'He opened the windows so that they could breathe better.'
Il volume descrive sommariamente il percorso di un manoscritto nella redazione delineando le diverse operazioni che devono essere compiute affinché esso si trasformi in un libro.	'The volume summarizes a manuscript's progress through editing, sketching the various operations which have to be carried out for it to become a book.'
Acciocché non si creassero equivoci, tutti i consiglieri erano stati invitati personalmente a partecipare alla prossima assemblea.	'That no misunderstandings should arise, all advisors had been personally invited to attend the next assembly.'

Perché is the commonest purpose conjunction in spoken Italian, while *affinché* is used mainly in writing. *Acciocché* is rare, and now found only in literary style. *Per* or *a* + present infinitive is used when the subject of the main and that of the purpose clause are one and the same, or when the subject of the purpose clause is indefinite personal (see 6.29):

Oggigiorno i giovani sono sempre meno disposti a emigrare per trovare lavoro.	'Nowadays young people are less and less prepared to emigrate to find work.'
Per rilassarsi non c'è niente di meglio che ascoltare Chopin.	'To relax there's nothing better than listening to C.'
L'aceto è ancora un mezzo validissimo per eliminare il calcare.	'Vinegar is still a very good way of getting rid of limescale.'

The preposition *a* tends to be used after *venire, correre, rientrare, tornare* and other verbs of movement. There is a difference, however, between using *a* and *per* in such cases, in that *a* is a rather 'neutral' form having relatively little association with purpose (note that its English equivalent is often 'and', rather than 'in order to'), whereas *per* emphasizes purpose:

Prima di andare a lavorare Gianni rientrò a salutare la madre.	'Before going to work G came back in to say/and said goodbye to his mother.'
Prima di andare a lavorare[7] Gianni rientrò per salutare la madre.	'Before going to work G came back in in order to say goodbye to his mother.'

Other sentence conjoiners introducing a purpose clause and followed by the infinitive are *allo scopo di, al fine di, in modo da* 'in order to', 'so as to':

---

[7]One would be unlikely to say *andare per lavorare* in much the same way as one would be unlikely to say 'go in order to work' in English.

Ho deciso di parlargli al fine di chiarire la situazione.	'I decided to talk to him in order to clarify the situation.'
Molte donne scelgono un lavoro part-time in modo da avere tempo per i figli.	'Many women choose a part-time job so as to have time for their children.'

Finally, note the structure *pur di* + present infinitive, which is used when the main clause expresses an extreme effort in order to do something (often by using expressions such as *fare qualsiasi cosa* 'to do anything', *combattere fino in fondo* 'fight to the end', *impegnarsi al massimo/il più possibile* 'be totally committed', etc.). The best English equivalent is something like 'just (to be able) to':

Pur di evitare al figlio la galera il pover'uomo non esitò a proclamarsi colpevole.	'Just to stop his son going to prison the poor man did not hesitate to declare himself guilty.'
Accetterei qualsiasi lavoro pur di guadagnare qualcosa.	'I'd take any job just to earn something.'

19.14 Concessive conjunctions and phrases: *benché, sebbene, ancorché, per quanto, quantunque, malgrado che, nonostante che, pur* 'although', 'despite the fact that', *seppure, anche se,* 'even if', etc.

These are used to contrast statements, or to say that something which is probably true does not affect the truth of some proposition, or to mention an exception to a statement already made. Note that in informal speech two coordinated sentences contrasted by using an adversative conjunction (like *ma*) are often preferred to a subordinate structure: *Non ho voglia di venire al cinema, ma ci vengo lo stesso visto che insisti* 'I don't want to come to the cinema, but I'll come anyway since you insist' is preferred to *Visto che insisti, vengo al cinema benché ne abbia poca voglia.* For the use of the subjunctive or indicative after these expressions, see 15.43.

Anna era il nome della ragazza, sebbene di solito la chiamassero Annichen o Annie.	'Anna was the girl's name, although she was usually called Annichen or Annie.'
Era l'ultima lite, almeno questo era chiaro. Ma per quanto l'avesse presentita da giorni e forse da settimane, nulla poteva placare l'ondata di rabbia e risentimento che gli stava montando dentro. [www]	'It was the last dispute, at least that was clear. But however much he had felt it coming for days and maybe weeks, nothing could placate the wave of rage and resentment building up within him.'
A considerarne lo sguardo, quantunque sia più giovane di lui, la fanciulla sembra incommensurabilmente più anziana, addirittura appartenente a una differente epoca. [www]	'If one considers her look, although she is younger than him, the girl seems immeasurably older, in fact as if she belongs to another age.'
Si sa bene che, malgrado ne abbiano l'apparenza, la balena non è affatto un pesce e che il pipistrello non è un uccello.	'It is well known that, despite appearances, the whale is no fish and the bat is no bird.'

Pur and *seppur(e)* mean 'although' but are followed by a gerund (*seppur[e]* can also be followed by a past participle):

Pur non amandola più, Andrea non aveva il coraggio di chiedere il divorzio.	'Although he no longer loved her, A did not have the courage to ask for a divorce.'

Pur facendo il possibile per mantenersi calmo, Giulio cominciava a perdere la pazienza.	'Although he did all he could to stay calm, G was beginning to lose his temper.'
Con questa opera l'autore ci introduce nel regno mentale della pazzia, dell'incapacità di governare i propri istinti seppur desiderando farlo.	'With this work the author takes us into the mental realm of madness, of inability to control one's own urges even though one wishes to do so.'
Filtravano nella penombra due raggi di sole; ed uno, crudele, andava a colpire il volto di Lavinia rivelando anche che i capelli, seppur in gran parte nascosti dal cappello, erano di quel mogano fasullo che dà la tintura. [www]	'Two shafts of sunlight filtered into the semi-darkness; and one, cruelly, went and fell across L's face revealing also that her hair, albeit largely concealed by her hat, were the fake mahogany colour produced by dyeing.'

Concessive *per* is mainly used in speech. In fact it corresponds closely to English concessive 'for', with the major difference that 'for', used in this way, can only be followed by a noun, whereas *per* is followed by a verb phrase containing an infinitive:

| *Tuo figlio è molto alto per avere solo dieci anni.* | 'Your son is very tall for a ten-year-old.' |
| *È proprio agile per essere così vecchio.* | 'He's really agile for such an old person.' |

Another concessive structure, 'not even', is *nemmeno, neppure, neanche, manco a* + infinitive, used only when the main clause is negative:

Non abiterei in un condominio nemmeno se mi pagassero!	'I wouldn't live in a condominium even if they paid me!'
Ad Adi, che resterà in casa e non andrà al tennis, però, non si sa che cosa dire. Neppure se uscire o no.	'But nobody knows what to say to A, who's staying at home and won't go to tennis. Not even whether to go out or not.'
Pierino non ha fatto i compiti. Non sa nemmeno dov'è il quaderno.	'P hasn't done his homework. He doesn't know where his exercise book is either.'

Manco a is used only in informal registers:

| *Nelle ore di punta non si trova un taxi manco a pagarlo oro!* | 'At rush hours you can't get a taxi for love nor money!' |

A costo di + infinitive is 'even if' (with overtones, as the expression suggests, of 'at any cost'):

| *Ti restituirò quello che ti devo a costo di lavorare giorno e notte.* | 'I'll give you back what I owe you even if I have to work night and day.' |

The expressions *tuttavia, nondimeno, pure, ugualmente, lo stesso* are sometimes used in the main clause to reinforce the contrast with the concessive clause:

| *Benché fosse ammalato, tuttavia l'anziano scrittore decise di uscire di casa per visitare un'esposizione di arte moderna.* | 'Although he was ill, the old writer decided in any case to get out and visit a modern art exhibition.' |

An idiomatic construction with concessive force is *avere un bel* + infinitive, which indicates that the action expressed by the infinitive was in vain, and is used in the following way:

| *Ebbe un bel gridare, non lo hanno sentito.* | 'Shout as he might, they didn't hear him.' |

Ho avuto un bel seguirlo di ristorante in ristorante, non ha mai rivelato niente.	'I followed him from restaurant to restaurant in vain, for he never revealed anything.'

19.15 Result conjunctions and phrases: *da* + infinitive, *così . . . che, tanto . . . che, di maniera (di modo) . . . che, al punto, a tal punto . . . che, talmente . . . che* + indicative

A result clause is usually preceded by an adjective (often *tale* 'such') or an adverb (*così, tanto, di maniera, a tal punto, talmente* 'so', 'so much so') in the main clause (see also 11.31):

Oggi fa così/tanto/talmente freddo che non ho proprio voglia di uscire.	'Today it is so cold that I really don't want to go out.'

When the adjective/adverb in the main clause is missing, the subordinate clause is introduced by the conjunctions *cosicché, sicché, di maniera che, di modo che, che, da*:

Vorrei incoraggiare moltissimo la lettura, cosicché diventi naturale prendere un libro in mano.	'I'd like to encourage reading very much, so that it becomes natural to pick up a book.'
Io sono sardo, quando sono qui a Roma mi chiamano 'il sardo', quando sono in Sardegna mi chiamano 'il romano', sicché non ho amici.	'I'm Sardinian, when I'm here in Rome they call me "the Sardinian", and when I'm in Sardinia they call me "the Roman", so that I don't have any friends.'
Il ragazzo tornò a casa bianco in faccia che sembrava morto.	'The boy came home so white-faced he seemed dead.'

In writing, *cosicché, sicché, di maniera che, di modo che* are separated by a comma from the main clause:

Appena vide arrivare la polizia il ragazzo tentò di scappare, cosicché fu chiaro a tutti chi fosse il colpevole.	'As soon as he saw the police arrive the boy tried to escape, so that it was clear to everyone who the guilty person was.'

Result clauses with *da* + infinitive are used only when the subjects of the main and the subordinate clause are coreferent, although in informal speech the constructions with the finite clause are always preferred:

Il traffico è così caotico nelle ore di punta da costringere gli automobilisti a lunghe cose.	'The traffic is so chaotic at rush hours that it forces/as to force long waits on motorists.'
Sono così stanco da non aver/che non ho nemmeno la forza di mangiare.	'I'm so tired that I don't even have the strength to eat.'

In the main clause adjectives (e.g., *tale*) and adverbs (e.g., *così, tanto, di maniera, a tal punto, talmente*) are found both in writing and in speech. The normal word order can be changed for emphasis (as it is in English), usually when the verb in the main clause is *essere* or when an auxiliary is used:

Così onesto e rassicurante sembrava l'uomo in divisa da poliziotto, che la vecchia donna non esitò a consegnargli la busta di documenti.	'So honest and reassuring did the man in the police uniform seem, that the old woman didn't hesitate to hand him the envelope with the documents.'

A tal livello di violenza sono arrivati oggi certi quartieri delle grandi città, che molti cittadini vorrebbero poter girare armati.	'Such a level of violence have certain areas of big cities reached today that many citizens would like to be able to go round armed.'
Tale era la mia paura che non osavo entrare nella stanza.	'Such was my fear that I dared not enter the room.'

Tale may either precede (more emphatically) or follow a noun:

Ho una tale voglia/voglia tale di rivedere la mia famiglia che se potessi salterei sul primo aereo.	'I have such a longing to see my family that if I could I'd jump on the first plane.'

Così, tanto, talmente can be used as adverbs or as modifiers followed by an adjective:

Arturo ruba la fidanzata del suo migliore amico e lo umilia talmente da indurlo a fare un gesto avventato e a nascondersi tra i barboni del parco.	'A steals his best friend's girlfriend and so humiliates him that he makes him make an impulsive gesture and hide among the tramps in the park.'
Le poltrone, come tutto il resto dell'arredamento nella hall dello Chateau, erano così/tanto/talmente grandi che chiunque ci si sedesse sembrava fatto in miniatura.	'The armchairs, like the rest of the furniture in the hall of the château, were so big that anyone who sat on them seemed to be a miniature.'
Scrivevo in modo così/tanto/talmente veloce che dopo mezz'ora ero costretto a fermarmi.	'I wrote so quickly that after half an hour I was forced to stop.'
Sophia Loren ieri ha firmato così tante copie del suo libro che alla fine si è detta davvero 'stanca ma felice'.	'SL yesterday signed so many copies of her book that at the end she said she was really "tired but happy".'

A tale livello/punto da + infinitive is adverbial 'so . . . that':

Ero stanco a tal punto da non desiderare altro che di dormire.	'I was so tired that all I wanted was to sleep.'
Ulisse [. . .] è un uomo scaltro, infedele, amato dalle donne, appassionato dell'avventura a tal punto da lasciare ben presto la fedele Penelope.	'Ulysses is a shrewd, unfaithful man, beloved by women, so enamoured of adventure as to leave his faithful Penelope very soon.'

Al punto 'to such an extent that' can be placed only at the end of the main clause:

La situazione in Kosovo si è deteriorata al punto da attirare l'attenzione anche di stati geograficamente lontani.	'The Kosovo situation has deteriorated to such an extent that it is attracting the attention even of geographically distant countries.'

19.16 Time conjunctions: 'when' *quando*, 'whenever' *ogni volta che, se*, 'while', 'as' *mentre, man mano che*, 'until' *finché/fino a che*, 'before' *prima che/di*, 'after' *dopo che/(di)*, 'as soon as' *appena, subito che*, 'since' *da quando*

'When' + verb is *quando* (interrogative *quando?*) + verb.

E quando i piccoli non possono lasciare il letto, sono le maestre ad andare da loro.	'And when the little ones can't leave their bed, the teachers go to them.'

> *Quando pensi di poter rileggere il testo?*   'When do you expect to be able to reread the text?'

In informal speech the final vowel of *quando* is frequently deleted when a word beginning with a vowel immediately follows and especially, it seems, where the following word is a form of *essere* or *avere*:

> *Quand'è che comincia lo spettacolo?*   'When is it the show starts?'
> *Quand'avevo quindici anni ci andavo ogni giorno.*   'When I was 15 I went there every day.'

'Whenever' + verb can be expressed by *ogni volta che* + verb (lit. 'every time that'):

> *Ogni volta che lo vedevo sembrava invecchiato di cinque anni.*   'Whenever I saw him he seemed 5 years older.'

Se, usually 'if', can also mean 'whenever'. In this sense it is usually followed by an indicative:

> *Se lo guardavo, cercava di nascondersi dietro il fazzoletto.*   'Whenever I looked at him, he would try to hide behind his handkerchief.'

Compare this with *Se lo guardassi, cercherebbe di nascondersi dietro il fazzoletto* 'If I looked at him/were to look at him, he would try to hide behind his handkerchief.'
'While' or 'as' + verb is usually *mentre* + verb (also *intanto che/frattanto che*):

> *Mentre mangiavi ho fatto una bella passeggiata.*   'While /As you were eating I had a nice walk.'

Simultaneous progression can be expressed by *man mano che, a mano a mano che, mano a mano che* + verb:

> *Man mano che spalava io continuavo a portare su carbone.*   'As he shovelled away I went on bringing up coal.'

'Before' + verb is *prima che* + subjunctive verb or *prima di* + infinitive; 'after' + verb is *dopo che* + indicative verb or either *dopo* or *dopo di* + infinitive of the auxiliary + past participle:

> *Bisognerebbe chiudere il cancello prima che entrino le pecore.*   'We'd better close the gate before the sheep get in.'
> *L'accampamento s'indovina prima d'arrivarci.*   'One can sense the encampment before getting to it.'
> *Dopo aver ammesso di aver detto in passato di essere 'nato cristiano' ...*   'After admitting he'd said in the past that he'd been "born a Christian" ...'
> *Dopo che avremo lavato la bandiera potremo issarla.*   'After we have washed the flag we'll be able to hoist it.'

'Until' + verb is generally *finché/fin che/fino a che* + *non* + verb (see 15.3 for an account of the use of *non* and of the subjunctive or indicative verb after *finché/fino a che*):

> *Aspettò sotto l'albero finché non smise di piovere.*   'He waited under the tree until it stopped raining.'

'For as long as' may be *finché/fino a che* + verb:

> *Continuò a camminare finché ne ebbe la forza.*   'He continued walking as long as he had the strength to.'

> *Perché finché fosse stato comandante della stazione di San Ginesio, noi saremmo dovuti rimanere nella caserma.*
>
> 'Because as long as he was commander of the San Ginesio station, we would have to remain in barracks.'

'As soon as' can be expressed by *appena* + verb (for the syntax of these expressions, see 15.11)

> *Appena entrò lo riconobbi.*
>
> 'As soon as he came in I recognized him.'

'Since' + verb is usually *da* + *quando* + verb:

> *Fin da quando aveva sei anni, aveva seguito suo fratello.*
> *I barattoli di metallo smaltato dove viene conservato, da quando era bambina, il prezioso granulato . . .*
>
> 'Since she was six, she had followed her brother.'
> 'The enamelled metal jars where the precious granulate has been kept since she was a child . . .'

19.17 Discourse markers

Conjunctions (*e, ma, allora*), adverbs (*cioè, praticamente*), interjections (*mah! beh!*) verb phrases (*figurati! guarda*), prepositional phrases (*in qualche modo*), interrogative phrases (*come dire*) occur – mainly in informal speech – as discourse markers. They indicate the attitude of the speaker, or make the hearer take a particular attitude to what the speaker is saying, or focus attention on a particular element of the utterance. Wherever they are placed in the sentence they are usually separated by a slight pause (or by a comma) from the words around them.

E 'and', *a parte questo* 'apart from that', *inoltre* 'moreover', *in aggiunta a* 'in addition to', *soprattutto* 'above all', 'especially', *allo/nello stesso tempo/momento* 'at the same time', *allo stesso modo, alla/nella stessa maniera* 'in the same way', *ugualmente* 'similarly', 'also', serve to introduce additional information to what has already been said:

> *A parte questo, va tutto bene.*
> *In RAI hanno cominciato tutti come giornalisti. Inoltre si sono occupati di trasmissioni culturali. Alla fine son diventati tutti conduttori.*
> *Ammesso che possano bastargli per avviare un simile programma. E, soprattutto, che gli elettori decidano di mandarcelo davvero, a Palazzo Chigi.*
>
> 'Apart from that, everything's fine.'
> 'At the RAI they all started out as journalists. Moreover they worked on cultural broadcasts. Finally they all became leaders.'
> 'Always assuming they suffice to launch such a programme. And, especially, that voters really do decide to send him to Palazzo Chigi.'

Comunque 'however', *nondimeno* 'none the less', *invece* 'instead', *al contrario* 'on the contrary', *d'altra parte, d'altro canto* 'on the other hand', *veramente* 'really', 'actually', introduce a sentence that contrasts with the previous one or gives another point of view:

> —*Vuoi una Margherita?*
> —*Veramente preferirei una Capricciosa.*
>
> 'Do you want a Margherita?'
> 'Actually I'd prefer a Capricciosa.'

> *Internet sta diventando sempre più un grande mercato elettronico. Nondimeno Internet continua a essere elitaria perché richiede l'utilizzo di un computer.*
>
> 'The Internet is increasingly a great electronic market. None the less the Internet is still elitist because it requires the use of a computer.'

In questo modo 'that way', *dunque* 'so', *di conseguenza* 'consequently', *come risultato (si ha che . . .)* 'as a result' (it turns out that . . .), *in tal modo* 'in that way', *con ciò* 'with that', *così* 'thus', *perciò* 'therefore', *quindi* 'so', *pertanto* 'therefore' introduce a sentence containing the result of what has been said previously:

Invita personalmente le autorità. In questo modo eviterai ogni equivoco.	'Invite the authorities personally. That way you'll avoid any misunderstanding.'
Lei non mi ama più. Dunque non ho più ragione di vivere.	'She doesn't love me any more. So I have no further reason to live.'

Second person imperatives of *guardare*, *vedere* and *sentire* are used to preface or point to an explanation:

Guarda, forse è meglio se ne parliamo.	'Look, perhaps it's better if we talk about it.'
Vede, lei dovrebbe solo dirmi se pensa che . . .	'You should just tell me if you think . . .'

Senti/senta (un po') 'Hey, I say', *Mi segui/segue?* 'Do you follow?', *Dimmi/Mi dica* 'Tell me', *Ehi* 'hey', *Dai* 'Come on', *Su, Allora* are used to draw attention:

Senta, le dispiace darmi un passaggio?	'I say, do you mind giving me a lift?'
Senti un po', dove sei stato ieri pomeriggio?	'Hey, where were you yesterday afternoon?'
Gianni, mi segui?	'G, are you with me?'
Mi dica, su, che cosa si intende con 'fonema'.	'Come on, tell me, what "phoneme" means.'

Beh, mah, insomma, ecco, dunque, allora are used to soften the contrast between the answer/comment and what has just been said, or avoid abruptness when changing the topic of conversation, or when starting to talk about a different aspect of it (e.g. *va bé/vabbè*, only in informal speech, *d'accordo, ora*):

Allora, da dove vogliamo cominciare quest'esame?	'Right, where do we start this exam from?'
Si può considerare che esista una vera e propria rivoluzione in atto? Mah, le rivoluzioni sono spesso questioni di punti di vista.	'May we take it that there's a real revolution under way? Well, revolutions are often a question of one's point of view. '
Beh, non sono d'accordo con te, ma rispetto la tua opinione.	'Well, I don't agree with you, but I respect your opinion.'
Beh, cosa sei venuto a fare?	'OK, what have you come to do?'
Dunque, ora parliamo di un altro argomento.	'Right, now let's talk about something else.'
Vabbè, vedo che sei stanco, allora andiamo a letto.	'OK, I can see you're tired, so let's go to bed.'
—*Dai, ora non farmi il moralista!*	'Come on, don't start moralizing at me now!'
—*Vabbè, ma ero ironico . . .*	'OK, but I was being ironic.'

A proposito 'by the way', is used to draw attention to a new topic of discussion:

—*Vieni a prendere Lucia a scuola?*	'Are you coming to pick up L at school?'
—*A proposito, ti ho portato i libri che mi avevi chiesto.*	'By the way, I've brought you the books you asked me for.'

Non so 'I don't know', *forse* 'perhaps', *come posso dire, come dire* 'How can I put it' are elements indicating that the speaker is not sure exactly how he or she can best express what follows:

Qui è bello ma, non so, tutto mi sembra così diverso.	'This is beautiful but, I don't know, everything seems so different.'
Mah, quel ragazzo, come posso dire, mi sembra un po' strano.	'Well that boy, how can I put it, strikes me as rather odd.'
Gli alimenti transgenici sono un po', come dire, una violenza fatta alla natura.	'Transgenic foodstuffs are a bit, so to speak, of a violation of nature.'

Appunto,[8] *per l'appunto* 'exactly so', *davvero, proprio* 'really', 'actually' are reinforcing elements:

—*Hai visto Riccardo?*	'Have you seen R?'
—*Appunto, sono venuto a dirti che è appena arrivato.*	'Exactly, I've come to tell you he has just arrived.'
Gianni, che sorpresa vederti! Pensavo appunto di telefonarti.	'G, what a surprise to see you! I was actually thinking of phoning you.'
—*Hai spiccioli?*	'Do you have any small change?'
—*Per l'appunto li ho dati tutti a mio figlio.*	'Actually I've given it all to my son.'
—*Ti piace ancora fare castelli di sabbia?*	'Do you still like building sand castles?'
—*Davvero, non puoi capire quanto mi rilassi!*	'Really you can't imagine how it relaxes me!'

Secondo me 'in my opinion', 'I reckon', *per conto mio* 'for my part', *direi* 'I'd say', *mi sembra* 'I think', 'it seems to me', *penso* 'I think', emphasize the role of the speaker. More formal are *se lei mi permette/consente, se mi è permesso/consentito/lecito* 'if you'll allow me':

Vendere la tua bella casa, per conto mio, è una gran stupidaggine.	'Selling your beautiful house, in my book, is a really stupid thing to do.'
Il conto, secondo me, è davvero salato!	'The bill, in my opinion, is really a bit steep!'
Vorrei fare una domanda, se mi è permesso, al Professor Ramat.	'I'd like, if I may, to ask Professor R a question.'

Mettiamo/diciamo/facciamo '[let's] say', *per esempio* 'for example', etc. are used to give examples:

Andrea, mettiamo, ti telefona stasera. Come fai se c'è anche tuo marito?	'Say A phones you this evening. What do you do if your husband's in too?'
Enrico Rossi, per esempio, è chiaramente avviato a una bella carriera politica.	'ER, for example, is clearly heading for a fine political career.'

No?, vero?, non è vero? 'is(n't) it?', *non ti sembra/pare?, non credi?* 'don't you think?', *non è così?* 'isn't that so?', *dico male?* 'am I wrong?', *mica male, eh?* 'not bad, eh?' are used in questions asking for confirmation from the person who is addressed ('tag questions'):

Vieni, no?	'You're coming, aren't you?'
Mi hanno proposto un lavoro a Roma: alloggio pagato, e cinque milioni netti al mese. Mica male, eh?	'I've been offered a job in Rome: free accommodation and five million a month after tax. Not bad, eh?'
Il candidato favorito alla presidenza della Repubblica è Emma Bonino, vero?	'The favourite candidate for President of the Republic is EB, right?'

---

[8]*Appunto* can also be used in answers:

—*Sei venuto per vedere Gianni?*	'Have you come to see G?'
—*Appunto.*	'Just so.'

No, certamente no, proprio no, no di certo, no di sicuro, no davvero, no e poi no, no no e poi ancora no, ma no! are used to emphasize that an answer is negative:

Non vengo di certo.	'I'm certainly not coming.'
—Telefoni a Marco stasera?	'Are you phoning M this evening?'
—No di certo, se mi vuole mi chiama lui.	'Absolutely not; if he wants me he can call me.'
—Allora, esci con Andrea domani?	'So, are you going out with A tomorrow?'
—No, no e poi ancora no. Abbiamo litigato e non voglio più vederlo.	'Not bloody likely. We've had a row and I don't want to see him again.'

Certo, di certo, sicuro, di sicuro, bene, benissimo, esatto, come no, (è) chiaro, senza dubbio, non c'è alcun dubbio, express approval:

—Vieni a cena stasera?	'Are you coming to dinner this evening?'
—Certo, non me la perderei per niente al mondo!	'Sure, I wouldn't miss it for the world!'

Purtroppo, sfortunatamente 'unfortunately', *peccato* '[that's a] pity/shame':

—Gianni è già uscito.	'G's already gone out.'
—Peccato, volevo salutarlo.	'A pity, I wanted to say hello to him.'
Purtroppo non posso uscire stasera.	'Unfortunately I can't come out this evening.'

Magari expresses a strong, but unfulfilled (and perhaps unfulfillable) desire. It may be equivalent to 'if only':

Magari avessero tutti lo stesso atteggiamento!	'If only they all had the same attitude.'

In informal usage, *magari* may be equivalent to 'perhaps', 'maybe' – but only where something desirable is being expressed:

Loro, magari, ti daranno un passaggio.	'Maybe they will give you a lift.'

It also functions as an interjection expressing enthusiastic wishes:

—Vuoi venire con noi al mare?	'Do you want to come to the seaside with us?'
—Magari!	'Oh yes!/I'll say!/Rather!'

19.18 Interjections

Interjections are extensively used to express emotions.

Ah, which is usually followed by a comma in writing, can express happiness or relief (in which case it is usually pronounced [aː], with a lengthened vowel), or apprehension, pain, anger (usually pronounced [a]):

Ah, guarda la tigre. Che bestia feroce!	'Ah, look at the tiger. What a fierce beast!'
Ai tre anni di età, finalmente, per noi maschietti, arrivava il momento di vestire da uomo. Ah, quel mio primo paio di pantaloncini!	'At age three the moment came at last for us little boys to dress like men. Ah, my first pair of little trousers!'

Eh can have a variety of uses:

- to reinforce what the speaker is saying (pronounced [e] or [ɛ]):

  Eh su, si faccia coraggio.　　　　　　'Come on, be brave.'
  Splendida serata, eh?　　　　　　　'Splendid evening, eh?'

- to express doubt, possibility, hope or approval (pronounced [e] or [ɛ]):

  Eh, non so proprio.　　　　　　　'Hmm, I don't rightly know.'
  Eh, presto starà meglio.　　　　　　'Hey, it'll be better soon.'

- to express surprise or incredulity (usually pronounced [ɛh] or [ɛʔ]):

  Eh? Ma che dici?　　　　　　　'Uh? What are you saying?'
  Eh? Non ci posso credere!　　　　　'Eh? I can't believe it!'

In informal language *eh* may be used with the same meaning as *eccomi* 'here I am', or to answer or inform the other person that what he or she said has not been perceived/understood:

—Lorenzo?　　　　　　　'Lorenzo?'
—Eh?　　　　　　　　'Yes [here I am]?'
—Se esci dimmelo per favore.　　'If you go out please tell me.'
—Eh?　　　　　　　　'Eh?'

Eh, già, and *eh, sì* are also used in conversation to indicate understanding or emphasize agreement:

Andai alla cassa della stazione e dissi alla　'I went to the station ticket counter and
signorina: 'Un biglietto!' La cassiera mi　said to the young lady: "A ticket!" The
guardò e disse calma calma: 'Eh, sì, ma per　cashier looked at me and said, very
dove, signore?'　calmly: "Quite, but where to, sir?"'
Primi giorni di scuola, le prime paure, le　'The first days of school, the first fears,
prime soddisfazioni, e poi . . . eh, già: le　the first satisfactions, and then . . . oh,
'prime pagine' da leggere . . .　yes: the "first pages" to read . . .'

Oh (and *oddio, oh Dio*), much as in English, can express compassion, doubt, wish, pain, boredom, surprise:

—Mi hai portato l'articolo?　　　'Did you bring me the article?'
—Oh Dio, l'ho lasciato a casa!　　'Oh God, I left it at home!'
—Vuoi un gelato?　　　　　'Do you want an ice cream?'
—Oh, un gelatino ci starebbe proprio bene.　'Oh, an ice cream would go down a
　　　　　　　　　treat.'

Oh, come mi sentii stringere dolorosamente　'Oh, how I felt my heart ache, that
il cuore, quella mattina!　morning!'

Ahi, ohi, express both physical and psychological pain, *ahi ahi, ohi ohi* regret, worry, concern. *Ahimé, ohimé* express psychological pain, 'alas'.

Ahi, mi sono tagliato con la scatoletta di　'Ouch, I've cut myself on the tuna tin!'
tonno!
Ahimé, ho capito che è inutile continuare a　'Alas, I've realized it's pointless to go on
pensare a lei.　thinking about her.'
Ahi ahi, la vedo brutta!　'Uh, oh, this looks nasty!'

Ohibò (oibò) expresses disapproval, disgust:

Ohibò, che roba è questa?　　　　'Ugh, what's this?'

Ehi (stressed on the 'e') is used to draw attention, and is usually followed by the name of the person addressed:

Ehi Woody Guthrie, ti ho scritto una canzone . . .	'Hey, Woodie Guthrie, I've written you a song . . .'

When it is not followed by the personal name, it may be pronounced with the stress on the 'i':

Ehi, un momento, io non sono per niente d'accordo.	'Hang on, I don't agree at all.'

Bah, chissà, forse express uncertainty and resignation, incredulity:

Bah, non so proprio cosa fare.	'Oh well, I really don't know what to do.'
Anche stasera non c'è niente di bello alla TV. Bah, quasi quasi vado a letto.	'There's nothing worth watching on TV this evening either. Oh well, I might just as well go to bed.'
—Tornerai per pranzo?	'Will you be back for lunch?'
—Chissà, dipende da quanto lavoro troverò in ufficio.	'Maybe, it depends on how much work I have at the office.'

Beh, always at the beginning of a sentence, can be used with a conclusive or an interrogative meaning:

Beh, se non dite altro me ne vado.	'Well, if you're not telling me anything else I'm off.'
Disegnare fumetti mi è sempre piaciuto perché pensavo che i disegnatori non dovessero alzarsi presto al mattino. Beh, in realtà non era solo questo . . .	'I've always liked drawing strip cartoons because I thought cartoonists didn't need to get up early in the morning. Well, in fact it wasn't just that . . .'
—Ciao . . . allora?	'Hi . . . well?'
—Mmm . . .	'Hmmm . . .'
—Tutto bene?	'Everything OK?'
—Beh, non saprei . . .	'Er well, I'm not sure . . .'

Boh expresses uncertainty, incredulity, disdain (or indifference – a kind of verbal shrug of the shoulders):

—Ma lei gli mette le corna?	'Is she deceiving him then?'
—Boh!	'Search me.'
—A che ora ci troviamo stasera?	'What time shall we meet this evening?'
—Boh! Fate voi.	'Dunno. You decide.'

Uffa, che noia, che barba, che scocciatura (also the rude *che palle*), *basta!, non (mi) va!,* express boredom, irritation and annoyance. These may also be expressd by *accidenti, accidempoli, accipicchia, acciderba* (the last three are old-fashioned):

Che scocciatura, piove e devo andare a fare la spesa.	'What a nuisance. It's raining and I have to go shopping.'
Uffa, ma la smetti di lamentarti?	'Oh, will you stop moaning?'

Accidenti,[9] *capperi, caspita* (which is a euphemism for the rude *cazzo*) can be used at a very informal level to convey surprise or amazement:

Caspita, ma è meraviglioso!	'Blimey, it's marvellous!'

---

[9]*Accidenti* can also express anger, as well as *che rabbia, che nervi/nervoso,* and *accipicchia,* which is very mild and rather old-fashioned. *Porco cane, porca miseria, porca puttana* are considered rude.

20

Word derivation

20.1 Word derivation: Compounds and conversion

Many Italian words are obviously 'made up of' or 'derived from' other existing words, but most 'word derivation' is best described in a dictionary rather than a reference grammar. This is because it is rarely the case that new words can be coined in simple and predictable ways from existing words, and existing derived words rarely have a meaning which can be simply and transparently related to the words from which they are derived. In short, there are very few reliable rules. Take the example of compound nouns and adjectives (aspects of whose grammar are described in 3.7 and 3.13). These are words made up of other, independently existing, words (nouns, adjectives, verbs and sometimes prepositions), and are usually written as a single word. The meaning of a compound can never be wholly deduced from the meaning of its component parts. An example of a relatively 'transparent' compound is *cassaforte* 'strong box', made up of *cassa* 'box' and *forte* 'strong', but still a *cassaforte* is not just any 'strong box', but specifically a box for the safe storage of valuables, a 'safe'; a *fermacarte* is clearly made up of the verb 'to stop' (specifically, the second person singular imperative form thereof) and the word for 'papers', but this is not some instruction to 'stop papers', or just any device for 'stopping papers', but specifically a 'paperweight'. At the other extreme, a by now wholly 'opaque' compound is *coprifuoco*, literally 'cover fire', but in fact a 'curfew'. So word derivation is sufficiently fraught with unpredictabilities that while non-native speakers should of course do their best to *learn* as many derived words as possible, they should be wary of trying to coin new ones themselves, and cautious in interpreting existing ones.

We should, however, mention one relatively straightforward and predictable method of word derivation, namely 'conversion', or the transferral of a word from the part of speech to which it normally belongs (verb, adjective, etc.) to some other part of speech without change in the structure of the word. Thus the masculine forms of adjectives may be used as nouns: *Mi piace il rosso* 'I like red', *Oseremo l'impossibile* 'We shall dare [try] the impossible' (see further 3.15 and 17.20), *Ha detto il falso* 'He told a lie', lit. 'He said the false'. Conversion of adjectives into nouns is used rather more extensively in Italian than in English, in that in Italian 'article + noun' is often used where English might employ 'article + adjective + thing':

L'importante è che tu l'abbia visto.   'The important thing is that you should have seen it.'

| *Il bello era che non sapeva che io ci sarei stato.* | 'The good [or 'unexpected'] thing was that he didn't know I'd be there.' |

Similarly, the infinitive may be used as an abstract noun generally identical in meaning to the verb: *il cantare* '(the act of) singing', *lo scendere* '(the act) of descending'. For further discussion of this use of the infinitive, see 15.24.

20.2 Affixation: prefixes and suffixes

A further and extremely important method of word derivation is affixation (attachment of prefixes and suffixes to existing words). Many prefixes can be freely attached to existing words to form new words, and the meaning of the resulting derived word is often simply the sum of the meanings of the prefix + base word, e.g., *ri* [prefix of repetition] + *aprire* 'open' gives *riaprire* 'to open again'. A few of the more transparent and freely usable prefixes (a more extensive list of them can be found in Dardano 1991: 152–6) are:

TABLE 20.A

anti 'against', 'anti-'	*anticomunista* 'anti-communist', *antimateria* 'antimatter', *antinfiammatorio* 'anti-inflammatory', etc.
ex- 'former', 'ex-'	*ex-marito* 'ex-husband', *ex-comunista* 'ex-communist', etc.
ri- 'repetition', 'again', 'back', 're-'	*riportare* 'bring back', *rifare* 'redo', *ridire* 'say again', etc. *Ri-* can also indicate 'intensification': *ripiegare* 'to fold up'. But in some cases the meaning of *ri-* is not transparent, e.g., *rimordere* not only 'to bite again', but also 'to cause remorse'.
pre- 'pre-', 'in advance'	*preannunciare* 'announce in advance', *preconfezionato* 'pre-packaged', etc.
stra- 'intensive', 'excessive', 'extra-'	*stravecchio* 'very old' (especially of liquor); *stracuocere* 'overcook', etc.
super- 'super', 'above'	*superuomo* 'superman', *superaffaticarsi* 'overstrain oneself', *superintelligente* 'superintelligent', etc.

Italian has an array of negative or 'privative' prefixes (*dis-, s-, de-, in-, a-*), but there is no systematic way of predicting which negative prefix will be used, so these negative forms have to be learned word by word:

- *s-* is often prefixed to words beginning with a consonant: *sfortunato* 'unfortunate', *sleale* 'disloyal', *scorretto* 'incorrect', 'improper', *sgradevole* 'unpleasant', *scortese* 'discourteous', 'rude', *sbucciare* 'peel' (a verb derived from the noun *buccia* 'peel'), etc. *S-* may also have an 'intensive', rather than a negative, value, e.g., *sbandierare* 'wave a flag about' (from *bandiera* 'flag'), *smartellare* 'hammer away' (from *martello* 'hammer'), etc.
- *dis-* rather than *s-* is often used before vowels: *disordinato* 'disordered', 'untidy', *disorganizzato* 'disorganized', *disadatto* 'unsuited', etc. But there is also *in-* (or *im-*): *inutile* 'useless', 'pointless', *inelegante* 'inelegant', *impossibile*

'impossible', etc. and sometimes (especially in words belonging to erudite registers) *a-: apolitico* 'apolitical', *asociale* 'asocial', etc. *De-* often indicates 'removal', e.g., *decaffeinare* 'decaffeinate'.

Suffixes are attached to the root of a noun or adjective (i.e., to the base word minus any unstressed vowel at the end of that word): *fiore (fior-)* 'flower' > *fioraio* (or *fiorista*) 'flower seller', *posta (post-)* 'post' > *postino* 'postman', *gomma (gomm-)* 'tyre' > *gommista* 'tyre salesman', *blu (blu)* 'blue' > *bluastro* 'bluish', etc. (an exception is *assenteismo* 'absenteeism'). Italian possesses hundreds of suffixes with an extremely wide variety of functions but, unfortunately, there is almost never a transparent 'one-to-one' relationship between suffix and function. That is to say that given a particular function one cannot predict which suffix will express it, or whether it will be expressed by a suffix at all; and given a particular suffix, one cannot say for sure what function it performs. For example, the suffix *-aio* is frequently found in derived 'agent' words meaning 'one who sells/deals in/makes/does X': e.g., *vinaio* 'wine seller' (*vino*), *orologiaio* 'clock maker' (*orologio*), *sellaio* 'saddler' (*sella*), but there is no predicting with which words *-aio* will be used: a 'postman' is *postino* (*posta*), 'road sweeper' *spazzino* (*spazzare*), a tyre salesman *gommista* (*gomma*), a gardener *giardiniere* (*giardino*), a warrior *guerriero* (*guerra*), a teacher *insegnante* (*insegnare*), a worker *lavoratore*[1] (*lavorare*), and so forth. The suffix *-ino* is widely used to express 'diminutiveness', e.g., *ragazzo* 'boy' *ragazzino* 'little boy', but we have already seen that *-ino* carries no connotation of 'diminutiveness' in *postino* 'postman', while *polsino* (from *polso* 'wrist') is not normally interpreted as 'small wrist' but as 'cuff' (of shirt, etc.). All this means that, while some generalizations may be possible, the safest approach to suffixes is to learn, word by word, the appropriate suffixal form and the meaning of the suffix in any particular context. The category of suffixal derivation of nouns from other nouns is very large, and to some degree addressed elsewhere in this section and below (see Dardano 1991: 145–8 for further examples). Notable because of their (relative) transparency are:

- *-ame* 'collectivity': *fogliame* 'foliage' (*foglia* 'leaf'), *pollame* 'poultry' (*pollo* 'chicken'), *bestiame* 'livestock' (*bestia* 'beast'), etc.
- *-eto* 'place where plants are cultivated, or found in abundance': *oliveto* 'olive grove' (*olivo* 'olive tree'), *canneto* 'reed bed' (*canna* 'reed'), etc.
- *-eria* 'place where some business or activity is carried out', especially when there are corresponding agent nouns in *-aio*: *orologeria* 'clock and watch shop' (*orologiaio*), *selleria* 'saddle shop', 'saddlery' (*sellaio* 'saddle maker'), also *falegnameria* 'carpenter's shop' (*falegname*), etc.

We list below (see also Dardano 1991: 136–48) just a few of the more common derivational suffixes, and the functions commonly associated with them:

Deriving adjectives from nouns and verbs:

- *-abile* (first conjugation transitive verbs), *-ibile* (transitive verbs of other conjugations): *mangiabile* 'eatable' (*mangiare*), *bevibile* 'drinkable' (*bere*),

---

[1]For agent nouns ending in *-tore*, such as *lavoratore* 'worker', feminine *lavoratrice*, and for other suffixes denoting females, see 3.12.

leggibile 'legible' (*leggere*). But note also the following, not derived from verbs: *papabile* 'capable of being made pope' (*papa* 'pope'), *tascabile* 'pocket-sized' (*tasca* 'pocket'), etc. But also, and unpredictably, *-evole*: *ammirevole* 'admirable' (*ammirare*), *lodevole* 'praiseworthy' (*lodare*), etc.

- *-ale*: *nazionale* 'national' (*nazione*), *invernale* 'pertaining to winter' (*inverno*), etc.
- *-ano*: *africano* 'African', *italiano* 'Italian', etc.
- *-ese*: *maltese* 'Maltese', *milanese* 'Milanese', etc.
- *-oso*: *pericoloso* 'dangerous' (*pericolo*), *amoroso* 'in love' (*amore*), *orgoglioso* 'proud' (*orgoglio*), etc.
- *-uto* (this suffix is particularly prominent in deriving adjectives from names of body parts, often with slightly pejorative connotations): *ossuto* 'bony' (*osso*), *nasuto* 'big nosed' (*naso*); also *occhialuto* 'bespectacled' (*occhiali*), *panciuto* 'pot-bellied' (*pancia*).

Deriving nouns from adjectives and verbs:

- *-esimo*: *umanesimo* 'humanism' (*umano*), *cristianesimo* 'Christianity' (*cristiano*), etc.
- *-ezza*: *bellezza* 'beauty' (*bello*), *amichevolezza* 'friendliness' (*amichevole*), etc.
- *-ino*: *perugino* 'Perugian', *tunisino* 'Tunisian', etc.
- *-io* (pronounced -['io], is attached to verb roots to derive nouns expressing a sustained or repeated activity, especially a noise): *mormorio* 'murmuring sound' (*mormorare*), *fruscio* 'rustling' (*frusciare*), *calpestio* 'tramp-tramp' (*calpestare*), *lavorio* 'persistent labour', 'industriousness' (*lavorare*), etc.
- *-ismo* (often correlates with 'agent' nouns in *-ista*): *nazionalismo* (*nazionalista*) 'nationalism', *socialismo* (*socialista*) 'socialist', etc. But note also *tennista* 'tennis player', derived from *tennis*, *cretinismo* 'stupid behaviour' (*cretino*).
- *-ità*: *moralità* 'morality' (*morale*), *nazionalità* 'nationality' (*nazionale*), *abilità* 'ability' (*abile*), etc.
- *-mento*: *affidamento* 'entrusting' (*affidare*), *apprendimento* 'learning' (*apprendere*), etc.
- *-ume* (typically pejorative and used typically of entities perceived as forming a mass or a group): *verdume* 'unpleasant green stuff', 'mould' (*verde*), *sudiciume* 'filth' (*sudicio*), *forestierume* 'blasted outsiders' (*forestiero*), etc.
- *-zione*: *determinazione* 'determination' (*determinare*), *amministrazione* 'administration' (*amministrare*).

Mention should be made also of what is sometimes labelled 'zero suffixation', where a noun is derived from a verb merely by using the bare root of the verb (plus, unpredictably, the masculine ending *-o* or feminine *-a*). For example, both *bonifica* 'reclamation [of land]' and *bonifico* 'credit payment' (from two different senses of the verb *bonificare*), *dedica* '[words of] dedication' (*dedicare*), *spaccio* 'dealing', 'distribution' (*spacciare*), *inoltro* 'forwarding' (*inoltrare*), *decollo* 'take off [aeroplane]' (*decollare*), *proroga* 'adjournment', 'rescheduling' (*prorogare*), etc. It is noteworthy that many 'zero suffixation' forms belong to the language of administration and bureaucracy.

Deriving verbs from nouns and adjectives:

A common device is *-izzare* (often corresponding to English '-ize')

- *-izzare*: *atomizzare* 'atomize' (*atomo*), *toscanizzare* 'Tuscanize' (*toscano*), *nazionalizzare* 'nationalize' (*nazionale*), etc.

But there are other possibilities, such as:

- *-eggiare*: *verdeggiare* 'be verdant' (*verde*), *toscaneggiare* 'speak/act like a Tuscan' (*toscano*), etc.

20.3 Feminine past participles in noun-formation, and the suffix *-ata*

The feminine past participle of verbs can be used as a noun, usually expressing the rapid, sudden completion of the action indicated by the verb: e.g., *dare una letta* 'to give a quick read through' (*leggere*), *fare una dormita* 'to have a quick nap' (*dormire*), *guardata* '(quick) glance' (*guardare*). Such forms may also indicate 'fullness', 'completedness', as in *farsi una bella mangiata* 'have a good eat', 'eat one's full' (*mangiare*), *spalata* 'shovelful' or 'act of shovelling away' (*spalare*), *sfregiata* 'slashing' (*sfregiare*), etc. But *-ata*, the first conjugation feminine past participle ending, can also be suffixed to nouns: *gomitata* 'dig with the elbow' (*gomito*), *pugnalata* 'stab' (*pugnale* 'dagger'), *cretinata*, *stupidata* 'stupid action' (*cretino*, *stupido*), *risata* '(burst of) laughter' (*riso*), *stronzata* 'nasty action', 'mean trick' (*stronzo* 'bastard', 'nasty person'), *spaghettata* 'spaghetti-eating session' (*spaghetti*), *cucchiaiata* 'spoonful' (*cucchiaio*), *occhiata* 'glance' (*occhio*), *boccata* 'mouthful' (*bocca*), even *videata* 'everything displayed on a (computer) screen' (*video*), etc.

Note the diminutive form of *risata* in the following:

In due o tre giorni Nino ebbe fatto amicizia *con loro e si parlavano a risatine e gomitate.*	'In two or three days, N had made friends with them and they were exchanging giggles and nudges.'

20.4 Evaluative suffixes

The so-called 'evaluative' suffixes have a rather special status. First, and unlike most suffixes, they usually do not change the basic meaning of the word to which they are attached and they never change the part of speech (verb, noun, adjective, etc.) to which the base word belongs. Second, *some* evaluative suffixes have a relatively high degree of productivity (i.e., they may be fairly readily combined with existing words to form new ones), and relatively transparent meanings, and it is on the more productive and transparent forms that we focus here.

The evaluatives are usually subdivided according to the labels 'augmentative', 'diminutive', 'pejorative' and what is known in Italian as 'vezzeggiativo', expressing endearment or affection. The commonest and most productive of these suffixes are: *-one* (augmentative), *-ino* (diminutive, 'vezzeggiativo') and *-uccio* (diminutive, 'vezzeggiativo'). There is also the somewhat less productive, *-etto*, the now rather unproductive *-ello* (diminutive and also 'vezzeggiativo'), and -*accio* (pejorative). To these we may add a few more suffixes which might be called 'attenuative', and roughly correspond to English '-ish' (e.g., -*astro*). These suffixes can be attached to nouns, adjectives, and to 'lexical' adverbs (see 13.3) such as *bene, male*: *tavolone, tavolino, tavoluccio, tavolaccio* (*tavolo* 'table'); *cattivone, cattivino, cattivuccio, cattivaccio* (*cattivo* 'bad'); *benone, benino, benuccio* (*bene* 'well'); *malaccio* (*male* 'badly'). It is even marginally possible to attach them to numerals, e.g., *un seuccio* 'a bare six' (from *sei*, the minimum pass mark in schools). They normally *follow* other, less productive, suffixes (e.g., *pennello* 'paintbrush', from *penna* 'pen', yields *pennellino* 'little paintbrush'; *cagnetto* 'little dog' yields *cagnettaccio* 'nasty little dog'; *leprotto* 'young hare' yields *leprottino* 'tiny young hare'). They cannot normally be attached to compound nouns and adjectives (one cannot say, for example, **cassapanchina* from *cassapanca*). In certain cases, the base to which the suffix is attached may be changed: when -*ino* is attached to a word ending in -*on(e)*, it generally takes the form -*cino* (e.g., *milione* 'million' *milioncino, camion* 'truck', 'lorry' *camioncino, bastone* 'stick' *bastoncino* 'little stick', 'chopstick'); note also *uomo* 'man' but *omino, ometto, omone, omaccio; cane* 'dog' but *cagnolino, cagnetto, cagnaccio; sasso* 'stone', 'rock' but *sassolino; libro* 'book' but *libriccino; ponte* 'bridge', *ponticello; vento* 'wind', *venticello*.

The transparency of the evaluative suffixes listed above should not be over-stated, for sometimes the meaning of -*ino*, -*one* forms is not straightforwardly related to the word from which they are derived: a *finestrino* is specifically the window of a vehicle (car, train, aeroplane), *tavolino* may mean specifically a 'desk used for study', or 'small table used for serving tea/as a bedside table', *testina* is a 'head' on a tape recorder, etc. (or just a 'small head'), *battaglione* is 'battalion', rather than a 'big battle', *cavalletto* is not a 'small horse' but an 'easel' or an 'A-frame', and a *cavalletta* is not a 'small mare', but a 'grasshopper', and so forth. There are some cases in which suffixation of -*ino* is blocked because an identical word ending in -*ino* already exists. Thus 'I'm going for a little walk round. I'll be back in about an hour' could be *Vado a fare un giretto. Tornerò fra un'oretta*, but not *Vado a fare un *girino*, nor *Tornerò fra un' *orina*, because *girino* means 'tadpole', and *orina* 'urine'! And -*etto* tends to be avoided, in favour of -*ino*, in words whose roots end in -*t* or -*tr*: *lettino* 'little bed', not **lettetto, fettina* 'little slice', not **fettetta, teatrino* 'little theatre' not **teatretto*; and -*ino* tends to be avoided with words ending in -*ino*: *cuscinetto* 'little cushion' rather than *cuscinino, cuginetto* 'little cousin', rather than *cuginino*. Some further examples where either -*ino* or -*etto* forms are blocked because an identical word already exists with a special meaning are: *forchetta* 'fork' (so *forca* 'gibbet', *forchina*), *mulino* 'windmill' (so *mulo* 'mule', *muletto*), *corpetto* 'bodice' (so *corpo* 'body', but *corpicino*), *manetta* 'handcuff' (so *mano* 'hand', *manina*). However, some words in -*etto* do not block the derivation of other, more transparent, words in -*etto*: *rosetta* 'washer (on a tap/faucet)' but also 'little rose' (*rosa*), *lametta* 'razor blade' or any 'small blade' (*lama*), *balletto* 'ballet' or any small dance (*ballo*).

In cases like those just described, where the suffix changes the basic meaning of the word, it is likely that the suffixed form is listed as well as the non-suffixed form in dictionaries, and can be freely used in any register. But it is a hallmark of spoken, informal Italian that evaluative suffixes are freely and spontaneously attached to nouns and adjectives without change in basic meaning. Such suffix-ation is unlikely to be encountered, say, in academic writing or in a public address, so that while *cavalletto*, which has an independent dictionary entry as 'easel', could freely occur in such contexts, use of *cavallaccio* (which has no separate dictionary entry) in an academic study on the evolution of the horse, or in a public announcement at a horse race, might produce much the same effect as saying 'gee gee' or 'damned horse' in the same contexts in English.

The fact that 'transparent' evaluative suffixation is characteristic of informal registers does not mean that it can be ignored by learners. A sense of the appropriate contexts for its use is an essential part of fluent command of Italian, even though such contexts are very difficult to define. What needs to be recognized is that the highly productive evaluative suffixes such as *-one*, *-ino*, *-etto*, *-uccio*, *-accio*, etc., do not primarily mean 'big', 'small', 'endearing', 'nasty', etc.; rather they tend to signal a certain attitude of 'informality', 'playfulness' or 'non-seriousness' towards what is being said (and not just to the word to which they are attached).[2] If there is a difference between *-ino* and *-etto*, however, it is that the latter *tends* to be perceived as less expressive of endearment and affection than the former, but it needs to be said that while this is apparently true in Tuscany, it may not be valid for the whole of Italy. Abundant use of diminutive suffixes is particularly characteristic of the language used to address small children, and does not necessarily imply that the suffixed nouns are 'small'. For example, an adult might say to a child:[3]

Hai trovato un posticino bellino.	'You've found a nice little place.' [to a child sitting on an adult's knees]
Alla zietta le fa male il dentino.	'Your auntie's toothie is hurting.'
Ma come sei grandina!	'My, how big you are!'

The diminutives may also convey 'understatement', a desire not to sound too direct or insistent, deference towards one's addressee, or irony:

Ho anche una casetta a Capri. Molto grande ma non è un granché.	'I also have a house on Capri. It's very big but doesn't amount to much.'
Avrei una domanda un po' difficilina da farti. Vorrei chiederti una sommetta di danaro.	'I've a ticklish question to ask you. I'd like to ask you for a sum of money.'
Gianni Agnelli qualche miliardino ce l'avrà da dare via.	'I guess GA must have the odd billion lire to give away.'
Le tigri? Non si scherza con quegli animaletti!	'The tigers? Don't mess around with those beasties!'

Use of *-one* (see 3.12 for more on *-one*) tends to convey playful exaggeration (often with the suggestion that what is being described is regarded as excessive):

M'ha fatto uno di quei suoi discorsoni.	'He delivered me one of those endless speeches of his.'
C'era un maledetto sassone in mezzo alla strada.	'There was a dirty great stone in the road.'

In the above examples there is no necessary implication that the speeches are actually 'long', or the stone 'big' (although such interpretations are perfectly

---

[2] But not necessarily, it should be said, levity or good humour. The *intent* behind such utterances can be entirely serious and even in some circumstances threatening.
[3] One may even encounter, in speech used by adults to children, such utterances as *Hai mangiatino?* for *Hai mangiato?* 'Have you eaten?'

possible). Rather, they may express the attitude that the actions or state of affairs described are excessive or unpleasant. Some *-one* forms which have separate dictionary entries are: *brontolone* 'grumbler' (*brontolare*) and *mangione* 'excessive eater' (*mangiare*), *amicone* 'crony' (*amico*), etc.

It is a curiosity of the *-one* suffix that it cannot normally be applied to an entity larger than a human being, unless that entity has actually been built by human beings. So one cannot say **cielone* 'big sky', **campone* 'big field', **spiaggione* 'big beach', but one can say *piazzone* 'big square', *stradone* 'big road', *canalone* 'big canal', and so forth.

The 'vezzeggiativo' *-uccio* usually conveys endearment, sympathy but sometimes pejorative nuances as well:

Quegli studenti sono tutti un po' debolucci.	'Those students are all a bit feeble.'
Quanto sono carini quei cappellucci con la piuma.	'Aren't those little hats with feathers nice.'

Note that when a child is born a common way of saying 'It's a girl' is *È una femminuccia*, but 'It's a boy' is *È un maschietto*.

The most productive pejorative suffix is *-accio*, which generally means 'unpleasant', 'nasty':

Questo vinaccio è imbevibile!	'This awful wine is undrinkable!'
Ha il viso coperto di brufolacci.	'His face is covered with nasty blackheads.'
Ha scoperto una lumacaccia nell' insalataccia!	'She's discovered a nasty slug in her awful salad!'

A number of other evaluative suffixes have a value between pejorative and 'attenuative' (the latter being close to English '-ish'). These are rather less productive than *-one*, *-ino*, etc., and less closely associated with 'non-seriousness'. The suffix *-astro* attached to nouns is strongly pejorative and often suggests inadequacy, inferiority, incompetence or amateurishness: e.g., *medicastro* 'quack', 'third-rate doctor' (*medico*), *poetastro* 'poetaster', 'scribbler of verse' (*poeta*), etc. Note also *automobilastro* 'bad driver', 'road hog' (corresponding to *automobilista*). Attached to an adjective, *-astro* has more 'attenuative' force, but sometimes with a suggestion of inadequacy. It is frequently attached to colour adjectives:

Aveva le mani giallastre.	'He had yellowish hands.'
Questo vino è un po' dolciastro.	'This wine is a bit sweetish/sickly.'
Quanto i tedeschi sono rossicci, carnosi, imberbi, tanto i fascisti sono neri, ossuti, con le facce bluastre e i baffi da topo.	'As the Germans are ruddy, chubby, and clean-shaven, so the fascists are swarthy and bony, with bluish faces and rat-like whiskers.'

The last example above introduces another attenuative adjectival suffix, *-iccio*, again moderately productive. *Rossiccio* is, roughly, 'a little bit red' (*rosso*), *bianchiccio* 'whitish'; *malaticcio* is 'sickly' (prone to illness) (*malato*); *appiccicaticcio* is '[irritatingly] sticky', 'liable to stick' (*appiccicare*), etc. It is extremely difficult to identify exact differences of meaning between the various 'attenuatives', or to predict exactly where they can be used. Among others are *-igno* (e.g., *gialligno* 'yellowy'), *-ognolo* (e.g., *azzurrognolo* 'bluey', 'bluish').

A useful list of further evaluative suffixes, many of which comprise combinations of two or more suffixes, such as *orsacchiotto* 'bear cub', 'teddy bear' (*orso*), *mostricciattolo* 'little monster' (*mostro*), may be found in Lepschy and Lepschy (1988: 176–82).

20.5 Verb suffixes

Certain suffixes can be attached to the root of a verb (the resulting suffixed verbs all belong to the first conjugation). They tend to indicate that the action expressed by the verb is frequently interrupted and intermittent, or inadequately and imperfectly performed. There are no rules regarding which suffix will be selected in such cases, and no rules to predict to which verbs these suffixes can be attached. Some examples are:

-erellare	*salterellare* 'leap about' (*saltare*), *trotterellare* 'trit-trot along' (*trottare*)
-ettare	*fischiettare* 'to whistle intermittently' (*fischiare*)
-ottare	*parlottare* 'mumble' (*parlare*)
-icchiare	*dormicchiare* 'snooze' (*dormire*); *studicchiare* (also *studiacchiare*) 'study in a desultory, unenthusiastic fashion' (*studiare*), also *costicchiare* 'to be a bit pricy' (*costare*)
-acchiare	*rubacchiare* 'indulge in petty theft' (*rubare*), *ridacchiare* 'snigger' (*ridere*), *vivacchiare* 'live hand to mouth', 'eke out an existence' (*vivere*)
-ucchiare	*mangiucchiare* 'nibble occasionally' (*mangiare*), *sbaciucchiare* 'neck' (prolonged kissing) (*baciare*)

21

Time expressions

For time adverbs, time prepositions and time conjunctions see 13.16, 11.32, 19.16.

21.1 Telling the time

To the question 'What time is it?', which may be either *Che ora è?* or *Che ore sono?*, one might reply:

È l'una.	'It's one (o'clock).'
Sono le sette.	'It's seven (o'clock).'
Sono le otto e mezza.	'It's half past eight.'
Sono le nove meno un quarto.	'It's a quarter to nine.'
Sono le quattro e un quarto.	'It's a quarter past four.'
Sono le cinque e ventisette.	'It's five twenty-seven.'
Sono le undici meno dodici.	'It's twelve (minutes) to eleven.'
È mezzogiorno.	'It's midday.'
È mezzanotte e un quarto.	'It's a quarter past midnight'.
etc.	

It will be seen that hours are specified as *feminine* (because *ora* is feminine) and are preceded by a feminine definite article. Both article and any accompanying verbs are plural if the number is greater than one (although one sometimes encounters the plural even with 'one': *Sono le una*). Accordingly, we find feminine plural agreement in phrases such as *Sono già suonate le sette* 'It has already chimed seven o'clock'/'Seven o'clock has already chimed'. Minutes, and fractions of hours, past the hour are preceded by *e*, those before the hour by *meno*. 'A quarter past/to ' is *e/meno un quarto*. 'Half past' may be either *e mezzo* or *e mezza*. The twenty-four-hour clock is generally used in official and public contexts (e.g., timetables, television listings), where it is not uncommon to include the word *ore*.

Lo spettacolo inizierà alle (ore) venti.	'The show will begin at 8 p.m.'
Il servizio verrà sospeso alle (ore) diciannove.	'The service will be suspended at 7 p.m.'

21.2 Periods of the day, days, months, seasons, years and centuries

TABLE 21.A

Periods of the day

mattina 'morning'	*di/la mattina* 'in the morning'	*stamattina* *stamani* *questa mattina* } 'this morning'
mezzogiorno 'midday'	*a mezzogiorno* 'at midday'	
pomeriggio 'afternoon'	*nel/di pomeriggio* 'in the afternoon'	*questo pomeriggio* 'this afternoon'
sera 'evening'	*di/la sera* 'in the evening'	*stasera* 'this evening' *questa sera* 'tonight'
notte 'night'	*di/la notte* 'at night'	*stanotte* 'last night' or *questa notte* 'tonight'
mezzanotte 'midnight'	*a mezzanotte* 'at midnight'	

There is some regional variation in the terms *pomeriggio* and *sera*. In much of Italy the division between them seems to occur, very approximately, at around five o'clock. But in the far south, *sera* often seems to denote 'afternoon' as well as 'evening', so that one may even say *buona sera* at 3 in the afternoon. Many Italians use *dopopranzo*, strictly the period immediately after lunch, to denote the whole afternoon. Note that 'tonight' is normally *stasera* or *questa sera*. The expressions *stanotte* and *questa notte* are used principally in contexts where the speaker wishes to emphasize that some event occurs at *night*, rather than in hours of daylight:

C'è la luna piena stanotte. Che ne dici di andare a caccia? — 'There's a full moon tonight. What about a bit of hunting?'

Days of the week

lunedì	'Monday'
martedì	'Tuesday'
mercoledì	'Wednesday'
giovedì	'Thursday'
venerdì	'Friday'
sabato	'Saturday'
domenica	'Sunday'

Except for feminine *domenica*, all day names are masculine.

To express 'on Friday' (etc.) (i.e., on the next or most recent Friday (etc.) relative to the time of speaking), the bare name of the weekday is used. To express habitual occurrence on a particular day ('on Fridays', etc., 'every Friday', etc.), the name of the day is preceded either by *di* or by the definite article:

Mario viene venerdì.	'M is coming on Friday.'
Mario viene di/il venerdì.	'M comes on Fridays.'
	'M comes every Friday.'
Esco domenica.	'I'm going out on Sunday.'
Esco sempre di/la domenica.	'I always go out on Sundays.'
Mercoledì ero impegnata.	'On Wednesday I was busy.'
Di/Il mercoledì ero impegnata.	'On Wednesdays I was busy.'

Il mercoledì ero impegnata, etc., with the article, could of course also mean 'On the Wednesday (of that week) I was busy'.

'Yesterday', 'tomorrow', etc.; 'the day before' and 'the day after', etc.:

avantieri/ieri l'altro/ier l'altro/l'altro ieri	'the day before yesterday'
ieri	'yesterday'
oggi	'today'
domani	'tomorrow'
dopodomani	'the day after tomorrow'

Also

ieri pomeriggio	'yesterday afternoon'
domani mattina (also *dommattina*)	'tomorrow morning'
ieri sera	'yesterday evening', 'yesterday night', 'last night'
domani sera	'tomorrow evening', 'tomorrow night'
etc.	

Note that *la notte scorsa* 'last night', means strictly 'in the night between yesterday and today', rather than 'yesterday evening'; it can also mean 'the night between the day before yesterday and yesterday'. *Oggi* in the wider sense of 'nowadays' sometimes appears as *oggigiorno*, *al giorno d'oggi*.

'The day before' or 'on the day before' is simply *il giorno prima*. For 'the day after' or 'on the day after' one may say *il giorno dopo* or *l'indomani* or *all'indomani*; 'on the day after' is *all'indomani (di)*.

Months

gennaio	'January'	*luglio*	'July'
febbraio	'February'	*agosto*	'August'
marzo	'March'	*settembre*	'September'
aprile	'April'	*ottobre*	'October'
maggio	'May'	*novembre*	'November'
giugno	'June'	*dicembre*	'December'

All names of months are masculine.

'In January' (etc.) is expressed by placing *in* or *a* before the name of the month:

Ho ricevuto la lettera in gennaio.	'I got the letter in January.'
I corsi riprenderanno ad ottobre.	'Classes start again in October.'

Seasons

primavera	'spring'	*in primavera*	'in (the) spring'
estate	'summer'	*d'estate*	'in (the) summer'
autunno	'autumn'	*in autunno*	'in (the) autumn'
inverno	'winter'	*d'inverno*	'in (the) winter'

Years

Names of calendar years are preceded by the masculine article: *il millenovecentonovantasei* (*il 1996*), *il milleduecentosessanta* (*il 1260*), *Nacquero tutti e due nel milleottocentotrentanove* (*nel 1839*) 'They were both born in 1839', etc. Names of years may be abbreviated by omitting specification of the century, as in English: *È nato nel '75* 'He was born in '75', *Tornò in Italia dopo la guerra, nel '46* 'She returned to Italy after the war, in '46'.

'In the (nineteen) thirties', 'in the (seventeen) forties', etc. is *negli anni (millen-ovecento)trenta, negli anni (millesettecento) quaranta,* etc. If only the decade is specified (*gli anni Trenta,* etc.), then the numeral normally takes a capital letter:

> *Conobbe la moglie nei primi anni Sessanta*   'He met his wife in the early sixties
> *grazie alla sorella Maruzza.*   thanks to his sister M.'

The abbreviations *a.C. (avanti Cristo)* and *d.C. (dopo Cristo)* correspond respectively to 'BC' and 'AD': *nel terzo secolo a.C., il settecentodue d.C.,* etc.

Centuries

Centuries may be expressed either by an ordinal numeral + *secolo* (e.g., *il quindicesimo secolo* 'the fifteenth century', *il ventunesimo secolo* 'the twenty-first century'), or – for centuries from the thirteenth until the twentieth inclusive – by reference to the number of 'hundreds' in the name of the century. Thus, *il Duecento* (or *il '200*) is the thirteenth century, that century whose dates all contain -*duecento*- (e.g., *il milleduecentoundici* '1211', *il milleduecentosessantacinque* '1265'); and likewise *il Trecento* (*il '300*) is the fourteenth century, and so forth up to *il Novecento* (*il '900*), the twentieth century. For the thirteenth century the term *il Dugento* is sometimes encountered. Note also the adjectives *duecentesco/duegentesco* '(pertaining to the) thirteenth century', *trecentesco, quattrocentesco,* etc. Apparently, no name of this kind is available to denote the twenty-first century.

21.3 Expressions of duration in -*ata*: *giornata, serata,* etc.

Italian has a range of terms emphasizing temporal duration which are formed by adding the feminine suffix -*ata* to common words indicating periods of time:

anno	'year'	*annata*
giorno	'day'	*giornata*
mattina	'morning'	*mattinata*
sera	'evening'	*serata*
notte	'night'	*nottata*

What principally distinguishes the -*ata* forms is that they are durative. They focus on the internal unfolding of the time period in question, on the activities which take place within it. Thus *Buongiorno!* and *Buonasera!* are salutations meaning 'Good day' and 'Good evening', but *Buona giornata* and *Buona serata* mean, for example, 'Have a good day's work', 'Enjoy your day' and 'Have a good evening's entertainment', 'Enjoy your evening'. Compare also:

> *Si chiude con questa ultima partita una*   'With this last match an extraordinary
> *straordinaria annata sportiva.*   sporting year draws to a close.'
> *Sono stati sessantanove i colpi partiti, nella*   'Sixty-nine shots were fired, during that
> *sconvolgente mattinata del primo marzo,*   harrowing morning on 1 March, from
> *dalla carabina calibro 22.*   the point-22 rifle.'
> *Quell'estate passammo delle giornate*   'That summer we had some magnificent
> *magnifiche sdraiati al sole.*   days lying in the sun.'
> *Che giornata!*   'What a day!' [e.g., 'What a hard day's
>   work!']
>
> *Purtroppo è stata una serata di pioggia.*   'Unfortunately it rained all evening.'
> *Dopo tante nottate di lavoro, non ne poteva*   'After so many nights spent working, he
> *più dalla stanchezza.*   was tired to death.'

Riuscì a finire il lavoro in mattinata.	'He managed to finish the job during the morning.'
Prima serata; seconda serata	[in television listings, respectively the programmes scheduled approximately between 8.30 and 10, and 10 and midnight]

Note that *mesata* has the special sense of 'a month's wages'.

21.4 Dates

Dates are specified in the following way: masculine singular definite article + cardinal numeral + month + year.

> *il cinque dicembre millenovecentosessantadue* 'the fifth of December 1962'

Except that for the 'first' of a month, the ordinal *primo* is used instead:

> *il primo gennaio millenovecentonovantasette* 'the first of January 1997'

Exactly the same formula is used to express the date on which an event occurs.

È nato il 5 dicembre 1962.	'He was born on 5 December 1962.'
Il tre maggio è morto mio zio.	'On 3 May my uncle died.'
Spero di tornare prima del primo marzo.	'I hope to return before 1 March.'

The preposition *di* is sometimes introduced between the number and the month (*il tre di maggio*, etc.), without any appreciable difference of meaning. The date at the head of a letter may be preceded by the article if the month is given as a word (e.g., *il 20 maggio 1998*); a now formal and old-fashioned usage in letter headings is to employ an archaic form of the masculine plural article, *li*, instead of *il* (e.g., *li 20 maggio 1998*).

To say 'in May of 1957' the month is preceded by *nel* but the year is not preceded by *del*: *nel maggio 1957*, etc.

To ask what date it is, one may say *Qual è la data (oggi)?* but one commonly encounters the phrase *Quanti ne abbiamo (oggi)?* literally 'How many do we have today?' (scil. how many days of the month?).

21.5 Ages

The usual formula for stating the age of a person, building, institution, etc. is *avere X anni* 'to be X (years old)':

Mario aveva ottantasette anni quando morì.	'M was 87 (years old) when he died.'
Fin da quando aveva sei anni aveva sentito quello strano dolore.	'Ever since she was 6 she had felt that strange pain.'

Expressions of the type 'to be 60' in the sense 'to turn 60 years old', 'to complete 60 years' are usually expressed by the verb *compiere* + number of years:

Mario compirà 60 anni domani.	'M will be 60/turns 60 tomorrow.'

Note also:

Mario ha 60 anni compiuti.	'M is in his sixty-<u>first</u> year.'

When an age is preceded by a preposition, then the masculine plural definite article is normally present as well:

Si sta avvicinando ai sessant'anni.	'He's approaching 70.'
Era ancora una ragazzina, tra i cinque e i sette anni.	'She was still a little girl, between five and seven.'

For the use of *-ina* with numerals generally, see 12.10. With ages it indicates approximation and can be used as follows:

È sulla sessantina.	'He's about 60.'
Avrà una ventina d'anni.	'She must be about 20.'

The adjective phrase 'X-year-old', and the noun phrase 'a/the X-year-old' can be derived in Italian by addition of the suffix *-enne* to the year number: *trenta* > *trentenne, sessantotto* > *sessantottenne*. Note that the final vowel of the number is removed when *-enne* is added (except *ventiseienne*, etc.). 'Ten-year-old' is *decenne*. The *-enne* forms occur particularly, but not exclusively, in journalistic prose:

Il nipote appena trentenne aveva già i capelli bianchi.	'The nephew [who was] barely thirty already had white hair.'
Sono praticamente innumerevoli gli esempi di ultrasettantenni al comando di questo o quell'altro apparato dello Stato.	'There are practically countless examples of over-seventy-year-olds in command of this or that state body.'
Furono aggrediti da due quindicenni.	'They were attacked by two 15-year-olds.'

There is no 'upper' limit on the ages to which *-enne* may be suffixed, but it is not normally used below 10 (*bienne* 'two-year-old', and *trienne* 'three-year-old' are restricted to scientific and technical usage), and seems for most Italians to be impossible for 1, 2, 3, 4, 5 and 8.

21.6 Expressions of frequency: 'twice a day', 'every five minutes', etc.

To express the frequency with which some event occurs, *volta, volte* 'time', 'times' is used. The period within which some event is repeated (e.g., 'three times a year') takes a definite article. It may optionally be preceded by the preposition *a*.

Devi prendere una di queste pastiglie tre volte al giorno/il giorno.	'You must take one of these pills three times a day.'
Vado a trovare i miei almeno due volte all'anno/l'anno.	'I go and see my parents at least twice a year.'

Ogni may also be used much as 'every' in English:

Passa un pullman ogni cinque minuti.	'A bus goes by every five minutes.'

'Every other day' may be expressed as *un giorno sì, l'altro no* or *un giorno sì e uno no*.

Interrogative 'how often?', 'how frequently?' is *ogni quanto?*:

Ogni quanto dai da mangiare al maiale?	'How often do you feed the pig?'

21.7 Time adjectives: 'last' *scorso*, 'next' *prossimo*, etc.; 'the late . . .' *il fu*; 'the then' *l'allora*

Scorso (also *passato*) 'last' refers to a period of time immediately preceding the period of speaking:

La settimana scorsa sono tornata al lavoro.	'Last week I went back to work.'
Quanto doveva essere diversa l'Italia del secolo scorso!	'How different the Italy of the last century [e.g., the Italy of the *nineteenth* century, assuming that the speaker is speaking in the *twentieth* century] must have been!'

For time preceding some moment other than the period of speaking, 'last' (i.e., 'last' in relation to 'then', rather than 'last' in relation to 'now') is *precedente* or *prima*:

Sapevo che eravate tornati la settimana prima.	'I knew you had come back the week before.'
Quanto doveva essere diversa l'Italia del secolo precedente!	'How different the Italy of the previous century [e.g., the Italy of the *eighteenth* century, viewed in relation to the *nineteenth* century by somebody speaking in the *twentieth*] must have been!'

Note that *scorso* and *precedente* must be distinguished from *ultimo*, which means 'latest' (*Sai l'ultima notizia?* 'Have you heard the latest news?'), or indicates the 'last', 'final' member of any series (*Chi fu l'ultimo re di Francia?* 'Who was the last king of France?').

Similar principles apply to 'next'. 'Next' is *prossimo*, for a period of time immediately following the period of speaking (i.e., 'next' in relation to 'now'):

L'anno prossimo mi trasferirò a Napoli.	'Next year I'll move to Naples.'
Il ritorno è previsto per il prossimo agosto.	'The return is planned for next August.'
Ho deciso di svendere tutto quanto nei prossimi giorni.	'I've decided to sell up everything in the next few days.'

But if 'next' refers to a period of time following some time other than the period of speaking (i.e., 'next' in relation to 'then', rather than 'next' in relation to 'now'), then it is *successivo* or *seguente* (usually corresponding to English 'the next', rather than 'next').

Arriverai il 3 dicembre e ripartirai la settimana successiva/seguente.	'You'll arrive on 3 December and you'll leave again the next week.'
Mi promise che me li avrebbe restituiti la volta successiva.	'He promised me he'd give them back to me the next time.'
È arrivato il lunedì e il venerdì successivo se n'è andato senza nemmeno salutarmi.	'He arrived on the Monday and the next Friday he left without even saying goodbye to me.'

The words *passato* and *venturo* are also available, respectively, as synonyms of *scorso* and *prossimo*.

Note also the adverbs *attualmente* 'at present', *recentemente* 'recently', *precedentemente* 'previously', *prossimamente* 'in the near future', *successivamente/susseguentemente* 'subsequently'.

L'altro may also be used to express a period of time preceding the period of speaking, but *l'altr'anno* can either mean 'last year' or 'the year before last'; while *l'altro giorno* can refer to any recent day except 'yesterday' (cf. English 'the other day'). One occasionally encounters *un altr'anno* with the meaning of 'next year'; otherwise, *un'altra settimana*, *un'altra volta*, etc., refer to any week/time in the future.

Note that the use of *questo* with the names of days of the week, months and seasons indicates proximity in time, but can refer either backwards or forwards in time:

Quest'aprile ha avuto un figlio.	'This (last) April she had a child.'
Quest'aprile avrà un figlio.	'This (next) April she'll have a child.'

The adjectivally used *fu* 'late', 'deceased' and *allora* 'then' are invariable and always precede the noun:

la fu Vittoria, regina d'Inghilterra	'the late Victoria, queen of England'
Alberto Rossi, l'allora presidente della società, diceva sempre che . . .	'AR, the then president of the society, always said that . . .'

22

Forms of address

22.1 Importance of selecting the correct address form

Italian has a range of pronouns, and corresponding verb forms, expressing what is expressed in English simply by 'you'. Not only is there a distinction in Italian between singular and plural addressees (for example, *Tu parli* 'You [singular] speak' vs. *Voi parlate* 'You [plural] speak'), but the form of the pronoun (and that of the verb) serves to express something about the nature of the relationship[1] (see 22.3) between speaker/writer and addressee (e.g., *Tu parli* used, say, in addressing a child vs. *Lei parla* used in addressing an adult stranger). The relevant distinctions are clearly made in the singular, less so for the plural (where, for example, *Voi parlate* could be used both to children and to adult strangers). If an adult uses *tu* inappropriately there is a serious possibility that offence could be caused (*tu* may sound too familiar and be perceived as lacking in respect or even arrogant). When in doubt, non-native speakers are strongly advised to use the more formal and distant *Lei* (and the corresponding third person singular verb form) in the singular, leaving it to the native speaker[2] to propose mutual use of *tu* (often by the phrase *Diamoci del tu!* 'Let's call each other *tu*' – see 22.3).[3]

22.2 Forms and syntax of pronouns and verb forms used in address

Before discussing the *uses* of the different address forms, we need to say something about their *forms*. *Tu* and *voi* are used exclusively as pronouns of address (see 6.2, 10.4 for the corresponding object, clitic and possessive forms *te, ti, tuo,*

---

[1]A more detailed overview of modern address forms may be found in Brunet (1987), Renzi, Salvi and Cardinaletti (1995: 350–75).

[2]However, there may be situations in which the native speaker feels unable to initiate use of *tu*, and the onus may be on the foreigner to do so. Use of *tu* cannot easily be initiated by an 'inferior' towards a figure whom the speaker regards (for whatever reason) as superior. For example, if two university professors meet for the first time, one of them a native speaker of Italian, but younger and perhaps less well-established, and the other a non-native speaker who is older and better established, the latter may feel that their shared profession licenses mutual *tu*, but it will usually have to be he or she, not the junior, who proposes using *tu*.

[3]Note the verbs *dare del tu (a qualcuno)* 'call [someone] *tu*', *dare del Lei (a qualcuno)* 'call [someone] *Lei*'.

voi, vi, vostro, etc.). When *tu* and *voi* are the subject of the verb, the correspond-ing second person singular and plural verb forms are respectively the second person singular (*Tu parli/dormi/sai,* etc.) and second person plural (*Voi parlate/ dormite/sapete,* etc.). In the (nowadays unusual) cases where *voi* is used as a *singular* form of address (see 22.4), adjectives and past participles always show singular agreement, with gender reflecting the sex of the addressee: *Voi vi siete alzato/alzata presto* 'You got up early'.

The remaining address forms, singular *Lei, Ella,* and plural *Loro* are remark-able in that, although they are used to mean 'you', they are actually identical in form to *third person* pronouns (see 6.2; 7.19) and take, respectively, third per-son singular and third person plural verb forms (*Lei* or *Ella parla/dorme/sa,* etc. and *Loro parlano/dormono/sanno,* etc.). Moreover, *Lei* and *Ella* are identical to third person *feminine* pronouns,[4] even though they are used equally in address-ing males and females. The direct object, indirect object and reflexive forms (*la, li, le (gli), si*) are exactly the same as for the third person pronouns *lei/ella* and *loro*:

Se la vedo, glielo darò senz'altro.	'If I see you, of course I'll give it to you.'
Lei è invitato a presentarsi presso questo ufficio entro il 20 maggio.	'You are requested to present yourself in this office by 20 May.'

Although *Lei* has the form of a feminine pronoun, the gender of adjectives (and of past participles) used with it reflects the sex of the addressee; use of fem-inine agreement when the addressee is male is nowadays extremely archaic, but the situation is different with *Ella* – see below:

Lei è davvero generoso [to a man]/*generosa* [to a woman] *a offrirmi il suo aiuto.*	'You are really generous to offer me your help.'
Cara professoressa/Caro professore, Lei è stata/stato davvero gentile.	'Dear professor, you have been really kind.'

The sole exception concerns the agreement of the past participle (see 14.23) with the direct object pronoun *la* (corresponding to *lei, ella*). In this case, the past par-ticiple is generally feminine, irrespective of the sex of the addressee:

Dottor Biagi, l'ho vista ieri in TV.	'Dr. B, I saw you on TV yesterday.'
Caro professor Rossi, se non ci fossimo incontrati l'avremmo certamente contattata per telefono.	'My dear professor R, if we hadn't met I would certainly have contacted you by phone.'

What the following examples reveal, also, is that the third person address pro-nouns (and the corresponding possessives) are sometimes written with a capital letter (particularly in formal and official correspondence). This applies even to clitic forms of the third person pronoun attached to the verb (see 6.3):

---

[4]The reason for the apparently peculiar use of third person (feminine) pronouns as second person address forms is to be sought in the history of the language (see Maiden 1995: 178f. for a brief account). The phenomenon originates in the use of 'honorific' noun phrases as ways of indicating respect, deference, admiration (cf. English phrases such as 'your hon-our', 'your worship', etc.). These honorific phrases tended to comprise feminine nouns (e.g., *la vostra signoria* 'your lordship', *la vostra eccellenza* 'your excellency'), which could also be signalled by the corresponding feminine third person pronouns *ella, lei,* etc.

La V. S. è pregata di presentarSi appena possibile.	'You are requested to present yourself as soon as possible.'
Professor Simone, La ringrazio molto per il Suo gentile invito. Sarò lieta di tenere una relazione ai Suoi studenti: mi faccia sapere il giorno che Le sembra più adatto. In attesa di risentirLa, La saluto cordialmente.	'Professor S, I thank you very much for your kind invitation. I shall be happy to give a talk to your students: let me know the day which seems most suitable to you. Waiting to hear from you, I greet you cordially.'

But the general trend in current usage seems to be towards use of *lei*, etc., with lower-case letters.

As is generally the case in Italian, subject pronouns are only used to give emphasis to the subject, and the identity of the subject is indicated by verb-endings alone. This applies equally to pronouns of address, so that the form of address being selected is often indicated only by the verb-ending: *Che cosa fai?* 'What are you [*tu*] doing?', *Che cosa fate* 'What are you [*voi*] doing?', *Che cosa fa?* 'What are you [*lei* or *ella*] doing?', *Che cosa fanno?* 'What are you [*loro*] doing?' Note that the third person singular verb-ending alone does not distinguish between *lei* and *ella*.

22.3 Uses of the address forms *tu* / *Lei* / *voi* / *Ella*

The second person singular *tu* implies intimacy, familiarity, closeness between speaker and addressee. It is commonly used between friends, members of the same family, and often between interlocutors who feel 'familiar' by virtue of belonging to the same profession or social group. The connotation of 'familiarity' in *tu* can also serve to express contempt (especially where the addressee is somebody one would normally call *Lei*). *Tu* is used in addressing children, animals, inanimate objects and others over whom the speaker has (or feels that he/she has) power or authority. It is normally employed, also, where the addressee is called by his/her first name:

Mamma, dove hai messo il mio accappatoio?	'Mummy, where have you put my bath robe?'
—Tu caschi dal sonno, ragazzo mio, —gli diceva l'omone, —non vorrai mica che ti porti in braccio?	'"You're so tired you're dropping, my lad," said the big man. "Are you sure you don't want me to carry you?"'
Ma sai che sei proprio un bel cagnone?	'Do you know you're a real bastard?'
Ti si seccasse la voce in gola, una buona volta!	'I wish your voice would dry up in your throat, for once.'
Vattene, non voglio più vederti.	'Go away, I don't want to see you again.'

God is nowadays addressed with *tu* (in more archaic usage, one also encounters singular *voi*):

Padre nostro, che sei nei cieli ...	'Our Father, Who art in heaven ...'
Signore, ti preghiamo per Antonella e Bernardo che oggi si sono uniti in matrimonio.	'Lord, we pray to Thee for A and B who are today united in wedlock.'

Tu is used (regrettably!) by people who feel that they are in authority and want to stress the importance of their power (some doctors and nurses in hospitals, some policemen, etc.), or to threaten and to show contempt:

Stai buono e fermo, devo farti un'iniezione.	'Be good and keep still. I've got to give you an injection.'
Alzati e seguimi dal Commissario.	'Get up and follow me to the Commissioner.'
Stai zitto o ti spacco il muso.	'Shut up or I'll smash your face in.'

In schools, and increasingly in universities, *tu* is used by teachers and professors when addressing students (who, however, generally use *Lei* in reply):

—*Lucia, per la prossima settimana devi prepararmi una relazione sull'Inghilterra.*	'Lucia, for next week you must prepare me a talk on England.'
—*Va bene maestra, non si preoccupi, la farò.*	'All right, miss, don't worry. I'll do it.'

Professional equals and members of the same club, political party, sports team, society, tend to use *tu*. Men, especially, tend to address the other person by using the surname instead of the first name, at least when they meet for the first time:

—*Caro Latini, conosci l'ingegner Ovi?*	'Dear Latini, do you know Mr Ovi, the engineer?'
—*Come no! Siamo entrambi membri della Commissione Fulbright.*	'Of course! We're both members of the Fulbright Commission.'
—*Come stai, Latini?*	'How are you, Latini?'
—*Bene grazie, e tu?*	'Fine thanks, and you?'

It is frequently the case that authors of books will address their reader as *tu*. Thus Calvino at the opening of a novel:

Stai per cominciare a leggere il nuovo romanzo Se una notte d'inverno un viaggiatore *di Italo Calvino. Rilassati. Raccogliti. Allontanati da ogni altro pensiero.*	'You are about to begin to read the new novel *Se una notte d'inverno un viaggiatore* by IC. Relax. Concentrate. Banish every other thought from your mind.'

The expression *diamoci del tu*, initiating use of mutual *tu* rather than *Lei*, is usually uttered by the older or more eminent person:

—*Buongiorno, professoressa. Il nostro meeting è alle 10, vero?*	'Good morning, Professor. Our meeting is at 10, right?'
—*Sì, ma se ci siamo già tutti possiamo cominciare. Ah, senti, diamoci del tu. Non ti dispiace, spero.*	'Yes, but if we are all already there we can begin. Oh, listen, let's call each other *tu*. I hope you don't mind.'
—*Anzi! Mi fa piacere.*	'Far from it! I'm delighted.'

Use of the third person singular *Lei* implies, first and foremost, social distance (non-familiarity) between interlocutors. *Lei*, contrary to what is sometimes stated, is not an inherently 'polite' address form. It may be used even when one is being rude to one's interlocutor. But use of *tu* in circumstances where *Lei* would be expected, and no permission has been given to use *tu*, can be extremely impolite. *Lei* is generally used to strangers, regardless of their age (unless the addressee is a child), or to persons whom one regards as superior (because they are in positions of authority, or are of a significantly greater age):

Scusi signora, le dà noia se fumo?	'Excuse me madam, do you mind if I smoke?'
Onorevole Facco Bonetti, mi permette di rivolgerLe qualche domanda?	'Honourable[5] FB, will you allow me to ask you some questions?'

---

[5]*Onorevole* is a title accorded to Italian members of parliament, but lacking a ready equivalent in English.

Lei conosce già Pisa, dottor Riotta?	'Do you already know Pisa, Dr R?'

Adult strangers meeting for the first time, especially in formal contexts, use mutual *Lei* (although young people tend to use mutual *tu*):

—*Professor Santangelo, ho il piacere di presentarle il professor Matarangolo.*	'Professor S, I'm pleased to introduce you to Professor M.'
—*Molto piacere professore, come sta?*	'Delighted to meet you professor. How are you?'
—*Bene grazie, e Lei?*	'Very well, thank you. And you?'
—*Sono lieto di conoscerla.*	'I'm very pleased to meet you.'

Lei is also used as a sign of respect towards subordinates, especially porters, cleaners, caretakers, etc.), and in corner shops. Note that in this case people may be addressed by the first name:

Sirio, senta, potrebbe venire domani a potare la siepe?	'Sirio, listen, could you come and trim the hedge tomorrow?'
Rossana, potrebbe farmi per favore 10 fotocopie di questa pagina?	'Rossana, could you please make me 10 photocopies of this page?'
—*Buongiorno Francesco.*	'Good morning Francesco.'
—*Buongiorno signora. Cosa le do stamani?*	'Good morning madam. What can I give you this morning?'
—*Mi dia un chiletto di vitello. Ma che sia morbido!*	'Give me a kilo or so of veal. But make sure it's tender!'
—*Non dubiti, nessuno la serve bene come me.*	'Don't worry, nobody serves you as well as I do.'

It is not impossible for both *Lei* and *tu* to be used to the same addressee in the same utterance, as a reflection, for example, of a changing attitude towards the addressee. In the following example, the abandonment of *Lei* in favour of *tu* corresponds to the speaker's growing loss of temper with the addressee:[6]

Guardi, se lei la prende su questo tono . . ., se lei dice . . ., ma va' al diavolo, idiota, cosa sto a perdere tempo qui con te . . .	'Look, if you're going to be like that about it . . ., if you say . . ., oh go to hell, you idiot, why am I wasting my time here talking to you . . .'

See 6.34 for the use of 'generic' *tu* even when addressing people one would otherwise call *Lei*.

Ella shares most of the functions of *Lei*, but is used only in extremely elevated, formal registers (cf. 6.26), and it usually – but not exclusively – shows feminine agreement regardless of the sex of the addressee:

Ci onoriamo di informarla che Ella è stata prescelta quale vincitrice del concorso letterario bandito dal nostro comune.	'We have the honour of informing you that you have been selected as winner of the literary competition announced by our commune.'
Eccellenza, con l'accettare la mia proposta Ella mi onora!	'Your excellency, by accepting my proposal you honour me!'

22.4 Singular *voi*

In earlier stages of the language, the second person plural pronoun *voi* was used as a *singular* address form performing the functions of modern *Lei* (compare the

---

[6]This example is taken from Renzi, in Renzi, Salvi and Cardinaletti (1995: 373).

singular use of *vous* in French). Remnants of this usage survive in some parts of Italy (for example rural Tuscany, especially when talking to old people), and in parts of southern Italy:

Nonna, volete ancora un po' di minestra?	'Grandmother, do you want a bit more soup?'
Venite Antonio, accomodatevi.	'Come here Antonio, sit down.'

Singular *voi* may also be used by old people to address God, saints, the Virgin Mary:

Madonnina mia, fatemi questa grazia!	'My little Lady, please grant me this!'
Dio mio, aiutatemi!	'My God, help me!'
Sant'Antonio, non mi abbandonate!	'St Anthony, do not forsake me!'

In general, the use of singular *voi* nowadays produces on Italians an effect of rusticity, old-fashionedness or foreignness (it is sometimes found, for example, in translations from languages like French, which regularly uses singular *vous*). Its use is best avoided altogether by non-native speakers.

22.5 *Voi* and *Loro* as plural address forms

The relation between *voi* and *Loro* in the plural is not the same as that between *tu* and *Lei* in the singular. Plural *voi* (and the corresponding second person plural verb form) is an all-purpose plural address form and generally corresponds both to singular *tu* and *Lei*:

Voi sarete le prime a saperlo, signore.	'You'll be the first to know, ladies.'
Cari amici, vi sarei grata se la smetteste di perseguitarmi con i vostri inviti a pranzo: siete molto gentili, ma io sono a dieta!	'Dear friends, I'd be grateful to you if you would stop pestering me with your invitations to lunch: you are very kind, but I'm on a diet!'
Entra pure, Andrea. Venga anche Lei, dottor Caputi. Accomodatevi. Avete tempo o andate di fretta? Vorrei parlarvi del nuovo progetto di ricerca appena approvato dal Consiglio di Dipartimento.	'Do come in Andrea. You come too, Dr Caputi. Take a seat. Do you have time or are you in a hurry? I'd like to talk to you about the new research project which has just been approved by the Departmental Council.'

Voi is also used in advertisements, TV, radio, newspapers, etc., where it is often hard to tell whether the intended addressee is singular or plural:

Realizziamo software per decisioni di successo. Decidete il vostro software con noi.	'We create software for successful decisions. Decide on your software with us.'
Alfa 166? Il vostro senso per gli affari vi dirà 'la voglio'.	'Alfa 166? Your business sense will tell you "I want it".'

The use of *Loro* (and the corresponding object clitic forms masculine *Li*/feminine *Le*; indirect object *Loro*, possessive *Loro*) involves a very high degree of formality, much higher that *Lei* does in the singular. It clearly indicates that the speaker wants to signal distance from the addressees, formality:

Sono convinta che Loro concorderanno con me sulla necessità di riesaminare la questione.	'I am certain that you will agree with me on the need to re-examine the matter.'

Mi diano le loro borse, per favore. Li/Le ritengo persone onestissime, ma ho l'obbligo di controllare il contenuto della borsa di chiunque esce da questo laboratorio.	'Please give me your bags. I believe you to be very honest people, but I'm obliged to check the contents of the bags of anyone leaving this laboratory.'
Mi dicano la verità. Forse il mio collega ha detto loro qualche malignità sul mio conto?	'Tell me the truth. Has my colleague told you something spiteful about me?'
Entrino pure. Mi scuso con loro se non ho molto tempo, ma ho un appuntamento con il Direttore fra quindici minuti.	'Do come in. I'm sorry if I don't have much time, but I have an appointment with the Director in fifteen minutes.'

Gender agreement with plural *voi* and *Loro* depends purely on the sex of the addressees; the direct object clitic forms of *Loro* are *Li* where the addressees are male and *Le* where they are female.

22.6 Other address forms: *la Signoria Vostra*, etc.

Forms such as *la Signoria Vostra* (often abbreviated *la S.V.*), *Vossignoria*, etc. are restricted to highly formal contexts (notably official and bureaucratic communications). Modifying adjectives and past participles are usually feminine even when males are addressed:

La Signoria Vostra è invitata a partecipare all'incontro che si terrà a Roma in occasione del Cinquantenario del Programma Fulbright.	'You are invited to take part in the meeting which will be held in Rome on the occasion of the fiftieth anniversary of the Fulbright Program.'
Vossignoria è pregata di passare in sala da pranzo.	'You are asked to go through to the dining room.'

Very frequent in the bureaucratic language is the use of *Le Signorie Loro* (abbreviated *le SS. LL.*):

Le SS. LL. riceveranno comunicazione ufficiale della loro destinazione da parte di questo Ministero entro il mese.	'You will receive official notification of your destination from this Ministry by the end of the month.'

22.7 Salutations, titles and address forms: *Ciao, bello!* vs. *Buonasera, signore*

Certain salutations are appropriate only for people whom one would address as *Lei* (or *Ella*). *Buonasera* 'good evening' and *arrivederla* 'goodbye' go only with *Lei*; *buongiorno* 'hello', 'good morning' goes only with *Lei*, except as the first greeting of the morning, when it may also be used to somebody one would address as *tu*. Other salutations are appropriate only to people whom one would call *tu*. For example *ciao* 'hello', 'hi' / 'goodbye', *ohé* 'hi', *salve* 'hello' could not be used when addressing someone one calls *Lei* : **Ciao, signora, si accomodi* 'Hi, madam, do sit down', is unacceptable, but *Ciao, Elena, accomodati* is fine. *Buonanotte* 'goodnight' and *arrivederci* 'goodbye' can be used equally with *tu* and *Lei*.

To a greater extent than seems to be the case in the English-speaking world, Italians are given to addressing people by appropriate professional titles, such as *professore, dottore, ingegnere*. Use of such titles always implies *Lei* (e.g., *Ingegnere, si accomodi*, not **Ingegnere, accomodati*).

23

Bibliography and references

The following lists both works cited in the text of this book, and some major works of reference on Italian grammar (the most useful general reference works are marked with an asterisk). The list is limited to works available in English or Italian (except Brunet 1978–, which is in French). A more detailed bibliography covering a great many areas of Italian grammar (especially syntax) may be found in Renzi (1988: 699–745), Renzi and Salvi (1991: 857–924), Renzi, Salvi and Cardinaletti (1995: 517–82).

Battaglia, S. and Pernicone, V. 1954: *La grammatica italiana*. Turin: Loescher-Chiantore.

Berruto, G. 1990: *Sociolinguistica dell'italiano contemporaneo*. Rome: La Nuova Italia Scientifica.

Brunet, J. 1978–: *Grammaire critique de l'italien*. [*1 Le pluriel* (1978). *2 L'article* (1979). *3 Le possessif* (1980). *4 Démonstratifs, numéraux, indéfinis* (1981). *5 Le genre* (1982). *6 L'adjectif* (1983). *7 La comparaison* (1984). *8 Les pronoms personnels* (1985). *9 Tu, Voi, Lei* (1987). *10–11 Les suffixes* (1991). *12 Un 'si' ou deux?* (1995).] Saint-Denis: Presses universitaires de Vincennes.

Bruni, F. 1992: *L'italiano nelle regioni: lingua nazionale e identità regionali*. Turin: UTET.

*Canepari, L. 1992: *Manuale di pronuncia italiana*. Bologna: Zanichelli.

Cinque, G. 1991: *Teoria linguistica e sintassi italiana*. Bologna: Mulino.

Dardano, M. 1978: *La formazione delle parole nell'italiano di oggi*. Rome: Bulzoni.

Dardano, M. 1991: *Manualetto di linguistica italiana*. Bologna: Zanichelli.

*Dardano, M. and Trifone, P. 1985: *La lingua italiana*. Bologna: Zanichelli.

*Fogarasi, M. 1983: *Grammatica italiana del Novecento*. Rome: Bulzoni.

Korzen, I. 1996: *L'articolo italiano fra concetto ed entità: uno studio semantico-sintattico sugli articoli e sui sintagmi nominali italiani con e senza determinante*. Copenhagen: Tusculanum.

Lepschy, G. 1964: I suoni dell'italiano – alcuni studi recenti. *L'Italia dialettale* **29**, 49–69.

Lepschy, G. 1989: Teoria e descrizione nella sintassi italiana. Reggenza, legamento e un uso di *ne*. *Romance Philology* **42**, 422–35.

Lepschy, G. 1992: Proposte per l'accento secondario. *The Italianist* **12**, 117f.

Lepschy, G. 1993: Altre note sull'accento secondario. *The Italianist* **13**, 266–8.

*Lepschy, A-L. and Lepschy, G. 1988: *The Italian Language Today*. London: Hutchinson.

Maiden, M. 1995: *A Linguistic History of Italian*. London: Routledge. [Revised and translated into Italian, 1998, *Storia linguistica dell'italiano*, Bologna: Il Mulino.]

Miklić, T. 1998: Uso cataforico del trapassato prossimo italiano: un espediente testuale per la messa in rilievo. *Linguistica* **38**,2, 183–95.

Palermo, M. 1998: Il tipo 'il di lui amico' nella storia dell'italiano. *Studi linguistici italiani* **24**, 12–50.

Price, G. (ed.) 1998: *Encyclopedia of the Languages of Europe*. Oxford: Blackwell.

*Renzi, L. (ed.) 1988: *Grande grammatica italiana di consultazione*. I *La frase. I sintagmi nominale e preposizionale*. Bologna: Il Mulino.

*Renzi, L. and Salvi, G. (eds) 1991: *Grande grammatica italiana di consultazione*. II *La frase. I sintagmi verbale, aggettivale, avverbiale. La subordinazione*. Bologna: Il Mulino.

*Renzi, L., Salvi, G. and Cardinaletti, A. (eds) 1995: *Grande grammatica italiana di consultazione*. III *La frase. Tipi di frase, deissi, formazione delle parole*. Bologna: Il Mulino.

Robustelli, C. 1995: La costruzione di 'fare' con infinito in italiano moderno. *Studi e saggi linguistici* **35**, 199–272.

Sabatini, F. 1997: Pause e congiunzioni nel testo. Quel *ma* a inizio di frase. In *Norma e lingua in Italia: alcune riflessioni fra passato e presente*. Milan: Istituto lombardo di scienze e lettere, 113–46.

*Serianni, L. 1988: *Grammatica italiana. Italiano comune e lingua letteraria*. Turin: UTET.

Visconti, J. 1996: 'Deverbal' conditional connectives in English and Italian. *The Italianist* **16**, 305–25.

Index